P9-CKN-222

SPORT PSYCHOLOGY

an introduction

Nelson-Hall Series in Psychology
Consulting Editor: **Stephen Worchel**
Texas A & M University

SPORT PSYCHOLOGY
an introduction

Arnold D. LeUnes
Jack R. Nation
Texas A & M University

NELSON-HALL nh **CHICAGO**

Copy Editor: Jean Scott Berry
Project Editor: Dorothy Anderson
Designer: Claudia von Hendricks
Cover Design: Claudia von Hendricks, Richard Meade
Production Manager: Claudia von Hendricks
Photo Editor: Stephen Forsling
Illustrations: Cynthia Schultz
Manufacturer: R. R. Donnelley & Sons Company
Cover Painting: *The Cosmology of Joy* by Ruyell Ho

Photo credits appear on p. 467.

LIBRARY OF CONGRESS CATALOGING-IN-PUBLICATION DATA

LeUnes, Arnold D.
    Sport psychology / Arnold D. LeUnes, Jack R. Nation.
        p.   cm.
    Bibliography: p.
    Includes index.
    ISBN 0-8304-1139-9
    1. Sports—Psychological aspects.   I. Nation, Jack R.   II. Title.
GV706.4.LL48 1989
796'01—dc19   88-29796
                                                                  CIP

Copyright © 1989 by Nelson-Hall Inc.
Reprinted 1990

All rights reserved. No part of this book may be reproduced in any form without permission in writing from the publisher, except by a reviewer who wishes to quote brief passages in connection with a review written for broadcast or for inclusion in a magazine or newspaper. For information address Nelson-Hall Inc., Publishers, 111 North Canal Street, Chicago, Illinois 60606.

Manufactured in the United States of America

10   9   8   7   6   5   4   3   2

CONTENTS

Explaining how a textbook comes about is not an easy task. Perhaps the genesis of this one goes back to a conversation the two of us had at the conclusion of our daily 3-mile jog, a ritual we began in 1974. We noted a very apparent gap in the literature with regard to texts in sport psychology. Those in existence had their merits but they were limited in perspective. The primary emphasis of some was on anxiety, arousal, and related topics. Even more common were texts with heavy emphasis on social psychology. None were really comprehensive in their coverage of the broad field of psychology as it relates to the sport environment.

Our first inclination was to try to put together a first-rate book of edited readings. Somehow, this approach did not meet the need for a comprehensive text that represented the best of theory, research, and application in sport psychology. Accordingly, we set out in December 1983 on a Herculean task.

Among the unique features of this text are:

- A presentation that is the most comprehensive to date. Too, the documentation of points made throughout the text is easily the most comprehensive of all available texts in the field of sport psychology. We believe that science advances best in the face of carefully chosen documentation. We have cited approximately 1,000 authoritative pieces of pertinent speculation, statistics, theory, research, and application.
- Highlights aimed at promoting interest in topics not covered in the main body of the text. The purpose of the Highlights is to enhance interest in new developments and to provide personal glimpses within the fields of sport and sport psychology.
- A healthy balance between theory and application. In general, the first half of the text is devoted to theoretical perspectives within psychology, whereas the balance applies these basics to content areas, such as women athletes, youth participants, coaches, and the fitness seeker.
- Unique coverage of black athletes and high-risk sports groups as well as females, youth participants, coaches, and fitness seekers. Also given extensive coverage is psychological assessment, an area of current interest as well as historical significance in sport psychology.
- A number of pedagogical aids woven into the text. Chapter outlines, highlighted key terms, extensive chapter summaries, student-oriented annotated bibliographies, and numerous Highlights, tables, and figures are included to assist the student in mastering the material.
- A 50-item Test Bank for each chapter. All questions are in the multiple choice format and were written by LeUnes, who was the author of the test bank that accompanied the seventh edition of the best-selling Coleman, Butcher, and Carson text in the area of abnormal psychology.

Though we have interacted on a continuous basis for the past five years in an effort to provide philosophical consistency, there have been clear-cut labor divisions throughout the text. Nation, with his expertise in the areas of behavioral applications, wrote chapters 3 and 4, which deal with basic learning principles, anxiety and arousal, performance enhancement, and anxiety reduction. He will be more than happy to take the plaudits associated with those two chapters. Accordingly, he will also take any heat generated as a result of his efforts. At the same time, LeUnes is responsible for both the success and the failure of the other eleven chapters. Of course, we hope the credits far outweigh the debits insofar as the text is concerned.

ACKNOWLEDGMENTS

This book would not have reached completion without the assistance of a number of devoted individuals, some at Nelson-Hall in Chicago and others at Texas A&M University in College Station. To them, we owe a substantial debt of gratitude. First of all, thanks are extended to the various Nelson-Hall contributors. Ron Warncke helped forge the initial agreement, and we appreciate his early efforts on our behalf. The encouragement and support provided by Steve Ferrara as publisher has been most gratifying; working with him has been a delight. Dorothy Anderson, senior editor, combined technical expertise with a low-key, "Don't worry about it—it will get done" attitude that

we impatient authors need to hear. Claudia von Hendricks created an attractive, functional design and Steve Forsling chose a rich assortment of pictures. Finally, Richard Meade provided high-quality promotional materials.

Next, we thank all those helpful persons at Texas A&M. Steve Worchel, our department chair, provided us with inspiration as well as technical assistance. The legwork done by a number of students in tying up the seemingly endless number of loose ends associated with writing a textbook is most appreciated. Significant among these contributors were Ginger Faught and Stacey Shaeffer, both recent graduates of Texas A&M University. The feedback from the students enrolled in the sport psychology classes over the past two years has been most helpful; with a little practice, they became adept at the review process, and their input is reflected throughout the work. Getting the manuscript typed in a professional style is a major undertaking; our efforts could not have been in better hands than those of Therese Marcellin, Lorraine Doherty, and Dianne Poehl. These young women will always be successful because they place a high premium on quality in everything they do. We were indeed fortunate to have had them on our team.

Clearly, the creation of a book such as this one represents a lot of time and work. We would certainly be remiss if we did not make mention of the continuous forebearance and encouragement that our wives and children have provided throughout. Our heartfelt thanks go to Judy LeUnes, Leslie, Natalie, Chay, Amy, Katie, and Lyndon, and Pat Nation, Shannon, and Derek.

SPORT PSYCHOLOGY
an introduction

With all my heart do I admire
Athletes who sweat for fun or hire,
Who take the field in gaudy pomp,
And maim each other as they romp;
My limp and bashful spirit feeds
On other people's heroic deeds.
        Ogden Nash,
            "The Face Is Familiar"

PART · ONE

BASIC CONCEPTS AND
BEHAVIORAL PRINCIPLES

Introduction to Sport Psychology

Sport is adventure, personal and vicarious. It is challenge, endeavor, and relaxation. It is, too, universal, and very few people have not succumbed to its lure, either as participant or spectator. (Brasch, 1970)

INTRODUCTION

That we live in an era of intense interest in sports is undeniable. On any given Saturday afternoon in early November, nearly two hundred major college and university football teams will tee up the proverbial pigskin before some several million adoring fans. At a point geographically removed from much of this pandemonium, a Curtis Strange, a Seve Ballesteros, or a Greg Norman will be capping off a year of professional golf with winnings of almost a million dollars. Concurrently, a Chi Chi Rodriguez or a Miller Barber will be pocketing earnings for the year of over $300,000 on the seniors (over fifty) version of the golf tour.

Somewhere, perhaps on the other side of the globe, a Martina Navratilova will cash in earnings in excess of $1.5 million on the women's professional tennis circuit. Meanwhile, in Reno or Manila or Atlantic City, top professional boxers will be matching their pugilistic skills for purses totaling upward of $10 million per fight! In a different arena, renegotiation of already lucrative contracts will be taking place in much of professional team sports, particularly in baseball, where money gained through arbitration has been considerable.

Another area of athletic expression involves the world community. The Olympic Games, of course, represent the epitome of athletic performance among the nations of the world. Such events as the World Games and the Pan American Games serve as tune-ups for the Olympics. International competition ranging from swimming to luge is virtually an everyday event in television sports programming. Many dollars and hours of effort are expended in behalf of sport as a manifestation of national

The world of sport is as diverse as its participants and its spectators. (Left) Athletes bear the Olympic torch at the opening ceremonies of the 1988 summer games in Seoul, South Korea; (right) players compete in the national tournament of the Wheelchair Basketball Association in Sacramento, California.

pride and prowess, and this is not likely to change in the foreseeable future.

At another level of amateurism, children and adolescents will be plying their skills each year in a dazzling array of youth programs—city-sponsored soccer leagues, peewee football, Little League baseball, and interscholastic athletics, to name only a few of the possibilities. Well over a million children are estimated to play soccer at some level or another; another sizable contingent plays baseball in one of the 8,500 leagues under Little League jurisdiction; yet another 6 million are involved in such inter-school competitions as football, basketball, and

baseball; the State of Texas, for example, fields almost one thousand public high school varsity football teams.

None of this takes into account the daily games or recreational events that involve so many millions, activities such as racquetball, recreational jogging, and the various aerobics exercises. The relationship of these activities to sport has been the subject of some academic argumentation, but the participants in question likely regard their activity as sport, sport as participant rather than as spectator. For a summary of sport involvement in the United States, see table 1.1.

Clearly, many of us are participants and spectators in the tremendously varied world of sport. The broad field of sport science should therefore do everything it can to enhance understanding and enjoyment of sport of every type and at all levels of complexity. The intent of the remainder of this book is to try to convey to the reader what psychologists and allied sport scientists know and have to say about sport. Unarguably, psychologists are relatively new to the scientific analysis of sport. For example, the first documented work of any note relating psychology to sport in the United States was a book written in 1926 by a University of Illinois psychologist, Dr. Coleman Griffith, and entitled *The Psychology of Coaching*. Griffith followed that with a companion volume in 1928 entitled *Psychology and Athletics*. In Europe, things began a bit earlier, but for all intents and purposes sport psychology is a newcomer on the academic and applied scene, worldwide. Perhaps Browne and Mahoney (1984, p. 606) have captured the essence of this youthful state of sport psychology: "Thus raised and nurtured in infancy by the single parent called Sport Sciences, with a modicum of child support from the (largely unrecognized) parent called Psychology, this exciting toddler named Sport Psychology is now attracting considerable professional and public attention." This youthfulness notwithstanding, let us

Table 1.1 Athletic Participation/Involvement in the United States

Attendance (in millions)

Auto racing	70.4
Thoroughbred and harness racing	69.3
College and professional football	49.9
Major league baseball	48.9
College and professional basketball	43.8

Television viewing of sports (in millions)

Professional football	63.2
Baseball	62.7
College football	48.9
Boxing	37.2
College basketball	36.2

Salaries (in millions)

Ozzie Smith, baseball	$2.34
Mike Schmidt, baseball	2.25
John Elway, football	1.5
Jim Kelly, football	1.5
Larry Bird, basketball	1.8
Moses Malone, basketball	1.6
Wayne Gretzky, hockey	0.825
Mike Bossy, hockey	0.61

Sports marketing expenditures

Corporations spend an estimated $6.2 billion annually to promote their products. Leading spenders include:

Philip Morris, $85 million
RJR Nabisco, $58 million
Anheuser-Busch, $50 million

Endorsement of athletic wear is a lucrative business for athletes. Among the top endorsers are:

Boris Becker, tennis, $5 million
Michael Jordan, basketball, $4 million
Greg Norman, golf, $4 million
Dennis Conner, sailing, $1.8 million

Fitness

Eight billion dollars is spent annually on active-wear, $1 billion on exercise equipment, $1 billion on athletic footwear, and $1 billion on athletic shoes.

An estimated 55 million walkers belong to 3,000 walking clubs. There are 15 walking shoes brands and 140 styles of walking shoes. *The Walking Magazine* has a circulation of 500,000.

An estimated 50 to 60 million people exercise on a regular basis.

Youth

Twenty million youngsters take part in some type of youth sport annually. In addition, 6.4 million boys and girls participate in interscholastic sports each year.

Miscellaneous

Gambling on athletic events may be as high as $500 billion annually. In professional basketball an estimated $100 million changed hands when a Detroit Pistons player beat the point spread with a 3-point shot at the buzzer. Similarly, an estimated $200 million changed hands when a Denver Broncos lineman scored a safety in the late minutes of a 1986 playoff game, again beating the point spread.

The growth of sports in the past 30 years has been phenomenal. The National Hockey League (NHL) began in 1960 with six teams; it now has 14. The National Basketball Association (NBA) has grown from 12 to 24 teams in roughly the same time. Major league baseball has expanded from 16 to 25 teams, and the National Football League has grown from 13 teams in 1960 to its present level of 28.

Don Pooley won $1 million for a hole-in-one at the 1987 Professional Golfer's Association (PGA) Bay Hill Classic in Orlando, Florida.

The 1987 payroll for major league baseball was $256 million.

Carl Lewis earns $25,000 to $35,000 per track appearance.

Earl Anthony and Mark Roth have career earnings in professional bowling of almost $1.3 million.

Ray Floyd, Tom Kite, Curtis Strange, Lanny Wadkins, and Tom Watson, among 1987 top money winners on the professional golf tour, all have career earnings in excess of $3 million. Strange won $925,000 in 1987 alone.

Nancy Lopez has career earnings of $1.7 million on the Ladies Professional Golfer's Association (LPGA) tour.

SOURCE: *Sports Illustrated; USA Today.*

proceed to some definitional matters that will help us understand just how sport and psychology have become so interrelated.

PSYCHOLOGY, A DEFINITION

Psychology as a scientific discipline began in 1879, making it one of the youngest of all the sciences. Some question whether psychology is, in fact, a science at all. These dissenters typically point to the relative sophistication of physics or chemistry to illustrate and strengthen their claims. However, a science is not necessarily measured by the extent of its knowledge base or by its age; rather, the method (the scientific method) used to arrive at its data base should be the critical determinant of what is and what is not a science. Anderson (1966, p. 4) defines the method as "the following of a set of rules for describing and explaining phenomenon: operational definition, generality, controlled observation, repeated observations, confirmation and consistency." Carrying Anderson's definition one step further, the role of prediction in science should not be omitted or underestimated; indeed, being able to accurately predict future events related to sport would constitute a rather utopian state!

Definitions of psychology prior to the 1950s stressed that psychology was the study of mental activity. Most definitions in the 1950s and 1960s emphasized that it is the scientific study of behavior, human or animal, with the latter contributing to generalizations about the former. Then an interesting transformation in our collective thinking began to occur; it became obvious that neither definitional stance was inclusive enough to capture the essence of the human organism. Hence, we began to see the emergence of a definition that led to a marriage of the two positions. A brief historical survey of definitions of psychology is presented in figure 1.1, with the following dated 1970:

Psychology is usually defined as the scientific study of behavior. Its subject matter includes behavioral processes that are observable, such as gestures, speech, and physiological changes, and processes that can only be inferred as thoughts and dreams.

Atkinson, Atkinson, and Hilgard define *psychology* similarly, but more succinctly as "the scientific study of behavior and mental processes" (1983, p. 15). They point out that their definition recognizes the significance of objectively studying behavior, yet it allows for the importance of mental processes that are more inferred than observed. They also say that devoting an inordinate amount of time to definitions can be counterproductive, and suggest that "we can get a better idea of what psychology is from looking at what psychologists do" (p. 15). We shall take heed of this admonition and do exactly as they suggest!

Psychologists are called upon today to serve in a diverse number of specialties and in an ever-increasing variety of settings. Table 1.2 will give the reader a feeling for the diversity of *specialties within professional psychology.*

WHERE DO PSYCHOLOGISTS WORK?

The major organization of psychologists in the United States is the *American Psychological Association (APA)*, made up of more than 65,000 psychologists. Founded in 1892, APA is commissioned by its membership to establish standards for professional behavior, create and oversee a code of ethics, regulate training, and, in general, lobby wherever needed for the betterment of the members, just to name a few of its aims or functions. According to data from APA published in 1981, approximately 43 percent of all psychologists work in a university, college, or medical school setting; private

Figure 1.1 A Brief Historical Survey of Definitions of Psychology

Psychology is the Science of Mental Life, both of its phenomena and of their conditions. . . . The phenomena are such things as we call feelings, desires, cognitions, reasoning, decisions, and the like. (William James, 1890)

Psychology has to investigate that which we call internal experience — our own sensations and feelings, our thoughts and volition — in contradistinction to the objects of external experience, which form the subject matter of natural science. (Wilhelm Wundt, 1892)

All consciousness everywhere, normal or abnormal, human or animals, is the subject matter which the psychologist attempts to describe or explain; no definition of his science is wholly acceptable which designates more or less than just this. (James Angell, 1910)

For the behaviorist, psychology is that division of natural science which takes human behavior — the doings and sayings, both learned and unlearned — as its subject matter. (John B. Watson, 1919)

As a provisional definition of psychology, we may say that its problem is the scientific study of the behavior of living creatures in their contact with the outer world. (Kurt Koffka, 1925)

Conceived broadly, psychology seeks to discover the general laws which explain the behavior of living organisms. It attempts to identify, describe, and classify the several types of activity of which the animal, human or other, is capable. (Arthur Gates, 1931)

Today, psychology is most commonly defined as "the science of behavior." Interestingly enough, however, the meaning of "behavior" has itself expanded so that it now takes in a good bit of what was formerly dealt with as experience . . . such private (subjective) processes as thinking are now dealt with as "internal behavior." (Norman Munn, 1951)

Psychology is usually defined as the scientific study of behavior. Its subject matter includes behavioral processes that are observable, such as gestures, speech, and physiological changes, and processes that can only be inferred as thoughts and dreams. (Kenneth Clark and George Miller, 1970)

Psychology is the scientific analysis of human mental processes and memory structures in order to understand human behavior. (Richard Mayer, 1981)

SOURCE: *Introduction to Psychology* (p. 14) by R. L. Atkinson, R. C. Atkinson, and E. Hilgard, 1983, New York: Harcourt, Brace, Jovanovich.

practice encapsulates another 15 percent, followed by employment in clinics or counseling centers (14 percent), work in government or industry (13 percent), and employment in hospitals (10 percent); another 5 percent ply their skills in public or private school districts. Due to rounding errors in the preceding figures, 0.7 of 1 percent of psychologists are not accounted for, and they report "other" as their work arena. These data, of course, only refer to APA-affiliated psychologists and are not pertinent to the sizable proportion of sport psychologists who come from backgrounds other than psychology.

Following this rather terse coverage of the field of psychology, it seems appropriate to explore the realm of sport and, later, sport psychology.

SPORT, A DEFINITION

Sport, like most things, is not characterized by a universally accepted definition. The interplay of sport with games, recreation, and play is such that a concise, universally agreed upon definition is difficult to piece together. A poignant summary of the problem of differentiating these various activities is provided by Zeigler (1973, pp. 345–346), who states:

Table 1.2 Major Subareas or Branches of Psychology

Subarea or Branch	Percentage of Psychologists	Major Focus/Interest
Comparative psychology	1%	Study various forms of behavior (e.g., sexual, parental) across different species
Consumer psychology	1%	Focus on consumer behavior—especially factors influencing consumer decisions (e.g., advertising, brand loyalty)
Environmental psychology	1%	Study effects of the physical environment (e.g., heat, noise, crowding) on behavior, feelings, and health
Physiological psychology	2%	Examine biological and physiological bases of behavior
Psychometrics	3%	Specialize in the administration and interpretation of various psychological tests
Developmental psychology	4%	Examine changes in physical state, cognitive abilities, and social behavior across the entire span of life
Social psychology	5%	Study all aspects of social behavior—everything from love and attraction to aggression and violence
Experimental psychology	7%	Study basic psychological processes such as perception, motivation, and cognition; often viewed as providing the basic foundation for other branches of psychology
Industrial psychology	8%	Various aspects of behavior in employment settings (e.g., work attitudes, work motivation, leadership); perform such tasks as designing effective methods of personal selection and improving workers' morale
School psychology	9%	Perform such activities as testing, guidance, and counseling primarily with students
Counseling psychology	10%	Assist individuals in dealing with a wide range of personal problems (e.g., personal adjustment, interpersonal relations, career plans)
Educational psychology	10%	Help design curricula and develop new methods of instruction; deal with special problems such as learning disabilities, the effects of school desegregation, etc.
Clinical psychology	29%	Study both the causes and the treatment of behavioral problems; conduct therapy and give psychological tests
Other (community psychology, psycho-pharmacology, humanistic psychology, etc.)	10%	Varied activities, depending upon subarea

SOURCE: *Understanding Behavior* (2d ed, p. 19-20) by R. Baron, D. Byrne, and B. Kantowitz, 1980, New York: Holt, Rinehart, and Winston.

In the 1967 *Random House Dictionary*, for example, the word "sport" is used thirteen ways as a noun, two ways as an adjective, six ways as an intransitive verb, and five ways as a transitive verb. Thus, we will offer here only two definitions which seem to be most applicable to the topic at hand:

1. an athletic activity requiring skill or physical prowess and often of a competitive nature, as racing, baseball, tennis, golf, etc.
2. diversion; recreation; pleasant pastime. The reader can be thankful that play, game, and athletics aren't being defined, as there are 74 ways in which the word "play" is used, and the terms "game" and "athletics" are employed in 23 and three ways, respectively.

Traditional definitions of sport are relatively narrow, and place much emphasis on what amounts to athletics in the strictest sense. For example, Harry Edwards (1973, pp. 57–58), the sport sociologist, defines sport as "activities having formally recorded histories and traditions, stressing physical exertion through competition within limits set in explicit and formal governing role and position relationships, and carried out by actors who represent or who are part of formally organized associations having the goal of achieving valued tangibles and intangibles through defeating opposing groups." Singer (1976, p. 40), in a fashion similar to that of Edwards, sees sport as "a human activity that involves specific administrative organization and a historical background of rules which define the objective and limit the patterns of human behavior; it involves competition and/or challenge and a definite outcome primarily determined by physical skill." On a similar but more elaborate note, Nixon (1984, p. 14) makes distinctions among play, recreation, games, and sport, and these differentiations may be seen in figure 1.2. To Nixon, *play* might be represented by children kicking a ball back and forth or engaging in a snowball fight, the latter being of some historical significance as we

Figure 1.2 Distinctions among Types of Physical Fitness

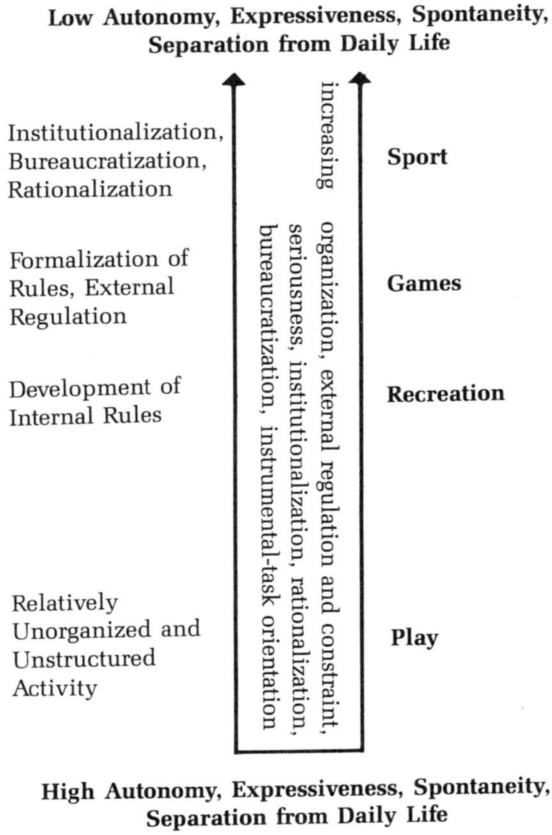

Low Autonomy, Expressiveness, Spontaneity, Separation from Daily Life

Institutionalization, Bureaucratization, Rationalization — **Sport**

Formalization of Rules, External Regulation — **Games**

Development of Internal Rules — **Recreation**

Relatively Unorganized and Unstructured Activity — **Play**

increasing organization, external regulation and constraint, seriousness, institutionalization, rationalization, bureaucratization, instrumental-task orientation

High Autonomy, Expressiveness, Spontaneity, Separation from Daily Life

SOURCE: *Sport and the American Dream* (p. 14) by H. Nixon, 1984, New York: Leisure Press.

shall see in chapter 2. *Recreation* might be personified by jogging or holiday skiing. *Games* are more formalized than either play or recreation, and a "pickup" game of basketball or a soccer match between neighborhood groups would be examples. As for *sport*, he says: "Sport is defined as an institutionalized competitive activity involving two or more opponents and stressing physical exertion by serious competitors who represent or are part of formally organized associations" (p. 13). Nixon further states that an activity is sport when "(a) it is characterized by relatively persistent patterns of social organization; (b) it is serious competition (whose outcome is not pre-arranged) between two or more opponents; (c) it stresses the physical skill factor; and (d) it occurs within a formal organizational framework of teams, leagues, divisions, coaches, commissioners, sponsorship, formalized recruitment and replacement of personnel, rule books, and regulatory bodies." A definitional stance that more closely approximates the spirit of this book is offered by Spears and Swanson (1983, p. 3):

> Sport will be considered to be the activities involving powers and skill, competition, strategy and/or chance, and engaged in for the enjoyment and satisfaction of the participant and/or others. This definition includes both organized sport and sport for recreational purposes. It clearly includes the component of sport as entertainment, which encompasses professional sport.

If we accept the ideas proposed by Nixon, Spears and Swanson, Edwards, and Singer, certain definitional properties of sport emerge. Among them are:

1. Any definition of sport is going to be possessed of a certain degree of ambiguity.
2. Rules or limits are an important part of the definitional process.
3. The role of history in defining sport seems to be most relevant.
4. The role of victory and defeat is a clear-cut aspect of defining sport.
5. Emphasis is placed on the physical exertion factor in competition.

Although the definitions mentioned to this point have considerable merit, they all fall short of the one we would propose, namely, a definition that incorporates a *"sport for all"* spirit. In a broadly conceived definition, the youngster in peewee football, the high school football star, the collegiate gymnast, the professional athlete, the Olympian, the summer slowpitch softball player who is competing with her friends, and the jogger who is merely trying to achieve and maintain fitness are all sport participants. It is in the spirit of "sport for all" that the remainder of this book will proceed.

SPORT PSYCHOLOGY, A DEFINITION

The problem of defining sport psychology is difficult and, at best, must be viewed as a multifaceted, hydra-headed monster. Certainly no shortage of argumentation has existed among concerned professionals over this important issue. One perspective on definition relies heavily on generalities that have an appealing ring but perhaps come up a bit short in terms of capturing the comprehensive nature of the task. Salmela (1981, p. 3) provides a definitional smorgasbord from which we may sample in an effort to arrive at some consensus about just what sport psychology is. He summarizes the definitions of sport psychology offered by several authorities in table 1.3.

In reacting to the broad and perhaps wordy definition of Sleet given in table 1.3, Whiting (1974) describes it as a regular ragbag, a term that can be applied to the totality. It is this *ragbag* issue that is creating such a problem in defining sport psychology and just what a sport psychologist is, does, and ought to do.

An alternate slant on this issue, and a reasonably straightforward one, is succinctly advocated by Martens (1980), who suggests that we operationally define sport psychology as what sport psychologists do. This simplistic stance is proposed because Martens essentially feels that sport psychology is too premature in its development to worry about a definition that

Table 1.3 Definitions of Sport Psychology

Morgan (1972)	The study of psychological foundations of physical activity.
Sleet (1972)	Not limited to the study of athletes or behavior in athletic competition. Sport psychology research is also interested in acquiring knowledge about crowd behavior, rehabilitation and therapy through physical activity, motor skill acquisition, play group dynamics, readiness, proprioception, motor educability, body image, personality, and physical ability, and the phenomenology of movement.
Singer (1978)	Science of psychology applied to sport.
Tutko (1979)	Study of behavior as it relates to sports and athletics.
Alderman (1980)	The effect of sport itself on human behavior.
Cratty (1983)	An applied subdivision of general psychology.

NOTE: The works listed in this table appear in References at the end of the chapter.

SOURCE: *The World Sport Psychology Sourcebook* (p. 3) by J. H. Salmela, 1981, Ithaca, NY: Mouvement Publications.

is rigorous or universally agreed upon. He further warns us that definitions arising from the podium (academia) are insufficient, and that good solid research in sport settings rather than laboratories should ultimately provide a sounder definition. The biggest flaw in Martens' reasoning, and one that will appear from time to time throughout this book, has to do with the problem of defining just *who* sport psychologists are; certainly no consensus exists on this question.

A lively exchange concerning definitional issues continues. For instance, Dishman (1983) points to an identity crisis in North American sport psychology. He argues that the defining of sport psychology as what sport psychologists do shortchanges the profession and hinders the development of useful theoretical and research models that are needed for the advancement of the discipline. He further calls for the creation of sport-related psychological models rather than a continued reliance on the time-honored clinical or educational models that have dominated sport psychology theory, research, and practice.

In view of the considerable ambiguity and argumentation about definitional matters, we shall accept, with reservations, the definition proposed by Martens (1980). The caveat forwarded by Dishman, however, must be recognized. Clearly, no field of endeavor, inside or outside of psychology, can prosper without increasing the sophistication of its theoretical, research, and applied bases. A compelling need exists to press on in the search for sport-related models that define the domain of sport psychology and, in turn, generate research and application that enhances the credibility of sport psychology as a valid scientific undertaking that can make a contribution to sport, worldwide.

WHAT DO SPORT PSYCHOLOGISTS DO?

Granting the acceptance of Martens' definition of sport psychology with all the attendant reservations, it seems appropriate to address our attention to exactly what it is that sport psychologists do. Of course, many teach and do research within university environments; others operate in a more applied milieu. One perspective on what both academic and applied sport psychologists do is provided for us by Nideffer, DuFresne, Nesvig, and Selder (1980, pp. 171–172). They state:

Dr. Shane Murphy, head of the U.S. Olympic Committee's sport psychology program, leads a group of figure skaters in relaxation exercises.

Sport psychologists are being asked to perform the following functions:

1. To *develop performance improvement programs*. This can be accomplished in a number of ways. Techniques like biofeedback, meditation, cognitive behavior modification, attention control training, mental rehearsal, progressive relaxation, autogenic training, hypnosis, and self-hypnosis are used to give the athlete greater control over physiological arousal and concentration.
2. To *use psychological assessment techniques*, including behavioral assessment, paper-and-pencil inventories, psychophysiological measures, and interviews for the selection, screening, and counseling of athletes.
3. To *improve communication* between athlete–coach, athlete–athlete, and coach–coach through the use of tests, group techniques, and individual consultation. The sport psychologist must be sensitive to the entire system or organizational structure in which both coach and athlete function; that is, they must be sensitive to the needs of each part of the system, yet be able to relate to all parts in an effective and ethical manner.
4. To *provide crisis intervention services*. At critical times, athletes or coaches may be temporarily unable to function, and the sport psychologist may be needed to help them quickly regain control.
5. To *provide consultative and program development services* for coaches, trainers, and others who work directly with athletes. Many times sport psychologists do not have the necessary relationship to provide services directly to athletes. The presence of the psychologist may be threatening and can interfere with the relation-

HIGHLIGHT 1.1
Reasons for Sport
Psychology

Why sport psychology? The answers to this question are numerous and reflect world-wide and time-honored fascination with sport and fitness. From the time of the early Greeks, and their emphasis on sport as an expression of beauty, to today, sport has occupied a prominent place in virtually every society. At least six factors have contributed to the evolution of the sport psychology profession.

The growth of sport psychology is closely linked to what often seems to be a national obsession with spectator sports. One of the challenges professionals face, however, is to see that participation be enjoyable, too — that we become as much a culture of doers as we are of watchers.

1. *The pursuit of excellence by athletes.* There are many indications that athletes are open to virtually anything that will allow them to perform at higher and higher levels. Performance enhancement techniques drawn from psychology have been applied widely. Unfortunately, this pursuit of excellence has a down side in the form of steroids, blood doping, and the use of stimulant drugs, to name just a few questionable practices.

2. *Sport as a political tool.* From the time of the first Olympic Games in 776 B.C., athletic achievement has been used as a means of promoting political ends, and the picture remains the same today. Sport psychologists are increasingly being asked by national governing bodies to assist in the development of elite athletes who will serve as international spokespersons for their country.

3. *High salaries in sport.* The fact that sport has become big business, one with a lot of money at stake, has helped propel sport psychology to the forefront. Superstar athletes and athletic organizations have prevailed upon sport psychologists to assist them in their search for excellence.

4. *Recognition gained from sport.* Sport can be viewed as a means of enhancing recognition and resultant feelings of self-worth; there is every reason to believe that sport psychology has something to offer in this regard. One of the proper functions of psychology, and therefore sport psychology, has been to assist people in the creation and maintenance of self-esteem.

5. *Spectator interest.* Millions of people are regular viewers of some sort of sport-related activity. The sport psychologist can enhance the value of this facet of sport by helping athletes maximize their talents as well as contributing to spectator enjoyment through, for example, suggestions for controlling violence at sport events. At the same time, efforts must be expended to make participation enjoyable too, so that we do not become a world of watchers rather than doers.

6. *The fitness movement.* Our fascination with athletics tends to obscure a significant facet of the human existence, that of the many manifestations of fitness. The sport psychologist has much to offer in terms of techniques for improving fitness and fitness activities as well as procedures for making the experience enjoyable enough to insure high rates of lifelong dedication to personal betterment through exercise.

ship coaches have with their athletes. Under these conditions, the sport psychologist may be more effective by teaching and supervising others in the delivery of service.

6. To *function as a therapist* or clinical psychologist. Frequently sport psychologists are asked to provide clinical rather than educational services. Although sport psychologists should be trained to recognize when an athlete has a severe psychological problem, they should not attempt to treat it. Instead, they should make a referral to a clinical psychologist or a psychiatrist who has experience working with athletes. The needs of the system or team are often in conflict with the needs of a severely disturbed athlete, and the sport psychologist who attempts to serve two masters will end up in a conflict of interest, losing both trust and credibility.

Obviously, sport psychologists are called upon to possess a myriad of skills, and at least two problems arise as a result. One has to do with training, and the other with ethical provision of services. As the reader has already noted, these are not totally separate issues. However, the training issue is focused on just who a sport psychologist is in terms of educational background. Must one be a Ph.D. with a license to practice psychology in order to function as a sport psychologist? Or can qualified physical educators practice sport psychology? The ethics issue relates more to performing within one's training and capabilities. In any event, these are critical issues that can only become more salient, and they will be dealt with later.

Before we leave this topic, some mention should be made of the United States Olympic Committee, which is acutely aware of the demands of being a sport psychologist and, concurrently, cognizant of the fact that no psychologist is capable of providing all of the services mentioned by Nideffer and his colleagues. More specifically, we are referring to a task force of eminent sport authorities who met in Colorado Springs, Colorado, in 1982 to draw up recommendations for the practice of sport psychology in the sports under the jurisdiction of the United States Olympic Committee (U.S. Olympic Committee, 1983). This panel of professionals (Kenneth Clarke, Russell Copelan, Dorothy Harris, Daniel Landers, Rainer Martens, Jerry May, William Morgan, Robert Nideffer, Bruce Ogilvie, Richard Suinn, Denis Waitley, and Betty Wenz) identified three broad areas engaged in by sport psychologists:

Clinical. Helping athletes who experience severe emotional problems and where intervention continues over an extended period of time. Examples of such problems include depression, anorexia, and panic. Clinical services also include crisis intervention, which involves helping an athlete who is in need of immediate intervention for an emotionally severe problem. Examples include helping a team member(s) who is experiencing interpersonal conflicts and an athlete who is experiencing severe stress at the competitive site. Clinical services also include helping individuals achieve personal growth—for example, preparation of career termination, coping with sudden success, and dealing with peer relationships.

Educational. Helping athletes to develop the psychological skills necessary for optimal participation in the sport. Examples include teaching athletes relaxation, concentration, and imagery skills. Educational services also emphasize

providing athletes with information that will enhance their participation in the sport. These generally are group-delivered rather than provided through individual athlete training.

Research. Research was designated as a separate component, although it is understood that research is inherent in clinical and educational activities. The important role that research plays in the total development of sport psychology activities was recognized. Within the USOC, a Human Subject Review Panel will be used to assure that HEW guidelines are followed (U.S. Olympic Committee, 1983, p. 5).

Although they state things in a slightly different format, the Nideffer et al. group and the Colorado Springs task force seem to generally agree on the issue of what a sport psychologist does or should be able to do.

TASKS OF THE SPORT PSYCHOLOGIST

Salmela (1981) has provided us with interesting coverage of just how sport psychologists spend their professional time. In his innovative work, *The World Sport Psychology Sourcebook*, Salmela has poignantly addressed himself to a number of important issues, not the least of which is a look at the professional tasks of sport psychologists. Three years of research involving contributors from more than forty countries gave Salmela some insights that he has shared with the sport psychology committee, and much of the discussion in the next few pages is attributable to his efforts.

In response to Salmela's questionnaire to sport psychologists in North America, the following activities and percentage of time devoted to each emerged:

1. Undergraduate teaching (20.5)
2. Consultation (15.7)
3. Graduate teaching (15.3)
4. Planning and doing research (15.3)
5. Writing and publishing (10.9)

The remaining time was divided between training of athletes or patients, administrative duties, and miscellaneous activities.

In general, the duties and responsibilities of the sport psychologist do not differ principally from those of psychologists (or other professors) with different specialties and interests. Teaching, research, writing, service, and administration all sound familiar to those of us in the professorial business!

Interestingly, Salmela took his research one step further and had each of his respondents rank the importance of five professional behaviors that arise out of the preceding tasks. Ranked by an average score on a 1 to 7 Likert-type format (1 = very important, 7 = very unimportant), the activities engaged in were as follows:

1. Carrying out new research (1.9)
2. Interpretation of existing research (2.1)
3. Education of coaches (2.1)
4. Preparation of athletes (3.0)
5. Talent identification (4.0)

The emphasis on research is apparent and should provide partial solace to Dishman (1983) and others.

The findings from North America are similar to those reported from Eastern European respondents in terms of rank order of importance. However, the values assigned by the Eastern European sport psychologists are indicative of a relatively equal and very strong commitment to all five activities (1.6 to research, 2.1 to interpretation of existing research, 2.2 to education of coaches, 2.3 to preparation of athletes, and 2.4 to talent identification).

Salmela also reports on the amount of time sport psychologists spend with various research and application populations. Nonathletes, developing athletes, top athletes, and retired athletes are ranked in that order by our North American contingent, with retired athletes receiving by far the least attention. Strikingly, nonathletes receive much less time in Eastern Europe, whereas top athletes are awarded a high priority. Developing athletes receive almost equal attention in Europe and North America. Retired athletes get less than 11 percent of the sport psychologists' time in Eastern Europe, and they fare only slightly better in North America, where the figure is 18 percent.

CONTENTIOUS ISSUES WITHIN SPORT PSYCHOLOGY

A number of problematic concerns within sport psychology include communication, licensure, credentialing, territoriality, and training. Each will be discussed in turn.

Communication

Much like the situation that existed in psychology in the 1940s and 1950s, anyone can now hang out the proverbial shingle and be called a sport psychologist. Such a situation has many pitfalls and problems, not the least of which is communication among interested professionals. Many sport psychologists today are actually physical educators who come primarily but not exclusively from a physical education or movement science background. They more often than not have been athletes, coaches, or trainers and have a unique perspective when compared with the academically trained psychologist. At the other end of the spectrum is the psychologist who ostensibly is well-trained in psychological matters but often brings a limited or nonexistent sport background to bear on the issues in the area of sport psychology. This disparity in sport and academic background lends itself to concomitant disparities in interests within sport psychology, and it may create communication breakdowns.

A related issue and one germane to the problem is the communication vacuum that often exists between sport psychology researchers and practitioners. To this point, Danish and Hale (1981, p. 96) have written:

> The failure of the two groups to communicate is not caused by the lack of opportunity but because of a lack of perceived common interests. The applied research and the practitioner groups within sport psychology barely communicate with each other because they lack a common framework for discussing their mutual interests. Given that these two groups do not communicate, it is not surprising that sport psychologists have little to say to physical educators and coaches.

Obviously, communication breakdowns among sport psychologists, physical educators, and coaches can be ill afforded, irrespective of sport experience and academic orientation.

Licensure

Yet another issue of considerable significance for both the present and the future is licensing. All fifty American states and the eight Canadian provinces have implemented licensing or certification laws that restrict psychological practice to people who have rather narrowly defined educational and experiential backgrounds and who have passed a licensing examination (Hess, 1977). By the nature of the various laws and the licensing examination, it would be a rare physical educator practicing sport psychology who could become licensed as a psychologist in any state or province.

This licensure problem has been discussed at considerable length by Brown (1982), Danish and Hale (1981), Danish and Smyer (1981), Dishman (1983), Gross (1978), Harrison and Feltz (1979), Heyman (1982), and Nideffer, Feltz, and Salmela (1982). The essence of their combined message is that licensing and the possibility of related malpractice problems is a

reality that merits attention. At the same time, little support exists for the notion that licensing is an infallible preventive measure or panacea for shoddy methods and practices. In the end, it is hoped that sport psychology will not suffer due to an overreliance on standards that have not been proven, and that some eventual rapprochement between licensing considerations and the practical matter of conducting sport psychology can be worked out to the satisfaction of all parties.

Credentialing

Not unrelated to the licensing issue is the question of credentialing. If in fact a license is not required in order to engage in sport psychology practice, surely some type of credentialing would be desirable. Many of the sport psychology professional organizations to be discussed later are currently engaged in efforts to arrive at some sort of credentialing standards. The issues involved are numerous and complex, and they are not likely to be resolved any time soon. Nevertheless, the desirability of such a process is clear if sport psychology is to advance its status in the broad world of sport.

Territoriality

Some mention should be made of territorial concerns. A number of professional organizations have a vested interest in regulating and promoting sport psychology (to be discussed later in the chapter), and the possibility of disputes over domain is a distinct reality. Arguments over turf will not materialize, in all likelihood, but an awareness of such a possibility is essential to an enlightened understanding of the issue of territoriality. Recent evidence from a survey conducted by LeUnes, Hayward, and Bourgeois (1988) provides partial support for the position that territorial wars are unlikely. These researchers asked 102 chairpersons of top-ranked clinical psychology programs to respond to a brief questionnaire about training, territoriality, credentialing, and attitudinal issues. The respondents in the LeUnes et al. study held very favorable views toward sport psychology and, in general, voiced no territorial predispositions. Substantial concern was expressed, however, about credentialing and licensure issues.

Training

As suggested, the training background of sport psychologists is highly variable. A decided minority of sport psychologists are psychologists by training; the United States currently has about three hundred people who call themselves sport psychologists, but fewer than thirty of them are actually trained as psychologists (Morgan, 1980). Nideffer, Feltz, and Salmela (1982, p. 4) view the situation from a most conservative perspective:

> Currently, close to one-half of the NASPSPA membership has identified its primary interest as "sport psychology." This group contains a majority of the "practitioners" and consists of about one hundred fifty people. Of these, fewer than fifteen are clinically trained. Of those who are clinically trained, less than three would describe themselves as clinicians who specialize in athletes.

In the study by Salmela (1981), mentioned earlier, a slightly different picture was drawn; 17 percent of his 252 North American respondents reported psychology as their major field of study. Another 62 percent came from physical education perspectives, leaving 21 percent reporting neither background. Whiting's rag-bag notion surfaces once again!

The ramifications of such a confused picture for the training of sport psychologists are considerable. Persons interested in the field have far too little commonality in training; on that point, there is agreement. Salmela, in taking this theme one step further, points to a severe deficiency in internship or related field-oriented experiences, particularly among the physical education people in his study, of whom only 21 percent report para-academic training. This figure is about 53 percent for the psychology group. Nideffer et al. (1980) add to this by indicating a failure of most sport psychology programs to provide much training at all in a broad variety of performance enhancement, assessment, intervention, and therapy areas. No major or clear-cut efforts to remedy this shortcoming have thus far emerged.

Granted the aforementioned training shortcomings, some beacons of light out there are giving it their best in an effort to turn out quality sport psychologists. Among them, according to Salmela (1981), are the University of Illinois, University of Wisconsin, Florida State University, Pennsylvania State University, and University of California at Los Angeles, or what Salmela calls *dominant institutions*. At the next echelon are what he calls *supporting universities*, and they are the University of Arizona, University of California (Berkeley), University of California (Davis), and University of Washington. Certainly, these rankings are only those of one individual, John Salmela. All systems of ranking universities and programs are subjective and open to criticism. Too, Salmela's rankings are in danger of becoming dated, though good programs tend to remain so over time. In any event, Salmela has provided an interesting point of departure for a wider discussion of training issues.

Clearly, training issues exist that need attention and resolution in order for the field to grow and prosper. Fortunately, people, programs, and universities are forging ahead in this quest. One group with definite notions about academic training and experiential background is the U.S. Olympic Committee, and a summary of their recommendations is provided in figure 1.3.

Figure 1.3 U.S. Olympic Committee Recommendations for Sport Psychologist Status

A group of sport psychologists met in 1982 to make recommendations to the U.S. Olympic Committee (USOC) concerning appropriate sport psychology practice related to those sports under USOC jurisdiction. They concluded that sport psychologists work in three broad areas—clinical, educational, and research—and the academic and training qualifications they recommended for each were as follows:

Clinical Sport Psychologist
■ Degree in clinical/counseling psychology or psychiatry from an American Psychological Association accredited or Liaison Committee on Medical Education (LCME) accredited university.
■ Meets the standards required for full membership in the American Psychological Association/American Psychiatric Association.
■ Psychologists must have a current license/certification. Psychiatrists must have a current license and be board-eligible in psychiatry. In addition, psychiatrists must be prescreened as having met minimum standards set for physicians engaged in USOC Sports Medicine programs.
■ Demonstrated experience as an athlete or coach or practitioner in the application of psychological principles to sports.
■ A personal interview with a Review Board member(s), if requested.

Educational Sport Psychologist
■ A doctorate in psychology or psychiatry or in a related field with background in psychology that would meet the standards required for full membership in the American Psychological Association.
■ At least three years of demonstrated postdoctoral experience as an athlete or coach or practitioner in the application of psychological principles to sports.
■ Reference letters from recognized institutions/organizations related to the applicant's teaching educational facilitation skills.
■ Personal interview with a Review Board member(s), if requested.

Research Sport Psychologist
■ A doctorate in psychology or psychiatry or in a related field with a background in psychology that would meet the standards required for full membership in the American Psychological Association in accordance with established guidelines.
■ Evidence of scholarly research contributions to the field of sport psychology.
■ Reference letters from recognized institutions/organizations related to research conducted by applicant.
■ A personal interview with a Review Board member(s), if requested.

SOURCE: "USOC Establishes Guidelines for Sport Psychology Services" by U.S. Olympic Committee, 1983, *Journal of Sport Psychology*, 5, 6.

SPORT PSYCHOLOGY PROFESSIONAL ORGANIZATIONS

A growing number of professional organizations represent sport psychologists and, at the same time, work for improving the profession for those who use the various services of the membership. Such concerns as licensure or credentialing, ethics in both research and practice, and training issues occupy a great deal of both time and energy for the leadership in the professional organizations. Eleven rather prominent organizations merit further elaboration; one is international in scope, nine are largely American in membership makeup, and one primarily represents the Canadian sport psychologists.

The International Organization

Many sport psychologists worldwide belong to the *International Society for Sport Psychology (ISSP)*, which was founded in 1965 by Feruccio Antonelli of Italy. ISSP was formed primarily as a forum for sport scientists from all over the world to engage in communication about sport and fitness, and as a means of breaking down some of the more general barriers that exist between people with differing philosophical and political views. To quote Salmela (1981, p. 45): "The ISSP's main contributions have come from its quadrennial conferences and from its publications." The quadrennial conferences have been held in Rome (1965), Washington (1969), Madrid (1973), Prague (1977), Ottawa (1981), and Copenhagen (1985) and have gener-

ated considerable interest among sport psychologists worldwide. ISSP publications are the *International Journal of Sport Psychology* and the *Sport Psychologist,* the latter published in conjunction with Human Kinetics Publishers. In brief, ISSP attempts to bridge the formidable language and political gaps that exist in order to promote the discipline of sport psychology for the world community; in doing so, it serves a most useful purpose.

HIGHLIGHT 1.2

Sport Psychology at the 1984 Olympic Games

Richard Suinn has described the involvement of American sport psychologists in the 1984 Olympics, and a number of interesting conclusions can be drawn from his informal survey of psychologists who worked in a variety of capacities prior to or during those games. First of all, eleven professionals were significantly involved wtih teams or individuals in Alpine skiing, archery and shooting, boxing, cycling, fencing, hunting, Nordic skiing, synchronized swimming, men's track and field, women's track and field, volleyball, and weight lifting. Second, services provided by this diverse cadre of sport psychologists were gratifyingly similar, covering the gamut of performance enhancement techniques as well as some crisis intervention. Interestingly, no one mentioned the use of hypnosis, often thought to be a big part of the sport psychologists' repertoire. A third point concerns responses to these enhancement procedures on the part of coaches and athletes. Anecdotal reports isolated several instances of success attributed to the work of various sport psychologists, but no systematic evaluation was possible. Fourth, and a very significant finding, was that no sport psychologist working the 1984 games was credentialed by the U.S. Olympic Committee; none was therefore able to provide on-site services during the actual competition. This forced several to set up shop outside the Olympic Village; others declined invitations to accompany their respective teams to the games. Sport psychologists from a number of other countries were conspicuous by their continued access to the Olympic Village and their athletes.

From these data, Suinn offers a number of recommendations for improving sport psychology within the U.S. Olympic movement and as a discipline in general. Most of his recommendations center around the dominant issues of communication, credentialing, and training discussed at length in this chapter. In summary, Suinn sees the developments of the 1984 Olympics as a historic moment for sport psychology, one that should result in greater involvement and formal recognition of the sport psychologist within the Olympic movement.

SOURCE: "The 1984 Olympics and Sport Psychology" by R.M. Suinn, 1985, *Journal of Sport Psychology, 7,* 321–329.

American Organizations

An influential national organization to which sport psychologists belong is the *North American Society for the Psychology of Sport and Physical Activity (NASPSPA)*. As of 1987, the organization was composed of 356 professional and 148 student members divided into three specialty areas: sport psychology, motor learning and control, and motor development. NASPSPA originated in 1965 with 10 charter members and has served since that time as a stimulus for professional activity among many American and some Canadian sport psychologists. The regard with which NASPSPA is held is best summarized by Salmela (1981, p. 121): "NASPSPA is the single most influential academic professional society in the world focusing upon the psychology of sport and physical activity."

Another organization of note is the *Association for the Advancement of Applied Sport Psychology (AAASP)*, which was formed through the leadership of John Silva in 1985. As of mid-1986, AAASP has a membership of 235 professionals and 206 students whose primary interest in sport psychology is in theory and research related to intervention and performance enhancement strategies, health psychology, or individual and group processes in sport and exercise settings. AAASP held its first annual national convention in 1986 at Jekyll Island, Georgia, and the interest demonstrated there indicates that AAASP will continue to be a force in shaping the future of sport psychology.

HIGHLIGHT 1.3
NASPSPA/AAASP
Presidents,
1967–1988

A list of the presidents of the North American Society for the Psychology of Sport and Physical Activity (NASPSPA) and the Association for the Advancement of Applied Sport Psychology (AAASP) reads like a Who's Who in American sport psychology, and it attests to the leadership qualities of these dedicated professionals.

NASPSPA		AAASP	
1967–1969	A. T. Slater-Hammel	1986	John Silva
1969–1971	B. J. Cratty	1987	Ronald Smith
1971–1973	E. Dean Ryan	1988	Robert Weinberg
1973–1974	Rainer Martens		
1974–1975	Dorothy Harris		
1975–1976	Don Kirkendall		
1976–1977	Waneen Wyrick Spirduso		
1977–1978	Richard Schmidt		
1978–1979	Harriet Williams		
1979–1980	Robert Christina		
1980–1981	Ronald Marteniuk		
1981–1982	Tara Scanlan		
1982–1983	Glyn Roberts		
1983–1984	Robert Schutz		
1984–1985	Richard Magill		
1985–1986	Daniel Landers		
1986–1987	Mary Ann Roberton		
1987–1988	Craig Wrisberg		

A potentially powerful organization also of recent vintage is the *Division of Exercise and Sport Psychology* within the American Psychological Association (APA). As of 1987, there were 437 APA members affiliated with Division 47. Just what role this division will play in future developments within sport psychology remains to be seen, but it may be a significant one.

The *American College of Sports Medicine (ACSM)* was started in 1953 and now boasts a membership of more than ten thousand scientists from a number of professions concerned with various aspects of sport. Approximately 30 percent of the membership are physicians interested in applying their medical expertise to sport and physical activity. A sizable segment of sport psychologists are members of this organization.

Perhaps 2,000 members of the *American Alliance for Health, Physical Education, Recreation, and Dance (AAHPERD)* report more than a passing interest in sport psychology. The remainder of the AAHPERD membership is devoted to a variety of subinterests within the broad domain of health, physical education, recreation, and dance.

ARENA—The Institute of Sport and Social Analysis is yet another sport-oriented enterprise. It takes a decidedly sociological and social-psychological orientation to the study of sport and publishes two journals dealing with sport and social issues.

The *North American Society for the Sociology of Sport (NASSS)* is made up of over two hundred sport sociologists, social psychologists, and sport scientists in general, all professing an interest in the ramifications of sport in the broader societal context. Speaking to the issue of the relationship between NASPSPA and NASSS and possible territorial concerns, Martens (1979, p. 96) offers the following tongue-in-cheek assessment: "Sport psychology will surely be a healthier field when we recognize that the internal psychological processes that

occur when people engage in sport must be understood within the social context of sport. Thus, rather than making war with sport sociologists, we must make love." Perhaps being friends is good enough!

Another organization of interest is the *North American Society for Sport History (NASSH)*, which has over seven hundred members. NASSH serves as the primary vehicle for scholarly interchange with regard to sport history. Given the relative youthfulness of sport psychology, it follows that we have a short history. Such is not the case with sport in general and NASSH devotes much effort to informing us about the historical perspective. Much of what will follow in chapter 2 is a product of the revelations penned by various members of NASSH.

A final American organization to be discussed is the *North American Society for Sport Management (NASSM)*. This organization held its first annual convention at Kent State University in Ohio in 1986 and attracted more than one hundred professionals interested in various aspects of sport management. Members of NASSM are devoted to the application of management theory and practice to sport, exercise, play, and dance settings. Publication of a journal devoted to sport management commenced in 1987 through the combined efforts of NASSM and Human Kinetics Publishers.

The Canadian Organization

Sport psychology in Canada is promoted primarily through the efforts of the *Canadian Society for Psychomotor Learning and Sport Psychology (CSPLSP)*. CSPLSP was founded in 1969, though it was a part of the Canadian Association for Health, Physical Education, and Recreation (CAHPER) until 1977. At present, CSPLSP represents approximately 125 sport psychologists in Canada (Salmela, 1981) in much the same manner that NASPSPA serves the interests of their American counterparts. Attempts have been made to merge

CSPLSP and NASPSPA, but these efforts have not been successful. Overall, relations between the two organizations remain cordial and cooperative. This cordiality is reinforced in part by the fact that some of the members of CSPLSP are also members of NASPSPA (and vice versa).

Among their other responsibilities, most of the organizations representing sport psychologists publish a journal dedicated to furthering the knowledge base in the world of scientific sport. A list of these as well as other publishers and publications is found in table 1.4.

Table 1.4 Major Sport Journals and Publishers

Sport psychology

Journal of Sport and Exercise Psychology	Human Kinetics Publishers
The Sport Psychologist	Human Kinetics Publishers
Journal of Applied Sport Psychology	Allen Press
Journal of Sport Behavior	University of South Alabama
International Journal of Sport Psychology	International Society for Sport Psychology

Sports medicine

Sports Medicine	ADIS Press International
British Journal of Sports Medicine	The British Association of Sport and Medicine
Medicine and Science in Sports and Exercise	American College of Sports Medicine
The Physician and Sportsmedicine	American College of Sports Medicine
Journal of Sports Medicine and Physical Fitness	Federation International de Medicine Sportive

Physical education

Research Quarterly for Exercise and Sport	McGraw-Hill Publishing Co.
The Physical Educator	Phi Epsilon Kappa
Journal of Physical Education, Recreation and Dance	American Alliance for Health, Physical Education, Recreation and Dance
Quest	Human Kinetics Publishers

Sport sociology

Sociology of Sport Journal	Human Kinetics Publishers
Journal of Sport and Social Issues	ARENA: Center for the Study of Sport in Society, Northeastern University
ARENA Review	ARENA: Center for the Study of Sport in Society, Northeastern University

Canadian

CAHPER Journal	Canadian Association for Health, Physical Education and Recreation
Canadian Journal of Applied Sport Science	Canadian Association of Sport Sciences

Sport history

Journal of Sport History	North American Society for Sport History

Sport management

Journal of Sport Management	Human Kinetics Publishers

Interdisciplinary

Journal of Applied Research in Coaching and Athletics	Academic Library

HIGHLIGHT 1.4
Sport Psychology in
Asia

Though sport psychology is a relatively young discipline, it has firmly established roots in the United States, Canada, and Europe. In Asia, however,
the development of sport psychology has varied considerably from country to country. The summaries here of the status of sport psychology in India
and Japan are based on articles by sport psychologists from those two
countries.

India. Though India has a rich history, of which sport is most certainly
an integral part, sport psychology is clearly a newcomer in that country.
The Indian Association of Sport Psychology was founded in 1977 but died
for lack of support and was replaced in 1985 by the Sport Psychology Association of India. The Netaji Subus National Institute of Sport (NIS) in Patiala
is, according to Bhattacharya, the premier sport institute in all of Asia.
The focus of the NIS has been on preparing elite athletes for international
competition, producing coaches for elite athletes, and related research.
Research topics of primary interest are personality variables, arousal, intelligence, and self-esteem. Other than a small cadre of academics, there are
no private practitioners in India with concentrations in sport psychology.
One ray of hope for the future of sport psychology in India was the creation of a separate sports ministry following the 1982 Asian Games, which
were held in New Delhi.

Japan. Sport psychology in Japan is much more developed than in India.
The roots of sport psychology can be traced back to 1924 with the creation of the National Institute of Physical Education in Tokyo. Though
other significant developments played a role in the evolution of the discipline, the formation of the Japanese Society of Sport Psychology (JSSP)
in 1973 was a major step forward. JSSP now has 210 members. At present,
thirty-one universities or colleges are involved at various levels in the training of sport psychologists. It is now possible to obtain a doctorate in sport
psychology. As in the United States, these doctoral programs are found
almost exclusively in departments of physical education. Mental aspects
of athletic performance are a dominant theme of writing and research in
Japan.

The future. The 1989 conference of the International Society for Sport Psychology (ISSP) scheduled in Singapore represents an attempt on the part
of that august body to bring Asian sport psychologists into a more prominent place in the world sport community. Events such as the 1989 ISSP conference send a clear signal to the rest of the world that Asian sport psychology
is an emerging force.

Sources: "Sport Psychology in India: Current Status and Future Directions" by B. B. Bhattacharya,
1987, *Sport Psychologist, 1,* 161–165; "The Development of Sport Psychology in Japan" by A. H.
Fujita, 1987, *Sport Psychologist, 1,* 69–73; "The Development of Sport Psychological Research in
India" by M. L. Kamlesh and J. Mohan, 1987, *Sport Psychologist, 1,* 257–261.

ORGANIZATION OF THE BOOK

Part One of this book, entitled *Basic Concepts and Behavioral Principles,* is concerned with the issues already discussed to this point, namely attempting to arrive at some degree of closure with regard to what sport is, what sport psychology is, and who may practice the discipline. Another important topic to be addressed in this section will be the history of sport. Sport has a long and fascinating history beginning, for all practical purposes, with the early Greeks. Brief detours into the history of psychology and physical education will also be made. Finally, an intensive discussion of the basic principles of human learning as they relate to sport and physical activity will be conducted. Included in this discussion will be such topics as classical conditioning, operant learning, cognitive learning, anxiety, and intervention and performance enhancement strategies.

Part Two, *Social-Psychological Dimensions,* represents a major thrust of the book. Such topics as attribution theory, need achievement, locus of control, self-concept, leadership, group cohesion, audience effects, and aggression and violence in the realm of sport constitute this portion of the book.

Part Three, *Personality and Assessment,* represents an attempt to look at the interaction between personality theory and research and the measurement of personality traits that may be related to sport performance. In the chapter on personality variables, such topics as sport personology, the high risk athlete, the elite performer, and the black athlete are discussed. With regard to assessment, much of the early sport psychology practice and research involved the measurement of psychological traits and subsequent attempts to relate them to sport performance. Such efforts have fallen into some disrepute. However, an argument can be made

for making better use of assessment techniques that are available as well as creating new and innovative tests in an effort to predict who will and who will not, who can and who cannot, and how selected individuals will perform at any given moment. It is far too early to abandon this potentially viable area of scientific inquiry.

Part Four, *A Wider Perspective,* allows us to take up selected topics not discussed at length earlier in the book. Certainly, the female performer merits attention; it can be argued that a separate consideration is not necessary, but our contention is that the state of development of women in sport is such that a chapter devoted exclusively to the topic is warranted. Another emerging area of interest is youth sport, in which there has been an explosion of theory, research, speculation, and controversy. Too, the psychological variables that impinge on effective coaching will be an important focal point in this section. Finally, a look at sport and physical activity for all would seem to be a logical wrap-up to the book. Millions of recreational joggers, softball players, swimmers, and others take part in health-related activities each day, and there are psychological antecedents and consequences related thereto.

SUMMARY

1. Sport is big business in this country and the world in general, and psychology has much to offer in terms of our understanding of athletic performance and its enhancement and to the general welfare of athletes at all levels of competitiveness.
2. Psychology is defined here as the scientific study of behavior and mental processes, simultaneously emphasizing the necessity for objectively viewing behavioral events and yet recognizing the exis-

tence of inferred but not observable mental events that affect human behavior.

3. Psychologists work in a variety of subspecialties and settings. Those most interested in sport psychology generally are academicians with a clinical, counseling, or educational specialty area. Research remains a central focus for many members of the sport psychology community.

4. Opinions as to what sport itself actually is are plentiful but not universally accepted. Those that emphasize history, explicit rules, formal organization, defined objectives, and achievement through competition seem to be popular. However, we would like to emphasize a "sport for all" approach as a philosophy for this book.

5. Sport psychology is not easily defined or explained. Martens' succinct definition of "sport psychology being what sport psychologists do" is accepted here with several caveats. Dissent with Martens' point of view is not unheard of, and the search for definitional closure goes on.

6. Sport psychologists perform a broad variety of services in academic and athletic settings. They include performance improvement, psychological assessment, communications enhancement, crisis intervention, consultation and program development, and clinical/therapeutic intervention.

7. American sport psychologists spend much of their time in teaching and research activities and in the training of athletes. They see carrying out new research and the interpretation of existing research as important parts of their job definition; they regard talent identification as their lowest priority.

8. A number of lingering problems continue to confront sport psychology, including communication, licensure, credentialing, territoriality, and training.

9. Communication problems persist between psychologists, who often lack academic training in sport science and actual playing or coaching experience, and physical educators, who are generally sophisticated in the academic and experiential aspects of sport but lacking in in-depth psychological training. Too, the failure of applied and research sport psychologists to maintain open lines of communication is problematic.

10. Licensure issues continue to be a source of concern. The state and provincial laws that regulate the independent practice of psychology could eventually cause some difficulties for sport psychologists who are not licensed. At this time, however, it does not appear that such restrictions will pose an immediate problem for sport psychology professionals.

11. Credentialing issues are a continuing source of contention within professional sport psychology organizations; several of them have appointed task forces that hope to establish credentialing standards for sport psychology in the near future.

12. Concern has been expressed that sport psychology may suffer territorial wars between the sport sciences and psychology. However, this does not seem to pose an immediate threat, a point that is substantiated by a recent survey of psychology department heads.

13. The training of sport psychologists is highly variable. Deficiencies in academic-related field experiences for graduate students are numerous. A number of leading academic institutions and the U.S. Olympic Committee offer suggestions for remedying these training shortcomings.

14. The International Society for Sport Psychology (ISSP) is the leading forum for communication among the world sport psychology community. The preponderance of the efforts of ISSP are dedicated to communication through the *International Journal of Sport Psychology* and

through worldwide conferences held every four years since 1965.

15. A number of professional organizations are open to North American sport psychologists; chief among them are the North American Society for the Psychology of Sport and Physical Activity (NASPSPA), the Association for the Advancement of Applied Sport Psychology (AAASP), and Division 47 of the American Psychological Association.

16. Canadian sport psychologists are represented by the Canadian Society for Psychomotor Learning and Sport Psychology (CSPLSP).

SUGGESTED READINGS

Chu, D. (1982) *Dimensions of sport studies.* New York: Wiley.

This book gives the reader an overview of sport psychology, sport sociology, sport history, and the philosophy of sport. It then relates the contributions of these subdisciplines to the rise of sport, women's issues, race and sport, sport and American education, and the Olympic Games.

Higgs, R. (1982) *Sports: A reference guide.* Westport, CN: Greenwood Press.

Chapter 13 in particular offers a brief summary of who the prominent people are, what the relevant information sources are, and a brief bibliography of salient books and articles on psychology of sport.

Leonard, W. (1980) *A sociological perspective on sport.* Minneapolis: Burgess.

Chapter 1 represents a good summary of statistics related to the interest in sport in America. Too, the reader is introduced to a definitional effort and a brief history of sport sociology.

Morgan, W.J. (1983) Toward a critical theory of sport. *Journal of Sport and Social Issues, 7,* 24–34.

Intended for the philosophically inclined, this article is an elaboration of Morgan's views on sport and national interest. Morgan sees sport as

essentially an instrument of the social order whose primary function it is to further the political and economic interests of the nation–states.

Vander Zwagg, H., & Sheehan, T. (1978). *Introduction to sport studies: From the classroom to the ball park.* Dubuque, IA: Wm. C. Brown.

Chapter 9 provides a good summary of what sport psychology is, a little on the history of the field, and what the major areas of research are. Chapter 11 is a unique coverage of career opportunities in the world of sport.

REFERENCES

Alderman, R. (1980) Sports psychology: Past, present, and future dilemmas. In P. Klavora & K. Wipper (Eds.), *Psychological and sociological factors in sport.* (pp. 3–19). Toronto: University of Toronto.

Anderson, B. (1966) *The psychology experiment.* Belmont, CA: Wadsworth.

Atkinson, R.L., Atkinson, R.C., & Hilgard, E. (1983) *Introduction to psychology* (8th ed.). New York: Harcourt Brace Jovanovich.

Brasch, R. (1970) *How did sports begin?* New York: David McKay.

Brown, J.M. (1982) Are sport psychologists really psychologists? *Journal of Sport Psychology, 4,* 13–18.

Browne, M., & Mahoney, M. (1984). Sport psychology. *Annual Review of Psychology, 35,* 605–625.

Cratty, B.J. (1983) *Psychology in contemporary sport* (2nd ed.). Englewood Cliffs, NJ: Prentice-Hall.

Danish, S.J. & Hale, B. (1981) Toward an understanding of the practice of sport psychology. *Journal of Sport Psychology, 3,* 90–99.

Danish, S.J., & Smyer, M. (1981) Unintended consequences of requiring a license to help. *American Psychologist, 36,* 13–21.

Dishman, R.K. (1983) Identity crisis in North American sport psychology: Academics in professional issues. *Journal of Sport Psychology, 5,* 123–134.

Edwards, H. (1973) *Sociology of sport.* Homewood, IL: Dorsey Press.

Gross, S. (1978) The myth of professional licensing. *American Psychologist, 33,* 1009–1016.

Harrison, R., & Feltz, D.L. (1979) The professionalization of sport psychology: Legal considerations. *Journal of Sport Psychology, 1,* 182–190.

Hess, H. (1977) Entry requirements for professional practice of psychology. *American Psychologist, 32,* 365–368.

Heyman, S.R. (1982) A reaction to Danish and Hale: A minority report. *Journal of Sport Psychology, 4,* 7–9.

LeUnes, A., Hayward, S.A., & Bourgeois, A.E. (1988) *Sport psychology: Movement of the 80's or flash in the pan?* Paper presented at annual convention of the North American Society for the Psychology of Sport and Physical Activity, Knoxville, Tennessee.

Martens, R. (1979) About smocks and jocks. *Journal of Sport Psychology, 1,* 94–99.

Martens, R. (1980) From smocks to jocks. A new adventure for sport psychologists. In P. Klavora & K. Wipper (Eds.), *Psychological and sociological factors in sport.* (pp. 20–26). Toronto: The University of Toronto.

Morgan, W.P. (1972) Sport psychology. In R.N. Singer (Ed.), *The psychomotor domain* (pp. 193–228). Philadelphia: Lea and Febiger.

Morgan, W.P. (1980) Test of champions. *Psychology Today,* July, 92–108.

Nideffer, R.M., DuFresne, P., Nesvig, D., & Selder, D. (1980) The future of applied sport psychology. *Journal of Sport Psychology, 2,* 170–174.

Nideffer, R.M., Feltz, D.L., & Salmela, J.H. (1982) A rebuttal to Danish and Hale: A committee report. *Journal of Sport Psychology, 4,* 3–6.

Nixon, H. (1984) *Sport and the American dream.* New York Leisure Press.

Salmela, J.H. (1981) *The world sport psychology sourcebook.* Ithaca, NY: Mouvement Publications.

Singer, R.N. (1976) *Physical education foundations.* New York: Holt, Rinehart and Winston.

Singer, R.N. (1978) Sport psychology: An overview. In W.F. Straub (Ed.), *Sport psychology: An analysis of athletic behavior* (pp. 3–14). Ithaca, NY: Mouvement Publications.

Sleet, D. (1972) Sport psychology. In *Psychosources. The psychology resources encyclopedia.* Del Mar, CA: CRM books.

Spears, B., & Swanson, R. (1983) *History of sport and physical education in the United States* (2nd ed.). Dubuque, IA: Wm. C. Brown.

Tutko, T.A. (1979) The identity of the sport psychologist. In P. Klavora & J.V. Daniel (Eds.), *Coach, athlete, and the sport psychologist* (pp. 40–43). Toronto: University of Toronto.

U.S. Olympic Committee (1983) USOC establishes guidelines for sport psychology services. *Journal of Sport Psychology, 5,* 4–7.

Whiting, H.T.A. (1974) Sports psychology in perspective. In J.D. Brooke (Ed.), *British proceedings of sports psychology* (pp. 1–11), Salford, England: University of Salford.

Zeigler, E.F. (Ed.). (1973) *A history of sport and physical education to 1900.* Champaign, IL: Stipes.

A Historical Perspective on Sport

INTRODUCTION

Sport, no doubt, preceded recorded history. However, the first Olympic Games staged in Greece in 776 B.C. represent an accepted landmark for the continuing inquiry into sport history. Prior to that time, there is only fragmentary evidence for the existence of sport.

Much of what we know about the history of sport is fragmentary and suppositional. *Archeological findings* have yielded mosaics, frescoes, paintings, textiles, works of art and sculptures, architecture, seal stones, ornaments, tablets, and other sources from which we have inferred much about sport history. Too, works such as Homer's *The Iliad* and *The Odyssey* are considered landmark pieces of literature to sport historians. Much later, church records tell us some about sport history in Roman times and beyond. Indeed, a rich legacy of materials exists from which to draw inferences but, in the final analysis, our earliest sport history must be considered suppositional or speculative. In any event, there is a sport history to review.

THE ANCIENT WORLD

Palmer and Howell (1973) indicate that the first archeological evidence for sport and games comes from the *Sumerian civilization* of 3000 to 1500 B.C., a society that arose between the Tigris and Euphrates rivers. Artifacts found there seem to indicate participation in boxing and wrestling events. Board games have also been discovered from this time period.

In reviewing a host of pertinent studies related to the *Egyptian civilization* (3000–1100 B.C.), Palmer and Howell cite evidence for the existence of acrobatics, tumbling, resistance exercise, yoga, tug-of-war, a kicking game, crawling games, and ball games. Simri (1973) mentions some evidence as early as 1500 B.C. for the existence of ball games. He cites a relief showing what appears to be a pharaoh holding a bat and ball (while two priests await a catch), knife throwing, wrestling, the swinging of weights, swimming, board games, and a host of other activities indicative of considerable emphasis having been placed on sport and physical activity by the early Egyptians. An inference made from findings in various tombs is that these activities were viewed as more suitable for the nobility, namely, kings, pharaohs, and noblemen. However, poor people did not leave tombs and artifacts to be pored over, so little is known about whether, in truth, only the nobility engaged in these activities and what their attitudes might have been about sport and games for the economically less fortunate.

Evidence from *ancient China* is supportive of the existence of sports. According to Sasijima (1973), ancient Chinese history begins around 1700 B.C. and can be broken into four dynasties as follows: Yin, 1700–1100 B.C.; Chou, 1100–256 B.C.; Chin, 221–207 B.C.; and Han, 202 B.C.–A.D. 8, A.D. 25–221. Of particular relevance to our discussion of sport history is the *stage of Chou*; as part of the proper education of its young people at that time, children were expected to be trained in the *six virtues* (wisdom, benevolence, goodness, righteousness, loyalty, and harmony), in the *six good actions* (honoring parents, being friendly to brothers, polite to relatives by marriage, neighborly, trustful, and sympathetic), and the *six arts* (rituals, music, archery, charioteering, writing, and mathematics) (Zeigler, 1973b). However, it appears that Chinese enthusiasm for physical activity was tempered in part because of the more quiet, cerebral, studious nature of the dominant religions in the East, namely, Taoism, Buddhism, and Confucianism. However, the founder of Buddhism, Prince Siddhartha (later known as Buddha) was, according to Rajagopalan (1973, p. 51), a "sportsman of no mean order." The prince was said to have excelled in a number of games and sports.

Rajagopalan further informs us that there is evidence in *India* for the existence of hunting, fishing, archery, wrestling, boxing, the javelin throw, running, swimming, jumping, digging, and dancing as early as 1500 B.C. As food for thought, he also mentions that marbles dating back to Neolithic times have been unearthed. Whether these marbles were used for recreation purposes, as weapons, or were valued for their aesthetic properties is most certainly not known.

A significant contribution to our understanding of sports in antiquity was made by the unearthing of the *Palace of Minos* in 1871. The Minoan times ran from roughly 3000 to 1200 B.C., and Minoans were people living on the isle of Crete during that period. Significant evidence was obtained from a variety of sources that points to the existence of such activities as tumbling, acrobatics, dancing, boxing, wrestling, hunting, archery, running, swimming, table games, sailing, and a host of so-called "taureador" sports (Howell, 1969; Palmer and Howell, 1973). The "taureador" sports are those that relate to bull grappling, bull vaulting, and other possible acrobatic events involving the bull. Bull grappling we now, of course, recognize as steer wrestling in our modern day rodeo! The "taureador" sports were apparently so dominant with the Minoans that Palmer and Howell (1973, p. 69) say: "The representations of the bull games far outnumber any other games in the Minoan period. The bull is a common subject of Minoan artists, and is shown to us on seal stones, frescoes, rhytons, plaster reliefs, bronze, rings, pendants, and vases." A particularly revealing source of information, and a neglected one, has been the seal stones that were essentially carved or engraved on clay. Not all dealt with physical activity but

Howell (1969) found twenty-five in the Ashmolean collection at Oxford University that were related to the various events suggested earlier.

THE GREEK CONTRIBUTION

Though the subject of considerable debate among historians, it appears that the Minoan civilization was destroyed by the Mycenaeans, or early Greeks, around 1400 B.C. Some two hundred years later, the Mycenaeans attacked and destroyed Troy. The Mycenaeans in turn, were vanquished by the Dorians. With the ascent to power of the Dorians, a "dark age" in Greek history began. Much of what we do know about the Dorian era has been generated by the epics and stories of and about the period, not the least of which were those by a blind Ionian poet named *Homer*. The writings of Homer have led sport history authorities (for example, Harris, 1973; Van Dalen, Mitchell, and Bennett, 1953; and Zeigler, 1973a, among others) to refer to this period, roughly 1200 to 700 B.C., as the *Homeric Age*. In actuality, Van Dalen et al. see the Homeric period in Greek history as running from prehistoric times to 776 B.C., the time of the first Greek Olympiad. They further break Greek history into the following three periods:

1. *Early Athenian.* This encompassed the period from 776 B.C. to the end of the Persian War in 480 B.C.
2. *Spartan.* This ran throughout the history of Sparta, roughly from the eighth century B.C. to the Macedonian conquest in 338 B.C.
3. *Later Athenian.* This was the period from 480 B.C. to the ultimate conquest of the Greek city–states by the Macedonians in 338 B.C. Except for its later stages, this has been called the "Golden Age of Greece."

Homeric Greece

Homer is believed to have written *The Iliad* and *The Odyssey* around 850 B.C. He essentially took various tales and legends transmitted by word of mouth and created our earliest documented literature. As a result, much of what is known about Greek life at the time of the Trojan War (1194–1184 B.C.), a ten-year struggle between the Greeks and the Trojans of Troy, is attributable to Homer. *The Iliad* has been called variously a "classic epic of war" (Stull, 1973, p. 121) and the "basic source of the Greek concept of manhood" (Stull and Lewis, 1968). These writers further suggest that *The Iliad* indeed is the first written account for sport historians to peruse. One of the unique features of *The Iliad* is its description of the so-called *funeral games,* so named because they were started by Achilles in honor of his slain companion and friend, Patroclus. The games were called to give the involved warriors a brief respite from war and to lift their mourning through physical competition. Such activities as wrestling, boxing, archery, chariot racing, sword fighting, javelin and discus throwing, and footracing characterized the funeral games.

As for *The Odyssey*, it recounts the trials and tribulations of Odysseus, a Greek hero at the battle of Troy who was absent from his Ithaca home for twenty years. The final forty-one pages are rich in information for the sport historian. Wrestling and boxing are prominently mentioned, as is an amalgam of the two, an event known as the *pankration* (pancratium). Harris (1972) parallels the pankration to judo while Binfield (1948) and Hackensmith (1966) interpret it as quite similar to jujitsu. Henry (1976) says that if historians are correct in their interpretation of the event, it "more closely resembles a gutter brawl than an athletic event" (p. 16). Also mentioned in *The Odyssey* are the diskos (discus) or weight throw, the javelin, ball games, the footrace, and archery.

Despite their allegedly apocryphal nature, *The Iliad* and *The Odyssey* must be regarded as brilliant works that have greatly contributed to our understanding of ancient Greece and its many facets, one very important aspect of which was sport. The ancient Greeks placed much value on sporting and physical activities, and their love for them influenced generations of Greeks, Romans, Macedonians, and others who were to follow them historically.

The Early Athenians

Nowhere can this reverence for sport and competition be better viewed than in the concept of the Olympic Games, first held in Olympus in 776 B.C. The initial games consisted of the *stadion*, or single course race, and they continued that way until the fourteenth Olympiad in 724 B.C., at which time a double course race, the *diaulos*, was added. A long course race, the *dolichos*, was added in 720 B.C., and wrestling and the pentathlon were added during the eighteenth games in 708 B.C. Twenty years later, boxing was added. The twenty-fifth Olympiad (680 B.C.) saw the addition of chariot racing. In the thirty-third games, horse racing and the pankration were added. In the sixty-fifth games (520 B.C.) the race in armor was included and, with minor variants, the games were to remain pretty much the same until their demise some one thousand years later (Yalouris, 1979). Hackensmith and Yalouris summarize the typical Olympic events from 520 B.C. to the end in A.D. 394 in table 2.1.

The early Olympic Games were characterized by *several unique features*. One is that the only material award for winners was a *crown of wild olive leaves*. However, Olympic heroes were greatly admired for their skills and the fame they brought to their home states, and rewards above and beyond the olive leaf crown were most certainly given to the top athletes once they returned to their homes upon completion of the games. Another interesting feature is that

Table 2.1 Typical Olympics, 520 B.C. to A.D. 394

Three combat events	Four running events	Pentathlon
Boxing	200 yards	Javelin
Wrestling	400 yards	Discus
Pankration	Distance	Long jump
	Race in armor	200-yard race
		Wrestling

SOURCE: *History of Physical Education* (pp. 43-50) by C. Hackensmith, 1966, New York: Harper & Row; *The Eternal Olympics: The Art and History of Sport* (pp. 155-231), edited by N. Yalouris, 1979, New Rochelle, NY: Caratzas Brothers, Pub.

HIGHLIGHT 2.1
Evolution of Events
of Early Olympic
Games

1st Olympiad (776 B.C.):	**Stadion (single course race)**
14th Olympiad (724 B.C.):	**Diaulos (double course race)**
15th Olympiad (720 B.C.):	**Dolichos (long course race)**
18th Olympiad (708 B.C.):	**Pentathlon and wrestling**
23d Olympiad (688 B.C.):	**Boxing**
25th Olympiad (680 B.C.):	**Tethrippon (four-horse chariot race)**
33d Olympiad (648 B.C.):	**Horse race and pankration (combination of boxing and wrestling)**
37th Olympiad (632 B.C.):	**Boys' footrace and wrestling**
38th Olympiad (628 B.C.):	**Boys' pentathlon (only for this Olympiad)**
41st Olympiad (616 B.C.):	**Boys' boxing**
65th Olympiad (520 B.C.):	**Race in armour**
70th Olympiad (500 B.C.):	**Apene (race of chariots drawn by two mules) (abandoned in the 84th Olympiad)**
93d Olympiad (408 B.C.):	**Synoris (two-horse chariot race)**
96th Olympiad (396 B.C.):	**Competitions for trumpeters and heralds**
99th Olympiad (384 B.C.):	**Tethrippon for foals**
128th Olympiad (268 B.C.):	**Synoris for foals**
131st Olympiad (256 B.C.):	**Foals' race**
145th Olympiad (200 B.C.):	**Boys' pankration**

SOURCE: *The Eternal Olympics: The Art and History of Sport* (p. 84), edited by N. Yalouris, 1979, New Rochelle, NY: Caratzas Brothers, Pub.

This detail from a sixth century B.C. vase painting reveals two characteristics of the Olympic games in ancient Greece: no women and no uniforms.

contestants after the fifteenth games (720 B.C.) *competed in the nude.* Harris (1972) offers two plausible explanations for what may seem to be an oddity to those of us of more modest inclinations. One is that in Homeric Greece, nude competition was not in vogue, but one runner lost his shorts in the middle of a race and proceeded to win handily, thereby setting a trend for his colleagues. Perhaps superstitious behavior is not the invention of the modern athlete! A second explanation has to do with a runner losing his shorts, an event that caused him to trip. He was killed in the subsequent fall, thereby causing the presiding magistrate to ban shorts for the remainder of that and later games. Neither explanation seems to overpower the other, and so readers may choose whichever pleases them most.

A third interesting feature of the early competition was the *stadium* itself. Archaeological evidence indicates that the typical Greek stadium was rectangular, perhaps 200 yards long and 25 to 40 yards wide, with a turning post at each end. Longer runs added to the Olympic Games in 724 and 720 B.C. required the contestants to make a series of abrupt turns at each end of the stadium. This was particularly true of the long event added in 720 B.C., which has been reported to be 2 to 3 miles (Binfield, 1978), or as long as 3,850 meters (Yalouris, 1979), and approximately a mile or perhaps even longer (Henry, 1976).

A final aspect of note is that *women were not allowed to participate* or, in most instances, even view the activities. Exceptions apparently were made in cases of virgins, who were allowed to be spectators. The penalty for violating this prohibition was to be flung from the highest cliffs of Mount Typaion (Yalouris, 1979). The one instance in which a female could be awarded an Olympic prize was in the equestrian events; owners rather than riders were crowned as victors.

The Spartan Period

The *Spartans*, according to Yalouris (1979), probably never numbered more than five thousand men. (Van Dalen et al. place the number at nine thousand). Yet they were a dominant military force for several centuries, an attestation

---

HIGHLIGHT 2.2
Milos of Kroton

The athletic world has a penchant for elevating its heroes to larger-than-life proportions, and the ancient Greeks apparently were no exception. The legendary wrestler, Milos of Kroton, represents a case in point. Milos (also variously cited as Milo and Milon) lived in Kroton, a Greek colony on the Italian boot, during the sixth century B.C. Milos won six consecutive Olympic wrestling championships from 536 to 512 B.C.; in addition, he was victorious in an additional twenty-six instances at the Isthmian, Nemean, and Pythian games, giving him a total of thirty-two national titles during his wrestling career.

As might be suspected, much folklore surrounded this heroic figure. Unbelievable feats of strength and equally unfathomable gastronomic excesses were attributed to him. Legend has it that Milos once carried a bull (or heifer) around the stadium at Olympia, slew it with his fists, and devoured it in its entirety before the day was over. Milos was also said to have eaten twenty loaves of bread at one meal; in another instance, he consumed the equivalent of nine liters of wine in a short time in order to win a bet.

In addition to his feats of strength and gastronomic excess, Milos was a student of Pythagoras and wrote a number of scholarly treatises of some importance. Too, he took up arms on occasion in order to defend Kroton from its enemies and was said to have been heroic in battle.

Milos' strength ultimately did him in. He apparently ventured one day into a nearby forest and noticed a partially cut tree which held the wedges that had been driven into it earlier. Milos tried to topple the tree, but managed only to get his hands trapped where the wedges once were. Unable to extricate himself from his inadvertent but self-imposed trap, Milos was attacked and killed by wild beasts.

SOURCES: *How Did Sports Begin? A Look at the Origins of Man at Play* (p. 398) by R. Brasch, 1970, New York: Davis McKay; "Perspective" by E. Burns, 1985, *Sports Illustrated*, Dec. 2, p. 8–12; *Sports in Greece and Rome* (pp. 71, 143) by H. Harris, 1972, Ithaca, NY: Cornell University Press; "Muscular Vegetarianism: The Debate Over Diet and Athletic Performance in the Progressive Era" by J. C. Whorton, 1981, *Journal of Sport History, 8*(2), 58–75; *The Eternal Olympics: The Art and History of Sport* (pp. 266–267) edited by N. Yalouris, 1979, New Rochelle, NY: Caratzas Brothers, Pub.

tion to their desire to produce the perfect warrior.

The Spartans lived among a group of slaves or serfs known as helots, numbering perhaps as high as 250,000, and unrest among these helots as well as the threat of outside invasion made it necessary for the Spartans to be fit and prepared for combat. Their excessive emphasis on militarism was undoubtedly warranted!

Physical activity to the Spartans was seen to be of value only in terms of its contribution to this *perfect warrior* concept. Unlike the Athenians, who saw physical competition as a beautiful and harmonious extension of oneself, the Spartans subjugated personal goals and achievements in order for the city–state (Sparta) to survive. In effect, there is a selflessness here that speaks well for the Spartan point of view.

Lest one thinks that the Spartan search for the perfect warrior was a narrow and one-sided effort, it should be noted that the Spartans were very successful in Olympic competition. Yalouris tells us that the first apparent Spartan victor was Akanthos, who won the *dolichos* (long course race) in the fifteenth Olympiad (720 B.C.). Further, eighty-one winners in the games between 720 and 576 B.C. were Spartans. Twenty-one of the thirty-six winners of the *stadion* (single course race) were Spartans. Interestingly, it was the Spartans who introduced nakedness among the Olympic competitors and also the practice of anointing themselves with oil prior to competition, a ritual that became quite common in later games.

In order for the Spartan citizen to meet the demands of the perfect warrior concept, training began early. At birth, children were taken before their elders for judgment, and the sickly were left on Mount Taygetus to die or be rescued by slaves (Hackensmith, 1966; Van Dalen et al., 1953). Spartan males were educated at home until their seventeenth birthday, at which time they became wards of the city–state for gradual training in the arts of manhood and good citizenship. Military training was inten-

sified each year and actual engagement in combat was not unusual by age twenty. A big part of all this preparation, of course, was in the physical domain. The Spartan citizen-soldier was expected to engage daily in a regimen of physical exercise until age thirty. At age fifty, retirement was allowed if military conditions were favorable for such an action. In addition to military training, a rather exacting regimen of diet and clothing was imposed. The boys went barefoot, wore the same tunic all year irrespective of hot or cold weather, and were fed meager rations. Stealing to supplement the diet was encouraged, as craftiness in such matters would be valued militarily. Bathing was not acceptable though swimming in nearby rivers or streams was apparently condoned. Beatings and flogging were commonplace as a means of character training.

Women were less regimented than men but were expected to take part in physical activities of a public nature until age twenty. At all times, women were expected to place a premium on personal fitness and appearance. Their exercise program was similar to that of the young men, that is, wrestling, javelin, discus, running, jumping, dancing, and a host of other conditioning games.

The fascination with fitness, competition, and militarism was not without cost. Rice, Hutchinson, and Lee (1969, p. 17) sum it up well:

> The Spartan system of physical and military training obtained the desired results: the army was the best in the world. Spartans never made the mistake of substituting specialization in athletics for the ultimate goal of specialization for war. For this pre-eminent military position they sacrificed personal liberty, individualism, home life, and the achievements of peace. Sparta did not contribute great drama, immortal verse, models of architecture, and inimitable sculpture but left such accomplishments to her more cultured neighbor, Athens.

Adding support to Rice and his colleagues is a statement from Forbes:

> The Spartan system of physical education achieved its limited aim and in that sense was a resounding success. Nearly every Spartan could glory in a splendid physique and in health unequaled elsewhere in Greece. Spartan courage, tenacity, and obedience were proverbial. If the battle of Waterloo was won on the playing-fields of Eton, surely Sparta's many battles were won on the playing-fields by the River Eurotas. Speaking of New Hampshire, Daniel Webster once said, "The Granite State makes men." Sparta made men.
>
> But the cost was high. Sparta deliberately neglected the education of the mind. In a country astonishingly rich in philosophers, Sparta had none. Poets were few—none of note after the seventh and sixth centuries. Books that deal in generalizing terms with the cultural contribution of Greece have little to say about Sparta. Such were the results of a one-sided educational system in the world's first totalitarian state. (1973, p. 138)

The Later Athenians

The later Athenian period, particularly the earliest portion, has been referred to as the *"Golden Age of Greece."* With the rather amazing defeat of a seemingly superior Persian army in 480 B.C., nearly fifty years of peace and unprecedented growth began. The city–state concept was in full force and was most effective; Sparta had achieved great status as a military power and Athens had become a mecca for artists, poets, writers, and the intelligentsia in general. Greece became, as a result of the Persian War and the ensuing good times, about as cohesive a "nation" as it ever had been in the past or would be in the future. A spirit of unity prevailed! In Athens, a greater expansion of the concept of democratic government gave the masses a larger say in matters related to their welfare. The base of wealth was ever-expanding and many citizens of Athens profited from this

economic bonanza. Tremendous emphasis in Athenian education was placed on greater enhancement of individual freedom, a fact that has not gone unchallenged as a contributor to the eventual fall of the Greek civilization.

Physical education became a matter of self-enhancement and self-expression; the utilitarian aspects of physical and military preparedness were overlooked. The individual took precedence over the welfare of the state. Rampant professionalism dominated sporting events, thereby encouraging spectatorism rather than participation. Amusement of the masses became preeminent. Plato (427–347 B.C.), a student of Socrates (470?–399 B.C.) and a leading social critic of his time, was particularly outspoken in his views of the decline of Greek values. He saw the real value of physical activity to lie in its moral education properties. Also, he was quite opposed to the professionalization of athletes. In any event, life was good for the Athenian of that period and the gradual softening of the city–state fiber went largely unnoticed until it was too late.

Prosperity was not to prevail for long. Athens, under the influence of Pericles, became involved in wars of aggression with other city–states, a situation that was to persist over a period of twenty-seven years beginning in 431 B.C. Eventually, the Spartans prevailed over the Athenians, who fell under Spartan domination. Meanwhile, a costly internecine conflict between the various city–states under Spartan rule and the Spartans themselves led to a rebellion in which the Spartans fell to a coalition army of city–states led by Thebes. The Spartans were subdued in 371 B.C., ending almost a century of Panhellenic internal conflict. This costly, long-term war rekindled the spirits of the aggressive Persians. In order to deal with this threat, Phillip II (382–336 B.C.), king of Macedonia in northern Greece, invaded what was left of the vulnerable Spartans and Athenians, thereby bringing them under Macedonian domination. The Greek empire

HIGHLIGHT 2.3
Quotes About Sport and Exercise from Prominent Men of the Early Greek Period

Socrates: "No citizen has a right to be an amateur in the matter of physical training; it is a part of his profession as a citizen to keep himself in good condition, ready to serve his state at a moment's notice."

Plato: "Gymnastics as well as music should receive careful attention in childhood and continue through life."

Plutarch: "The exercise of the body must not be neglected; but children must be sent to schools of gymnastics. This will conduce partly to a more handsome carriage and partly to an improvement of their strength."

Euripides: "Of all the countless evils through Hellas, there is none worse than the race of Athletes."

Aristotle: "The education of the body must precede that of the intellect."

Galen: "He is the best physician who is the best teacher of gymnastics."

SOURCE: *A Brief History of Physical Education* (5th ed., pp. 26–27), by E. Rice, J. Hutchinson, and M. Lee, 1969, New York: Ronald.

effectively came to an end in 338 B.C. The legacy it provided, however, would influence sport and physical activity throughout the next seven hundred years and, ultimately, throughout the broader historical context.

While preparing to deal with the ominous Persians, King Phillip was assassinated and his son, Alexander the Great (356–323 B.C.), took charge of the Macedonians. Though only twenty-three years old, he was able to marshal forces that not only dealt effectively with the Persians but were able to conquer Asia Minor, Egypt, and India. Alexander was consolidating his empire when he was stricken with a disease that took his life at the age of thirty-four. Significantly, in his eleven-year odyssey sports and competition and Greek culture in general were spread far and wide by his troops. Alexander himself was reportedly a good athlete, although he seldom competed because he felt that kings should compete only against other royalty. As his conquests grew, so did the Hellenization of the lands to the east, and soon sport arenas and athletic festivals sprang up in profusion.

THE ROMANS

By 500 B.C. there were two thriving civilizations in Italy, the *Etruscan* and the *Greek*. The Greeks occupied, as part of their expansionism policy, the southern part of Italy, while the Etruscans occupied that part of Italy generally north of the Tiber River. Little is known of the origin of the Etruscans and none of their literature has survived; what we know of them comes from the Roman and Greek writers and from the elaborate and ornately decorated tombs in which the Etruscans buried their dead.

Wall paintings and sculptured reliefs clearly indicate that the Etruscans held the Greeks in high esteem and were attracted to their love of sport. Harris (1972) tells us that the Etruscans did not slavishly follow the Greek sporting traditions as exemplified by the fact that their athletes apparently competed in shorts. Too, they possessed more of a streak of cruelty as indicated by their interest in gladiatorial fights and what Harris calls wild beast shows. Howell and Sawula (1973) point out that the most popular activity for the Etruscans was chariot racing, but dance, music, javelin, discus, boxing, wrestling, jumping, running, horse racing, acrobatics, and table games were also significant to them. They make no mention of the wild beast shows mentioned by Harris, and so no firm conclusion can be drawn about the importance or even the presence of such events. The Etruscans ceased to be a major power by the end of the fourth century B.C., but their influence on the Romans was considerable.

In 500 B.C. no one could have envisaged the *Romans* dominating the Mediterranean world within three hundred fifty years. In a long series of acts of aggression against their neighbors, including the Etruscans, the Romans enhanced their base of power. By 275 B.C. they had dominated their neighbors and set up a city–state rule that would have been the envy of the less unified Greeks. Corsica, Sicily, Sardinia, and Spain came under Roman rule in the Punic Wars. Finally in 146 B.C., the Greeks fell to the Romans.

By the time the Greeks fell, much of their creative genius had degenerated. The energetic, industrious Romans, at the peak of their power and prosperity, revived much of this lost vitality. Van Dalen et al. (1953) draw a nice comparison between the people of the two cultures:

> The Latin possessed a serious, industrious personality and a natural executive ability. On the other hand, he lacked the sparkling, aesthetic genius and the capacity for deep philosophical contemplation of the Greek. The empire builders were not proficient in pure art forms, did not fashion new lights of philosophical thought, or evolve new concepts of scientific truths. Nevertheless, the Western world is deeply indebted to the Romans for their practical contributions to mankind. Although the Greeks were the more profound and versatile thinkers, the Romans were the more energetic and efficient "doers." (P. 76)

For the early Romans, particularly in those years of military conquest, physical education was aimed at producing a better soldier. The Greek preoccupation with aesthetics, grace, beauty, and harmony was looked upon as a bit frivolous and not at all conducive to developing toughness and strength of character. Unlike the Spartan youth educated in military barracks or the Athenian educated in the gymnasium, the Roman child was constantly under parental tutelage. Around age seventeen, the males were expected to join the military service for a period of thirty years. At all times, physical fitness was expected. Work at activities (i.e., farming) that were intrinsically physically taxing contributed to fitness, but it remained the responsibility of the family to insure the fitness of their offspring.

Popular activities at the time included table games, ball games, horse races, chariot races, dancing, running, jumping, fencing, and javelin throwing. Of particular interest were the ball games. Roman youth appear to have engaged in an early version of what is now known as handball. The name used for the game was *harpastum*, also known as *phaininda* (Van Dalen et al., 1953; Young, 1944). Evidence indicates that involved youths would hit a ball with an open hand against a wall for the eventual return by one or more other competitors.

As the Roman Empire expanded, a period of great prosperity was achieved. People had more money and leisure time than in the past, and their demand for leisure activities increased. Self-serving individualism, unrest among the masses, governmental corruption, outright despotism, and a decay in morality and religious values were at work in creating the rottenness that would eventually doom the proud Romans.

Physical fitness took on a new look. Professionalization of both the military and the athletes led to a rather fragmented philosophy about the whole issue. Fitness for the military

"Thumbs down!" is the crowd's verdict in this nineteenth century interpretation of gladiatorial combat in ancient Rome. Insatiable Romans continually sought variations on their bloodthirsty theme: dual combat was soon replaced by battles involving hundreds of gladiators and later by combat between humans and wild animals.

and for athletes seemed sensible, but little incentive was seen by the ordinary citizen for more than the most cursory fitness. The Romans, like the Greeks earlier, became spectators rather than participants.

The ever-increasing decay of national values and the lowered emphasis on participation led to events that appealed to many Romans, events that still serve as measures of how decadent a society can become. A small indicator can be found in the general rejection of Greek sporting tradition by the Romans. As an example, running, throwing, and jumping were generally boring to the Romans, but wrestling, boxing, and the pankration were more exciting. To

enhance the thrill of boxing, the gloves were "enhanced" by adding pieces of lead or iron, and two or three potentially lethal spikes were added to the glove knuckles. One of the more dramatic events was *chariot racing*. Though conceived in a high spirit, it reached new depths in Rome. Cheating, pushing, cutting in front of opponents, and hitting opponents when possible were all acceptable behaviors. Because of the nature of the various dangerous sports engaged in by the Romans, there were many injuries and deaths. Substantial gambling added to the drama of these events (and perhaps the decadence). Race drivers, perhaps above all others, were revered in all of Rome;

Rice et al. (1969) tells us that if a slave somehow became a highly successful driver, he was given freedom. If a free man, he was given monetary rewards. *Diocles,* a Spaniard, was cited as an example of what could lie in store for the successful driver (called an auriga). Diocles won the equivalent of almost $2 million over a twenty-four-year period in which he won 1,462 of 4,257 races!

A step up in appeal to our most primitive side and a step down in terms of the values of sportsmanship was the *gladiatorial event.* Though these events were popular among the Etruscans, the Romans did not revive them until the middle of the second century B.C. At first, the gladiatorial competition was restricted and was conducted for the entertainment of the wealthy and engaged in primarily by prisoners of war who preferred risking death to slavery. However, demand became so high that schools for gladiators were instituted, and professionalization of the combat was under way. As time went on, watching two combatants fight it out to the death was not enough, so new wrinkles were added. Scores of men were pitted against each other; the arena was flooded and mock naval battles were staged in which many were killed; wild animals were brought in and killed

---

HIGHLIGHT 2.4
Nero as Athlete

The typical perception of the character of the Roman emperor, Nero, is quite negative; almost invariably, his name is associated with evil. Stories about his propensities for cruelty, both true and apocryphal, do him no favor; this is particularly true where the early Christians were concerned. However, it is the contention of Mouratidis that historical accounts of the life of Nero are distorted because they have been written almost exclusively by his enemies, hardly an impartial panel. His negative image has been furthered by the fact that he avidly embraced the Greek love and admiration for athletic glory, thereby offending many Romans who were not Christians. The combination of offending both the Christians and the Roman power structure led, according to Mouratidis, to a less than objective accounting of Nero's behavior.

Nero was born in A.D. 37, ascended to power as emperor seventeen years later, and died at age thirty in the year A.D. 68. During his short reign, he tried to Hellenize sport (and Roman life in general) by bringing it into line with earlier Greek philosophy and practice. He instituted schools for athletic participants and masterminded the construction of a magnificent gymnasium for athletic expression. Nero also attempted to humanize the gladiatorial event by ruling that no combat be conducted to the death of one of the participants. As a participant himself, Nero was fascinated with chariot racing and wrestling, events in which he apparently made periodic public appearances, much to the chagrin of the ruling class and to the glee of the proletariat in Rome. This catering to the masses while offending both the ruling class in Rome and the increasingly numerous and powerful Christians, in the name of Hellenizing sport and the arts in Rome, played a role in his ultimate demise, both physically and historically.

SOURCE: "Nero: The Artist, the Athlete, and His Downfall" by J. Mouratidis, 1985, *Journal of Sport History, 12,* 5–20.

by their natural predators; eventually men and animals were pitted against each other. These latter two events were named the *venationes*, or the hunt for wild beasts.

The Roman Empire began in 31 B.C. and ended in A.D. 476, a period of more than five hundred years. The decline of the Roman Empire, according to Rice et al. (1969), can be attributed to a number of interrelated factors. Depopulation due to a lowered birth rate brought about by instability of the institution of marriage, gladiatorial game deaths, incessant civil wars, and a high suicide and homicide rate all were instrumental in weakening the structure of the civilization. Add general physical and moral decay and economic ruin to the preceding liabilities and all the ingredients for decline are present. Too, the rise in influence of Christianity was a factor of considerable importance. The final nail was driven in the Roman Empire coffin by the Teutonic barbarian invaders from Northern Europe.

THE MIDDLE AGES

With the fall of Rome, a period of historical darkness began. Not until the discovery of the New World one thousand years later was the darkness essentially lifted.

One beacon of brightness in the gathering twilight of culture was found in the *Byzantine Empire* to the east. Much of the Greek culture, language, and love of sport had been preserved in Constantinople. At the same time, much of the Roman approach to law and governance was subscribed to. Christianity was the dominant religion of the Byzantines. Obviously, they borrowed from the Greeks, Romans, and Christians alike. The Byzantine Empire endured from approximately the fourth century A.D. to 1453, when Constantinople fell to invading forces.

Among the favorite activities of the Byzantines was chariot racing, an activity that was to last until the twelfth century. Much of what was done in Constantinople was copied from the model provided by the Romans. To quote Schrodt (1981, p. 44): "Chariot races were the most important events in the life of the ordinary Byzantine citizen, and race days were occasions for excessive gambling, roistering, eating, and shouting—providing a particular kind of excitement and entertainment not available to him in any other facet of his life." Shades of our Super Bowl weekend!

The hippodrome in which the chariot races were held was also used for public executions. Understandably, the Christian leaders were not fond of any of the proceedings in the hippodrome, whether races or executions.

By the fifth century A.D. the Byzantines had lost their fascination with gladiatorial contests and *venationes*, and these activities ceased to be. Schrodt indicates that even at their acme, the *venationes* of the Byzantines appeared to be more acrobatic and less sadistic and cruel than the Roman versions.

Within the Byzantine time and territorial purview came the *demise of the Olympic Games*. It is generally agreed that Theodosius I (346?–395) decreed that the games be ended in 394 because of what he viewed as pagan idolatry. The games were not to take place again until 1896, a period of more than one thousand five hundred years. Theodosius, himself a Christian, felt that the games glorified the paganism of body worship associated with the Greeks and should be abolished. This assertion by Theodosius has led Brasch (1970, p. 414) to say: "While one religion had given birth to the Olympic Games, in the name of another they were destroyed."

In the West, the barbaric Teutons were establishing themselves; during the fifth century, the Visigoths occupied Spain, the Vandals seized North Africa, Gaul came under the domination of the Franks and Burgundians, and the Anglo-Saxons took over Britain. The result of this influx of barbarians was the creation of an intellectual vacuum in a previously cultured world; language and learning languished. Civilization as it was known at that time was in decline. The barbarians lived in crude dwellings, wore equally crude clothes, and were essentially farmers and herders of sheep and cattle. What these invaders lacked in language and worldly sophistication, however, was compensated for by a stable family life, industriousness, physical vitality, and intense loyalty to friends and an equal capacity for cruelty to those whom they disliked. The barbarians infused a physical vigor into the decadent Roman life. The Teutons were to eventually acquire the more aesthetic skills for which the Romans and, more particularly, the Greeks were known, and the combination of physical vitality and intellectual growth created a backdrop for the development of Western Europe and, ultimately, the New World. Many of us in the Western Hemisphere are descendants of these early barbarians.

While the barbarians were dominant in the West and the Byzantines were a force to reckon with in the East, a movement of major influence was itself showing strength, and this was *Christianity*. Most of the early Christians were unshakable in their belief in Jesus as savior; they believed strongly in a better life hereafter, and suffering in this life was immaterial or expected. Martyrdom in the name of Christianity was a virtue. These Christians also firmly rejected the debauchery and degradation of the Romans; they felt that life was best lived in service to the soul, not the body. This early belief pattern was to have profound repercussions for physical activity for more than one thousand years, and even today we find people who are guilt-ridden if they have a good time, as if there were something evil about worldly pleasures.

Because their belief patterns ran counter to the licentiousness of the Romans, many Chris-

tians suffered indignities and cruelties that only served to reinforce rather than dissipate their piety. The end result of much of this piety was an increasing disenchantment with the physical side of man, and nowhere is this better seen than in the extremism of the *ascetics* of the early Middle Ages, which roughly covered the period from the sixth to tenth centuries. The ascetics personified the ultimate in Christian rejection of bodily worship and, conversely, the acceptance of sacrifice and suffering. The ascetics lived as hermits in caves or other primitive surroundings where suffering could be maximized; they fasted, prayed, and meditated; they tormented themselves with physical discomfort by sleeping on beds of nails or by beating themselves into exhaustion. It is no small wonder that their fanaticism often led them to bizarre behavior fed by hallucinations brought on by the interaction of prolonged meditation, contemplation, pain, sleeplessness, and virtual starvation. Needless to say, physical activity of a healthful nature had no place in the life of the ascetics!

A more rational approach to worship was seen in the *monasteries* organized in Europe by Saint Benedict in the early part of the sixth century. These monasteries were set up so that those who wished to live a holy life minus the distractions of the secular world could do so. Strict discipline centered around manual labor, reading, study, and prayer. Work was seen as meeting their physical needs, and much of their labor centered around construction of the monasteries themselves. Again, physical education per se had no place. Historians and historians of sport should be thankful to the monks, however, because much of what we know about significant periods of our history is available to us as a result of their thorough record keeping and preservation of previously generated literature.

In the latter part of the Middle Ages, approximately the eleventh to the thirteenth century, the *Age of Chivalry* came to fore as an influential force in reviving interest in physical activity. The feudal estates of the Age of Chivalry, which probably originated with the Germanic tribes of the tenth and eleventh centuries, were presided over by landlords who placed much emphasis on fitness for military and competitive tournament purposes; physical preparedness for combat and competition was the watchword of the day. Broekhoff (1968, p. 24) points to the interplay of militarism and physical activity: "Physical education has always been held in high esteem at times in which a society recognizes the need for physical action." The core of chivalric training was physical education, with the intellect virtually neglected; many of the knights were poorly educated or illiterate (Moolenijzer, 1968). Early education took place at home; at age seven, a son of the nobility was taken from his home to serve a baron or king as a page; at fourteen, he became a squire and served an apprenticeship to a knight by caring for his horse and acting as shield bearer in combat. At age twenty-one, he became a full-fledged knight. Preparatory to knighthood, some emphasis was placed on the arts and social graces, but the majority of the time from age seven on was devoted to horsemanship, swordsmanship, and hunting. Perhaps the best summary of what was expected in the training for knighthood is reflected in a prose passage by Rothe near the end of the fifteenth century (Neumann, 1936):

> The arts all seven which certainly at all times a perfect man will love are: he must ride well, be fast in and out of the saddle, trot well and canter and turn around and know how to pick something up from the ground.
>
> The other, that he knows how to swim and dive into the water, knows how to turn and twist on his back and on his belly.
>
> The third, that he shoots well with crossbows, arm, and handbows; these he may well use against princes and dukes.
>
> The fourth, that he can climb fast on ladders when necessary, that will be of use in war, in poles and ropes it is also good.

> The fifth art I shall speak of is that he is good in tournament, that he fights and tilts well and is honest and good in the joust.
>
> The sixth art is wrestling also both fencing and fighting, beat others in the long jump from the left as well as from the right.
>
> The seventh art: he serves well at the table, knows how to dance, has courtly manners, does not shy away from board games or other things that are proper for him.

Obviously, the prospective knight was expected to be proficient in various aspects of horsemanship, swimming and diving, archery, climbing, fencing, wrestling, jumping, dancing, and table games.

One outgrowth of all this fascination for readiness for war and fitness for competition was the *joust* (bouhourt). In its original form, both the horse and the rider were as protected as was possible considering that the purpose of the event was to dislodge one's competitor from his horse. As time went on, a simple joust was not sufficient; blunt instrumentation was replaced with sharp and lethal lances and all other safeguards were largely dropped. Too, touring professionals, called "jousting bums" by Moolenijzer, started taking over the event, leading, in part, to its demise as a sporting event in the first part of the sixteenth century.

The overall effect of chivalry, however, was to elevate physical activity to a position of importance again; it remained for subsequent generations to arrive at a balance between the physical and intellectual so revered by the early Greeks.

THE RENAISSANCE

During the fourteenth to sixteenth centuries, there was a major reawakening of interest in language, culture, arts, and education, and this renaissance had considerable influence on sport and physical activity. A major part of this rebirth was the establishment of universities, such as those found in Paris, Salerno, and Bologna. Loosely structured and attended by a rather ragtag clientele, these early universities placed much emphasis on grammar, logic, mathematics, and scholarly debate and essentially accorded no place for organized physical activities. As a consequence, much youthful energy was spent in confrontations with the local populace, pranks, fights among themselves, and other shenanigans. All in all, however, these universities presaged an age of intellectual inquiry that was to end the Dark Ages.

Concomitant with this reawakening of interest in knowledge was the growth of free trade and mercantilism, the lessening of the strength of the feudal estates, and an increasing secularism. Gunpowder was developed and this was to change the course of warfare drastically; the printing press was invented by Gutenberg; Columbus sailed to the New World; and his Portuguese and Spanish peers were quite involved in their various discoveries all over the globe.

Though still fettered with much ecclesiasticism and the remnants of chivalry, breakthroughs in thinking and to some extent in physical activity were being made in Italy by Vittorino da Feltra (1378–1446), Martin Luther (1483–1540) in Germany, Juan Luis Vives (1492–1540) in Spain, Michel de Montaigne (1533–1592) and François Rabelais (1490–1553) in France, Sir Thomas Elyot (1490?–1546) in England, Paracelsus (1493–1541) in Switzerland, and Copernicus (1473–1543) in Poland. These influential scholars were not rabid proponents of physical exercise in the early Greek and Roman sense, but they did see a place for physical fitness in the scheme of things for the healthy, well-rounded individual. This stance, of course, was a big departure from the asceticism and monasticism of the early Middle Ages.

THE REFORMATION

In addition to the continuing influence of the writings of each of the great thinkers of the Renaissance period, the rapidly enlarging world was starting to feel the effects of people like Galileo (1564–1642) with his popularization of the telescope (among other things), Isaac Newton (1642–1727) and his concept of gravity, and the eloquence of Sir Francis Bacon (1561–1626) on educational issues. Too, John Milton (1608–1674), John Locke (1632–1704), and Jean Jacques Rousseau (1712–1778) bridged the gap between the Age of Reformation and the Age of Enlightenment. Though not much was happening during this period with regard to physical activity, the Reformation is clearly an important historical period.

THE AGE OF ENLIGHTENMENT

Recognition of the dignity and rights of each person and emphasis on the ability to think analytically and critically marked the Age of Enlightenment. England was operating under a form of democracy, making it unique at that time. The French and the new Americans in New England were becoming aware that education for all was a worthy goal, and it should be neither a responsibility of the church nor the right of only the wealthy or noble. These flames were fanned by educational reformers such as Rousseau, Johann Heinrich Pestalozzi (1746–1827), and Pestalozzi's European disciples: Friedrich Froebel (1782–1852), Johann Friedrich Herbart (1776–1841), and Phillip Emanuel von Fellenberg (1771–1844).

Rousseau's beliefs, summarized in *Emile* (1762), were a break with tradition. He opposed the formal learning so characteristic of schools of that time, which stressed Latin, Greek, and mathematics; and Rousseau heretically insisted that play, games, manual arts, and nature studies would be more educational. Unlike Locke and Rabelais, who were proponents of physical education in the schools, but for military and health reasons, Rousseau viewed such a requirement as part of the total development of the child and young adult of school age. It is also interesting to note that Rousseau, according to Gerber (1968), was also a proponent of sport as a means of promoting national unity.

Even more heretical than his opposition to formal learning was Rousseau's insistence that the nature of man is good and not sinful, as had been emphasized for so many previous centuries. He was to have a profound impact on education and philosophy beyond anything he could ever imagine.

Pestalozzi, in turn, was greatly influenced by Locke and Rousseau, and he passed down to his disciples his emphasis on physical education within the total school curriculum. Though all of these disciples practiced variations of what Locke and Rousseau had suggested, they were *in toto* proponents of games and physical activity within the academic life of the child.

Thanks in part to the collective efforts of great men, from Copernicus and Rabelais to Locke and Rousseau, there developed a veritable explosion of activity all over Europe in the eighteenth and nineteenth centuries. The Germans, under the guidance of physical educators such as Johann Christoph Friedrich Guts Muth (1759–1839), Friedrich Ludwig Jahn (1778–1852), and Adolf Spiess (1810–1858), developed active programs in *gymnastics*, which were, in reality, broadly based programs of physical fitness. The Germans also contributed the *playground movement* in the latter part of the nineteenth century. The Danes and the British were also very active in the promotion of play, games, and various physical activities.

COLONIAL AMERICA

The settling of Jamestown, Virginia, in 1607 and Plymouth, Massachusetts, in 1620 signaled the beginning of the *colonial period* in American history. Though Leonard (1984) says the times were not as stark and monotonous as some would have us believe, the period nevertheless had its rigors; the soil had to be tilled, the forests cleared, houses built, and protection against the elements had to be generated. Strong prohibitions were placed on play and sport, partially due to persistent threats to survival and because of religious admonitions to avoid idleness and abuse of precious work time.

Among the early settlers were the *Puritans*, who were particularly opposed to sports because of their interference with what the Puritans considered proper piety. In some ways, the Puritans were a throwback to the ascetics of the Middle Ages; they truly resented the "worldliness" of sport. To counter their influence in England prior to their departure to the New World, King James I issued a proclamation known as the *Book of Sports*, which was a statement that parts of divine services of any kind should be devoted to games, play, feasts, and physical activity. Puritans in both England and the colonies tenaciously fought the *Book of Sports*, continually trying to protect the Sabbath from levity.

Though influential, the Puritans were not the only *Sabbatarians*; evangelical groups neither Anglican nor Puritan sprang up all over the colonies, not the least of which was the Society of Friends (Quaker) sect, founded by George Fox in the early eighteenth century. The Quakers, the Puritans, and other evangelicals were powerful forces in opposing sports and physical activity.

Nevertheless, sports and games flourished. Influential men of the period, such as Benjamin Franklin (1706–1790) and Samuel Moody (1727?–1795), called for physical activity as a health and character builder. The *taverns*, much to the chagrin of the Pilgrims, became a focal point for social life and sponsored card games, billiards, bowling, and rifle and pistol competitions. Cockfighting and horse racing were not unknown in the colonies. Other popular activities were skittles (bowling), cricket, football (more soccer than football as we now know it), golf (called "goff"), shinny, rounders, ninepins, swimming, and tennis (Rice et al., 1969; Struna, 1981).

In Maryland, the colonials paid lip service to Sabbatarianism, generally going their merry way, enjoying fox hunting, yachting, and "ball and long bullets," the latter a game involving the throwing of cannonballs for distance (Kennard, 1970, p. 393). Gambling related to these sporting events was not at all unusual; particularly prominent was betting on horse races. Rader (1983) tells of a southern colonial named William Byrd III who was such an inveterate gambler that, after depleting the considerable family fortune amassed by his father, he committed suicide at an early age.

In 1732, the first sport social club, the Schuylkill Fishing Company, was organized in Philadelphia for purposes of allowing its members to hunt and fish on the Schuylkill River and to demonstrate that work and play could in fact be mutually advantageous to individual well-being.

A significant part of the colonial period was the Revolutionary War, fought from 1775 to 1783. According to Ledbetter (1979), several features characterized the games, play, and sport of the warriors of the Revolution. One is that most of what we know is gleaned from diaries and records of officers; few enlisted men kept notes on their activities. A second feature is that the army had no specific athletic and recreation program so that the soldiers had to improvise as they went. Also, competition between units was not stressed as a means of maintaining morale. A third feature is that most of the war effort was curtailed in the cold months, so that much spare time was available for recreational purposes. A fourth feature is that seldom did winning or losing matter; competition for the sake of recreation was paramount and there was much spontaneity in the generation of diversions.

According to Ledbetter, games and sports of the Revolutionary War included wicket, cricket (an ancestor of baseball), shinny (a cousin of field hockey), football, fives (handball), ninepins, billiards, shuffleboard, boxing, horse racing, cockfighting, sleighing, snowball fighting, skating, swimming, sailing, and wrestling.

THE CIVIL WAR PERIOD

Between the Revolutionary War and the Civil War, sports clubs similar to the Schuylkill Fishing Company proliferated; universities such as Harvard instituted wrestling and football, boxing clubs were springing up, and various forms of racing gained in popularity. The fervor associated with horse racing gave impetus to Stephen Foster (1826–1864) to extol its virtues in his popular song, "Camptown Races," generally considered to be the first popular song with a sport theme (Leonard, 1984).

In 1843, Yale University started a collegiate rowing club, and a year later Harvard did the same. This interest in rowing eventually led to America's first intercollegiate sport, boating, in 1852 (Lewis, 1967; Spears and Swanson, 1983). The first competitive race was held on Lake Winnipesaukee in New Hampshire and was won by Harvard. These regattas continued to grow in popularity, and a number of other universities created competitive teams. The sport of boating was to set a precedent for intercollegiate competition that has now reached staggering proportions.

Boating was the first inter-collegiate sport to gain widespread popularity. By the time members of Harvard's crew posed for this photo in 1875, Harvard and Yale had been competing in regattas for almost twenty-five years.

The Civil War, despite its immense brutality, had numerous moments of levity insofar as sport goes. Sport at the outbreak of the fighting was in a period of unprecedented acceptance. Many of the Puritan and Pietist proscriptions against sport had been diluted or ignored. Great surges in inventions, wealth, urbanization, and industrialization were at hand, and were altering our society greatly (Lucas, 1968). So it seems natural that sports should be such a big part of the nonfighting aspect of the life of the Civil War soldier.

According to Fielding (1977a): "In the beginning, the Civil War was a holiday which freed American youth from the shackels [sic] of responsibility. The soldier was recruited amidst a revival atmosphere. In his home town the call went out, the speeches were made and the whiskey flowed" (p. 145). In this atmosphere, it should not be surprising that the typical recruit had little patience with drill, ceremony, pomp, circumstance, and military maneuvers.

Fielding (1977b) conveniently divides the life of the Union soldier into four aspects, and talks of the typical activities that took place in each. The initial conscription into the army was arduous but boredom crept in when training was light. Competitive activities engaged in generally had a military purpose, hence shooting, horse races, and drilling were emphasized. Later, boxing, wrestling, footraces, fencing, and football were allowed. In addition to assisting training and relieving boredom, the various activities also enhanced group solidarity, which was a real plus for the trainers of the raw recruits. Holidays on or near the battlefield were a second part of the soldier's life, and recreation was generally similar to that of the boot camp period. One sport that was added here that did not seem to be present in early training was baseball. According to Crockett (1961, p. 341), it was a welcome addition: "Baseball appears to have been the most popular of all action sports engaged in by 'Billy Yank' and 'Johnny Reb.'" Betts (1971) indicates that prisoners of war passed time playing baseball. He also cites a case of a $100 challenge game played in Virginia between Army of the Potomac factions from New York and New Jersey. Betts further mentions a game between Union soldiers in Texas who were playing outside friendly lines. Rebel soldiers attacked them, wounding and capturing the centerfielder and scattering the other participants.

A third dimension of soldiering was the winter camp experience. In cold weather, soldiering diminished considerably and free time escalated. Cockfights were popular, but perhaps the most exciting events for the soldiers were snowball fights (Crockett, 1961; Fielding 1977b). These snowball fights became so sophisticated in certain instances that complex plans of attack along military lines were developed and weapons stockpiled. Some of these battles were quite long and so bitterly fought that serious injuries became commonplace, and the activity had to be reduced in intensity or stopped.

The final facet of soldier life was centered around lulls in the fighting. Cockfights, football, and baseball were quite popular, along with most of the activities mentioned in the other phases. Crockett (1961) says the soldiers

of the Union and Confederacy alike engaged in thirty-four different sports and recreation practices during the conduct of the war. The typical Civil War firefight was at close quarters due to limitations in the accuracy of the rifles and pistols and as a result of much use of swords and knives. In the infighting process, many verbal exchanges accompanied the fighting, and tempers flared as a result. Fielding (1977b) cites several instances in which combat was actually stopped so that combatants angered by these verbal exchanges could settle their disputes on neutral ground between the Union and Confederate soldiers through boxing. Once the issue was settled by fisticuffs, the war would be resumed!

THE TECHNOLOGICAL REVOLUTION

Prior to the Civil War and, more particularly, in the forty years that followed it, great changes took place in the American way of life. Population explosion was to take place; 17 million people lived in the United States in 1840 whereas there were 50 million by 1880 (Spears and Swanson, 1983). Immigration was rampant, initially by northwestern Europeans and later by Catholics and Jews from Southern and Eastern Europe (Rader, 1983). The blacks freed by the Emancipation Proclamation of 1863 were yet to be assimilated. North-South relations were strained. The effects of the technological revolution were being felt throughout the fabric of America. And sport was not exempt from these reverberations.

A particularly informative handling of these various social forces is provided by Betts (1953). He states that a number of factors contributed to the new direction in sport from 1850 to 1900, and among them were the decline of Puritan orthodoxy, the influence of the new immigrants, frontier emphasis on manliness and strength, the English athletic movement, and the contributions of energetic sportsmen. In figure 2.1, Betts further cites a number of products of this new technology as shaping the direction of sport.

Significant athletic events of the era included the founding of the New York Athletic Club in 1868, which was the first attempt to bring amateur athletics under a unified umbrella and led ultimately to the formation of the *Amateur Athletic Union (AAU)* in 1888. The first professional baseball team, the Cincinnati Red Stockings, was founded in 1869; tennis was introduced to the country in 1874; the National Baseball League was formed in 1876 with eight original participants; the United States Lawn Tennis Association was formed in New York in 1881; basketball was invented in 1891 by Dr. James Naismith of Springfield, Massachusetts; the first relay race in track and field was run in 1893, and this event was America's unique contribution to the sport; and the first American marathon race was held in Massachusetts in 1897.

A particularly noteworthy event of the time was the *reinstitution of the Olympic Games* in Athens, Greece, in 1896. The modern games were the product of the leadership of a Frenchman, Pierre de Fredy, Baron de Coubertin. Spears and Swanson (1983) indicate that he was by no means the first to try, merely the one who succeeded. With the exception of the war years in 1940 and 1944, the games have continued to be held and have, despite many political problems, grown in popularity.

All in all, the period from 1850 to 1900 was one of dramatic changes in the American way of life and one of great growth in all facets of sporting events.

1900 TO PRESENT

At the risk of neglecting the past ninety years, only a few high spots will be touched upon

Figure 2.1 Impact of Technological Advances on Sport

1. *Railroads.* The railroad companies made fairly extensive travel distinctly possible. The various railroad companies sponsored travel to athletic events in order to spur ticket sales. The Harvard–Yale boat races were put together by a railroad company that promised to transport and defray all expenses of the participants (Lewis, 1967). The rail companies were also instrumental in popularizing baseball, horse racing, and boxing.

2. *Telegraphy.* The development of telegraphy led to a great expansion in the transmission of sport information between cities, and by 1870 many metropolitan newspapers reported sport news. The first sport section in a newspaper was created in New York by William Randolph Hearst just before the year 1900.

3. *Innovations in printing.* Various improvements in the printing process allowed for better newspapers, journals related to sport only, and books with sport themes.

4. *Sewing machine.* The sewing machine allowed for more diverse and higher quality athletic goods.

5. *Incandescent lighting.* Improved quality of lighting expanded the sport day by allowing for nighttime events at a higher quality than that provided by gas lighting. Electrification created the environment for the growth of basketball and volleyball.

6. *Vulcanization of rubber.* The advent of vulcanized rubber had far-reaching consequences for the development of the ball so central to most sports. Pneumatic tires revolutionized cycling and harness racing and were to ultimately have great impact on automobile racing in the 1900s.

7. *Miscellany.* The stop watch, percussion cap, ball bearings, camera, movies, telephone, typewriter, and phonograph are just a few other products of the industrial revolution that were to enlarge the role of sport in the life of the American participant and spectator.

SOURCE: "The Technological Revolution and the Rise of Sport, 1850–1900" by J. Betts, 1953, *Mississippi Valley Historical Review, 40,* 231–256.

Fashionable New Yorkers took quickly to the new game of lawn tennis after 1880. Here, a quartet of well-dressed women enjoy the game in Brooklyn's Prospect Park.

from this period. The historical antecedents of most of the topics we will be dealing with in the remaining chapters have short histories, almost always from some point in the 1900s, so much of the history of this period will be woven into the various topical elaborations in chapters to follow. There are, however, some high points that merit immediate attention.

America went from a concern with national issues only to a nation of great worldwide influence in the 1900s, and this assumption of power was to affect sport. Olympic participation was only one case in point; others include the creation of the Davis Cup competition in tennis and international pistol competition in 1900.

Internally, a crisis of major proportions was brewing in intercollegiate football that eventu-

ally necessitated intervention by *President Theodore Roosevelt (1858–1919)* in 1905 in order to arrive at some determination of the future of that game, which had become so brutal in the eyes of many critics. Lewis (1969) covers the situation well, but issues a warning that Roosevelt's role has been reported so variously by so-called authorities that one must use caution in adopting a doctrinaire view of just what the President actually did. Roosevelt, of course, believed strongly in the value of physical activity and saw football as "the most valuable of all team sports because it provided each individual with opportunities to test his courage" (Lewis, 1969, p. 719). Yet there were many dissenters because of injuries, deaths, cheating and general brutality associated with the sport. After a number of meetings with interested parties from Yale, Harvard, Princeton, New York University, and members of the rules committee of the Intercollegiate Athletic Association of the United States, agreements were reached as to the future of football in what Lewis describes as "probably the single most important event in the history of intercollegiate sport" (p. 724). Lewis goes on to point out that President Roosevelt's role in the discussions was significant but not crucial and that he did not, as some would have us believe, save the game because it was never really threatened; the desire to reform the game was there, not an intent to abolish it. Four years after the tempest, the *National Collegiate Athletic Association (NCAA)* was formed (in 1910) and is the prime governing force in college athletics at present.

As an interesting side note, while the talks were going on, the president's son Theodore, Jr., a freshman at Harvard, was injured in the Yale game. Despite the fact that the boy's nose was broken and he suffered assorted cuts and bruises, the president did not waver in his dedication to the values of football and to fairness in the debate over its status (Lewis, 1969).

Another interesting event of the times had to do with prohibitions against Sunday participation in sport, the so-called *Blue Law of 1794*, which was a holdover from the days of the Puritans and the evangelicals of the colonial period. After World War I, sports became a virtual obsession with Americans, and increasingly were engaged in on the Sabbath. Jable (1976) relates that in 1919 the Philadelphia Park Commission started allowing sports such as baseball, tennis, and golf to be played on Sundays in parks under its jurisdiction. The Philadelphia Sabbath Association took the issue to court, and the battle was on.

A big test of the Blue Law was made by the Philadelphia Athletics professional baseball team when they scheduled a Sunday afternoon game in August of 1926. The game was played and was viewed as a success by the team management, but the Sabbatarians promptly took them to court for their violation of the Sabbath and won an injunction against any further such indiscretions.

The stock market crash of 1929 put a well-documented strain on the economy of the country and, in the search for relief from the economic plight of their citizens, Philadelphia and Pennsylvania politicians and other officials turned again to Sunday sport as a partial solution. Again, Sabbatarians, such as the Friends of the Proper Observance of the Sabbath, took umbrage at this increasing encroachment on the sanctity of the final day of the week. However, laws were passed that allowed local option voting on Sunday sports. Philadelphia and Pittsburgh voters approved the option by a 7 to 1 majority, and on November 12, 1933, the Pittsburgh Steelers (known then as The Pirates) lost to a team from Brooklyn 32–0 before 12,000 supporters while the Eagles of Philadelphia were playing the vaunted Chicago Bears to a 3–3 tie before 20,000 fans. The Blue Law of 1794 was defeated and the Sabbatarians dismayed. Perhaps the issue is best summed up by Jable (p. 363): "Eighteenth-century customs were not compatible with twentieth-century behavior."

Another issue of note is chronicled by Zingale (1977), who summarizes much of what *Dwight D. Eisenhower* (1890–1969) did for public attitudes and behaviors related to physical fitness and sports during his presidency from 1952 to 1960. Himself an athlete at the United States Military Academy at West Point (member of the baseball and football squads), Eisenhower maintained a lifelong love of sport and fitness. Testing conducted by physical educators during the early 1950s revealed then 58 percent of young people in the United States were deficient in one or more of six aspects of strength and flexibility, compared to only 9 percent of their European counterparts. Dismayed by these findings, the president called

HIGHLIGHT 2.5
Collegiate Football
During World War II

During World War II, collegiate football was forced to adapt to a number of conditions that greatly altered its conduct. Among these adaptations:

1. Night games were banned on both coasts because of the threat of attack by enemy forces.
2. The 1942 Rose Bowl, one of the premier events in all of sport, was played in Durham, North Carolina, instead of its traditional home in Pasadena, California. Again, the fear of an enemy attack on the east or west coasts led to the decision to temporarily move the game.
3. More than 60 colleges abandoned football in 1942, and 149 more did so in 1943. Among the 1943 dropouts: Auburn, Baylor, Florida, Harvard, Kentucky, and Tennessee.
4. Because of the draft, military bases were able to field teams that were often superior to most of the college teams. Four of these military teams were ranked in the top ten in collegiate football in 1943.
5. In 1944, some universities renewed their football programs. The military academies at West Point and Annapolis became football powers as they were able to stockpile outstanding players from other universities in the name of military preparedness.

SOURCE: "College Football During World War II: 1941–1945" by T. Harbrecht and C. R. Barnett, 1979, *Physical Educator, 36,* 31–34.

for a convention of experts on fitness. In June, 1956, the conference on Youth Fitness was convened, and a number of far-reaching recommendations were made. Too, the *President's Council on Youth Fitness* was formed. This infusion of presidential clout into the fitness realm must be regarded as a landmark event. The subsequent involvement on the part of President John F. Kennedy (1917–1963) was significant also.

The years since the 1950s, which Twombly (1976) calls the *Electronic Age* of sport, have seen an amazing involvement in physical activity. The growth in interest and involvement has been spectacular, as has a preoccupation with being a spectator rather than a participant. The latter situation is a source of considerable concern for critics of our modern lifestyle; references from neophytes and experts alike are constantly being made to the parallels

between contemporary physical softness and that of the decadent Romans of two thousand years ago. The growth of collegiate and professional sport has been phenomenal in the past thirty years. Equally dramatic has been the rise in the sophistication and influence of television; many see television as a corrupting force in sport in a variety of ways.

All things considered, sport and physical activity are a big and fascinating business today, far removed in many ways from their origins, but nevertheless a powerful social force.

A BRIEF HISTORY OF PHYSICAL EDUCATION

Paralleling and interacting with the history of sport and physical activity is the *physical edu-*

cation movement in the United States. Though there were proponents of what might be construed as physical education among the early colonists, perhaps the early German and Swedish immigrants who brought with them an enthusiasm for gymnastics in the early 1800s were our earliest physical educators. Catharine Beecher (1800–1878), daughter of the well-known preacher Lyman Beecher, sister of Harriet Beecher Stowe, the author of *Uncle Tom's Cabin,* and sister of the renowned reformer Henry Ward Beecher, was an early proponent of physical activity for women. She wrote two books advocating fitness in women, *Course of Calisthenics for Young Ladies* (1832) and *A Manual of Physiology and Calisthenics for Schools and Families* (1856). Among other things, her work was instrumental in the creation of the *first physical education program for women* at Vassar College, in 1865.

In 1861, the *first collegiate men's physical education program* had been established at Amherst College and, significantly for the time period, was called the Department of Physical Education. It was not until the 1920s that physical education would completely supplant physical culture as the preferred term for addressing these kinds of activities and departments. In any event, the department was chaired by Dr. Edward Hitchcock (1828–1911), and the program stood alone for twenty years as an example for all to emulate. By 1965, there would be 539 colleges and universities offering professional preparation in physical education (Lee, 1983).

Another significant milestone for 1861 was the publication of the first physical education journal by Diocletian (Dio) Lewis (1823–1886), an eminent physical educator of the time, which was entitled *Gymnastics Monthly and Journal of Physical Culture.* A year later, Lewis published a significant book, *The New Gymnastics for Men, Women, and Children.* Another significant publication for professionals in the field was the *American Physical Edu-*

cation Review (1896), which later became the *Journal of Health and Physical Education* in 1930, the *Journal of The American Association for Health, Physical Education, and Recreation* in 1949, the *Journal of Health, Physical Education, and Recreation* in 1955, the *Journal of Physical Education and Recreation* in 1976, and the *Journal of Physical Education, Recreation and Dance (JOPERD)* in 1982. Another significant physical education journal, the *Research Quarterly,* was founded in 1930 and became the *Research Quarterly for Exercise and Sport* in 1980; the interested reader is referred to an article by Park (1980) that summarizes its first fifty years. A journal for coaches, the *Athletic Journal,* began publication in 1919.

On the educational front, the *first state to pass a law requiring physical education in the public schools* was California in 1866, primarily as a result of the efforts of John Swett of the Rincon School (Hoepner, 1970). It was quite a while before other states followed suit; by 1930, 36 states had laws requiring physical education in the schools. By 1916, however, physical education had reached a level of importance that allowed for the appointment of the first state supervisor of physical education, Dr. Thomas Storey (1875–1943) of New York. Not coincidentally, New York University and Columbia University conferred the first Doctor of Philosophy degrees in physical education in 1924.

As events unfolded, there was a growth in the number and influence of professional organizations within physical education. In 1885, the American Association for the Advancement of Physical Education was created; in 1903, it became the American Physical Education Association; in 1937 the name was changed to the American Association for Health and Physical Education; the word "Recreation" was added to the title in 1938; the word "Association" was replaced by "Alliance" in 1975; and the official name as of now is *The American Alliance for Health, Physical Education, Recreation, and Dance (AAHPERD).*

Another organization, the College Physical Education Association (CPEA), was formed in 1897, followed by Amy Homans' (1848–1933) creation, the National Association for Physical Education of College Women in 1910, and Phi Epsilon Kappa, the professional fraternity of physical educators, in 1913. At the same time these organizations were lending their influence to the cause of physical fitness, organizations such as the Playground Association of America (1906), the Boy Scouts (1910), the Girl Scouts (1912), and the Campfire Girls (1912) were springing up to further emphasize the broad concepts of fitness and recreation.

Though the list of leaders is virtually endless, we would be remiss if a few of the more eminent contributions were not mentioned. In 1880, Dr. Dudley Sargent (1849–1924) was appointed Director of Hemenway Gymnasium at Harvard. Dr. Sargent, a physician (as were most of the early pioneers in physical education), was an early promoter of strength testing and was said to have administered 50,000 anthropometric tests in his career (Hackensmith, 1966). In 1890, Dr. Luther Gulick (1865–1918) devised the first athletic achievement test, which dealt with the pentathlon event in track. In 1904, R. *Tait McKenzie* (1867–1938) became head of the Department of Physical Education at Pennsylvania University, where he distinguished himself for twenty-seven years. In addition to his scholarly and leadership qualities, McKenzie was a most accomplished sculptor, and he was perhaps the first since the early Greeks to use athletics as a medium. His works became world famous, leading Lee (1983, p. 203) to say: "No one of modern times has bound the profession of physical education to the glories of its ancient heritage as did R. Tait McKenzie through his art work."

Two other leaders of note, Clark Hetherington (1870–1942) and Jesse Feiring Williams (1886–1966) published books in 1922 that called for a movement away from the militaristic and moralistic gymnastic influence of the Germans and Swedes and toward the establishment of a physical education by and for the United States, one that educated the whole person. This call ushered in a new era for physical education. Too, the influence of eminent educators, psychologists, and philosophers of that time was instrumental in shaping not only our views of physical education but our vision of education and life in general. Among them were people like John Dewey (1859–1952), G. Stanley Hall (1846–1924), William James (1842–1910), and E. L. Thorndike (1874–1949).

The cause of physical education was greatly served by the events of World Wars I and II. The fitness deficiencies among our youth that were so graphically illustrated by medical exams, coupled with the need for fitness for those accepted into military life, gave added impetus to the physical education movement. Too, events of the Korean War and fitness test results amassed by physical educators in the 1950s and 1960s and presented to Presidents Eisenhower and Kennedy only served to strengthen the case.

Two other recent events that have been most salient in their far-reaching effects are the *Civil Rights Act of 1964* and *Title IX* of the Educational Amendment Act of 1972. These acts militated against discrimination due to race or sex and have facilitated the integration of women and minorities into the mainstream of American life, including physical activity and sport.

A BRIEF HISTORY OF PSYCHOLOGY

Most historians in psychology attribute the beginning of psychology as a scientific endeavor to the year 1879. At that time the German Wilhelm Wundt (1832–1920) had started a laboratory in Leipzig aimed primarily at the study of psychophysiological phenomena.

According to Roediger, Rushton, Capaldi, and Paris (1984), Wundt was a prolific writer who published some 50,000 pages of professional papers.

Prior to the establishment of the Leipzig laboratory, German scientists such as Hermann Ebbinghaus (1850–1909), Hermann von Helmholtz (1821–1894), and Gustav Fechner (1801–1887) were systematically studying various psychophysical phenomena. Fechner published a book, *Elements of Psychophysics,* in 1860, and this is considered to be one of the earliest of all psychology texts.

In 1870, Sir Francis Galton (1822–1911), an Englishman, published *Hereditary Genius,* a book that was to spur eventual interest in the development of psychological tests. In 1880, another prominent figure, G. Stanley Hall, was appointed president of Clark University. Hall was the leader of a child-study movement that had considerable impact on educational practices; he also started in 1887 the first psychology journal, the *American Journal of Psychology,* which still exists today. In 1890, William James published his two-volume work entitled *Principles of Psychology,* a twelve-year labor of love (Benjamin, Hopkins, and Nation, 1987). Out of James' work would grow a historical school of thought known as *functionalism.* Functionalism, as opposed to the structuralist camp of the early psychophysicists with their emphasis on the elements of mental life, was more interested in the uses or functions of the mind. John Dewey, who administered an influential experimental school at the University of Chicago from 1896–1903, was also a leading functionalist.

An alternate method of looking at human behavior was proposed in 1913 by John B. Watson (1878–1958). Watson outlined his revolutionary *behavioristic approach* in a paper entitled "Psychology as the Behaviorist Views It." He advocated that scientists should study observable behavior not unobservable mental processes or the murky mystical mentalisms of the structuralists and functionalists. Reinforcement of a sort was provided for Watson's viewpoint in the same year (1913) by E. L. Thorndike, who outlined his behavioristic notions in a treatise entitled *Educational Psychology.* Subsequent behaviorists, including Clark Hull (1884–1952), Edward Tolman (1886–1961), and Edwin Guthrie (1886–1959), provided further fuel for the behaviorist fires with their varied but behavioral theories. The present-day leader of the behavioral movement is the eminent Harvard psychologist, B. F. Skinner (1904–). Skinner has eloquently outlined his position in such offerings as *Behavior of Organisms* (1938), the fictional *Walden Two* (1948), and *Beyond Freedom and Dignity* (1971). All of these American behaviorists are indebted to the work of the Russian physiologist, Ivan Pavlov (1849–1936), who demonstrated the nature of classical conditioning in the late 1800s.

Another powerful force in the history of psychology has been the *psychoanalytic model* of Sigmund Freud (1856–1939). Over the past eighty years much has been said on both points of view as to the efficacy or validity of psychoanalysis, but it has served to spur much research into personality theory, psychopathology, and psychotherapy techniques.

As a protest to the pessimism of the analysts, American psychologists such as Abraham Maslow (1908–1970) and Carl Rogers (1902–1987) have championed the *humanistic movement,* an approach with strong emphasis on optimism and individual initiative. The humanists, like most psychologists, owe a heavy debt to philosophy; humanism is traceable to the works of Rousseau.

On a more atheoretical tack, the *testing movement* has been influential. In 1902 two French physicians, Alfred Binet (1857–1911) and Theodore Simon (1873–1962), created the first paper-and-pencil test of intelligence. This objective measure of intelligence sparked a revolution that was to generate literally thousands of tests designed to measure every psychological trait and capability imaginable. Many of the significant tests pertinent to sport psychology are discussed in chapter 9.

A modern point of emphasis in the field of psychology includes the study of physiological bases for behavior and investigation of mental or cognitive events that shape behavior. The structuralists and functionalists are essentially defunct; the Freudians are small in number and suspect in scientific validity; the humanists, though a bit fuzzy scientifically, have their devotees, and behaviorism is thriving though modified to place more credence in less observable behaviors, that is, mental events.

SUMMARY

1. Much of what we know about sport in ancient times has been gathered from analysis of various archeological findings to include mosaics, frescoes, paintings, textiles, works of art, sculpture, ornaments, tablets, architecture, and seal stones.

2. Artifacts dated to the period 3000–1500 B.C. seem to indicate that boxing, wrestling, and board games were engaged in by the Sumerians. An even broader representation of activities is yielded by the Egyptians of the same time period. The early Chinese were apparently avid participants in sport, as were the Indians of 1500 B.C.

3. The unearthing of the Palace of Minos in 1871 showed that the Minoans of 3000 to 1200 B.C. engaged in many activities, but the so-called "taureador" sports (bull-grappling and related activities) seemed to dominate their interest.

4. Much of what we have learned about early Greek activities has been gleaned from the *Iliad* and the *Odyssey*, the twin creations of the blind Ionian poet, Homer. It is gener-

ally agreed that the two were written about 850 B.C., and both reveal the Greek love of sport.

5. The date of the first Olympic Games has been fixed as 776 B.C. It was not until the 14th Olympics that more than one event was held; a second running event was added in 724 B.C., and a long race was added in 720. By the sixty-fifth games in 520 B.C., the games had been enlarged to include wrestling, boxing, the pankration, four running events, and the pentathlon. This format was to last until the demise of the games in A.D. 394.

6. Olympic winners won a crown of wild olive leaves for their victories. They competed in the nude (after 720 B.C.), and women were, with few exceptions, not allowed to compete in or view the games. The penalty for violating this rule was death to the offender.

7. The people of the city–state of Sparta, unlike their contemporaries in Athens who saw physical activity as a glorification of the entire human organism, viewed physical activity as a means of furthering military preparedness. They emphasized the "perfect warrior" concept, and physical activity was aimed at meeting this ideal. In the process, many Spartan athletes were successful in the Olympic Games and other sports events.

8. The defeat of the Persians in 480 B.C. ushered in the "Golden Age of Greece." Great harmony existed between the various Greek city–states. As time wore on, internecine wars broke out. Energies and resources were strained, and the Greeks could not withstand external invasions, falling to the Macedonians. The Greek empire ceased to exist as a power in 338 B.C., though the overall effect it had on culture has never ceased.

9. The Romans ascended to power over all of the Mediterranean world in 146 B.C. The early Romans, much like the Spartans, viewed physical activity as a means of

preparing men for combat. Many sports and games were played; one of them, harpastum, appears to be the earliest version of what is now known as handball. As time wore on, the Romans came to view activity and fitness as the province of the professional army and the full-time athletes. A period of physical neglect set in and, coupled with a deterioration in the overall quality of life values, laid the framework for the ultimate demise of the Romans.

10. Gladiatorial events and *venationes*, fights between animal predators or man and predator, became very popular in meeting the decadent needs of the later Romans. The Roman Empire ended in A.D. 476, when the barbarian Teutons from the north took over.

11. The Middle Ages was a period of about one thousand years characterized by the development of Christianity, many wars, devastating diseases, and a dearth of intellectual advancement. One early exception was found in the Byzantines in the East; they carried on many of the Greek aesthetic and athletic traditions. Chariot racing was most popular, though gladiatorial events and *venationes* were well-received; apparently they were not as violent as those staged by the Romans, however. The Olympic Games died at the decree of the Byzantine ruler, Theodosius I, in A.D. 394 because of their supposed worship of pagan practices.

12. The growth of Christianity led to a rejection of most of the Greek and Roman worship of sport and physical activity. The body was seen as secondary to the soul; the ultimate here can be seen in the self-imposed pain and indignities of the ascetics, and the quiet, monastic, worshipful, reflective lifestyle of the monks of the sixth century A.D.

13. The Age of Chivalry, from the eleventh to the thirteenth century, was an important time for physical competition. The core of chivalric training was physical education. Physical fitness was the rule, as was illiteracy. Swordsmanship, horsemanship, and physical preparedness for competition and combat were greatly valued.

14. The Renaissance—the age of Martin Luther, Paracelsus, and Rabelais—was a period of rebirth of ideas but not a major period in sport and physical fitness. Jousting, however, dominated the period.

15. The Reformation, dominated by ideas from luminaries like Galileo, Newton, Bacon, and Locke, was not marked by great advances in physical activity, though the stage was being set for a veritable explosion of such endeavors.

16. The Age of Enlightenment was dominated by Pestalozzi, Rousseau, Froebel, and Herbart, all of whom espoused to varying degrees and in different ways the importance of physical activity to the overall well-being of a child. Their influence over the past two hundred years has been inestimable; physical educators continue to pay homage to these pioneers.

17. The early colonials in America were consumed with concerns of safety and piety, and all physical activities had to conform to these demands. However, by 1700, games and sports were flourishing; taverns became a focal point for social life, offering a broad array of games, sports and gambling activities. This profligacy offended the Pietists and Sabbatarians of various religious persuasions, and the conflict between fun and the forces of evil was on, a conflict that is still being staged today.

18. The Revolutionary War was a time of immense interest in recreational diversions and fitness for both military preparedness and for relief from the boredom of a war.

19. The Civil War, despite its bloodshed and well-documented inhumanity, was replete with sport and physical activity. Baseball was popular among troops on both sides. Competition within and sometimes between the armies was continual.

20. Prior to the Civil War, and most certainly afterward, a technological revolution of major proportions took place, with multiple effects on the face of sports. Population growth, rapid urbanization, and the development of such advances as the sewing machine, the light bulb, the camera, vulcanized rubber, the railroad, telegraphy, and innovations in printing revolutionized the face of America and its sport involvement.

21. The development of intercollegiate sports, the creation of professional baseball leagues, the increasing fascination with football, the development of the Amateur Athletic Union (AAU), and the reinstitution of the Olympic Games in 1896 are only a few of the sports landmarks between 1850 and 1900.

22. A crisis in American football required the intervention of President Theodore Roosevelt in 1905. Attacks were being made in Pennsylvania against laws that prohibited Sunday sport involvement. The two world wars signaled more need for physical fitness in American youth. All of these affected modern sports. Too, the expansion of sports created by television and professional sports becoming a big business have had significant effects.

23. The history of physical education is one of significant events and of people who have moved the field along to its present state of importance.

24. Psychology, officially beginning in 1879 with Wundt in Leipzig, has been influential in many spheres of American life, and its influence on sport and physical activity is significant.

Time Line

B.C.

850	Homer writes the *Iliad* and the *Odyssey*.
776	First Olympic Games are conducted.
520	Sixty-fifth Olympic Games establishes format for rest of competitions until games end in A.D. 394.
146	Greek Empire falls to the Romans.

A.D.

394	Theodosius I declares that the Olympic Games must cease because of their glorification of bodily paganism.
476	Roman Empire falls to the invading Teutons.
1000–1200	Age of Chivalry places much emphasis on knightly combat as sport.
1300–1500	The Renaissance period is characterized by reawakening of interest in physical activity, though it is largely informal.
1618	King James I issues proclamation known as *Book of Sports*.
18th Century	Rousseau espouses virtues of physical activity as part of total development of the person; he is also a proponent of sport as a means of promoting national unity. The roots of the German playground movement are established.
1732	Schuylkill Fishing Club is established in Philadelphia, and remains the oldest sporting organization in America.
1810	Tom Molineaux, a black, engages Tom Cribb in first interracial boxing title fight in history.
1831	*Course of Calisthenics for Young Ladies*, by Catherine Beecher, is published.

continued

Time Line—continued

1846	First recorded baseball game is played in Hoboken, New Jersey.	**1895**	William Randolph Hearst starts the first newspaper sport page.
1852	First intercollegiate sporting event takes place between rowing crews from Harvard and Yale.	**1896**	The Olympic Games are reinstituted in Athens, Greece.
1861	First college physical education program for men is instituted at Amherst College.	**1897**	The first American marathon race is run in Massachusetts.
1865	First physical education program for females is started at Vassar College.	**1900**	Women take part in Olympics for the first time.
1866	California becomes the first state to pass a law mandating physical education in public schools.	**1901**	The first bowling tournament is held in Chicago, Illinois.
1868	New York City Athletic Club is formed.	**1903**	The World Series in major league baseball is played for the first time.
1869	Rutgers and Princeton play the first intercollegiate football game.	**1904**	The Olympic Games are held for the first time in America in St. Louis.
1871	Palace of Minos is unearthed, yielding valuable artifacts for sport historians and others.	**1905**	The Intercollegiate Athletic Association is formed, laying the groundwork for creation of the National Collegiate Athletic Association (NCAA).
1872	Bud Fowler is the first black professional baseball player.	**1905**	President Teddy Roosevelt convenes a meeting of major university presidents to reduce violence in football.
1874	Tennis is introduced to America.		
1876	The first intercollegiate track meet is conducted in Saratoga, New York.	**1911**	The first Indianapolis 500 takes place.
1876	A. G. Spalding becomes the first major sporting goods corporation.	**1913**	Jim Thorpe is stripped of medals won in the 1912 Olympics because he had played professional baseball in 1909 and 1910.
1882	Handball is introduced to the United States.	**1913**	The forward pass is introduced in football.
1883	Moses Fleetwood Walker becomes the first black major league baseball player.	**1916**	The Professional Golfer's Association (PGA) is formed.
1886	*Sporting News* is published for the first time.	**1917**	The National Hockey League (NHL) is created in Canada.
1887	Legal betting takes place at a racetrack in New York State.	**1919**	The first coaching journal, *Athletic Journal*, is published.
1888	The Amateur Athletic Union (AAU) is formed.	**1920**	The first play-by-play account of a football game takes place as Station WTAW of College Station, Texas, broadcasts Texas-Texas A&M game.
1889	Walter Camp selects the first college football all-American team.		
1891	Basketball is invented by Dr. James Naismith in Springfield, Massachusetts.	**1926**	Gertrude Ederle becomes the first woman to swim the English channel.
1891	A world high jump record is set by W. B. Page at 6 feet 4 inches.	**1928**	Women take part in track and field at the Olympics for the first time.

Time Line—continued

1928	The United States Volleyball Association is formed.
1932	Mildred (Babe) Didrikson dominates women's track and field at the Olympic Games.
1933	Didrikson makes her debut in professional basketball.
1935	The first night game in major league baseball is played in Cincinnati.
1935	Hialeah (Florida) Race Track employs an electronic eye to determine race winners.
1936	The Rodeo Cowboy Association is formed under the name of Cowboy's Turtle Association.
1938	The first intercollegiate gymnastics championships are held.
1939	Little League baseball begins.
1939	A college baseball game between Columbia and Princeton becomes the first televised sport event.
1940	The Olympic Games are cancelled until 1948 because of World War II.
1941	Ohio State University hosts the first college fencing championships.
1945	Five college players from Brooklyn College admit taking bribes to throw a basketball game.
1947	Jackie Robinson breaks the color barrier in professional baseball.
1947	Babe Didrikson wins the British Open golf championship.
1948	Fred Morrison invents the Frisbee.
1949	The National Basketball Association (NBA) is formed from two other leagues.
1949	The Ladies Professional Golfer's Association (LPGA) is formed.
1950	Black players are admitted to professional basketball.
1951	The Soviet Union files to take part in the 1952 Olympics.
1954	*Sports Illustrated* begins publication.

1954	The Fellowship of Christian Athletes (FCA) is initiated.
1954	Roger Bannister posts the first mile run in under four minutes in Oxford, England (3:59.4).
1961	Mickey Mantle becomes the highest paid player in the American League at $75,000.
1962	Wilt Chamberlain scores 100 points in an NBA game.
1965	The so-called eighth wonder of the world, the Astrodome, opens in Houston.
1966	The first football Super Bowl is staged.
1971	The Association for Intercollegiate Athletics for Women (AIAW) is formed.
1972	Title IX of the Educational Amendments Act opens up sports for females.
1972	The Boston marathon has its first female entrant.
1973	A New Jersey court allows girls to play Little League baseball.
1975	Frank Robinson is hired as the first black manager in major league baseball.
1976	Janet Guthrie is the first woman to compete in the Indianapolis 500.
1979	Women reporters are allowed in athletic dressing rooms after games for interviews.
1980	Olympic Games are held in Russia, the first time they have been hosted by a Communist country. The United States boycotts the games.
1980	Entertainment and Sports Programming Network (ESPN) begins broadcasting television.
1982	Commemorative stamps honoring Bobby Jones and Babe Didrikson Zaharias are issued by the U.S. Postal Service.
1983	The United States Football League (USFL) is formed.
1984	Olympics are held in Los Angeles, and Russians return the U.S. boycott of the 1980 Games in Moscow.
1987	Ben Johnson of Canada runs 100 meters in world record time of 9.84 seconds.

Basketball inventor James Naismith takes a shot at the first "hoop"—a peach basket.

Gertrude Ederle dons a thick coat of grease to ward off the cold before swimming the English Channel in 1926. Ederle, the first woman to brave the channel, beat the men's record by nearly two hours.

SUGGESTED READINGS

Berryman, J. (1982) Important events in the history of American sports: A chronology. In R. Higgs (Ed.), *Sports: A reference guide* (pp. 227–267). Westport, CN: Greenwood Press.

> Berryman has compiled a thorough and readable chronology of sport events from 1618 to mid-1981. The reader can quickly become familiar with sport history by reading Berryman's work.

Brasch, R. (1970) *How did sports begin?* New York: David McKay.

> Brasch details the development of 43 separate sports and the Olympic Games in this 434-page volume.

Higgs, R. (1982) *Sports: A reference guide.* Westport, CN: Greenwood Press.

> In addition to a chapter on the history of sports, Higgs has chapters on sports and art and literature, as well as an excellent appendix on important research centers, collections, and directories within the United States and Canada.

Twombly, W. (1976) *200 years of sport in America: A pageant of a nation at play.* New York: McGraw-Hill.

> Twombly divides the history of sport into four ages, Pastoral (1776–1865), Passionate (1866–1919), Golden (1920–1945), and Electronic (1946–1976), and provides approximately fifteen vignettes per age in both prose and pictures as a means of documenting the progression of sport over the past two hundred years.

Yalouris, N. (1979) *The eternal Olympics: The art and history of sport.* New Rochelle, NY: Caratzas Brothers, Publishers.

> The prose in this book is informative and the pictures captivating. There are 156 illustrations, primarily from early Greek times and secondarily from the Roman era. A list of all known Olympic winners from 776 B.C. to A.D. 369 is also provided.

REFERENCES

Benjamin L.T., Hopkins, R., & Nation, J.R. (1987) *Psychology.* New York: Macmillan.

Betts, J. (1953) The technological revolution and the rise of sport, 1850–1900. *Mississippi Valley Historical Review, 40,* 231–256.

Betts, J. (1971) Home front, battlefield, and sport during the Civil War. *Research Quarterly, 42,* 113–132.

Binfield, R. (1948) *The story of the Olympic Games.* London: Oxford University Press.

Brasch, R. (1970) *How did sports begin? A look at the origins of man at play.* New York: David McKay.

Broekhoff, J. (1968) Chivalric education in the Middle Ages. *Quest,* Monograph XI (Winter), 24–31.

Crockett, D. (1961) Sports and recreational practices of Union and Confederate soldiers. *Research Quarterly, 32,* 335–347.

Fielding, L. (1977a) Sport as a training technique in the Union Army. *The Physical Educator, 34,* 145–152.

Fielding, L. (1977b) Sport and the terrible swift sword. *Research Quarterly, 48,* 1–11.

Forbes, C. (1973) The Spartan Agoge. In E.F. Zeigler (Ed.), *A history of sport and physical education to 1900* (pp. 133–138). Champaign, IL: Stipes.

Gerber, E. (1968) Learning and play: Insights of educational protagonists. *Quest,* Monograph XI (Winter), 44–49.

Hackensmith, C. (1966). *History of physical education.* New York: Harper & Row.

Harris, H.A. (1972) *Sport in Greece and Rome.* Ithaca, NY: Cornell University Press.

Harris, H.A. (1973) The spread of Greek athletics. In E.F. Zeigler (Ed.), *A history of sport and physical education to 1900* (pp. 139–153). Champaign, IL: Stipes.

Henry, B. (1976) *History of the Olympic Games.* New York: Putnam's.

Hoepner, B. (1970) John Swett's experience with physical exercise at the Rincon School: Foundation for the first state physical education law in the U.S. *Research Quarterly, 41,* 365–370.

Howell, M. (1969) Seal stones of the Minoan period in the Ashmolean Museum, Oxford, depicting physical activities. *Research Quarterly, 40,* 509–517.

Howell, M.L., & Sawula, L.W. (1973) Sports and games among the Etruscans. In E.F. Zeigler (Ed.), *A history of sport and physical education to 1900* (pp. 79–91), Champaign, IL: Stipes.

Jable, J.T. (1976) Sunday sport comes to Pennsylvania: Professional baseball and football triumph over the Commonwealth's archaic blue laws, 1919–1933. *Research Quarterly, 47,* 357–365.

Kennard, J. (1970) Maryland colonials at play: Their sports and games. *Research Quarterly, 41,* 389–395.

Ledbetter, B. (1979) Sports and games of the American Revolution. *Journal of Sport History, 6,* (3), 29–40.

Lee, M. (1983) *A history of physical education and sports in the USA.* New York: Wiley and Sons.

Leonard, W. (1984). *A sociological perspective of sport* (2nd ed.). Minneapolis: Burgess.

Lewis, G. (1967) America's first intercollegiate sport: The regattas from 1852 to 1875. *Research Quarterly, 38,* 637–648.

Lewis, G. (1969) Theodore Roosevelt's role in the 1905 controversy. *Research Quarterly, 40,* 717–724.

Lucas, J.A. (1968) A prelude to the rise of sport: Antebellum America, 1850–1860. Quest, Monograph XI (Winter), 50–57.

Moolenijzer, N. (1968) Our legacy from the Middle Ages. Quest, Monograph XI (Winter), 32–43.

Neumann, H. (Ed). (1936) *Der Ritterspiegel.* Halle, Germany: Max Niemeyer.

Palmer, D., & Howell, M.L. (1973) Sports and games in early civilization. In E.F. Zeigler (Ed.), *A history of sport and physical education to 1900* (pp. 21–34). Champaign, IL: Stipes.

Park, R. (1980) The *Research Quarterly* and its antecedents. *Research Quarterly for Exercise and Sport, 51,* 1–22.

Rader, B. (1983) *American sports from the age of folk games to the age of spectators.* Englewood Cliffs, NJ: Prentice-Hall.

Rajagopalan, K. (1973) Early Indian physical education. In E.F. Zeigler (Ed.), *A history of sport and physical education to 1900* (pp. 45–55). Champaign, IL: Stipes.

Rice, E., Hutchinson, J., & Lee, M. (1969) *A brief history of physical education* (5th ed.). New York: Ronald.

Roediger, H., Rushton, J., Capaldi, E., & Paris, S. (1984). *Psychology.* Boston: Little, Brown.

Sasijima, K. (1973) Early Chinese physical education and sport. In E.F. Zeigler (Ed.), *A history of sport and physical education to 1900* (pp. 35–44). Champaign, IL: Stipes.

Schrodt, B. (1981) Sports of the Byzantine Empire. *Journal of Sport History, 8(3),* 40–59.

Simri, U. (1973) The ball games of antiquity. In E.F. Zeigler (Ed.), *A history of sport and physical education to 1900* (pp. 93–99). Champaign, IL: Stipes.

Spears, B., & Swanson, R. (1983) *History of sport and physical activity in the United States* (2d ed.). Dubuque, IA: Wm. C. Brown.

Struna, N. (1981) Sport and colonial education: A cultural perspective. *Research Quarterly for Exercise and Sport, 52,* 117–135.

Stull, G.A. (1973) The athletic events of *The Odyssey.* In E.F. Zeigler (Ed.), *A history of sport and physical education to 1900* (pp. 121–131). Champaign, IL: Stipes.

Stull, G.A., & Lewis, G. (1968) The funeral games of the Homeric Greeks. Quest, Monograph XI (Winter), 1–13.

Twombly, W. (1976) *200 years of sport in America: A pageant of a nation at play.* New York: McGraw-Hill.

Van Dalen, D., Mitchell, E., & Bennett, B. (1953) *World history of physical education.* Englewood Cliffs, NJ: Prentice-Hall.

Yalouris, N. (Ed.). (1979) *The eternal Olympics: The art and history of sport.* New Rochelle, NY: Caratzas Brothers, Publishers.

Young, N. (1944). Did the Greeks and the Romans play football? *Research Quarterly, 15,* 310–316.

Zeigler, E.F. (Ed.). (1973a). *A history of sport and physical education to 1900.* Champaign, IL: Stipes.

Zeigler, E.F. (1973b). Historical foundations: Social and educational. In E.F. Zeigler (Ed.), *A history of sport and physical education to 1900* (pp. 11–19). Champaign, IL: Stipes.

Zingale, D. (1977). "Ike" revisited on sport and physical fitness. *Research Quarterly, 48,* 12–18.

3

Behavioral Principles and Applications

INTRODUCTION

An athlete rarely excels in a given sport due only to his or her natural gifts. The natural endowment surely plays a major role as a determinant of athletic performance, but skill development is equally essential to establishing a competitive profile. Basic to the notion of athletic development is the idea that the environment shapes, polishes, and directs the course of sport behaviors. In other words, what we learn about a sport often dictates how we perform in a sport, and ultimately it determines at what level we participate in sport activities. In this chapter we shall discuss some of the basic learning processes that underlie the acquisition of selected athletic skills. And we shall see that in many instances trainers and coaches can intervene to alter these processes and thereby produce a more talented sport performer.

In psychology, the term "learning" is a generic label embracing a wide range of environmental conditions that function to change behavior through experience (Tarpy, 1983). Our coverage will focus on three major types of learning and examine the role of each in sport. The three learning categories are: *classical conditioning*, *operant learning*, and *cognitive learning*.

CLASSICAL CONDITIONING

Classical conditioning is a form of learning that has its scientific roots in Russia. The renowned psychologist Ivan Pavlov was among the first investigators in this area and classical conditioning is most commonly associated with his name (Pavlov, 1927). Traditionally, the procedure shown in figure 3.1 is used to describe the conditions that are necessary for learning to take place. First, a primary eliciting stimulus, called an unconditioned stimulus (UCS), is presented. It reflexively evokes a response, labeled appropriately an *unconditioned response* (UCR). Note that this relationship is biologically prepared; that is, experience is not necessary for the occurrence of the behavior. Subsequently a neutral event called a conditioned stimulus (CS) is paired with the UCS, and after several such pairings the CS comes to produce a conditioned response that it did not previously trigger. An example is what happens when a person sees lightning and then immediately hears a loud clap of thunder. The thunder (the UCS) makes him or her shiver (the UCR) and, because of the close temporal relation between lightning and thunder, a flash of lightning elicits a similar fright response.

Despite the enormous popularity of classical conditioning as a subject area for experimental psychologists, there has not been widespread application of classical conditioning techniques in the sport and physical education realms. When applications are made, they generally fall in the area of stress alleviation or some other method of controlling the discomfort that sometimes comes with competition (see Smith, R.E., 1984). For instance, it is not uncommon to find immensely gifted sport competitors who become so acutely anxious before a big meet, or a critical game, that they lose sleep, vomit, and so forth. Such reactions lower the physical and mental status of the athlete to a point at which his or her ability to perform is compromised. When this sort of private misery occurs, a form of classical conditioning called *reciprocal inhibition* may prove helpful (Craighead, Kazdin, and Mahoney, 1981). This counterconditioning technique involves training the athlete to think about the upcoming competition in a supportive, relaxing context. By pairing the stressful thoughts with behavioral events that are incompatible with the anxiety reaction, the former anxiety-

Figure 3.1 The Procedure for Obtaining Classical Conditioning

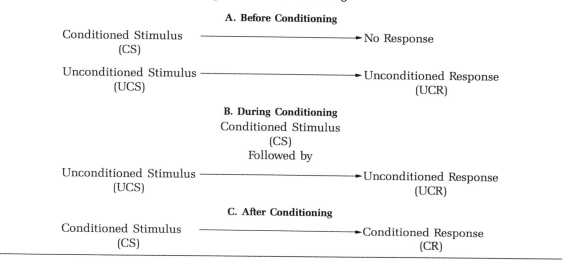

A. Before Conditioning

Conditioned Stimulus ——————————————→ No Response
(CS)

Unconditioned Stimulus —————————————→ Unconditioned Response
(UCS)   (UCR)

B. During Conditioning
Conditioned Stimulus
(CS)
Followed by

Unconditioned Stimulus —————————————→ Unconditioned Response
(UCS)   (UCR)

C. After Conditioning

Conditioned Stimulus ——————————————→ Conditioned Response
(CS)   (CR)

eliciting mental events (thinking about the gymnastics routine, rehearsing the game strategy) evoke relaxation and an attitude of confidence. Now, instead of discomfort, the athlete feels comfortable when he or she thinks about the approaching competition. Such approaches have been used successfully in helping many different types of athletes (Cox, 1985). We discuss this topic in much greater detail in chapter 4.

Other possible uses of classical conditioning methodologies in sport include memory aids and cues that might facilitate recall of particular performance strategies. Along these lines, the importance of the learning context becomes apparent (Smith, S.M., 1979; 1984). For example, psychologists have known for years that we remember better when we recall information under the precise conditions under which it was learned (see Smith, 1979). Trouble arises when we learn in one situation and perform in another. Perhaps this is because the requisite behaviors have been classically conditioned to relevant stimuli in the environ-

ment. When the stimuli are reinstated, performance improves due to the added benefits associated with multiple retrieval cues. For the athlete, this may translate into better execution and a more effective competitive posture. It follows that coaches and trainers would be wise to make special arrangements for their athletic progeny to acquire basic skills under fundamentally the same circumstances of their expected uses. This might mean practicing on the game field as opposed to a remote practice area, working out with an audience present, wearing the same uniform for practice as in actual competition, and so forth.

Unfortunately, systematic studies of the viability of such classical conditioning applications have not been undertaken. Perhaps a serious test of these predictions would be excessively expensive and logistically cumbersome. Nonetheless, classical conditioning is a learning system that likely has greater relevance to sport than heretofore realized, and future developments in this important area are needed.

OPERANT LEARNING

In contrast to the paucity of research on classical conditioning and sport, there has been a veritable explosion of experimental work on the

The merits of negative reinforcement are open to question. These basketball players may go on to win after being reprimanded by their coach during half-time, but chances are they will do so chiefly to avoid another bout with their coach's temper.

application of operant techniques in the area of sport behavior (see Donahue, Gillis, and King [1980] for a review). Operant learning, or operant conditioning as it is also called, is a set of principles set forth by B.F. Skinner of Harvard University. Unlike classical conditioning, for which the important feature for learning is temporal contiguity, for operant learning it is the consequence or outcome of responding that dictates behavioral development (Schwartz, 1984).

Basic Principles

Although operant behavior and the vast research that relates to it are exceedingly complex, the basic tenets of the operant position can be expressed rather simply (see figure 3.2). First, there is the common reward procedure that is known in psychology circles as *positive reinforcement.* Positive reinforcers are events (stimuli) that, when produced by a response, increase the probability of occurrence of that response. An example is when someone performs well on a given task and receives praise or recognition. According to the principle of positive reinforcement there is a good chance he or she will behave similarly in the future. *Negative reinforcement,* by contrast, is a second operant procedure wherein behavioral probability increases when the response prevents or terminates an aversive stimulus. Performing at a certain level to avoid the unkind remarks of an excessively harsh and wrathful coach illustrates the use of negative reinforcement. Opponent processes to these reinforcement techniques are *punishment* and *omission* training, each of which operates to weaken behavior. The former involves the delivery of aversive stimulation contingent upon some behavior; the latter is said to take place when a response results in the loss of a scheduled reward event. In either case, the impact is a negative one that is designed to diminish the strength of responding.

Figure 3.2 Four Basic Training Procedures Used in Operant Conditioning

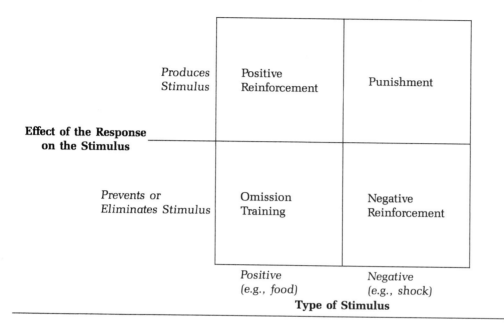

	Positive (e.g., food)	Negative (e.g., shock)
Produces Stimulus	Positive Reinforcement	Punishment
Prevents or Eliminates Stimulus	Omission Training	Negative Reinforcement

Effect of the Response on the Stimulus

Type of Stimulus

Behavior Coaching Techniques. Although the application of operant conditioning concepts has been made under a variety of labels, one of the more elaborate descriptions of the potential uses of such methods was introduced by Martin and Hrycaiko (1983) under the rubric of "effective behavioral coaching." The definition of effective behavioral coaching (EBC) is "the consistent application of principles of behavioral psychology for the improvement and maintenance of athletic behavior" (p. 10). A cardinal operant principle endorsed by EBC is the identification of target behaviors. In this case, this means the specific detailed measurement of selected athletic performances. Rather than rely on impressions and poorly defined criteria for evaluating the effectiveness of certain training strategies, a coach should prepare a preliminary list of behaviors that are the goal of the training manipulation. Such precision provides better clues to the validity of new techniques. Martin and Hrycaiko suggest the following as an example list for a coach of a group of young persons in an age-group competitive sport:

I. Desirable behaviors by athletes and practices:
  A. Attendance at practice
  B. Good listening to instruction (in groups and individually)
  C. Practice of proper skill technique following instruction
  D. Practice of proper components of good technique during endurance training
  E. Continuous repetition of skill without frequent stopping
  F. Practice of skills with the intensity and speed at least equal to that required in the final desired performance
  G. Practice of relaxation techniques and imagery (so that they might be used just prior to competition)

II. Desirable behaviors by athletes at competition:
  A. Muscle relaxation and imagery to prepare to compete
  B. Good skill performance leading to measurable performance improvement (e.g., time, distance)
  C. Good team spirit and mutual support of group members
  D. Desirable sportsmanlike behaviors and minimal behavior problems (e.g., shaking hands, emotional control after losing or poor officiating). (Martin and Hrycaiko, 1983, p. 11)

Once the specific target behaviors have been identified, the appropriate reinforcement procedure should be implemented. It is the consequence of responding that is thought to regulate future response probabilities. Therefore, the coach or trainer should provide the appropriate positive or negative experiences consequent to the performance of desired or undesired athletic responses.

One of the more elegant reports demonstrating the potential use of behavioral coaching methods has been provided by Allison and Ayllon (1980). These researchers examined the efficacy of the behavioral coaching method relative to standard methods of coaching youth football. The procedure for behavioral coaching involved the use of verbal instructions and feedback in a systematic way with four male athletes. When the athlete executed a blocking motion properly, the coach blew a whistle and told the player, "great, way to go." Incorrect blocking techniques were met with verbal reprimands while the player was in a frozen position. Furthermore, the player was given explicit instruction using the coach as a model and later was asked to imitate the proper techniques. This behavioral method contrasted with the standard method primarily in terms of consistency. In the standard method, the coach did not often provide encouragement and when verbal rewards were given they were not enthusiastically offered.

Figure 3.3 shows the results of this attempt to judiciously apply an operant learning strategy. Obviously, the four individuals tested performed better when they received behavioral coaching than standard coaching. The praise following the desirable response can be interpreted as positive reinforcement in this case. Similarly, the verbal reprimands can be interpreted as punishment for the incorrect response. The idea is that these environmental events were contingently related to selected target behaviors.

The comparative effectiveness of positive reinforcement and punishment was assessed in a differential reinforcement study of coaching tennis skills (Buzas and Ayllon, 1981). Under one set of conditions, three female students (ages 13–14) from a physical education class at a junior high school were corrected with routine criticism when they made errors in executing three tennis skills—forehand, backhand, and serve. Performance under this correction procedure defined *baseline*, an operant term used to describe stable response rates when a specified set of conditions is employed. After a period of time, a *differential reinforcement* procedure was introduced whereby the coach selectively ignored errors but systematically praised correct performance. The results of this study revealed that all three girls increased in the execution of appropriate tennis skills by two to four times the baseline rates when coached using this differential reinforcement approach. Positive reinforcement was a more desirable tactic than punishment. Although different findings might occur with older age groups or other special populations, it is doubtful that aversive training procedures ever are preferred over positive techniques, at least when they are used in isolation (see Highlight 3.1).

In another area of athletic competition, Shapiro and Shapiro (1984) extended the use of behavioral coaching techniques to include skill acquisition in track. Using the previously

Figure 3.3 The Percentage of Trials in Which Football Blocks Were Executed Correctly as a Function of Standard Coaching and Behavioral Coaching Techniques

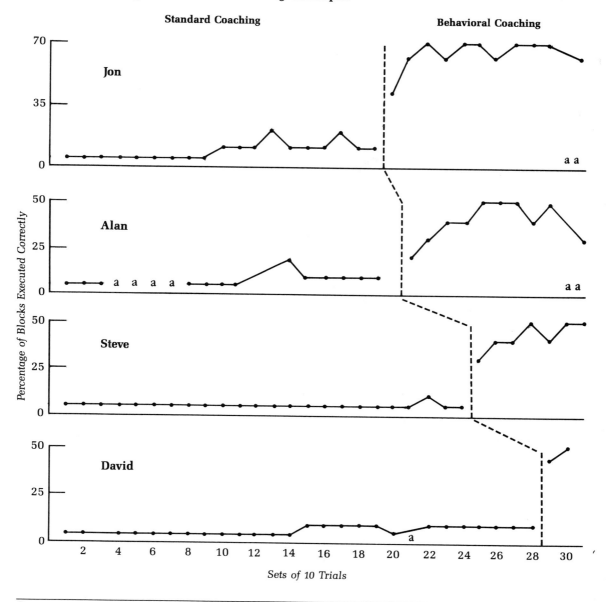

SOURCE: "Behavioral Coaching in the Development of Skills in Football, Gymnastics, and Tennis" by M.G. Allison and T. Ayllon, 1980, *Journal of Applied Behavior Analysis, 13,* 297–314.

HIGHLIGHT 3.1
Why Punish?

As a defensive end for a high school football team in the Midwest, Jason R. was no standout, but he was a reliable player with good judgment. At least this was the usual pattern, but one that Jason failed to conform to during last Friday night's game against an opponent from a neighboring town. It was an absolutely horrid evening with a spate of missed assignments, poor tackling techniques, and penalties. Now it is Monday afternoon practice, and experience tells Jason that he will pay the price for his shortcomings; he must suffer the physical abuse of his coach, and the embarrassment of being singled out for punishment.

"You're worthless, kid," the coach screamed. "I might as well have stood a dummy out there. You let that jerk beat you all night long. Do you know what it means to hit somebody? Try this sometime!" (Jason is flattened by the enraged coach.)

"I'm warning you, you execute the way you did Friday night, and I'll execute you. I'll be on the sideline waiting for you. Count on it!" the coach wailed.

For the uninitiated, this vignette may sound farfetched, but for anyone who has participated in athletics, it is likely all too familiar. It is just another example of the use of a coaching strategy predicated on fear and intimidation. How many times have we seen a coach shout negative comments to a player when a mistake is made, only to quietly look past positive performances? The player under such circumstances putatively learns through relief, and perhaps the system works. But the truth is that virtually no systematic research on this style of behavioral intervention has been attempted (Donahue et al., 1980). In one or two of the few studies that include a negative condition approximating this approach, more desirable results were obtained with positive reinforcement. Then why the widespread use of harsh tactics? Perhaps years of modeling aggressive coaches who win has spawned a generation of athletic trainers and coaches who have adopted the policy of "Do it right, or else!" Whatever the reasons for their use, a more serious scientific look into the use of popular aversive conditioning techniques is badly needed.

Even if the gap between research and practice were lessened in the area of aversive control, we must nonetheless question the wisdom of continuing to use an approach that creates stress and negative self-images. How is Jason likely to feel after being publicly disgraced in front of his teammates? Even if his performance does improve, he is not likely to forget the ridicule and open contempt heaped on him by his coach. Along these lines, the famous Harvard behaviorist B.F. Skinner has cautioned against excessive use of punishment and negative reinforcement in controlling behavior (Skinner, 1971) on the grounds that such procedures evoke unwanted emotional by-products. Along with control come anger and aggression; although these traits may be only moderately destructive within the bracketed framework of certain sport environments, they clearly may have a more negative impact on civilized society as a whole. To even the most ardent supporter of sport, aversive techniques that achieve the desired results would not likely appear useful when they sacrifice personal dignity and perceptions of self-worth. Perhaps coaches would be better advised to employ positive reinforcement techniques. As philosopher Henry David Thoreau remarked, "There are few exceptions where it is better to punish a sin than to reward a virtue."

Sources: "Behavior Modification in Sport and Physical Education: A Review" by J.A. Donahue, J.H. Gillis, and K. King, 1980, *Journal of Sport Psychology, 2,* 311–328; *Beyond Freedom and Dignity* by B.F. Skinner, 1971, New York: Knopf.

described procedures employed by Allison and Ayllon (1980), conditioning, form, and starts in the blocks improved for high school track athletes. The end result was decreases in running times for two events (110m and 200m).

Elsewhere, the development of swimming skills has been the focus of attention for operant applications including behavioral coaching techniques. The procedure of shaping was used to modify the form of an incorrect kicking motion in the front crawl swimming motion of a novice swimming student at Dalhousie University (Rushall and Siedentop, 1972). *Shaping* is an operant technique that involves the selective reinforcement of successive approximations to a goal behavior. When teaching an animal to press a lever to receive food, for example, it is most improbable that the animal will begin pressing the lever immediately upon placement in the apparatus. Typically, the animal is given reinforcement (food) for just moving toward the lever, then for touching the lever with some part of its body, and eventually the criterion for an actual lever press is introduced. Gradually, the animal is shaped into performing the desired response. Similarly, the young swimmer mentioned above was shaped into executing a more acceptable flutter style kick. The specific operant procedure used to accomplish the intended result is described below:

> The desired terminal behavior was to effect an acceptable form of the flutter kick. The consequences used were (1) a light was shone in the swimmer's face every time he performed an incorrect kick, (2) only lengths performed to criterion were recorded on the swimmer's progress chart each being worth double the normal amount, and (3) the coach discussed the subject's performance after each session. The performance criterion was gradually made more stringent for the subject to record a satisfactory length. Initially, four [unacceptable] kicks per length were allowed to be deemed satisfactory. This was reduced to a complete absence of kicks in the fourth practice session. The most attention time required of

the coach for the process was to observe 20 laps of swimming in each of the four sessions. (Rushall and Siedentop, 1972, p. 149)

The findings showed that the number of incorrect swimming kicks systematically decreased with increasing sessions and the associated elevated criteria. Closer inspection of exactly what happened in this study perhaps would be instructive. The shaping component of the operation, of course, is contained in the more stringent performance criterion implemented gradually over sessions. That is, initially reinforcement (gaining a satisfactory evaluation) was attainable when as many as four errors were made, but eventually performance had to be error free. But there is another principle at work here. Can you identify it? What is the operant procedure being used to control the swimming of the student? Recall that in earlier discussions we said that *omission training* involves the removal of a scheduled reinforcement contingent upon the occurrence of an unwanted behavior. Under such circumstances, reinforcement is given when the response is not present; that is, when it is omitted. This is basically what was required of the swimmer. Reinforcement was given not for executing a certain number of correct actions, but rather it was given for the absence of incorrect actions. Such a modification procedure clearly illustrates the uses and advantages of applying one of the several types of operant methods described earlier.

More recently, Koop and Martin (1983) have used a behavioral coaching strategy to teach swimming that emphasized negative consequences of incorrect performances as well as positive consequences of correct performances. Specifically, three male and two female swimmers ranging from 7 to 12 years of age received a tap on the shoulder with a padded stick when errors in specific strokes were made during a lap. In addition, when laps were swum correctly, the trainer shouted "Good" or "That's great! You're really getting that arm right." This technique produced a systematic decrease in errors of selected swimming strokes. So, at least for swimming, a variety of behavioral coaching methods appear to produce performance benefits.

Public Recordings. The performances of swimming athletes has also been studied using a "public recording" reinforcement procedure (Donahue et al., 1980). Public recordings are essentially just that; they are the displaying formal evaluations in such fashion that how well the athlete did, or how poorly, is apparent to all. When we do something well, generally speaking, we want someone to know about it, and athletics is no exception. The positive reinforcement is in the satisfaction that goes with posting a good score on the public record.

An investigation by McKenzie and Rushall (1974) evaluated the impact of checking off completed work units on a program board that was presented publicly. Eight members of a swimming team were asked to record the number of laps swam during successive 1-minute periods in a series of uninterrupted swims. When a certain level of output was achieved, the swimmers checked off the appropriate box on a program board located where other swimmers could see it. In this particular investigation, the intervention strategy (the public recording manipulation) was introduced after a baseline control period, and then it was discontinued. This design, called an *ABA design*, permits the experimenter to evaluate the effectiveness of the modification procedure. Specifically, one would expect that to the extent to which the intervention (B) produced superior results relative to baseline conditions (A), then there should be a pattern of improvement under B but a subsequent decline under A. Otherwise, the improvement registered during the period of intervention might just reflect practice efforts or something else unrelated to the behavioral manipulation. Regarding the findings reported by McKenzie and Rushall (1974), the results were in

the expected direction. Specifically, all eight swimmers had 20 to 30 percent more work output in the intervention phase than the baseline period. Moreover, when the public recording procedure was discontinued the output of seven of the eight swimmers decreased substantially.

The use of public recordings as an applied operant technique raises some interesting theoretical questions. Not the least of the issues here relates to the very nature of the reinforcement process. Is the intervention grounded to positive reinforcement or negative reinforcement? At first glance, it appears to be positive in nature, because the person enjoys the satisfaction of showing the world how well she or he performed. But there is also the possibility that a negative incentive is the true motivational source responsible for any noticed improvement in performance. Surely the person does not want to suffer the embarrassment and potential ridicule attendant to a poor showing. To avoid the possibility of such derisive experiences, an athlete may perform at a high level not to gain recognition but to insure his or her acceptance into a support group. In other words, the response avoids an aversive situation that would otherwise occur. This is clearly negative reinforcement, and many psychologists have suggested that this sort of control is stronger than that accomplished by positive means (Geen, Beatty, and Arkin, 1984).

Regardless of the exact nature of the social reinforcement process underlying the effects observed in coaching swimmers by McKenzie and Rushall (1974), even more dramatic results may occur with material rewards. Rushall and Pettinger (1969) found that thirty-two members of a swimming team increased lap production more when the rewards involved candy or money than they did when the coach's attention served as reward. Thus, while many incentives can be used to modify athletic performance, evidently some consideration should be given to the selection of the particular events that are to function as reinforcement outcomes.

Changing Coaching Behaviors. Operant procedures can be used to modify the behavior of coaches as well as athletes. Indeed, Dickinson (1977) has expressed forcefully the need to implement techniques for changing coaching behavior. Among the recommendations for change are increases in the frequency with which positive comments are offered and greater clarity with regard to specific sport behaviors that are required for excellence. In other words, coaches should use more positive reinforcement and provide better instruction.

Rushall and Smith (1979) attempted to show that the quality and quantity of feedback statements could be increased through self-recording techniques. The subject in this investigation was a thirty-two-year-old senior male swimming coach. Self-recording of "reward and feedback behaviors" was accomplished with the use of sheets that contained columns indicating types of feedback (effort, skill, task execution, performer interaction), and thirty-one key words, all of which could be checked. During several coaching sessions, the subject was signaled at the end of successive 5-minute intervals to count the frequency with which he was giving verbal rewards and relevant feedback. This self-recording process, which in essence is reinforcing the coach for performing goal behaviors that define high quality coaching, produced the desired result. The frequencies of emission of verbal comments and feedback increased dramatically over the course of the study.

An adjunctive element to the Rushall and Smith (1979) project is worthy of mention. Realistically, one cannot expect a coach to continue to keep detailed personal records indefinitely. It is just too time consuming to keep track of the frequency with which specific verbal remarks are registered, and so forth. So how can we expect the target behaviors to survive when the intervention processes are removed? Fortunately, operant conditioners have perfected a procedure called *fading*, which assures persistence even beyond the point at which the behavioral manipulation is discontinued. The fading strategy used by Rushall and Smith involved gradually "leaning" or stretching the reinforcement schedule so that the required 5-minute interval counts became less and less frequent. The high production of the target behavior continues in such a case but the control of the higher quality coaching performance falls under the influence of other stimuli, such as witnessing improvement in the athletes themselves, greater comradeship, and so forth. In effect, a temporary control device is exchanged for a more enduring one. A follow-up period of observation conducted by Rushall and Smith indicated that their fading techniques were successful in achieving the purpose of transferring stimulus control from the checklist to the performance of the swimmers.

Conditioned Reinforcement. Yet another operant procedure that may prove useful for training athletes is *conditioned reinforcement*. Conditioned reinforcers are stimuli that, when paired with a primary reinforcer, come to possess the same control properties as the primary reinforcer (Martin and Pear, 1988). An example in a more traditional laboratory setting is when a tone is paired with a primary reward object such as food, and then the previously neutral tone acquires the ability to strengthen behavior it is made contingent upon. That is, the subject works for the previously neutral event (the conditioned reinforcer) because it has been correlated with reward.

In applied situations, a common training rationale based on conditioned reinforcement is the *token system* (Kazdin, 1977; Thomas and Miller, 1980). In such a system, an object of some sort is given to the subject when the appropriate behavior is executed. For example, a plastic disk might be given to a child suffering from a speech difficulty upon the successful production of a word phase. At some point, the token (the disk) can be exchanged for a more meaningful object such as a toy or food. Research has shown that this form of conditioned reinforcement is an effective way to modify behavior, and it has the advantage of not satiating the subject (Martin and Pear, 1988).

Two investigations have indicated that token systems can be used to alter athletic skills. In a study by Jones, reported in Donahue et al. (1980), the subjects of the manipulation were participants in a basketball camp. Because the objective of most basketball coaches is to outscore the opponent, it seemed reasonable to select "points scored" as the target behavior. The staff employed three different training routines. First, all members of a given basketball squad were rewarded with an "Olympic ring" each time their team scored 20 points. With 80 points in a single game, four rings were given to each player on the team. Later, these rings could be redeemed for food or rewards. Secondly, the players were placed on the same sort of token system, but it was predetermined that no rings would be dispensed. A third condition simply scored the games in the standard way, and no token system was even suggested. The findings from this study revealed that players scored more points under the Olympic ring contingency than either of the other conditions. Evidently, the operant strategy of token reinforcement was an effective behavioral control device.

Nine members of a professional basketball team were subjects in a token system intervention that used money as the conditioned reinforcer (money, after all, is a sort of token because it has value only when it can be exchanged for something of greater worth). The players were given financial rewards for efficient offensive performance. An efficiency average (EA) served as the target measure. In this study, an *ABAB* design was used in which the intervention following the initial baseline was discontinued but subsequently reinstated. Each time the token intervention was instituted,

three players with the highest EAs received monetary payments. The result showed that six of the nine players increased their offensive production during the first intervention and of these six, four decreased in performance during the return to baseline. All four players subsequently improved again when the final intervention was introduced. So, consistent with findings in other studies using token systems, conditioned reinforcers did have a positive influence on athletic performance.

Although it seems clear that token systems have a legitimate place in the development of sport skill, the use of such tangible rewards to control behavior is not without opposition. The concern over the use of such techniques stems from evidence indicating that, following the removal of a recently introduced reward, response rates decline to levels below those consistently maintained prior to the introduction of the rewarding event (Lepper, Greene, and Nisbett, 1973). For instance, consider what may happen with the aforementioned use of rings to reinforce high point production in basketball games. How will the athletes react when their high outputs no longer render the rings? Will they abandon the activity altogether because the payoff is no longer there? Unfortunately, there is a good chance that this will be the case.

Lepper and Greene (1978) have suggested that such negative patterns following reward removal may in fact relate to *overjustification.* According to this view the introduction of an external reward forces a person to review the value of the activity, and the amount of worth attached to the behavior often is defined according to the degree of extrinsic gain. Ultimately, when the external reward is taken away, the person concludes that the entire reason for responding is gone. What this may mean to a coach is that, if external reinforcement manipulations are to be used, some agenda should exist for shifting to more realistic controlling stimuli. Earlier in this chapter we talked about fading as a psychological principle. Here is another instance in which such a procedure could prove useful.

Premack Principle. When tokens or other types of tangible rewards are not used for behavior modification, the opportunity to engage in a preferred activity can act as reinforcement. In learning circles this approach is often referred to as the *Premack Principle* (Premack, 1962). The idea is that any behavior that is independently more probable than some other behavior can be used as a reward to strengthen the lower probability response. For example, a child presented with the task of completing his or her arithmetic assignment may be offered the chance to play with the classroom gerbil, subject to meeting the academic contingency. Basically, the behavior is the reinforcer in this procedure and in that sense the Premack Principle departs somewhat from the traditional operant format.

The potential effectiveness of a Premack training operation in the area of athletics and sport is evident from a study by Kau and Fisher (1974). The purpose of this research was to demonstrate that the preferred activity of engaging in various social activities could be used as a reinforcement for the less probable activity of jogging in an aerobics program. The results of the study indicated that over a four-week course, sharp increases in jogging were apparent. Interestingly, weight loss and other natural reinforcers took over and the program was judged to be successful beyond the point of the intervention. At any rate, in at least some cases the opportunity to perform a response that is deemed desirable can be used successfully as a behavioral method for athletic training.

One of the great advantages of the Premack approach is that the program is individually tailored to meet the needs of each person. Not all people enjoy doing the same things. For some people, the opportunity to immerse

themselves in a social situation may be outright offensive. Rather than be forced to engage in what he or she views as trivial social interactions, the person may prefer a private moment in a sauna. The point is that, according to the Premack Principle, targeted behavioral rates can be increased in both individuals as long as the responses occasion the opportunity to do what they enjoy. The bottom line for the coach is: Find out what the athlete likes to do and make the opportunity to do it contingent upon the execution of the desired sport skills.

Response cost. One operant technique not yet mentioned is *response cost*. Response cost is a procedure whereby undesirable behaviors are penalized by taking away a reward object already in the possession of the person. The rewards are regained when appropriate behaviors are exhibited. This approach differs slightly from omission training in that response cost involves rewards that have already been obtained, whereas omission training involves scheduled rewards that were never given. A response cost procedure used by Wysocki, Hall, Iata, and Riordan (1979) was successful in getting seven of eight college students to increase aerobic exercising, and the benefits were still apparent at a twelve month follow-up.

Feedback. We have seen that a number of different applications of operant learning are possible in the world of sport. Curiously, all of the studies reported in this chapter have one feature in common. That feature is *feedback*. There was always knowledge of results, whether it was in the form of a public record, a tangible object, attention, or the chance to engage in a preferred activity. Considering the demonstrated utility of providing feedback to athletes in controlled experimental settings, it is not altogether a surprise that coaches and trainers have used films and the even more immediate feedback afforded by videotaping (Penman, 1969). When an athletic participant receives information about what and how he or she has done, in whatever form, chances are that person's skill development will benefit.

Also, we note that in one recent study of feedback that examined endurance in a laboratory setting, Hall, Weinberg, and Jackson (1987) found that the nature of the feedback stimulus is important in determining performance. Specifically, feedback given during training is preferred to feedback given at the end of training. Apparently, the value of moment-to-moment results is greater than the final result, at least as it relates to athletic performance as an adjunct of behavior.

Training Variables

Session Length. Training variables that are known to affect operant performance have also attracted the interest of applied sport psychology investigators. One such variable with the potential for having profound impact on the acquisition of sport skill is the length and spacing of practice sessions. What are the optimal durations for teaching new skills? Should the practice sessions occur close together or should they be widely spaced with long rest intervals? These were a few of the questions taken under consideration in an article by Sanderson (1983). The psychology of learning literature would argue that *distributed practice* (widely spaced training trials with long periods of rest) should be superior to *massed practice* (cramming training sessions into a short time frame). But as Sanderson notes, the only conclusion that can be drawn for the development of sport skill is that "somewhere between too little rest and too much lay off is the desired condition for practice" (p. 121). A great deal depends on the skill being developed and the nature of the instruction process. In general, it is safe to say that aspects of performance requiring gross motor skills (catching a baseball, blocking tech-

nique in football, and so forth) survive over longer periods of time than events that have mental components (reading keys, using appropriate cognitive strategies, and so forth). Accordingly, coaches should be alert to the different types of training programs that may be most suitable for introducing a particular skill.

Schedules of Reinforcement. Another variable that may influence the efficacy of athletic training operations is *schedule of reinforcement*. It is widely accepted that *intermittent reinforcement* occasions greater persistence than *continuous reinforcement* (Nation and Woods, 1980). This means that when a target response is rewarded half the time but is not rewarded on the other half of the trials (intermittent reinforcement), the response will continue for a greater time period after reward is no longer available than would be the case had the response been rewarded every time it occurred. An example is the child who learns to throw a tantrum in order to get what he or she wants from a parent. If the parent is inconsistent, that is, occasionally he or she gives in but not always, the child is essentially on an intermittent reinforcement schedule. Be assured that the parent will have greater difficulty extinguishing this tantrum behavior by finally ignoring it altogether than would have been the case had the tantrum response consistently been reinforced (had the child always got his or her way).

To date only a few studies of sport behavior have examined the possible utility of intermittent reinforcement as a tool for insuring response persistence (see Donahue et al., 1980). But there is little doubt that such schedules can serve the coach or training staff. An offensive lineman who learns that he will fail once in awhile, nonetheless learns to keep trying. A tennis player, having learned that most but not every strategically placed serve will be a winner, acquires an attitude of perseverance. To be sure, intermittent reinforcement schedules are accomplished to some degree according to the natural order of competition. But training experiences in this area need not be haphazard; rather, schedules can be judiciously programmed to produce the intended result.

Learned Helplessness

Perhaps one of the most exciting links between operant phenomenon and the sport realm rests with the concept of *learned helplessness*. Learned helplessness is said to occur when an organism previously exposed to an aversive noncontingency exhibits a deficit in the acquisition of a subsequent operant behavior (Maier and Seligman, 1976). This means that when animals or people are placed in situations in which they have no control over their success or failure rate, they do poorly on other unrelated tasks even though their chances for success might be good. An example in the animal laboratory is the rat that is exposed to shock and cannot turn the shock off regardless of its activity. Later, when this animal is exposed to shock in another environment in which the shock could be terminated by something as simple as a lever press, no responses are attempted (Seligman and Beagley, 1975). It's as if the rat has learned that it is helpless with respect to controlling the environment and carries this expectancy of uncontrollability with it into new learning situations even though the reward conditions have improved dramatically. Similarly, humans often show depression and other types of performance anomalies once they have experienced a series of failures due to circumstances they view as largely outside their control (Abramson, Seligman, and Teasdale, 1978). The person comes to expect failure and, not surprisingly, does fail.

Psychologist Carol Dweck has written on the potential parallels between learned helplessness as a laboratory phenomenon and certain problem athletes (Dweck, 1980). The issue seems to center on how the sport participant reacts to his or her own encounters with failure. When a person becomes preoccupied with failure and assumes personal responsibility for it, chances are greater for helplessness. Dweck uses the example of heavyweight boxer Dwayne Bobick, who had a near perfect record but eventually was knocked out in the first round. He subsequently lost every fight. According to helplessness theory (cf. Abramson et al., 1978), such a result in a "success only" person is not unexpected. Because there has been no experience with failure and interpolated success, failure signals only more setbacks, and negative forecasts only build on themselves. Ultimately, a losing attitude (helplessness) emerges.

What is preferred may be a mastery-oriented attitude toward failure. When a person uses a personal disappointment as a "psyching-up" mechanism, and struggles even harder, then the chances for an eventual triumph increase appreciably. It has been recommended that intermittent reinforcement schedules of the sort described earlier could help immunize individuals against feelings of helplessness (Nation and Massad, 1978). The belief is that failure experienced in the context of aggregate success builds an attitude of persistence, and therein preempts helplessness. One has only to look to Dweck's example of Ben Hogan to appreciate what a positive attitude in the face of adversity can do for a competitor. Despite a conspicuous lack of natural talent, years of defeat, and a severe auto accident that nearly killed him, a dedicated Hogan came back to become perhaps the greatest golfer ever. Clearly, failure is perceived differently by different people.

On a purely commonsense level, all of this points to the need to make players, especially young ones, feel as if they are winners. A young athlete constantly berated and criticized by a coach or parent will think only of losing and feel helpless about winning. In Highlight 3.1 we addressed the issue of aversive control and concluded that, even though it may be effective, it is also potentially destructive, both to the individual and society. Rather than criticize, a better strategy might be to build real confidence by teaching children how to handle failure in a realistic fashion.

COGNITIVE LEARNING

Over the past decade the psychology of learning has witnessed a resurgence of interest in the uniquely mental aspects of behavior (Kirschenbaum and Wittrock, 1984). Several years ago, terms such as "the mind," "beliefs," and "mental activity" were considered unobservables and therefore they were events outside the purview of scientific psychology. More recently, psychologists have been more accepting of the cognitive position, and processes such as imagery, rehearsal, and causal ascription have become primary areas of focus (see Weinberg, 1984). Evidence even indicates that such cognitive events are crucial for the elite athlete (cf. Mahoney, Gabriel, and Perkins, 1987).

Imagery

Cognitive learning theory and its applications have certainly gained increased visibility in the sport environment in recent years. Silva (1982) has reviewed much of the work that has been done in the area of cognitive intervention and he finds that in many instances use of cognitive strategies has enhanced performance. Imagery and mental rehearsal, for example, have been shown to improve the performances of athletes ranging from gymnasts (Meyers, Schleser, Cooke, and Cuvillier, 1979) to downhill skiers (Suinn, 1972). With the skier, for example, the competitor was told to imagine actually going down the slope, each turn was made mentally, and the athlete raced successfully to the finish line. Just thinking through the task actually produced benefits; that is, times improved after only a few sessions.

A similar cognitive intervention was used for improving the performance of a male varsity college basketball player (Meyers and Schleser, 1980). In actual game situations, the following coping mechanisms were used: coping instructions patterned after Meichenbaum (1977) (refer to chapter 4) were implemented so that self-reinforcement statements were given for successful performances, attribution for failure was shifted from self-blame to effort requirements and external demands, and so forth. Also, the athlete was taught to relax and imagine successful scenes in increasingly problematic situations. The athlete imagined failure situations as well, but he was able to cope with the setbacks during the imagery session. These procedures were practiced first in a noncompetitive environment, but later prior to pregame warmups and even during the game when there was a break in the action. Figure 3.4 shows the points-per-game record for the basketball player before the cognitive intervention (pretreatment) and after the intervention (posttreatment). Clearly, significant improvement in performance did occur following the introduction of the cognitive strategies. Although not reflected in figure 3.4, shooting percentage (field goal) increased from 42 percent to almost 66 percent.

Hall and Erffmeyer (1983) employed a modified version of Suinn's (1972) cognitive training as a technique for enhancing free throw accuracy among ten highly skilled female members of an intercollegiate basketball team. The technique, termed visuomotor behavioral rehearsal (VMBR), basically consists of (a) an initial relaxation phase, (b) visualizing performance during a specific stressful situation, and (c) actually performing the skill in a simulated environment. In the Hall and Erffmeyer study (rare in that an actual control manipulation was carried out), a group of girls was simply

Figure 3.4 Points per Game for the 28-Game Season before (Pretreatment) and after (Post-treatment) the Introduction of a Cognitive Intervention Technique

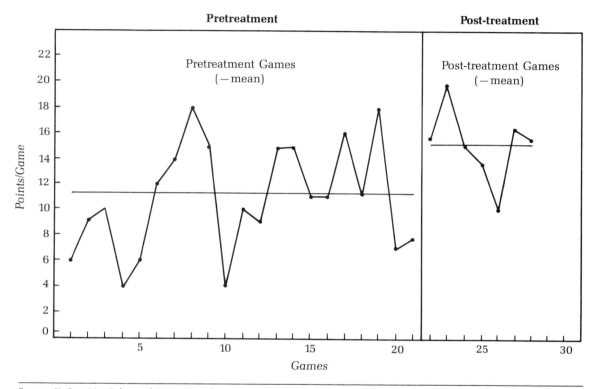

SOURCE: "A Cognitive Behavioral Intervention for Improving Basketball Performance" by A. W. Meyers and R. Schleser, 1980, *Journal of Sport Psychology, 2,* 69–73.

trained to relax and visualize excellent foul shooting. A second group (the VMBR condition) viewed a color videotape of a model female basketball player executing ten consecutive foul shots with perfect form. Because the model was viewed from behind, it was relatively easy for each girl to imagine that she was the one actually shooting the free throws. After the tape, girls in the VMBR condition were asked to close their eyes and again view themselves as shooting without errors in form or consequence.

The findings from this interesting study indicated that watching the tape had a more dramatic impact on performance than imagery training alone (see figure 3.5). Specifically, the percent of free throws made rose sharply during a five-day post-test period following treatment for the VMBR athletes, but there was no corresponding increase among the girls who had merely learned to relax and use visual imagery (no modeling). These findings are of special significance because they suggest that the use of more traditional imagery techniques may be limited. Certainly such approaches may be at a disadvantage without some sort of visual aid that may assist in the process of image formation.

Figure 3.5 A Comparison of Pretest and Post-Test Foul-Shooting Percentages of Groups Experiencing a Visuo-Motor Behavioral Rehearsal (VMBR) Intervention or Relaxation Training Only

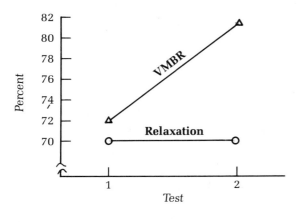

SOURCE: "The Effects of Visuo-Motor Behavior Rehearsal with Videotaped Modeling on Free-Throw Accuracy of Intercollegiate Female Basketball Players" by E.G. Hall and E.S. Erffmeyer, 1983, *Journal of Sport Psychology*, 5, 343–346.

So, despite the many experiments that show positive mental rehearsal and imagery effects (Corbin, 1972; Harris and Robinson, 1986), in some cases imagery and mental practice have failed to produce positive results. A study by Andre and Means (1986), for instance, detected no differences in motor performance between controls and mental practice groups that were instructed to utilize normal or slow-motion imagery techniques. In order to account for such inconsistencies in the literature, many researchers of sport psychology have begun to examine individual traits that could dispose a person to react favorably or unfavorably to imagery manipulation. Too, proper training is needed. Imagery training is varied, and many coaches may not know enough about it to effectively train their athletes. Consequently, in an effort to standardize sport imagery training, and therein provide some consistency in gaug-

ing the value of the technique, specific conditions that facilitate sport imagery training have been set forth (see Highlight 3.2).

Psyching-up Strategies

Of all the intervention strategies that are rooted to the traditions of cognitive psychology, perhaps none has received more attention than psyching-up techniques. The term "psyching-up" is often used in athletic circles by coaches, players, and others close to the competition. Despite the nebulous features associated with such an unscientific term, it connotes some very specific ideas. When a player "psychs up," a state of cognitive and mental readiness is gained that affords the athlete a psychological advantage. Cognitive elements are brought forth in such polished form that physical precision results. Tension, alertness, and even nausea have all been shown to contribute to optimum behavioral expression in sport. In conventional vernacular, the player must develop "a winning attitude."

Only recently has the systematic literature on psyching-up begun to take shape. Weinberg (1984) has proposed that the varied techniques that form the corpus of this literature can be categorized as invoking (a) attentional focus, (b) self-efficacy statements, (c) relaxation, (d) imagery, or (e) preparatory arousal. While some approaches are characterized by more than one area, others focus exclusively on one dimension.

The seminal paper on psyching-up was written by Shelton and Mahoney (1978). In a test of influence of the psyching-up strategy on motor performance, thirty Olympic-style weightlifters were instructed to psych up or simply count backward prior to performing on a hand dynamometer task designed to measure grip strength. The results indicated that the athletes who were permitted to use their own methods for getting themselves psyched up showed dramatic increases in performance, whereas their control counterparts (the counting backward condition) either registered no improvement or actually exhibited performance decreases.

These findings were extended by Weinberg, Gould, and Jackson (1980) in a study that examined task specificity and psyching-up. Three different motor tasks (isokinetic leg strength, stabilometer balance, speed-of-arm-movement) were employed and careful measurements were taken on each task after a psych-up manipulation. The results indicated that while isokinetic leg-strength performance was facilitated by the psych-up strategy, the other two behaviors were largely unaffected by this intervention. It would seem, therefore, that only certain types of response systems are likely to benefit from psych-up techniques.

Along other lines, Weinberg, Gould, and Jackson (1981) have observed that the changes in the motor systems affected by psych-up strategies are relatively independent of the duration of the interval during which the psyching-up takes place. Specifically, while leg-strength performance increased above a baseline level following instructions to use whatever psych-up technique the subject might select, the length of time the subject engaged in this exercise was of little consequence. Such findings are of interest because they are at odds with much of the traditional psychological literature on arousal and performance.

Documentation of the validity of psyching-up strategies for increasing athletic performance in field situations is provided by Caudill, Weinberg, and Jackson (1983). Using college sprinters and hurdlers off the North Texas State University Track team, performance was evaluated for each of sixteen athletes under both psych-up and control conditions. The findings revealed that significantly better performances did occur for fifteen of the sixteen athletes under the psych-up as opposed to the control condition. Apparently, the increased effectiveness associated with psyching-up, assumed by coaches, players, and sport practitioners, is genuine and confirmable.

Current Issues

Recent studies have focused on the range and scope of influence of cognitive techniques. Increasing evidence indicates that cognitive approaches are most likely to be effective when the athletic skill has a large cognitive component. Ryan and Simons (1983), for instance, found that mental practice facilitated learning of a low motor task with a heavy cognitive component but had no effect when the cognitive aspects of the task were reduced. Such findings imply that some athletic tasks such as tackling in football, or serving in volleyball or tennis, may not benefit from cognitive learning interventions. Or, as Feltz and Landers (1983) note, if positive effects are to be achieved in such sports using cognitive methods, then considerably more time should be allocated to the intervention (p. 46).

Another topic of heated debate has centered on what Schmidt (1982) has labeled "the initial learning hypothesis." The position taken here is that cognitive interventions are most likely to enhance performance during the early stages of skill acquisition. Perhaps this could be due to a greater reliance on cognitive components at this stage; that is, you still have to think about it before you execute it. In any case, the implication is that elite athletes (athletes already performing at a high level of efficiency) would be better off invoking an alternative strategy. And this notion does have some support (Schmidt, 1982, pp. 458–462). But the findings are far from conclusive in this area and any remarks made must be considered tentative.

Even if externally imposed cognitive intervention strategies are shown to be of limited value for elite athletic performers, there can be little doubt that internal cognitive processes are

HIGHLIGHT 3.2
Sport Imagery
Training

Many successful athletes from a variety of sport areas have noted that they imagine the execution of a sport skill before they actually perform. High jumper Dwight Stones, for example, reports that he would close his eyes prior to a jump and mentally pace through his steps and then see himself carrying over the crossbar. Golfer Jack Nicklaus often rehearses a putt in his mind before he steps over the ball, and tennis star Chris Evert uses imagery for polishing key techniques on the court.

Although both elite performers and beginners may practice imagery training to some extent, not many people are ever likely to develop this skill to its potential. For one thing, it is often self-taught, and for another it is not likely to be systematized. The practical use of sport imagery training could perhaps be enhanced by directing greater attention to the conditions that facilitate its development. Some of the more important conditions are suggested below.

1. *Vividness and controllability.* Images are likely to prove most beneficial when they are colorful, realistic, and involve the appropriate emotions. Actual recollections of previous performances provide an anchor for building comparisons, and they make images of future performances seem more believable. When the downhill skier really sees the slope, his or her mental executions are more likely to result in real improvements. Also, it is essential that the skier be able to control the presence of the image. That is, he or she must be able to turn it on and off in order to use it to advantage. In certain circumstances, images may be distracting and divert the athlete's focus from the task immediately at hand. Knowing when to use imagery is as important as knowing how to use it.

2. *Practice.* Imagery is a skill that can be learned. Although some people are better at visualizing events than others, everyone can improve his or her mental functioning along these lines. This is not to say, however, that improvement is likely to come about quickly or without effort. Often, athletes must mentally practice for months before they become proficient in the use of imagery techniques. Short sessions with long rest intervals are preferred; repetition is absolutely required.

3. *Attitude and expectation.* Imagery is most likely to benefit those who believe in it. If an athlete rejects the approach as nontraditional, it is not likely to be of much value. If used at all, the technique should be approached with the recognition that it is a legitimate skill and, like any other skill, can be learned in time, within the ability of the learner.

4. *Previous experience.* Some evidence exists that experienced athletes may gain more than beginners from imagery training. The reason is not clear. It may be because the more experienced performer has already mastered basic physical skills and thus is able to allocate more attention to mental processes.

5. *Relaxed attention.* A relaxed state of mind during imagery training seems to facilitate the effectiveness of training. A person who is fully relaxed is better able to attend to the integrity of an image, with the result that images are more vivid and easier to control.

High-jumper Dwight Stones closes his eyes prior to a jump, and sees himself clearing the crossbar. Although the practice of imagery training is familiar to athletes at all levels, it's unlikely that many develop the skill to its potential.

6. *Internal versus external imagery.* **Although the scientific evidence is still out, the notion that an internal perspective results in more favorable images than an external one has intuitive appeal. To see someone else perform successfully is one thing; it is something else again to visualize oneself accomplishing the same feat. If for no other reason, the image should likely include oneself because it is desirable for the image to overlap as much as possible with the real-life situation.**

SOURCE: "Conditions That Facilitate the Development of Sport Imagery Training" by D. Smith, 1987, *Sport Psychologist, 1,* 237–247.

important to performance of truly gifted athletes. Indeed, there is even evidence that internally based cognitive strategies can be used to differentiate more successful competitors from their less successful counterparts (Mahoney and Avener, 1977). Several years ago, a suspicion among researchers was that many world class long distance runners were using "dissociative" strategies that permitted them to block out the pain and torment of the final, most stressful part of the race. For example, for the closing few miles a marathoner might count backward from some set value, or think about an unrelated, pleasant activity, and thereby shut out the agony associated with finishing. It was left to Morgan and Pollack (1977) to assess scientifically the validity of such dissociative processes among elite long distance runners. Contrary to what many people in sports expected, the better runners adopted an "associative" task-demand/body-monitoring cognitive strategy, and it was the less talented runner who was more likely to dissociate. The more competent runner, it seems, is more likely to "stay in tune with bodily signals." That is, should something go wrong it is advantageous

Greg Louganis immediately before his final platform dive at the 1988 Summer Olympics. Louganis won the gold in the event, becoming the first man to win two gold medals for diving in consecutive Olympics.

to detect the problem immediately so that appropriate corrective action can be taken. This may mean engaging some sort of compensatory mechanism or ceasing any further activity altogether in order to avoid irrepairable damage.

Elsewhere, greater concentration ability, success in dreams, reported self-confidence, and self-instructional behavior have been reported by successful gymnasts (Mahoney and Avener, 1977) and racquetball players (Meyers, Cooke, Cullen, and Liles, 1981), at least relative to less successful athletes in the same sport. Also, it seems that "champion" status athletes in these sports handle situational anxiety better than the less skilled athlete. So, even though the value of cognitive learning manipulations introduced by coaches or trainers may on occasion be questioned, there is clearly evidence to indicate that internal cognitive mechanisms are important to the ultimate success of even the most gifted athletic participant.

We have now discussed some of the possible sport applications of learning processes in three major areas: classical conditioning, operant learning, and cognitive learning. Each of these areas has an immense basic literature, and only a few of the many uses of the knowledge base in this area have been suggested by sport psychologists. Oversights are especially great in the areas of classical conditioning, considering the demonstrated value of procedures in this area regarding other attempts at human behavior modification (see Wolpe, 1982). Finally, the technology of behavioral psychology must be appreciated by coach and player alike for the athlete to reach his or her athletic potential.

SUMMARY

1. Classical conditioning, operant learning, and cognitive learning are three major types of learning that have influenced sport.
2. In classical conditioning a primary eliciting stimulus called an unconditioned stimulus (UCS) reflexively produces a response called an unconditioned response (UCR). When a neural stimulus, called a conditioned stimulus (CS), is paired with the UCS, the CS comes to evoke a conditioned response (CR) similar to the UCR.
3. Despite a large literature on classical conditioning, it has been an overlooked area in the psychology of sport.
4. In operant learning, positive reinforcement refers to the strengthening of behav-

ior by presenting an event following responding. Conversely, negative reinforcement refers to the strengthening of behavior by removing an event following responding. Punishment and omission training both weaken responding, but different operations are involved with each procedure.

5. Behavioral coaching techniques involve the application of learning principles to situations involved with training athletic competitors. Differential reinforcement, shaping, and reinforcement are a few of the learning principles that have been used in this area.
6. Public recordings involve the placement of formal evaluations in a display in an effort to reward or punish athletic performances.
7. In addition to emphasizing behavioral techniques for the purpose of changing the athlete's performance, behavioral manipulations can also be used to modify the behavior of coaches. Feedback statements about the frequency with which positive and negative criticism is given especially have produced positive results.
8. Conditioned reinforcers are neutral stimuli that, when paired with primary reinforcers, come to act as primary reinforcers. Token systems illustrate one potential use of conditioned reinforcers.
9. The Premack Principle states that a high probability behavior can be used as a reward for the occurrence of a lower probability response. The advantage of this approach is that rewards are defined on an individual basis.
10. Session length and schedules of reinforcement are two training variables discussed in the chapter. As a rule, widely spaced trials work better when gross motor skills are the target of training. Also, persistence in responding is greater when intermittent rather than continuous reinforcement is used.

11. Learned helplessness occurs when an expectancy of uncontrollability emerges following exposure to an aversive noncontingency. Many athletes fail because they anticipate failure. One way to prevent learned helplessness is to incorporate success and failure experiences into the training program.

12. Cognitive learning theory involves the study of the mental aspects of behavior. Recently, sport psychology has witnessed an increased interest in cognitive learning as it relates to treatment intervention and performance enhancement.

13. Mental practice techniques that make use of cognitive manipulations have produced positive results, but a number of issues are yet to be reconciled. Among them are the restrictions on *when* and *where* the techniques can be applied in sport, and there is some question about the usefulness of the approach when the elite athlete is being trained.

SUGGESTED READINGS

Catania, A.C. (1984) *Learning.* Englewood Cliffs, NJ: Prentice-Hall.

This textbook provides low-level but comprehensive coverage of learning and conditioning principles. Theoretical as well as empirical issues are discussed. Among the topics covered are schedules of reinforcement, conditioned reinforcement, and the nature of stimulus control. In many instances applied examples are provided so that the reader can see how learning processes relate to real-world experiences.

Lutzker, J.R., & Martin, J.A. (1981) *Behavior change.* Monterey, CA: Brooks/Cole

This book is an overview of how learning concepts can be used to change behavior in clinical and educational settings. A number of treatment interventions are discussed and ethical concerns are raised that relate to the use of behavioral control techniques. Unlike the more basic texts on learning, this book focuses on practical applications of learning principles. Among the topics covered are shaping, token-economy systems, and fading techniques. Although the book deals mostly with therapy issues, it is research-based and provides many references for the interested reader.

Schwartz, B. (1984) *Psychology of learning and behavior.* New York: W.W. Norton.

A more advanced coverage of classical conditioning and operant learning is presented in this popular textbook than is provided in this chapter. It will be of interest to students whose specific concern is to develop sophistication in the learning area. Although there is some application to practical settings, the book focuses on laboratory issues and theoretical matters. Writing for the more advanced student, Schwartz has assumed some understanding of experimental design.

Seligman, M.E.P. (1975) *Helplessness.* San Francisco: W.H. Freeman.

This is a nonacademic coverage of the concept of helplessness as it relates to depression and the stresses of everyday life. It is tied to research, but the reader need not be a student of experimental psychology to understand it. The basic notion that lack of control resulting from an environmental noncontingency can produce deficit performance is linked to a variety of phenomena in everyday life, and even to death, in some instances.

Skinner, B.F. (1971) *Beyond freedom and dignity.* New York: Knopf.

The classic work by one of the foremost authorities on learning addresses the problems associated with the use of aversive control techniques. The author calls into question the wisdom of using punishment and negative reinforcement when other procedures are available. The implications of this work for coaching and other areas that make use of aversive techniques become clear as the author spells out the unfortunate consequences associated with negative stimulation. The recommendation by Skinner is that we substitute positive reinforcement for negative reinforcement, and omission training for punishment.

REFERENCES

Abramson, L.Y., Seligman, M.E.P., & Teasdale, I.D. (1978) Learned helplessness in humans: Critique and reformulation. *Journal of Abnormal Psychology*, 87, 49–74.

Allison, M.G., & Ayllon, T. (1980) Behavioral coaching in the development of skills in football, gymnastics, and tennis. *Journal of Applied Behavior Analysis*, 13, 297–314.

Andre, J.C., & Means, J.R. (1986) Rate of imagery in mental practice: An experimental investigation. *Journal of Sport Psychology*, 8, 124–128.

Buzas, H.P., & Ayllon, T. (1981) Differential reinforcement in coaching tennis skills. *Behavior Modification*, 5, 372–385.

Caudill, D., Weinberg, R., & Jackson, A. (1983) Psyching-up and track athletes: A preliminary investigation. *Journal of Sport Psychology*, 5, 231–235.

Corbin, C.B. (1972) Mental practice. In W.P. Morgan (Ed.), *Ergogenic aids and muscular performance* (pp. 68–84). New York: Academic Press.

Cox, R.H. (1985) *Sport psychology: Concepts and applications*. Dubuque, IA: Wm. C. Brown.

Craighead, W.E., Kazdin, A.E., & Mahoney, M.J. (1981) *Behavior modification: Principles, issues, and applications*. Boston: Houghton Mifflin Company.

Dickinson, J.A. (1977) *A behavioral analysis of sport*. Princeton, NJ: Princeton University Press.

Donahue, J.A., Gillis, J.H., & King, K. (1980) Behavior modification in sport and physical education: A review. *Journal of Sport Psychology*, 2, 311–328.

Dweck, C.S. (1980) Learned helplessness in sport. In K.M. Newell & G.C. Roberts (Eds.), *Psychology of motor behavior and sport—1979* (pp. 1–11). Champaign, IL: Human Kinetics.

Feltz, D.L., & Landers, D.M. (1983) The effects of mental practice on motor skill learning and performance: A meta-analysis. *Journal of Sport Psychology*, 5, 25–57.

Geen, R.G., Beatty, W.W., & Arkin, R.M. (1984) *Human motivation: Physiological, behavioral and social approaches*. Boston: Allyn and Bacon.

Hall, E.G., & Erffmeyer, E.S. (1983) The effects of visuo-motor behavior rehearsal with videotaped modeling on free-throw accuracy of intercollegiate female basketball players. *Journal of Sport Psychology*, 5, 343–346.

Hall, H.K., Weinberg, R.S., & Jackson, A. (1987) Effects of goal-specificity, goal difficulty, and information feedback on endurance performance. *Journal of Sport Psychology*, 9, 43–54.

Harris, D.V., & Robinson, W.J. (1986) The effects of skill level on EMG activity during internal and external imagery. *Journal of Sport Psychology*, 8, 105–111.

Kau, M.L., & Fisher, J. (1974) Self-modification of exercise behavior. *Journal of Behavior Therapy and Experimental Psychiatry*, 5, 213–214.

Kazdin, A.E. (1977) *The token economy: A review and evaluation*. New York: Plenum.

Kirschenbaum, D.S., & Wittrock, D.A. (1984) Cognitive-behavioral interventions in sport: A self-regulatory perspective. In J. Silva & R. Weinberg (Eds.), *Psychological foundations of sport* (pp. 81–98). Champaign, IL: Human Kinetics.

Koop, S., & Martin, G.L. (1983) Evaluation of a coaching strategy to reduce swimming stroke errors with beginning age-group swimmers. *Journal of Applied Behavioral Analysis*, 16, 447–460.

Lepper, M.R., & Greene, D. (1978) *The hidden cost of reward: New perspectives on the psychology of human motivation*. New York: Halsted.

Lepper, M.R., Greene, D., & Nisbett, R.E. (1973) Understanding children's intrinsic interests with intrinsic awards: A test of the "overjustification" hypothesis. *Journal of Personality and Social Psychology*, 28, 129–137.

Mahoney, M.J., & Avener, M. (1977) Psychology of the elite athlete: An introductory study. *Cognitive Therapy and Research*, 1, 135–141.

Mahoney, M.J., Gabriel, T.J., & Perkins, T.S. (1987) Psychological skills and exceptional athletic performance. *The Sport Psychologist*, 1, 181–199.

Maier, S.F., & Seligman, M.E.P. (1976) Learned helplessness: Theory and evidence. *Journal of Experimental Psychology: General*, 105, 3–46.

Martin, G.L., & Hrycaiko, D. (1983) Effective behavioral coaching: What's it all about? *Journal of Sport Psychology*, 5, 8–20.

Martin, G.L., & Pear, J. (1988) *Behavior modification: What it is and how to do it*. Englewood Cliffs, NJ: Prentice-Hall.

McKenzie, T.L., & Rushall, B.S. (1974) Effects of self-recording on attendance and performance in a competitive swimming training environment. *Journal of Applied Behavior Analysis, 7,* 199–206.

Meichenbaum, D. (1977) *Cognitive behavior modification.* New York: Plenum.

Meyers, A.W., Cooke, C., Cullen, J., & Liles, L. (1981) Psychological aspects of athletic competitors: A replication across sports. *Cognitive Therapy and Research, 5,* 29–33.

Meyers, A.W., & Schleser, R. (1980) A cognitive behavioral intervention for improving basketball performance. *Journal of Sport Psychology, 2,* 69–73.

Meyers, A.W., Schleser, R., Cooke, C., & Cuvillier, C. (1979) Cognitive contributions to the development of gymnastic skills. *Cognitive Therapy and Research, 3,* 75–85.

Morgan, W.P., & Pollack, M.L. (1977) Psychology characterizations of the elite distance runner. *Annals of the New York Academy of Sciences, 301,* 382–403.

Nation, J.R., & Massad, P. (1978) Persistence training: A partial reinforcement procedure for reversing learned helplessness and depression. *Journal of Experimental Psychology: General, 107,* 436–451.

Nation, J.R., & Woods, D.J. (1980) Persistence: The role of partial reinforcement in psychotherapy. *Journal of Experimental Psychology: General, 109,* 175–207.

Pavlov, I.P. (1927) *Conditioned reflexes.* London: Oxford University Press.

Penman, K. (1969) Relative effectiveness of teaching beginning tumbling with and without an instant replay videotape recorder. *Perceptual and Motor Skills, 28,* 45–46.

Premack, D. (1962) Reversability of the reinforcement relation. *Science, 136,* 235–237.

Rushall, B.S., & Pettinger, J. (1969) An evaluation of the effect of various reinforcers used as motivators in swimming. *Research Quarterly, 40,* 540–545.

Rushall, B.S., & Siedentop, D. (1972) *The development and control of behavior in sports and physical education.* Philadelphia: Lea and Febiger.

Rushall, B.S., & Smith, K.C. (1979) The modification of the quality and quantity of behavioral categories in a swimming coach. *Journal of Sport Psychology, 1,* 138–150.

Ryan, E.D., & Simons, J. (1983) What is learned in mental practice of motor skills: A test of the cognitive-motor hypothesis. *Journal of Sport Psychology, 5,* 419–426.

Sanderson, F.H. (1983) Length and spacing of practice sessions in sport skills. *International Journal of Sport Psychology, 14,* 116–122.

Schmidt, R.A. (1982) *Motor control and learning: A behavioral emphasis.* Champaign, IL: Human Kinetics.

Schwartz, B. (1984) *Psychology of learning and behavior.* New York: W.W. Norton and Company.

Seligman, M.E.P., & Beagley, G. (1975) Learned helplessness in the rat. *Journal of Comparative and Physiological Psychology, 88,* 534–541.

Shapiro, E.S., & Shapiro, S. (1984) Behavioral coaching in the development of skills in track. In J. Silva & R. Weinberg (Eds.), *Psychological foundations of sport* (pp. 81–98). Champaign, IL: Human Kinetics.

Shelton, T.O., & Mahoney, M.J. (1978) The content and effect of "psyching-up" strategies in weight lifters. *Cognitive Therapy and Research, 2,* 225–284.

Silva, J.M. (1982) Competitive sport environment: Performance enhancement through cognitive intervention. *Behavior Modification, 6,* 443–463.

Smith, R.E. (1984) Theoretical and treatment approaches to anxiety reduction. In J.M. Silva & R.S. Weinberg, (Eds.), *Psychological foundations of sport* (pp. 157–170). Champaign, IL: Human Kinetics.

Smith, S.M. (1979) Remembering in and out of context. *Journal of Experimental Psychology: Human Learning and Memory, 5,* 460–471.

Smith, S.M. (1984) A comparison of two techniques for reducing context-dependent forgetting. *Memory and Cognition, 12,* 447–482.

Suinn, R.M. (1972) Behavioral research for ski racers. *Behavioral Therapy, 3,* 519–520.

Tarpy, R.M. (1983) *Principles of animal learning and motivation.* Glenview, IL: Scott, Foresman and Company.

Thomas, D.L., & Miller, L.K. (1980) Helping college students: Democratic decision-making versus experimental manipulation. In G.L. Martin and J.G. Osborne (Eds.), *Helping in the community: Behavioral applications* (pp. 180–240). New York: Plenum.

Weinberg, R.S. (1984) Mental preparation strategies. In J.M. Silva & R.S. Weinberg (Eds.), *Psychological foundations of sport* (pp. 145–156). Champaign, IL: Human Kinetics.

Weinberg, R.S., Gould, D., & Jackson, A.V. (1980) Cognition and motor performance: Effects of psyching-up strategies on three motor tasks. *Cognitive Therapy and Research, 4,* 239–245.

Weinberg, R.S., Gould, D., & Jackson, A.V. (1981) Relationship between the duration of the psych-up interval and strength performance. *Journal of Sport Psychology, 3,* 166–170.

Wolpe, J. (1982) *The practice of behavior therapy.* New York: Pergamon.

Wysocki, T., Hall, G., Iata, B., & Riordan, M. (1979) Behavioral management of exercise: Contracting for aerobic point. *Journal of Applied Behavior Analysis, 12,* 55–64.

4

Anxiety, Arousal, and Intervention

INTRODUCTION

Virtually every person who has been intimately involved with sport recognizes the importance of motivational influences on athletic performance. Both coaches and players commonly attribute success to "being up" or failure to "being down." Intensity, commitment, and level of alertness often dictate the style and eventual outcome of sport performance.

Despite the obvious advantage of individual readiness and determination, the negative consequences of extreme excitement cannot be ignored. As we shall see, gearing up for an athletic contest will produce benefits up to a point and then further increases in motivation may actually be counterproductive. To better understand this basic principle, one needs to focus on the subtle but exceedingly important difference between arousal and anxiety. *Arousal,* as it is commonly invoked, refers to an all-inclusive, well-ranging continuum of psychological activation (Sonstroem, 1984). By way of contrast, *anxiety* is generally regarded as a negatively charged emotional state that is characterized by internal discomfort and a feeling of nervousness. This is not to say that anxiety is independent of arousal; quite to the contrary, anxiety contributes to the overall arousal state, but anxiety in many instances must be dealt with as a special case of activation. For example, the impact of anxiety in sport is apparent from empirical studies of national championship wrestlers who reported they felt excessive stress prior to competition (Gould, Horn, and Spreeman, 1983), as well as numerous anecdotal accounts of the debilitating effects of tension.

In this chapter, we shall explore the determinants of arousal and anxiety, the effect of these variables on sport performance, and finally strategies designed to promote performance via the alleviation of anxiety.

DETERMINANTS OF ANXIETY AND AROUSAL

Because of the diverse nature of anxiety formation, both physiological and psychological causes must be considered. Each of these aspects of anxiety and arousal is important to the ultimate expression of the behavior—biological and mental events work in concert to produce changes in athletic performance. With a better grasp of this interaction, we are in a position to gain in our awareness as to how to manipulate arousal so that sport performance is enhanced.

Neurophysiological Mechanisms

Although a detailed description of the body components that comprise the physiological substrate of anxiety is beyond the scope of this book, two of the major contributors to arousal phenomena can be specified: brain mechanisms and the autonomic nervous system (ANS). Curiously, as noted by Hatfield and Landers (1983), only recently have sport psychologists come to recognize the importance of studying these systems. Although the intricate workings of the central nervous system (CNS), of which the brain is a part, remain a mystery for neuroscientists, the peripheral nervous system (PNS), which includes the ANS, is much better understood. Nonetheless, theory and methodology in sport psychology have only recently made advances in extrapolating basic psychophysiologic research findings to the athletic realm.

Regarding brain structure and functions, the *cerebral cortex,* the *hypothalamus,* and the *reticular formation* represent the most critical substructures related to anxiety and arousal (Carlson, 1986). The cerebral cortex is the convoluted mass of neural tissue shown in figure 4.1 that makes up the outer covering of the

Figure 4.1 Human Brain Structures Important for Arousal and Anxiety

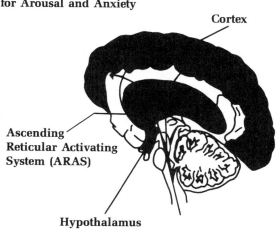

Cortex

Ascending
Reticular Activating
System (ARAS)

Hypothalamus

brain. Cortex comes from the Latin word meaning "bark," and it has the same rough appearance. Here higher intellectual functions take place, and here cognitive representations of anxiety are fashioned. When a gymnast mulls over his or her nervousness prior to a vault, cortical activation determines the manner by which the arousal state is translated into constructive determination and focus. It is at the cortical level that the experience of anxiety is interpreted as a relevant emotional phenomenon.

The hypothalamus is another forebrain structure that has been linked to arousal. When certain areas of the hypothalamus are surgically destroyed, a decrease in the level of behavioral action occurs, and sleep often ensues. Conversely, electrical stimulation of discrete regions within the hypothalamic area have been shown to cause increased excitement (Benjamin, Hopkins, and Nation, 1987). Although few studies of the role of the hypothalamus in sport behavior have been conducted, the fact that this structure is so integrally involved in the control of the endocrine system

(which prepares the body for both psychologically and physically demanding circumstances) would suggest that hypothalamic functions are vital determinants of athletic proficiency.

The reticular formation is a complex system of ascending and descending collaterals that extend from the lower brain stem throughout the midbrain area. Although the precise function of the reticular formation is difficult to ascertain, the available evidence suggests that it serves as an alarm system to awaken the rest of the brain (Cotman and McGaugh, 1980). When an incoming signal arrives at the level of the reticular formation, cortical centers are alerted that new information is on the way. Appropriately, when the reticular formation functions appropriately, new (sensory) information is processed attentively and arousal results (Lykken, 1968). Yet, when the reticular formation is rendered dysfunctional, loss of attention and even sleep occurs. It follows from these observations that the reticular formation should be involved in any situation in which alertness is at a premium, as is the case for athletic participation.

As indicated, the autonomic nervous system (ANS) is also very much involved in arousal functions. It is largely through this ANS network of neural fibers that bodily reactions to environmental stressors are expressed. Of special interest is the interaction between the ANS and the endocrine system, which consists of glands such as the adrenals, thyroid, and the master controlling gland called the pituitary. They release their respective secretions (hormones) into the bloodstream in order to prepare the body for emergency situations. The provocation for this hormonal discharge often comes from stress-mediated ANS activation. For example, immediately prior to a critical dive in an aquatics competition, a participant may feel anxious and nervous. Consequently, the ANS excites the adrenals, forcing the systematic distribution of the hormone epinephrine. Also known as adrenalin, epinephrine energizes the person and accents his or her state of physical and mental readiness. Accordingly, the interplay between the nervous system and the endocrine system serves to enhance performance. In this instance anxiety and arousal increase the chances for success by triggering physiological reactions that contribute to a positive individual athletic profile.

Psychological Mechanisms

Although biological processes are central to the experience of anxiety, clearly cognitive and behavioral aspects of stress reactivity also must be addressed (Borkovec, 1976). How athletes, and everyone else for that matter, think about threatening events may determine both the level of felt discomfort and the course of action for alleviating the tension. Occasionally, people become so preoccupied with their negative thoughts that they are unable to resolve even routine crises, with the end result that their confidence about handling stress diminishes (Meichenbaum, 1977). Of course, this process evolves into a negative circular spiral in which one disastrous encounter precipitates yet another, and on it goes. The ultimate fate of such recurrent episodes is a form of emotional debilitation that may require psychological intervention. Further discussion of this topic will appear later in the chapter.

With respect to coping strategies, it is important to distinguish between two different types of anxiety. *State anxiety,* as defined by Spielberger (1972), is a transitory form of apprehension that varies in intensity, commensurate with the strength of the fear-eliciting cue. When a young girl is required to perform a recital in front of a live audience for the first time, she may exhibit obvious signs of nervousness, including trembling, perspiration, and high distractibility. Similarly, a professional tennis player who has never before played at Wimbledon may be overwhelmed by the crowds at

center court, and his or her performance may be adversely affected. In instances such as these when highly skilled performers suffer bouts of anxiety, the emotional reaction is one that is likely to be peculiar to that specific circumstance. The young pianist may have no difficulty performing in small groups or in front of friends, and surely the professional tennis player feels at ease amidst more familiar surroundings. This sort of situational apprehension occurs in all of us from time to time.

Recent developments in the state anxiety literature have focused on the multidimensional nature of the phenomenon. Specifically it has been proposed that state anxiety actually consists of two components, *cognitive state anxiety* and *somatic state anxiety.* The former is characterized by worry and emotional distress whereas the latter is more physiologically based, i.e., rapid heart rate, clammy hands, and so on. In support of the notion that these two aspects of state anxiety should be dealt with as independent constructs, Karteroliotis and Gill (1987) have demonstrated that the two variables are influenced differentially at different stages of competition, although they do tend to follow the same general temporal course. Along other lines, Gould, Petlichkoff, Simons, and Vevera (1987) have shown that athletic performance is more strongly affected by somatic state anxiety than cognitive state anxiety. In any event, there is apparently reason to suspect that state anxiety as it relates to sport is a multidimensional issue, and future work in this area should help clarify the relations that each of these components has with competitive athletic behavior.

Compared to state anxiety, *trait anxiety* is a more enduring form of anxiety (Spielberger, 1972). Persons with trait anxiety (A-trait persons) project a profile that reflects nonspecific anxiety proneness. A broad range of life situations are perceived as threatening, and the individual's reaction to such events is commonly disproportionate to the actual fear properties of the stimulus. With this type of anxiety disturbance, the person may be haunted by fears of the most trivial phenomena. In its extreme form, the A-trait condition may render the individual dysfunctional and incapable of responding at all.

In terms of the relations between state and trait anxiety and competitive athletic performance, one theoretical formulation that has guided research in this area has been proposed by Martens, Gill, Simon, and Scanlan (1975). The theory posits that state anxiety registered by a person in a competitive situation is determined by the person's perception of the likelihood of success. The prediction is that when sport outcomes are contingent on lower levels of anxiety, athletes who are uncertain of their ability, and thus more likely to feel anxious, are also more likely to perform poorly. Consistent with this prediction Gerson and Deshaies (1978) examined batting averages of female varsity intercollegiate softball players participating in the National Women's Intercollegiate Softball tournament and found that, indeed, higher precompetitive state anxiety was associated with lower batting averages. Perhaps the expectancy of performing poorly more than lack of ability per se leads to the athlete's poor performance.

Supporting evidence also comes from field investigations of golf performance (Weinberg and Genuchi, 1980). Because golf is a game that requires precision, coordination, and the integration of fine muscle movements, it is especially appropriate for studying the effects of anxiety on athletic performance. Excessive levels of anxiety may interfere with the execution of golfing responses that must occur within a relative narrow range of expertise. Weinberg and Genuchi found that high A-trait persons were more likely to experience elevated state anxiety on Day 1 and Day 2 of a competitive collegiate golf tournament than persons low in trait anxiety. Further, it was shown that high state anxiety levels and expectations of performing poorly were related to how well the

golfers did in the tournament. Better performances were associated with low anxiety and worse performances were associated with high anxiety.

Additional evidence that favors the idea that competitive anxiety may be a principal determinant of athletic proficiency comes from studies of youth sport (Passer, 1983). When 316 male youth soccer participants were evaluated with respect to competitive trait anxiety, it was discovered that players' performance expectancies, anticipated affective reactions to success-failure, and expectancies for criticism, were all influential in determining how well the child played. The greater the anxiety (i.e., the more dismal the expectations for being successful), the less effective were the youth participants, at least as rated by their coaches with respect to overall ability. Moreover, failure seems to be potentially more devastating, psychologically speaking, for youngsters who demonstrate high competitive trait anxiety. Such children worried more about their performance and were more apprehensive about evaluations by peers than children who registered low anxiety. The disquieting aspect of these findings, of course, is that a vicious cycle may form. The child who is anxious and expects to perform poorly does so, and consequently experiences greater perceived ridicule, which leads to increased apprehensiveness about competitive situations.

Brustad and Weiss (1987) extended Passer's (1983) research on patterns of competitive trait anxiety by examining female athletes and male athletes in different sports. Interestingly, when boy baseball players were evaluated, the boys who registered high competitive trait anxiety reported lower levels of self-esteem and more frequent worries, in much the same fashion as the youth soccer players mentioned earlier. For girl softball players, however, no significant relationships were found between levels of competitive trait anxiety and cognitive variables. Apparently, competition in sport takes on different meanings for girls and boys.

Studies have shown that highly skilled parachutists exhibit low levels of anxiety prior to a jump. Would a neophyte share this skydiver's cool?

Two other important variables that seem to be important with respect to modulating the intensity of the anxiety reactions in children and adult competitors are the skill level of the competition and the relative time to competition (see Huddleston and Gill, 1981, for a review). In a study of parachutists (Fenz, 1985), for instance, it was observed that highly skilled parachutists actually exhibit low levels of anxiety immediately prior to a jump. Conversely, parachutists who are not yet accomplished jumpers experience extreme levels of anxiety just before the jump. The studies discussed

earlier, beginning with Martens et al. (1975), would lead us to believe that the high anxiety before the jump may prevent the poor parachutists from gaining in skill development. Additional work by Fenz (1985) and Mahoney and Avener (1977) indicates that the discrepancies in skill level that foster differential anxiety reactions in athletes are particularly important as the person approaches closer to the competition. However, Huddleston and Gill (1981) failed to confirm this idea. In their study involving track and field competitors, athletes did show greater levels of anxiety as their respective events drew nearer, but this was uniformly true for highly skilled athletes (those who reached national qualifying standards during the season) and for less skilled athletes.

At odds with the relatively large literature that argues that competitive trait anxiety negatively affects athletic performance, Scanlan and Passer (1979) have shown that competitive performance expectancies, but not competitive trait anxiety, relate to athletic ability. In a field study involving ten- to twelve-year-old female soccer players, intrapersonal factors affecting players' pregame personal performance expectancies were first identified. Subsequently, the impact on each player of winning or losing the game was determined, and the interaction of the game outcome with intrapersonal variables was assessed by determining each player's expectations for a hypothetical rematch, ostensibly with the same opponent. The results showed that winning players held higher expectancies for themselves and their team than did losing players or players who had tied. Similarly, players with greater ability were higher in self-esteem than their less proficient counterparts. But high and low competitive trait-anxious players evidenced similar profiles with respect to performance expectancies. This pattern of results calls into question the validity correlated with athletic competency. Performance expectancies and general self-attitude would appear to be more directly related to how well an athlete performs than the anxiety events they are purported to mediate (Martens, 1974).

Drive Theory and the Inverted U-Hypothesis

Until this point in the chapter, we have focused on the negative consequences of heightened anxiety and arousal. But as nearly every coach and athlete knows, when an athlete is totally tension free, concentration may wane and thoughts may wander from the task at hand. Consequently, a superior athlete may be outperformed by a less competent athlete, due simply to motivational and attentional deficiencies. What is required for optimal performance may be a moderate level of anxiety, sufficiently high to sharpen the athlete's focus but not so intense that it encumbers his or her execution.

The idea that increases in anxiety, and ultimately in arousal, increase performance up to a point, and that further anxiety impairs performance, is an important consideration for the *drive theory* of learning and behavior first advanced by Yale psychologist Clark Hull more than forty years ago (cf. Hull, 1943). This formulation states that behavior potential $_sE_r$ is a multiplicative function of drive (D) and habit strength ($_sH_r$); specifically:

$$_sE_r = D \times {_sH_r}$$

In the Hullian tradition, the concept of *drive* related to a nonspecific motivational force that served to energize responding. At the animal level, drive was defined operationally as the number of hours of deprivation of food, water, sex, and so forth. But in dealing with humans, drive functions were often interpreted within the broad realm of arousal (cf. Benjamin, Hopkins, and Nation, 1987). Sources of drive included conflict and tension (anxiety) that inspired the person to seek their reduction. Within this context, motivational (drive) variables were viewed as intervening states, the

expression of which was observed in overt actions. Consequently, linear increases in performance would be expected commensurate with increases in anxiety and arousal.

By way of contrast, habit was viewed as associative as opposed to a motivational variable. This means that habit is determined by learning principles, which include the process of reinforcement as described in detail in chapter 3. Notice the s and r subscripts on the symbol for habit. This suggests that habit strength is peculiar to a specific stimulus (s) and response (r). Because different habits are likely to vary in strength due to different learning experiences, they are predictably going to interact with a given amount of drive. Habits that are strong, and thus high in the habit hierarchy, will contribute to substantially greater values of $_sE_r$ (the tendency to make the response) than lesser habit values, due to the multiplicative nature of the drive and habit relationship. Consequently, when there are clear discrepancies in habit strength, increased drive should have a facilitating effect by pushing the excitatory potential values ($_sE_r$) of correct responses (high habit) well above some threshold for responding, while incorrect responses (low habit) and their corresponding excitatory potential values remain below threshold.

A quite different picture emerges, however, when the different habits involved in a situation are of similar strength. In such cases higher drive levels may interact with habit to produce excitatory potential products that are all above threshold. Thus, response competition would occur and behavioral interference would be expected. A better strategy might be to keep drive levels low, so that the movement of specific habits (and the excitatory potential values linked to them) across the threshold could be controlled.

This complex prediction of the Hullian rationale was empirically tested many years ago by one of Hull's most distinguished students, Kenneth Spence. Spence reasoned that in an easy task, in which the habit differentiates between correct and incorrect responses are likely to be sizable, higher drive level should result in better performance. Conversely, in a difficult task, in which the respective habit strengths for correct and incorrect behaviors are not likely to be great, high drive should produce worse performance, because of the behavioral interference alluded to in the preceding paragraph. The formal test of this important line of thought came from Spence, Farber, and McFann (1956). In this study, subjects were presented with easy or difficult word lists. Anxious (high anxiety) subjects learned the easy list faster whereas nonanxious (low anxiety) subjects learned the difficult list faster.

These data confirmed some of the precise predictions of the Hullian model. But they further challenged some of the assertions made by a doctrine that had its origins much earlier. As long ago as 1908, Yerkes and Dodson described the relation between psychological activation and performance as an inverted-U (see figure 4.2). This *inverted-U hypothesis* states that there is an optimal level of arousal for every behavior, values above and below which are likely to create poor performance. It follows that in some cases intensely motivated performers are going to do well, but in other cases those same individuals are going to have trouble.

As it relates to sport, the inverted-U hypothesis predicts that athletes may become so "psychologically charged" that they are unable to perform efficiently (Bunker and Rotella, 1980). Precompetitional hype is a familiar tool used by sport practitioners, ostensibly to "get athletes ready to play." But implicit in the message of the inverted-U formulation is the notion that such a strategy can be excessively used and it may actually backfire. When a long jump competitor gets so psyched up that he or she "ties up" going down the runway, arousal is translated as anxiety and it becomes counterproduc-

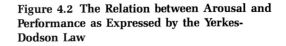

Figure 4.2 The Relation between Arousal and Performance as Expressed by the Yerkes-Dodson Law

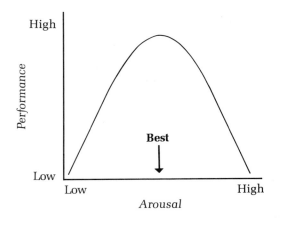

tive. A preferred approach would be to relax so that the appropriate response could be executed. This is not to say that motivational enhancement techniques are valueless, of course, because a moderate level of excitement may be needed to maintain attention and generate the best performance.

Because the basic tenet of the inverted-U hypothesis proposes that the optimum point of arousal varies as a function of task characteristics, different sports are likely to demand different levels of arousal for the best results. In a game such as golf, in which fine motor behaviors are at a premium, a lower point of optimal arousal is expected relative to, say, wrestling, in which delicate performances are not judged to be so critical. Even for the same sport, the nature of the requisite behaviors may dictate different levels of psychological activation for the best result. In football, for instance, a highly aroused defensive lineman capering before an opponent may be appropriately cast. But a quarterback who must make instantaneous decisions may not be served so well by high levels of arousal. The point is that behavioral features must be considered when defining optimal arousal levels in sport.

Also, as graphically depicted in figure 4.3, skill level is likely to dictate disparate points of optimal arousal. For a beginning athlete, the inverted-U account of the relation between arousal and performance predicts a lower optimum range than would be the case for intermediate or advanced players. When a shooter in a rifle competition is new to the sport, high levels of excitement may have a diverting influence and make it difficult to sustain a steady aim. For a more experienced participant, however, the same high level of arousal may channel attention and contribute positively to the task.

A considerable amount of space in the literature on arousal/performance interactions has been devoted to professed differences in the predictions made by either drive theory or the inverted-U hypothesis (see Sonstroem, 1984). The common assertion is that drive theory predicts that well-learned tasks involving established habits should always reflect performance facilitations as anxiety (arousal) increases. On the other hand, the inverted-U hypothesis argues that behaviors, however well they are learned, will be impaired at some point, given a sufficiently high level of anxiety and arousal.

Clearly, great numbers of research articles can be brought forth in support of each of the claims. Wankel (1980), for instance, studied drive manipulations in motor performance tasks by varying audience size. In this sort of investigation modeled after Zajonc's social facilitation theory (Zajonc, 1965), increased numbers of observers are alleged to increase drive (anxiety) and therein facilitate responding. But the report by Wankel revealed that audience size had no effect on pursuit rotor tracking. Further, dispositional differences in anxiety were negatively correlated with performance; high anxious subjects performed more poorly than low anxious subjects. Yet despite

Figure 4.3 Application of Yerkes-Dodson Law to Rifle Shooters of Various Skill Levels

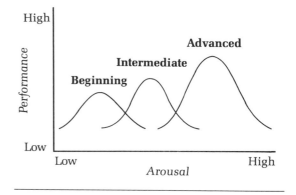

such reports Landers (1980) comments that "[an] obstacle in the way of advocating abandonment of drive theory is the overall success this theory has had in the area of social facilitation research." Such statements are vigorously in agreement with the predictions of drive theory as it is described earlier.

In terms of tests of the validity of the position taken by the inverted-U hypothesis, Martens and Landers (1970) assigned high, moderate, or low anxious male youths to a motor tracking task under conditions of high, moderate, or low stress. Supporting evidence from physiological measures (heart rate, palmar sweating) confirmed the differences in the three different stress conditions. The overall pattern of results was highly favorable to an inverted-U type model. Specifically, it was shown that the moderate stress condition was associated with better motor performance than either low- or high-stress conditions. Further, Martens and Landers observed that boys with moderate A-trait scores performed better on the tracking task than either low A-trait or high A-trait boys.

Similar findings were reported by Klavora (1977) in a field study that used Canadian male high school basketball players as subjects.

Precompetition state anxiety scores for 145 boys were obtained for each player throughout the second half of a season. Following the completion of each of the games, the respective coaches were asked to rate the performance of each basketball player in terms of whether his performance could be described as poor, average, or outstanding. When the performance ratings were presented as a function of the individual athlete's level of state anxiety, a profile emerged that was of the general form of the inverted-U. That is, the rating of outstanding was most likely to be achieved when the player reported a moderate level of stress. When players indicated either low or high levels of state anxiety, they were more likely to perform at a poor or average level.

To date, one of the more compelling articles related to establishing the validity of the inverted-U curve has been written by Sonstroem and Bernardo (1982). In this study that involved thirty female university varsity basketball starters off six different teams, an athlete's lowest, median, and highest pregame state anxiety values across three games of a double-elimination basketball tournament held at Brown University were used to define low, moderate, or high anxiety levels. Also, the effects of trait anxiety were investigated. Performance during the competition was determined by total points scored and an overall value that was generated for each player by the linear combination of shot percentage, rebounds, points, assists, steals, fouls, and turnovers committed. As with the previous studies, the performance measures were examined as a function of registered anxiety. The intrasubject results appeared to be remarkably consistent with the inverted-U hypothesis. Not only did total points and game performance (see figure 4.4) follow a quadratic trend (first increasing, then decreasing) as a function of state anxiety, but this general pattern held across low, moderate, and high trait anxiety

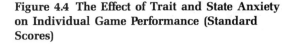

Figure 4.4 The Effect of Trait and State Anxiety on Individual Game Performance (Standard Scores)

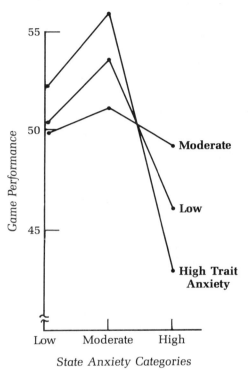

Source: "Intraindividual Pregame State Anxiety and Basketball Performance: A Re-Examination of the Inverted-U Curve" by R.J. Sonstroem and P. Bernardo, 1982, *Journal of Sport Psychology, 4,* 235–245.

comparisons. Thus, the robustness of the effect of anxiety, and therein arousal, would seem to be substantial.

Considering the great amount of support for the inverted-U position, there is reason to question the value of a perhaps oversimplistic account of the relationship between arousal and sport performance that is predicted solely on a single drive principle such as Hull's. And, as noted by Martens (1974), other problematic issues exist:

1. The drive theory hypothesis should be rejected for the reason that "it is not testable for motor behavior because of the inability to specify habit hierarchies for motor performance."
2. The evidence essentially provides equivocal support for the drive theory.
3. The inverted-U hypothesis supersedes the drive theory hypothesis because arousal levels may not have been of sufficient magnitude to cause a performance decrement in studies finding a positive linear relationship between arousal and performance.
4. The psychophysiological theories of activation and attentional theories, such as Easterbrook's (1959) cue utilization theory, are more viable alternatives for explaining the inverted-U relationship.

Although Landers (1980) has contested some of the points raised by Martens (1974), at this point it seems relatively clear that whatever theory of arousal/performance interactions ultimately prevails, it will have to incorporate elements that can explain why a little excitement in sport is not enough and a lot is too much. Coaches and other sport practitioners must constantly monitor athletes and determine the optimal motivational level that is required for specific events conducted under given conditions. Perhaps the greatest difficulty in the entire area associated with motor behavior and athletic participation is matching peak arousal and the onset of the competition.

Along other lines, people vary substantially in terms of what they see as the optimal level of arousal. As Highlight 4.1 indicates, some individuals thrive on a level of stimulation that would overwhelm most others.

In this first section, we have reviewed some of the biological and psychological features that are believed to be most important to the formation of anxiety. Additionally, we have seen that anxiety viewed as a source of arousal can have a positive effect in the sport arena. But there is no dismissing the debilitating impact that intense stress and excessive emotional reactivity can have on an amateur or professional career. In the next section, we shall discuss several of the treatment strategies that have been used as intervention techniques designed to alleviate excess tension. For the sport psychologist, the ability to lower and control anxiety within tolerable limits is one of the most important services that he or she can provide.

INTERVENTION STRATEGIES: ANXIETY ALLEVIATION

For some athletes, even the most stressful situations are approached with the same emotional outlook as a walk in the park. In a nationally televised college basketball game between two of the nation's top twenty ranked teams, a point guard was observed to yawn during a timeout 3 seconds before the game's end. With the team leading by only one point, his relaxed style would seem to be unexpected, especially because this same guard had to convert two free shot opportunities following the timeout in order to assure a victory for his team. He made both free throw attempts and withdrew to the locker room without ceremony.

Such examples are rife in the lore of amateur and professional athletics, but the truth is that a sizable number of highly skilled players are prone to anxiety bouts that prevent them from performing at the level of their ability. When a player "chokes" in a game situation, the effect may be to make it more difficult to execute freely when a similar circumstance is reinstated. The resulting vicious loop in which anxiety precludes success and failure increases anxiety may render the athlete dysfunctional unless something is done to break the cycle. In some instances this intervention may take the form of a program designed to increase

HIGHLIGHT 4.1
The Thrill of It All

Sensation seeking refers to the notion that some individuals prefer extraordinarily high levels of stimulation to moderate levels of stimulation. For these persons, "living life on the edge" is a personal orientation and a framework for evaluating the worth of prospective life endeavors. In terms of the discussion presented in this chapter on the relation between arousal and performance, such people would have optimal points of arousal that would shift the peak of the inverted-U to a point far in advance of the norm.

The literature associated with the relationship between sports activities and sensation seeking has by and large concentrated on the sports such people select. For example, sky divers (Hymbaugh and Garrett, 1974), auto racers, (Zuckerman, 1983), and hang gliders (Straub, 1982) all exhibit unusually high sensation-seeking scores. This could, of course, reflect a need to engage in risky sport activities. But it also may be due simply to the fact that sensation seekers are more likely to try a greater number of sport activities, low risk as well as high risk. To further clarify this issue, Rowland, Franken, and Harrison (1986) recently administered Zuckerman's (1979) Sensation Seeking Scale to 97 male and 104 female undergraduate students. The results indicated that persons scoring high on the scale tend to become more involved in more sports, but that persons scoring low on the scale are more likely to remain with the sport for a longer period. Also, a positive correlation was found between sensation seeking and participation in risky sports. So, it appears that both increased activity and a desire to get involved with high risk sports characterize the sensation seeker. Arousal levels that would be excessive for most people evidently just keep such persons from becoming bored.

SOURCES: "Sensation-seeking among Skydivers," by K. Hymbaugh and J. Garrett, 1974, *Perceptual and Motor Skills, 38,* 118; "Sensation Seeking and Participation in Sporting Activities," by G.L. Rowland, R.E. Franken, and K. Harrison, 1986, *Journal of Sport Psychology, 8,* 212–220; "Sensation Seeking among High and Low-risk Male Athletes" by W.F. Straub, 1982, *Journal of Sport Psychology, 4,* 246–253; *Sensation Seeking: Beyond the Optimal Level of Arousal* (p. 1–30) by M. Zuckerman, 1979, Hillsdale, NJ: Erlbaum; "Sensation Seeking in Sports," by M. Zuckerman, 1983, *Personality and Individual Differences, 4,* 285–293.

the player's mental toughness. In other types of treatment, conditioning techniques can be used that produce the desired behaviors independent of cognitive mediation. The models discussed in the next few pages represent some of the more popular methods available for changing mental or behavioral reactions to anxiety-evoking situations.

Classical Conditioning Techniques

One of the oldest and most widely accepted accounts of the causes of anxiety is predicated on the principles of classical conditioning (Mowrer, 1960). Recall from our discussion in chapter 3 that classical conditioning involves the continuous association of an unconditional stimulus (US) and a conditioned stimulus (CS). Regarding fear (anxiety) development, a CS is believed to be paired with a fear-eliciting US; consequently the CS acquires the ability to elicit a conditioned fear reaction (the CR). Fear, then, mediates performance by virtue of occasioning behaviors that are compatible with or oppositional to selected voluntary behaviors.

In terms of what this conditioned fear mechanism means in sport, apprehensiveness is likely to be engendered when a competitor associates poor performance in pressure situations with peer disappointment and even ridicule. Especially in sports like rifle shooting and golf, which require highly skilled fine motor behaviors, the situation (the CS) evokes a level of anxiety (the CR) that in turn produces muscle tightness, nervousness, an unsteady hand, and other reactions that prevent the synchronous flow of the appropriate movements. Here, the fact that anxiety occurs at all runs counter to successful performance. What is necessary is a strategy designed to disrupt the chain of events that has produced the anxiety, or conditioned fear, as it is more often referred to in the psychology literature.

Extinction. From a learning point of view, one of the surest ways to eliminate classically conditioned fear is to place it on *extinction*. This process would mean presenting the conditioned fear-eliciting cue (the CS) in the absence of the threatening event (the US). Because the CS is inherently neutral, repeated exposure with no US pairing will result in the diminution of the response strength of the CR. Simply stated, the CS cannot stand alone. When this extinction approach is employed in a therapeutic realm it is called *flooding* (refer to Martin and Pear, 1988, for a more detailed discussion).

Because flooding is an intervention technique that is likely to provoke extremely high levels of anxiety, especially in the early stages of treatment, it must be used cautiously (Smith, 1984). Consider what a 30- to 40-minute flooding session may involve. As a professional baseball player you are asked to imagine that you are batting in the bottom of the ninth inning with your team trailing by a single run. The count is three balls and one strike. You swing and miss; fans shout derisive remarks, players on the field taunt you, and you

sense the complete rejection of other team members. Again you swing and again you miss the ball, which clearly was thrown out of the strike zone. The game is over, you have failed, and you are alone.

The purpose of such forced exposure to unkindness, of course, is to permit the patient (player) to encounter such thoughts within the relatively safe confines of the therapy environment. Ultimately, the amount of fear and anxiety that are triggered by such threatening images should diminish. But intense unpleasantness is surely going to be the rule in the initial treatment sessions, and judiciousness on the part of the therapist is essential.

A variant of flooding that is preferred by many psychologists is *implosive therapy* (Stampfl and Levis, 1967). This technique incorporates many of the same features of flooding but it includes a hierarchy of fear-eliciting images that each person judges to reflect those aspects of his or her personal situations that are most and least threatening. Accordingly, the therapist is free to systematically work through the list, extinguishing the anxiety to items lower in the hierarchy before proceeding to more tension-laden images. Using this technique combined with clinical insights into the psychodynamic undercurrents that contribute to the disorder, the successful practitioner can help alleviate stress symptoms (Foa et al., 1983), and this can be accomplished without undue felt anxiety.

Despite the widespread use of extinction techniques in applied settings in general, a few attempts have been made to employ the treatment regimen in sport settings, either in laboratory or field studies (Smith, 1984). Many sport psychologists are disinclined to use an approach that is so fundamentally geared to aversive conditioning. Nonetheless, flooding and implosion have on occasion produced real benefits when alternatives have failed to reduce anxiety and they should be considered as part of the arsenal for effecting behavior change.

Counterconditioning. A classical conditioning therapy procedure that is favored over the extinction approaches, at least by sport psychologists, is *counterconditioning*. In counterconditioning, there is no attempt to eliminate the anxiety evoked by the CS. Rather the objective is to use an antagonistic US to condition competing responses to the CS that will interfere with the existing CR (fear, anxiety). If a person is given sufficient retraining, or counterconditioning, the newly acquired conditioned behaviors will replace the older fear reaction as the dominant response tendency. The basic components of counterconditioning are graphically illustrated in figure 4.5.

The aim of any counterconditioning treatment initiative is redefining the behavioral consequences of anxiety. For the athlete, this means changing habits with respect to how stressful situations are handled. Consider the apocryphal case of Vernon Smith. Vernon is a nineteen-year-old male on the college varsity track team. He is an immensely talented high jumper who has the potential for developing into a national class competitor. Yet his performance is often erratic, and he seems to especially have trouble in those meets that would bring him the greatest recognition. Closer inspection reveals that a major factor in Vernon's mercurial performance record is stress. He suffers intense feelings of discomfort and tension in big meets. He imagines that he will embarrass himself by stumbling on his approach to the bar, and that thousands of people will see him as foolish and miscast. To ensure that he does not fall, he approaches the bar tentatively, thus avoiding shame but guaranteeing a substandard jump.

Treatment in this case involves *relaxation training*. In this procedure, the person learns to make a series of physiological reactions that include decreased muscle tone, lowered heart rate, slower respiration, and an increase in the production of alpha brain wave patterns. With respect to the treatment of Vernon, once he has

Figure 4.5 The Basic Model of Counterconditioning Used in Behavior Therapy

Note: (A) The original associations involve a weaker stimulus-response connection (e.g., anxiety reaction) and a stronger stimulus-response connection (e.g., relaxation). (B) When the stimuli that cause each response are paired, the stronger of the two responses begins to connect to the weaker stimulus as well as the stronger stimulus. (C) Eventually, the originally weaker response is replaced with the new, stronger response (e.g., the previously anxiety-eliciting stimulus now evokes relaxation).

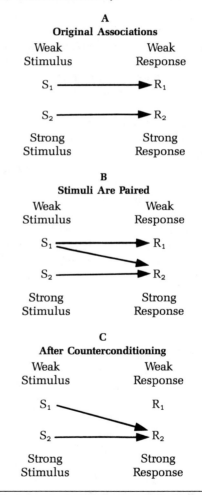

SOURCE: *Psychology*, by L. T. Benjamin, J. R. Hopkins, and J. R. Nation, 1986, New York: Macmillan.

mastered the art of relaxation, he is enjoined to think about a competitional scene that creates anxiety. When the anxiety is super-ordinate, Vernon is asked to switch off that scene and focus again on relaxing. According to the basic tenets of counterconditioning, the relaxation response will eventually bond to those stimulus events that previously were associated with tension. When Vernon begins a jump, thoughts of disaster that previously caused him to tighten up, now evoke relaxa-tion, and performance should improve.

An assortment of relaxation techniques such as the one prescribed for Vernon are used in modern behavior therapy, and all are variations of the *progressive relaxation procedure* origi-nated by Edmond Jacobson (1938). In this tech-nique, which begins with each patient lying on his or her back with arms extended to the side, selected muscle groups are first tensed and then slowly relaxed. Then the same proce-dure shifts to other major muscles. The pur-pose of this approach is to help patients identify the various muscle systems within the body and to teach them to discriminate be-tween tense and relaxed muscle conditions. Most of the time during the session should be devoted to relaxation training, which is more difficult to accomplish. Acquisition may be slow at first, but after a few months athletes and most other patients learn to evoke a relaxation response in just a few seconds (Nideffer, 1981).

Although relaxation is a common compo-nent of many counterconditioning operations, numerous other behaviors are suitable for treat-ing anxiety disorders. Humor, sexual arousal, and incongruous images have all been used successfully to alter a person's reaction to a fear-eliciting situation. Indeed, one of the more popular versions of counterconditioning ther-apy, known as *systematic desensitization*, recommends the inclusion of a range of responses that formally compete with anxiety (Wolpe, 1982). The systematic desensitization model appeals to many treatment specialists

because it embraces a hierarchical arrangement of anxiety arousing events, with low anxiety items at the bottom of the list and high anxi-ety items at the top. One example of such a list has been presented by Smith (1984). The case (a hypothetical one) involves an acute anxiety reaction experienced by a male basketball player when presented with high pressure game situations. The hierarchy in this existence was of the form:

5. Preparing to shoot a free throw, with 1 second left in the championship game and your team trailing by 1 point (high anxiety scene)
4. Sitting in the locker room before the game as your coach tells you how important this game is (moderately high anxiety scene)
3. Walking toward the arena where the game will be played (moderate anxiety scene)
2. Getting up from bed in the morning and thinking of the game that evening (moder-ately low anxiety scene)
1. Thinking about the fact that the game will be played in two days (low anxiety scene)

Treatment would involve taking the lowest anxiety scene and pairing it with relaxation, or an amusing idea, or some other conflicting behavior. Once the scene no longer evoked an anxiety response, and instead produced the relevant counterconditioned behavior, treat-ment would proceed to the next step (moder-ately low anxiety scene) and the process would be recapitulated. Eventually, the patient would work upward through the list until completion. The advantage of such a strategy is that it makes counterconditioning easier to achieve. Because items low on the list necessarily evoke minimal fear and tension, they are more sus-ceptible to disruption. In classical condition-ing terms this means that the CR strength is likely to be low relative to that of the compet-ing response elicited by the antagonistic US (refer back to figure 4.5). Further attempts at counterconditioning involving more intense fear-eliciting cues will be accomplished with greater ease because of the gains made lower in the hierarchy.

To summarize the application of classical conditioning techniques in treating sport-related anxiety disorders, one approach (extinction) is intended to eliminate anxiety altogether, whereas the other (counterconditioning) aims to replace the conditioned anxiety reaction with a more tolerable alternative. Although the extinction procedures have the advantage of total removal of anxiety, the counterconditioning techniques have been more thoroughly investigated (see Winter, 1982). With either approach, athletic performance should be facilitated and life should be a bit more comfortable in general for participants.

Instrumental Conditioning Techniques

Previously, we have considered only treatment regimens that are based on classical conditioning principles. In this section we discuss the relevance of instrumental procedures (refer to chapter 3) for treating anxiety reactions that actively interfere with the execution of motor behaviors in sport.

Reinforced Practice. The procedure known as *reinforced practice* (refer to Leitenberg, 1976) is one instrumental approach that has been used with success in the treatment of anxiety related disorders. The central idea underlying this approach is that reinforcement can be administered in such a fashion that responses incompatible with the typical anxiety behaviors are strengthened. For example, a person who has a fear of snakes may be asked to approach a snake that is placed in a glass enclosure at a set distance across the room. Successively closer steps toward the snake are identified by numbered strips of tape on the floor. A 1 may correspond to an initial step, a 2 to the next,

and so on up to, say, 14, which is at the point of the enclosure. Each time the patient moves closer to the snake he or she is rewarded by the therapist with verbal praise or some tangible evidence of approval. A record is kept of the patient's progress, and he or she sees the graphic representation reflecting improvement. By learning to approach a feared object, the patient loses his or her phobia.

Although this procedure has not been applied in any systematic way in a sports setting, it could easily be adapted to fit the demands of the athletic environment. Rewarding mental approaches to a crowded area, for instance, may prove to be helpful for a gymnast who fears a large audience. Or reinforcing a young batter who fears a pitched baseball for making increasingly more aggressive swings may decrease anxiety and may increase hitting performance in the process. This is a potentially rich area for sport psychology research and some worthwhile information along these lines clearly is needed.

Biofeedback. Perhaps the most common intervention technique based on the principles of instrumental learning is a procedure that has come to be known as *biofeedback*. Known in the experimental psychology literature as "instrumental conditioning of autonomic behaviors," this area had its origins with Neal Miller at Rockefeller University (Dicara, 1970; Miller, 1978). Challenging a long-standing axiom that instrumental techniques were restricted to voluntary, somatically controlled responses, Miller and his colleagues observed under a variety of experimental conditions that animals could learn to control heart rate, digestive procedures, salivation output, and a host of other internal responses. Before long, practitioners were employing reinforcement techniques to treat everything from migraines to excess muscle tension caused by stress. Today, biofeedback procedures are commonly recommended for treating anxiety.

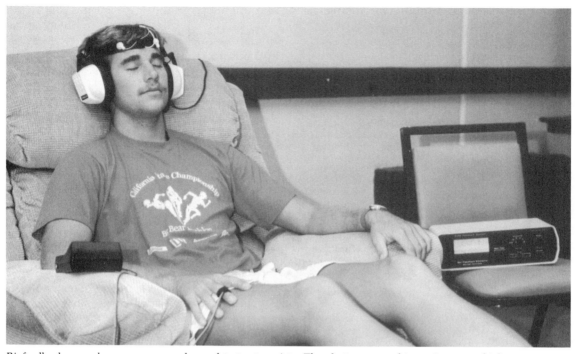

Biofeedback procedures are commonly used to treat anxiety. The electromyographic equipment, which measures skin temperature and muscle tension level, will help this triathlete learn to relax.

Often biofeedback training involves the inclusion of some sort of electronic gadgetry that signals the patient that an appropriate autonomic response has occurred. And the use of such biofeedback devices in treating athletes has produced convincing results. DeWitt (1979), for example, used an electromyographic procedure to assist football players in learning to relax. The electromyograph is equipped with electrodes that can be placed at selected muscle sites. These electrodes sense the degree of muscle contraction, and the information is presented in either digital or analog form on a display screen. By focusing on the feedback from the screen, players were able to decrease muscle tension and preempt excessive arousal.

In a more recent investigation by DeWitt (1980), cognitive therapy was combined with biofeedback training in an attempt to lower stress among university football and basketball players. Cognitive approaches to treatment focus on restructuring thought processes and self-perceptions and as a rule have been valuable treatment tools in traditional clinical settings. Using the techniques of mental rehearsal and cognitive restructuring along with electromyographic feedback, DeWitt decreased muscle tension in a laboratory setting for six varsity football players and twelve varsity basketball players. Moreover, the players' performance efficiency improved dramatically following the intervention. Although this study provides no clues as to the differential effects of cognitive therapy versus biofeedback training, it does provide evidence that performance increases parallel reductions in muscle tension brought about by biofeedback sessions.

Elsewhere, Daniels and Landers (1981) conducted an investigation of a squad of shooters who were given either verbal instructions or auditory biofeedback training. The findings revealed that the shooters who were given biofeedback training improved more and maintained greater consistency than their counterparts who received only verbal statements about their performance. Additionally, the biofeedback groups exhibited greater control over the automatic pattern, thus validating the relation between internal autonomic control

and enhanced shooting performance.

Despite forceful arguments by many sport practitioners about the desirability of using biofeedback techniques (Bird and Cripe, 1986), only a few experimental demonstrations of potency of the approach have occurred in actual field studies. Although supporting evidence from well-controlled laboratory investigations of motor performance are somewhat

---

HIGHLIGHT 4.2

Does Biofeedback Really Work?

The appropriateness of biofeedback as an intervention technique is complicated by a recent report by Dworkin and Miller (1986) that reverses the position taken by the founder of the area. Miller and his colleagues ran more than two thousand animals in a series of experiments designed to replicate some of the seminal biofeedback studies, and the result was an inability to reproduce the earlier effects. The unreliability of biofeedback as an intervention procedure with human behavior disorders has also been an item for fiery debate.

Certain treatment specialists seem to be more likely than others to obtain positive results. Although differing techniques and levels of expertise may contribute to the discrepant results to some degree, it is most remarkable that many therapists never report improvement for their patients on a consistent basis. This has triggered a steady flow of accusations about fraudulent reporting and embellished accounts of the successes of biofeedback training.

This biofeedback controversy is no less heated in the realm of sport intervention. In a recent report on enhancing human performance (Druckman and Swets, 1987), quite negative conclusions were reached about the efficacy of biofeedback training techniques. It seems that when a positive result is obtained it often turns out to be a fluke. Because performance enhancement is noted in one instance, or in one individual, does not mean that it will be seen again in the same situation, or with other performers. The lack of reliable findings from case to case has caused many treatment specialists to turn away from biofeedback and pursue other behavioral change strategies.

Still, it likely would be a mistake to presume that biofeedback is contraindicated as an intervention technique in sport. As shown elsewhere in this chapter, biofeedback training apparently is valuable in certain situations. Perhaps it would be a better idea to drop the indictment and focus on defining the boundaries and conditions under which the technique actually does work.

SOURCES: *Enhancing Human Performance: Issues, Theories, and Techniques* (p. 14–34) by D. Druckman and J.A. Swets, 1987, Washington, DC: National Academy Press; "Failure to Replicate Visceral Learning in the Acute Curarized Rat Preparation" by B.R. Dworkin and N.E. Miller, 1986, *Behavioral Neuroscience, 100,* 299–314.

helpful (French, 1978), what is needed are experiments with athletes who are actually attempting to function under intense stress. Also, there is the very serious issue of the reliability of the effects (see Highlight 4.2).

Cognitive Techniques

Whereas the foregoing interventions focused on behavioral techniques evolving out of the basic literature on classical conditioning and instrumental learning, cognitive intervention strategies are designed to restructure the way the athlete thinks about competition. Attitudes, impressions, and other covert mental operations are not only acknowledged to exist, they are the targets of change. Thus, rather than attempt to modify the behavior, cognitive approaches aim to alter thought processes (cognitions) and therein influence responding (athletic performance).

One cognitive strategy that is grounded to an empirical treatment framework is called *stress inoculation* therapy (Meichenbaum, 1977). With this regimen the person learns an appropriate coping strategy for dealing with the negative emotional fallout that comes with periodic bouts of acute anxiety. Typically, a person who suffers from debilitating stress becomes preoccupied with self-deprecating personal statements and the feeling that his or her defense system is collapsing. In the stress inoculation approach, the idea is to get the patient to recognize the pattern of events that characterizes the anxiety attack and then to use those cues as signals for making adaptive coping responses. Such a treatment is designed to redirect anxiety-mediated behavior and to formally teach a patient how to deal with stress. Three stages are generally involved in the retraining experience: (1) the experiential conditions of anxiety are clarified for the patient, so that the onset of the negative mood state is easier to identify; (2) re-education regarding the determinants and dynamics of the stress response must take place; and (3) appropriate coping behaviors are practiced, and then used when stress occurs. Thus, stress becomes a stimulus for the execution of functional behavior.

In athletics, the original format has been altered only slightly to produce four stages (see Long, 1980). In the initial phase, discussions are held with the athlete about the particular feelings he or she has in certain competitive situations. The therapist explains the impact that such feelings are likely to have on performance. The intent of this period is to increase the athlete's awareness of the unique physical and mental reactions that constitute stress. In the second phase, the educational program is intensified and the athlete learns about the basic self-regulation skills. It is not unusual during this period to administer the training in small groups. During the third phase, specific coping behaviors are prescribed and the athlete is taught to transform negative thoughts into positive self-statements. For instance, a player might be instructed to react to an image of choking under pressure with a private statement such as, "Just relax, you can do this. You have handled tougher situations, so just get on with doing your job." By converting negative self-statements to positive verbal commands, the individual develops a more practical coping style. Finally, in the fourth and last stage recommended by Long's version of stress inoculation training, the athlete has a chance to implement his or her new strategy in graded stress situations. Successively more threatening competitive circumstances are presented in imaginal form, and then actual athletic situations are instated. Even though the athlete's fears may not subside, his or her reaction to them may be dramatically changed.

Another cognitive treatment regimen that has proven to be of value for treating anxiety in sport is based on Bandura's (1977) *self-efficacy theory*. This theory purports that performance will be determined jointly by the strength of the person's conviction that he or she has the competency to execute the skills that are demanded by the situation and the responsiveness of the environment. One determinant of responding, which might be called "self-confidence," is *efficacy expectation*. A second variable is known as *outcome expectation*. The differential effects that these two types of expectancy are likely to have on responding is profiled in figure 4.6. The term efficacy expectancy refers to the person's belief about his or her own ability. "Can I even do this? Sure, other people are good at this sort of thing, but what am I capable of doing?" Because efficacy expectancies are integrated to the person's perception of self-worth, they often constitute the target for behavioral change in therapy. It really makes little difference that an individual possesses talent if that person is convinced of his or her inability to succeed. Remediation in this case must take the form of enhancing self-esteem and making patients believe they are winners, not losers. Conversely, with outcome expectancy the person's beliefs relate to predictions about the likelihood that rewards will occur, even when efficacious responses are made. In this instance, it is not that the individual does not believe in himself or herself; rather, the situation is viewed as

harsh and unresponsive: "Why bother with responding if nothing happens?" Obviously, this type of expectancy problem dictates a different intervention approach than that required in the case of efficacy expectation difficulties.

As Feltz (1984) indicates, efficacy expectancies may be of greater importance in the mediation of athletic performances than outcome expectancies. When a player loses confidence, his or her perceptions about the payoff ratio in the environment may be incidental. For example, a golfer may be acutely aware of the need to take the ball from right to left out on the fairway. But questions about his or her ability to accomplish this feat may be intrusive, and may prevent the athlete from executing the swing appropriately. Although a detailed review of the major sources of influence on efficacy expectation is beyond the scope of our coverage, Feltz notes that performance accomplishments (one's own mastery experiences), vicarious experience (information obtained by watching others), verbal persuasion (the opinions of others), and emotional arousal (the person's perception of his or her anxiety status) all contribute to the formation of efficacy expectations.

The experimental literature on self-efficacy has centered on the relation between self-

---

Figure 4.6 Relations of Efficacy Expectations and Outcome Expectations to the Individual, the Individual's Behavior, and Behavioral Outcomes

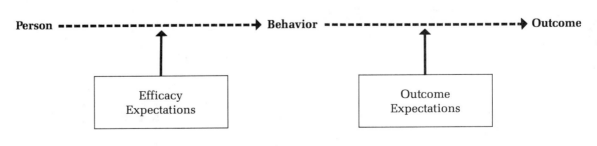

confidence and athletic achievement. Performance in competitive gymnastics, for instance, has been found to vary as a function of one's efficacy expectations (Lee, 1982). In this investigation of fourteen female athletes, individual gymnasts' expectations about how well they thought they could do in competition were determined to be a better predictor of their actual performance than their previous competition scores. Curiously, the athlete's coach made even more accurate predictions about the athlete's ultimate performance score than either the athlete or the past record. This overall pattern was particularly apparent when the participants were more experienced and of greater natural ability. Similar findings have been reported by Feltz, Landers, and Raeder (1979) in a laboratory study of motor behavior.

In other empirical tests of Bandura's self-efficacy theory, Weinberg, Gould, and Jackson (1979) conducted a study of high or low self-efficacy men and women using a muscular leg-endurance task. A confederate was said to be either a varsity track athlete who exhibited higher performance on a related task (the high self-efficacy condition) or an individual suffering from a knee injury who exhibited lower performance on a related task (the low self-efficacy condition). With the experiment rigged so that subjects lost to the confederates in competitive trials, the findings revealed that subjects in the high self-efficacy manipulation maintained leg extensions for longer periods of time than those in the low self-efficacy manipulation. The results from self-report questionnaires administered after the experiment confirmed that confidence was a major factor in determining individual performance.

More recent experiments relating self-efficacy to performance have been concerned with induction procedures that may change efficacy expectations, thus modulating athletic outcome. Along these lines, Kavanaugh and Hausfield (1986) have examined the role of mood in optimal sport performance. Elevations

in mood may alter what athletes think they can achieve. Accordingly, competitive efficacy should be enhanced when athletes are made happy as compared to cases in which a sad state is induced. Using an audiotape that asked some subjects, but not others, to visualize winning $10,000 from a lottery, performance on handgrip (dynamometer) task was observed to be positively influenced by an elevated mood state. However, the increases in motor performance that paralleled improvements in mood did not appear to be related to changes in efficacy expectations. So, at this point, the proposed mediational link between mood/self-efficacy and athletic performance is uncertain.

Although the relation of self-efficacy to anxiety is often implicitly stated in such basic research projects, serious attempts at documenting the assumed tie between these two phenomenon are scant (see Duncan and McAuley, 1987). One report that does pertain directly to this issue comes from a study by Lan and Gill (1984). In this experiment, subjects performed either easy or difficult tasks and cognitive worry, somatic anxiety, self-confidence, and heart rate were measured concurrently. The easy task generated higher self-confidence (self-efficacy) and lower anxiety whereas the opposite pattern was produced by the difficult task. Such findings of an explicit link between anxiety reduction and a self-efficacy intervention forcefully argue for the validity of this cognitive strategy as a treatment device in the sport realm. What is needed, of course, are more systematic field studies in this area.

Hypnosis

Hypnosis has been defined as an altered state of consciousness characterized by increased acceptance of suggestion. Despite connotations of voodoo and deception, hypnosis has a lengthy history that suggests it is an effective method for controlling anxiety (Rotella, 1985).

Yet scientists remain uncertain about how this mysterious procedure benefits patients suffering from anxiety disorders. Some argue that hypnosis is nothing more than increased concentration, whereas others advocate that trance states alleviate basic tensions arising out of underlying psychic conflicts. Whatever the mechanism, sport psychologists have shown that hypnosis is a viable technique for inducing a relaxed state that is crucial to success in sport.

Krakauer (1985) reports a long list of professional athletes who have been helped with hypnotic procedures. Former heavyweight boxing champion Ken Norton used a hypnotist to help him prepare for his fight with Muhammad Ali, a fight which he would win. In baseball, hypnotist Harvey Misel has intervened on behalf of more than fifty major league players, among them Bill Buckner when he was playing for the Chicago Cubs. Buckner had been in a batting slump that had brought his average 20 points below his normal performance. After a few sessions with hypnosis, Buckner increased his batting performance so dramatically that he was named National League Player of the Month.

A number of analysts of therapeutic models in sport have advanced the notion that the true strength of hypnosis rests with the athlete's belief that the procedure works (Rotella, 1985). If the athlete approaches the competitive situation with a positive frame of mind, confidence is increased, and as we observed in earlier discussion, this in itself can improve performance efficiency. Still, negative scientific reports failing to confirm the alleged usefulness of hypnosis in sport are not uncommon (Greer and Engs, 1986), so that skeptics continue to question the validity of the procedure.

Even more controversial than hypnosis are meditation procedures such as *yoga*, *Zen*, and *transcendental meditation* (TM). Such procedures teach people to relax by excluding distracting images from consciousness. By narrowing the concentration of the individual and restricting the range of mental activity, task requirements are given greater attention and performance should improve accordingly. Yet, because the precise goals of intervention are not clearly delineated in such procedures, gauging psychological growth during treatment is often difficult. Consequently, it is virtually impossible to determine parallels between performance changes and mental progress. Not surprisingly, there has been a scarcity of empirical reports that establish the role that TM and other meditational procedures may play in the treatment of anxiety disturbances among athletes.

A FINAL NOTE

In this chapter we have seen that techniques are available that decrease arousal with the result that better sport performances occur. But arousal levels can fall too low, and performance deteriorates. The real issue for the coach or practitioner is identifying the level of tension that maximizes the athlete's attention and maintains his or her concentration. At what point do we pull in the reins, and how much control is required? Has the player peaked too soon, and how long can optimal arousal levels be expected to be sustained? As most coaches know already, the answers to these questions are individually determined. Nonetheless, some of the features covered in this chapter may help with respect to improving our judgments about arousal and athletic performance.

SUMMARY

1. Arousal is an all-inclusive term referring to psychological activation. Anxiety is generally regarded as a negatively charged emotional state.

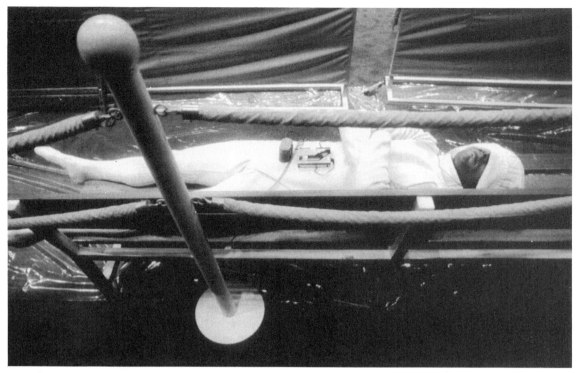

An Italian fencer meditates before the pentathlon in the 1988 Olympics. Although the effectiveness of meditation in sports is unclear, this athlete can relax by eliminating distracting images from his consciousness.

2. The cerebral cortex, the hypothalamus, and the reticular formation are brain structures important to the expression of anxiety.
3. State anxiety is a transitory form of apprehension that varies in intensity. Trait anxiety is a more enduring variable that reflects nonspecific anxiety proneness.
4. The drive theory of learning and performance posits that arousal will interact positively with well-established behaviors but negatively influence behaviors with weaker habit strength. By contrast, the inverted-U hypothesis states that all behaviors (low or high habits) will increase as arousal increases, up to a point; further increases in arousal will result in performance deterioration.
5. Sensation seeking refers to the notion that some persons prefer extraordinarily high levels of stimulation to moderate levels of stimulation. Some evidence exists that such persons just prefer more activity of any type, threatening or otherwise.
6. Flooding and implosive therapy are two intervention techniques based on the principles of classical conditioning. In each of these procedures, extinction is used as a method for anxiety alleviation.
7. Relaxation training employs the technique of counterconditioning to replace anxiety reactions to fear-eliciting cues with calmness. The end result is that the athlete's performance improves. A variant of this procedure is called systematic desensitization.
8. Reinforced practice is an intervention procedure based on the principles of instrumental conditioning. The idea is to reward

the person for systematic approaches toward an anxiety-provoking stimulus.

9. One of the most popular methods for treating anxiety is an instrumental technique known as biofeedback. Ostensibly, this approach uses reward outcomes (feedback) to change the probabilities of autonomic behaviors. However, recent research questions the validity of the early claims along these lines.

10. Two of the better known cognitive models for treating anxiety in sport are stress inoculation and self-efficacy. The former aims to teach an appropriate coping style, the latter focuses on increasing self-esteem.

11. Among the various procedures designed to alter consciousness and thereby relieve anxiety, hypnosis is probably the best known. Hypnotic techniques have been used successfully in the treatment of athletes, but the reasons for change are poorly understood. Yoga, Zen, and transcendental meditation (TM) are examples of other meditational strategies that have been used as intervention techniques.

SUGGESTED READINGS

Corsini, R.J. (1979) *Current psychotherapies.* Itasca, IL: Peacock.

This book of readings covers a broad range of treatment and practices. Details about behavioral and cognitive techniques are provided, and information is presented about how to select the appropriate intervention. While one type of treatment may be ideal for one disorder or subpopulation, it may be unsuitable and not recommended in other cases.

Lazarus, R.S., & Folkman, S. (1984) *Stress, appraisal, and coping.* New York: Springer.

This volume presents a focused and penetrating account of stress as a transaction between the person and the environment. In addition to examining the role of social forces in the creation of

stress, the book outlines appropriate ways of dealing with stress. The reading level is moderate and should not present a problem for the unsophisticated reader.

Selye, H. (1976). *The stress of life.* New York: McGraw-Hill.

Selye is the king of anxiety research and this book spells out his position on the topic. Selye adopts the fundamental position that stress and anxiety arise out of circumstances in which a person feels pressured to be someone he or she is not. When individuals are required to behave in a manner that is basically oppositional to their nature, or go at a pace that is inappropriate for them, the result is anxiety and discomfort.

REFERENCES

Bandura, A. (1977) Self-efficacy: Toward a unifying theory of behavioral change. *Psychological Review, 84,* 191–215.

Benjamin, L.T., Hopkins, R., & Nation, J.R. (1987) *Psychology.* New York: Macmillan.

Bird, A.M., & Cripe, B.K. (1986) *Psychology and sport behavior.* St. Louis: Times Mirror/Mosby.

Borkovec, T.D. (1976) Physiological and cognitive processes in the regulation of anxiety. In G.E. Schwartz & D. Shapiro (Eds.), *Consciousness and self-regulation: Advances in research* (pp. 141–180). New York: Plenum.

Brustad, R., & Weiss, M.R. (1987) Competence perceptions and sources of worry in high, medium, and low competitive trait-anxious youth athletes. *Journal of Sport Psychology, 1,* 97–105.

Bunker, L., & Rotella, R. (1980) Achievement and stress in sport: Research findings and practical suggestions. In W.F. Straub (Ed.), *Sport psychology: An analysis of athlete behavior.* Ithaca, NY: Mouvement Publications.

Carlson, N.R. (1986) *Psychology: The science of behavior.* Boston: Allyn and Bacon.

Cotman, C.W., & McGaugh, J.L. (1980). *Behavioral neuroscience.* New York: Academic Press.

Daniels, F.S., & Landers, D.M. (1981) Biofeedback and shooting performance: A test of disregulation and systems theory. *Journal of Sport Psychology, 2,* 288–294.

DeWitt, D.J. (1979) Biofeedback training with university athletes. In *Proceedings of the Biofeedback Society Annual Meeting*. Denver, CO: The Biofeedback Society.

DeWitt, D. (1980) Cognitive and biofeedback training for stress reduction with university athletes. *Journal of Sport Psychology, 2,* 288–294.

Dicara, L. (1970) Learning in the autonomic nervous system. *Scientific American, 22,* 30–39.

Duncan, T., & McAuley, E. (1987) Efficacy expectations and perceptions of causality in motor performance. *Journal of Sport Psychology, 9,* 385–393.

Easterbrook, J.A. (1959) The effects of motion on cue utilization and the organization of behavior. *Psychological Review, 66,* 183–201.

Feltz, D.L. (1984) Self-efficacy as a cognitive mediator of athletic performance. In W.F. Straub & J.M. Williams (Eds.), *Cognitive sport psychology: Personal growth to peak performance* (pp. 114–148). Lansing, NY: Sport Science Associates.

Feltz, D.L., Landers, D.M., & Raeder, U. (1979) Enhancing self-efficacy in high avoidance motor tasks: A comparison of modeling techniques. *Journal of Sport Psychology, 1,* 112–122.

Fenz, W.D. (1985) Coping mechanisms and performance under stress. In D.M. Landers & R.W. Christina (Eds.), *Psychology of sport and motor behavior II* (pp. 64–84). University Park, PA: College of HPER, The Pennsylvania State University.

Foa, E.B., Grayson, J.B., Steketee, G.S., Doppelt, H.G., Turner, R.M., & Latimar, P.R. (1983) Success and failure in the behavioral treatment of obsessive-compulsives. *Journal of Consulting and Clinical Psychology, 51,* 287–297.

French, S.N. (1978) Electromyographic biofeedback for tension control during gross motor skill acquisition. *Perceptual and Motor Skills, 47,* 883–889.

Gerson, R., & Deshaies, P. (1978) Competitive trait anxiety and performance as predictors of precompetitive state anxiety. *International Journal of Sport Psychology, 9,* 16–26.

Gould, D., Horn, T., & Spreeman, J. (1983) Perceived anxiety of elite junior wrestlers. *Journal of Sport Psychology, 5,* 58–71.

Gould, D., Petlichkoff, L., Simons, J., & Vevera, M. (1987) Relationships between Competitive State Anxiety Inventory-2 subscale scores and pistol shooting performance. *Journal of Sport Psychology, 9,* 33–42.

Greer, H., and Engs, R. (1986) Use of progressive relaxation and hypnosis to increase tennis skill learning. *Perceptual and Motor Skills, 63,* 161–162.

Hatfield, B.D., & Landers, D.M. (1983) Psychophysiology—A new direction for sport psychology. *Journal of Sport Psychology, 5,* 243–259.

Huddleston, S., & Gill, D.L. (1981) State anxiety as a function of skill level and proximity to competition. *Research Quarterly for Exercise and Sport, 52,* 31–34.

Hull, C.L. (1943) *Principles of behavior.* New York: Appleton-Century-Crofts.

Jacobson, E. (1938) *Progressive relaxation.* Chicago: University of Chicago Press.

Karteroliotis, C., & Gill, D.L. (1987) Temporal changes in psychological and physiological components of state anxiety. *Journal of Sport Psychology, 9,* 261–274.

Kavanaugh, D., and Hausfield, S. (1986) Physical performance and self-efficacy make happy and sad moods. *Journal of Sport Psychology, 8,* 112–123.

Klavora, P. (1977) An attempt to derive inverted-U curves based on the relationship between anxiety and athletic performance. In D.M. Landers & R.W. Christina (Eds.), *Psychology of motor behavior,* (pp. 369–377). Champaign, IL: Human Kinetics.

Krakauer, J. (1985) Hypnosis. *Ultrasport, 2,* 22–27.

Lan, L.Y., & Gill, D.L. (1984) The relationship among self-efficacy, stress responses, and a cognitive feedback manipulation. *Journal of Sport Psychology, 6,* 227–238.

Landers, D.M. (1980) The arousal-performance relationship revisited. *Research Quarterly for Exercise and Sport, 51,* 77–90.

Lee, C. (1982) Self-efficacy as a predictor of performance in competitive gymnastics. *Journal of Sport Psychology, 4,* 405–409.

Leitenberg, H. (1976) Behavioral approaches to treatment of neuroses. In H. Leitenberg (Ed.), *Handbook of behavior modification and behavior therapy* (pp. 41–64). Englewood Cliffs, NJ: Prentice Hall.

Long, B.C. (1980) Stress management for the athlete: A cognitive behavioral model. In C.H. Nadeau, (Ed.), *Psychology of motor behavior and sport* (pp. 111–119). Champaign, IL: Human Kinetics.

Lykken, D. (1968) Neuropsychology and psychophysiology in personality research. In E.F. Borgatta &

W.W. Lambert (Eds.), *Handbook of personality theory and research* (pp. 16–41). Chicago: Rand McNally.

Mahoney, M.J., & Avener, M. (1977) Psychology of the elite athlete: An exploratory study. *Cognitive Therapy and Research, 7,* 135–141.

Martens, R. (1974) Arousal and motor performance. *Exercise and Sport Science Reviews, 2,* 155–188.

Martens, R., Gill, D., Simon, J., & Scanlan, T. (1975) Competitive anxiety: Theory and research. Proceedings of the seventh Canadian Psycho-Motor Learning and Sport Psychology Symposium, Quebec City (October).

Martens, R., & Landers, D.M. (1970) Motor performance makes stress: A test of the inverted-U hypothesis. *Journal of Personality and Social Psychology, 16,* 29–37.

Martin, G., & Pear, J. (1988) *Behavior modification: What it is and how to do it.* (3d ed.). Englewood Cliffs, NJ: Prentice-Hall.

Meichenbaum, D.M. (1977) *Cognitive behavior modification: An integrative approach.* New York: Plenum.

Mowrer, O.H. (1960) *Learning theory and behavior.* New York: Wiley.

Miller, N.E. (1978) Biofeedback and visual learning. *Annual Review of Psychology, 29,* 373–404.

Nideffer, R.M. (1981) *The ethics and practice of applied sport psychology.* Ithaca, NY: Mouvement Publications.

Passer, M.W. (1983) Fear of failure, fear of evaluation, perceived competence, and self-esteem in competitive-trait anxious children. *Journal of Sport Psychology, 5,* 172–188.

Rotella, R.J. (1985) Strategies for controlling anxiety and arousal. In L. Bunker & R.J. Rotella (Eds.), *Sport psychology* (pp. 185–195). Ann Arbor, MI: McNaughton and Gunn.

Scanlan, T.K., & Passer, M.W. (1979) Factors influencing the competitive performance expectancies of young female athletes. *Journal of Sport Psychology, 1,* 151–159.

Smith, R.E. (1984) Theoretical and treatment approaches to anxiety reduction. In J.M. Silva & R.S.

Weinberg (Eds.), *Psychological foundations of sport* (pp. 157–170). Champaign, IL: Human Kinetics.

Sonstroem, R.J. (1984) An overview of anxiety in sport. In J.M. Silva & R.S. Weinberg (Eds.), *Psychological foundations of sport* (pp. 104–117). Champaign, IL: Human Kinetics.

Sonstroem, R.J., & Bernardo, P. (1982) Intraindividual pregame state anxiety and basketball performance: A re-examination of the inverted-U curve. *Journal of Sport Psychology, 4,* 235–245.

Spence, K.W., Farber, I.E., & McFann, H.H. (1956) The relation of anxiety (drive) level to performance in competitional and noncompetitional paired-associated learning. *Journal of Experimental Psychology, 52,* 296–305.

Spielberger, C.D. (1972) *Anxiety: Current trends in theory and research* (Vol. 1). New York: Academic Press.

Stampfl, T.G., & Levis, D.J. (1967). Essentials of implosive therapy: A learning theory based psychodynamic behavioral therapy. *Journal of Abnormal Psychology, 72,* 496–503.

Wankel, L.M. (1980). Social facilitation of motor performance: Perspective and prospective. In C.H. Nadeau, W.R. Halliwell, K.M. Newell, & G.C. Roberts (Eds.), *Psychology of motor behavior and sport—1979* (pp. 41–53). Champaign, IL: Human Kinetics.

Weinberg, R.S., & Genuchi, M. (1980). Relationship between competitive trait anxiety state anxiety and golf performance: A field study. *Journal of Sport Psychology, 2,* 148–154.

Weinberg, R.S., Gould, D., & Jackson, A. (1979) Expectations and performance: An empirical test of Bandura's self-efficacy theory. *Journal of Sport Psychology, 1,* 320–331.

Winter, B. (May 1982) Relax and win. *Sports and athletes,* pp. 72–78.

Wolpe, J. (1982). *The practice of behavior therapy.* New York: Pergamon.

Zajonc, R.B. (1965) Social facilitation. *Science, 149,* 269–274.

PART · TWO

SOCIAL-PSYCHOLOGICAL
DIMENSIONS

Cognitive Dimensions of Sport

INTRODUCTION

In addition to the behavioral perspectives of sport performance presented earlier, the cognitive model offers much food for thought scientifically. At the peak of the fascination with behavioral explanations for our actions, the cognitive psychologists found themselves in disfavor. However, an acceptance of cognitive variables as mediators of behavior has become reputable and has spawned considerable research in its behalf. Geen, Beatty, and Arkin (1984, p. 11) refer to this change in the acceptance of consciousness and thinking as the "cognitive revolution."

Four interrelated cognitive concepts will be discussed in this chapter and, though not totally exhaustive of the possible topics within cognitive psychology, they do represent major research thrusts within the sport domain. Accordingly, attribution theory, need achievement, locus of control theory, and self-esteem/ self-concept variables will constitute the intellectual menu for the next several pages.

ATTRIBUTION THEORY

A topic of relatively recent but continuing interest to sport scientists is attribution theory, which was first advanced by Fritz Heider (1944, 1958). Representing a move toward a more cognitive approach to psychology, attribution theory essentially deals with the "naive psychology" of the average person and how he or she interprets behavior. These behavioral inferences may take two forms, either causal or dispositional attributions. *Causal attributions* are inferences as to why something happened; for example, tennis players playing as a doubles team may attribute their success to their capacity for teamwork. As for *dispositional attributions*, we are dealing with inferences about some quality or trait that an individual may possess. The football player who plays at a level generally above his apparent ability is said to be a "winner" or an "overachiever." Both causal and dispositional attributions represent an attempt on the part of laypersons and professionals alike to explain both their behavior and that of those around them. By engaging in such attributions, a measure of psychological closure is achieved, integrity and self-esteem are maintained, and a degree of order is achieved in the environment. Such is the function of our continuous behavioral attributions.

According to Geen, Beatty, and Arkin (1984), attributions are subject to a number of biases, and these must be taken into account when dealing with related theory, research, or application. One source of error is *informational bias* and this comes about as the result of discrepancies between what we know about ourselves, what we know about others, and what they know about us. As a result, misunderstanding of motives and behavior takes place. A second error source is *perceptual bias*. Briefly stated, we cannot perceive ourselves as others do because we cannot observe ourselves and are more prone than others to make external as opposed to personal attributions about life events. A final source of problems is *motivational bias*, and here we are dealing primarily with defensive attributions. Of particular interest to sport researchers has been the notion of the self-serving attribution bias. In this situation, the person involved assumes too much personal responsibility for success and too little for failure. We are all prone, in our athletic endeavors, to see victory or success as due to ability or effort and defeat or failure as attributable to poor officiating, faulty equipment, unfavorable weather conditions, and bad luck. More will be said on this topic later.

Attribution Theory Models

In general, two models of attribution theory have been advanced and have caught the fancy of theorists and researchers. They are cognitive and functional (Brawley and Roberts, 1984).

The Cognitive Model. The cognitive model is based on an integration by Weiner (1974, 1980) of Heider's work and that of Julian Rotter and his locus of control theory. Weiner's formulation in its simplest form essentially asserts that task outcomes (O) in any achievement-related activity is a function of ability (A), effort (E), task difficulty (T), and luck (L):

$$O = f(A,E,T,L)$$

This formula allows for an assessment of success or failure through evaluation of level of ability, amount of effort expended, the difficulty of the task at hand, and the strength and direction of luck or chance factors confronted (Weiner, 1980).

These causal antecedents for behavior suggested by Weiner (i.e., ability, effort, task difficulty, and luck) allow for inferences about achievement outcomes.

Ability Antecedents. According to Weiner (1980), ability antecedents are primarily drawn from past experience with success ("I can") or failure ("I cannot"). High academic achievement often leads to an inference that a person is "smart" or is "a brain" just as general speed and agility may lead to the conclusion that the person possessing these qualities is a "good all-around athlete."

Effort Antecedents. The amount of effort put forth in order to achieve is an important variable though there is not necessarily a one-to-one correspondence between the two. If that were so, the student who studies the most would

always make the highest grade. In the athletic realm, as will be discussed later in more detail, the black athlete is often perceived as successful not due to effort but to natural or innate ability, an obviously erroneous but common attribution.

Task Antecedents. If many succeed at a task, it is seen as easy, whereas the opposite is true when few succeed. Running the hurdles without embarrassing or injuring oneself is seen as a major accomplishment by many, and such a task is generally seen as difficult because so few can do it. The same can be said for the pole vault. The role of concensus information in assessing task difficulty is of paramount importance, though objective factors— such as length, complexity, and novelty—also enter into the overall process of judging task antecedents.

Luck Antecedents. The flip of the coin, the luck of the draw, and various weather events in outdoor sports are examples of things that are perceived as chance or luck attributions contributing to success or failure in achievement situations. And we are prone to bring luck attributions to bear on losing efforts. For example, Mann (1974) asked spectators at a football game why the winning team had triumphed over its opponent. Ninety-three percent of the winner's fans cited superior play as the reason for victory, whereas the loser's fans in 50 percent of the cases cited bad luck as the cause of their team's defeat.

An expanded list of reasons for success and failure related to ability, effort, task difficulty, and luck is presented in table 5.1. Carrying this work a step further, we see that Weiner has expanded beyond the elements of ability, effort, task difficulty, and luck to include stability and locus of causality in what becomes a two-dimensional taxonomy, represented in figure 5.1. As can be seen, ability and effort are internal and task difficulty and luck are external.

Table 5.1 Some Cues Utilized for Inferences Concerning the Causes of Success and Failure

Causes	Cues
Ability	Number of successes, percentage of success, pattern of success, maximal performance, task difficulty
Effort	Outcome, pattern of performance, perceived muscular tension, sweating, persistence at the task, covariation of performance with incentive value of the goal
Task difficulty	Objective task characteristics, social norms
Luck	Objective task characteristics, independence of outcomes, randomness of outcomes, uniqueness of event

SOURCE: *Human Motivation* (p. 332) by B. Weiner, 1980, New York: Holt, Rinehart and Winston.

At the same time, ability and task difficulty are seen as stable whereas effort and luck are unstable or changing over time. A number of possible inferences can be drawn. Among them are:

1. The low ability athlete who loses would expect to lose in future events because of his or her perception of ability as stable. Defensiveness could be expected to enter in here, thereby salvaging self-esteem by attributing failure to any of the other three elements of effort, task difficulty, or luck.
2. Winning or losing attributable to changeable elements such as effort or luck offer something for both successful and less successful sport participants in that the latter may view more effort as a means of reversing losing, and the former may see that luck can change things in a negative way so that they, too, may expend more effort in order to neutralize chance events. The latter is typified by the coach who pushes his already successful team to even greater effort with exhortations such as, "The harder I work, the luckier I get," or "I believe in luck and the harder I work, the luckier I get," or "Good luck is what happens when preparation meets opportunity."

Though Weiner has expanded his model beyond the two-dimensional framework in recent years, it is the most influential in terms of creating research in sport psychology (Brawley and Roberts, 1984).

In an effort to expand Weiner's work in the sport realm, Roberts and Pascuzzi (1979) have offered a more inclusive model, which is described in figure 5.2. Roberts and Pascuzzi arrived at their formulation through a study they conducted at the University of Illinois using 346 male and female undergraduate students. Subjects were asked to respond to eight stimulus items aimed at determining causal attributions for success or failure as a player and as a spectator. Only 45 percent of the subjects' attributions fell into Weiner's four elements of ability, effort, task difficulty, and luck. Frieze (1976), in a study of an academic environment, found that 83 percent of all attributions were within Weiner's four elements, leading Roberts and Pascuzzi to conclude that perhaps the two-dimensional model is more applicable to academic than sport environments.

Though all other factors reported by Roberts and Pascuzzi can be seen in figure 5-2, it is interesting to note that psychological factors (such as motivation, anxiety, and arousal), practice, and unstable ability factors related to day-by-day performance variations were cited so often by the subjects in the study.

Though Roberts and Pascuzzi's work is an extension of the Weiner two-dimensional model and, in general, is characteristic of the kind of research spawned therefrom, Weiner's updated *three-dimensional taxonomy* has not gone unnoticed by sport researchers. The three-dimensional taxonomy (Weiner, 1979, 1980)

Figure 5.1 Dimensions and Elements of Weiner's Two-Dimensional Taxonomy (1972)

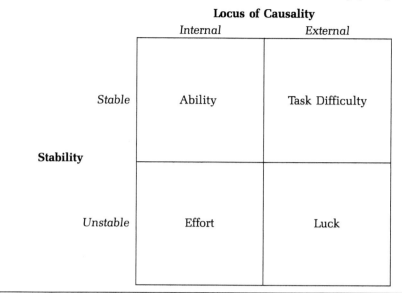

Locus of Causality

	Internal	*External*
Stable	Ability	Task Difficulty
Unstable	Effort	Luck

Stability

SOURCE: "Attribution in Sport: Research Foundations, Characteristics, and Limitations" by L. R. Brawley and G. C. Roberts, 1984, in J. M. Silva and R. S. Weinberg, eds., *Psychological Foundations of Sport* (pp. 197–213), Champaign, IL: Human Kinetics.

Figure 5.2 Dimensional Categorization of Sport-Relevant Attributions

Locus of Control

	Internal	*External*
Stable	Ability	Coaching
Unstable	Effort Psychological Factors Unstable Ability Practice	Luck Task Difficulty Teamwork Officials

Stability

SOURCE: "Causal Attributions in Sport: Some Theoretical Implications" by G. C. Roberts and D. Pascuzzi, 1979, *Journal of Sport Psychology*, 1, 203–211.

adds to the stability and locus of causality dimensions a third leg, that of controllability (events are seen as either controllable or uncontrollable). The three-dimensional model can be seen in table 5.2. Consistent with the new addition to the earlier models, antecedents such as effort would be viewed as controllable whereas ability has a strong element of uncontrollability. In terms of the originally stated concepts of ability, effort, task difficulty, and luck, a perusal of table 5.2 will yield the following generalizations:

1. Individual ability is internal, stable, and uncontrollable.
2. Individual effort is internal, stable or unstable, and controllable.
3. Task difficulty is external, stable, and uncontrollable.
4. Luck is external, unstable, and uncontrollable.

Generalizations can also be made about the contributions of others (teammates, opponents) with regard to the success-failure dichotomy, and these are also revealed in table 5.2.

Considerable research has been generated in an effort to evaluate the three-dimensional taxonomy. Illustrative of one of the earlier attempts to test the three-dimensional model is the work of Gill, Ruder, and Gross (1982). Using both field and laboratory experiments (two each), Gill and her associates gathered a total of 352 open-ended attributions by simply asking their subjects, once they had completed actual or laboratory competitions, to respond to the question, "What is the most important reason for your team's winning or losing in today's match?" The preponderance of responses indicated an emphasis on internal, unstable, and uncontrollable attributions in team competition. References to teamwork were the most frequent attributions and the traditional attributional elements of ability, effort, task difficulty, and luck were not particularly salient. This suggests that research in team sports would do well to focus on causal dimensions rather than the more traditional attributions.

As a caveat related to their work, Gill and associates suggest that coding difficulties and psychometric weaknesses associated with the open-ended format are problem areas of note. In this connection, Elig and Frieze (1979) are critical of open-ended measures when compared to other more objective methods. To partially deal with this problem, Gill et al. suggest that the Causal Dimension Scale (Russell, 1982) might be useful to future researchers with a penchant for more objective measures of attributions. The Causal Dimension Scale is presented in table 5.3.

Table 5.2 A Three-Dimensional Taxonomy of the Perceived Causes of Success and Failure

	Controllable		Uncontrollable	
	Stable	*Unstable*	*Stable*	*Unstable*
Internal	Stable effort of self	Unstable effort of self	Ability of self	Fatigue, mood, and fluctuations in skill of self
External	Stable effort of others	Unstable effort of others	Ability of others; task difficulty	Fatigue, mood, and fluctuations in skill of others; luck

SOURCE: *Human Motivation* (p. 347) by B. Weiner, 1980, New York: Holt, Rinehart and Winston.

Table 5.3 The Final Causal Dimension Scale

Instructions: Think about the reason or reasons you have written above. The items below concern your impression or opinions of this cause or causes of your outcome. Circle one number for each of the following scales.

1. Is the cause(s) something that:

Reflects an aspect of yourself	9	8	7	6	5	4	3	2	1	Reflects an aspect of the situation

2. Is the cause(s):

Controllable by you or other people	9	8	7	6	5	4	3	2	1	Uncontrollable by you or other people

3. Is the cause(s) something that is:

Permanent	9	8	7	6	5	4	3	2	1	Temporary

4. Is the cause(s) something:

Intended by you or other people	9	8	7	6	5	4	3	2	1	Unintended by you or other people

5. Is the cause(s) something that is:

Outside of you	1	2	3	4	5	6	7	8	9	Inside of you

6. Is the cause(s) something that is:

Variable over time	1	2	3	4	5	6	7	8	9	Stable over time

7. Is the cause(s):

Something about you	9	8	7	6	5	4	3	2	1	Something about others

8. Is the cause(s) something that is:

Changeable	1	2	3	4	5	6	7	8	9	Unchanging

9. Is the cause(s) something for which:

No one is responsible	1	2	3	4	5	6	7	8	9	Someone is responsible

NOTE: A total score for each of the three subscales is arrived at by summing the responses to the individual items as follows: (1) locus of causality—items 1, 5, and 7; (2) stability—items 3, 6, and 8; (3) controllability—items 2, 4, and 9. High scores on these subscales indicate that the cause is perceived as internal, stable, and controllable.

SOURCE: "The Causal Dimension Scale: A Measure of How Individuals Perceive Causes" by D. Russell, 1982, *Journal of Personality and Social Psychology, 42,* 1137–1145.

Accordingly, McAuley and Gross (1983) and McAuley (1985) have taken the challenge of Gill and her collaborators by utilizing the *Causal Dimension Scale* in their respective research efforts. In the McAuley and Gross study, sixty-two male and female undergraduates who were enrolled in a physical education skills class in table tennis served as subjects. Upon completion of matches between same-sex players, thirty-one winners and thirty-one losers of each sex were identified. All subjects were admin-istered the Causal Dimension Scale. Winners and losers alike made attributions that were internal, unstable, and controllable, though winners used more of them than losers. McAuley and Gross also reported high reliability coefficients for the dimensions of locus of causality and stability, but the controllability dimension had lower reliability than expected. Reservations were expressed about the latter scale's applicability to sport research as a result.

The second study by McAuley was conducted with fifty-two women's intercollegiate gymnasts as subjects. Each gymnast was judged on the traditional gymnastic events (vault, balance beam, uneven parallel bars, floor exercises). Each was asked how she felt she had done in each event prior to finding out her scores, and all subjects then completed the Causal Dimension Scale. Among the more salient findings were that high success gymnasts made more internal, stable, and controllable attributions for their performance; made significantly more stable attributions on all four events; made more internal attributions on two events (vault, balance beam); and made more controllable attributions on all events except the floor exercise. Perceived success was seen as a more powerful predictor of causal attributions than actual performance scores. Impressions of success for all gymnasts were lowest for the balance beam, an event many believe to be the hardest of the group of exercises to accomplish successfully.

Future research in this area will undoubtedly focus more on Weiner's three-dimensional model, and further utilization and refinement of Russell's Causal Dimension Scale can be expected. Too, self versus team attributions will be more intensively scrutinized in an effort to shed light on individual and team dynamics.

The Functional Model. The functional or motivational model posits that the motivation to maintain or enhance feelings of self-esteem is at the core of attributional efforts. This is, of course, the *self-serving attributional bias* mentioned earlier, whereby feelings of self-worth are maintained or enhanced through attributing success to internal factors (ability, effort) and failure to external events (task difficulty, luck).

Early studies by Iso-Ahola (1975, 1977) and Roberts (1975) were supportive of the existence of a self-serving attributional bias in Little League baseball players. Essentially all of the preceding three studies indicated that evalua-

For many athletes defeat or failure is rationalized in such a way as to maintain self-esteem. These Little Leaguers might well offer a variety of explanations as to just how this particular play occurred: one player might credit ability and effort, while another might chalk it up to good luck.

tions of self and team are disparate; players from unsuccessful teams tended to be rather critical of team ability and effort but did not view losing as an indictment of their own ability and work output. Conversely, players from successful teams made both self- and team-serving attributions (Bird and Brame, 1978; Roberts, 1975). However, Bird and Brame, in their study of female collegiate basketball players, found consistency between self- and team-serving attributions on effort but not on ability. Winners generally saw the team as possessing more ability than they themselves did individually. In a later study, Bird, Foster, and Maruyama (1980) introduced another variable into the process, namely, team cohesion. Cohesive teams in women's collegiate basketball demonstrated greater agreement on team- and self-attributions than did low cohesive teams. However, there were no differences in either ability or effort attributions between the two groups, though low cohesive teams made greater luck and lesser task attributions for their performance than for that of the team.

Bukowski and Moore (1980), in a bit of a disclaimer, found little evidence for the existence of a self-serving bias in their study of seventy-seven Canadian youth attending an overnight camp who participated in a camp "Olympics" made up of a variety of physical activities. Too, luck and task difficulty were not seen as particularly salient by their subjects.

Two days prior to competing in the "Olympics," each contestant was asked to rate how important certain factors would be in terms of succeeding in the upcoming events. Ratings were on a 5-point scale ranging from 1 (important) to 5 (not important). A second rating was made one day after the camp competition was concluded. Results from the two administrations can be seen in table 5.4.

In general, there is agreement between pre- and postcompetition evaluations, though equipment came under careful scrutiny by the competitors in both the attributions for success and failure conditions. Too, the quality of officiating was seen as increasingly critical in the attributions for failure condition.

Overall, trying hard (effort), being good athletes (ability), being interested in competing, and good officiating were seen as very important to success in the post-test condition. On the other hand, having lots of luck (luck) and because the events are easy (task difficulty) were viewed as less important to success.

Table 5.4 Mean Ratings of Attributions for Success and Failure

Attributions for Success	M	*Attributions for Failure*	M
Trying hard	1.23/1.29	Not trying hard	1.84/1.84
Good officiating	1.61/1.63	Bad officiating	2.07/2.42
Being good athletes	1.61/1.66	Not being interested in competing	2.08/1.98
Being interested in competing	1.67/1.58	Not being interested in winning	2.22/2.07
Being in a good mood	1.80/2.06	Being in a bad mood	2.30/2.55
Having good leaders	1.84/1.91	Having bad leaders	2.32/2.52
Being interested in winning	1.97/2.04	Being poor athletes	2.52/2.27
Having good equipment	2.44/2.76	Having poor equipment	2.77/3.25
Having lots of experience	2.55/2.67	Having no experience	3.30/3.28
Being smart	2.95/2.89	Perceiving the events as hard	3.43/3.27
Perceiving the events as easy	3.68/3.79	Not being smart	3.58/3.29
Having lots of luck	3.66/3.81	Having bad luck	4.00/3.79

The number to the left of the slash is the item's mean rating from the postevents evaluations and the number to the right of the slash is the item's mean rating based on the pre-events evaluations. Sixty-nine subjects provided postevents evaluations, seventy subjects provided pre-events evaluations.

Source: "Winners' and Losers' Attributions for Success and Failure in a Series of Athletic Events" by W. Bukowski and D. Moore, 1980, *Journal of Sport Psychology*, 2, 195–210.

Another failure to support the existence of the self-serving attributional bias is provided by Mark, Mutrie, Brooks and Harris (1984). Mark et al. reported results from two studies, one with fifty-nine squash players in a national tournament and the second with twenty-six racquetball players participating in an open tournament in Pennsylvania. In general, winners and losers in both situations did not differ in their attributions on locus of causality dimensions. Winners, as opposed to losers, did make more stable and controllable attributions, however.

By way of summary, it would appear that evidence for the existence of a self-serving attributional bias is inconclusive. At a very commonsense level, however, it seems to be a viable concept. In view of the significance of such a bias in terms of its protective role with regard to self-esteem, further research on the issue would seem useful. Mark and his colleagues do suggest that research in the area could profit from more real-life as opposed to contrived, novel test situations in the laboratory; from better measures of attribution, such as Russell's Causal Dimension Scale; and from less emphasis on team as opposed to individual success.

Future Directions

Excellent reviews containing suggestions for future work in the realm of attributions and sport are offered by Brawley and Roberts (1984); Mark, Mutrie, Brooks, and Harris (1984); and Rejeski and Brawley (1983). All parties show common concerns about such research, and their suggestions may be summarized as follows:

1. Let the athlete define the causal attributions, not the experimenter. Only recently has the relevance of subject not experimenter definition been seen as important (Bukowski and Moore, 1980; Roberts and Pascuzzi, 1979). The biggest step in this direction of subject definition of attributions has been the use of the Causal Dimension Scale mentioned earlier; it clearly lets the subject define the causes of his or her achievement behavior. There appears to be generally universal agreement as to its efficacy in future research.

2. Much emphasis has been placed on winning and losing and they have been equated with success or failure; it is certainly likely that the two pairings are not equivalent. Many an athlete has won and seen his or her performance as a failure, and many losses have been viewed as successes. The win/lose dichotomy is simply too narrow a definition of success or failure.

3. The team versus individual attribution becomes blurred because of team mores, folkways, pressures, and concerns. Attributions for success and failure are complicated greatly by team pressures to present oneself in ways that may or may not represent one's true ascriptions for those matters. The need for further studies of group dynamics on attributional concerns is clearly accentuated here.

4. The role of perceived ability as a moderator of causal ascriptions has been studied fairly thoroughly but has not been exhausted.

5. There seems to be universal agreement that research in the area of youth sport represents a considerable gap in the attributional research. How this deficiency might be rectified in view of the tendency of young people to make few or primitive attributions is quite problematic.

6. The original Weiner model is too limited and should be replaced with more updated models emphasizing elements far more broad than ability, effort, task difficulty, and luck.

7. Too heavy a reliance has been placed in past attributional research on the use of college students, and team sports have been studied

Losing need not be equated with failure, nor should winning necessarily be paired with success.

far more often than have individual sports. More research with individual athletes is called for.

One potentially useful tool in separating team and individual attributions is the *Wingate Sport Achievement Responsibility Scale (WSARS)* of Tenenbaum, Furst, and Weingarten (1984). This sport-specific instrument showed a low but positive correlation between team and individual attributions, thereby suggesting a separation of the two for future research purposes. Much remains to be done in validating the WSARS, but it seems to be a good addition to the scientific arsenal of the sport researcher.

NEED FOR ACHIEVEMENT

Closely related to our discussion of attribution theory is the concept of need for achievement, often expressed as *n ach*.

Murray's Contribution

Inquiry into the need to achieve is generally thought to have begun in the late 1930s with the work of the accomplished Harvard personality theorist, Henry Murray. It was Murray's position that people differ in their need "to overcome obstacles, to exercise power, to strive to do something difficult as well and as quickly as possible" (Murray, 1938, pp. 80–81). This striving he called the need for achievement. Murray devised the very popular projective test of personality, the *Thematic Apperception Test (TAT)*, as a means of measuring variations in human motivation. The TAT has become, over the past fifty years, one of the most popular projective tests available to psychologists and psychiatrists working in clinical settings. The TAT is made up of twenty stimulus cards into which subjects are asked to project hidden personality themes or dimensions through fantasy stories. These fantasy stories are, in turn, analyzed by specialists in thematic analysis who

categorize the various response themes. The TAT has undergone revision over the years and is still used in clinical work and research studies, though its use in the latter has been sparse to nonexistent in sport psychology. An example of a TAT card can be seen in figure 5.3.

The McClelland-Atkinson Model

Murray's pioneering efforts were further advanced through the efforts of David McClelland and associates in the early 1950s (McClelland, Atkinson, Clark, and Lowell, 1953). McClelland and his associates revised and added considerable sophistication to the scoring procedure of the TAT, and they have greatly extended Murray's original premises. Though they have engaged in several collaborative efforts, much of the work of McClelland and Atkinson has proceeded independent of one another. The net effect of their independent efforts, however, has led Cox (1985) and others to refer to their work as the *McClelland-Atkinson model*. We, too, shall approach the topic of need for achievement from that perspective.

Basically, the McClelland-Atkinson model takes the position that motivation to achieve is a function of the relative strengths of the motive or tendency to approach success and the motive or tendency to avoid failure. Atkinson (1957) calls these simply hope of success and fear of failure. In any event, goal-directed or achievement behavior is mediated by the joint action of the two motives regardless of the terminology used. Atkinson proposes that quantification can be brought to bear on the issue, and suggests that three factors *must* be considered in making the determination of hope of success. These three determinants are as follows:

1. Motivation to achieve success = M_s
2. Perceived probability of success = P_s
3. Incentive value of success $(1 - P_s) = In_s$

With the tendency to achieve or hope of success expressed as T_s, the following formula emerges:

$$T_s = M_s \times P_s \times In_s$$

With regard to fear of failure, again three forces are at work:

1. Motive to avoid failure = M_f
2. Probability of failure $(1 - P_s) = P_f$
3. Negative incentive value of failure = In_f

Again, a formula emerges to help quantify fear of failure where this tendency is expressed as T_f:

$$T_f = M_f \times P_f \times In_f$$

In turn, Atkinson indicates that these two motives, hope of success and fear of failure, are additive, resulting in a formula for total motivation as follows:

$$T_s + T_f = (M_s \times P_s \times In_s) + (M_f \times P_f \times In_f)$$

This total score, which is called resultant achievement motivation (RAM), allows for prediction of individual motivation in a variety of settings, not the least of which is sport.

A view of how the mathematics of the formula work is provided in table 5.5, which calculates the tendency to succeed and the tendency to avoid failure under varying conditions of task difficulty. Several noteworthy points emerge from a thorough reading of table 5.5. Most salient among them are:

Figure 5.3 (facing page) Sample TAT Card

Source: *Thematic Apperception Test* by H. A. Murray, 1943, Cambridge, MA: Harvard University Press.

Table 5.5 Calculations of T_s and T_{-f} for Five Levels of Task Difficulty When $M_s > M_F$, When $M_F > M_s$, and When $M_s = M_F$

	Task (P_s)	($M_s \times P_s \times In_s$)	+	($M_F \times P_f \times In_f$)	=	$T_s + T_{-f}$
$M_s > M_F$,	A (.9)	(5 × .9 × .1)	+	(1 × .1 × −.9)	=	.36
where $M_s = 5$	B (.7)	(5 × .7 × .3)	+	(1 × .3 × −.7)	=	.84
and $M_F = 1$	C (.5)	(5 × .5 × .5)	+	(1 × .5 × −.5)	=	1.00
	D (.3)	(5 × .3 × .7)	+	(1 × .7 × −.3)	=	.84
	E (.1)	(5 × .1 × .9)	+	(1 × .9 × −.1)	=	.36
$M_F > M_s$,	A (.9)	(1 × .9 × .1)	+	(3 × .1 × −.9)	=	−.18
where $M_F = 3$	B (.7)	(1 × .7 × .3)	+	(3 × .3 × −.7)	=	−.42
and $M_s = 1$	C (.5)	(1 × .5 × .5)	+	(3 × .5 × −.5)	=	−.50
	D (.3)	(1 × .3 × .7)	+	(3 × .7 × −.3)	=	−.42
	E (.1)	(1 × .1 ×. 9)	+	(3 × .9 × −.1)	=	−.18
$M_s = M_F$,	A (.9)	(5 × .9 × .1)	+	(5 × .1 × −.9)	=	0
where $M_s = 5$	B (.7)	(5 × .7 × .3)	+	(5 × .3 × −.7)	=	0
and $M_F = 5$	C (.5)	(5 × .5 × .5)	+	(5 × .5 ×− .5)	=	0
	D (.3)	(5 × .3 × .7)	+	(5 × .7 × −.3)	=	0
	E (.1)	(5 × .1 × .9)	+	(5 × .9 × −.1)	=	0

SOURCE: "Motivational Determinants of Risk Taking Behavior" by J. Atkinson, 1957, *Psychological Review*, 64, 359–372.

1. Maximum motivation occurs when task difficulty is .5 for conditions in which motivation to succeed surpasses fear of failure, even though success and failure are equally likely. Athletic teams made up of highly talented players with a high need for achievement thrive on competition with the better teams. Conversely, there is little to excite them when playing weaker teams; weak task difficulty demands simply do not inspire achievement motivation.

2. In conditions where the tendency to avoid failure (M_f) is greater than the tendency to succeed (M_s), maximum motivation will occur at either the .1 or .9 difficulty level. Accordingly, athletes at each point would select to play either under conditions in which success is a virtual guarantee or, paradoxically, under conditions where failure is likely. In the latter case, because task difficulty is so high, no loss of face or stature is associated with defeat. If you are a duffer on the golf course, losing to the city or course champion in a head-to-head confrontation is not likely to be deflating.

Intrinsic Versus Extrinsic Motivation

An important addition to this model was made by Atkinson (1974) when he incorporated the notion of *extrinsic motivation* (M_{ext})to the motivational prediction formula. Money, verbal praise, pats on the back, medals, trophies, and other awards all constitute sources of extrinsic motivation, and their relevance to performance has not gone unnoticed.

Deci (1975) has suggested that the interplay of intrinsic and extrinsic motivation can be explained through his *cognitive evaluation theory*. Essentially Deci states that intrinsic motivation is a function of the degree of competency, self-determination, and feelings of self-worth that are created by sport competition. In turn, these intrinsic qualities are lessened or greatened by two external reward characteristics, control and information. In the control aspect, we are essentially dealing with a locus of causality artifact; that is, the extent to which the sport participant views his or her rewards as residing internally greatly determines how much an activity is enjoyed. Briefly stated, when a player perceives that a sport is no longer played for the intrinsic enjoyment felt, and conversely is now being played for a trophy or medal, intrinsic motivation may decrease. How often have the fans and the sports writers decried the performance decrement in the first year after a professional athlete has signed a secure and financially lucrative contract? Though these decrements may vary from performer to performer, they do serve notice that internal motivation can decrease when external rewards become more salient.

Insofar as the informational aspect is concerned, participation that increases feelings of self-worth and self-determination due to the message it transmits to the player is seen as facilitating intrinsic motivation. When these coveted qualities are not created, external rewards decrease intrinsic motivation. A player who is voted Most Valuable Player (MVP) on his team is being afforded information as to his worth and competence; this should lead to considerable intrinsic motivation. On the other hand, a player who wins a trophy as part of a championship team to which he or she frankly contributed little is getting a very different message about worth and competence. Further athletic participation, for this competitor, may greatly be a function of the extrinsic reward associated with the activity.

The controlling and informational aspects of rewards are not mutually exclusive; they do interact to effect intrinsic motivation. For example, the high school athlete who is playing football because it is expected by his father and because of expectancies created by the prevailing football climate but who is also doing well at the task may feel that he is getting positive information about himself though he is primar-

ily playing to please others; it might be expected that his intrinsic motivation would be lessened, thereby giving increased importance to external rewards.

To put the issue of intrinsic and extrinsic motivation in a succinct manner, Weinberg (1984, p. 182) says: "If the controlling aspect is more salient, rewards will decrease intrinsic motivation whereas if the informational aspect is the more salient aspect and provides positive information about one's competence, rewards can enhance intrinsic motivation."

Enjoying sport and physical activity for internal reasons is preferable to liking them for external ones. This is not to denigrate or downplay the role of external rewards; they are real, sometimes very powerful, and likely to be with us as sport motivators for quite some time. Weinberg (1984) offers five ways to enhance intrinsic motivation, and they are:

1. Coaches and others involved in physical activity should structure their activities in ways that guarantee a certain amount of success. People are not successful in everything they do every time they do it, and such should and will not be the case in sport. But some success should be assured. Weinberg cites the example of the 10-foot-high basket for youth basketball players. In the case of very young novices, few successes can be achieved with the 10-foot goal; on the other hand, lowering the goal a few feet creates a situation that is conducive to success.

2. Athletes should be allowed more of a role in goal setting and decision making. This granting of responsibility coincides with the locus of causality concern of Deci (1975); athletes who are a part of the decision-making process should feel more in control, which should, in turn, be conducive to the development and maintenance of intrinsic motivation. Using the input of older, more experi-

enced players to guide the development of younger teammates would be an example in which this principle is applicable.

3. Praise is a facilitator of intrinsic motivation. Players whose role is of lesser influence are just as much in need of praise as are the team stars. Role players or substitutes need to feel that they also contribute to overall team goals. Your senior author can recall a high school experience in which this principle was brutalized. A third-team linebacker named Hall who never played in any of the games made a bone-jarring tackle in a midweek scrimmage. Excitedly, Hall awaited the expected praise. Once the pile was sorted out and the coach could determine the involved parties, his response was "Oh, hell, it was only Hall!" This, of course, was temporarily devastating to the player and was a source of considerable bitterness some six years later when Hall graduated from college. *All* players need periodic reinforcement for desirable behavior!

4. Realistic goals feed the players' feelings of competence, which is translated into intrinsic motivation. Despite what many would mistakenly have us believe, winning is not everything. Playing well, improving on previous skill levels, and further social development are desirable goals and need to be stressed. Everyone cannot win; there will be losers on the scoreboard. But these win/loss statistics are far from the only standards with which to measure success.

5. Variation in content and sequence of practice drills helps generate intrinsic motivation. Boredom is one enemy of sport participation; when it is no fun, people drop out or stay on only for extrinsic rewards. Practices do not need to be repetitious nor do they have to be exercises in stamina or drudgery. The mark of a good practice is not measured by the amount of time, repetition, or drudgery involved. At the extreme, some practices do not even have to be practices.

One highly successful high school football coach in the Gulf Coast region of Texas takes his team fishing once or twice a year in lieu of the usual activities. Everyone fishes, food is cooked on the beach, and a spirit of camaraderie is generated. And boredom and drudgery are avoided.

Clearly, a number of ways exist to create, maintain, and even enhance intrinsic motivation. A little creativity coupled with a lot of knowledge of human motivation can be a significant force in creating a positive atmosphere for competition at all levels.

Other Contributions

Before we leave the theoretical aspects of need for achievement, three additional contributions should be mentioned. One is the contribution of Raynor (1969), who posited the concept of *perceived contingency*. Essentially, the role of present behavior on future goals is the concern of Raynor. At every level of competition, the player with future ambitions in a particular sport must be aware of what his or her present athletic behavior means for future participation. Thus, both immediate and future expectancies of success and failure are the focus of Raynor's work.

A second contribution is that of Mehrabian, who has developed a much used measure of *N ach*, the *Mehrabian Scale of Achieving Tendency* (Mehrabian, 1968; 1969). The original scale was made up of twenty-six items with separate items for each sex. Items such as "I think more of the future than the present or past" and "I would rather work on a task where I alone am responsible for the final product than one in which many people contribute to the final product" are representative of Mehrabian's approach to measuring *n ach*. Though it has been used in a number of sport studies (Dunleavy and Rees, 1979; Henschen, Edwards, and Mathinos, 1982; Reid and Hay, 1979), the technique is not without its critics. McClelland (1985, p. 217) states: "There is little justification for using it as a substitute for the fantasy N Achievement score, which has been extensively validated." Granting that McClelland is partial to the fantasy measure of *n ach* (i.e., the Thematic Apperception Test), the Mehrabian scale is not beyond criticism. Nevertheless, Mehrabian's work has been well received in both sport and nonsport research on achievement motivation.

A third noteworthy offering to our present discussion is that of Horner (1968). Horner introduced the idea of *fear of success (FOS)*, a problem of achievement motivation particularly associated with females. Because of socialization practices, females express themselves differently in achievement situations, particularly in those involving males. This topic will be addressed in detail in chapter 10.

LOCUS OF CONTROL

Closely intertwined with attribution theory and need for achievement is the concept of *locus control*. Rotter (1966), a social learning theorist with a cognitive bent, gave initial impetus to the notion that has spawned so much research. For example, Throop and MacDonald (1971) put together a bibliography of locus of control research that contained 339 studies for the period 1966 to 1969 alone. Rotter (1975) cited more than six hundred I-E studies prior to 1975. To Rotter, locus of control was conceived as a generalized expectancy to perceive reinforcement as contingent upon one's behavior (internal) or as the result of forces outside one's control and related to luck, chance, fate, or powerful others (external).

The I-E Scale

In order to measure the various dimensions of locus of control, Rotter (1966) developed the *I-E*

Scale. The scale itself is made up of twenty-nine items, six of which are used as fillers. Subjects are asked to respond to each of the twenty-nine items by choosing between two alternative statements. Scores range from 0 to 23, with higher scores denoting externality. *Sample items from the Rotter scale are represented below:*

   a. In the case of the well prepared student there is rarely if ever such a thing as an unfair test.
   b. Many times exam questions tend to be so unrelated to course work, that studying is useless.

   a. There is too much emphasis on athletics in high school.
   b. Team sports are an excellent way to build character.

The I-E Scale has not gone unnoticed by sport researchers, though findings have been somewhat equivocal.

Perhaps the first locus of control study utilizing the I-E Scale in sport was conducted by Lynn, Phelan, and Kiker (1969). Lynn et al. administered the I-E scale to thirty basketball players (group sport), thirty gymnasts (individual sport), and thirty nonparticipants in sport; all were twelve to fifteen years of age and matched for intelligence. Group sport participants were significantly more internal than were members of the other two groups. Finn and Straub (1977) used the I-E Scale in a study of highly skilled female softball players from the Netherlands (N = 35) and the United States (N = 44). Statistically significant differences (.01) were noted, with the Dutch players being more external than their American counterparts. Further analyses also showed that American pitchers and catchers were significantly more internal than the Dutch battery-mates as well as groups of Dutch infielders and outfielders. Correlational analyses of the relationship of locus of control to height, weight, years of playing experience, playing position, and position in batting order failed to produce significant differences. As a caveat, Finn and Straub point to potential problems related to translating the I-E Scale to the Dutch language. Hall, Church, and Stone (1980) used the Rotter scale with twenty nationally ranked weight lifters. Firstborn lifters were more external than later borns, but all were basically internal when compared to overall norms reported by Rotter.

Other more complex studies involving the I-E Scale have been conducted by Hall (1980) and Scheer and Ansorge (1979). Hall administered the locus of control measure and the Spielberger State-Trait Anxiety Inventory (STAI) to three hundred subjects at the University of Virginia. Two groups of thirty-two subjects were then selected to take part in a motor task based on whether or not they were internal (scores of 0 to 6) or external (scores of 16 to 23). Subsequent analyses revealed, among other things, that externals were significantly higher than internals on trait anxiety. Laboratory manipulations of success and failure revealed that internals made more internal attributions for failure; this finding, of course, is consistent with much of the attributional locus of control literature.

In the Scheer and Ansorge study, ten national- or regional-level female gymnastic judges served as subjects. Based on I-E Scale results, five were designated as internals (M = 5.8) and five as externals (M = 15.4). They were then asked to evaluate videotapes of the 1977 Region VI AIAW Gymnastics Championships in four Olympic events. In all, forty gymnasts were rated by the ten judges. Data analysis revealed that external judges were more susceptible to their own preconceived expectancies for athletic performance than were internal evaluators. Based on their findings, Scheer and Ansorge suggest that the I-E Scale might eventually become a part of the process for selecting the most qualified officials for championship athletic events.

On the other side of the coin, at least four studies have failed to support the validity of the I-E Scale. Celestino, Tapp, and Brumet (1979) found no differences between seventy-four finishers and twenty-three nonfinishers in male marathoners in New York. They did find, however, a small (.28) but significant correlation between internality and order of finish. Di Giuseppe (1973) divided 167 high school freshmen into four groups: team sports, individual sports, intramural sports, and no athletic involvement. No significant differences were noted among the four groups. Gilliland (1974) divided ninety San Jose State University males and females into five groups related to sports involvement. Again, various analyses by sex and by athletic activity or nonactivity revealed no differences in locus of control. Finally, McKelvie and Huband (1980) studied various college athletes (N = 92) and nonathletes (N = 93) and concluded that no systematic relationship exists between athletic participation and locus of control.

Despite the preceding disclaimers, it would appear that Rotter's I-E Scale remains a useful instrument for future investigations of the locus of control concept.

Levenson's Multi-Dimensional Approach

A more recent and increasingly popular measure of locus of control has been provided by Levenson (1973). Reacting to both personal considerations (Levenson, 1981) and a body of growing research indicating that these were problems associated with Rotter's original conceptualization (e.g., Collins, 1974; Gurin, Gurin, Lao, and Beattie, 1969; and Mirels, 1970), Levenson arrived at a multidimensional locus of control measure that tapped into *internality* and two dimensions of externality, *powerful others* and *chance*. Her feeling was that Rotter's notion of externality was greatly confounded by the fact that one could be external on the I-E Scale and yet arrive at that point through greatly different avenues; that is, the individual who views external causation as a function of chance or luck events may be very different from one who perceives causality as a function of powerful others in the environment. Hence, the creation of what we shall call hereafter the *IPC Scale*.

The refined IPC Scale is made up of twenty-four items, eight of which load respectively on the Internal, Powerful Others, and Chance dimensions. Responses are made based on a 7-point Likert scaling procedure with scores on all three dimensions ranging from 0 to 48. Representative items for each of the dimensions include:

1. *Internal.* "When I make plans, I am almost certain to have them work."
2. *Powerful Others.* "In order to have my plans work I make sure that they fit in with the desires of people who have power over me."
3. *Chance.* "It's not wise for me to plan too far ahead because many things turn out to be a matter of good or bad luck."

According to Levenson (1981, p. 18) the IPC Scale was designed to differ from Rotter's I-E scale in five important ways:

1. The items are presented as a Likert scale instead of in a forced-choice format, so that the three dimensions are more statistically independent of one another than are the two dimensions of Rotter's scale.
2. The I, P, and C subscales make a personal–ideological distinction. All statements are phrased so as to pertain only to the person answering. The subscales measure the degree to which an individual feels he or she has control over what happens, not what the person feels is the case for "people in general."
3. The items in the scales contain no wording that might imply modifiability of the specific issues. The factors of personal versus ideological control and system modifiability were found by Gurin et al. (1969) to be contaminating factors in Rotter's I-E Scale.

4. The I, P, and C scales are constructed in such a way that there is a high degree of parallelism in every three-item set.
5. Correlations between items on the new scales and the Marlowe-Crowne Desirability Scale are negligible and nonsignificant.

Levenson (1981, p. 18) further offers the following interpretive caution:

A word of caution about interpretation is necessary. High scores on each subscale are interpreted as indicating high expectations of control by the source designated. Low scores reflect tendencies not to believe in that locus of control. We cannot interpret a low I Scale score as indicating that a subject believes in chance; we can say only that this subject does not perceive him or herself as determining outcomes. Empirically, one could score high or low on all three scales; that is, a person could say he or she was personally in control yet also say that life is a random series of events controlled by powerful others. Rarely has such a profile been obtained. Before one could interpret such a seemingly inconsistent profile one would have to give serious consideration to the presence of confounding factors (e.g., acquiescence response set or random responding).

Perhaps the first sport studies using the IPC Scale, and certainly the most extensive to date, were made by LeUnes, Nation, and Daiss (Daiss, LeUnes, and Nation, 1986; LeUnes and Nation, 1982; Nation and LeUnes, 1983a, 1983b). Summing across these four studies of 108 major university football players and two groups of college students not playing football, the following more salient results were reported:

1. In comparing the traveling squad of this football team (N = 60) with an equal number of college students who had lettered in football in high school but were not playing collegiate football and yet another equal group of college students who had never won an athletic letter ("nonathletes"), the college football players were significantly

more powerful others oriented (.05) than their two peer groups. This powerful others finding suggests that coaches undoubtedly play a significant role in the lives of collegiate players; their athletic careers literally are in the hands of these "powerful others" coaches.

2. In looking at differences across playing positions, no significant findings were noted.

3. In terms of black/white differences, two findings of statistical significance (.05) were isolated. Black defensive linemen were more internal than white offensive linemen and, more significantly, black players overall were more chance-oriented than white players. Given the relatively sad state of racial affairs that currently exists in the United States and given the history of blacks overall, this finding comes as no great surprise.

4. In a five-year follow-up of the 34 out of 108 who were freshmen in 1980 when the original data were collected, 16 had stayed with the football program for either four or five years and 18 had departed. The chance score of the "stayers" was 19.39 while "leavers" scored 11.65, a difference that is significant at the .001 level. Before they ever played a down of football, players who ultimately stayed appeared to have an early realization of the vagaries of a college football career. Apparently, they were aware of the role of chance factors (coaching decisions, academic difficulties, bad luck in the form of injury, and other unpredictables) in determining their ultimate success.

Other more recent applications of the Levenson scale have been made by McCready and Long (1985) and Whitehead and Corbin (1985). It is anticipated that the appeal of Levenson's multidimensional approach will increase, and greater use of her instrument will be made in sport in the future. Studies such as that of Blau (1984) and Bourgeois, Malatich, LeUnes and Mendoza (1985), in which the factorial superiority of the IPC over Rotter's I-E Scale is demonstrated, lend credibility to such a notion.

Locus of Control Measurement with Youth

Nowicki and Strickland (1973) have created a scale for measuring locus of control in children and, though their work has been applied rather widely with children in general, its use in youth sport has been sparse. Anshel (1979) and Morris, Vaccaro, and Clarke (1979) represent two such studies. Anshel used the forty-item Nowicki-Strickland Scale with fifty-seven fifth graders and eighty eighth-grade students in Florida. Based on locus of control scores, thirty-two subjects were assigned by age and internality-externality scores to one of four groups of sixteen each. All subjects took part in a pursuit rotor task in which success and failure conditions were randomly determined. Overall, older subjects, as expected, were superior to the younger ones on the motor task. Too, older subjects were more internal than their younger peers. Thirdly, high internals in both age groups performed better than high externals under positive as opposed to negative feedback conditions; however, negative feedback adversely affected the motor performance of high internals but facilitated that of high externals. In general, Anshel's work supported previous locus of control work with youth in other settings of a nonsport nature.

As for Morris et al., they administered the Nowicki-Strickland Scale to twenty competitive swimmers (seven to seventeen years of age). When their scores were compared with norms published for similar aged youth by Nowicki and Strickland (1973), the swimmers were significantly more internal than their nonathletic age mates.

Though it offers promise, little of late has been done with the Nowicki-Strickland Scale and with young athletes' attributions in general. More work needs to be done to get a more learned perspective on attribution and locus of control in young athletes.

SELF-CONCEPT/SELF-ESTEEM/ SELF-ACTUALIZATION

Yet another aspect related to attribution, achievement, and locus of control is *self-concept* or *self-esteem*, terms we shall use interchangeably. Self-concept or self-esteem, like each of the preceding terms, is a hypothetical construct used to describe a personality variable. We cannot see self-esteem any more than we can view an electrical current, but we can infer it based on behavioral predispositions and occurrences in the same way that electricity can be defined by its effects. Before defining and discussing self-concept/self-esteem, however, a historical review of self theory would set the stage for an appropriate discussion of the topic.

Self Theory

According to Hamachek (1971), the first awakening of interest in *self theory* can be traced to the works of the French mathematician and philosopher, Rene Descartes. Descartes' notions, in turn, were scrutinized by the likes of Leibnitz, Locke, Hume, and Berkeley. With the turn of the twentieth century, interest in the self was primarily vested in the works of William James and Sigmund Freud. Freud's conception of the ego has served as a beginning point for all discussion of the self since he first proposed it, though the concept of the self has certainly been stretched beyond the limits proposed originally by Freud. James gives us a flavor of his feelings about the self with the following passage:

> I am not often confronted by the necessity of standing by one of my empirical selves and relinquishing the rest. Not that I would not, if I could, be both handsome and fat and well-dressed, and a great athlete, and make a million a year, be a wit, a bon-vivant, and lady-killer, as well as a philosopher, a philanthropist, statesman, warrior, and African explorer, as well as a "tone-poet" and saint. But the thing is simply impossible. The millionaire's work would run counter to the saint's; the bon-vivant and the philanthropist would trip each other up; the philosopher and lady-killer could not keep house in the same tenement of clay . . . to make any one of them actual, the rest must more or less be suppressed. . . . So the seeker of his truest, strongest, deepest self must review the list carefully, and pick out the one on which to stake his salvation. All other selves thereupon become unreal, but the fortunes of this self are real. Its failures are real failures, its triumphs real triumphs, carrying shame and gladness with them. . . .
>
> I, who for the time have staked my all on being a psychologist, am mortified if others know more psychology than I. But I am contented to wallow in the grossest ignorance of Greek. My deficiencies there give me no sense of personal humiliation at all. (1890, p. 91)

This quotation serves to remind us of several aspects of the self that will be entertained shortly.

With the advent of the behavioral movement in the late 1800s and the early 1900s, it became unfashionable or unscientific to spend one's time studying what might be viewed as mystical imponderables, so self theory became temporarily passé. However, much has been made of the conception in the past forty years. Gordon Allport, one of those most instrumental in furthering the revival, summarized the revolution as follows:

> In very recent years the tide has turned. Perhaps without being fully aware of the historical situation, many psychologists have commenced to embrace what two decades ago would have been considered a heresy. They have re-introduced self and ego unashamedly and, as if to make up for lost time, have employed ancillary concepts such

as self-image, striving, and many other hyph-enated elaborations which to experimental positi-vism still have a slight flavor of scientific obscenity. (1955, pp. 104–105)

Since that time, self-theory has been greatly promoted by the noted works of Maslow (1954) and Rogers (1961).

As is evidenced from the last sentence in the quote from Allport, many terms have been used to describe essentially the same thing. In an effort to clarify the issue, we shall discuss, in turn, definitions of the self, self-concept, and self-esteem.

The Self

Jersild (1952) tells us that a person's *self* "is the sum of all he can call his. The self includes, among other things, a system of ideas, attitudes, values, and commitments. The self is a person's total subjective environment; it is the distinc-tive center of experience and significance. The self constitutes a person's inner world as dis-tinguished from the other world consisting of all other people and things." Calhoun and Acocella (1983, p. 38) define the self accord-ingly: "The *self* may be defined as a hypothet-ical construct referring to the complex set of physical processes of the individual." These authors go on to describe five aspects of the self:

1. The physical self: the body and its biologi-cal processes
2. The self-as-process: the perception, re-sponse, problem-solving, and action com-ponent of the self
3. The social self: people and roles (father, stu-dent, Republican, industrious worker, lead-er, wife, and so on)
4. The self-concept: what Calhoun and Aco-cella call the "mental self-portrait"
5. The self-ideal: what the person could be if all barriers were down

It is clear from the preceding that the self-structure is multidimensional.

The Self-Concept

Martens (1975) tells us that the *self-concept* (the "mental self-portrait" of Calhoun and Acocella) has three important components: cognitive, affective, and behavioral. The *cognitive com-ponent* refers to self-descriptive terms that we apply to ourselves, words such as bright, attrac-tive, slow, athletic, and so forth. The *affective component* in the formula refers to how we feel about the totality of cognitive ascriptions we have made about ourselves, and it is often referred to as self-esteem. The *behavioral aspect* refers to our tendencies to behave in ways consistent with the other aspects of the self. The behavioral component is perhaps what Jourard (1974, p. 153) had in mind when he defined the self-concept as a self-fulfilling prophecy:

> When a person forms a self-concept, thereby defining himself, he is not so much describing his nature as he is making a pledge that he will continue to be the kind of person he believes he is now and has been. One's self-concept is not so much descriptive of experience and action as it is prescriptive. The self-concept is a commitment.

From the perspective of the behaviorist, posi-tive experiences lead to enhanced feelings of worth that lead to positive experiences that lead to enhanced feelings of worth, and so on. Unfortunately, the same is true if the word "negative" is inserted for "positive" in the for-mulation. Coaches, particularly but not exclu-sively in youth sports, should take heed of the implied admonition!

Some mention of one other perspective of self-concept is warranted. Calhoun and Aco-cella (1983) tell us that the self-concept is made up of knowledge, expectations, and evaluative dimensions. The knowledge dimension translates to what we think we know about ourselves. Expectations are what we aspire to or could be. The evaluative dimension measures what we are (knowledge) against what we could be (expectations) and manifests itself as "what-I-should-be." This determination to be, Calhoun and Acocella call self-esteem.

Self-Esteem

Derlega and Janda (1981) tell us that *self-esteem* is a more specialized concept than self-concept but admit that distinctions are of the hairsplitting variety; Calhoun and Acocella (1983) view self-esteem as the measurement of what we are against what we could and should be; Martens (1975) sees it as an affective evaluation of self; Hamachek (1971) appears to largely agree with Martens. Thus, subtle evaluative distinctions can be made between self-concept and self-esteem, but as Derlega and Janda (1981) point out, terms such as "good self-concept," "favorable self-image," "high self-concept," "favorable self-image," and "high self-esteem" have much in common in that they all refer to positive self-evaluations. The literature in sport psychology, sparse as it may be, seems to indicate that there is little quarreling with the Derlega and Janda position.

Self-Concept Research in Sport Psychology

Martens (1975) summarizes the literature related to self-concept and physical activity and issues a call for more research. Unfortunately, his request has fallen largely on deaf ears. Sport psychologists have shown little interest in the relationship between the two variables, though most would agree that sport and physical activity serve to enhance positive feelings of self-worth. Certainly, what little research that exists has been conducted with minimal regard for a theoretical tie. Perhaps an exception is found in the self-serving attributional bias in

which defeat or failure is rationalized in such a way as to maintain self-esteem. As noted earlier, even this self-serving attributional bias idea has not gone unchallenged.

Early research in self-concept and self-esteem centered around the relationship of esteem and physical appearance or concerned itself with the relationship between physical activity and attitudes about the self (e.g., Hellison, 1970; Ludwig and Maehr, 1967; Read, 1969; Zion, 1965). In general, these various

Studies show that male university undergraduates who participate in regular weight-training activities have healthier self-concepts than students who work out little or not at all.

investigations found that physical activity has a facilitative effect on self-esteem, particularly when positive experiences are provided. These generalizations are particularly true for youth sport, which we shall take up in greater detail later. Overall, the research in the 1960s and 1970s was loosely associated and largely atheoretical.

One of the more recent and continuing efforts in this area has been that of Tucker (1981, 1982a, 1982b, 1982c, 1983a, 1983b, 1983c, 1983d, 1984) with his research on self-concept and weight training. By way of summarizing across these nine reports, the following trends were noted:

1. Standard instrumentation was the Tennessee Self-Concept Scale (Fitts, 1965), the Body Cathexis Scale (Secord and Jourard, 1953), the Eysenck Personality Inventory (Eysenck and Eysenck, 1968), and the Perceived Somatotype Scale (Tucker, 1982a).
2. All subjects were male university undergraduates primarily in beginning weight-training classes as compared to samples of students from a wide variety of major fields of study with little or no involvement with weights.
3. The subjects who participated in regular weight-training activities had healthier self-concepts than did students who worked out little or not at all. Body satisfaction scores also were enhanced by weight training.
4. Evidence for somatotype theory (Sheldon, 1942), particularly the mesomorphic body build, as a moderator of self-concept and body satisfaction was also found. Though Tucker's work has been conducted with similar subjects and measures, generalizing from weight training to all domains of sport and physical activity may be hazardous. Nevertheless, he has added to our knowledge of the relationship of self-concept to at least one sport.

Self-Actualization

Related to our discussion is the *self-actualization motive* of Maslow. It seems only natural that sport and physical activity would be an important part of what Maslow considers self-actualization: "man's desire for self-fulfillment, namely, to the tendency for him to become actualized in what he is potentially" (1970, p. 46). Carrying this definition a step further, Maslow (cited in Gundersheim, 1982, p. 187) says:

> We may define it as an episode or a spurt in which the powers of the person come together in a particularly efficient and intensely enjoyable way, and in which he is more integrated and less split, more open for experience, more idiosyncratic, more perfectly expressive or spontaneous, or fully functioning, more creative, more humorous, more ego-transcending, more independent of his lower needs, etc. He becomes in these episodes more truly himself, more perfectly actualizing his potentialities, closer to the core of his Being, more fully human.

Certainly, these self actualizing feelings and notions have been attributed to sport by players, coaches, and spectators. And it would seem that sport would be a perfect forum for the manifestation of self-actualizing behavior. The available research, however, has shown little relationship between actualization and sport. Gundersheim (1982), in the introduction to a research report, cited eight references prior to 1980, none of which found any relationship between the two variables. Gundersheim goes on to report on a study he did with 339 male and female university athletes and nonathletes. Numerous cross-sport, cross-sex and sport and nonsport comparisons were made based on results from the *Personal Orientation Inventory (POI)* (Shostrom, 1963), a noted measure of self-actualization. The only significant difference found was between male and female athletes; the females were more actualized. Ibrahim and Morrison (1976), using the POI, found a tendency for male and female high school and college athletes to be average or above on self-actualization. Interestingly, and sympto-

HIGHLIGHT 5.1
Maslow's Concept of
Self-Actualization

Abraham Maslow devoted most of his professional life to an in-depth analysis of normal personality, undoubtedly in response to a psychology that was fascinated with a far more sensational facet of the human condition, that of psychopathology. His optimistic view of the organism was in sharp contrast to the pessimism of the psychoanalytic model of the Freudians. Among Maslow's major contributions to our understanding of human behavior is the concept of *self-actualization.* To Maslow, the self-actualized person is someone who has achieved a sense of personal harmony or unity and has maximized his or her potentials across a broad spectrum. In order for this actualization of personality to take place, the individual must have come to grips with and mastered a *hierarchy of needs.* This hierarchy is arranged from the more prepotent fundamental needs through the psychological needs to the need for self-actualization. A pictorial representation of the needs hierarchy tells us much about the dynamic, ongoing process of self-actualization.

Clearly, the lowest but most compelling needs in the hierarchy are the *physiological* ones; the need for food, water, and warmth, as examples, is quite powerful. Assuming that these lower level needs are met, the *safety* needs come into play. A realization that we are generally safe from harm within normal limits gives us the freedom to pursue the *love and belong-*

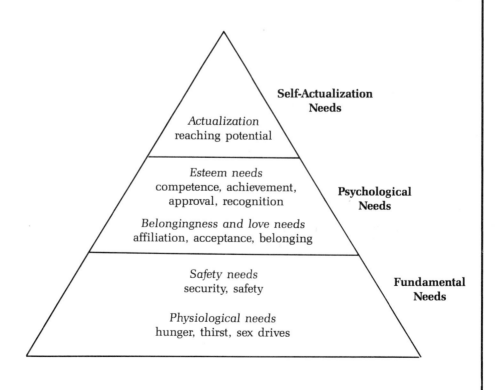

ingness needs, or the feeling that we are loved and accepted by whatever individual standards we use to gauge such acceptance. Out of this acceptance grows a feeling of *esteem,* a belief that we are not only accepted or loved but also that we are respected for our capabilities. If all of the preceding levels of needs are in good order, we are free to achieve the maximization of potential called *self-actualization.* It is easy to lapse into a pattern of thinking that would suggest that the various needs in the hierarchy are met in a step-by-step, static progression. Clearly, the process is ongoing and dynamic and is always in a potential state of flux. Sudden regressions in service of the basic or *deficiency* needs can interfere with the achievement of the growth or *meta-needs,* which is Maslow's explanation for the various adjustment difficulties. Although Maslow's work is not without its critics, the emphasis on the positive, on growth, and on the capacity for change has made an indelible and lasting impression on our views of human behavior.

SOURCES: *Encounters with the Self* (3d ed., pp. 94–96) by D. Hamachek, 1987, New York: Holt, Rinehart, and Winston; *Fundamentals of Abnormal Psychology* (pp. 71–72) by R. Suinn, 1984, Chicago, IL: Nelson-Hall.

matic of the confused self-concept literature in sport psychology, the athletes they studied scored significantly lower than their nonathletic peers on eight of the fifteen dimensions of the Tennessee Self-Concept Scale.

All things dealing with self-theory (constructs such as self-concept, self-esteem, and self-actualization) have been neglected despite the obvious implications sport has for the development of feelings of self-worth. Too, the research done has been marked by isolated pockets of work done here and there with widely assorted subjects who have been assessed with a wide assortment of instruments, mostly conducted in the absence of a unifying theoretical framework. Suffice it to say, more work needs to be done in this important area of self theory.

SUMMARY

1. Four interrelated cognitive variables—attribution, need achievement, locus of control, and self-esteem/self-concept—have been of considerable interest to psychologists inside and beyond the sport realm.

2. Attribution theory owes a considerable debt to the impetus provided in the 1940s and 1950s by the theory and research generated by Fritz Heider.

3. Two general models, cognitive and functional, have been of interest to attribution theory researchers. The cognitive approach, owing much to Julian Rotter, talks of four causal antecedents for behavior: ability, effort, task difficulty, and luck. More contemporary theorizing, such as that of Weiner, has demonstrated that the original model is too simplistic. Accordingly, Weiner posits, in addition to the stability and locus of control dimensions mentioned earlier, a third dimension, that of controllability.

4. The Causal Dimension Scale of Russell (1982) offers a new and possibly superior way to measure sport attributions.

5. The functional model takes the position that maintenance or enhancement of self-esteem is at the core of attributional effort.

HIGHLIGHT 5.2

Tests of Achievement Motivation, Attributions, and Self-Concept/ Self-Esteem

Mark Anshel (1987) has compiled a most comprehensive and useful list of psychological assessment devices that have been applied in the sport setting. His compilation covers tests used in such areas as achievement motivation, aggression, anxiety, arousal, attention, attitude, attributions, burnout, coaching effectiveness, cognitive strategies, cognitive style, competitiveness, expectancies, imagery, leadership, learned helplessness, locus of control, mood, morality and ethical behavior, motivation, observations, perceived exertion, precompetition, pressure, personality, relationships, running, satisfaction, self-concept/self-esteem, self-disclosure, self-efficacy, sensation seeking, sex roles, sport socialization, and stress. Of particular interest to the present discussion is the coverage devoted to achievement motivation, attributions, and self-concept/self-esteem. The following scales have been cited and briefly discussed by Anshel.

Achievement Motivation:
- *The Achievement Motivation Questionnaire,* a measure of McClelland's concept of achievement motivation
- *A Questionnaire Measure of Individual Differences in Achieving Tendency,* which measures an adult's preferences toward seeking and being motivated by achievement situations
- *Fear of Success Scale,* which measures the extent to which one avoids or feels uncomfortable with success
- *Sports Behavior Scale,* a measure of achievement and affiliation
- *Competition-Related Motives Scale,* which measures motives to approach success and avoid failure

Attributions:
- *Attributional Style Scale,* which determines the attributions of subjects as a function of helplessness and depression
- *The Causal Dimension Scale,* a measure of the attributional aspects of causality, stability, and control
- *Wingate Sport Achievement Responsibility Scale,* a sport-specific scale that measures attributional dispositions toward success and failure

Self-Concept/Self-Esteem:
- *Children's Self-Concept Scale,* a measure of self-esteem based on peer popularity
- *Coopersmith Self-Esteem Inventory,* which measures self-esteem as a function of the home and school environment
- *Rosenberg Self-Esteem Scale,* which measures generalized feelings of self-worth
- *Martenik-Zaichkowsky Self-Concept Scale,* a measure of self-concept in children
- *Self-Description Questionnaire III,* a measure of thirteen areas of self-concept among late adolescents and young adults
- *Washington Self-Description Questionnaire,* a measure of self-esteem that can be used with all age groups
- *Tennessee Self-Concept Scale,* which is a most popular multidimensional measure of self-concept
- *Test for Self-Esteem,* a measure of self-esteem in adults

SOURCE: "Psychological Inventories Used in Sport Psychology Research" by M. Anshel, 1987, *Sport Psychologist, 1,* 331–349.

This position statement has led to formulation of a controversial concept known as the self-serving attributional bias, whereby success is attributed internally (ability, effort) and failure is attributed externally (task difficulty, luck).

6. Future directions in attribution research in sport should focus on the athlete as the definer of causal attributions, not the researcher. Too, winning and losing have too long served as the only indices of success or failure; future research should look more at performance. Thirdly, team versus individual attributions need to be viewed separately. Fourth, perceived ability as opposed to actual ability as a moderator of attributions bears additional scrutiny. Fifth, youth sport suffers from a dearth of research. Sixth, the original Weiner model seems limited and needs expansion. Finally, basing attributional generalizations on studies largely conducted with college students seems narrow in scope.

7. Henry Murray introduced the concept of the need to achieve to the psychological literature. He also devised a projective test, the Thematic Apperception Test (TAT), to measure the construct.

8. McClelland and Atkinson have advanced a model for need for achievement that has been scrutinized continually in the sport psychology literature. Intrinsic versus extrinsic motivation has, in turn, played a big part in the total picture of unraveling the need for achievement in athletics and physical activity.

9. Raynor's concept of perceived contingency, Mehrabian's Scale of Achieving Tendency, and Horner's fear of success formulation are related phenomena that bear on the need for achievement literature.

10. Locus of control, a creation of Julian Rotter, continues to be a salient personality variable in sport research. The unidimensional I-E Scale of Rotter has been a very popular instrument for the measurement of internal or external locus of control. Though the literature is generally supportive of the construct, there is a body of research that does not vindicate the I-E Scale.

11. Hanna Levenson, in response to Rotter's early work, developed a multidimensional scale of locus of control. The primary difference in the two scales has to do with their unidimensional versus multidimensional nature, with particular variation reported by Levenson on the external aspect.

12. The measurement of locus of control in youth has been largely the province of Nowicki and Strickland. The inability of the very young athlete to make a variety of attributions has plagued the locus of control research in youth sport.

13. The relatively sparse, confused, and atheoretical research in the area of self-esteem and self-concept has generated an image of an overlooked research domain.

14. Significant literature contributions in self-theory have been advanced by Freud, James, Maslow, and Rogers, to name only a significant few.

15. Definitions of what constitutes the self are varied. Dimensions such as the physical self, the self-as-process, the social self, the self-concept, and the self-ideal have generally received some degree of universal acceptance.

16. Distinctions in the literature between self-concept and self-esteem are largely ambiguous and confused, hence in general use herein of the two terms as synonymous.

17. Sport research in self theory has been a bit sparse and without direction. Nine studies by Tucker relating self-concept and body type to weight lifting represent the most congruent research in the area; Tucker has consistently found a strong relationship between muscular fitness through weight lifting and self-concept.

18. Maslow's conceptualization of the self-actualization motive has been most significant in psychology. However, no consistent relationship between sport and physical activity and self-actualization has been noted.

of the highlights of the paper is the point made by the author that physical activity in and of itself may not be sufficient to enhance feelings of worth; however these outcomes are made much more likely when reward from significant others becomes a part of the formula.

SUGGESTED READINGS

Bostian, L., & Gardner, I. (1981) Achievement motivation and the athlete. *International Journal of Sport Psychology, 12,* 204–215.

These authors summarize much of the theory and research related to the concept of need achievement. Of particular interest, however, is their coverage of practices designed to enhance achievement motivation during the recruiting process, through scheduling strategies, in preseason and practice situations, during actual game competition, and during the off-season.

Fineman, S. (1977) The achievement motive construct and its measurement: Where are we now? *British Journal of Psychology, 68,* 1–22.

Fineman summarizes twenty-two different psychology measures of the need to achieve.

Hamachek, D. (1987) *Encounters with the self* (3d ed.). New York: Holt, Rinehart and Winston.

This exceptionally readable book does a splendid job of presenting the history of self-theory as well as providing many helpful hints to enhance the self-concept in the home, the schools, and elsewhere. A portion of chapter 7 is devoted to enhancing the self-concept through fitness.

Hergenhahn, B. (1984) *An introduction to theories of personality* (2d ed.). Englewood Cliffs, NJ: Prentice-Hall.

Hergenhahn reviews fourteen different theories or perspectives on personality. Of particular interest is the material in chapter 14 that deals with Maslow's theory of self-actualization.

Sonstroem, R. (1982). Exercise and self-esteem: Recommendations for expository research. *Quest, 33,* 124–139.

Soenstrom cites seventy references related to the interplay of self-esteem and physical activity. One

REFERENCES

Allport, G. (1955) *Becoming.* New Haven: Yale University Press.

Anshel, M. (1979) Effect of age, sex, and type of feedback on performance and locus of control. *Research Quarterly, 50,* 305–317.

Atkinson, J.W. (1974) Strength of motivation and efficiency of performance. In J.W. Atkinson & J.O. Raynor (Eds.), *Motivation and achievement* (pp. 193–218). Washington, DC: V.H. Winston.

Bird, A.M., & Brame, J. (1978) Self versus team attributions: A test of the "I'm OK, but the team's so-so" phenomenon. *Research Quarterly, 49,* 260–268.

Bird, A.M., Foster, C., and Maruyama, G. (1980) Convergent and incremental effects of cohesion on attributions for self and team. *Journal of Sport Psychology, 2,* 181–194.

Blau, G. (1984) Brief note comparing the Rotter and Levenson measures of locus of control. *Perceptual and Motor Skills, 58,* 173–174.

Bourgeois, A.E., Malatich, J., LeUnes, A., & Mendoza, J. (1985) *A comparison of the Rotter and Levenson locus of control measures.* Unpublished manuscript.

Brawley, L.R., & Roberts, G. (1984) Attribution in sport: Research foundations, characteristics, and limitations. In J.M. Silva & R.S. Weinberg (Eds.), *Psychological foundations of sport* (pp. 197–213). Champaign, IL: Human Kinetics.

Bukowski, W., & Moore, D. (1980) Winners' and losers' attributions for success and failure in a series of athletic events. *Journal of Sport Psychology, 2,* 195–210.

Calhoun, J., & Acocella, J. (1983) *Psychology of adjustment and human relationships* (2d ed.) New York: Random House.

Celestino, R., Tapp, J., & Brumet, M. (1979) Locus of control correlates with marathon performances. *Perceptual and Motor Skills, 48,* 1249–1250.

Collins, B. (1974) Four components of Rotter internal-external scale. *Journal of Personality and Social Psychology, 29,* 381–391.

Cox, R. (1985) *Sport psychology: Concepts and applications.* Dubuque, IA: Wm. C. Brown.

Daiss, S., LeUnes, A., & Nation, J.R. (1986) Mood and locus of control of a sample of college and professional football players. *Perceptual and Motor Skills, 63,* 733–734.

Deci, E. (1975) *Intrinsic motivation.* New York: Plenum.

Derlega, V. & Janda, L. (1981) *Personal adjustment: The psychology of everyday life* (2nd ed.). Glenview, IL: Scott, Foresman.

Di Giuseppe, R. (1973) Internal-external control of reinforcement and participation in team, individual, and intramural sports. *Perceptual and Motor Skills, 36,* 33–34.

Dunleavy, A., & Rees, C.R. (1979) The effect of achievement motivation and sports exposure upon the sports involvement of American college males. *International Journal of Sport Psychology, 10,* 92–100.

Elig, T., & Frieze, I. (1979) Measuring causal attributions for success and failure. *Journal of Personality and Social Psychology, 37,* 621–634.

Eysenck, H.J., & Eysenck, S.B.G. (1968) Manual for the *Eysenck Personality Inventory.* San Diego, CA: Educational and Industrial Testing Service.

Finn, J., & Straub, W.F. (1977) Locus of control among Dutch and American women softball players. *Research Quarterly, 48,* 56–60.

Fitts, W. (1965) Manual: *Tennessee Self-Concept Scale.* Nashville, TN: Counselor Recordings and Tests.

Frieze, I. (1976) Causal attributions and information seeking to explain success and failure. *Journal of Research in Personality, 10,* 293–305.

Geen, R., Beatty, W., & Arkin, R. (1984) *Human motivation: Physiological, behavioral, and social approaches.* Boston: Allyn and Bacon.

Gill, D.L., Ruder, M., & Gross, J. (1982) Open-ended attributions in team competition. *Journal of Sport Psychology, 4,* 159–169.

Gilliland, K. (1974) Internal versus external locus of control and the high-level athletic competitor. *Perceptual and Motor Skills, 39,* 38.

Gundersheim, J. (1982) A comparison of male and female athletes and nonathletes on measures of self-actualization. *Journal of Sport Behavior, 5,* 186–201.

Gurin, P., Gurin, G., Lao, R., & Beattie, M. (1969) Internal-external control in the motivational dynamics of Negro youth. *Journal of Social Issues, 25,* 29–53.

Hall, E. (1980) Comparison of post performance state anxiety of internals and externals following failure or success in a simple motor task. *Research Quarterly for Exercise and Sport, 51,* 306–314.

Hall, E., Church, G., & Stone, M. (1980) Relationship of birth order to selected personality characteristics of nationally ranked Olympic weight lifters. *Perceptual and Motor Skills, 51,* 971–976.

Hamachek, D. (1971) *Encounters with the self.* New York: Holt, Rinehart and Winston.

Heider, F. (1944) Social perception and phenomenal causality. *Psychological Review, 51,* 358–377.

Heider, F. (1958) *The psychology of interpersonal relations.* New York: Wiley.

Hellison, D. (1970) Physical education and the self-attitude. *Quest, 13,* 41–45.

Henschen, K., Edwards, S., & Mathinos, L. (1982) Achievement motivation and sex-role orientation of high school female track and field athletes versus nonathletes. *Perceptual and Motor Skills, 55,* 183–187.

Horner, M. (1968) *Sex differences in achievement motivation and performance in competitive and noncompetitive situations.* Unpublished doctoral dissertation, University of Michigan, Ann Arbor.

Ibrahim, H., & Morrison, N. (1976) Self-actualization and self-concept among athletes. *Research Quarterly, 47,* 68–79.

Iso-Ahola, S. (1975) A test of attribution theory of success and failure with Little League baseball players. *Mouvement, 7,* 323–327.

Iso-Ahola, S. (1977) Effects of team outcome on children's self-perceptions: Little League baseball. *Scandinavian Journal of Psychology, 18,* 38–42.

James, W. (1890) *Principles of psychology, I.* New York: Henry Holt & Company.

Jersild, A. (1952) *In search of self.* New York: Teachers College Press, Columbia University.

Jourard, S. (1974) *Healthy personality: An approach from the viewpoint of humanistic psychology.* New York: Macmillan.

LeUnes, A., & Nation, J. (1982) Saturday's heroes: A psychological portrait of college football players. *Journal of Sport Behavior, 5,* 139–149.

Levenson, H. (1973) *Reliability and validity of the I, P, and C Scales: A multidimensional view of locus of control.* Paper presented at 81st Annual Convention of the American Psychological Association, Montreal.

Levenson, H. (1981) Differentiating among internality, powerful others, and chance. In H. Lefcourt (Ed.), *Research with locus of control construct,* Vol. I (pp. 1–39). New York: Academic Press.

Ludwig, D., & Maehr, M. (1967) Changes in self concept and stated behavioral preferences. *Child Development, 38,* 453–467.

Lynn, R., Phelan, J., & Kiker, V. (1969) Beliefs in internal-external control of reinforcement and participation in group and individual sports. *Perceptual and Motor Skills, 29,* 551–553.

Mann, L. (1974) On being a sore loser: How fans react to their team's failure. *Australian Journal of Psychology, 26,* 37–47.

Mark, M.M., Murtrie, N., Brooks, D.R., & Harris, D.V. (1984) Causal attributions of winners and losers in individual competitive sports: Toward a reformulation of the self-serving bias. *Journal of Sport Psychology, 6,* 184–196.

Martens, R. (1975) *Social psychology and physical activity.* New York: Harper and Row.

Maslow, A. (1954) *Motivation and behavior.* New York: Harper and Row.

Maslow, A. (1970) *Motivation and behavior* (2nd ed.) New York: Harper and Row.

Maslow, A. (1971) *The farthest reaches of human nature.* New York: Viking Press.

McAuley, E. (1985) Success and causality in sport: The influence of perception. *Journal of Sport Psychology, 7,* 13–22.

McAuley, E., & Gross, J. (1983) Perception of causality in sport: An application of the Causal Dimension Scale. *Journal of Sport Psychology, 5,* 72–76.

McClelland, D. (1985) *Human motivation.* Glenview, IL: Scott, Foresman.

McClelland, D., Atkinson, J., Clark, R., & Lowell, E. (1953) *The achievement motive.* New York: Appleton-Century-Crofts.

McCready, M., & Long, B.C. (1985) *Locus of control, attitudes toward physical activity, and exercise adherence.* Paper presented at the Annual Convention of North American Society for Psychology of Sport and Physical Activity, Gulfport, Mississippi.

McKelvie, S., & Huband, D. (1980) Locus of control and anxiety in college athletes and non-athletes. *Perceptual and Motor Skills, 50,* 819–822.

Mehrabian, A. (1968) Male and female scales of the tendency to achieve. *Educational and Psychological Measurement, 28,* 493–502.

Mehrabian, A. (1969) Measure of achieving tendency. *Educational and Psychological Measurement, 29,* 445–451.

Mirels, H. (1970) Dimensions of internal vs. external control. *Journal of Consulting and Clinical Psychology, 34,* 226–228.

Morris, A., Vaccaro, P., & Clarke, D. (1979) Psychological characteristics of age-group competitive swimmers. *Perceptual and Motor Skills, 48,* 1265–1266.

Murray, H.A. (1938) *Explorations in personality.* New York: Oxford Press.

Murray, H.A. (1943) *Thematic Apperception Test.* Cambridge, MA: Harvard University Press.

Nation, J.R., & LeUnes, A. (1983a) Personality characteristics of intercollegiate football players as determined by position, classification, and redshirt status. *Journal of Sport Behavior, 6,* 92–102.

Nation, J.R., & LeUnes, A. (1983b) A personality profile of the black athlete in college football. *Psychology, 20* (3/4), 1–3.

Nowicki, S., & Strickland, B. (1973) A locus of control scale for children. *Journal of Consulting and Clinical Psychology, 40,* 148–154.

Raynor, J.O. (1969) Future orientation and motivation of immediate activity: An elaboration of the theory of achievement motivation. *Psychological Review, 76,* 606–610.

Read, D. (1969) *The influence of competitive and noncompetitive programs of physical education on body-image and self-concept.* Paper presented at the Association for Health, Physical Education and Recreation National Convention, Boston, Massachusetts.

Reid, R., & Hay, D. (1979) Some behavioral characteristics of rugby and association footballers. *International Journal of Sport Psychology, 10,* 239–251.

Rejeski, W.J., & Brawley, L.R. (1983) Attribution theory in sport: Current status and new perspectives. *Journal of Sport Psychology, 5,* 77–99.

Roberts, G.C. (1975) Win-loss causal attributions of Little League players. *Mouvement, 7,* 315–322.

Roberts, G.C., & Pascuzzi, D. (1979) Causal attributions in sport: Some theoretical implications. *Journal of Sport Psychology, 1,* 203–211.

Rogers, C. (1961) *On becoming a person.* Boston: Houghton Mifflin.

Rotter, J. (1966) Generalized expectancies for internal versus external control of reinforcement. *Psychological Monographs, 80,* No. 1 (Whole No. 609).

Rotter, J. (1975) Some problems and misconceptions related to the construct of internal versus external control of reinforcement. *Journal of Consulting and Clinical Psychology, 43,* 56–67.

Russell, D. (1982) The Causal Dimension Scale: A measure of how individuals perceive causes. *Journal of Personality and Social Psychology, 42,* 1137–1145.

Scheer, J., & Ansorge C. (1979) Influence due to expectations of judges: A function of internal-external locus of control. *Journal of Sport Psychology, 1,* 53–58.

Secord, P., & Jourard, S. (1953) The appraisal of body-cathexis: Body-cathexis and the self. *Journal of Consulting Psychology, 17,* 343–347.

Sheldon, W.H. (1942) *The varieties of human temperament.* New York: Harper.

Shostrom, E. (1963) *Personal Orientation Inventory.* San Diego, CA: Educational and Industrial Testing Service.

Tenenbaum, G., Furst, D., & Weingarten, G. (1984) Attribution of causality in sport events: Validation of the Wingate Sport Achievement Responsibility Scale. *Journal of Sport Psychology, 6,* 430–439.

Throop, W., & MacDonald, A. (1971) Internal-external locus of control: A bibliography. *Psychological Reports, 28,* 175–190.

Tucker, L.A. (1981) Internal structure, factor satisfaction, and reliability of the Body Cathexis Scale. *Perceptual and Motor Skills, 53,* 891–896.

Tucker, L.A. (1982a) Relationship between perceived somatotype and body cathexis of college males. *Psychological Reports, 50,* 983–989.

Tucker, L.A. (1982b) Effect of a weight-training program on the self-concept of college males. *Perceptual and Motor Skills, 54,* 1055–1061.

Tucker, L.A. (1982c) Weight training experience and psychological well-being. *Perceptual and Motor Skills, 55,* 553–554.

Tucker, L.A. (1983a) Self-concept: A function of self-perceived somatotypes. *Journal of Psychology, 113,* 123–133.

Tucker, L.A. (1983b) Effect of weight-training on self-concept: A profile of those influenced most. *Research Quarterly for Exercise and Sport, 54,* 389–397.

Tucker, L.A. (1983c) Muscular strength: A predictor of personality in males. *The Journal of Sports Medicine and Physical Fitness, 23,* 213–220.

Tucker, L.A. (1983d) Muscular strength and mental health. *Journal of Personality and Social Psychology, 45,* 1355–1360.

Tucker, L.A. (1984) Trait psychology and performance: A credulous viewpoint. *Journal of Human Movement Studies, 10,* (1), 53–62.

Weinberg, R.S. (1984) The relationship between extrinsic rewards and intrinsic motivation in sport. In J.M. Silva & R.S. Weinberg (Eds.), *Psychological foundations of sport* (pp. 177–187). Champaign, IL: Human Kinetics.

Weiner, B. (Ed.). (1974) *Achievement motivation and attribution theory.* Morristown, NJ: General Learning Press.

Weiner, B. (1979) A theory of motivation for some classroom experiences. *Journal of Educational Psychology, 71,* 3–25.

Weiner, B. (1980) *Human motivation.* New York: Holt, Rinehart and Winston.

Whitehead, J., & Corbin, C. (1985) *Multidimensional locus of control scales for physical fitness behaviors.* Paper presented at Annual Convention of the North American Society for the Psychology of Sport and Physical Activity, Gulfport, Mississippi.

Zion, L. (1965) Body concept as it relates to self-concept. *Research Quarterly, 36,* 490–495.

Leadership, Cohesion, and Audience Effects

INTRODUCTION

The sport scientist with an interest in social psychology will find much to captivate him or her in the area of athletics. Sports teams literally abound with social-psychological components. Leadership is but one of them. No one in sport questions the role of the coach as leader; less scientific interest has been expressed in players as leaders, and this represents an area for future exploration. Too, it is widely believed that cohesive teams are, for whatever reason, successful ones. It is usually the coach (or leader) who is expected to forge these cohesive and successful units. In the process of leading and generating team cohesion, we find that athletic performance is moderated by the effects of being around other participants, being evaluated by significant others, or being cheered by friendly supporters, all of which falls under what might be called audience effects. It is this threesome from the social psychology literature from which we will compose this chapter.

LEADERSHIP

Psychologists have studied the ubiquitous concept of leadership for more than 80 years. Though much has been learned overall, there are still as many definitions and ideas of what constitutes leadership as there are experts to generate them. Burns (1978, p. 2) states unequivocally that "leadership is one of the most observed and least understood phenomena on earth."

Though leadership has always been recognized as an important part of the sport process, it has been scientifically addressed for only about 10 years. All of us are familiar with individuals within the sport context who have established a winning tradition through their leadership capabilities. The football fans of the 1970s can attest to the leadership of Roger Staubach in making the Dallas Cowboys a perennial power. He never believed the Cowboys were going to lose and the effect on his teammates was obviously highly positive. At one time Staubach's ability to play in the National Football League had been widely questioned inasmuch as he had incurred a five-year military obligation as a function of his enrollment in the U.S. Naval Academy. Near the end of his service obligation, your author (LeUnes) expressed concern about the effects of the long hiatus. An acquaintance who had played with Staubach at the Naval Academy took exception, suggesting that Staubach would become a force in the NFL primarily but not exclusively because of his leadership ability. As the ex-teammate said, "If Roger wanted you to do it, it was simple. You did it! We knew he was right, and we would have done anything he asked. He's the greatest leader I have ever seen." Obviously, Staubach's admirer/ex-teammate knew what he was talking about. Many of us, Cowboy fans or not, have thrilled to his last-ditch efforts and exhortations in snatching victory from apparent defeat; Staubach rallied his mates to wins on twenty-three occasions after trailing in the fourth quarter, and fourteen of those comebacks came in the last two minutes or overtime!

The annals of sport are replete with similar examples, and this has led to an awakening of interest in the relationship of sport and leadership. Before examining the topic of leadership, however, a review of the more general conceptualizations and research contributions is in order.

A Brief History

According to Bass (1981), discussion of leadership dates back to the time of Plato, Caesar, and

The annals of sport are filled with athletes who have spurred their teammates on to victory in the eleventh hour. Football fans of the 1970s can attest to the leadership of Roger Staubach in making the Dallas Cowboys a perennial power. On no less than twenty-three occasions the quarterback rallied his teammates to win after trailing in the fourth quarter, and fourteen of these comebacks occurred in the last two minutes or overtime.

Plutarch. Also, the ancient Chinese and Egyptians wrote of leadership. Homer's *Iliad* provides us with an early Greek reference on the topic; Agamemnon represented justice and judgment, Nestor exemplified wisdom and counsel, Odysseus personified shrewdness and cunning, and Achilles was the prototype for valor and action. Most, if not all, of these qualities we expect and admire, now as then, in our leaders.

In a more contemporary vein, leadership studies in this country probably began around the turn of the twentieth century (Bass, 1981). These early efforts have generated theorizing and research that has continued unabated for the better part of eighty years. Though many theories have been advanced, we shall undertake only a few that seem to be more relevant to past and future sport applications.

Leadership Theories

Trait Theory. One early theory, generally known as the "great-man theory," posits that great men shape history through their leadership. These great leaders would then be leaders in any situation because they possess the traits that make for leadership. The development of psychological tests added impetus to the great-man notion because traits could be objectively measured, at least in theory. In actuality, the great-man, or trait, approach suffers considerably under scrutiny. According to Carron (1980), the only trait that successfully holds up upon inspection is intelligence; Bass (1981) cites twenty-three studies supportive of the position that leaders are intellectually brighter than so-called followers. Bass cites only five references to the contrary, but also mentions five more indicating that large disparities in the intelligence of leaders and others can actually militate against successful leadership. If the latter position is true, too much intelligence could be detrimental.

Even though intelligence does appear to be a consistent trait of leaders, comprehensive literature reviews (e.g., Campbell, Dunnette, Lawler, and Weick, 1970; Mann, 1959) show only modest correlations between intelligence and leadership, relationships sufficiently modest so as to lead Carron (1980) to conclude that less than 10 percent of task performance can be explained by the leader's intellectual ability. Too, Cattell (1946) has pointed out that intelligence taken separately is still a multifaceted trait made up of a lot of other characteristics, such as wisdom, maturity, and perseverance, to name only a few.

Lest we be guilty of throwing out the baby with the bathwater, we should not prematurely discard trait theory. A wiser course would be to integrate trait theory into other more comprehensive ones that take into account other leadership variables. More contemporary theorists do exactly that; they see leadership as a function of the interaction of the leader, the followers, and the situation. One conceptualization of this interactive perspective is that of Hollander (1978), who speaks of a "locus of leadership." As can be seen in figure 6.1, this locus is the point at which there is a convergence of leader, follower, and situational variables. Charming in its simplicity, the Hollander model provides a convenient springboard for discussing variants of this general theme that have had more application within sport.

Fiedler's Contingency Model of Leadership Effectiveness. Fiedler (1967) proposed an interactive model that places emphasis on both traits and situational variable as predictors of leadership. Much is made in Fiedler's model of type of leadership; leaders are seen as task oriented and autocratic or interpersonally oriented and democratic. A second key aspect of contingency theory is the favorableness of the group-task situation. This favorableness arises out of three subfactors: leader-member interactions, task structure, and the power position of the leader. Fiedler asserts that the task-oriented or directive leader will be more influential in either of two conditions: (1) when task structure is loose and unfavorable and (2) when task structure is rigid and favorable. On the other hand, the interpersonally oriented leader will be most effective in situations neither too loose nor too rigid and of intermediate favorableness. A visual representation of the Fiedler model can be seen in figure 6.2.

By way of summarizing points made so far, Carron (1980, p. 115) offers the following:

> The main tenets of the Contingency Theory are that: group-work situations differ in their degree of favorableness; individual leaders vary along a continuum from task to person orientation; and any individual can be an effective leader provided his/her leadership style coincides with a situation of appropriate favorableness.

Figure 6.1 Locus of Leadership

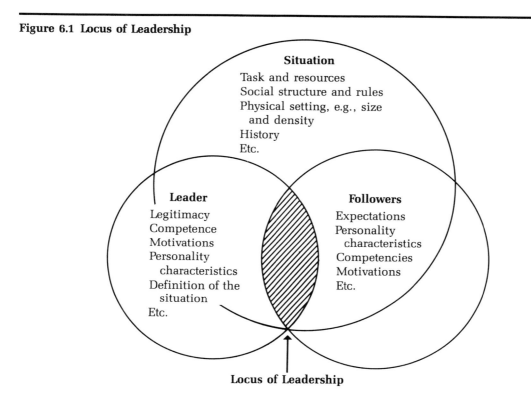

Locus of Leadership

NOTE: The arrows indicate the social exchange that occurs between leader and followers. The shaded area (locus of leadership) represents the intersection of three elements involved in leadership—the situation, the leader, and the followers. Some relevant attributes of each element are listed.

SOURCE: *Leadership Dynamics* by E.P. Hollander, 1978, New York: Free Press.

Fiedler's approach to leadership and its determination has utilized a technique known as the Least Preferred Co-Worker Scale (LPC). Bipolar adjectives, sixteen to twenty in number, are used. Typical items from the LPC include the following:

Friendly							*Unfriendly*
8	7	6	5	4	3	2	1

Efficient							*Inefficient*
8	7	6	5	4	3	2	1

Respondents who react in a relatively favorable way to the least preferred co-worker stimuli are then viewed as interpersonal or people oriented whereas those with highly negative responses are seen as task oriented.

Some attempts have been made to apply the contingency model to sport. The payoff has not been very big in these efforts. Possibly, contingency theory simply has little applicability. Other hypotheses include the paucity of studies in the area (Cox, 1985) and the lack of variation in situational favorableness created by applying the theory to teams homogeneous in

Figure 6.2 Fiedler's Contingency Model of Leadership (1967)

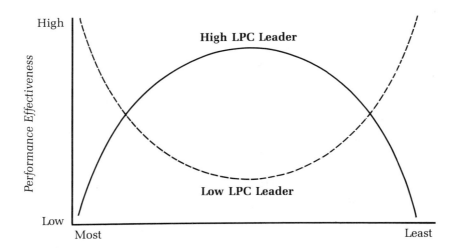

Situational Favorableness

Leader Member Relations	Good	Good	Good	Good	Poor	Poor	Poor	Poor
Task Structure	Structured		Unstructured		Structured		Unstructured	
Leader Position Power	Strong	Weak	Strong	Weak	Strong	Weak	Strong	Weak

SOURCE: *Social Psychology of Sport* (p. 114) by A.V. Carron, 1980, Ithaca, NY: Mouvement Publications.

type of sport and organizational context (Chelladurai, 1984a).

Concerning the shortage of studies aimed at testing the theory, Cox (1985a) has stated that only two studies have been conducted bearing on this point. Chelladurai (1984) set the figure at seven whereas Carron (1980) cited three studies of contingency theory. Irrespective of the numbers, all of these sources agree that little if any support for the efficacy of Fiedler's model exists within the sport context. All

equally agree that the issue has not been sufficiently studied to the point that the case should be closed to future research efforts.

Three consistently cited sport-related studies of the contingency model, all of which used the LPC as the measure of leadership style, are those of Inciong (1974), Danielson (1976), and Bird (1977). Inciong, in his study of forty-three high school basketball teams, found correlations between performance effectiveness and situation favorableness to be sufficiently low so as to warrant rejection of the theory. Danielson, studying forty minor league hockey coaches, concluded that leadership in hockey may have peculiar properties that differ from those in business and industry, where the Fiedler model may be more applicable. Bird studied female intercollegiate volleyball coaches and players, and she found no support for Fiedler's formulation.

Path-Goal Theory. As opposed to the trait-oriented approach of Fiedler, House (1971) has popularized a situation-specific leadership model known as the path-goal theory. Emphasis in the path-goal theory is placed on the leader as a catalyst for or facilitator of follower success. Cox (1985) indicated that the basic function of the leader is to provide a "well-lighted path" for subordinates. House and Dessler (1974, p. 31) state: "The motivational function of the leader consists of increasing personal pay-offs to subordinates for work-goal attainment, and making the path to these easier to travel by clarifying it, reducing road blocks and pitfalls, and increasing the opportunities for personal satisfaction en route." A relatively simple representation of this relationship can be seen in figure 6.3.

Another key aspect of path-goal theory is concerned with the situational nature of leadership; that is, leadership effectiveness should largely be a function of situational variables. Situational variables of significance include (1) subordinate characteristics (i.e., personality, ability) and (2) environmental demands placed upon subordinates that impinge on their job effectiveness and needs (i.e., the task, formal structure of the organization, and the primary work group). Of particular significance for sport research is the nature of the task at hand. Path-goal theory posits that tasks can be categorized in terms of routineness/variability, dependence/interdependence, and inherent satisfaction/nonsatisfaction (Carron, 1980). Given that these three dimensions do exist, it becomes clear that situational demands on sport leaders (usually coaches) will require much diversity on their part if they are to be effective. The routineness of the usual practice session as opposed to game conditions varies greatly. Task interdependence is highly variable; coaching a track sprinter may be very

Figure 6.3 Path-Goal Model of Leadership

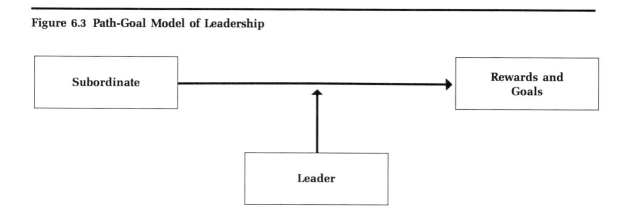

SOURCE: *Social Psychology of Sport* (p. 117) by A.V. Carron, 1980, Ithaca, NY: Mouvement Publications.

different from molding a sophisticated offensive scheme in football. Too, satisfaction will surely vary from practice to game conditions or from sport to sport.

Although appealing in a commonsense way, path-goal theory has not generated much research in or out of the sport domain. One notable exception in sport is reported by Chelladurai and Saleh (1978). Their study was conducted with 160 physical education students, and partial support for the theory was gained to the extent that members of team sports had a preference for leaders who would improve their individual performances through training as well as facilitate improvement through clarification of the relationships among team members.

One other test of path-goal theory has been reported by Vos Strache (1979), who investigated leadership style of coaches as perceived by female basketball players from twenty-nine universities. Players on winning teams perceived their coaches to be high in the more technical aspects of coaching (e.g., persuasion, production emphasis), but this was not the case with players from losing teams, who viewed their coaches as high on tolerance. Vos Strache interpreted these results as supportive of the path-goal theory notion that the main role of the coach is as a catalyst or facilitator.

Life Cycle Theory. Life cycle theory, or what Carron (1980) prefers to call situational theory, is a situation-specific approach to leadership that places greater emphasis on subordinate behavior than on that of the leader (Hersey and Blanchard, 1969, 1977). In the life cycle model, great reliance is placed on the maturity level of subordinates in determining group task success and personal fulfillment. Maturity is viewed by Hersey and Blanchard as a combination of the need to achieve, a willingness to accept the responsibility for goal attainment, and the ability to profit from experiences. It is generally accepted that young athletes just beginning in sport would be low in maturity and therefore would be high in the need for relations-oriented leadership. As the person progresses through the various ages and sport stages, the maturity level would increase and task-related needs would become more important. Finally, at the professional or world class level, both the need for task behavior and relations behavior would be low due to the sophistication of the athletes. This relationship, a sport-related variant of the original life cycle theory, has been proposed by Chelladurai and Carron (1978) and is visually represented in figure 6.4.

Partial support for this formulation has been provided by Neil and Kirby (1985). These investigators asked 128 elite and 77 novice Canadians (average age 20.3 years) involved in rowing, canoeing, and kayaking to respond to a leadership questionnaire. Overall, differences indicated that the novices preferred a coach who explained how each athlete fit into the total picture, helped new members adjust, did not place unnecessary barriers between him- or herself and team members, did little things to facilitate player satisfaction, and who could rule in a decisive fashion when necessary. No gender differences were noted.

The Functional Model. Another model of leadership that warrants some elaboration is the *functional model,* as proposed by Behling and Schriesheim (1976). Though tested little in sport, the face validity of the functional model is appealing for future sport applications. Essentially, the functional model posits that any group lives or dies based on the satisfaction of two functions, expressive and instrumental. The *expressive function* has to do with social and emotional aspects whereas the *instrumental function* is task-related. The leader who is trying to meet the expressive needs of subordinates would be concerned with how they interact, or with cohesion, or with morale factors. On the other hand, the leader deal-

Figure 6.4 Life Cycle Model of Leadership

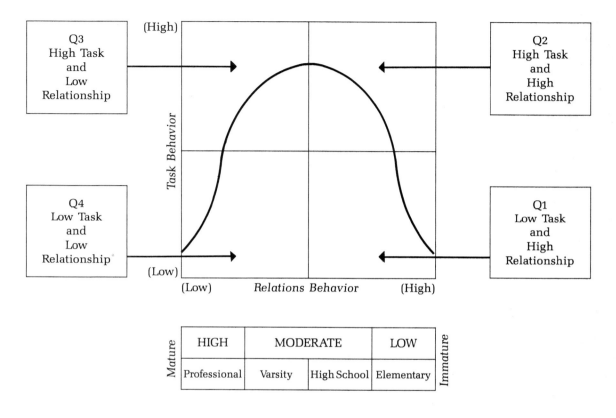

SOURCE: *Social Psychology of Sport* (p. 121) by, A.V. Carron, 1980, Ithaca, NY: Mouvement Publications.

ing with the instrumental function would be concerned with task achievement. Cox (1985) cites a possible application of the functional model to a coaching situation by suggesting that the task-oriented head coach often selects an assistant who is excellent in the expressive function, one who relates well, who takes the psychological pulse of the team and individual players and rounds off the rough edges that are sometimes created in the pursuit of skill acquisition and, ultimately, success in sport. Another example at the player level might involve the selection of team co-captains who

in some way strike a balance between the instrumental and expressive functions; certainly some player-leaders are task-oriented while others serve to meet the social-psychological needs of their peers.

One test of the idea has been made by Rees (1983). Twenty-three collegiate intramural basketball teams answered questionnaires designed to measure leadership development in their respective organizations. In general, Rees found moderate correlations between both functions, thereby failing to lend support to the theory. Rees also found integration of the two roles to be more the norm than was differentiation. These results are further supported by work done by Rees and Segal (1984) with varsity football teams. Though otherwise untested and not particularly supported, the functional model does have an appeal for future research that is intriguing.

The Multidimensional Model. In series of papers on leadership, Chelladurai proposed a *multidimensional model of leadership* that is at the forefront in sport-related leadership research (Chelladurai, 1984b; Challadurai and Carron, 1978). This model is presented in figure 6.5. As can be seen, the model proposes three states of leader behavior: actual leader behavior, preferred leader behavior, and required leader behavior. *Actual leader behavior* is behavior that is engaged in irrespective of norms or subordinate preferences. *Preferred leader*

behavior is behavior that subordinates would like to see in the leader. Finally, *required leader behavior* is behavior expected of the leader on a more formal basis, such as organizational demands. In any athletic situation, but particularly as it becomes more advanced and formalized, the leader is expected by the organization to behave in certain ways. The leader, usually the coach, is expected to select players, organize practices, create a disciplined atmosphere, meet the press and the public, and otherwise engage in a host of other leader-related behaviors. At the same time, the players have expectancies for competence, humaneness, and fairness from the coach. The coach in turn has to lead in a way that is consistent with his or her own goals, ability, and personality; these will, of course, dictate much of his or her actual leadership. The antecedents of leader behavior as proposed by Chelladurai

Figure 6.5 A Multidimensional Model of Leadership

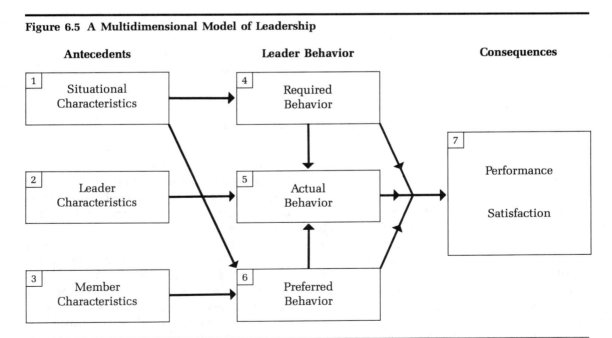

Source: "Leadership in Sports," by P. Chelladurai, 1984, in J.M. Silva and R.S. Weinberg, eds., *Psychological Foundations of Sport* (p. 338), Champaign, IL: Human Kinetics.

will be the leader characteristics, the subordinate characteristics, and the situation. The interaction of these antecedents with the various leader behaviors results in performance and satisfaction at varying levels. According to Chelladurai (1984a), the major proposition of the model is that performance and satisfaction will ultimately be determined by the degree of congruence among the three states of leader behavior.

To test the essential proposition just stated, Chelladurai developed the *Leadership Scale for Sports (LSS)* (Chelladurai and Saleh, 1978; 1980). The 1980 effort, which was an attempt to refine the 1978 effort, resulted in a forty-item scale with five dimensions of coaching behavior. A total of 485 subjects from various Canadian universities (in both studies) responded to the scale; roughly half of the participants were physical education students of both sexes with the other half being male athletes in basketball, rowing, track and field, and wrestling. The physical education students

were asked to indicate their respective favorite sports. The athletes responded similarly but were also asked to indicate the actual behavior of their coaches. Appropriate statistical analyses yielded five dimensions of coaching leadership behavior: training and instruction, democratic behavior, autocratic behavior, social support, and positive feedback. Chelladurai and Saleh (1980) further categorized the five dimensions into one direct task factor (training and instruction), two decision-style factors (democratic and autocratic behavior), and two motivational factors (social support and positive feedback). An elaboration on these dimensions is provided in table 6.1.

Efforts aimed at validating the innovative Chelladurai and Saleh measure have been relatively rare. Chelladurai and Carron (1981) have attempted to extend the LSS to youth sport. High school wrestlers (n = 54) and basketball players (n = 193) were administered the LSS (the preferred leadership dimension) and, with the exception of the autocratic behavior subdimen-

Table 6.1 The Leadership Scale for Sports (LSS)

Dimension	Description
Training and instruction behavior	Coaching behavior aimed at improving athletes' performance by emphasizing and facilitating hard and strenuous training; instructing athletes in the skills, techniques, and tactics of the sport; clarifying the relationship among the members; and structuring and coordinating the members' activities
Democratic behavior	Coaching behavior that allows greater participation by athletes in decisions pertaining to group goals, practice methods, and game tactics and strategies
Autocratic behavior	Coaching behavior that involves independent decision making and stresses personal authority
Social support behavior	Coaching behavior characterized by a concern for the welfare of individual athletes, positive group atmosphere, and warm interpersonal relations with members
Rewarding (positive feedback) behavior	Coaching behavior that reinforces an athlete by recognizing and rewarding good performance

SOURCE: "Leadership in Sports" by P. Chelladurai, 1984, in J. M. Silva and R. S. Weinberg, eds., *Psychological Foundations of Sport* (p. 332), Champaign, IL: Human Kinetics.

sion, the applicability of the LSS to high school sport was supported. Incidentally, the autocratic behavior scale was not particularly salient in the 1980 work of Chelladurai and Saleh.

Chelladurai and Carron (1983) had sixty-seven high school midget, sixty-three junior, sixty-three senior, and sixty-nine university basketball players complete the "preferred leader behavior" version of the LSS. The goal of the research was to assess the relationship between maturity as defined by level of competition and preferences for training and instruction (task-oriented) and social support (relationship-oriented) approaches to leadership style. In general, findings with regard to both training and instruction and social support were the opposite of what was predicted; that is, preference for both increased rather than decreased with maturity. Several methodological problems are raised by this study. One has to do with maturity. The definitional range from high school to the university level is quite narrow and may not accurately reflect increases in maturity. A second relates to sport as a mechanism for fostering maturity. Chelladurai and Carron (1983) point out that sport is largely an autocratic enterprise that may run counter to the development of maturity. Sage (1978, p. 225), quoting ex-pro football player George Sauer, offers food for thought on this issue.

> The traditional pattern of training for self-discipline is exposed for the joke that it is by former All-Pro football player George Sauer [see Scott, 1971] who said, "It's interesting to go back and listen to the people on the high school level talk about sport programs and how they develop a kid's self-discipline and responsibility. I think the giveaway, that most of this stuff being preached on the lower levels is a lie, is when you get to college and professional levels, the coaches still treat you as an adolescent. They know damn well that you were never given a chance to become responsible or self-disciplined. Even in

the pros you are told when to go to bed, when to turn off your lights, when to wake up, when to eat, and what to eat." It is ironic, but pitifully illustrative of how traditional sports practices, which claim to develop self-discipline, keep those who have been exposed to these methods the longest, the pros, in virtual bondage.

A more recent effort by Chelladurai (1984b) bears on the issue of congruence mentioned earlier. Canadian university athletes (eighty-seven basketball players from ten teams, and fifty-seven track and field athletes from six teams) took part in the study. The LSS was used to assess leadership behavior by coaches. Both the preferred and the perceived variants of the LSS were used. Briefly, training and instruction and positive feedback were the most prevalent dimensions of leadership behavior that bear on athlete satisfaction. To quote Chelladurai (1984a, pp. 338–339):

> The discrepancy between athletes' perception of coaching behaviors and their preferences for specific behaviors was significantly correlated with their satisfaction with leadership, team performance, and overall involvement. Although the pattern of relationships between the discrepancies in the five dimensions of leader behavior and the satisfaction measures varied in the three sport groups studied (basketball, wrestling, and track and field), the relationship between discrepancy in training and instruction and satisfaction with leadership was similar in all three groups. That athletes' satisfaction with leadership increased as the coach's perceived emphasis on this dimension also increased was considered to be consistent with the task-oriented nature of athletics. Another finding of their study highlights the effects of situational differences. Basketball players were satisfied even when the coach's positive feedback exceeded their preferences (linear relationship), while the wrestlers were dissatisfied with discrepancy in either direction (curvilinear relationship). Such discrepancy did not have any effect in the track and field group.

Recently, Chelladurai (1986) administered the LSS to 229 collegiate and other adult athletes in India in an effort to establish its utility in other countries. Though limited by the fact that only Indian athletes proficient in the English language were able to participate in the study, the reliability of the LSS was demonstrated.

All things considered, it would appear that Chelladurai and his colleagues have generated a model worthy of future consideration. Leadership in sport is a critical issue, one not nearly expended in terms of theory and research. The coach as leader is a common theme that needs considerable expansion.

Player Leadership. A completely overlooked area of leadership in sports is that generated by the players themselves. Good player leadership may transcend bad coaching and, in turn, add much when the coaching leadership is superb. A pioneering effort in this area has been offered by Yukelson, Weinberg, Richardson, and Jackson (1983) in a study of collegiate baseball and soccer teams. Though limited in scope and more correlational than causal, preliminary support is generated for the notion of player leadership. Significant correlations were found between leadership status and coaches' ratings of performance, eligibility, and locus of control. Leaders in both sports were generally viewed as excellent performers by the coaches, were more experienced, and tended to be more internal than external on Rotter's I-E Scale. Much more work in this neglected area of leadership needs to be done.

GROUP COHESION

Shaw (1976, p. 11) defines a group as "two or more persons who are interacting with one another in such a manner that each person influences and is influenced by each other person." Carron (1980, p. 233) states that "a group is not simply a crowd of people—a group is characterized by purposive interaction in goal directed and/or interpersonal behavior." Carron and Chelladurai (1981) further assert that the factors that most saliently separate the group from the random gathering of individuals is the degree of attraction, commitment, and involvement of the individual members related to the collective totality. This triumvirate—attraction, commitment, and involvement—is the essence of cohesion.

The term cohesion is derived from the Latin word *cohaesus,* which means to cleave or stick together (Carron, 1984), and the theme of sticking together is at the core for most definitions of the term. The resistance of the group to disruptive forces (Gross and Martin, 1952) and the total field of forces causing members to remain within a group (Festinger, Schachter, and Back, 1950) are two early examples from the general psychology literature that lend additional attestation to the theme of sticking together. In sport, Carron (1984, p. 341) views cohesion as a "dynamic process that is reflected in the group's tendency to stick together while pursuing its goals and objectives."

In the eyes of coaches and players at all levels of sophistication, team cohesion seems both highly desirable and extremely necessary to ultimate team success. Coaches are expected to forge cohesion among their players through a host of actions, and this expectancy has not gone unnoticed by members of the coaching profession. Silva (1982), in a national survey, found that the issue of how to create and maintain cohesion in sport teams was the most frequently cited concern among coaches he polled. Players also point to cohesion as a necessary condition for excellence. For example, quarterback Danny White of the Dallas Cowboys undoubtedly spoke for many an athlete when he said: "This is not a game you can

Many coaches and players see unity as integral to team success. For years a closely knit team, the Pittsburgh Pirates, generated an excitement and family spirit that helped them win the 1979 World Series. Team leader Willie Stargell (number eight, upper left) was voted the series' Most Valuable Player.

be successful at on nothing but raw talent. Sooner or later, the team that works together and supports each other is going to come out on top" (Stowers, 1985, p. 20).

The issue of team unity also extends to the fans. A particularly noticeable example is seen in the baseball World Series championship team of 1979, the Pittsburgh Pirates. Led by the team leader, Willie Stargell, the Pirates generated excitement and unity seldom seen in the annals of sport. To quote Dickey (1982, p. 264):

The "Family" was the big news in the National League in 1979, and one of the great stories in baseball history.

It started one rainy spring day in Pittsburgh. The Pirates had been in the habit of playing the Sister Sledge record, "We Are Family," in the clubhouse before and after games. During a rain delay that day, the song was played over the public address system and the fans started singing it. The song became the team's anthem and it forged a bond between fans and players.

No team ever deserved the family nickname more. For years the Pirates had been a close knit team, largely because of Wilver ("Willie") Stargell.

The examples given here notwithstanding, the relationship between cohesion and team success is less than clear. The popular literature is replete with examples of teams who appeared to be disharmonious but successful. The Oakland A's teams of the early 1970s fought among themselves and with their controversial owner, Charles O. Finley, who was no shrinking violet when it came to a fight with those above or below him. Yet the A's won three consecutive World Series titles in 1972, 1973, and 1974. The New York Yankees of 1978 were reputedly a group of malcontents, and yet they won the World Series that year.

On a more scientific level, a study by Lenk (1977) is instructive. Lenk worked with a 1960 Olympic champion rowing team from Germany. Though the team was highly successful by most standards, team unity was minimal according to Lenk. In summing up his observations, Lenk (p. 12) says: "The strength of achievement of the crew even increased in the two years in which the crew existed, parallel with the strength of conflict in its increase. The crew was not beaten at all and won the Olympics in 1960. Sports crews can, therefore, perform top athletic achievements in spite of strong internal conflicts." To put it another way, Lenk (p. 38) said: *"Even fierce social internal conflicts in top performance rowing crews need not noticeably weaken their achievement strength and capacity if these conflicts do not really blow up the crew."*

These examples of both positive and negative reflections on cohesion only serve to illustrate its complex and controversial nature. And the issue of whether or not togetherness is in fact necessary for athletic success only touches the tip of the iceberg insofar as the issue of cohesion is concerned. Let us now address some of the more relevant issues related to team cohesion.

Models of Team Cohesion

Carron (1984) suggests that there are three outstanding conceptual issues related to cohesion and they, in turn, are suggestive of three cohesion models. The first of these is the *pendular model*, which hypothesizes that team cohesion operates in a pendular fashion with the amount of cohesion in a constant state of oscillation. This can be illustrated by an example from high school basketball. During the initial tryout period, a sense of cohesion comes from merely being a part of what all expect will become a well-oiled machine capable of winning most if not all of its games. Too, the mental and physical demands being made on all participants to perform well are a force for cohesion. After a short time, however, athletes will be broken into subgroups for certain parts of the overall workout; that is, the guards become identified, as are the forwards and centers. Drills and skills somewhat unique to each group are stressed, and one's competition for a starting spot on the team is more clearly identified. At this point, team identity and cohesion are lessened. As skills develop, as players are selected, and as the team is put back together to form a whole, cohesion among team members should again increase. This increase in togetherness will be particularly true as actual game competition begins and feelings of "we" are heightened. During the course of the season, events may arise that lessen the team's cohesion and the pendulum may swing in the direction of disunity. These waxings and wanings of cohesion thus continue to resemble a pendulum.

A second proposal by Carron is a *linear model*, and it states that cohesion progresses in a linear fashion as teams go through various developmental phases. These stages have been identified by Tuckman (1965) as *forming, storming, norming,* and *performing.* The basic tenet of Tuckman's formulation is that cohesion progresses in a linear fashion from its most primitive state (forming), proceeding from there to conflict and polarization (storming) to resolution of these problems and the institution of a more cooperative stance (norming) to the final stage in which goal attainment is paramount (performing).

A third model is the *life cycle model,* which emphasizes a somewhat "cradle to grave" approach to group formation. In this model, initial formative efforts or encounters are followed by a period in which limit testing predominates. This testing process is followed by the creation of a system of expected behaviors or norms which, in turn, lead to a phase or production in which goal attainment is emphasized. Finally, the group will face its eventual death through separation or dissolution.

The similarities in the three models appear to be considerable, and none has emerged as superior to the others. Carron (1984) is quick to point out that, regardless of the model preferred, the element of dynamism that pervades each of them is most noticeable. Cohesion is definitely not a static, lockstep sort of entity.

Factors Impinging on Group Cohesion

Inasmuch as cohesion is a dynamic process, a number of forces must be at work in creating it. There are at least four factors of note.

Group Size. One of the correlates of cohesion is group size. As is intuitively obvious, the problems of handling a golf team are very different from those associated with a university football team that is allowed by NCAA rules to award ninety-five scholarships to players. In view of the demands in football, much reliance is placed on individual assistant coaches as catalysts for cohesion within their respective offensive or defensive subdomains.

As a group becomes larger, communications problems will almost certainly arise. Too, it is easy to get lost in the shuffle. Coaches (as well as player-leaders) must be alert to both communication difficulties and feelings of depersonalization. Another negative outgrowth of too much size is the feeling that the individual can slack off because the group will collectively make up the difference. It may be tempting, for

instance, to go at half-speed for a few plays in football on the assumption that the other ten players will pick up the slack. Such a mentality, if pervasive, sounds like a prescription for team failure.

Related to slacking off are two social-psychological concepts known as the *Ringelmann Effect* and *social loafing.* The *Ringelmann Effect* is named after a German psychologist who observed some fifty years ago that average effort decreases with an increase in group size. To demonstrate this, Ringelmann observed individuals and groups of two, three, and eight persons engaged in a rope-pulling task. Eight-person groups pulled only 49 percent of the average individual force. Three-person groups pulled 85 percent of the average individual force, and two-person groups only 93 percent. Ingham, Levinger, Graves and Peckham (1974) resurrected the work done over a half-century ago and found essentially the same results as Ringelmann.

This motivation decrement as a function of increasing group size has been called *social loafing* by Latané (Latané, 1973; Latané, Williams, and Harkins, 1979). Of particular interest to Latané and his colleagues has been the role of identifiability and resultant evaluation potential in group situations (Williams, Harkins, and Latané, 1981). When groups are large, evaluation potential drops as each individual's contribution becomes blurred by that of the whole. The origins of glitches in the system are unclear because of the inability to correctly identify the sources of poor group performance. Though Latané et al. have conducted group research in a number of situations, one particularly relevant to our concerns within sport is most intriguing. Latané, Harkins, and Williams (1980), through a creative series of experimental manipulations, were able to deal effectively with the identifiability issue in a study of intercollegiate swimmers. Latané and his colleagues asked sixteen swimmers to take part in both individual and relay swimming events. All swimmers participated in two 100-meter freestyle events as individuals and then swam one lap in each of two 400-meter freestyle relay races. Identifiability was manipulated by announcing or not announcing individual lap times. In the low identifiability condition, individual times were faster (61.34 seconds) than were the corresponding relay times (61.66 seconds), all of which is suggestive of social loafing. However, under the high identifiability condition, individual times were slower (60.95 seconds) than were the relay times (60.18 seconds). The announcing of individual times evidently does much to eliminate social loafing. Too, the high identifiability condition appears to serve as a social incentive to perform.

Inasmuch as sport teams are highly susceptible to social loafing, it behooves researchers to continue looking into this phenomenon, which is a potential source of performance decrements within sport.

The Task. The task at hand for the sport teams is another correlate of cohesion. Obviously, all sports do not require the same degree of cooperative effort among and between members. Cox (1985) refers to an *interactive–coactive continuum* to explain this relationship. *Interactive sports* are those in which close teamwork is required for success whereas coactive sports require little individual interaction. In turn, Cox talks of low and high means interdependence, a conceptual framework created by Goldman, Stockbauer, and McAuliffe (1977). *Coactive tasks* exemplify low means interdependence and interactive tasks personify high means interdependence. Sports such as golf or riflery require little team interaction, and interdependence is therefore low. On the other hand, basketball and volleyball require that all players depend on each other for success, and interdependence is high. As is almost always the case, the coaction-interaction dichotomy is not steadfast. Some sports (softball and rowing) involve aspects of both coaction and interaction and involve a moderate amount of interdependence. For a summary of the coaction-interaction and means/interdependence relationship, see table 6.2.

Table 6.2 Coaction-Interaction and Means-Interdependence Relationship

Coacting teams	*Mixed Coacting-interacting*	*Interacting teams*
Low means–interdependent tasks:	**Moderate means–interdependent tasks:**	**High means–interdependent tasks:**
Archery	American football	Basketball
Bowling	Baseball/softball	Field hockey
Field events (track)	Figure skating	Ice hockey
Golf	Rowing	Rugby
Riflery	Track events	Soccer
Skiing	Tug-of-war	Team handball
Ski jumping	Swimming	Volleyball
Wrestling		
	Degree of task cohesion required:	
Low	Moderate	High

Source: *Sport Psychology: Concepts and Applications* (p. 278) by R. H. Cox, 1985, Dubuque, IA: Wm. C. Brown.

When interdependence and interaction are high, a fertile source for team cohesion exists. For instance, team success in basketball requires a great deal of interaction. Guards set up plays, forwards set picks and get into position to shoot or rebound, and the center serves as a catalyst for all of this action. No one is successful if all are not doing their part. In this milieu, cohesion is highly desirable.

Team Tenure. The length of time that a team stays together is an important aspect of cohesion. Donnelly (1975) talks of a team *"half-life"* (Donnelly, Carron, and Chelladurai, 1978). Donnelly analyzed data on six major league baseball teams from 1901 to 1965 and concluded that a half-life of five years was most desirable for success, thereby suggesting that cohesion does not take place instantaneously but requires time and nurturance. In Donnelly's study, a half-life was considered to be the amount of time it took for the starting roster of a particular team to turn over by 50 percent. From this, Donnelly arrived at the five-year figure by studying the win-loss records and the player turnover rates. Though caveats are necessary in terms of how relevant this finding is to other teams and sports, Donnelly's work is suggestive of a temporal force in team cohesion. More work needs to be done in the area of team tenure.

A related phenomenon is team stability. Keeping players together for reasonable periods of time would seem to be a necessary first step in creating a cohesive atmosphere. Some evidence indicates that stability does in fact contribute to performance success. Essing (1970) found correlations of .62, .58, and .47 between continuity of team lineups and success in the win–loss column in eighteen soccer teams. Veit (1970), also studying soccer teams, found a correlation between team success and player turnover. Perhaps Zander (1976, pp. 974–975) sums it up best: "Poorly performing organizations typically release more members than do organizations that are succeeding—this is demonstrated at the end of a professional sports season when losing teams rid themselves of managers and players, while winning teams leave well enough alone."

None of the preceding opinions and assertions addresses the circular nature of the stability-cohesion issue. Are stable teams more cohesive or are cohesive teams more stable? Perhaps future research efforts will shed light on this issue.

Satisfaction. A decided circularity is seen in cohesion and individual or team satisfaction. Satisfaction could either be a cause or an effect of group cohesion. An important third leg of relevance here is performance success, and there are two noteworthy models for viewing the interaction between satisfaction, success, and cohesion. An early model by Martens and Peterson (1971) posits a circular relationship with performance success leading to satisfaction which, in turn, leads to team cohesion. A second model from Williams and Hacker (1982) hypothesizes that performance success leads to both satisfaction and team cohesion, that team cohesion can lead to satisfaction, but that satisfaction in and of itself leads nowhere in terms of either success or cohesion. A representation of both of these models can be seen in figure 6.6.

In brief, the two models agree on the existence of a relationship between performance success, satisfaction, and team cohesion but the direction of causality constitutes a fundamental point of disagreement between them. Based on the Williams and Hacker model in particular, Cox (1985) urges continuation of efforts aimed toward maintaining team cohesion on the part of coaches. Cox also urges researchers to continue to study this interrelationship, and suggests that the Sport Cohesion Instrument (SCI) (Yukelson, Weinberg, and Jackson, 1984) may be the most effective way to go in terms of measuring team cohesion.

Figure 6.6 Two Models of the Relationship among Performance, Satisfaction, and Cohesion

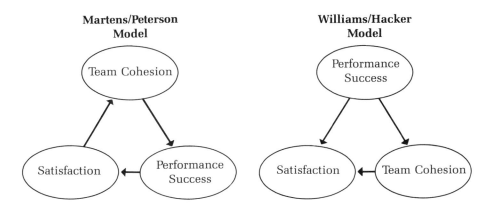

SOURCE: *Sport Psychology: Concepts and Applications* (p. 283) by R.H. Cox, 1985, Dubuque, IA: Wm. C. Brown.

Granted that there are other correlates of group cohesion, suffice it to say that group size, task demands, group stability, and satisfaction are important considerations and give the reader some insights into the complexity of the issue.

Measures of Team Cohesion

Four instruments have emerged to measure cohesion in sport. Perhaps the first of these measures was the *Sports Cohesiveness Questionnaire (SCQ)* (Martens and Peterson, 1971). The SCQ has been by far the most popular measure used in sport cohesion research, having been a part of at least twelve published studies (Widmeyer, Brawley, and Carron, 1985). The SCQ can be seen in table 6.3, and is made up of seven questions. The first five heavily load on social cohesion whereas the final two are more task related.

Three recent alternatives to the SCQ have been provided in the form of the *Task Cohesiveness Questionnaire (TCQ)* (Gruber and Gray, 1981, 1982); the previously mentioned *Sport Cohesion Instrument (SCI)* (Yukelson et al., 1984); and the *Group Environment Questionnaire (GEQ)* (Carron, Widmeyer, and Brawley, 1985; Widmeyer et al., 1985). The TCQ consists of seventeen items and measures six dimensions of team cohesion, whereas the SCI contains twenty-one items loading on four dimensions. Time will tell concerning the efficacy of these two measures, but they appear to be promising due to their emphasis on direct measures of cohesion and the fact that both are relatively equally weighted toward task and social cohesion.

However, the publication of the GEQ in 1985 offers a critical look at cohesion theory and assessment while offering perhaps the soundest cohesion measure yet developed. Widmeyer and his colleagues are quite critical of other measures of cohesion, primarily because they are largely atheoretical. Widmeyer et al. also argue that, in addition to theory problems, too little has been done to validate the psychometric properties of cohesion measures used up to this time. Widmeyer and his associates go on to unequivocally state that the lack of conceptual clarity and inadequate measurement procedures add up to equivocal results,

Table 6.3 Sports Cohesiveness Questionnaire

Categories	Items	Questions
Individual-to-individual relationships	Interpersonal attraction	1. On what type of friendship basis are you with each member of your team?
	Personal power or influence	2. How much influence do you believe each of the other members of your team has with the coach and other teammates?
Individual-to-team relationships	Value of membership	3. Compared to other groups that you belong to, how much do you value your membership on this team?
	Sense of belonging	4. How strong a sense of belonging do you believe you have to this team?
	Enjoyment	5. How much do you like competing with this particular team?
The group as a unit	Teamwork	6. How good do you think the teamwork is on your team?
	Closeness	7. How closely knit do you think your team is?

SOURCE: "Group Cohesiveness as a Determinant of Success and Member Satisfaction in Team Performance" by R. Martens and J. Peterson, 1971, *International Review of Sport Sociology, 6,* 49–61.

which they see as the current status of cohesion research in sport.

The GEQ was created in response to the existing inadequacies of other measures. It is an eighteen-item questionnaire responded to along a nine-point continuum from "strongly agree" to "strongly disagree."

The GEQ measures four dimensions of the group member's perceptions of group cohesiveness: group integration–task; group integration–social; individual attractions to the group–task; individual attractions to the group–social (Widmeyer et al., 1985).

Recent studies by Brawley, Carron, and Widmeyer (1987) have demonstrated the validity of the GEQ. In their 1987 article, Brawley and his associates report the results of three studies in which the GEQ was used. In all three instances, the validity of the GEQ was upheld, but the authors issued the customary call for other cohesion researchers to get busy and assist in further validation studies of their most promising instrument.

Widmeyer and his colleagues assert that the GEQ is an improvement over existing measures because it incorporates both existing group cohesion theory from social psychology and sound psychometrics. Whether the authors of the GEQ are correct in their assertion will be answered by research conducted over the next several years, but the instrument looks most promising.

Two Final Notes

Two additional issues warrant discussion. One has to do with the *issue of circularity,* particularly as it relates to the cohesion-performance distinction. Perhaps the ultimate question revolves around whether cohesion facilitates performance or whether performance dictates cohesion. Studies within sport by Landers, Wilkinson, Hatfield, and Barber (1982), Ruder and Gill (1982), and Williams and Hacker (1982) all lend support to the notion that the direction of causality is more likely to be from

"Even a solitary workout may be accompanied by an unseen audience, a group of people residing in the mind of the performer. This audience, the athlete knows, stands ready to judge his or her performance at some future time, harshly or with kindness and praise." (Cratty, 1981)

performance to cohesion than vice versa. If the assertion of these researchers is so, team cohesion may well have been traditionally overrated as a cause of success. Nevertheless, coaches should strive for cohesive units, but also maintain an awareness of the significance of task success in shaping the coveted spirit of togetherness.

A final point related to cohesion (and very much related to the issue of circularity) is the negative side of the coin. Cohesion is not altogether a positive; if overdone, it may lead to conformity and lessened task success. Individuality may be suppressed, self-

deception may become more likely, and cliques may be formed. The Klein and Christiansen (1969) and Fiedler (1967) studies, which showed that basketball players who are close friends tended to pass more often to each other to the detriment of the collective effort, demonstrate the dangers of cliques within a team. The role of the coach in creating a winning *and* cohesive atmosphere is essential and will be explored at greater length in chapter 12.

AUDIENCE EFFECTS

Anyone who has participated in any form of athletics is acutely aware of what it is like to be evaluated by others. We aspire to perform well because of internal forces, such as personal desire to excel, but we are also impelled to success because of pressures generated by those who are interacting at one level or another with us. Our peers serve as one point of evaluative reference; coaches are also formidable forces; and audiences for which we may demonstrate our skills serve as a third evaluative source. Too, as Cratty (1981, p. 191) has pointed out: "Even a solitary workout may be accompanied by an unseen audience, a group of people residing psychologically and socially in the mind of the performer. This audience, the athlete knows, stands ready to judge his or her performance at some future time, harshly or with kindness and praise."

The interaction between internal motivational and external evaluative forces is most complex and intriguing, and a number of theorists and researchers in and out of sport have tried to shed light on the tangled web of audience effects on human performance. This fascination with audience effects owes a great debt to research that has been done over the years in what is known as social facilitation.

HIGHLIGHT 6.1
Obstacles to
Effective Team
Performance

Team cohesion and team performance have been the subjects of much arm-chair speculation and scientific research. An assumption underlying most sport teams is that the participants who work together and get along most harmoniously will prevail over those who are torn by petty jealousies or, at the extreme, out-and-out dissension. Merrill Melnick is among those who believe that, all other things being equal, small groups (teams) function best in the absence of disharmony. Accordingly, Melnick has identified six obsta-cles to effective team performance and offers a few suggestions for dealing with these potential sources of group inefficiency.

1. *"Groupthink."* Groupthink is a powerful force that arises in cohesive groups and is characterized by a tendency to be overoptimistic and undervigilant. Melnick cites the example of a female Soviet mountain climbing team that had been strongly discouraged from attempting a climb of Peak Lenin in the Russian Parmirs, a range on the USSR-China border. The groupthink process that dominated in this instance was that the group was invincible precisely because it was a strong, cohesive group and would prevail against all odds. In the face of inadequate equipment and dismal weather, eight of the team members died during the ill-fated attack on Peak Lenin. Maintaining group uncertainty about goal outcome and the encouragement of participatory decision making and exploration of all facets of the issues at hand are suggested by Mel-nick as possible remedies for a problem that is not easily resolved.

2. *Cliques.* Clique formation can be a considerable impediment to group effectiveness, and athletic teams are quite susceptible to such subgroup formation. Few other small groups are made up of people who may con-tribute little or nothing to group success, and cliques are not uncom-mon as a result. Vigilance in monitoring the development of cliques and the skillful utilization of all team members are suggested as ways of deal-ing with potentially deviant subgroup formation.

3. *Negative Affect.* Whether it is essential for teammates to like each other is a contentious issue. Such a state does not appear to be absolutely essen-tial but is probably more important in interdependent teams, where individual players must continually rely on each other, than in such sports as bowling or tennis. One effective and neglected method for monitoring the development of negative affect on a team is the sociogram.

4. *Psychological Homogeneity.* For quite some time, team success and psy-chological homogeneity in personality makeup were believed to go hand in hand. It is now clear that team chemistry is more likely a product of the meshing of a variety of personality types, and future research in isolating this chemistry is called for.

5. *Value/Norm/Sanction Incompatibility.* Team values, such as hustle, are dictated by the group. Norms imply conformity to these group-dictated values. Sanctions imposed for not displaying these values, such as not running out a ground ball in baseball, are a third part of the team idio-culture. It is assumed that a harmonious relationship among this tril-ogy will positively influence team dynamics. Conversely, disharmony

should exert a negative influence on the team. Greater team morale and productivity should result when team members are an integral part of setting team values, norms, and sanctions.

6. *Distributed Leadership.* Focused leadership exists when all group members agree on the leadership hierarchy. When disagreement exists on this issue, leadership is said to be distributed. If a stable social environment is indeed necessary for group effectiveness, then distributed leadership provides a confused picture. Therefore, clarifying the leadership structure and providing clear-cut roles within that structure for all team members should result in increased group effectiveness.

SOURCE: "Six Obstacles to Effective Team Performance: Some Small Group Considerations" by M. J. Melnick, 1982, *Journal of Sport Behavior, 5,* 114–123.

Social Facilitation

To Zajonc (1965, p. 269), social facilitation "examines the consequences upon behavior which derive from the sheer presence of other individuals." Zajonc also classifies social facilitation research into two basic paradigms: audience effects and coaction effects. *Audience effects* are those created by observing behavior in front of passive spectators, and *coactive effects* are behavioral effects occurring as a result of the presence of other individuals engaging in the same activity.

Early Research. Social facilitation research dates back to the work of Triplett (1898). In what Allport (1954) calls the first experiment in social psychology, Triplett studied bicycle racers under a variety of conditions and concluded that the presence of others actually facilitated performance. In the same study, Triplett also showed that adolescents could spin a fishing reel-like device more rapidly when working with another individual than when working alone. Allport (1924) was another significant figure in social facilitation research and is, in fact, given credit for coining the term (Cox, 1985; Wankel, 1984). In 1933, the mere presence hypothesis received its first significant challenge as a result of research

reported by Pessin (1933). Pessin noted that college students learned nonsense syllables better when alone than in the presence of others. In 1935, Dashiell, a protégé of Allport, added some refinements to his mentor's suggestion that there is no such thing as a pure alone or pure coaction situation because of the intrusion of internal psychological mediators. Too, Dashiell observed that the presence of others tended to speed up performance rate but not accuracy of response. This latter point served as a precursor to the substantial contribution of Zajonc, though thirty years elapsed in the process.

The Work of Zajonc. In 1965, Zajonc published a pivotal paper in which he outlined his approach to social facilitation. Borrowing heavily from Hull-Spence drive theory, Zajonc suggests that the mere presence of an audience heightens physiological arousal, which in turn enhances the likelihood that the individual will emit his or her dominant response in social situations. To quote Zajonc (1965, p. 270), "The emission of these well-learned responses is facilitated by the presence of spectators, while the acquisition of new responses is impaired." This expostulation, according to Zajonc, means that performance is enhanced and learning hindered by the presence of others. Based on these kinds of predictions, it would follow that audiences would have differential effects on sport performance as a function of skill level, with young athletes most adversely affected by audiences and highly skilled ones least affected. A visual representation of this hypothesis can be seen in figure 6.7.

The evidence for Zajonc's work is generally strong, and several studies in the area of motor behavior are supportive (Hunt and Hillery, 1973; Landers, Brawley, and Hale, 1978; Martens, 1969). However, the Zajonc model in sports is not without its limitations, and other alternative conceptualizations have arisen as a result.

Other Drive Theories. Cottrell (1972) has taken exception to Zajonc's mere presence hypothesis, and suggests that drive is facilitated by the presence of someone who can evaluate performance. This presence Cottrell calls *evaluative*

apprehension. Through socialization experiences, the individual comes to anticipate positive or negative outcomes as a result of the presence of evaluative others. This emphasis on the critical audience is a point of separation between Cottrell's work and that of Zajonc; Zajonc would suggest that the uncertainty created by the presence of an audience would increase arousal as opposed to Cottrell's emphasis on evaluation effects as the cause of an increased drive state. As is the case with the Zajonc model, some support for the Cottrell approach has been generated in the area of motor behavior (e.g., Haas and Roberts, 1975; Martens and Landers, 1972). All in all, however, the research on the Cottrell model has been equivocal and rather scant of late.

Other drive theories of note include those of Sanders, Baron, and Moore (1978) and Guerin and Innes (1982). Sanders et al. view *attentional conflict* as the cause of drive; that is, the presence of people who can provide

Figure 6.7 Audience Effects on Athletes at Various Skill Levels

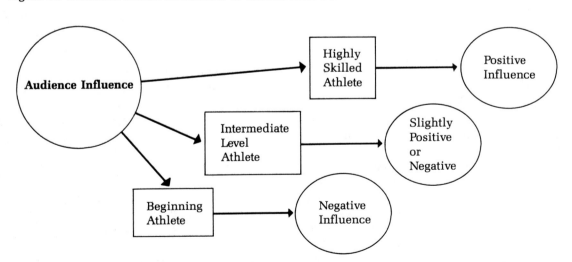

Source: *Sport Psychology: Concepts and Applications* (p. 247) by R.H. Cox, 1985, Dubuque, IA: Wm. C. Brown.

social comparison data that will conflict with attention to the task at hand serves as a source of generalized drive. Guerin and Innes suggest a *social monitoring theory*, which posits that the presence of others who cannot be visually monitored or the presence of others who are unfamiliar, unpredictable, or threatening increases drive. According to Bond and Titus (1983, p. 266), "Drive will not be increased by the mere presence of innocuous others if those others can periodically be monitored. According to this social monitoring theory, the individual should be less affected by the presence of coactors than by the presence of spectators because coactors are more predictable."

An Evaluation of Drive Theory. Wankel (1984) suggests that drive theory has been dominant in social facilitation research partially because of its generally parsimonious nature. On the other hand, Wankel states that the various drive theories are too mechanistic to be of value in trying to explain complex human behavior. Sanders (1981) indicates that the various drive models have much overlap and are generally not comprehensive enough to explain socially facilitated behavior. Cox (1985) raises objections to drive theory on relevancy grounds; although important from a research viewpoint, noninteractive audiences used in drive theory studies are far less relevant to sport than interactive ones. Most athletic situations are characterized by interactions between coaches and athletes and spectators.

Because of the preceding charges, calls for other approaches to explaining social facilitation have been made (Geen and Gange, 1977; Landers, 1980; Wankel 1984). Each of these authorities has issued a call for more cognitive explanatory models. Several models of recent vintage, however incomplete, have responded to the challenge. We shall take a brief look at three of them.

Alternative Nondrive Theory Models. Duval and Wicklund (1972) have posited a model that stresses *objective self-awareness.* In theory, the performer who is self-aware should be motivated to reduce discrepancies that arise from the disparities between actual and ideal task performance.

Another formulation is that of Bond (1982), who proposes a *self-presentational model.* The Bond approach contends that the motivation to project an image of competence in the presence of others will facilitate performance. Whereas the drive theorists equate drive with physiological arousal, Bond sees possible embarrassment as the source of arousal (Bond and Titus, 1983).

An *arousal-cognitive information processing model* is a third approach. Within sport, Landers (1980) and Wankel (1984) are proponents of the model because it represents a step away from the mechanistic drive theory and places emphasis not only on the energizing effects of social factors but also on the informational or cognitive aspect.

Though intuitively appealing, the cognitive models have, for the most part, been of recent creation and little has been done to test them within sport. Perhaps future efforts will be directed toward confirming or disconfirming these cognitive approaches, thereby shedding light on the complex issue of social facilitation.

Interactive Audience Effects on Sport Performance

As stated earlier, the preponderance of sport interactions are with an active audience as opposed to the passive audience so prominent in social facilitation research. The effects of supportive versus nonsupportive audiences, audience size, and viewer sophistication are only a few of the interactive forces at work in shaping athletic behavior. Of the preceding, far more is known about the supportive audience than the other variables. This supportive audience generally is viewed in athletics as constituting the home advantage, a topic of considerable interest to spectators, athletes, coaches, sport announcers, and sport scientists. The remainder of our discussion will be devoted to this effect.

The Home Advantage. Much is made in the media of the so-called *home court advantage.* A rule of thumb in basketball, according to Jimmy (The Greek) Snyder, is that the home court is worth 3 to 7 points to the home team. In major league baseball, the goal often seems to be to win big at home and break even on the road. While one can speculate that, for the visitors, the demands of travel, disrupted schedules, and unfamiliar surroundings are causes of the home advantage, fans typically believe that their support of the home team is at the heart of the edge enjoyed by their beloved minions. Such is, in fact, probably the case.

The first significant study of the home advantage was conducted by Schwartz and Barsky (1977). Their data analysis was made on 1,880 major league baseball games played in 1971, on 182 professional football games played that same year, on 542 National Hockey League games from the 1971–1972 season, and on 1,485 college basketball games played from 1952

through 1966 by the big five in Philadelphia (LaSalle, Pennsylvania, St. Joseph's, Temple, and Villanova). The percentage of games won by the home teams in each of these sports can be seen in table 6.4. Clearly, a home advantage is reflected, with the edge being greatest in basketball. Too, hockey teams profit from playing at home, particularly if tie games are excluded; the winning percentage for the home team in hockey then becomes 64. All things considered, Schwartz and Barsky concluded that the source of this advantage was social support from a friendly audience.

In another significant study, Varca (1980) lends support to the idea of the home advantage. Varca used game statistics for all men's basketball games in the Southeastern Conference for the 1977–1978 season in arriving at his conclusions as to why the home advantage exists. Varca's main hypothesis was that differences in aggressive play between the home team and visitors could account for the advantage. Simply stated, *functionally aggressive play* by the home team and *dysfunctionally aggressive play* by the visitors accounts for the edge afforded the home team. *Functionally aggressive play* to Varca includes skill in rebounding, stealing the ball from opponents, and blocking shots, whereas *dysfunctionally aggressive play* was limited to personal fouls,

Table 6.4 Percentage of Games Won by Home Team in Four Sports

Home Team Outcome	Sport				
	Baseball (1971)	Professional Football (1971)	College Football (1971)	Hockey (1971–1972)	Basketball (1952–1966)
Win	53% (989)	55% (100)	59% (532)	53% (286)	82% (290)
Lose	47 (891)	41 (74)	40 (367)	30 (163)	18 (64)
Tie	— —	4 (8)	1 (11)	17 (93)	— —
Total	100% (1,880)	100% (182)	100% (910)	100% (542)	100% (354)

Number of games in parentheses.

SOURCE: "The Home Advantage" by B. Schwartz and S. F. Barsky, 1977, *Social Forces, 55,* 641–661.

a generally detrimental force in basketball. As predicted, the home team was superior in all three of the functional behaviors, and the visitors were guilty of more fouls (dysfunctional aggression) than were the home teams. Varca gave the credit to arousal states generated by the friendly, supportive audiences at the various home courts, with the arousal being channeled positively by the home team and negatively by the visitors.

Yet a third study of the home advantage, and one similar to that of Varca, was conducted by Silva, Andrew, and Richey (1983). In their study of the home and away performance of the North Carolina Tarheels and their Atlantic Coast Conference basketball opposition over a ten-year period, Silva et al. arrived at the conclusion that performance decrements by visiting teams were more influential than performance increments by home teams in explaining the home court edge.

Based on the results of the three preceding pieces of research, it does seem clear that a home advantage in a number of fairly advanced sport settings is a reality. Major league baseball, football, and hockey teams and collegiate basketball teams do indeed seem to profit from playing at home. However, a recent study by Baumeister and Steinhilber (1984) adds a most provocative caveat to this conclusion. These researchers looked at baseball's World Series for the years 1924 through 1982 and the

National Basketball Association championship playoffs games from 1967 through 1982 in an effort to see if the home audience is in fact a positive force in the final or deciding games. In both instances, they found the home field or court advantage to be valid for early games in the playoffs but not for the games that actually determined the ultimate winner. Of particular interest to Baumeister and Steinhilber was the source of this effect; was the home team choking or were the visitors merely playing unusually well? In baseball, they chose fielding errors to analyze because their low mutual determinacy makes them a relatively pure measure of choking. In the first two games of the series, the visiting team made the most errors; in the seventh game, it is reversed, with the home team committing the most errors. The difference in errors noted in the seventh game is significant at the .01 level of confidence. These data are reflected in table 6.5.

In basketball, free throw shooting was chosen for analysis, and the results follow those of baseball. In games one through four of a seven-game playoff, the home team shot about the same as the visitors but the tables again turned in game seven, with the visitors having an edge that was statistically significant. These data are available in table 6.6.

Yet another analysis made by Baumeister and Steinhilber was of the NBA semifinal and championship series, again from 1967 through

Table 6.5 Fielding Errors in World Series Games, 1924–1982

Games	Errors per game		Errorless games	
	Home	*Visitor*	*Home*	*Visitor*
1 and 2	0.65	1.04	33	18
7	1.31	0.81*	6	12**

*p. = <.01

**p. = <.02

SOURCE: "Paradoxical Effects of Supportive Audiences on Performance under Pressure: The Home Field Disadvantage in Sports Championships" by R. F. Baumeister and A. Steinhilber, 1984, *Journal of Personality and Social Psychology*, 47, 85–93.

Table 6.6 Free Throw Performance in NBA Playoffs, 1967–1982

Performance	Home	Visitor
Games 1–4:		
Success (scored)	3368	3412
Failure (missed)	1303	1266
Scoring percentage	.72	.73*
Last (7th) game:		
Success	873	937
Failure	391	328
Scoring percentage	.69	.74**

*p. = not significant
**p. = <.01

SOURCE: "Paradoxical Effects of Supportive Audiences on Performance Under Pressure: The Home Field Disadvantage in Sports Championships" by R. F. Baumeister and A. Steinhilber, 1984, *Journal of Personality and Social Psychology, 47*, 85–93.

1982. In games one through four, the home team won 70.1 percent of the contests; in series decided in the seventh game, the home court advantage dropped to 38.5 percent. Clearly, the home team advantage does not exist in critical games at the highest levels of professional basketball.

Baumeister and Steinhilber feel that the presence of supportive others may actually be more harmful than helpful in some situations. This performance decrement is seen as choking on the part of the home team. Further support for this idea is offered by Baumeister, Hamilton, and Tice (1985) in a laboratory experiment with college students.

Gayton, Matthews, and Nickless (1987) have taken the work of Baumeister and Steinhilber to the Stanley Cup playoffs in the National Hockey League (NHL) for the years 1960 through 1985 and obtained very different results. They found no support for a significant home court advantage at any level in the NHL playoffs. Additionally, the choking phenomenon alluded to by Baumeister and Steinhilber did not occur in those series that went to a

seventh game. In the twelve playoffs that went to a seventh and deciding game, the home team won seven.

Considering the provocative nature of the findings of Baumeister and his colleagues as well as Gayton and his collaborators, more research needs to be done to shed additional light on a fascinating facet of audience effects, namely, the home advantage.

A Final Note. The home advantage is perhaps more clearly understood than other facets of audience effects. Audience size, audience sophistication, gender effects, team identification factor, and audience density are also important aspects of the overall audience issue. Much work remains to be done in clarifying these and other parameters that impinge on the audience effects issue.

SUMMARY

1. Leadership, cohesion, and audience effects represent three variables within social psychology that have intrigued scientists inside and outside of sport.

2. The discussion of leadership dates back to the time of Plato, Caesar, and Plutarch. Early Chinese and Egyptian writings also reflect an interest in leadership. Leadership studies have been pursued in this country for about eighty years.

3. The trait theory of leadership (the great-man theory) takes the position that leaders are leaders by nature, and would be leaders in most if not all situations. Support for the great-man perspective is equivocal.

4. Fiedler's contingency model incorporates both traits and situational variables into the leadership formula. Much is made in Fiedler's theory of type of leadership and

HIGHLIGHT 6.2
Basking in Reflected
Glory (BIRG)

We all like to be associated with a winner, and a 1976 report of three studies conducted by Robert Cialdini and his associates has added an element of scientific verification to the notion. In the first of the three studies, Cialdini and associates sought support for the existence of a phenomenon known as "basking in reflected glory" (BIRG) by covertly observing the apparel worn to introductory psychology classes by students from seven universities with major football programs. Essentially what the observers did was look for the wearing of various paraphernalia (buttons, T-shirts, jackets, sweatshirts) that displayed the school name, team nickname or mascot, or university insignia on Mondays after football games. Students clearly tended to wear more school-related paraphernalia on Mondays after wins than after losses, a finding that was interpreted as lending support to BIRG.

In the second experiment, an examination of pronoun usage served as the mechanism for studying BIRG. Simply stated, it was hypothesized that students would respond to wins with increased use of the pronoun *we* and to losses with greater use of the pronoun *they*. In order to more covertly test this hunch, students were contacted by telephone and the investigators identified themselves as employees of a "Regional Survey Center"; the subjects were asked to respond to six questions about campus life in general. Students were then given feedback that placed them in success or failure groups irrespective of how well they actually did on the six questions. They were then asked to respond to questions about their teams' recent football games, half of which had been won and half lost. Two hypotheses were generated by the experimental manipulations just described; one was that team wins would result in more *we's* than would losses. The second hypothesis was that the effect of the first hypothesis would be greater for those who had "failed" the test from the so-called Regional Survey Center. The latter supposition was based on the idea that those who had "failed" the campus events test would want to enhance themselves in the eyes of the investigators by associating themselves with positive entities, such as a team victory the previous Saturday. Clear support for BIRG was found in both instances. There was strong support for the use of the pronoun *we* and an even stronger relationship was noted when the respondents' public prestige was in jeopardy.

The third experiment arose out of the results of the previous manipulations of BIRG. Specifically, the investigators were curious as to how the students would respond when they were told that the phone calls were from either a University Survey Center or a Regional Survey Center. The idea here was that the students would demonstrate a stronger BIRG response to the regional than to the local center. The rationale for this hypothesis rested in the supposition that BIRG would be stronger when the respondent had a stronger link to the prestigious object than did the observer. The likelihood that a local caller would have a reasonably similar degree of identification was thought to be quite high; on the other hand, an outsider would not be so likely to have the same emotional investment in the admired object, and identifying with the source of prestige would enhance their perception in the eyes of the more geographically and presumably emotionally remote caller. By way of paraphrasing the authors, little prestige is to be gained from bragging about the virtues of California weather to another Californian; however, relating the same message to someone from states with more severe weather conditions might be more image enhancing. As expected, confirmation for BIRG was again demonstrated.

Overall, support for BIRG in all three studies was most evident, and the results were viewed as providing support for the importance of perceived esteem of others. Alternatively, however, an explanation for the results that is couched in terms of enhancing the self-concept might also be a viable one. Cialdini and his associates contend that BIRG is best explained in terms of its enhancing effects on social image, but the interplay between social image and self-image cannot be ignored.

SOURCE: "Basking in Reflected Glory: Three (Football) Field Studies" by R. B. Cialdini, R. J. Borden, A. Thorne, M. R. Walker, S. Freeman, and L. R. Sloan, 1976, *Journal of Personality and Social Psychology, 34*, 366–375; *Psychology of Sports: A Social Psychological Approach* (pp. 326–328) by S. E. Iso-Ahola and B. Hatfield, 1986, Dubuque, IA: Wm. C. Brown.

situational favorableness as predictors of leadership. Research within sport has been sparse and not especially supportive of Fiedler's approach.

5. Path-goal theory suggests that the leader is a catalyst for group success and satisfaction. Again, research within sport has been scant but the issue of the efficacy of path-goal theory has not been determined.

6. Life cycle theory places much reliance on the motivational and maturity level of subordinates to attain group goals. There is some support within the sport literature for the life cycle formulation.

7. A model with little research support so far, but one of intuitive appeal, is the functional approach of Behling and Schriesheim. Instrumental and expressive functions are emphasized, with the former referring to task-related aspects and the latter to social and emotional needs of the group members.

8. The multidimensional model is currently at the forefront of sport leadership research and has been advanced by Chelladurai, Carron, and Saleh in a series of studies. Quite a bit of interest has been generated by the multidimensional model, and research and refinement are continuing.

9. Group cohesion is generally but not universally considered to be essential to success in sport. The term itself comes to us from the Latin word *cohaesus* and refers to a group organized around purposeful behavior.

10. Three models—the pendular, the linear, and the life cycle—are suggested by Carron as representative of current thinking about group cohesion.

11. Group size is a correlate of cohesion, and cohesion is generally lessened as groups increase in size. The Ringelmann Effect and social loafing are two key terms here, both referring to the failure of groups to increase performance at a one-to-one ratio with increases in group size.

12. The task at hand greatly affects group cohesion. Cox talks of an interactive-coactive dichotomy to partially explain differences in task demands across sport.

13. The length of time that a team stays together affects cohesion. Research by Donnelly suggests that there is indeed an

optimal length of time for cohesion to develop and subsequently dissipate.

14. Two models, one by Martens and Peterson and the other by Williams and Hacker, are used to illustrate the relationship between task performance, cohesion, and satisfaction.

15. Four measures of team cohesion have emerged. They are the Sport Cohesiveness Questionnaire, the Task Cohesiveness Questionnaire, the Sport Cohesiveness Instrument, and the Group Environment Questionnaire. The GEQ has not been used extensively in sport studies, but there is some suggestion that it will eventually supplant the other three measures.

16. The circularity of the cohesion-performance relationship is troublesome, but the available evidence supports a performance success to cohesion sequence rather than vice versa. Too, cohesion does have some potentially negative aspects, and an awareness of them is important to all involved in team cohesion.

17. Audience effects on athletic performance represent an area of considerable scientific interest, getting its impetus from early social facilitation research.

18. Triplett, in 1898, was the first to study social facilitation, though the term was coined in 1924 by Allport.

19. A reawakening of interest in social facilitation took place in 1965, prompted by a pivotal paper in *Science* by Zajonc. To Zajonc, the mere presence of others increases arousal that facilitates well-learned responses and hinders the acquisition of new ones. Zajonc's mere presence theory has sparked much controversy and resultant research and theory.

20. Cottrell, while agreeing with Zajonc on several issues, disagreed with the mere presence formulation and suggested that evaluative apprehension generated by others viewing behavior is at the heart of the issue. Other recent theories have been advanced by Sanders, Baron, and Moore and by Guerin and Innes.

21. Critics of the various drive theories indicate that they are too mechanistic to explain complex human behavior. Too, the typical research in the drive theory area deals with noninteractive audiences whereas the typical sport situation involves an interactive one, thereby rendering much of the drive theory research inapplicable to sport psychology.

22. Alternate and more current theories take a more cognitive approach to the topic of social facilitation. Though little used so far, these newer approaches are appealing to sport scientists.

23. The best understood of the many aspects of the interactive audience is perhaps the advantage provided by the home crowd.

24. Research is supportive of the existence of a home advantage, though the studies so far have been either with professional hockey, baseball, and basketball teams or with collegiate basketball teams. Recent research by Baumeister and Steinhilber suggests that this advantage does not extend to championship games in the baseball World Series or the National Basketball Association (NBA) playoffs.

25. Size, density, sophistication, gender effects, and team identification factors are important aspects of audience effects and warrant more attention in the future.

SUGGESTED READINGS

Bass, B. (1981) *Stogdill's handbook of leadership*. New York: Free Press.

A veritable compendium, Bass is a must for the student of leadership. There are 617 pages of text devoted to virtually every aspect of leadership, and the serious researcher or student will find literally 190 pages of references on the topic.

Edwards, J. (1979) The home-field advantage. In J. Goldstein (Ed.), *Sports, games, and play: Social and psychological viewpoints* (pp. 409–438). Hillsdale, NJ: Lawrence Erlbaum Associates.

> Edwards offers data on the home advantage in several sports and attempts to clarify why the advantage exists. He concludes his informative chapters with a quotation that summarizes his conclusions about the home advantage in sport: "If the goal is to win, then, indeed, there is no place like home" (p. 436).

Greer, D. (1983) Spectator booing and the home advantage: A study of social influence in the basketball arena. *Social Psychology Quarterly, 46,* 252–261.

> Greer provides supportive data for earlier findings of Schwartz and Barsky while serving up a good review of other research findings on the home advantage. The possible role of officiating in facilitating the home advantage is also explored.

Maccoby, M. (1984) Leadership needs of the 1980s. In W. Rosenbach & R. Taylor (Eds.), *Contemporary issues in leadership* (pp. 305–317). Boulder, CO: Westview Press.

> Maccoby discusses three styles of leadership that have evolved in the United States over the past two hundred years. These three are independent craftsman (late eighteenth century to the Civil War), the paternalistic empire builder (post-Civil War to the 1950s), and the gamesman (from 1960 to the present). Implications of these styles for the future are discussed.

Melnick, M. J. (1983). A selected bibliography of psychosociological factors related to athletic performance. *Physical Educator, 40,* 92–94.

> The author cites sixty-one studies dealing with such topics as leadership and a number of group-related variables including cohesion. The references are subdivided by sport, with twelve different ones cited. This bibliography represents a nice collection of pertinent articles.

REFERENCES

Allport, F. H. (1924) *Social Psychology.* Boston: Houghton Mifflin.

Allport, G. (1954) The historical background of modern social psychology. In G. Lindzey & E. Aronson (Eds.), *Handbook of social psychology* (pp. 3–56). Reading, MA: Addison-Wesley.

Bass, B. (1981) *Stogdill's handbook of leadership.* New York: Free Press.

Baumeister, R. F., Hamilton, J., & Tice, D. (1985) Public versus private expectancy of success: Confidence booster or performance pressure? *Journal of Personality and Social Psychology, 48,* 1447–1457.

Baumeister, R. F., & Steinhilber, A. (1984). Paradoxical effects of supportive audiences on performance under pressure: The home field disadvantage in sports championships. *Journal of Personality and Social Psychology, 47,* 85–93.

Behling, O., & Schriesheim, C. (1976) *Organizational behavior theory, research, and application.* Boston: Allyn and Bacon.

Bird, A. M. (1977) Development of a model for predicting team performance. *Research Quarterly, 48,* 24–32.

Bond, C. F. (1982) Social facilitation: A self-presentational view. *Journal of Personality and Social Psychology, 42,* 1042–1050.

Bond, C. F., & Titus, L. J. (1983) Social facilitation: A meta-analysis of 241 studies. *Psychological Bulletin, 94,* 265–292.

Brawley, L. R., Carron, A. V., & Widmeyer, W. N. (1987) Assessing the cohesion of teams: Validity of the Group Environment Questionnaire. *Journal of Sport Psychology, 9,* 275–294.

Burns, J. M. (1978) *Leadership.* New York: Harper & Row.

Campbell, J., Dunnette, M., Lawler, E., & Weick, K. (1970) *Managerial behavior, performance, and effectiveness.* New York: McGraw-Hill.

Carron, A. V. (1980) *Social psychology of sport.* Ithaca, N.Y.: Mouvement.

Carron, A. V. (1984) Cohesion in sport teams. In J.M. Silva and R.S. Weinberg (Eds.), *Psychological foundations of sport* (pp. 340–351). Champaign, IL: Human Kinetics.

Carron, A. V. & Chelladurai, P. (1981) The dynamics of group cohesion in sport. *Journal of Sport Psychology, 3,* 123–139.

Carron, A. V., Widmeyer, W. N., & Brawley, L. R. (1985) The development of an instrument to assess cohesion in sport teams: The Group Environment Questionnaire. *Journal of Sport Psychology, 7,* 244–266.

Cattell, R. (1946) *Description and measurement of personality.* New York: World Book.

Chelladurai, P. (1984a) Leadership in sports. In J.M. Silva & R.S. Weinberg (Eds.), *Psychological foundations of sport* (pp. 329–339). Champaign, IL: Human Kinetics.

Chelladurai, P. (1984b) Discrepancy between preferences and perceptions of leadership behavior and satisfaction of athletes in varying sports. *Journal of Sport Psychology, 6,* 27–41.

Chelladurai, P. (1986) Applicability of the Leadership Scale for Sports to the Indian context. In J. Watkins, T. Reilly, & L. Burwitz (Eds.), *Sport science* (pp. 291–296). New York: E. & F. N. Spon Ltd.

Chelladurai, P., & Carron A. V. (1978) *Leadership* (Monograph). Ottawa: Canadian Association of Health, Physical Education and Recreation.

Chelladurai, P., & Carron, A. V. (1981) Applicability to youth sport of the leadership scale for sports. *Perceptual and Motor Skills, 53,* 361–362.

Chelladurai, P., & Carron, A. V. (1983) Athletic maturity and preferred leadership. *Journal of Sport Psychology, 5,* 371–380.

Chelladurai, P., & Saleh, S. (1978) Preferred leadership in sports. *Canadian Journal of Applied Sport Sciences, 3,* 85–92.

Chelladurai, P., & Saleh, S. (1980) Dimensions of leader behavior in sports: Development of a leadership scale. *Journal of Sport Psychology, 2,* 24–35.

Cottrell, N. B. (1972) Social facilitation. In C. G. McClintock (Ed.), *Experimental social psychology* (pp. 185–236). New York: Holt, Rinehart and Winston.

Cox, R. H. (1985) *Sport psychology: Concepts and applications.* Dubuque, IA: Wm. C. Brown.

Cratty, B. J. (1981) *Social psychology in athletics.* Englewood Cliffs, NJ: Prentice-Hall.

Danielson, R. R. (1976) Leadership motivation and coaching classification as related to success in minor league hockey. In R. Christina and D. Landers (Eds.), *Psychology of motor behavior and sport* (Vol. II, pp. 183–189). Champaign, IL: Human Kinetics.

Dashiell, J. F. (1935) Experimental studies of the influence of social situations of the behavior of individual human adults. In C. Murchison (Ed.), *A handbook of social psychology* (pp. 1097–1158). Worcester, MA: Clark University Press.

Dickey, G. (1982) *The history of National League baseball since 1876.* New York: Stein & Day.

Donnelly, P. (1975) An analysis of the relationship between organizational half-life and organizational effectiveness. Paper completed for an advanced topics course, Department of Sport Studies, University of Massachusetts, Amherst.

Donnelly, P., Carron, A. V., & Chelladurai, P. (1978) *Group cohesion and sport* (Sociology of Sport Monograph Series). Ottawa, Ontario: Canadian Association for Health, Physical Education, and Recreation.

Duval, S., & Wicklund, R. (1972) *A theory of objective self-awareness.* New York: Academic.

Essing, W. (1970) Team line-up and team achievement in European football. In G. Kenyon (Ed.), *Contemporary psychology of sport* (pp. 349–354). Chicago: Athletic Institute.

Festinger, L., Schachter, S., & Back, K. (1950) *Social pressures in informal groups.* New York: Harper.

Fiedler, F. (1967) *A theory of leadership effectiveness.* New York: McGraw-Hill.

Gayton, W. F., Matthews, G. R., & Nickless, C. J. (1987) The home field advantage in sports championships: Does it exist in hockey? *Journal of Sport Psychology, 9,* 183–185.

Geen, R., & Gange, J. (1977) Drive theory of social facilitation: Twelve years of theory and research. *Psychological Bulletin, 84,* 1267–1288.

Goldman, M., Stockbauer, J., & McAuliffe, T. (1977) Intergroup and intragroup competition and cooperation. *Journal of Experimental Social Psychology, 13,* 81–88.

Gross, N., & Martin, W. (1952) On group effectiveness. *American Journal of Sociology, 57,* 533–546.

Gruber, J., & Gray, G. (1981) Factors patterns of variables influencing cohesiveness at various levels of basketball competition. *Research Quarterly for Exercise and Sport, 52,* 19–30.

Gruber, J., & Gray, G. (1982) Responses to forces influencing cohesion as a function of player status and level of male basketball competition. *Research Quarterly for Exercise and Sport, 53,* 27–36.

Guerin, B., & Innes, J. (1982) Social facilitation and social monitoring: A new look at Zajonc's mere presence hypothesis. *British Journal of Social Psychology, 21,* 7–18.

Haas, J., & Roberts, G. (1975) Effects of evaluative others upon learning and performance of a complex motor task. *Journal of Motor Behavior, 7,* 81–90.

Hersey, P., & Blanchard, K. (1969) *Management of organizational behavior.* Englewood Cliffs, NJ: Prentice-Hall.

Hersey, P., & Blanchard, K. (1977) *Management of organizational behavior: Utilizing human resources.* Englewood Cliffs, NJ: Prentice-Hall.

Hollander, E. P. (1978) *Leadership dynamics.* New York: Free Press.

House, R. (1971) A path-goal theory of leader effectiveness. *Administrative Science Quarterly, 16,* 321–338.

House, R., & Dessler, G. (1974) The path-goal theory of leadership: Some post hoc and a priori tests. In J. Hunt & L. Larson (Eds.), *Contingency approaches to leadership* (pp. 29–62). Carbondale, IL: Southern Illinois University Press.

Hunt, P., & Hillery, J. (1973) Social facilitation in a coaction setting: An examination of the effects over learning trials. *Journal of Experimental Social Psychology, 9,* 563–571.

Inciong, P. (1974) *Leadership style and team success.* Unpublished doctoral dissertation, University of Utah.

Ingham, A., Levinger, G., Graves, J., & Peckham, V. (1974) The Ringelmann effect: Studies of group size and group performances. *Journal of Experimental Social Psychology, 10,* 371–384.

Klein, M., & Christiansen, G. (1969) Group composition, group structure and group effectiveness of basketball teams. In J. W. Loy and G. S. Kenyon (Eds.), *Sport, culture, and society* (pp. 397–408). London: Macmillan.

Landers, D. M. (1980) The arousal-performance relationship revisited. *Research Quarterly for Exercise and Sport, 51,* 77–90.

Landers, D. M., Brawley, L., & Hale, B. (1978) Habit strength differences in motor behavior: The effects of social facilitation paradigms and subject sex. In D. M. Landers and R. W. Christina (Eds.), *Psychology of motor behavior and sport, 1977* (pp. 420–433). Champaign, IL: Human Kinetics.

Landers, D. M., Wilkinson, M., Hatfield, B., & Barber, H. (1982) Causality and the cohesion–performance relationship. *Journal of Sport Psychology, 4,* 170–183.

Latané, B. (1973) *A theory of social impact.* St. Louis, MO: Psychonomic Society.

Latané, B., Harkins, S., & Williams, K. (1980) *Many hands make light the work: Social loafing as a social disease.* Unpublished manuscript, The Ohio State University.

Latané, B., Williams, K., & Harkins, S. (1979) Many hands make light the work: The causes and consequences of social loafing. *Journal of Personality and Social Psychology, 37,* 823–832.

Lenk, H. (1977) *Team dynamics.* Champaign, IL: Stipes.

Mann, R. D. (1959) A review of the relationship between personality and performance in small groups. *Psychological Bulletin, 56,* 241–270.

Martens, R. (1969) Effects of an audience on learning and performance of a complex motor skill. *Journal of Personality and Social Psychology, 12,* 252–260.

Martens, R., & Landers, D. M. (1972) Evaluation potential as a determinant of coaction effects. *Journal of Experimental Social Psychology, 8,* 347–359.

Martens, R. & Peterson, J. (1971) Group cohesiveness as a determinant of success and member satisfaction in team performance. *International Review of Sport Sociology, 6,* 49–61.

Neil, G., & Kirby, S. (1985) Coaching styles and preferred leadership among rowers and paddlers. *Journal of Sport Behavior, 8,* 3–17.

Pessin, J. (1933) The comparative effects of social and mechanical simulation on memorizing. *American Journal of Psychology, 45,* 263–281.

Rees, C. R. (1983) Instrumental and expressive leadership in team sports: A test of leadership role differentiation theory. *Journal of Sport Behavior, 6,* 17–27.

Rees, C. R., & Segal, M. (1984) Role differentiation in groups: The relationship between instrumental and expressive leadership. *Small Group Behavior, 15,* 109–123.

Ruder, M. K., & Gill, D. L. (1982) Immediate effects of win-loss on perceptions of cohesion in intramural and intercollegiate volleyball teams. *Journal of Sport Psychology, 4,* 227–234.

Sage, G. H. (1978) Humanistic psychology and coaching. In W. Straub (Ed.), *Sport psychology: An analysis of athlete behavior* (pp. 148–161). Ithaca, NY: Mouvement.

Sanders, G. (1981) Driven by distraction: An integrative review of social facilitation theory and research. *Journal of Experimental Social Psychology, 17,* 227–251.

Sanders, G., Baron, R., & Moore, D. (1978) Distraction and social comparison as mediators of social facilitation effects. *Journal of Experimental Social Psychology, 14,* 291–303.

Schwartz, B., & Barsky, S. F. (1977) The home advantage. *Social Forces, 55,* 641–661.

Scott, J. (1971) *The athletic revolution.* New York: Macmillan.

Shaw, M. (1976) *Group dynamics: The psychology of small group behavior* (2nd ed.) New York: McGraw-Hill.

Silva, J. M. (1982) *The current status of applied sport psychology: A national survey.* Paper presented at American Alliance for Health, Physical Education, Recreation, and Dance Convention, Houston.

Silva, J. M., Andrew, A., & Richey, S. (1983) *Game location and basketball performance variation.* Paper presented at the North American Society for the Psychology of Sport and Physical Activity Annual Convention, Michigan State University, East Lansing, Michigan.

Stowers, C. (1985) Danny White: Back in the saddle again. *Inside Sports,* October, 18–23.

Triplett, N. (1898) The dynamogenic factors in pacemaking and competition. *American Journal of Psychology, 9,* 507–533.

Tuckman, B. (1965) Developmental sequence in small groups. *Psychological Bulletin, 63,* 384–399.

Varca, P. (1980) An analysis of home and away game performance of male college basketball teams. *Journal of Sport Psychology, 2,* 245–257.

Veit, H. (1970) Some remarks upon the elementary interpersonal relations within ball game teams.

In G. Kenyon (Ed.), *Contemporary psychology of sport* (pp. 355–362). Chicago, IL: The Athletic Institute.

Vos Strache, C. (1979) Players' perceptions of leadership qualities for coaches. *Research Quarterly, 50,* 679–686.

Wankel, L. M. (1984) Audience effects in sport. In J. M. Silva and R. S. Weinberg (Eds.), *Psychological foundations of sport* (pp. 293–314). Champaign, IL: Human Kinetics.

Widmeyer, W. N., Brawley, L. R., & Carron, A. V. (1985) *The measurement of cohesion in sports teams: The group environment questionnaire.* London, Ontario: Sports Dynamics.

Williams, J. M., & Hacker, C. (1982) Causal relationships among cohesion, satisfaction, and performance in women's intercollegiate field hockey teams. *Journal of Sport Psychology, 4,* 324–337.

Williams, K., Harkins, S., & Latané, B. (1981) Identifiability and social loafing: Two cheering experiments. *Journal of Personality and Social Psychology, 40,* 303–311.

Yukelson, D., Weinberg, R. S., & Jackson, A. V. (1984) A multidimensional group cohesion instrument for intercollegiate basketball teams. *Journal of Sport Psychology, 6,* 103–117.

Yukelson, D., Weinberg, R. S., Richardson, P., & Jackson, A. V. (1983) Interpersonal attraction and leadership within collegiate sport teams. *Journal of Sport Behavior, 6,* 28–36.

Zajonc, R. B. (1965) Social facilitation. *Science, 149,* 269–274.

Zander, A. (1976) The psychology of removing group members and recruiting new ones. *Human Relations, 10,* 969–987.

Aggression and Violence in Sport

INTRODUCTION

That we live in a world replete with acts of aggression or violence is undeniable. The media are filled daily with examples of man's inhumanity to man (and animals); in the United States, senseless murders occur at the rate of one every twenty-three minutes, a rape is committed every six minutes, and a case of aggravated assault occurs every forty-nine seconds (Coleman, Butcher, and Carson, 1984). Instances of child and wife abuse are so numerous as to stagger the imagination. To quote Straus, Gelles, and Steinmetz (1980, p. 3):

> Drive down any street in America. More than one household in six has been the scene of a spouse striking his or her partner last year (1979). Three American households in five (which have children living at home), have reverberated with the sounds of parents hitting their children. . . . Over all, every other house in America is the scene of family violence at least once a year.

In addition to these more notorious manifestations of aggression, our ears are filled with the many sounds of violence. Angry mates exchanging unpleasantries, teenage groups jousting with each other verbally, harried cab drivers shouting at each other over traffic snarls, and angry fans at sporting events hurling epithets at each other or at some carefully chosen player target are everyday occurrences. On other continents, wars seem at times to be a dime a dozen, and brutality arising out of racial, ethnic, or religious disputes is commonplace. We indeed appear to live in an aggressive world, and this aggression often spills over into the realm of sport in a variety of ways. For a brief *chronology of recent sport violence*, the reader is referred to table 7.1. These manifestations of aggression in sport will constitute the intellectual menu for the remainder of the chapter.

AGGRESSION DEFINED

To put it mildly, the term aggression is a ubiquitous one. On the one hand, aggression is an admired trait in our society. The person from the ghetto who works hard to become a success or the highly motivated young business executive with lofty ambitions is thought to be aggressive. The general belief is that they would not be where they are without some aggressiveness. Captains of American industry are widely held in esteem for their aggressive qualities. This type of aggression is labeled as prosocial by social scientists.

On the other side of the coin are the people whose aggressions result in much pain and suffering for others, aggression gone awry. This tawdry end of the aggression continuum is of much interest to social scientists of all persuasions because of the emotional and monetary toll involved. This type of aggression is known as *antisocial.*

Somewhere generally but not exclusively in the middle of the scale is aggression in sport. Most of the examples of aggression in the athletic world are not criminal acts, but they are of concern because people do get hurt in the process. In the case of the occasional deaths associated with sport violence, most of these involve unruly fans rather than the players, and we shall address this issue shortly. But first let us proceed with a definition of aggression.

According to *Webster's New Twentieth Century Dictionary* (1984), aggression is derived from the Latin *ad* and *gradi* (to step) or from *aggredi* (to attack, to go to). Taking these etymological roots and putting them into a psychological context, we define aggression in terms of several properties to include aversiveness, intent, and victim unwillingness (Geen, Beatty, and Arkin, 1984). The first step in an aggressive act is the delivery of an aversive stimulus to another person. This aggressive stimulus

Table 7.1 A Recent Chronology of Sports Violence

1968	A riot at a soccer match in Buenos Aires, Argentina, kills 74 and injures at least 150 more.
1971	Celebration over the World Series triumph of the Pittsburgh Pirates leaves two dead. An additional dozen rapes are linked to the "celebration."
1971	Soccer rioting in Kayseri, Turkey, kills 400 and injures 600.
1971	Soccer riot in Glasgow, Scotland, kills 66 and injures 140.
1973	Paul Smithers, a seventeen-year-old hockey player, is convicted of manslaughter after killing an opposing player in a Toronto, Canada, parking lot following a hockey game.
1975	David Forbes of the NHL Boston Bruins is charged with aggravated assault by use of a dangerous weapon after attacking an opponent during a hockey match. After more than a week of testimony and 18 hours of jury deliberation, Forbes is acquitted.
1975	*Nabozny v. Barnhill* lawsuit is lodged when a youth soccer goalie is kicked in the head by an opponent.
1976	*Bourque v. Duplechin* lawsuit is filed when a twenty-year-old baseball infielder suffers a broken jaw and eight loosened teeth after being taken out on a double play by an opponent.
1976	*Hogensen v. Williamson* lawsuit is filed when a junior high football player suffers a neck injury when assaulted by his coach at practice.
1977	Rudy Tomjanovich of the NBA Houston Rockets suffers critical facial and skull injuries during a brawl when attacked by Kermit Washington of the Los Angeles Lakers.
1978	Daryl Stingley of the NFL New England Patriots is left quadriplegic after sustaining a crippling blow from Jack Tatum of the Oakland Raiders.
1982	Twenty-five policemen are hospitalized in Tallahassee, Florida, after fights erupted at the end of the Florida-Florida State college football game.
1984	Celebrations over the World Series triumph by the Detroit Tigers fans leave 16 injured and much related property damage to stores, businesses, and police cars.
1985	Soccer rioting in Brussels, Belgium, kills 38 and injures 437 others.

might take the form of a verbal insult, a punch in the nose, or a bullet in the back. A second property of aggression has to do with *intent.* The person who is being aggressive must intend to do harm to the victim. The thief who hits you over the head in order to steal the contents of your wallet or handbag is being aggressive; his intent is to do you harm. On the other hand, physicians often inflict pain upon their clients, but the intent is to cure or heal rather than harm. Thirdly, aggression involves an *unwilling victim.* Few of us have any desire to be hit over the head for a few dollars. However, there are masochists who willingly accept the infliction of pain from others; again, as in the case of the physician, this would not constitute aggression.

Cox (1985) adds a fourth dimension to the previous three, namely *expectancy of success.* Little aggression would likely take place in the absence of some reasonable assurance that the act would be successful in some way.

All things considered, it appears that aggression is defined as the infliction of an aversive stimulus upon one person by another, an act committed with intent to harm, one perpetrated against an unwilling victim, and done with the expectancy that the behavior will be successful.

Dimensions of Aggression

Now that we have arrived at a definition of aggression, a brief look at some related dimen-

HIGHLIGHT 7.1
A Longitudinal
Study of Prosocial
and Aggressive
Behavior

Leonard Eron in 1987 completed a twenty-two-year study of prosocial and aggressive behavior that began in 1960 when more than six hundred third graders (ages seven to nine) from one county in New York were interviewed and tested along with 75 percent of their parents. Aggression was assessed through peer nominations by the use of such questions as "Who pushes or shoves children?" Prosocial behaviors were gathered in the same way with questions such as "Who says 'excuse me' even if they have not done anything bad?" and "Who will never fight even when picked on?" Three salient correlates of aggression that were picked up through the testing and parent interviews were: (1) the less nurturant and accepting the parents were, the higher the levels of aggression displayed; (2) the more the child was punished for aggression, the more aggressive he or she was at school; and (3) the less the child identified with the parents, the higher the aggression displayed.

At the end of ten years, a follow-up was conducted through interviewing 427 of the original subjects. Perhaps the most salient conclusion reached at that juncture was that those who were aggressive in the third grade were three times more likely to have police records at age nineteen than were those not so rated.

Twenty-two years after the original study, 414 of the original subjects were again interviewed. The correlation between aggression in the third grade and aggression displayed in the intervening twenty-two years was .46, a hefty figure. On the other hand, prosocial third graders strongly tended to be prosocial adults as exemplified by educational and occupational attainment, low levels of antisocial acts, and overall good mental health. Aggression at age eight, unfortunately, predicted social failure, psychopathology, aggression, and low educational and occupational attainment.

Clearly, Eron's results add to the literature that points to early childhood antecedents of both prosocial behavior and aggression in adults.

Source: "The Development of Aggressive Behavior from the Perspective of a Developing Behaviorism" by L. Eron, 1987, *American Psychologist, 42,* 435–442; "A 22-Year Longitudinal Study of Aggression and Prosocial Behavior," 1988, *Psychology Update,* Winter, pp. 4–7.

sions is in order. Accordingly, let us consider five such aspects of aggression.

Provoked Versus Unprovoked. Akeem Olajuwon of the Houston Rockets and Mitch Kupchak of the Los Angeles Lakers were ejected from their 1986 National Basketball Association playoff game for exchanging punches, a fracas that led to both benches coming to the aid of their respective teammates. To quote Olajuwon:

"He threw the first punch and I could not help it" ("Sampson Answers a Prayer", 1986, p. 3B). If we assume that Akeem has the facts of the matter straight, we can say that his aggressive act was generated by the actions of his opponent. This, then, would be an example of *provoked aggression.* On the other hand, had a vandal randomly selected either of these two athletes' automobiles in the parking lot for an act of vandalism, the aggression would be considered unprovoked aggression. This random sort of aggression is less likely to affect the sport world than is the provoked variety. Many acts of aggression in sport take place as a result of some sort of verbal or physical provocation.

Direct Versus Indirect. Had our vandal broken the windshield or snapped off the radio antenna or slashed the tires of Olajuwon's automobile while he was playing against the Lakers because of frustration with his or her overall life situation, the aggression would have been indirect. This variety of aggression is commonly referred to as *displaced aggression;* that is, the aggression is directed at a source other than the one that created the need to aggress. However, had our villain been at the Rockets–Lakers game and become incensed because Olajuwon attacked his or her favorite player, left the arena early, and sought out Olajuwon's car based on prior knowledge as to its type and whereabouts, then we have a clear-cut case of *direct aggression.*

Physical Versus Verbal. Singling out Olajuwon and Kupchak for further analysis, we note that their altercation obviously attained physical proportions. In all likelihood, there had been a fair number of verbal exchanges between the two prior to the outbreak of physical aggression. More of the verbal than the physical type of aggression probably occurs in sport. Fortunately, we tend to talk more than we fight.

Adaptive Versus Maladaptive. In some cases aggression in sport may be adaptive. Our suspicion is that a certain amount of aggression is adaptive due to the physical nature of such activities as basketball, football, or hockey. An athlete in these sports probably cannot function without establishing the fact that he (or she in some cases) will not be pushed around and intimidated. This is not to condone the kinds of borderline sportsmanship and rules infractions that take place, but to merely point

Hockey players recognize that they will be pushed around and intimidated. But blatant high-sticking is clearly counter to the spirit of the sport.

out that, given the way the games are played and officiated today, an athlete simply must be aggressive. However, blatant high-sticking in hockey or fistfights on the basketball court have little adaptive value and should be considered counter to the spirit of sport.

Hostile Versus Instrumental. Aggression may also be viewed in terms of the reinforcement that is sought through its use. For example, it is generally known by those who play high-level slowpitch softball that the pitcher is inordinately vulnerable to being hit by the batted ball due to sheer physical proximity to home plate and the ample force applied to the ball by a strong and skilled hitter. Some players try to take advantage of this vulnerability by hitting the ball directly at or near the pitcher. To truly enjoy hitting the pitcher for the sake of it would be *hostile aggression;* that is, the reward here is seeing the person in physical pain. An acquaintance of one of your authors awards any of his players who intentionally hits the pitcher a six-pack of his favorite beer, clearly a hostile aggressive act. In the case of *instrumental aggression,* it would be perfectly acceptable to hit the pitcher not so much as to inflict pain or injury but more to promote a winning effort. Winning in instrumental aggression, simply stated, is a more important goal than the infliction of harm or injury. In both hostile and instrumental aggression, the deviance is rewarded, which of course increases the likelihood of its subsequent occurrence.

Hostile Aggression, Instrumental Aggression, and Sport Assertiveness

A fine line separates the various types of aggression and assertiveness in the sport situation, and these differences are reflected in figure 7.1. As can be seen, both types of aggression involve the intent to harm; such is not the case in sport assertion. The three concepts can further be separated on the dimension of winning versus harming; in *hostile aggression,* the goal is to harm; in *instrumental aggression,* it is to win; and in *assertiveness,* it is to play with as much enthusiasm, force, and skill as possible. Finally, the hostile assertive athlete is characterized by much anger whereas the athlete using instrumental force does so without anger; in sport assertion, anger is not an issue. Unusual force and energy expenditure are, however. The constitutive or formal rules (Silva, 1981) of the game matter in assertion, whereas they are violated, at least in spirit, by acts of aggression, regardless of type.

To illustrate how assertiveness might differ from the two types of aggression, let us return to our slowpitch softball example. A batter who is being assertive rather than aggressive real-

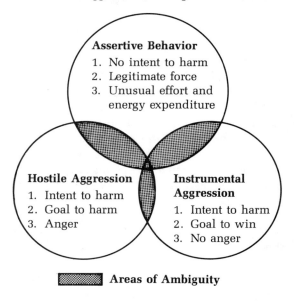

Figure 7.1 Relationship among Hostile Aggression, Instrumental Aggression, and Sport Assertiveness

Assertive Behavior
1. No intent to harm
2. Legitimate force
3. Unusual effort and energy expenditure

Hostile Aggression
1. Intent to harm
2. Goal to harm
3. Anger

Instrumental Aggression
1. Intent to harm
2. Goal to win
3. No anger

▨ **Areas of Ambiguity**

Source: *Sport Psychology: Concepts and Applications* by R.H. Cox, 1985, Dubuque, IA: Wm. C. Brown: "Assertive and Aggressive Behavior in Sport: A Definitional Clarification" by J.M. Silva, 1979, in C.H. Nadeau, W.R. Halliwell, K.M. Newell, and G.C. Roberts, eds., *Psychology of Motor Behavior and Sport—1979* (p. 199–208), Champaign, IL: Human Kinetics.

izes when he enters the batter's box that there are several distinct advantages well within the rules and the spirit of the game that are available by hitting at or near the pitcher. For one thing, the pitcher is very close to home plate. For another, he is often the poorest fielder in the infield. Also, a relatively vast expanse of territory must be covered by all fielders in the middle of the diamond. This would indicate that a well-hit drive in the area of the pitcher would be an intelligent decision. Should the pitcher take a shot or two off his body, those are the breaks of the game.

This illustration serves to indicate that there are arguable or ambiguous areas of overlap among hostile and instrumental aggression and assertiveness. The three are not completely distinct entities. For example, the forceful but clean and legal tackle in football can be viewed as assertive in that no intent to harm was involved. In view of the generally violent nature of the game of football, it may be argued that all tackles are acts of aggression. Equally plausible, however, is the hypothesis that all of them are merely examples of assertiveness. As for the goals sought, it is probably a truism that most if not all football players hold winning in higher regard than hurting their opponents. As for the third area of overlap, the anger as seen in aggression and the force and expenditure of energy in assertion are hard to separate. Collision sports, such as football, are possessed of a certain amount of controlled anger, something Kiester (1984) says can be put to constructive use. He cites the example of Conrad Dobler, the now retired offensive lineman for the St. Louis Cardinals, who achieved a great deal of notoriety through his brinksmanship exploitation of the rules and constructive use of anger. Much of his success he attributed to being able to do things verbally and physically that greatly angered his opponents, thereby distracting them from the task at hand, namely, playing their positions as well as they were expected to perform. John McEnroe, the tennis great, was also a master at turning anger to his advantage through distraction of the opposition.

Inferring whether aggressiveness or assertiveness has taken place in any particular event is a judgment call all the way. Contact or collision sports, such as football, offer many legitimate opportunities to injure and yet stay within the rules. Certain kinds of blocks, such as the crackback, can be applied legally and yet be intended to injure; a number of serious knee injuries owe their genesis to the crackback block. In baseball, the legal brushback pitch and the illegal and potentially life-threatening beanball are very difficult to distinguish. Often, these examples from two sports are labeled as aggressive or assertive based not on the behaviors themselves but on more subtle cues.

Tennis pro John McEnroe is famous for his skill at using anger to distract his opponents. But the contentious star is frequently less effective with tennis officials; McEnroe vents his spleen over calls made during the 1987 U.S. Open.

For instance, stares, glares, hand gestures, and verbal exchanges in temporal proximity to the crackback block or the brushback pitch could be used to determine whether the behavior was aggressive or assertive.

Aggression and Violence: One and the Same?

In defining aggression, it is appropriate to look at the relationship between aggression and

HIGHLIGHT 7.2
Bredemeier's
Conceptualization of
Aggression and Its
Measurement in
Sport

Brenda Jo Bredemeier has had a considerable impact on the way that sport psychologists and sociologists view aggression in the sporting context. She takes the position that any definition of aggression arises out of an implicit or explicit moral judgment, and research in the area must address these moral concerns. An important by-product of her continuing theorizing and research on sport aggression is a sport-specific measure known as the Bredemeier Athletic Aggression Inventory (BAAGI). The BAAGI is composed of one hundred items that purport to measure instrumental (goal-related) and reactive (injurious, harmful, or violent) aggression. Though recent investigations of the validity of the BAAGI have been equivocal (e.g., Wall and Gruber, 1986; Worrell and Harris, 1986), the instrument and the expostulations of Bredemeier are provocative and continue to spur research and theorizing about the nature of aggression in sport.

SOURCE: "Psychological Inventories Used in Sport Psychology Research" by M. Anshel, 1987, *Sport Psychologist, 1*, 331–349; "The Assessment of Reactive and Instrumental Athletic Aggression" by B. J. Bredemeier, 1975, in D. M. Landers, *Psychology of Sport and Motor Behavior II* (pp. 71–83), State College, PA: The Pennsylvania State University; "Athletic Aggression: A Moral Concern" by B. J. Bredemeier, 1983, in J. Goldstein, ed., *Sports Violence* (pp. 47–81), New York: Springer-Verlag; "Athletic Aggression: An Issue of Contextual Morality" by B. J. Bredemeier and D. L. Shields, 1986, *Sociology of Sport Journal, 3*, 15–28; "Relevancy of Athletic Aggression Inventory for Use in Women's Intercollegiate Basketball: A Pilot Investigation" by B. R. Wall and J. J. Gruber, 1986, *International Journal of Sport Psychology, 17*, 23–33; "The Relationship of Perceived and Observed Aggression of Ice Hockey Players" by G. L. Worrell and D. V. Harris, 1986, *International Journal of Sport Psychology, 17*, 34–40.

violence. Some researchers argue that to fail to make distinctions between them is to obscure some very important points (Bredemeier, 1983; Silva, 1984). For instance, Silva asserts that the failure to properly deal with the definition of sport aggressiveness has created disarray, leading him to propose that "confusion will be the epitaph of this research area" (Silva, 1979, p. 200). We are nevertheless of the opinion that the terms aggression and violence are sufficiently similar as to be equated within the present context. Accordingly, we would like to proffer the definition of violence proposed by Terry and Jackson (1985, p. 27): "Violence is defined as harm-inducing behavior bearing no direct relationship to the competitive goals of sport, and relates, therefore, to incidents of uncontrolled aggression outside the rules of sport, rather than highly competitive behavior within the

rule boundaries." The differences between this definition and the universally accepted one of aggression are minimal, and we shall use them interchangeably hereafter.

THEORIES OF AGGRESSION

Efforts at arriving at an understanding of our aggressive nature have taken many forms. One emphasizes the role of *genetics*. Though there is some evidence from the animal world in terms of the breeding of fighting cocks or fighting dogs, little substantiation for a genetic hypothesis exists in the human domain. Perhaps the closest example in humans is the chromosomal theory of aggression and criminality. In the 1960s it was hypothesized that many examples of criminality could be explained on the basis of such a chromosomal abnormality, the theory being that males with this abnormality were predisposed to a life of crime by chromosomal factors over which they had little or no control. Evidence gathered since then has cast much doubt on such a simplistic explanation for complex human behavior. Another theory that has provoked much inquiry concerning genetic factors has been the Darwinian notion of *survival of the fittest*. Based on this notion, it has been suggested that aggression exists in order to guarantee survival of any given species!

A third approach to understanding aggression has been to look at the role of various *neurological structures*, such as the hypothalamus, the limbic system, and temporal lobe pathology. A morbid but fascinating case of temporal lobe pathology is represented by Charles Whitman. In 1966, Whitman killed his wife and his mother in separate stabbings and then killed fourteen people and injured twenty-four others while perched atop the tower of the administrative building at the University of Texas (Austin). His lack of a history of violence coupled with a postmortem autopsy finding of what appeared to be a brain tumor led authorities to suspect temporal lobe pathology as a likely etiological factor in his aggressive acts. All things considered, however, there is no conclusive support for neurological processes as a major cause of aggression. Certainly, further research in the area is indicated.

Yet a fourth viewpoint has to do with *hormones*. There is some concensus that certain hormonal agents are involved in an interactive fashion with learned and cognitive factors in producing aggressive acts. Hamburg (1971), for instance, has related the increase in testosterone in males around the age of nine years to an escalation in aggressive acts as they become teenagers. In females, the ratio of estrogen to progesterone has been associated with irritability and hostility, particularly around the

menstrual period. Dalton (1961; 1964) has linked this increase in hostility to increased criminal acts outside and increased behavior problems inside the prison environment. Other hormonal precursors or mediators of aggression include hypoglycemia, allergies, alcohol, and drugs, such as amphetamines (Franken, 1982).

Two other significant approaches to unraveling the mystery of the genesis of aggression view aggression as cathartic or as a facilitator of antisocial acts.

Cathartic Approaches

The notion of reducing aggression through allowing its expression is neither novel nor unappealing. All of us at times have probably subscribed to the idea that "letting off steam" or "getting it off of our chests" is a constructive way of dealing with pent-up emotion. The release we feel at these times is often referred to as catharsis, which comes from the Greek *kathairein*, meaning "to cleanse." As used in the ensuing discussion, *catharsis* will refer to the release of aggressive tendencies through their expression. A number of theorists—including Freud, Lorenz, Ardrey, and Dollard and Miller and their associates—have generated scholarly explanations that are in line with the catharsis hypothesis.

Instinct Theory. Instinct theory has its origin in the expostulations of Sigmund Freud. Freud hypothesized that we are all possessed of a powerful life wish (Eros) and a potent death wish (Thanatos), with the former manifested in the sex drive and the latter in the need to aggress. Because the death wish involved self-destructiveness, the avoidance of harm to oneself could be avoided by aggressing against others. These tendencies toward self-destruction and harm avoidance Freud viewed as instinctual. Given Freud's hypothesis, it should come as no surprise that we live in such a stressful and war-torn world. Out of all of this, aggression is seen as being dissipated by its expression.

Alternative instinctive theories have been proposed by such contemporary ethologists as Ardrey (1966) and Lorenz (1966). Both theorists posit that man is like any other animal with the same need to aggress. For Lorenz, aggression is an instinctive behavior that persists because it facilitates the survival of the species. Because of its innate nature, it does not have to be learned. Ardrey talks in terms of *territoriality*, or the tendency of all animals to drive intruders out of their chosen territory. Territoriality is clearly seen in the behavior of animals, but is more nebulous in humans. However, the way we construct our dwellings, our locks, our fences, and our "beware of dog" or "no solicitors allowed" signs all point to defense of our territory. Our watchfulness with our young children and the increasing freedom we grant them as they mature are reminiscent of the ways animals treat their young.

Frustration–Aggression Hypothesis. Another approach with cathartic leanings is the *frustration–aggression model,* first proposed by Dollard, Doob, Miller, Mowrer, and Sears (1939). Though having similarities with previous models, the theory of Dollard et al. differs in that learned experiences rather than instinctive tendencies are emphasized. Their hypothesis is that frustration, or the blocking of motivated or goal-directed behavior, leads to aggression. Conversely, aggression is always preceded by frustration. Though this provocative hypothesis has served as the spark for a great deal of research over the past fifty years, it has fallen on rather hard times. For one thing, it greatly oversimplifies the issue by stating that frustration always leads to aggression, and vice versa. Secondly, in view of the rich abundance of other possible explanations, to assume that frustration is the only cause of aggression is too simplistic.

The Social Learning Approach

A point of view that seriously calls into question the basic tenets of the various cathartic theories is *social learning theory,* of which Bandura (1973) is a prime architect. Essentially, this theoretical stance asserts that aggression is reinforced rather than alleviated or lessened by aggression. Two primary mechanisms are at work here, namely, *reinforcement* and *modeling.* Instances in which unacceptable or aggressive behavior are reinforced increase rather than reduce the likelihood of their future occurrence, which is consistent with everything the behaviorists have validated in their theorizing, research, and application. Aggressive acts on the part of players that are reinforced by either tacit approval or by failure to punish on the part of a coach or parent may be seen as acceptable and therefore are reinforced. As for modeling, parents are usually the first sources of identification that a child has. A parent who displays aggression serves as a model for aggressive acts on the part of the child. The Little League coach who verbally attacks the umpires is likely to have the same effect on his young charges. Too, the aggressive athlete serves as a negative model for youthful admirers. As will be discussed in chapter 11, reinforcement and modeling of aggression are not to be glorified by people involved with young athletes in particular.

Catharsis or Social Learning?

The issue of cathartic versus enhancing effects of aggression is a complex one, and no easy answers are at hand. Perhaps the complexity of the whole issue is best illustrated by the furor generated over violence in television, whether in sport or otherwise. If the cathartic school of thought is correct, viewing television violence should decrease its incidence in the real world; if Bandura and his followers are correct, aggression as seen on television should promote rather than discourage aggression. No doubt the issue is far from resolved, and heated debate over both the theories and their application to sport and television violence will continue for quite a long while.

Our personal stance is that the role of learning in the development of human behavior can-

not be dismissed, and its relationship to aggression and violence is no exception. Perhaps our viewpoint is best expressed by Montagu (1975, pp. 438, 449):

No matter who or what was responsible for making us into what we have become, that does not for a moment relieve us of the responsibility of

---

HIGHLIGHT 7.3
The National Survival Game

An interesting movement that has received extensive media coverage is the activity known as *The National Survival Game.* It essentially is an adult make-believe war with pellet guns and wounds that never bleed. Cahill (1981, p. 23) describes the games as a "grandiloquent version of capture the flag" and that is precisely the major task of the survival game. The games are typically conducted on large plots of land for several hours at a time, and winners are determined by number of flags captured and/or number of "kills" made. The combatants are armed with guns that propel paint pellets at the various adversaries. Goggles are usually worn to protect the eyes, and camouflage outfits are commonplace.

Are these players macho men who are sick, twisted, perverted, demented, fascist, and fascinated by violence, as has been suggested by some, or are they simply people who are in search of a new sporting dimension? Little is actually known in the way of a definitive answer, but Joy Reeves has shed some light on the issue. She enlisted the help of the public relations director of the National Survival Games and was able to gather questionnaire data on 252 players (15 were females) from around the country. In general, Reeves found the participants to be young, unmarried, almost exclusively Anglo, and well-educated. Slightly over half were not hunters; an equal number indicated that they did not own a handgun. Two-thirds had scouting experience, but only 26 percent had been in the armed forces. Most had taken part in sports as children, and there was a slight tendency toward conservatism among the respondents. A factor analysis of the satisfactions derived from the games yielded one factor that centered around the comradeship offered, and a chance to test one's mental and physical skills. A second factor loaded on pretending to be in the military and a chance to dissipate built-up hostility or aggression. The third factor focused on a sense of achieving and control. Reeves also built a measure of sex role orientation into her questionnaire and, contrary to the macho image the games might project, traditional men played the games significantly less frequently than did nontraditional men.

Reeves is quick to state that her findings are more suggestive than definitive, but she has given us a look at an interesting activity, the National Survival Game..

SOURCE: "The Survival Game" by T. Cahill, 1981, *Outside*, Oct., pp. 23–26; "The Survival Game: Who Plays and Why" by J. B. Reeves, 1986, *Sociology of Sport Journal, 3*, 57–61.

endeavoring to make ourselves over into what we ought to be. . . . To suggest that man is born ineradicably aggressive, warlike, and violent is to do violence to the facts. To maintain that he is innately already "wired" or "programmed" for aggression is to render confusion worse confounded, to exhibit a failure to understand the pivotally most consequential fact about the nature of man. That fact is not that man becomes what he is predetermined to become, but that he becomes, as a human being, whatever—within his genetic limitations—he learns to be.

FACTORS PROMOTING AGGRESSION

A virtually unlimited number of factors may cause or facilitate aggression. Some are of a physical nature: heat, noise, and crowding. Others, such as modeling, reinforcement, and deindividuation, are psychological forces. At the sociological level, one of the more interesting phenomena is hooliganism. Too, no discussion of aggression and violence would be complete without a look at the role of the various media in promoting such misbehavior.

Physical Factors

Three physical factors contribute in a complex fashion to create or promote aggressive acts. They are heat, noise, and crowding.

Heat. There has been some research substantiation for the assumption that tempers tend to flare proportionally to increases in temperature. However, research by Baron (1977) has cast some doubt on this linear explanation; he suggests that the relationship between heat and acts of aggression is actually curvilinear. This relationship is shown in figure 7.2. As can be seen, aggressive episodes are low in frequency at the temperature extremes; too high or too low temperature actually serves to limit the kinds of

Figure 7.2 Relationship between Temperature and Aggression

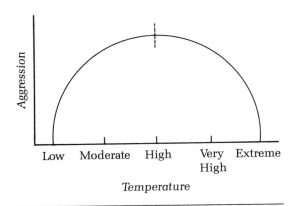

SOURCE: *Human Motivation* (p. 294) by R.E. Franken, 1982, Monterey, CA: Brooks/Cole.

arousal and human interaction that lead to violence. Clearly, there may be an optimal temperature in which aggression flourishes. Further substantiation for this curvilinear explanation was offered by Baron and Ransberger when they demonstrated its existence in a study of temperature and the incidence of riots in large U.S. cities. This relationship between temperature and riots is presented in figure 7.3. Obviously, riots are linked to temperature in a curvilinear fashion. Riots are infrequent below temperatures of 55° and above 95°F. How all this relates to sport violence is unclear because of a paucity of research on temperature and sport behavior. Undoubtedly, however, those hot baseball or soccer stadia or those steamy, sweaty, smoke-filled basketball arenas must in some way contribute to instances of player or fan aggression that take place from time to time.

Noise. Though there is little research in the area of noise and sport violence, the roar of the crowd is likely to be a factor in increasing arousal. Concomitantly, the likelihood of aggression is greater in heightened states of

Figure 7.3 Relationship between Ambient Temperature and Riots

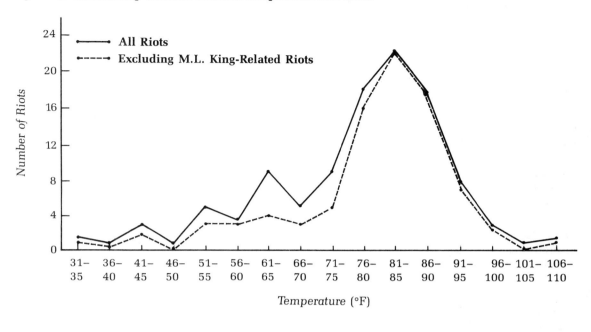

SOURCE: "Ambient Temperature and the Occurrence of Collective Violence: The 'Long Hot Summer' Revisited" by R. Baron and V. Ransberger, 1978, *Journal of Personality and Social Psychology, 36,* 351–360.

arousal. Part of the home advantage so well documented in sport and discussed in chapter 6, is the noise factor. Basketball coaches intentionally place the visitors' bench behind the home team's band, and football cheerleaders exhort the home crowd to drown out the opponent's signals. Although the intent in these instances is not to create aggression, noisy outbursts such as these can promote already existing hostile feelings or emotions.

Donnerstein and Wilson (1976) have demonstrated a link between noise and aggression, though not in a sport setting. They exposed students to either 55- or 95-decibel bursts of noise while the students were administering electric shocks to a confederate of the researchers. Students exposed to the higher noise level delivered more shock to the confederate than did the low noise intensity group. If we can extrapolate from the results of this research to the world of athletics, we can infer a possible relationship between noise and aggression. Perhaps Franken (1982, p. 290) says it best: "Noise does not seem to evoke aggression by itself. Rather, noise simply facilitates this behavior if it has already been evoked." Obviously, more sport-related research linking noise and aggression needs to be conducted.

Crowding. Rathus and Nevid (1980) indicate that the world population doubled between 1930 and 1975, predict it should double again to around 8 billion people by the year 2010, and suggest that if such a growth rate were to continue, there would be 128 billion people looking for elbow room on this planet in the year

2150. In and of itself, this does not represent a problem of crowding according to Berkowitz (1986), but more one of density. Density is thought of as the actual amount of physical space and the people filling it whereas crowding is the psychological stress response created by the problems of density. How all of this relates to aggression is not clear. Freedman (1975), after reviewing the available research, concluded that crowding itself is not a causative factor in aggression, but is most definitely a facilitator when the propensity for hostility already exists.

What emerges from the research in heat, noise, and crowding is the conclusion that they are more facilitators than causes of aggression; that is, they interact with other variables to produce aggression in situations in which the propensity for hostile action already exists. One does not have to look far in the world of sport to find applications for this generalization. The heat generated by the sun and/or lots of warm bodies coupled with the roar of the crowd and accentuated by a moving, shoving mass of people has contributed to more than one act of sport violence.

Psychological Factors

A number of psychological variables are related to the expression of aggression. Though modeling and reinforcement were discussed briefly earlier in this chapter, a more detailed elaboration on them will be made. Too, the role of external rewards will be discussed. Finally, the effects of deindividuation and becoming inured to violence will be accorded proper mention.

Vicarious Reinforcement and Modeling. According to Silva (1984, p. 268), one of the main promoters and maintainers of aggressive behavior in sport is *vicarious reinforcement* or what he calls "the tendency to repeat behaviors that we observe others rewarded for perform-

ing." A related concept is vicarious punishment. In defining the term, Silva says: "We are less likely to perform a behavior that we have seen another individual being punished for doing."

To Bandura (1973), the acquisition of behavior through either vicarious reinforcement or vicarious punishment is greatly mediated by model and observer similarity, by reward and punishment intensity, by setting similarity, and the status of the model being observed. As might be expected, the greater the similarity between the model and the observer, the greater is the likelihood of any given behavior being repeated. Reward value is rather obvious in this context; something meaningful to an individual is likely to be pursued with vigor. Also, if the setting in which a behavior is to be performed is similar to that in which it was originally observed and vicariously reinforced, the greater the transfer will be. Finally, the status of the model for the observer is critical; young aspiring athletes emulate their heroes, which of course is one of the reasons why positive role models should be promoted and negative ones downplayed.

The relationship of these variables advanced by Bandura to aggression in sport is reasonably obvious. Youngsters viewing aggressive models with whom they strongly identify and whose sport they themselves play are prone to believe that aggression is an acceptable behavior. Trial and reinforcement, coupled with the strengthening properties of the previous vicarious reinforcement, lay a firm foundation for the maintenance of aggressive sport behavior.

Direct External Rewards. Bandura (1973) has identified four forms of external reward that are operative in human interactions, and their applicability to sport is undeniable. One is *tangible reward*. Perhaps the most powerful of these tangible rewards is money. If being aggressive means more money in the personal coffers, then aggression it shall be. In a highly publicized incident from the football world in the 1970s, some members of the coaching staff at a major university in the Southwest offered various amounts of money to players on the specialty teams for tackles, breaking up wedges, kicks into the end zone, and so forth. Being particularly assertive (if not aggressive) was highly prized and rewarded accordingly. As the reader may suspect, this external reward system was met with disfavor among the various organizations that govern the conduct of intercollegiate athletics. Money is not the only tangible reward available; intimidation of opponents or officials in order to gain an advantage is not unknown to sport, and it serves as a powerful reinforcer for some athletes and coaches.

A second external reward is *status reward;* being aggressive in many sports carries with it a certain amount of respect and recognition among peers. Too, the use of nicknames connoting and reinforcing aggression (Killer, Assassin, Dr. Death, Enforcer) are liberally applied from a variety of sources to those who characterize higher levels of aggressive demeanor. This somewhat deviant form of recognition only furthers aggression in these athletes as their nicknames become a sort of self-fulfilling prophecy. You cannot be an "assassin" without working hard at it!

A third external reward, one whose relation to sport is less clear, is *expression of injury.* It is possible that hurting an opponent may actually promote aggression; it seems equally plausible that injury infliction may act to inhibit displays of aggression. Research in and outside of sport has not sufficiently established just what the effects are. For some athletes, hopefully a minority, the sight of blood from an opponent is probably reinforcing because it is evidence that the aggressive act worked. A sport such as boxing, in which intent to hurt is so manifest, would seem to be a prime example of the reinforcing properties of injury infliction.

A fourth and final reinforcer cited by Bandura is *alleviation of adverse treatment.* Aggression that reduces aggression on the part of the opponent is reinforcing. Establishing one's territory is inherent in this consideration, and failure to be aggressive in defending what one has is likely to be frowned upon by all involved parties, including the opposition. Loss of self-esteem and status with others is at stake here. We are reminded of the case of Paul Mulvey, a National Hockey League player who refused his coaches' order to take part in a brawl between his team, the Los Angeles Kings, and that of the opposition, the Vancouver Canucks. Mulvey's reticence to fight was poorly received by his peers and the team management, and because of his violation of the eye-for-an-eye norms of hockey, he soon found himself out of the league altogether. Such violations of the aggressive norm simply are not to be tolerated in contact sports.

Deindividuation. Another contributor to aggression, and one unstudied but not unrelated to sport, is *deindividuation.* The concept of deindividuation was introduced by Festinger, Pepitone, and Newcomb in 1952 and highlighted by research conducted by Zimbardo (1969). Deindividuation refers to the notion that, as density increases, personal identity and evaluation decreases and conformity to group dictates increases. The loss of identity or sense of belonging, in turn, promotes the incidence of aggressive acts. When the individual can no longer be separated from the mass and, concomitantly, individual responsibility for proper behavior is diluted, then deindividuation has taken place. Unfortunately, no research has attempted to relate deindividuation to aggression in sport. Too, the issue has not been satisfactorily resolved in research with nonsport groups. As has been the case with so many other variables, to make a case for singular causation is difficult when most human behavior is dictated in a complex fashion. In any event, loss of personal responsibility for behavior would appear to be explanatory in at least some cases of sport aggression.

Inurement to Violence. According to a widely held supposition, we have become so accustomed to violence in our daily lives that it no longer exerts a negative effect on us. The media report incredible numbers of acts of individual and group violence every day, and incidents of sport aggression are often highlighted. This exposure to violence on a continual basis tends to inure us to aggressive acts, thereby raising our tolerance for such behaviors.

Sociological Considerations

One of the more interesting phenomena associated with sport is soccer violence, something that has come to be known as *hooliganism*. From all appearances, it is a social class-related behavior and merits further attention. The *role of the various media* in fostering and promoting aggression is also a significant sociological consideration and will be addressed at length.

Hooliganism. According to *Webster's New Twentieth Century Dictionary*, a *hooligan* is "a young ruffian, especially a member of a street gang; hoodlum." The same source defines hooliganism as "the behavior or character of a hooligan; rowdiness; vandalism." Accordingly, the term hooliganism has been used extensively to refer to the behavior of soccer fans in Britain (Dunning, 1983; Dunning, Maguire, Murphy, and Williams, 1982; Marsh, Rosser, and Harre, 1978). Dunning (1983) indicates that hooliganism, in the eyes of those who engage in it, has become an accepted, almost normal part of professional soccer. Hooliganism's most central feature, the thing that marks it most, is physical violence. Sometimes hooligan violence is directed toward the players, at other times the officials and, more often than not, at rival fan groups. The violence may take the form of close hand-to-hand combat, the use of weaponry, or aerial bombardment from a distance. The fact that darts, coins, beer cans, and petrol bombs have been used as weapons is indicative of the intent to harm that is so integral a part of our definition of violence or aggression. In an effort to curb some of these hostilities, officials have resorted to segregating various fan groups by penning them together in separate areas within the stadium.

Dunning's opinion is that the behavior of football (soccer) hooligans is dominated by a misplaced attempt to demonstrate masculinity, with an exaggerated emphasis on toughness and ability and willingness to fight. He further asserts that the rival groups are recruited principally from the rougher segments of the working class populace. Dunning also feels that the soccer games themselves may merely serve as a forum for rival gangs to conduct their long-standing feuds; that is, fighting appears to be more important than watching the soccer match. Curry and Jiobu (1984, p. 250) sum it up as follows: "For the soccer hooligan, the soccer stadium is a battlefield, not a sports field." A final noteworthy observation by Dunning concerns the conformity to group dictates that characterizes the various hooligan gangs. Hooligans tolerate little individuality from gang members, and they reinforce group identification and conformity through ritualized songs and chants that they engage in at the matches. One of the more benign of these chants is provided by Marsh, Rosser, and Harre (1978, p. 66):

In their slums,
In their Nottingham slums,
They look in the dust bin for something to eat,
They find a dead cat and think it's a treat,
In their Nottingham slums.

Incidentally, the theme of most of these incantations is enhancement of masculinity.

Hooliganism has become an almost accepted part of professional soccer. Perhaps the ultimate act of hooliganism occurred in 1985 in Brussels, when drunken Britishers attacked rival Italian fans. A collapsing safety barrier killed nearly forty people and injured over four hundred.

Perhaps the ultimate contemporary act of hooliganism occurred in 1985 in Brussels, Belgium, when 38 people were killed and 437 injured by a group of young Britishers. Severe sanctions were sought against these people; 26 British participants were prosecuted for manslaughter ("Soccer," 1988). Some ways of controlling these hooligans will be entertained later in this chapter as a part of the overall recommendations for controlling aggression or sport violence.

The Media. Much ado has been made concerning the role of the media in the glorification of violence. Of particular concern has been the sex and violence issue as it relates to young, impressionable children, but the role of the media in promoting violence through their handling of sport has most certainly not gone unnoticed. Bryant and Zillman (1983, p. 197) have summarized part of our inconsistent feelings with regard to media portrayals of violence in sport with the following questions: "Why

does the public *tolerate* such extensive violence in its favorite spectator sports? Or is it the wrong question? Better, perhaps, why do people *desire*, why do they *demand* so much violence in their spectator sports?"

In answer to their own query, Bryant and Zillman offer three theories as to why people enjoy aggression in sports. One possible clue has to do with the *catharsis hypothesis*. Though the scientific support for the catharsis view is not strong, its popular appeal to the wider society is considerable. Its acceptance by the media has been largely with open arms. From cathartic theory it follows that engaging in or viewing aggression lessens aggression; if this is the case, then the more violence we observe, the more cathartic the effect will be. The media therefore provide us with as much blood and gore as we can tolerate, all the while assuring us that our aggressive needs will be even more ameliorated by these megadoses of violence.

A second explanation for our enjoyment of violence in sports has to do with *assertive dominance* over others, a viewpoint popularized in the psychological literature by Adler (1927). The need to be assertive and to dominate others, according to this theory, is among the strongest of human motivations. Opportunities for the expression of these strivings for assertion and dominance abound in such sports as basketball, football, hockey, and soccer, and the vicarious viewing of these dominance moves should account for some of our enjoyment of sport aggression. And, as we noted earlier in the cathartic approach, the greater the dominance displayed within the rules, the greater the enjoyment should be for the fans.

A final theory focuses on competition, or the *enjoyment of drama*. As Bryant and Zillman say, the catch phrase "The human drama of athletic competition" captures the essence of this theory. In this context of human drama, aggression is seen as exemplifying the ultimate in competition. The athlete who aggresses is only trying his best to win, and his aggression is proof positive of that fact. Part of our fascination with thrill or high risk sports in which the contestants actively risk serious injury or death may lie not in our perversity but in the high drama realm. Participants who are willing to tempt the fates so severely may represent the ultimate in intensity (i.e., competitiveness) for the spectators. An alternate and probably more widely accepted view is that people enjoy the high risk sports because of the likelihood of serious injury or death to the participants. It is hoped that this unproven perspective sells the human organism short.

No concensus is apparent as to which of the three theories is most valid, but general agreement exists with regard to the notion that sports violence has entertainment value. Three studies by Jennings Bryant and various colleagues have lent credibility to the supposition that spectators like violence in sports. In the first study, Comisky, Bryant, and Zillman (1977) looked at the sport of ice hockey because of its rough and tumble nature. In the Comisky et al.

research, the effect of color commentary was studied in terms of its relationship to viewer enjoyment. As can be seen in figure 7.4, enjoyment of play was not a function of actual roughness but rather one of perceived roughness; that is, color commentary emphasizing how rough play was when it actually was not and the downplaying of very rough play greatly affected spectator enjoyment.

Figure 7.4 Viewers' Perceptions of Roughness of Play in Ice Hockey as a Function of Broadcast Commentary

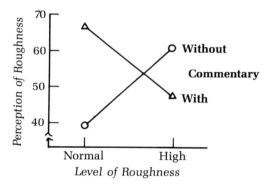

Viewers in the no commentary condition (circles) correctly perceived the depicted rough play as rough—that is, as rougher than normal play. In contrast, viewers in the commentary condition (triangles) perceived the normal play that was associated with commentary stressing roughness and idleness as rougher than the actually rough play that was associated with commentary ignoring roughness. Enjoyment of play proved to be a function of perceived roughness.

SOURCE: "Sports Violence and the Media" by J. Bryant and D. Zillman, 1983, in J. Goldstein, ed., *Sports Violence* (p. 202), New York: Springer-Verlag.

In the second study (Bryant, Comisky, and Zillman, 1981), professional football served as the sport under scrutiny. Male and female viewers were asked to rate their enjoyment of preselected plays from National Football League (NFL) games. As can be seen in figure 7.5, enjoyment increased as a function of concomitant increases in rough play. This was true for both sexes but was statistically significant for males only. Apparently, football fans like aggressive play from their warriors.

Figure 7.5 Viewers' Enjoyment of Plays of Televised Football as a Function of Degree of Roughness and Violence Involved

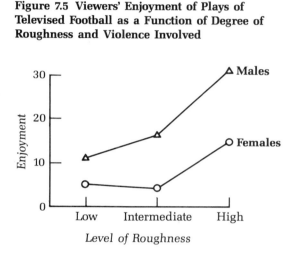

SOURCE: "Sports Violence and the Media" by J. Bryant and D. Zillman, 1983, in J. Goldstein, ed., *Sports Violence* (p. 201), New York: Springer-Verlag.

The third study (Bryant, Brown, Comisky, and Zillman, 1982) was done with the less violent sport of tennis as target, and the variable manipulated was how much or how little tennis players were perceived to like each other. Enjoyment of a tennis match was clearly a function of perceived enmity; when players were perceived as intensely disliking each other, enjoyment was high. Such was not the case when the tennis adversaries were thought to be friends. Competitiveness was also seen as much more intense when supposed enemies were playing each other. This material is presented in figure 7.6.

Figure 7.6 Viewers' Enjoyment of Identical Play in Tennis as a Function of Perceived Affect between the Players

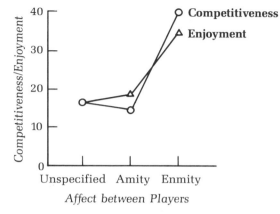

SOURCE: "Sports Violence and the Media" by J. Bryant and D. Zillman, 1983, in J. Goldstein, ed., *Sports Violence* (p. 203), New York: Springer-Verlag.

Collectively, these three studies suggest that fans really do like violence in their sports fare. How far this enjoyment of violence extends is unclear, however. Within limits, aggression is seen as acceptable and enhances spectator enjoyment. However, there must be a limit to this affinity for aggression. Russell (1986) suggests that the acceptance of violence is curvilinear; that is, fans enjoy aggression within limits but are not willing to endure excessive violence. Perhaps future research will answer this question, though obvious logistical and ethical problems are associated with such an undertaking. Manufacturing violence under laboratory conditions to see how far people would go before they would draw the line is impractical. Too, it is hoped that sport violence would not escalate to the point that we would have a real-world laboratory for the study of injurious or sadistic acts in sports.

Bryant and Zillman (1983) suggest that the media exploit violence in three ways. One is in the *coverage of violent plays.* How many times can you recall seeing a bone-jarring and injurious tackle in football replayed? Or the injury to Daryl Stingley of the NFL New England Patriots that left him permanently paralyzed? Or the devastating blow to the face of Rudy Tomjanovich of the NBA Houston Rockets by Kermit Washington of the Los Angeles Lakers? One encouraging development in this area, however, is the general policy of the various television networks not to give coverage to fights and other misbehaviors by players or fans at sporting events.

A second media exploitation method is to give articles the status of *features.* Many of our print media articles focus on violence; it is difficult to pick up a newspaper or any of the popular sport magazines without encountering a featured article on sport violence per se or one glorifying it in some form or fashion.

Finally, *promotions,* or promos, in television programming are exploitative. The filming of deaths in various high risk sports, such as automobile or power boat racing, and using the footage later to promote upcoming events in those sports appears to be pandering, as Bryant and Zillman so aptly put it, to some rather base human emotions.

CRITICAL SPORT-RELATED SITUATIONS AFFECTING AGGRESSION

A number of game-related variables have an impact on the expression of aggression. Summing across a number of studies, Bird and Cripe (1986) and Cox (1985) have provided us with five critical situations that affect aggression in sport.

Point Spread

When the score is close, aggressive acts will be in relative abeyance because a penalty suffered

at a critical juncture in a game can be decisive in determining the eventual winner. Also, when there is a substantial disparity in the score, aggression tends to be less because arousal is not so salient. Aggression is most likely to occur at a point midway between the two extremes.

Home/Away Factor

As was discussed in chapter 6, a general home advantage apparently exists in most sports. One of the more provocative hypotheses used to account for this purposed edge has been advanced by Varca (1980), who found that home basketball teams were more assertive in terms of rebounds, blocked shots, and steals, whereas the visitors were charged with more fouls. These results from Varca's work suggest some sort of dysfunctional use of assertion (if not aggression).

Outcome

Winning or losing makes a difference in frustration level, needless to say. Winners tend to display less aggression than losers. Temperamental outbursts on the part of losing players are reasonably common occurrences. They lend some support to the frustration-aggression hypothesis discussed earlier if one can assume that losing is in fact frustrating, an assumption that is probably a safe one in most instances.

League Standing

Though there are some conflicting data concerning this issue, concensus exists on the point that first place teams commit fewer aggressive acts than do their competitors. The real point of contention in this area concerns the other teams. For example, Volkamer (1971) found in a study of soccer teams that the lower a team was in the standings, the more likely it would engage in aggression. Russell and

Drewry (1976), studying Canadian hockey teams, found that the teams trailing the league leader most closely were actually the most aggressive. Again, however, the two studies are in agreement as to lower levels of aggression on the part of the first place teams.

Period of Play

In a study of hockey players, Cullen and Cullen (1975) found that aggression increased in a linear function for winning teams and in a curvilinear mode for losing units; that is, losing teams were lowest in aggression at the beginning and end of play, with most of the aggression occurring in the middle of the match. Winning teams, on the other hand, displayed more aggression as the game went on. This latter finding has drawn support from Russell and Drewry (1976) in their study of hockey teams.

Clearly, critical events and junctures in various sports partially determine the frequency and intensity of aggression. However, their relationship to sport aggression is far from understood and more research in these situational variables is needed. Too, broadening the data base beyond hockey and soccer, which have dominated so far, would be most illuminating.

VIOLENCE IN SELECTED SPORTS

Though many athletic events possess much propensity for violence on the part of players and/or spectators, three that have captured our imaginations—boxing, football, and hockey—will be elaborated on in the next several pages.

Boxing

Virtually no other sport besides boxing has as its avowed purpose the infliction of harm on the opposition; the clear intent in boxing is to render the other person in the ring unconscious if at all possible. Very little pretense is made about boxing skill, artistry, and outpointing the opponent. Boxing has been, continues to be, and will probably always be the subject of much controversy and public outcry. The sport is besieged on virtually every front; powerful lobbying directed toward cleaning up or abolishing boxing is being conducted by the powerful American Medical Association, and their protestations have not fallen on deaf ears at the national level of politics. Given that boxing has long been viewed as a brutal, barbarian spectacle, and given also that calls have been made for its abolition for several thousand years, the present brouhaha is unlikely to change much if anything.

As was noted in chapter 2, ancient Greek and Roman pugilists went to great lengths to subdue the enemy, including such machinations as wrapping their hands in rawhide and adding lead weight or metal spikes to their gloves. One legendary figure, Theagenes of Thasos, reputedly won one thousand four hundred championships and killed as many as eight hundred of his opponents in the process over a twenty-year career.

The modern era of boxing began in the 1800s in Great Britain and the United States, and it initially took the form of bare-knuckled brawls. Fights generally lasted until someone quit or was beaten into bloody submission. Though the contemporary version is slightly more humane, boxing remains a brutal sport. Perhaps the violence is best summarized by a quote from an anonymous boxer: "I don't want to knock him out. I want to hit him, step away, and watch him hurt. I want his heart" (Yeager, 1979, p. 124).

Interestingly, psychologists know very little about the psychological makeup of boxers. Virtually no psychological data exist on this intriguing group of athletes. Armchair speculation abounds but very little substantial data are

An example of the life-threatening potential of professional boxing occurred during the 1982 WBA lightweight championship fight in Las Vegas. In the fourteenth round, Ray "Boom-Boom" Mancini knocked out South Korean Duk-Koo Kim (left), who lapsed into unconsciousness and suffered extensive brain damage. Kim, who remained on life-support systems and never regained consciousness, was declared legally dead by a Nevada judge three days later.

available. In view of the considerable controversy that surrounds the sport, it would appear to be a fertile area for future research by social scientists.

Football

Though not as controversial as boxing, football is not without its critics. And the criticisms are not without some foundation in fact. Mueller and Schindler (1984) report injury data from 1931 through 1983 indicating that 893 deaths over that time period were attributable directly (e.g., head injury) to football, 572 of which occurred at the high school level. An additional 465 deaths were caused indirectly (e.g., fatalities caused by systemic failure as a result of exertion while playing the game, particularly heart failure and heat stroke). In 1983, there were 13 deaths, 10 of which were at the high school level. The per capita death rate for high school players was 0.30 per 100,000 players, and 0.00 for collegians. Clarke and Braslow (1978), partially in response to critics of football, reported statistics indicating that deaths attributable to football in 1964 in high school and college players occurred at about the same rate as did nonfootball related causes of death. In 1974, statistics indicated that deaths in football had actually decreased when compared with the 1964 data.

Aside from the fatalities associated with the sport, the problem of serious injury is of much concern. Atyeo (1979) points out that 30 players a year are rendered quadriplegic by football injuries. Yeager (1979) offers substantiation for these data in his reporting of figures from Pennsylvania's National Head and Neck Injury Registry, which indicates that 81 young men were rendered quadriplegic in a three-year period ending in 1977. In all likelihood, most of these football fatalities and injuries were inflicted within the limits of the rules and spirit of the game; that is, they were tragic responses to assertive rather than aggressive actions though, as indicated previously, a fine line exists between the two behaviors. All of these injury data underscore just how violent the game of football really is. No one knows how many injuries were the result of aggressive acts.

The National Football League (NFL) personifies the worst in the area of football violence. The NFL projects its injury rate each year at 100 percent. In other words, it is anticipated that all one thousand two hundred players will be injured to some degree during each season. Some of this grim injury projection is undoubtedly related to aggression. Perhaps the following quote from Dave Peurifory of the Green Bay Packers says it all:

It's vicious and barbaric. They try to make it safe, but they can't. It's like playing tag on a highway. You can try to make it safe, but sooner or later, it's going to get you. They draft the biggest, meanest, nastiest players they can find and line them up. Nice guys can't play this game. There is no way a nice guy can make it. Smart guys can't play this game. You have to be on a low mentality. It's like butting your head into a brick wall. . . . I'm no different. I'm just as bad as the rest. I'm on a different level during the season as opposed to the off-season. Football is not conducive to a good vocabulary and being articulate. I'm a degenerate, just like the rest. ("Page Three", 1985)

Similar quotes abound on the violent mentality so pervasive among professional football players. One of the all-time greats, Jerry Kramer, also of the Green Bay Packers, was quoted as follows in his autobiography:

Forrest Gregg tackled Andrie just as he crossed the goal line, and I was only a step or two behind Forrest, and I suddenly felt the greatest desire to put both my cleats right on Andrie's spinal cord and break it. We had been victimized by these stupid plays—scooped up fumbles, deflected passes, blocked kicks, high school tricks—so many times during the season that I felt murderous. I'd never in my career deliberately step on a guy, but I was so tempted to destroy Andrie, to take everything out on him, that I almost did it. A bunch of thoughts raced through my mind— I'd met Andrie off the field a few times and I kind of liked him—and, at the last moment, I let up and stepped over him. (Kramer and Schaap, 1969, p. 257)

These expressions of aggressive tendencies are indicative of just how violent the game of football can be, and little is being done about the precarious situation. Football, like boxing, runs along with many critics and few restraints on its violent ways.

Hockey

It is widely believed, and probably with good reason, that ice hockey is a violent sport. Perhaps Rodney Dangerfield, the stand-up comedian with the never-ending supply of one-liners, says it best: "I went to a fight the other night and a hockey game broke out." To the casual observer, the sport looks unusually rough. The players look rather haggard, few are in possession of their front teeth, speed of movement is breathtaking, sticks seem to be flying everywhere, and bodies are sacrificed with reckless abandon. The resulting perception is one of institutionally condoned mayhem.

Penalty calls would seem to support this perception; penalties for the 1987–1988 season were up by 1,275 at midseason. At the same juncture, there were 794 fighting penalties, one more than all of the 1986–1987 season ("Penalty Box," 1988).

Smith (1986) provides a typology with which to analyze sport violence in general. Smith's typology is based largely on material drawn from the legal area and has relevance to hockey. The first type of violence he refers to as *body contact*. In this instance, the body blocks, checks, and blows are inherent in the sport and the risks involved are accepted as part of the game by the participants. In legal terms, the players are consenting to receive such blows. Hockey, of course, is filled with a variety of physical acts that fall under the game rules but border on violence.

A second category of misbehavior is *borderline violence*. The frequent fistfights that break out in hockey would be an example. Potentially, serious injury could result from these altercations, but they seldom do. And if such an eventuality were to occur, it would be regarded as "part of the game" in all likelihood. Smith (1982, p. 294) quotes an unidentified NHL player as follows on this issue: "I don't see any violence in two players dropping their gloves and letting a little steam escape. I think that's a lot better than spearing somebody. I think it's an escape valve because you know yourself pressure builds up and there's no other way to release it and if fighting is not allowed then another violent act will occur." Players involved might be fined, but legal involvement is unlikely. The legal community tends to stay away from acts of this type within sport because the public mandate to do anything about it is not present.

The third leg in Smith's typology is *quasicriminal violence*, which involves both the formal rules and the informal norms of the game. Serious injury is apt to be involved and the legal authorities are likely to step in and impose penalties beyond what the league structure might levy. The most notable case of this type of violence in hockey involved David Forbes of the Boston Bruins and Henry Boucha of the Minnesota North Stars. Both players were sent to their respective penalty boxes simultaneously during a particularly heated match, and they exchanged verbal unpleasantries while in exile. Upon reentering the ice, Forbes assaulted Boucha with his hockey stick, causing extensive damage to Boucha's vision in one eye. Forbes was fined and barred from play for a short period, but was later charged by a Minnesota grand jury with assault with a deadly weapon. After much testimony and eighteen hours of jury deliberation, a mistrial was declared. As an interesting postscript, Boucha filed a civil suit against the Boston Bruins and the NHL, and an undisclosed amount of money was awarded to him in an out-of-court settlement (Smith, 1986).

The final category suggested by Smith is *criminal violence*. Here, the violation is such that the league sanctions will generally be transcended and the courts become involved from the outset. A case reported by Runfola (1974) is still regarded as a legal classic in sport violence. Paul Smithers, a seventeen-year-old youth league player, became so upset with game-related events that he carried the hostilities with him to a Toronto parking lot after a game. An opposing player was killed and young Smithers was convicted of manslaughter as a result of the melee.

That we have gradations of violence as indicated in Smith's typology is apparent. What is less clear is why these various kinds of behavior have become such an integral part of hockey. A number of possible explanations have been advanced by various authorities, one of which implicates the already beleaguered *mass media*. Without beating previously stated points to death, the media tend to promote violence in hockey. A prominent example is an article by O'Malley (1977), in which he perhaps unwittingly extols violent actions in a tribute to one of the all-time greats, Gordie Howe, on the occasion of his fiftieth birthday. O'Malley (p. 40) writes:

> It's not as if he played some Caspar Milquetoast game, shying away from the corners, relying on speed and finesse. He is of the generation that disdains the now accepted protection of helmets and he never was one to skate from a fight. After he was nearly killed from a check into the boards by Ted Kennedy of Toronto Maple Leafs—a skull operation saved his life—he returned as one who knows it is better to give than to receive, that retribution is best administered quickly and decisively. With Lou Fontinato of New York Rangers he participated in what many regard as the greatest hockey fight in the history of the NHL. Fontinato was the terror of the league then, intimidating everyone, pulverizing even the mighty Rocket Richard, but Howe destroyed him in that fight. He broke his nose, splattered Fontinato's blood over his face and jersey, and Fontinato never was as terrifying again.

Perhaps more troublesome than this sort of gratuitous glorification of violence involving adults is its impact on children, who are supposedly learning sport skills and sportsmanship. Research from a number of sources indicates that youth players admire aggressive players and learn much from these role models in terms of illegal or violent play. Smith (1982) reports a list of things young players learn from watching violent behavior by their role models who are playing on television. They are summarized in figure 7.7.

A second substantive explanatory mechanism for the learning of violence is the role of *significant others*. Parents, coaches, and peers are generally significant others in the lives of children. Parents are often intensely involved in the activities of their children, and their approval of violence, tacit or otherwise, is positively related to the incidence of violent behaviors in their children (Clark, Vaz, Vetere,

Figure 7.7 Illegal Actions Young Players Learn from Watching Professional Hockey

I learned spearing and butt-ending.

You sort of go on your side like turning a corner and trip him with a skate.

Charging. You skate towards another guy who doesn't have the puck and knock him down. Or coming up from behind and knocking him down.

Sneaky elbows, little choppy slashes Bobby Clarke style.

Hitting at weak points with the stick, say at the back of the legs.

Coming up from behind and using your stick to hit the back of his skates and trip him.

Butt-end, spearing, slashing, high sticking, elbow in the head.

Put the elbow just a bit up and get him in the gut with your stick.

Along the boards, if a player is coming along you angle him off by starting with your shoulder then bring up your elbow.

The way you "bug" in front of the net.

Clipping. Taking the guy's feet out by sliding underneath.

Sticking the stick between their legs. Tripping as they go into the boards.

I've seen it and use it: when you check a guy, elbow him. If you get in a corner you can hook or spear him without getting caught.

Giving him a shot in the face as he's coming up to you. The ref can't see the butt-ends.

How to trip properly.

Like Gordie Howe, butt-ends when the ref isn't looking.

SOURCE: "Social Determinants of Violence in Hockey: A Review" by M. D. Smith, 1982, in R. Magill, M. Ash, and F. Smoll, eds., *Children in Sport* (p. 298), Champaign, IL: Human Kinetics.

and Ward, 1978; Smith, 1979). Players also translate coaches' approval into aggression. Vaz and Thomas (1974) found a statistically significant relationship between insistence by coaches on being rough and aggressive and subsequent willingness to resort to unusual aggression on the part of youth participants. As for peer influence, youth hockey players live in an increasingly aggressive subculture in which masculinity and defense of territory are valued highly. To demonstrate this point, Smith (1979) reported the extent to which players agree with violent statements as a function of increasing age. These data are presented in table 7.2. It is apparent that the approval of violence in this instance is linear, with an increase in acceptance as a function of increasing age. Magnify these data considerably because of the stakes involved and you get an index of what the NHL represents in terms of violent norms and resulting misbehavior. Terry and Jackson (1985) report that more than thirty-one player minutes per game over a ten-year period in professional hockey were spent in the penalty box as a result of rule violations. The figure for the years 1981 through 1983 averaged nearly thirty-five minutes. This sort of violation of the rules is reinforced by findings of Widmeyer and Birch (1984) in a study of 1,176 professional hockey games over a four-year period; among other things; they found a correlation of .48 between games won and penalties in the first period of play. Setting an aggres-

sive tone early appears to be a productive strategy. Too, results from Russell (1974), in which a correlation of .43 was found between hockey assists and acts of hostile aggression, further add fuel to the raging fires of hockey violence.

RECOMMENDATIONS FOR CURBING VIOLENCE IN SPORT

Many recommendations have been made aimed at curtailing aggression in athletic events. The ensuing discussion will integrate the suggestions of a number of authorities to include Bird and Cripe (1986), Cox (1985), Freischlag and Schmidke (1979), Lefebvre, Leith, and Bredemeier (1980), Mark, Bryant, and Lehman (1983) and Nighswander and Mayer (1969). These recommendations will cover a broad front as the solution to the problem of sport violence must be a systems approach involving all interested parties. Accordingly, things that can be accomplished by management, the media, game officials, coaches, and players will be addressed.

Table 7.2 Acceptance of Violence as a Function of Age

	Minor Midget through Juvenile (N = 169)	PeeWee through Bantam (N = 313)	Junior B and Junior A (N = 122)
If you want to get personal recognition in hockey it helps to play rough. People in hockey look for this.	52	70	88
Roughing up the other team might mean getting a few penalties, but in the long run it often helps you win.	51	64	74
Most people in hockey don't respect a player who will not fight when he is picked on.	31	42	59
To be successful, most hockey teams need at least one or two tough guys who are always ready to fight.	43	57	84

SOURCE: "Social Determinants of Violence in Hockey: A Review" by M. D. Smith, 1982, in R. Magill, M. Ash, and F. Smoll, eds., *Children in Sport* (p. 304), Champaign, IL: Human Kinetics.

HIGHLIGHT 7.4
A Glossary of Sports Violence

Beanball A baseball deliberately thrown by the pitcher at a batter's head.

Board checking In ice hockey, throwing an opponent violently against the "boards," the wall that forms the boundary around the rink.

Brushback A baseball deliberately aimed by the pitcher at a batter's body, ostensibly to force him back from the plate.

Butt-ending Poking an opponent with the butt end of a hockey stick.

Chop block An especially vicious football technique in which one player, usually a lineman, straightens an opponent up while a teammate blocks down on his knees.

Clothesline A football tackle in which the ball carrier is hooked from one side or behind by an arm around the neck.

Crackback A football block in which an offensive player, usually a receiver feigning movement away from his own backfield, doubles back and at the last moment throws himself in front of the charging defensive player.

Crosschecking Using the hockey stick with both hands to block across the upper body of an opponent.

Earholing In football, a player's deliberate aiming of the top of his helmet at the hole in the side of an opponent's helmet.

Enforcer A term used in arena sports such as ice hockey and basketball to describe a player skilled in intimidating or, if need be, actually fighting with opponents.

Giving the bone In football, using the outside of the forearm to smash an opponent, usually in the head, as he runs toward the aggressing player.

Hand checking In basketball, using hand contact to control the movement of an opponent.

Head slap In football, using the open hand to hit the side of an opposing player's helmet.

High sticking In ice hockey, striking an opponent with the stick carried above shoulder height.

High tagging In baseball, purposely trying to hit a base runner in the head while tagging him out.

Jamming In football, hitting or running into an opposing pass receiver to throw him off his pattern.

Leg whipping In football, a lineman's use of his leg to trip an oncoming rusher from the side or behind.

Rake blocking In football, a technique in which a lineman jerks up his head from an opponent's chest, raking his face mask into the opponent's chin.

Raking In rugby, deliberately running over a fallen opponent with cleated rugby shoes.

Rip-up In football, a forearm uppercut, usually administered by either an offensive or a defensive lineman with the intent of catching an opponent under the chin.

Roundhouse In football, smashing an opposing player in the head with the inside of the forearm, usually from behind.

Spearing In ice hockey, poking an opponent with the point of the stick; in football, driving the top of the helmet into a player who is down.

Spikes high In baseball, trying to avoid being tagged out by aiming the spikes high while sliding into a base.

Tunneling In basketball, hitting a shooter or rebounder in the lower body while he is off the floor..

SOURCE: *Seasons of Shame: The New Violence in Sports* (pp. 248–249) by R. Yeager, 1979, New York: McGraw-Hill.

Management

At the highest level of intervention is the management structure of sport, and there are at least five innovations that they could implement in an effort to slow down the apparent escalating pace of violence.

1. *Abolish or control the use of alcoholic beverages at sporting events.* Abuse of alcohol interferes with good judgment. Most of us have attended a sporting event at which our enjoyment was lessened by one or several persons under the influence of alcohol. Alcohol abuse has been repeatedly linked with acts of sport-related vandalism in this country and hooliganism in Europe.

   American baseball represents a case in point. According to Gammon (1985), 77 percent of all fights among fans in major league baseball occur in the least expensive seats; additionally 69 percent take place at night, and 70 percent in the last four innings when the effects of alcohol would be most pronounced. Major League owners have responded in an effort to combat this problem by creating nondrinking sections in ten of the twenty-six stadiums ("Alcohol-Free," 1987). Certainly, this move is in line with results of a poll conducted by *USA Today* in which 42 percent of the respondents voted for the creation of nondrinking sections. An additional 14 percent were for a total alcohol ban ("Yes beer," 1987).

2. *Deal swiftly and firmly with acts of spectator aggression.* Management should take a very firm stand. Players and nonaggressive fans should be protected from those who would interfere with their right to participate in or watch sport. Cox (1985) has suggested that barring the flagrant first-time or chronic offender would not be a bad course of action for those having the power to do so.

3. *Make sports more of a family affair.* Perhaps professional baseball has done as much in this area as anyone with its sponsorship of family nights, cap or travel bag nights for children, and similar promotions. Certainly, bringing more of a family orientation to baseball and other sports should reduce aggressive behavior. This idea might be facilitated by reducing the price of tickets for families and by offering creative promotions that would be attractive to adults and children alike.

4. *Monitor the behavior of coaches.* Management should hold coaches accountable for their actions (or inaction) when they encourage or fail to penalize their players for aggressive acts. Athletes who are convinced that aggression on their part will meet with censure from the coaches are less

likely to engage in aggressive acts. Coaches are powerful others in the eyes of players and they should act the part insofar as acceptance of sport violence is concerned.

5. *Monitor the behavior of players.* Managers should make players aware of the fact that violence will not be condoned at the upper levels of the organization, whether peewee or professional. Penalties for violating institutional policy should fit the crime; as Cox (1985) notes, a $300 fine for a professional player who makes a half million dollars per year hardly serves as a deterrent to future misbehavior.

The Media

As stated earlier, the role of the media in promoting sports violence is a continuing source of interest for social and behavioral scientists. Though its effects are subject to argument, the media could collectively assist in at least three ways in defusing potentially violent episodes in sports.

1. *Do not glorify aggressive athletes for children and, conversely, provide as much coverage of counter examples to aggression as is possible.* There are many sensitive and humane athletes in the sports world, and every attempt should be made to present them in as favorable a light as possible to young people. Conversely, athletes who openly espouse aggression should be given as little media visibility as possible. Somehow, watching some oversized professional football player threatening to break someone's head if he does not purchase a certain product or subscribe to a particular sports magazine serves no healthy purpose that we can see. Such unadulterated nonsense provides a poor example for young players (as well as for those of us a bit older).

2. *Refrain from glamorizing violence.* Progress has been made, particularly in refusing to give airtime or print to fan misbehavior. The same restraint should apply in cases of player aggression against each other. The 1986 National Basketball Association (NBA) finals serve as a case in point. The celebrated altercation between Ralph Sampson of the Houston Rockets and Jerry Sichting of the Boston Celtics was replayed over and over on television and rehashed for days, especially in the Houston and Boston press. Little of value is accomplished by such media sensationalism.

3. *Do not attempt to promote hostility between teams.* There is already plenty of healthy rivalry in sports, and more than enough ego and money riding on the outcome, so that the media need not feed into the system. Sport is not war but it can be made to appear that way with a little assistance from the various media.

Game Officials

Umpires, referees, and line judges are an important part of various sport events. They are charged with the responsibility for making important split-second decisions and rule interpretations that can greatly affect game outcomes. As a result, they can be a catalyst for arousing emotions conducive to player or spectator violence. Two procedures for improving officiating are suggested.

1. *Eliminate perceived officiating injustices.* Mark and his associates (1983) indicate that officials get themselves into hot water with players or spectators because they are perceived as having committed an injustice either in terms of applying a rule inaccurately or unfairly or as a result of a perception that the game itself is unfair, irrespective of officiating excellence. In the first case, judgment calls and decisions as to rule infractions are predominant. Certainly, blown calls or misapplied rule

interpretations can trigger violence. In the second case, judgments and interpretations are secondary to the fact that the rules of the game themselves are seen as unfair. Sometimes an official can be dead right about a call and still inflame the players or audience because they perceive the overall situation as unfair.

Going a step further, Mark and his colleagues suggest that the incidence of rules infractions can be reduced and the resultant violence lessened through proper implementation of two types of penalties, equity based and deterrent based. *Equity-based punishment* is an "eye for an eye"; for example, a basketball player fouled while in the act of shooting will be awarded not one but two shots. This is equity. As for *deterrent-based penalties*, the probation for illegal recruiting in intercollegiate sports is an increasingly prominent example; the hope is that these penalties will deter further excesses. With the proper use of both equity- and deterrent-based penalties, perhaps violence in sports can be brought within acceptable limits.

2. *Take part in workshops on aggression and violence in sport.* Obviously, clinics would be most useful for people who officiate the sports in which aggression is likely. Intuitively, it is recognized that some officials exercise more control over games than others; however, this is not to say that these same control measures cannot be taught. There will always be gradations of control over the way games are played, but all officials can be schooled better in the anticipation, recognition, and control of potentially explosive situations.

Coaches

Coaches are important determinants of the course of violence in sports. Coaches who espouse notions such as that expressed by a prominent college basketball coach ("Defeat in sports is worse than death because you have to live with defeat") or that of an equally esteemed professional football coach ("To play this game you must have fire in you, and there is nothing that stokes the fire like hate") are partially to blame for setting a tone for violence in sport. However, ways exist to improve on the current situation.

1. *Encourage athletes to engage in prosocial behavior.* There is much to be said for the athlete who treats the opponent with respect. A verbal give and take or a friendly handshake before and after a game can only serve to reduce violence. The coach should reinforce nonviolence, as when an athlete takes a very assertive blow without resorting to very aggressive types of retaliation. As Cox (1985, p. 234) says: "Acts of great self-control *must* be identified and strongly reinforced."

2. *Participate in workshops on aggression and violence.* Like officials, coaches should acquire an awareness of the counterproductive nature of sport violence, not only in their own immediate situations but also in terms of society as a whole. As the proponents of social learning theory would say, "Violence begets violence."

Players

Ultimately, the individual player must assume most of the responsibility for reducing aggressive behavior. Individual initiative in controlling aggressive urges must not be sold short. It is the responsibility of each player to remain under control. To try to sell anything less than that is to abrogate each person's responsibility for emotional self-governance. We are all too quick to project the blame on our provocateurs, but such projections should in no way be

Ultimately, each player is responsible for reducing aggressive behavior.

accepted or reinforced. Accordingly, each player should volunteer to take part in programs aimed at helping them cope with aggressive feelings and actions. Visual imagery and mental practice are two techniques that should be valuable in learning greater emotional control.

Overall, if a carefully orchestrated effort is generated by management, the media, spectators, coaches, and players, a substantial reduction in sport violence could be effected. However, so long as social conditions that transcend sport are in effect, the task will be difficult; sport cannot do it alone. Nevertheless, we in sport should willingly do our part. We can have an impact on violence in sport and hope that our efforts generalize to the society as a whole.

VIOLENCE IN FEMALE ATHLETES

The general psychology literature strongly indicates that women are less prone than men to resort to the use of physical aggression when provoked. The literature in sport psychology relevant to this issue is virtually nonexistent. Female involvement in the sports most likely to evoke aggression is either nonexistent (e.g., professional football or boxing) or limited (e.g., soccer or hockey). As a consequence, female athletes are spared being involved in activities in which spectators or players are apt to lose control over their emotions. Generalizations about female athletes and aggression are therefore difficult to make; simply put, if they are not confronted with the stimuli most likely to evoke aggression, they will not display it. As women move more and more into the competitive realm, perhaps we shall see an increase in aggression on their part. The issue remains unresolved at this time.

SUMMARY

1. We live in a violent world, one replete with examples of man's inhumanity to man.

2. Aggression is defined as the infliction of an aversive stimulus upon one person by another, an act committed with intent to harm, one perpetrated against an unwilling victim, and done with the expectancy that the behavior will be successful.

3. Aggression may be viewed from a number of perspectives to include provoked versus unprovoked, direct versus indirect, physical versus verbal, adaptive versus maladaptive, and hostile versus instrumental.

4. Hostile aggression, instrumental aggression, and sport assertion are differentiated by intent or lack of intent to harm, by the nature of the goal that is valued, and by the presence or absence of anger or unusual effort and energy expenditure. Nevertheless, the distinctions among the three behaviors can be quite blurred in many sport situations.

5. Though there are differences in the eyes of some, we shall use the terms aggression and violence interchangeably because of the substantial overlap in their definitional properties.

6. Theories of aggression have been advanced that emphasize certain physical predispositions to include genetics, neurological structures, and hormonal influences.

7. Cathartic approaches to explaining aggression emphasize the release of aggressive tendencies through their expression. Various instinctive theories, such as those advanced by Freud, Lorenz, and Ardrey as well as the frustration–aggression hypothesis of Dollard and Miller are examples of cathartic theories.

8. Bandura has challenged the cathartic theory with his social learning approach, in which the role of reinforcement and modeling are emphasized. The social learning approach stresses the fact that aggression is made more likely by its expression as opposed to the cathartic notion of reduction through expression.

9. Our shared opinion is that the social learning approach has the most to offer in terms of understanding aggression.

10. Factors promoting aggression include physical, psychological, and sociological forces.

11. Heat, noise, and crowding are three physical factors affecting aggression. Though there is much research in the general application of these variables to the human condition, little has been done in the sport realm and their respective roles are poorly understood.

12. Vicarious reinforcement and modeling, external rewards, deindividuation, and becoming inured to violence are four psychological variables that have been studied as they relate to aggression.

13. The person who has been reinforced for aggression or who has seen it work for others, particularly in role models, is more prone to try it to see if it works for him or her.

14. External rewards of significance include tangibles (money, intimidation), status rewards (aggressive nickname), expression of injury, and alleviation of aversive treatment (evading coaches' wrath by being aggressive), and each is likely to facilitate aggression.

15. Deindividuation is a process whereby individual conformity to group dictates

increases as personal identity and evaluation decreases.

16. Becoming inured to violence may be occurring because we are so inundated with violence through the media. The ramifications for sport are considerable.

17. Significant sociological forces at work in creating and promoting violence are hooliganism and the media.

18. Hooliganism is a term used for the misbehavior of British fans at soccer matches. Displays of masculinity underscore much of the fan violence there; the participants are in actuality working-class gangs more intent on fighting than watching soccer. The culmination of hooliganism occurred in Belgium in 1985 in a riot in which 38 people were killed and 437 injured.

19. The media have not been spared criticism when it comes to sport violence. Why the American sports fan appears to thrive on a media diet of violence remains unanswered. Theories include catharsis, the assertion of dominance, and the enjoyment of the drama.

20. The media have been described as encouraging violence in three ways, namely, giving excess coverage to violent plays, featuring stories that glorify violence, and using promos depicting violence as a way of selling future sporting events.

21. Five sport-related variables influence the way violence is expressed. Point spread, the home/away factor, outcome, league standing, and period of play all are pertinent to an understanding of the way in which violence works in sport.

22. Three sports have been singled out for further elaboration because of their violent properties: boxing, football, and hockey.

23. Boxing is clearly the best example of a sport in which the avowed purpose is to inflict intentional harm on the opponent. In other sports, that intent is at least hidden behind sport assertiveness. Little is known of the psychological makeup of boxers.

24. Injury data suggests that football is, if not violent, a very dangerous sport at the high school and intercollegiate levels. At the professional level, manifestations of hostile thoughts and violent actions abound.

25. A sport that has been researched more than others, thanks primarily to the Canadian sport psychologists, is ice hockey. Using a typology suggested by Smith (1986), hockey can be analyzed for violence in four ways, each of which has some legal overtones. One is body contact in which aggressive acts are consented to by those who play the game. Borderline violence exists in the form of fistfights, and this is seen as "part of the game." In quasi-criminal violence, serious injury is involved and so are the courts in most cases. Finally, criminal violence, such as the Smithers case in which a youth player killed an opponent in the parking lot after a game, is the fourth leg in the Smith typology.

26. The media and the encouragement from significant others are viewed as prime contributors to violence in hockey.

27. Recommendations for curbing violence in sport involve changes in the way the games are viewed by management, the media, the officials, the coaches, and the players themselves.

28. Management needs to curb alcohol abuse at sports events, deal swiftly and firmly with fan violence, try to make sports more of a family affair, more effectively monitor coaching behavior with regard to the encouragement of aggression, and monitor players better to reduce aggressive acts.

29. The media needs to be sure that it is not glorifying violence, particularly where children are involved. Children need to see more prosocial and less antisocial

behavior from their sport heroes. Player and fan violence should never be played up, and trying to stoke the fires of hostility between players or teams is to be discouraged.

30. Sport officials are important in the controlling of sport violence. Useful goals include making the rules fairer and clearer to reduce perceived injustices; training officials in rule interpretation and application; and having officials attend clinics on the anticipation, recognition, and control of violence.

31. Coaches should encourage prosocial behaviors on the part of their athletes, and exceptional cases of emotional control in adverse circumstances should be reinforced. Too, coaches should attend clinics on violence management.

32. Ultimately, individual players must assume much of the responsibility for aggressive behavior. Taking part in emotional control exercises, such as visual imagery and mental practice, are strongly encouraged.

33. Little is known about aggressive sport behavior on the part of female athletes.

SUGGESTED READINGS

Bushman, B., & Bertilson, H. (1985) Psychology of the scientist: Frequently cited research on human aggression. *Psychological Reports, 56,* 55–59.

Seven major journals in social psychology and personality were reviewed over a three-year period (1980–1982) to determine books and articles that authors most often cited when writing about aggression. Bushman and Bertilson selected 35 references for discussion in their paper on the basis of the frequency with which they were cited. Most often cited in books was Baron's 1977 text, *Human aggression,* followed by Bandura's *Aggression: A social learning analysis,* and *The*

physiology of aggression by Buss. Berkowitz (40), Baron (37), Zillman (32), and Bandura (31) were the most frequently cited authorities in all types of publications. Overall, this paper would be a good starting point for those interested in reading about or researching the topic of aggression.

Goldstein, J. (Ed.). (1983) *Sports violence.* New York: Springer-Verlag.

Though several of the contributions to Goldstein's volume were cited frequently in the text of this chapter, a number of other important readings should appeal to the serious student of sports violence. This reader represents the starting point for any discussion of the topic because of the depth and breadth of coverage it gives to violence in sports.

Rainey, D. (1986) A gender difference in acceptance of sport aggression: A classroom activity. *Teaching of Psychology, 13,* 138–140.

The author gave three psychology classes examples of six sport competition situations and asked the students to rate the acceptability or unacceptability of each. Substantial sex differences were noted, with males endorsing nearly twice as many of the aggressive acts depicted. This exercise can easily serve as a springboard for discussing aggression in sport and in society as a whole.

Segrave, J., Moreau, C., & Hastad, D. (1985) An investigation into the relationship between ice hockey participation and delinquency. *Sociology of Sport Journal, 2,* 281–298.

Samples of Canadian youth hockey players and of nonathletes were compared to see if hockey serves in any way to ease the problem of delinquency. No differences were found between the two groups in terms of overall delinquency rates but hockey players reported a higher rate of delinquency of a physically violent nature.

Underwood, J. (1979) *The death of an American game.* Boston, MA: Little, Brown.

Underwood, a staff writer for *Sports Illustrated,* laments the impending death of college football because of the cheating, the brutality, and the loss of a sense of collegiality that have become the norm. Chapter 2, entitled "The Brutality," is particularly pertinent to the topic of aggression in sport, and a great deal of anecdotal material is put forth by Underwood.

REFERENCES

Adler, A. (1927) *The theory and practice of individual psychology*. New York: Harcourt Brace.

Alcohol-free seating not solution to some. (1987) *USA Today*, June 29, p. 7C.

Ardrey, R. (1966) *The territorial imperative: A personal inquiry into the animal origins of property and nations*. New York: Atheneum.

Atyeo, D. (1979) *Blood and guts: Violence in sports*. New York: Paddington Press.

Bandura, A. (1973) *Aggression: A social learning analysis*. Englewood Cliffs, NJ: Prentice-Hall.

Baron, R. (1977) *Human aggression*. New York: Plenum.

Baron, R., & Ransberger, V. (1978) Ambient temperature and the occurrence of collective violence. The "long hot summer" revisited. *Journal of Personality and Social Psychology, 36*, 351–360.

Berkowitz, L. (1986) *A survey of social psychology*. New York: Holt, Rinehart and Winston.

Bird, A. M., & Cripe, B. (1986) *Psychology and sport behavior*. St. Louis, MO: C. V. Mosby.

Bredemeier, B. J. (1983) Athletic aggression: A moral concern. In J. Goldstein (Ed.), *Sports violence* (pp. 47–81). New York: Springer-Verlag.

Bryant, J., Brown, D., Comisky, P. W., & Zillman, D. (1982) Sports and spectators: Commentary and appreciation. *Journal of Communication, 32*(1), 109–119.

Bryant, J., Comisky, P., & Zillman, D. (1977) Drama in sports commentary. *Journal of Communication, 27*(3), 140–149.

Bryant, J., Comisky, P. & Zillman, D. (1981) The appeal of rough-and-tumble play in televised football. *Communication Quarterly, 29*, 256–262.

Bryant, J., & Zillman, D. (1983) Sports violence and the media. In J. Goldstein (Ed.), *Sports violence* (pp. 195–211). New York: Springer-Verlag.

Clark, W. J., Vaz, E., Vetere, V., & Ward, T. A. (1978) Illegal aggression in minor league hockey: A causal model. In F. Landry and W. A. R. Orban (Eds.), *Ice hockey: Research, development and new concepts* (pp. 81–88). Miami, FL: Symposium Specialists.

Clarke, K., & Braslow, A. (1978) Football fatalities in actuarial perspective. *Medicine and Science in Sports, 10*(2), 94–96.

Coleman, J. C., Butcher, J., & Carson, R. (1984) *Abnormal psychology and modern life* (7th ed.). Glenview, IL: Scott, Foresman.

Comisky, P., Bryant, J., & Zillman, D. (1977) Commentary as a substitute for action. *Journal of Communication, 27*, 150–153.

Cox, R. H. (1985) *Sport psychology: Concepts and applications*. Dubuque, IA: Wm. C. Brown.

Cullen, J., & Cullen, F. (1975) The structural and contextual conditions of group norm violation: Some implications from the game of ice hockey. *International Review of Sport Sociology, 10*, 69–78.

Curry, T. J., & Jiobu, R. (1984) *Sports: A social perspective*. Englewood Cliffs, NJ: Prentice-Hall.

Dalton, K. (1961) Menstruation and crime. *British Medical Journal, 3*, 1752–1753.

Dalton, K. (1964) *The pre-menstrual syndrome*. Springfield, IL: Charles C. Thomas.

Dollard, J., Doob, L., Miller, N., Mowrer, O., & Sears, R. (1939) *Frustration and aggression*. New Haven, CN: Yale University Press.

Donnerstein, E., & Wilson, D. (1976) Effects of noise and perceived control on ongoing and subsequent aggressive behavior. *Journal of Personality and Social Psychology, 34*, 774–781.

Dunning, E. (1983) Social bonding and violence in sport: A theoretical-empirical analysis. In J. H. Goldstein (Ed.), *Sports violence* (pp. 129–146). New York: Springer-Verlag.

Dunning, E., Maguire, J., Murphy, P., & Williams, J. (1982) The social roots of football hooligan violence. *Leisure Studies, 1*, 139–156.

Festinger, L., Pepitone, A., & Newcomb, T. (1952) Some consequences of de-individuation in a group. *Journal of Abnormal and Social Psychology, 47*, 382–389.

Franken, R. E. (1982) *Human motivation*. Belmont, CA: Wadsworth.

Freedman, J. (1975) *Crowding and behavior*. San Francisco, CA: W. H. Freeman.

Freischlag, J., & Schmidke, C. (1979) Violence in sports: Its causes and some solutions. *Physical Educator, 36*, 182–185.

Gammon, C. (1985) A day of horror and shame. *Sports Illustrated*, June 10, pp. 20–35.

Geen, R., Beatty, W., & Arkin, R. (1984) *Human motivation: Physiological, behavioral, and social approaches.* Boston, MA: Allyn and Bacon.

Goldstein, J. (Ed.). (1983) *Sports violence.* New York: Springer-Verlag.

Hamberg, D. (1971) Recent research on hormonal factors relevant to human aggression. *International Social Science Journal, 23,* 36–47.

Kiester, E. (1984) The uses of anger. *Psychology Today, 18*(7), 26.

Kramer, J., & Schaap, D. (1969) *Instant replay.* New York: Signet.

Lefebvre, L., Leith, L., & Bredemeier, B. (1980) Models for aggression assessment and control. *International Journal of Sport Psychology, 5,* 102–110.

Lorenz, K. (1966) *On aggression.* New York: Harcourt, Brace & World.

Mark, M. M., Bryant, F. B., & Lehman, D. R. (1983) Perceived injustice and sports violence. In J. Goldstein, (Ed.), *Sports violence.* New York: Springer-Verlag.

Marsh, P., Rosser, E., & Harre, R. (1978) *The rules of disorder.* London: Routledge and Kegan Paul.

Montagu, A. (1975) Is man innately aggressive? In W. Fields and W. Sweet (Eds.), *Neurological symposium on neural bases of violence and aggression* (pp. 431–451). St. Louis, MO: Warren H. Green.

Mueller, F., & Schindler, R. (1984) Annual survey of football injury research, 1931–1983. *Athletic Training, 19,* 189–192, 208.

Nash, O. (1980) Confessions of a born spectator. In R. Dodge (Ed.), *A literature of sports.* Lexington, MA: D. C. Heath.

Nighswander, J., & Mayer, G. (1969) Catharsis: A means for reducing elementary school students' aggressive behaviors. *Personnel and Guidance Journal, 47,* 461–466.

O'Malley, M. (1977) Some day they'll retire Gordie Howe's sweater—If, of course, he takes it off. *Macleans, 90 (26),* 40.

Page three. (1985) *Houston Chronicle,* July 12, p. 3–3 .

Penalty box fills fast. (1988) *USA Today,* Jan. 26, p. 6C.

Rathus, S., & Nevid, J. (1980) *Adjustment and growth: The challenges of life.* New York: Holt, Rinehart and Winston.

Runfola, R. (1974) He is a hockey player, 17, black and convicted of manslaughter. *New York Times,* Oct. 17, p. 2–3.

Russell, G. W. (1974) Machiavellianism, locus of control, aggression, performance, and precautionary behaviour in ice hockey. *Human Relations, 27,* 825–837.

Russell, G. W. (1986) Does sports violence increase box office receipts? *International Journal of Sport Psychology, 17,* 173–183.

Russell, G. W., & Drewry, B. R. (1976) Crowd size and competitive aspects of aggression in ice hockey: An archival study. *Human Relations, 29,* 723–735.

Sampson answers a prayer. (1986) *Bryan-College Station (TX) Eagle,* May 23, p. 3B.

Silva, J. M. (1979) Assertive and aggressive behavior in sport: A definitional clarification. In C. H. Nadeau, W. R. Halliwell, K. M. Newell, and G. C. Roberts (Eds.), *Psychology of motor behavior and sport—1979* (pp. 199–208). Champaign, IL: Human Kinetics.

Silva, J. M. (1981) Normative compliance and rule violating behavior in sport. *International Journal of Sport Psychology, 12,* 10–18.

Silva, J. M. (1984) Factors related to the acquisition and expression of aggressive sport behavior. In J. M. Silva and R. S. Weinberg, (Eds.), *Psychological foundations of sport* (pp. 261–273). Champaign, IL: Human Kinetics.

Smith, M. (1979) Towards an explanation of hockey violence: A reference-other approach. *Canadian Journal of Sociology, 4*(2), 105–124.

Smith, M. (1982) Social determinants of violence in hockey: A review. In R. Magill, M. Ash, & F. Smoll (Eds.), *Children in sport* (pp. 294–309). Champaign, IL: Human Kinetics.

Smith, M. (1986) Sports violence: A definition. In R. Lapchick (Ed.), *Fractured focus: Sport as a reflection of society* (pp. 221–227) Lexington, MS: D. C. Heath.

Soccer. (1988) *Bryan College Station (TX) Eagle,* Jan. 9, p. 2B.

Straus, M., Gelles, R., & Steinmetz, S. (1980) *Behind closed doors: Violence in the American family.* New York: Anchor/Doubleday.

Terry, P. C., & Jackson, J. J. (1985) The determinants and control of violence in sport. *Quest, 37,* 27–37.

Varca, P. (1980) An analysis of home and away performance of male college basketball teams. *Journal of Sport Psychology, 2,* 245–257.

Vaz, E., & Thomas, D. (1974) What price victory? An analysis of minor hockey league players' attitudes toward winning. *International Review of Sport Sociology, 2*(9), 33–53.

Volkamer, N. (1971) Investigations into the aggressiveness in competitive social system. *Sportswissenschaft, 1*, 33–64.

Widmeyer, W. N., & Birch, J. S. (1984) Aggression in professional ice hockey: A strategy for success or a reaction to failure? *Journal of Psychology, 117*, 77–84.

Yeager, R. (1979) *Seasons of shame: The new violence in sports.* New York: McGraw-Hill.

Yes beer or no beer? (1987) *USA Today*, Oct. 1, p. 9C.

Zimbardo, P. (1969) The human choice: Individuation, reason, and order versus deindividuation, impulse, and chaos. In W. Arnold & D. Levin (Eds.), *Nebraska Symposium on Motivation* (Vol. 17, pp. 237–307). Lincoln: University of Nebraska Press.

PART · THREE

PERSONALITY AND ASSESSMENT

8

Personality Variables and Sport

INTRODUCTION

The study of personality has intrigued psychologists for most of the twentieth century. Sport psychologists have been no exception; according to Ruffer (1975, 1976a, 1976b), almost six hundred original studies of the relationship of personality to sport performance had been conducted by the mid-1970s alone. By way of update, Fisher (1984) sets the figure at well over one thousand. Though considerable skepticism has been expressed about the type and quality of inquiry done in many of those investigations, the quest for the link between sport and personality continues unabated. This interest arises out of a desire to find better answers to questions of importance to sport scientists, questions such as:

1. What personality variables are at work in producing the choking response in the face of competitive pressure?
2. What personality variables may contribute to good leadership from coaches and players?
3. Can personality tests be used to identify elite youth athletes at an early age so that they can be given the best of training for future athletic development?
4. Does sex role orientation relate in any way to performance among female athletes?
5. What unique features, if any, compel people to seek new experiences by jumping out of airplanes or diving into oceans, seas, bays, and lakes?
6. Are there personality predictors that might be of use in promoting fitness and exercise adherence?

These questions represent a scant few of the multitude that might be asked with regard to the personality–sport performance relationship. Before attempting to answer some of them, we would like to anchor the chapter discussion (and the remainder of the book) to a definition of personality, a discussion of various theories of personality that have guided thought and research, some reflections on argumentative issues, and suggestions for improving research in sport. We will then discuss what is presently known about three selected sport populations: the black athlete, the high risk sport participant, and the elite performer.

PERSONALITY DEFINED

Lazarus and Monat (1979 p. 1) define personality as "the underlying, relatively stable, psychological structure and processes that organize human experience and shape a person's activities and reactions to the environment." Essentially, what Lazarus and Monat refer to is the notion that a *core* personality exists and is more or less "the real you." In other words, there are core components of personality by which you know yourself and are known by others, and these are generally quite stable and unchanging. For the most part a healthy self-concept is stable and unchanging, just as is being aggressive. Similarly, being warm and friendly and trusting of others are core traits. They may be buffeted by life events, but generally will withstand these trials and tribulations with little alteration. The core you, simply put, does not change much once it is set. Think of your parents or grandparents as examples; how much are they changing or likely to change their basic patterns of reacting to life? Not much, we suspect!

Looking at only the personality core as a means of explaining behavior clearly has limitations; there is much more to each of us than a set psychological core. Allport (1937, p. 48) provides us with a way of incorporating more into the personality than the static core traits by offering the following definitional stance: "Personality is the dynamic organization within the individual that determines his unique adjustments to his environment." Though a bit laced with sexist language, Allport's time-tested work in the area of personality theory and research provides us with an additional facet or component of the personality, that of *peripheral states*. This is not to deny the considerable influence of the psychological core, but Allport's emphasis on dynamism allows for more changeable peripheral states to exert an influence on behavior. Some aspects of our personalities are always in a state of flux. For example, our responses to religious, political, or racial issues are often subject to variability. Too, daily events take their toll in such areas as depression, anxiety, and other related mood states. The dynamic interaction between the core (trait) and peripheral (state) portions of each of us composes the essence of what is known as personality.

Hollander (1967) has taken the discussion a step further by talking about a psychological core, typical responses, and role-related behaviors (see the schematic representation in figure 8.1). Hollander has maintained the core as conceptualized earlier in this discussion and broken the peripheral portion into *typical responses* and *role-related behaviors*. We respond to typical daily events with fairly predictable behaviors, but in ways that are more amenable to change than are the core traits. In other words, typical responses operate at a level slightly less entrenched than the core. Role-related behaviors are the most superficial, therefore malleable, aspect of the personality. Each of us is called upon everyday to fulfill a number of different roles, and we accomplish them in ways that get us by but are not always representative of our true core predispositions. How many times have you had to refrain from stating your true opinion about a life event because role expectations did not allow for honest expression?

Figure 8.1 Hollander's Model of Personality Structure

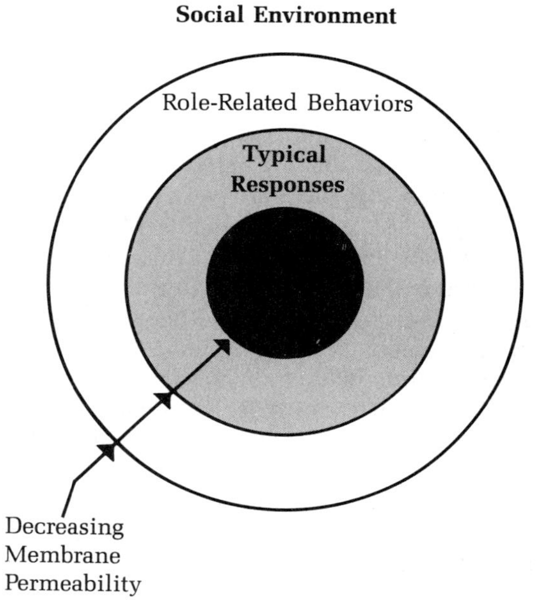

SOURCE: *Principles and Methods of Social Psychology* (p. 278), by E.P. Hollander, 1967, New York: Oxford University Press.

One final point about Hollander's model merits our attention. The social environment is a constant source of impact and pressure on adjustment. Role-related behaviors are the most susceptible to the influence of the social environment, whereas typical responses and the psychological core are increasingly less affected. This relationship can also be seen in figure 8.1.

THEORIES OF PERSONALITY

Theories concerning the nature of personality are numerous, all striving to explain why the human organism behaves as it does. These various theories have guided further theorizing and research about personality, and we will examine six of them.

Biological Theories

One theory advanced to account for behavior is the *constitutional theory* of William Sheldon (Sheldon 1940; 1942). Sheldon's theory takes the position that there are basic *somatotypes*, or body types, that are predictive of personality. For instance, Sheldon's *ectomorph* is characterized by leanness and angularity of build, and responds behaviorally with a high level of activity, tension, and introversion. The classic *mesomorph* is likely to be very muscular and athletic, and responds to environmental stimuli with aggression, risk taking, and leadership. It follows logically that team leaders would emerge from such a somatotype. Finally, the *endomorph* has a more round body type and reacts behaviorally with joviality, generosity, affection, and sociability. Jolly Old Saint Nick most closely serves as the prototype for the endomorphic individual. Clearly, the three somatotypes are stereotypes and, as such, they suffer from all of the shortcomings and criticisms of such a conceptualization. The reader is referred to Eysenck, Nias, and Cox (1982) for a review of Sheldon's theory as it relates to sport.

More closely related to sport is Dishman's *psychobiological theory* (Dishman, 1984), which is gaining acceptance as a means of predicting exercise adherence. Dishman's contention is that biological factors, such as body composition, interact with psychological variables, such as motivation, to produce an index of exercise compliance. More elaboration on Dishman's work will be made in chapter 13.

Psychodynamic Theory

One of the more well-developed, complex, and controversial theories about human behavior is the *psychoanalytic theory* of Sigmund Freud. The cornerstone of Freud's theory is that humans are inherently bad and, if left to their own devices, will self-destruct. This pessimism has fueled Freudian thought since its formative days in the late 1800s and early 1900s. The psychoanalytic model is an *intrapsychic* one; that is, the *psyche* is made up of an id, an ego, and a superego, with the id and superego in a constant state of conflict over control of the psyche. The arbiter of this eternal dispute is the ego, and its strength is a prime determinant of adjustment. Should the id win the intrapsychic conflict, a hedonistic thrill seeker in constant search of pleasure is produced. Should the superego become dominant, a dogmatic moralist is the end result. When the ego is able to arbitrate a healthy rapprochement between the pleasure-seeking id and the moralistic superego, a healthy, well-adjusted person is produced.

Unfortunately, the psychoanalytic model has focused almost exclusively on pessimism and pathology, and this preoccupation with abnormality has served to limit its applicability to the more normal manifestations of behavior. Inasmuch as sport participants, on the whole, appear to have no more and no fewer psychological problems than do nonparticipants, the Freudian model has limited utility for the sport psychologist. On a broader scale, however, psychoanalytic thought has served as an impetus for a mammoth amount of research and theory.

Humanistic Theory

A view counter to the Freudian model is that of the *humanists*. Beginning in the eighteenth century with the writings of the French philosopher, Jean Jacques Rousseau, all the way to the recent works of Abraham Maslow and Carl Rogers, humanists have adopted a stance that is diametrically opposite to that of the psychoanalysts. To the humanist, the nature of man is basically good and behavior, rather than being determined by deep, dark psychic forces, is free. The capacity for growth and change is at the heart of this personal freedom. In the analytic model, badness must be kept in check by laws, rules, mores, and folkways if the person is to adjust properly. Thus, when a person turns out bad, it is because society has failed. To the humanist, society with all its strictures is seen as a potential corruptive force; when a person turns out bad, it is because society interfered in some way with this natural expression of goodness.

Rogers accounts for the ultimate in adjustment with his concept of the *fully functioning person*. In Maslow's terminology, the person who maximizes his or her potentials across a broad spectrum of human endeavors has achieved *self-actualization*. Recall the discussion of self-actualization in chapter 5.

The Behavioral Model

A view counter to the previous models is that of the *behaviorists*. Behaviorism owes its origins to the work of Pavlov in Russia in the late 1800s and of Watson in the United States in the early 1900s. Modern behaviorists believe that behavior is inherently neither good nor bad; rather, it is the product of an interaction between genetic endowment and learned experience. This stance relegates the goodness-badness issue to its proper place in the eyes of the behaviorist, namely, in the realm of philosophy. With regard to the issue of freedom versus determinism, behaviorists are somewhat like the analysts in that they feel that behavior is determined. However, they differ on the mechanism by which behavior is stamped in. Traumatic childhood events are crucial to the analyst; to the behaviorist, reinforced early experiences are critical. Behaviorists also differ from analysts in their views of the extent to which these childhood experiences are changeable at a later point in time. In the view of the behaviorist, if a behavior can be learned, it can be unlearned, though not necessarily easily.

The behavioral approach has been warmly embraced by sport psychology. The behavioral coaching procedures discussed earlier represent one contribution from the behaviorists. The emphasis on modeling and social reinforcement as espoused by Bandura represents a second major offering. Most certainly, the performance enhancement and anxiety reduction strategies so integral to improving sport performance have had considerable impact on sport psychology practice and research. Finally, the use of reinforcement principles as a means of facilitating exercise adherence is another valuable contribution. In brief, the behavioral model, with its emphasis on learning new productive behaviors and unlearning old counterproductive ones, has been a bright beacon of light for sport psychology and the field of psychology as a whole.

Trait Theory

Much research in sport has been triggered by the trait (or factor) approach to personality as advanced by such psychologists as Gordon Allport, Raymond Cattell, and Hans Eysenck. Trait theorists contend that personality is best understood in terms of enduring traits or predispositions to respond in similar ways across a variety of situations. This is not to say that behavior is invariable; however, a strong tendency exists to respond in persistent, predictable, and measurable ways. Out of this belief has arisen a host of psychometric instruments that have purported to assess these various traits. (In chapter 9, Psychological Assessment, we shall elaborate on the more prominent trait measures.) Much sport research (and controversy) has been generated by trait psychology.

The Interactional Perspective

In an attempt to bring some clarity to the issue of personality within sport, an interactional model has emerged. The interactional perspective suggests that behavior is, in fact, an interaction of the person and the environment. The interactive model is summed up by a simple formula advanced more than fifty years ago by Kurt Lewin (1935), as follows: $B = f(P,E)$. A significant point here is that traits are still viewed as pertinent determinants of behavior, but not nearly so salient as the purists in trait psychology would suggest. Another important issue is the emphasis on environmental variables and their interaction with traits.

The simplicity of the Lewin model is very deceptive. Human behavior is never simply explained, and behavior exhibited while participating in sports is no exception. For example, trying to predict when a basketball player is going to "choke" in a critical moment of an important game is no small task. Undoubtedly, there are some trait-related predispositions to respond poorly in competitive situations that are pertinent to the present analysis. Equally important, situational variables—such as heat, crowd noise, too little sleep the night before, a possible touch of the flu, and the taunting of the unfriendly crowd—all impinge on performance. The secret to the long-range success of the interactional model would therefore appear to lie in its ability to isolate the traits and situational variables that are relevant to particular sport behaviors.

PROBLEMS IN SPORT PERSONALITY RESEARCH

The utility of personality measures in sport personality research, or what Martens (1975; 1981) refers to as *sport personology*, has been limited by a number of factors that may be viewed as conceptual, methodological, and interpretive.

Conceptual Problems

The failure to think in conceptual terms when devising investigations has led to a variety of difficulties that impinge on the quality of sport personology research and the reliance that can be placed on resulting findings.

Theoretical Versus Atheoretical Research. Much of the research in sport personology has proceeded in the absence of any driving theoretical framework. All too frequently, psychological assessment devices have been selected for a variety of sometimes sound but more often unsound reasons and administered to the most available captive audience of athletes. From this shaky research design have emerged published studies purporting to be descriptions of the personality of the athlete. The problems inherent in such a shotgun approach to data collection, analysis, and reporting are numerous. Ryan (1968, p. 71) characterized this chaotic situation (what Morgan [1980a, p. 52] prefers to call a "state of confusion") very well more than twenty years ago:

> The research in this area has largely been of the "shotgun" variety. By this I mean the investigators grabbed the nearest and most convenient personality test, and the closest sport group, and with little or no theoretical basis for their selection fired into the air to see what they could bring down. It isn't surprising that firing into the air at different times and different places, and using different ammunition, should result in different findings. In fact, it would be surprising if the results weren't contradictory and somewhat contrary.

Cox (1985, p. 20) sums up the situation this way:

> A large percentage of the sports personality research has been conducted atheoretically. That is, the researchers had no particular theoretical reason for conducting the research in the first

HIGHLIGHT 8.1
The Credulous-
Skeptical Argument

William Morgan published a pivotal paper in 1980 in which he elaborated on what he considered to be a crucial problem in sport personology, that of the call by a number of authorities in the field to abandon the trait approach. Morgan contended that to do so would be to throw the baby out with the bathwater, so to speak. He suggested that the problem was not so much with the trait approach as with the way it had been applied in sport research. Out of this scholarly exchange emerged the *credulous–skeptical argument.* Morgan intimated that the *skeptical* camp was made up of "knowledge brokers," authorities such as Fisher (1977), Kroll (1976), Martens (1975), Rushall (1975), and Singer and associates (1977), all of whom were calling for the abandonment of the trait approach within sport psychology. Morgan used the term "knowledge brokers" because of their tendency to cite only studies disconforming trait studies in their own research. At the other extreme were those who took the *credulous* position, spokespersons such as Ogilvie and Tutko (1966), who were willing to accept the power of the trait approach in predicting sport accomplishment.

Morgan has since suggested that the skeptical/credulous dichotomy is in fact a pseudo-argument, one that needs to be set aside in favor of a more interactional position incorporating traits, states, and situations into the predictive formula for sport behavior. Important in this position is awareness that it is still too early to abandon the trait approach in sport personology.

SOURCE: "Sport Personality Assessment: Fact, Fiction, and Methodological Re-examination by A. C. Fisher, 1977, in R. E. Stadulis, C. O. Dotson, V. L. Katch and J. Shick, eds., *Research and Practice in Physical Education* (pp. 188-204), Champaign, IL: Human Kinetics; "Reaction to Morgan's Paper: Psychological Consequences of Vigorous Physical Activity and Sport" by W. Kroll, 1976, in M. G. Scott, ed., *The Academy Papers* (pp. 30-35), Iowa City, IA: American Academy of Physical Education; "The Paradigmatic Crisis in American Sport Personology" by R. Martens, 1981, *Sportwissenschaft, 5,* pp. 9–24; *Problem Athletes and How to Handle Them* by B. C. Ogilvie and T. A. Tutko, 1966, London: Pelham Books; "Alternative Dependent Variables for the Study of Behavior in Sport" by B. Rushall, 1975, in D. M. Landers, ed., *Psychology of Sport and Motor Behavior II* (pp. 49–59), College Park: The Pennsylvania University; "Psychological Testing of Athletes" by R. N. Singer, D. Harris, W. Kroll, R. Martens, and L. J. Sechrest, 1977, *Journal of Physical Education and Recreation, 48,* 30–32.

place. They just arbitrarily selected a personality inventory, tested a group of athletes, and proceeded to "snoop" through the data for "significant" findings.

That so few answers about sport personology have emerged from so many studies is therefore not surprising. Gill (1986, p. 34) says: "If researchers do not ask meaningful questions, their efforts cannot produce meaningful answers." If sport personology is to advance our understanding of this significant aspect of sport, future research must be driven by meaningful questions that are byproducts of sound theoretical underpinnings.

Failure to Operationalize. One reason for the conflicting results within sport personology studies undoubtedly has to do with the inconsistency with which terms are defined from study to study. For example, what does the term "elite athlete" mean? It could easily be argued that only professional athletes are elite. On the other hand, this would eliminate the so-called amateur Russian hockey players participating in the Olympic Games. If one wanted to broaden the definition of elite athlete, all Olympians might be a useful standard. The inclusion of substandard Olympic performers such as Eddie "The Eagle" Edwards, the ski jumper from Great Britain who participated in the 1988 Winter Olympics in Calgary, would cast serious doubt on such a definitional stance. This issue will resurface later in the chapter, when the elite athlete is discussed more fully; the elite athlete serves here as a point of departure for illustrating the difficulties in operationalizing sport-related terms. Equally problematic in the research have been terms like athlete, nonathlete, nonparticipant, youth athlete, sportsman, and so forth. The need for proper definition of terms does indeed warrant greater attention in the design of future studies.

Methodological Problems

Above and beyond the conceptual problems just discussed, a host of methodological shortcomings have plagued the sport personology research, not the least of which has been *sampling* inconsistencies. For example, many studies have used college athletes and nonathletes from the United States as subjects for a variety of comparisons. The problems of defining the terms athlete and nonathlete notwithstanding, there is little assurance that college athletes and nonathletes from different universities going to school in different geographic locations are similar in personality makeup. The probability that the varsity athlete and nonathlete from Stanford (or Slippery Rock), for instance, is representative of all college students is low. Limits in generalizing results in these situations are present; we shall examine the implications of the generalization problem shortly.

A second methodological problem has to do with *data analysis*. Too much reliance has been placed on *univariate analysis* of results and too little on *multivariate approaches*. Essentially, univariate approaches to data analysis compare two or more groups on one variable and, as such, are useful. However, they provide what Silva (1984, p. 65) calls a "snapshot" of the subject being studied without capturing the interactions that take place between or among the variables being studied. Consequently, a fuller picture of the relationship between or among events is portrayed through multivariate methods.

Response distortion represents a third methodological problem in sport personology research. A number of issues must be addressed when administering psychological assessment devices to sport participants, not the least of which is response distortion. Sports participants, like other groups of people, respond to psychological assessment in a variety of ways. It would be naive to think that all responses to psychological inventories are completely honest and void of distortion. Careless responding, faking bad, and faking good are but a few of the possible ways in which a subject may distort data gathered from trait, state, or sport-specific inventories. The serious researcher should employ, wherever possible, measures to detect these various response distortions. Trait, state, and sport-specific assessment techniques, as well as one of the possible sources of response distortion, will be discussed in chapter 9.

Too few studies have been made of the *interactional model* that incorporates traits, states, and situations, and this omission represents a fourth methodological difficulty. As the earlier discussion of the various models of personality indicated, the interactional approach offers the most in terms of long-term return in sport personology.

A fifth methodological consideration is the absence of virtually any *longitudinal research* in sport psychology. The problem is bad enough in psychology generally, though the recent work of Eron (1987) on aggression mentioned in chapter 7 represents a most heartening exception. Unfortunately, sport psychology is virtually devoid of research looking at sport populations over extended periods of time. Youth sport and the sport for all movement, just to name two areas of inquiry, lend themselves beautifully to such an approach.

Finally, the *"one-shot"* method of data collection merits mentioning. At times, collecting data on a one-time basis may be useful. However, conducting intensive investigations of sport samples is advocated in most cases. The benefits to the discipline, the investigator(s), and the sport participants being sampled are undoubtedly going to be greater in most cases with the in-depth approach.

Interpretive Problems

Two prime areas of concern that interfere with proper communication of research findings in the area of interpretation include *faulty generalizations* and *inferring causation from correlation*.

Faulty Generalizations. As mentioned earlier, generalizing from one study to another has been problematical in sport personology. For example, generalizing about sport participants taking part in team activities based on data collected from those involved in individual sports is treacherous at best; the same can be said for generalizing from the reverse situation. Equally shaky are generalizations made between various age groups, different sexes, and participants from different countries, just to name a few. Another of the more common sources of error in sport personology research has to do with generalizations made among the various assessment devices. Tests, such as the Eysenck Personality Inventory (EPI) (Eysenck and Eysenck, 1963) and the Minnesota Multi-

phasic Personality Inventory (MMPI) (Hathaway and McKinley, 1943), have little in common philosophically and yet are often used for comparative purposes.

Inferring Causation from Correlation. A persistent problem in all of psychology (and life in general) is inferring causation from correlated things. A high correlation between events does not per se infer a cause and effect relationship between them. Eating pickles and death are correlated. Almost everyone eats pickles and everyone eventually dies, and this implies a high correlation; to infer that the eating of pickles causes death would be to misinterpret the data. To infer that the existence of a personality trait causes sport performance of a certain level of sophistication is also fraught with danger. The cause of sport performance is determined by many factors. To attribute too much to a certain personality trait may be stretching the data too far. This is not to say that traits are not important; rather, it is an admonition to beware of attributing too much to a given trait! The earlier call for more multivariate procedures in sport research is underscored here.

PERSONOLOGICAL STUDIES OF SELECTED SPORT POPULATIONS

In addition to the personality variables entertained to this point, we shall consider three additional sport dimensions. Rather than look at individual personality variables, however, we shall look at three sport groups and the research related to them. They are the black athlete, the high risk sport participant, and the elite performer. The rationale for addressing this admittedly broad content area is that these groups are of considerable interest to sport scientists, observers, and fans alike.

The Black Athlete

The overrepresentation of black athletes in many sports (e.g., football, basketball, track, boxing) has generated a great deal of interest on the part of professionals and laymen alike. What factors seem to account for this seeming black dominance in some sports? Is it true that the black athlete is physically superior to the white competitor or are the answers to be found in sociocultural and/or psychological explanations? These and other questions we will attempt to answer in our treatment of this provocative area.

A Brief History. Blacks were first brought to the New World from Africa; the first contingent arrived in 1619 at the English colony of Jamestown, Virginia. Initially, they were brought not as slaves but as indentured servants who were theoretically free at the end of their agreed upon period of servitude. In practice, however, most were made slaves, initially on a more-or-less informal basis, and later, through legislation. This formal enslavement began in the mid-1600s and continued until the Emancipation Proclamation of 1862. The value of these slaves to the economy of the United States, and particularly states located in the South, was a significant force in the creation and maintenance of slavery.

An extensive literature review of recreation engaged in by blacks living on southern plantations prior to 1860 is provided by Wiggins (1977). The form and substance of the recreation varied greatly depending on the personality and philosophy of the individual plantation owners. Wrestling, boxing, footraces, cockfights, hunting, fishing, boat races, and dancing were all popular pastimes. Related to dancing and music was an activity described by Wiggins as *"patting juba,"* a rhythmic patting or clapping of the hands as a substitute for musical instruments when none were available. All in all, much of the sport and recreation of the pre–Civil War period was tied to the rural life and the work circumstances that prevailed.

After the Civil War, the black athlete began to emerge through the sports of baseball, horse racing, and boxing. Chu (1982) indicates that the first black to play professional baseball was John (Bud) Fowler, who played for New Castle, Pennsylvania, in 1872. Following the lead of Fowler was Moses Fleetwood Walker, who played for the Toledo (Ohio) Mudhens in 1883, thereby making Walker the first black to play in the major leagues. Eitzen and Sage (1978) indicate that Fleetwood was joined by his brother, Weldy Wilberforce Walker, and together they were the first to play major league baseball. Rader (1983) indicates, by way of elaboration, that Moses preceded his brother Weldy by several months, with Weldy joining the team very late in the season. As one might suspect, the presence of the Walkers did not go unnoticed. Members of the Richmond, Virginia, team sent the following message to the Toledo, Ohio, manager prior to a game between the two teams:

> We, the undersigned, do hereby warn you not to play Walker, the negro catcher, the evening that you play in Richmond, as we could mention the names of 75 determined men who have sworn to mob Walker if he comes on the grounds in a suit. We hope you will listen to our words of warning, so that there will be no trouble; but, if you do not, there certainly will be. We only write to prevent much bloodshed, as you alone can prevent. (Peterson, 1970, p. 23)

Peterson provides us with additional insight into the difficulties faced by black ballplayers with another quote from a white player in 1888:

> While I myself am prejudiced against playing on a team with colored players, I still could not help pitying some of the poor black fellows that play in the International League. Fowler used to play second base with the lower part of his legs

encased in wooden guards. He knew that every player that came down to second base on a steal would head in for him and would, if possible, throw the spikes into him. . . . About half the pitchers try their best to hit these colored players when at bat. (p. 41)

Though these vignettes indicate that much remained to be done in race relations and sport, baseball stayed integrated, however troubled, until the 1890s, at which time it became totally segregated and remained so until 1945, when Jackie Robinson joined the Montreal Royals, a farm club of the parent Brooklyn Dodgers.

Curry and Jiobu (1984) indicate that perhaps twenty to thirty blacks formed an elite cadre of post–Civil War jockeys, with one of them riding in the first Kentucky Derby in 1876. Another, Willey Sims, eventually won both the Belmont Stakes and the Kentucky Derby. Another prominent name of the era was Pike Simms, a winner of the Futurity. Coakley (1982) cites a number of factors that led to the demise of the black jockey toward the end of the nineteenth century; among them were the Jim Crow laws that supposedly guaranteed separate but equal rights or protections, a white jockeys' union, a racist press, and assignment to slower horses. Over a short period of time the black jockey found himself relegated to less prestigious positions such as trainer or stable boy. By 1900, the elite black jockey was a historical relic.

Boxing was, and remains, a somewhat different story. Beginning with Tom Molineaux in 1800, blacks have fared relatively well, at least when compared with other sports. Though blacks have been discriminated against, they have been allowed to compete on a relatively continuous basis in boxing.

The controversial Jack Johnson won the heavyweight championship of the world in 1908 by defeating the white champion, Tom Burns. Refusing to fit into the white man's preselected mold for blacks, Johnson lived life in the fast lane. He had a penchant for flashy clothes and flashy women, had a succession of girlfriends, generally white, and married two different white women. These interracial relationships created many difficulties for Johnson, and he eventually fled the United States. Following Johnson as a great black boxer was the legendary Joe Louis, blessed with great ability and a more acceptable (to the white establishment) lifestyle. Louis has been succeeded by a series of black champions who have reigned for the better part of three decades.

With the integration of Jackie Robinson into the baseball major leagues in 1947, blacks became more and more a part of the athletic scene. Blacks were allowed in the National Basketball Association in 1950; Althea Gibson embarked on the professional tennis circuit in 1959; Bill Russell became the first black head coach in professional basketball in 1966; in 1968, professional baseball hired its first black major league umpire in Emmit Ashford; and Frank Robinson became the first black manager in the major leagues in 1975.

According to Eitzen and Sage (1978), blacks represent 12 percent of the American population. Blacks reached that same figure in professional baseball in 1957, basketball in 1958, and football in 1960. Since that time, blacks have been proportionately overrepresented to the point that by 1985 they held 75 percent of the professional basketball positions, while their numbers in football and baseball were 54 percent and 20 percent respectively (Coakley, 1986).

The Success of Black Athletes. In trying to account for the increasing numerical superiority and performance dominance of blacks in the more visible sports, at least three possible explanations exist. They are *genetic, social/ cultural*, and *psychological*. Each in turn will be examined.

Despite the presence of figures such as baseball's Jackie Robinson and boxing's Joe Louis, it has only been recently that blacks have been proportionately overrepresented in a few professional sports.

Genetic or Other Biological Explanations. It has long been suggested that apparent black superiority in sport is due to genetic or other biological influences. Coakley (1982, p. 265) offers an excellent summary of these differences. They are generally as follows:

1. Compared to whites blacks have longer legs and arms, shorter trunk, less body fat, more slender hips, more tendon and less muscle, a different heel structure, wider calf bones, more slender calf muscles, greater arm circumference, and more of the muscle fibers

HIGHLIGHT 8.2
Proportional Racial
Representation
Across Different
Sports

Although considerable evidence supports the numerical and performance superiority of blacks in many of the more visible sports, the picture is not so vivid if one takes the larger perspective. Snyder and Spreitzer (1983), building on earlier work conducted by other sport sociologists, have given us a schematic representation of black involvement across a number of types and levels of sport.

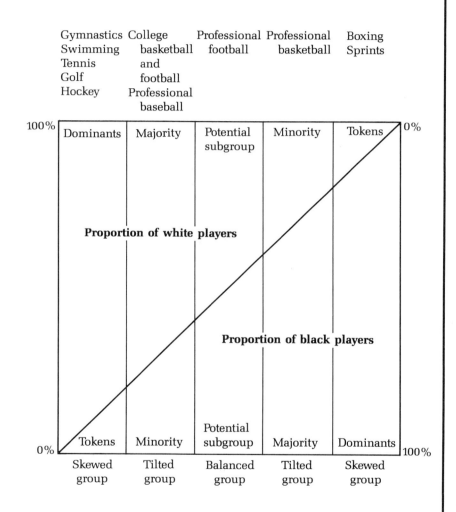

Skewed groups are those in which black or white domination is at or near 100%; gymnastics and golf for whites and boxing and track sprints for blacks are representative. The ratio for **tilted groups** is about 65:35, with

professional baseball loading in favor of whites and professional basketball for blacks. Professional football is an example of a sport that is *balanced*.
Obviously, exceptions exist between and within the various sports, but the
Snyder and Spreitzer conceptualization captures the essence of the issue
of so-called black domination of sport, which is clearly quite situational.
However, the visibility of such sports as football, basketball, boxing, and
track and field tend to give a distorted image of black domination of sport.

SOURCE: *Social Aspects of Sport* (2d ed., p. 175) by E. E. Snyder and E. A. Spreitzer, 1983, Englewood Cliffs, NJ: Prentice-Hall.

needed for speed and power and fewer of
those needed for endurance.

2. Compared to whites blacks mature more
   rapidly, their lung capacity is lower, they are
   more likely to have hyperextensibility (be
   "double jointed"), they dissipate heat more efficiently (they sweat more), they tend to become
   chilled more easily in cold weather, and they
   have superior rhythmic abilities.

As is pointed out by Coakley, as well as Chu
(1982) and Leonard (1984), a number of
problems are associated with these conclusions. First of all, most of what we have learned
about black athletes has been gathered from
studies, controlled and anecdotal, of relatively
superior athletes; nowhere are blacks with average, limited, or no athletic ability taken into
account. Second, what the designation *black*
means scientifically is subject to interpretation.
It is likely that a fair number of blacks have
white ancestors, particularly in light of some
of the practices that apparently transpired on
the plantations of pre–Civil War America (and
a number of people labeled as white undoubtedly have black ancestors). While the concept
of black has relatively clear-cut political overtones, its scientific validity is suspect. As Coakley so saliently states: "The notion that 'a black
is a black is a black' has created enough
problems on the street without letting it guide
scientific research in the laboratory" (p. 265).

A third problem has to do with the unexplained relevance of many of these supposed
superiorities to sport performance. By way of
explanation, if the first proposition offered by
Coakley were true, it would be most troublesome to explain how two prominent sprinters
of the late 1950s and early 1960s (and college
teammates at Abilene Christian University in
Abilene, Texas), Bobby Morrow and Bill Woodhouse, were world class caliber. Morrow was
relatively tall and lean, almost leonine in grace.
Woodhouse, perhaps aptly named, was short,
stocky, and very powerful. How could these
two diverse body types be so closely paired in
terms of excellence? How could Curtis Dickey
and Rod Richardson, both sprinters at Texas
A&M University, have claimed so many indoor
NCAA sprint titles between them, given their
physical diversity? Dickey, at 6 feet 2 inches
and 215 pounds, and Richardson, at 5 feet 8
inches and 150 pounds, had relatively little in
common except skin color and speed. Carrying this reasoning a step beyond, how could
Jimmy Howard, the American record holder in
the high jump (white, 6 feet 5½ inches, 175
pounds) and Franklin Jacobs (black, 5 feet
8 inches, 150 pounds) have had so much in
common as world class high jumpers? Interestingly, blacks are known as "leapers" and whites
are thought to be afflicted with "white man's
disease," and yet of the top ten high jumpers

in the world in 1985, nine were white, and the other one was an oriental ("High Jump" 1985).

A fourth problem concerns generalizations made about all sports that are based on a select few. The disproportionate representation of blacks in football, basketball, baseball, and boxing obscures the fact that many sports are dominated by other groups of athletes. For instance, Japanese-Americans, who constitute less than 1 percent of our total population, comprise in excess of twenty percent of the top AAU judo competitors (Phillips, 1976). No one has really come forth with a genetic explanation for this. As has been so beautifully stated by Robertson (1981, p. 91):

> Nobody proposes genetic factors, for example, to explain why East Germany has produced so many excellent swimmers, why Canadians do well at hockey, why Japanese-Americans are disproportionately represented in judo—or, for that matter, why the British are hopeless at baseball, while white Americans are equally inept at cricket. In each case, it is easy to see cultural factors, not genetic ones, are at work.

A final and most interesting genetic/biological explanation for black superiority states that survival of the fittest and selective breeding among slaves both while en route to this country and subsequent to entry is the real cause. This Darwinian hypothesis presupposes that the survivors of the admittedly brutal trip from Africa to America were physically stronger than those who died, thereby creating a superior gene pool among the survivors, a superiority, of course, that has been transmitted generationally. This rather myopic survival of the fittest notion does not take into account the fact that intelligence and cunning may have been critical contributors to survival and also greatly exaggerates the significance of speed and physical quickness as significant influences. Given the many problems associated with a genetic or biological explanation, per-

haps other avenues of exploration should be traversed. Accordingly, let us look at social/cultural influences.

Social/Cultural Influences. Black superiority in sports (or more appropriately, some sports) appears to be best explained in terms of social influences. Among them are discrimination in its various manifestations and what has been termed the "*sport opportunity structure*" (Eitzen and Sage, 1978). This discrimination has its roots in indentured servitude, slavery, and Jim Crow laws. At no point has some form of discrimination failed to exist; Moses Fleetwood Walker felt it, Jackie Robinson felt it, and athletes of today are not exempt from its effects. In the world of sports, discrimination is manifested in the form of stacking, a phenomenon whereby blacks are relegated to certain peripheral positions in sports such as football and baseball, whereas white players are seen in abundance in the more central positions. For example, most quarterbacks are white, most flankers or wide receivers are black. Yet another example is seen in baseball, where pitchers are predominantly white, whereas outfielders are often black.

Pioneers in this area of research were Loy and McElvogue (1970), who found that 83 percent of major league infielders (central) in 1967 were white whereas 49 percent of the outfielders (peripheral) were black; 96 percent of all catchers and 94 percent of pitchers were white. A reexamination of stacking in 1975 found few changes (Eitzen and Sage, 1978). Ninety-six percent of pitchers and 95 percent catchers were white, data almost identical to the 1967 findings; 49 percent of the outfielders were black and 76 percent of infielders were white, the latter being the only area of change but still overwhelmingly white. In a recent update using statistics from 1970 and 1984, Medoff (1986) indicates that there are indeed some slight shifts away from stacking. For instance 87 percent of pitchers were white in

1984 as oppposed to 91 percent in 1970. In the case of catchers, however, there has been a retrograde movement over the years; 88 percent were white in 1970 as opposed to 96 percent in 1984. The largest changes are among infielders and outfielders. Infielders (excluding first basemen) were 68 percent white in 1967 and 60 percent in 1984. With regard to outfielders, the figures over time read 36 percent white in 1970 and 30 percent in 1984. Though these figures are heartening for the most part, Medoff's study dealt only with starters and not the entire team rosters. Too, as has been noted by Yetman (1987), there were gains made against stacking from 1970 to 1984, but only to the extent of a 3 percent increase overall in black playing in the central positions.

In football, the data look amazingly similar to baseball. Central positions, despite the influx of blacks since 1960, remained largely white in 1975. According to Eitzen and Sage (1978), 84 of 87 quarterbacks in professional football, 69 of 70 punters, and 26 of 26 placement holders were white in 1975. Best (1987), using data from the 1982 season, found a similar effect: 78 of 80 quarterbacks, 56 of 56 kickers, and 45 of 47 offensive centers were white. The suggestion appears to be that blacks, for a host of unverified reasons, are just not suited for these varied duties. On the other hand, running back, wide receiver, and defensive back are particularly suited to the black athlete; 55 percent of running backs, 65 percent of wide receivers and 67 percent of defensive backs in the NFL in 1975 were black. The intimation here is that speed, good hands, and reckless abandon devoid of intense mental activity are of the essence and are frequently found in blacks.

Unsubstantiated biases have indeed become fact, causing coaches to select athletes for some positions and discouraging athletes from even aspiring to others. How many white track athletes in this country have been charmed into middle distance events because the sprints belong to the blacks? Conversely, how many blacks have been discouraged from running distances because of the perception that blacks are sprinters, not distance runners? Evidence, however arguable, from Africa suggests that blacks in fact can excel at distance running. Why is it that we have no great black pole vaulters? Surely speed, upper body strength, and gymnastic ability are not restricted to white athletes. Our own biases have led us into a self-fulfilling prophecy stance that validates them. If we don't have blacks running distances and if they continue to excel in the sprints, there will always be ample reason to suspect that they are not good at longer distances. Perhaps Edwards (1973, p. 322) sums it up best: "The white athletes who do participate in sports operate at a psychological disadvantage because they believe blacks to be inherently superior as athletes. Thus, the white man has become the chief victim of his own lie."

An interesting by-product of this tendency to stack and to stereotype is that few black athletes are being groomed for positions of leadership, such as coaching, when their playing days are over. Another by-product of the sport opportunity structure is lowered earnings for the black athlete due to shorter careers when compared to those of whites. Shorter careers also mean that many do not qualify for the relatively lucrative retirement benefits associated with professional sports. This latter point has been substantiated by results from research on professional football by Best (1987).

Also at work is some sort of a belief pattern that generally supports the notion that sport is the ticket to success for the black in America. Blacks are greatly underrepresented in most vocational areas, and role models for young blacks in the broad work arena are quite limited. On the other hand, black role models in sport are abundant. However, job opportunities in sport are quite limited. In sports to which blacks traditionally have gravitated — namely, football, baseball and basketball — jobs are scarce. Football at the professional level employs fifteen hundred people per year, basketball three hundred, and major league baseball approximately six hundred, yielding a total of about twenty-four hundred available jobs. Given that white athletes will fill well over half of these slots, job opportunities in professional sport are few. Harry Edwards has indicated that the likelihood that a black youth will be struck by lightning while walking down the street is greater than his or her chances of being a part of the glamor of professional sport. To put it another way, Lapchick (quoted in "Bulletin Board," 1985) says that the odds of a high school athlete, black or white, playing in professional sport are 12,000 to 1. Phillips (1988) indicates that this figure may be more like 25,000 to 1. Leonard and Reyman (1988) place the odds at 14,000 to 1 for males and 250,000 to 1 for females. Professional sports are for the chosen few.

The rather paradoxical result of discrimination, stacking, and the expectancy that sport can serve as a mechanism for black mobility is that a large number of exceptional black athletes have emerged. This excellence has been labeled as black superiority but in no way addresses the problem of what happens to those who do not excel and are left in the lurch with no sport career and few vocational opportunities elsewhere.

Psychological Explanations. Precious few investigations have dealt with the black athlete or black/white differences in psychological functioning. However, an excellent summary of a study conducted by Tutko in the early 1970s reported by Chu (1982) is most interesting. According to Chu, three hundred coaches were asked to rate black and white athletes on five dimensions: orderliness, exhibitionism, impulsivity, understanding, and abasement or humility. Most coaches indicated that they expected the blacks to be low on orderliness, understanding, and abasement and high on exhibitionism

and impulsivity. Subsequent results reported by Edwards (1973) indicated that the reverse was true in every case. In the same vein, Williams and Youssef (1975) found that college football coaches stereotyped blacks as possessing physical speed and quickness and being high in achievement motivation, whereas white players were viewed as more reliable, more mentally facile, and possessing superior thinking ability. Because these stereotypes are held by college coaches, it is not surprising that practices such as stacking have been so well documented.

Worthy and Markle (1970) have provided an interesting slant on the issue of psychological differences with their study of self-paced versus reactive activities within sport. They theorized that whites would excel at *self-paced activities*, such as golf or bowling or pitching a baseball, and blacks would star at *reactive tasks* such as boxing, tackling in football, or hitting a baseball. Using athletes from college basketball and professional football, baseball, and basketball, Worthy and Markle concluded that blacks indeed do excel at reactive tasks and whites at self-paced tasks. Dunn and Lupfer (1974), studying young soccer players, are supportive of Worthy and Markle. However, Jones and Hochner (1973) have criticized Worthy and Markle on methodological grounds. Too, Leonard (1984) has suggested that if there is no validity to the Worthy and Markle position, then they must account for the underrepresentation of blacks in clearly reactive activities, such as tennis, squash, fencing, auto racing, and skiing.

Other than the works reported earlier, one of the few studies aimed at black–white differences was conducted by Nation and LeUnes (1983). In a study of fifty-five college football players, significant differences were found on several dimensions. Among them were:

1. As measured by the Profile of Mood State (POMS), white players were significantly higher in vigor ($<.05$).

2. On the California F-Scale, blacks tended to be more authoritarian than whites, though differences were not particularly pronounced.
3. As for locus of control, black football players scored higher on the chance dimension (<.05). In view of the racist nature of our society and of sport, this finding should not be particularly surprising. Blacks, athlete or nonathlete, may well be justified in their belief that life is a chance event.
4. Black football players as seen from the perspective of the Sport Mental Attitude Survey (SMAS) (LeUnes and Nation, 1982), tend to impute responsibility for mental preparation to the coaching staff (<.05), feel confident about performing well even when depressed (<.01), are able to overlook poor past performances (<.05), and view physical not psychological factors as paramount in explaining athletic performance (<.05). Given the lack of data concerning the validity of the SMAS, these findings must be regarded as tentative. In any event, it does appear that there may be psychological differences between white and black football players. How these possible differences translate into performance, however, remains an unanswered question.

Summary. The black athlete is apparently only minimally understood, psychologically. The stark paucity of research in this area is most noticeable. From the sociocultural view, it does appear that much of the superior performance of black athletes in selected sports can be attributed to the job opportunity structure and, often but not always, subtle discrimination that forces them into certain roles that have largely been preselected for them by the long-term effects of racism. Success in these predetermined roles then leads to reinforcement on the part of both blacks and whites that, indeed, the black athlete is superior to the white.

As for genetic or biological theories, we are all too quick to point out that excellence in sport on the part of blacks is "in the genes" but we never explain Nordic skiing superiority or Japanese gymnastics excellence in terms of a particular race-related gene. The overall effect of the perpetuation of this notion is to create a form of discrimination that places blacks in the position of never having their achievements viewed as the product of intelligence, dedication to excellence, and long hours of arduous practice. Much remains to be done in sport and in the society as a whole in completely integrating black athletes and blacks in general into the mainstream of everyday American life.

The High Risk Sport Participant

Another fascinating area of sport competition, in which high risks of injury or death are an integral part, includes sport parachuting (skydiving), hang gliding, and scuba diving. Some would argue that football and boxing should be included as high risk sports in view of the injuries and deaths associated with them. Granting that any classification system is arbitrary, we shall confine our discussion to the three activities: sky diving, hang gliding, and scuba diving.

One way of conceptualizing high risk activities is provided by Tangen-Foster and Lathen (1983). These investigators sent a questionnaire to chairpersons of 120 physical education departments, primarily in large universities, asking a number of questions about their respective involvements in courses that would be considered a part of the "risk revolution" going on in America today; 73 responses were returned and analyzed. Ninety-six percent of the respondents viewed parachuting as "high" or "extraordinary risk," followed by 92 percent for hang gliding, and 64 percent for rock climbing. Scuba diving was viewed in this capacity by 32 percent of the respondents. In any event, we have isolated a few activities that have been viewed as dangerous or high risk to varying degrees. Their selection is based on two factors, their relative dangerousness and the availability of literature concerning them.

Sport Parachuting.

USPA Secretary Killed While Making Stunt Jump

On Friday, Jan. 14, Joe Svec, 35, secretary of the United States Parachute Association, was killed in a tragic skydiving accident during filming of a stunt sequence for "The Right Stuff," a film version of Tom Wolfe's best-selling novel about test pilots and astronauts.

Skydiving cameraman Rande Deluca of Big Sky Films was jumping with Svec at the time, and reported seeing no problems. Deluca quit filming at approximately 3500 feet and turned and tracked away to open a distance away from and above where Svec planned to open. Svec was seen by Doc Johnson, an experienced jumper, to turn face-to-earth (he had been facing upward, flying on his back during the filming sequence) and fall flat and stable until impact. Despite very careful analysis and medical tests, no explanation has been found for the accident.

The sequence being filmed depicts famed test pilot Chuck Yeager (first man to break the sound barrier) ejecting from an experimental aircraft. During the fatal jump, however, Svec was wearing no particularly cumbersome or otherwise "odd" gear (except perhaps his helmet) which might have inhibited his movements or reactions.

Svec had achieved meteoric success during his six years as a skydiver and USPA Board member. He began as a well-known figure in the Houston area, at the Spaceland Center and other Texas drop zones. He was elected as a write-in candidate for Conference Director in 1978 and published the very popular Southwest Swooper newsletter, which featured "Don DePloy" who had an opinion about almost every subject in the skydiving world, cleverly drawn and cleverly written. Svec became a National Director in 1980 (when Eric Pehrson succeeded him in the Conference Director slot) and was elected USPA's secretary that same year.

RW meet director of the National Championships in 1980, Svec also competed on various teams and served as Leader of the U.S. National Skydiving Team which won gold medals "across the board" at the World Meet in Zephyrhills in 1981.

As his friends would tell you, Joe Svec was truly a "Renaissance man," with a tremendous collection of skills and achievements. Little known, for example, was his generosity: he funded other people's skydiving teams when they ran out of money in order to permit them to compete in the Nationals and in world competitions. He was a true hero—he held some sort of record as Vietnam's luckiest combat veteran, having returned to combat repeatedly (with and without the Army's permission) after having acquired seven Purple Hearts that the government knew about and a total of more than 20 battle wounds. He served with the Special Forces in their most secret and difficult assignments, where he operated almost exclusively behind the enemy lines for months at a time.

When finally his wounds got to him, he was MED-EVAC'ed to Tripler General Hospital in Honolulu, where he stayed after his recovery and became a successful political cartoonist for the Honolulu Star Bulletin. His interest in politics and his wry humor combined to help him create a series of memorable cartoons and satirical articles, some of which appeared in the pages of PARACHUTIST.

Joe was principally involved in making El Capitan jumping legal (briefly, in 1980) and led the first Park Service-approved jump off the famed cliff. Perhaps one of his greatest disappointments was when a short time later actions by others caused Yosemite's policy to declare cliff jumping out of bounds. More recently Svec became a stunt jumper for the "Fall Guy" television show and this led directly to his commitment to "stand in" for one of the actors in the dangerous sequences to be filmed for the cinema version of Wolfe's best-seller.

Joe was buried by family and friends in a somber ceremony on a wind-swept afternoon on Tuesday, Jan. 18 in Houston, TX. USPA President Larry Bagley led a delegation of USPA officials who joined with hundreds of friends at the ceremony in the cemetery chapel. "This is one of the biggest services we've ever had," was the comment of one of the officials present. (Ottley, 1983, p. 35)

The preceding account points out the perils of parachuting. If an experienced jumper like Joe Svec is at risk, what do the statistics tell us about the novice in the sport? Data from *Parachutist*, the official publication of the United States Parachute Association (USPA), for the years 1973 through 1986, are presented in figure 8-2. Of the twenty-four 1985 fatalities, seven died because they did not pull their ripcord or pulled too low, lending support to the advocates of automatic activation devices (AADs). One fatality in 1982 involved a jumper with 5,300 jumps (Correll, 1983), showing the need for vigilance on the part of all participants. A breakdown of 1985 fatalities by experience level can be seen in figure 8-3. Given the considerable dangerousness of sport parachuting, why is it so attractive to so many people of all ages and walks of life? The ensuing discussion will perhaps shed some light on this perplexing and difficult question.

Physiologically, there is no question that the jumper is in a state of arousal. Fenz and Epstein (1967), Fenz and Jones (1972), Hammerton and Tickner (1968), and Powell and Verner (1982) have variously reported elevations in heart rate (HR), galvanic skin response (GSR), respiration rate, anxiety, and self-reports of fear responses in both novice and experienced parachutists. In the Powell and Verner research, twenty naive college-level parachutists were studied. Using the State-Trait Anxiety Inventory (STAI) as a means of measuring anxiety, Powell and Verner found a correlation of .78 between performance as first-time parachutists and fear rating, heart rate change, and state and trait anxiety, thereby accounting for 61 percent of the variance in performance. These novice parachutists were well below the mean on trait anxiety when compared with 484 undergraduate students reported on in the test manual. Heart rate change between control and jump conditions

Figure 8.2 U.S. Skydiver Deaths, 1973–1987

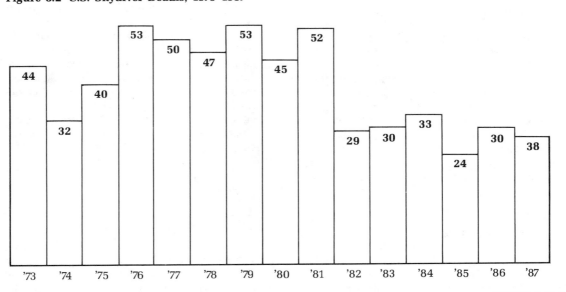

SOURCE: "1982 Fatalities Reflect Best Record Since 1971" by J. Correll, 1983, *Parachutist*, *24* (4), 27–30; "Twenty-Four Is Still Too Many" by P. Sitter, 1986, *Parachutist*, *27* (7), 28–32; "1986 Fatality Summary: Ignoring the Basics" by P. Sitter, 1987, *Parachutist*, *28* (7), 18–23.

Figure 8.3 Skydiving Fatalities by Experience Level, 1985

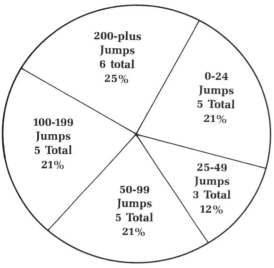

SOURCE: "Twenty-Four Is Still Too Many" by P. Sitter, 1986, *Parachutist*, 27 (7), 28–32.

rose 81 percent, similar to the 96 percent increase reported by Fenz and Epstein. Johnson (1980) reported nearly 120 percent change above resting levels in power boat racers just prior to competition. Additionally, Powell and Verner found that low state anxiety is associated with better performance than is high anxiety. Finally, they make a case for good training methods as a means of reducing both competitive anxiety and, more importantly, injuries and deaths.

Beaumaster, Knowles, and McLean (1978), in a study of the sleep patterns of twenty-seven skydivers, found differences in anxiety of experienced versus novice jumpers, with the latter scoring higher on an anxiety measure. No differences between the two groups on the Neuroticism and Extraversion scales of the Eysenck Personality Inventory (EPI) were

found, nor were either of the groups dissimilar to student sample norms reported in the test manual.

Continuing the psychological theme, parachutists are viewed variously as sensation seekers (Zuckerman, 1971; Zuckerman, Kolin, Price, and Zoob, 1964) or as stress seekers (Johnsgard, Ogilvie, and Merritt, 1975). A study by Hymbaugh and Garrett (1974) reported earlier in chapter 4, lends support to the sensation seeking notion. Twenty-one skydivers were compared with twenty-one nondivers on the Zuckerman Sensation Seeking Scale (SSS); the divers scored significantly higher than did the nondivers. In a similar vein, Johnsgard et al. studied forty-three male members of the USPA, all of whom had made at least one thousand jumps. Data gathered from the Edwards Personal Preference Schedule (EPPS), the Minnesota Multiphasic Personality Inventory (MMPI), and the Sixteen Personality Factor Questionnaire (16 PF) were analyzed. On the EPPS, parachutists demonstrated high needs for achievement, dominance, exhibition, courage, and heterosexual expression. Conversely, they had little need for deference or order. This psychometric composite gives us a picture of the parachutist as achievement oriented, desirous of being the center of attention, needing change with little concern for orderliness, and being independent and unconventional. MMPI results showed mild elevations on the Mania and Psychopathic Deviate Scales, findings similar to those of Fenz and Brown (1958). These MMPI elevations would suggest that parachutists are highly motivated and unconventional individuals, both of which also came out in the EPPS data. 16PF results showed the USPA members tested to be quite intelligent, happy-go-lucky, expedient, and not particularly influenced by group dictates.

Overall, Johnsgard et al. create an image of the parachutist as an intelligent, independent, achievement-oriented, and generally well-adjusted individual, an image contrary to that provided but not advocated by Ogilvie (1974), who summarizes some psychologically unhealthy stereotypes of skydivers and other stress seekers. According to these stereotypes, sensation seekers do the things they do as counterphobic reactions, as a means of fear displacement, as supermasculinity ploys, or because of an unconscious death wish. The available data simply do not support such assertions.

Hang Gliding

Obituary — Ian Middleton Pryde

Ian Pryde died as the result of a Gliding accident on the Dunstan Mountain range, 24th January, 1984, whilst competing in the New Zealand National Championships.

Ian was an achiever, and only recently expressed the opinion that one must live each day as if it were a bonus. That is exactly how he lived his life.

Dedicated to Gliding from the early sixties, Ian in his younger days was an Olympic yachtsman of world renown.

His extreme competitiveness, developed in yachting, was carried on into Gliding. He flew for New Zealand in the 1972 and 1976 World Championships, was New Zealand Open Champion in 1976 and winner of the N.Z. 15 Metre class in 1981.

He first crewed for a New Zealand pilot at a World Championship in Poland in 1968, and was a consistent supporter for New Zealand at almost every World event since.

An extremely successful businessman, Ian was a Papakura City Councillor for 20 years, was Chairman of the St. Stephens Maori Boys' and Victoria Maori Girls Colleges for 12 years. A Rotarian and a member of the Masonic Lodge.

One of the instigators of the Matamata Soaring Centre, he steered that Gliding Organisation into a very strong position. As President of the Auckland Gliding Club, and by his very inspiration in land and other deals, he directed the club into its own debt free airfield, almost in the middle of the city. He lifted the morale of the club to the point where it is now the strongest in New Zealand, and the Drury airfield will always be a living tribute to his drive, energy, ability and dedication.

Many a New Zealand Sailplane owner has Ian to thank for rebuilds to accident damaged sailplanes. His ability with his hands and his knowledge of fibre-glass construction will truly be missed. He was always very willing to help an owner in trouble. At his own time and expense he went to Germany to learn how to do it. Many who now have the skills in New Zealand have been taught by Ian.

Always outspoken, always making reasoned sense, he had a failing in not dotting all the "i's" and crossing the "t's" but we all accepted this, a small price for the magnificent "plus's" he scored for New Zealand and its Gliding fraternity.

He would achieve most things. I think he had vague dreams of sailing off into the sunset in a great ocean racer, but that was not to be. His great ambition was for a New Zealander to turn in an exceptional performance at a World Gliding Championship.

The whole New Zealand movement extends their sympathy to his wife Ruth and to Philip and Annette. We all share your loss. (Finlayson, 1984, p. 21)

This obituary notice taken in 1984 from the *New Zealand Gliding Kiwi*, the official publication of that country's hang-gliding association, serves as a reminder of the dangers inherent in the sport. Further substantiation of this point is seen in the fact that *Kiwi*, in addition to its periodical obituary section, also routinely contains sections known as "Safety Officers Column" and "Sailplane Accident Briefs." The most prominent American publication for gliding enthusiasts, *US Hang-Glider*, is very similar to *Kiwi* in many respects but has discontinued the routine reporting of accidents and deaths for fear of alienating or scaring potential enthusiasts. Such items are now reported only annually.

Research has shown that the risk of death in hang-gliding may exceed the Canadian suicide rate and the death by automobile rate for young American males. Despite these dire statistics, no data supports the stereotype that these "stress seekers" harbor an unconscious death wish.

Brannigan and McDougall (1983) paint a relatively grim picture of the hazards involved in hang gliding, pointing out that the risk of death in the sport probably exceeds the suicide rate for all ages in Canada and the death by automobile rate of young American males. Brannigan and McDougall also point to a death rate in hang gliding of 65 per 100,000, and also are of the opinion that the statistics in hang gliding are undoubtedly understated.

As is true for sport parachuting, a strong positive correlation exists between experience and accident rates. Even so, some notable participants feel that hang gliding is misrepresented in terms of risk. For example, Willard (1978, p. 26) quotes Dr. G. M. Yuill, a neurologist and a member of the British Hang-gliding Association, as follows: "I believe this sport is no more dangerous than horse riding, rockclimbing, potholing, or motorcycle racing, and with training may probably be rendered less hazardous than any of these sports."

Outside of the rather observational data reported by Brannigan and McDougall, little of a psychological nature has been done with hang gliders. Brannigan and his associate observed seven groups of hang gliders from southern Ontario and upper New York and Pennsylvania in an effort to better understand what it is that makes the hang glider tick. Several observational and tentative conclusions were drawn. Among them were:

1. Hang gliders tend to be single male Caucasians in their mid-twenties.
2. They tend to come from every walk of life, though students seem to be most frequent participants.
3. Most get into the activity through a friend.
4. Being a member of the subculture is a powerful force in maintaining their involvement.
5. Most believe that hang gliding is not without risk but they don't view it as a dangerous activity.
6. A "rush," a "blast," "visceral pleasure," and "a high" are often used to describe the experience.
7. A number of participants are able to turn their interest into a vocation as manufacturer, teacher, dealer, designer, test pilot, photographer, or writer.
8. People who give up the sport do so primarily because of accidents and secondarily due to job demands or marital considerations.

Scuba Diving

A moderately experienced eighteen-year-old female sports diver was diving in a flooded gravel pit (fresh water) and had been at a depth of 22 metres (72 ft.) for approximately seven minutes when her mouthpiece ceased to function correctly. She made an emergency rapid ascent from this depth during which she was thought to have inhaled water.

At the surface she was found to be apnoeic, cyanosed, and unconscious. However, she responded quickly to mouth-to-mouth resuscitation and was taken ashore in the head down and legs elevated position. At this time she had no symptoms and it was arranged for her travel by car to hospital for a "check-up." She then sat up, and suddenly developed pain in the right shoulder with associated weakness of movement, visual impairment and reduction in sensation, paraesthesiae, and weakness of both legs. She was immediately transferred to the decompression chamber available at the site and at this point,

the Leicester Royal Infirmary Accident Flying Squad was called out.

None of the members of the Flying Squad had any experience of diving personally. A member of the team could not enter the chamber without risking problems, in particular nitrogen narcosis. There was also lack of space in the chamber and uncertainty as to the length of time the patient ought to stay in. Subsequent management was, therefore, based on the history, a very distant view through a porthole of the patient and an intercom connection with the experienced diver in the chamber with the patient. The medical staff at HMS Vernon were contacted for their advice in the initial management. Later they offered direct help by sending one of their team members to enter the chamber and assess the patient directly. The treatment regime was set up with intravenous Dexamethasone 12 mg, followed by 8 mg six hourly and immediate recompression to an equivalent depth of 50 metres (165 ft. sea water) on air for thirty minutes. Thereafter the patient was slowly decompressed following a fairly standard table.

With this management, immediate improvement and gradual full recovery occurred. The patient left the chamber after 37½ hours and then transferred to the Leicester Royal Infirmary where a CAT scan, chest X-ray and thorough neurological examination was carried out. These did not reveal any abnormality. She was discharged home forty-eight hours after her admission to the hospital with no sign of any residual neurological impairment. (Ballham and Allen, 1983, pp. 7–8)

Again, as we noted in parachuting and hang gliding, the dangers of high risk sport participation are ever present. Much of the research on scuba diving, a sport involving some 2 million enthusiasts, has centered on the relationship between anxiety and various aspects of scuba training and performance. Griffiths and his associates (Griffiths, Steel, and Vaccaro, 1978, 1979, 1982; Griffiths, Steel, Vaccaro, and Karpman, 1981) have provided us with a fair amount of information. Summing across all four of the Griffiths *et al.* studies, the following conclusions seem warranted:

1. The subjects were college students or YMCA divers, and all were novices.
2. The State-Trait Anxiety Inventory (STAI) was used in every case.

In the 1978 work, twenty-nine beginning divers (college students) had resting trait and state anxiety scores significantly below college norms for the scale, but moderate increases in state anxiety were noted during the testing phase. The authors did note that anxiety levels were not sufficiently elevated to yield a meaningful indicator of stress that could ultimately prove to be life threatening in an underwater crisis situation. Related to this, Egstrom and Bachrach (1971) indicate that most underwater deaths are due to panic. In their second study, Griffiths and associates used sixty-two beginning scuba divers from the YMCA training program. Four performance indicators were used, and no relationship was found between performance and anxiety on simple tasks, but such was not the case on more complex tasks, thereby indicating that anxiety does in fact interfere with satisfactory performance of complex activities.

The 1981 study was conducted with fifty college scuba divers who were subsequently broken into three groups, one receiving biofeedback (N = 19), one receiving meditation (N = 14), and a control group (N = 17). Each group was asked after receiving the treatment condition to undertake an underwater assembly task borrowed from the U.S. Navy. Neither treatment group performed better than the control group, but state and trait anxiety as measured by the STAI were both significantly related to performance. In the 1982 research, the investigators chose to use the S-R Inventory of General Trait Anxiousness (Endler and Okada, 1975) and the STAI. Subjects were beginning scuba students. Based on results obtained, the authors concluded that the S-R Inventory is more useful than the STAI trait measure in predicting anxiousness prior to underwater

testing. Other than this, it was determined that respiration rate is an effective measure of underwater stress in beginning divers, something also suggested by Bachrach (1970).

Two other studies have attempted to look at personality variables other than anxiety. One, by Weltman and Egstrom (1969), looked at personal autonomy as measured by the Pensacola Z-scale in 147 scuba trainees at the University of California at Los Angeles. The Z-scale failed to differentiate among trainees and two other campus groups (engineering students and Peace Corps volunteers) nor did it separate successful trainees and dropouts.

In the second study by Heyman and Rose (1979), twenty-nine male and sixteen female college divers were administered the STAI, the Sensation-Seeking Scale, Rotter's I-E scale and the Bem Sex Role Inventory (BSRI) (Bem, 1974). Overall, scuba participants were lower on trait anxiety, more adventurous, more internal, and more masculine in sex role orientation than student norms for these dimensions. Also, state and trait anxiety was not related to performance, internals made more dives than externals, and surprisingly, there was an inverse relationship between sensation seeking and depth of dives. One might expect sensation seekers to dive deeper but such was not the case.

Correlates of High Risk Sport Participation.
Beyond the various correlates mentioned in specific association with the three high risk activities of parachuting, hang gliding, and scuba diving, at least two others deserve special attention. One is sensation seeking, the other birth order effects.

Sensation seeking is a construct first advanced by Zuckerman and associates (Zuckerman, Kolin, Price, and Zoob, 1964). Their notion was that psychological theories proposing that the human organism is basically a drive or tension reducer were limited; rather, they posit the notion of "optimal stimulation," which takes into account large individual variations in the need for stimulus reduction. Hence, the concept of sensation seeking.

The fifth revision of Zuckerman's test came out in 1984 (Zuckerman, 1984). The various editions of the *Sensation Seeking Scale (SSS)* seek to measure four subdimensions of sensation-seeking. They are:

1. *Thrill and Adventure Seeking (TAS)* — The desire to engage in thrill seeking, risk, adventurous activities such as parachuting, hang gliding, mountain climbing, and so forth.
2. *Experience Seeking (ES)* — Seeking arousal through mind and sense and nonconforming lifestyle.
3. *Disinhibition (Dis)* — Release through partying, drinking, gambling, and sex, generally regarded as more traditional sensation seeking outlets.
4. *Boredom Susceptibility (BS)* — Aversion for repetition, routine, and dull and boring people; restlessness when escape from tedium not possible.

Though the SSS has been linked to any number of psychological constructs outside sport (Zuckerman, 1971), it has generally been a valid assessment tool within the sporting context, particularly in studies of high risk athletes. As stated earlier, Hymbaugh and Garrett (1974) found skydivers to be significantly higher in sensation seeking than a matched sample of nondivers. Straub (1982) studied 80 male athletes who participated in hang gliding (N = 25), automobile racing (N = 22), and bowling (N = 25). As might be expected, the bowlers scored significantly lower (.01 level) on the total score and two of the four subdimensions when compared with the other two groups. Table 8.1 reflects these data in their entirety. In response to the question "Do you consider your sport to be a high-risk activity?" 67 percent of the hang gliders, 50 percent of the auto racers, and none of the bowlers said yes, though 63 percent of the hang gliders and 41 percent of the auto racers reported having been injured at some point in their careers. The studies mentioned here are not exhaustive of the available literature but are supportive of the use of the SSS with athletes in high risk activities.

Another correlate of high risk sport is *birth order effects*. The relationship of birth order to a variety of human behaviors has been a popular area of investigation, and sport has not been exempt from this research. Nisbett (1968) asked a group of judges to rank the most dangerous sports offered at Columbia University; football, soccer, and rugby were so designated. He then

Table 8.1 Sensation Seeking Data on Hang Gliders, Automobile Racers, and Bowlers

Test components	Hang gliders (n = 33)		Auto racers (n = 22)		Bowlers (n = 25)		F
	M	SD	M	SD	M	SD	
TAS	8.12	1.92	7.41	2.56	6.28	2.68	4.35*
ES	5.42	2.26	5.18	1.84	3.56	2.27	5.83**
Dis	5.06	3.04	5.73	2.19	4.40	2.16	1.56
BS	2.67	1.95	4.32	1.89	3.16	1.77	5.17**
Total	21.27	2.29	22.64	2.12	17.40	2.22	3.79*

*p<.05.

**p<.01.

SOURCE: "Sensation Seeking among High and Low-Risk Male Athletes" by W. F. Straub, 1982, *Journal of Sport Psychology*, 4, 246–253.

asked nearly three thousand undergraduates from Columbia, Yale, and Penn State (about twenty-four hundred were from Columbia) and a sample of professional athletes from the New York Mets (baseball) and the New York Giants (football) to respond to a questionnaire on birth order. Firstborns were overrepresented in all cases, but they were less likely to have participated in high risk sports. Nisbett (p. 352) says: "The underrepresentation of firstborns in the dangerous sports is not a pronounced effect but it is a consistent one. In high school, college, and professional athletics, firstborns are less likely to play the high-risk sports."

In a similar vein, Longstreth (1970) asked students enrolled in two semesters of child development to respond to a seven-point continuum question in which Response 1 was "Physically very conservative at age 12; tended to avoid dangerous activities and rough games; preferred sedentary activities" and Response 7 was "Physically very daring at age 12; never turned down a physical challenge; always ready for rough and tumble with plenty of bruises and cuts to show for it." Like Nisbett, Longstreth found firstborns overrepresented in his classes but underrepresented at the "rough and tumble" end of the continuum; 59 percent of firstborns rated themselves at the conservative end of the scale. Sex differences were noticeable, with 62 percent of the males and 41 percent of the females scoring a 5, 6, or 7 on Longstreth's question.

Yiannakis (1976) compared sixty-seven firstborn college students with ninety-nine later-borns concerning their preference for such sports as judo, football, lacrosse, skydiving, ski jumping, and motorcycle racing. In general, firstborns tended to avoid the high-risk activities. Casher (1977), in a study of 127 Ivy League varsity athletes, lends strong support to previous findings with her observation that participation in dangerous sports is significantly related to birth order. In addition to the general underrepresentation of firstborns, Casher found

a statistically significant number of third-borns in dangerous sports. Nixon (1981, p. 12), in a study of Vermont collegians, found a "weak tendency for male firstborns to be less attracted than male later-borns to playing risky sports." Nixon also found that males showed a pronounced preference over females for participating in or watching risky sports.

All things considered, birth-order effects appear to be relevant to our understanding of high risk sports; firstborns consistently appear to be underrepresented. Most of the writers mentioned here account for this apparent underrepresentation in terms of child-rearing practices, the consensus being that firstborns are often treated differently from subsequent children within the family. Firstborns may have their needs met in more conventional ways whereas later-born children are forced to resort to nontraditional activities in order to achieve a measure of success and parental and peer approval. Though speculative, this seems to be the gist of the most accepted explanation.

The Elite Athlete

Research on elite athletes has been unfocused at best. Access to elite populations in which much is at stake for the athlete is understandably limited. Nevertheless, some information about top-flight performers is available.

Kroll's Personality-Performance Pyramid. One of the more creative and sport-specific ways of conceptualizing the relationship between personality and performance is provided by Kroll (1970). His formulation is summarized by Silva (1984) in terms of the *personality–performance pyramid,* which can be seen in figure 8.4. Kroll's model would predict a great deal of heterogeneity among athletes at the entry level and considerable homogeneity at the elite level, though differences would still exist at any and all levels. Part of this similarity could be attributable to preselection variables for sport,

Figure 8.4 The Personality-Performance Pyramid

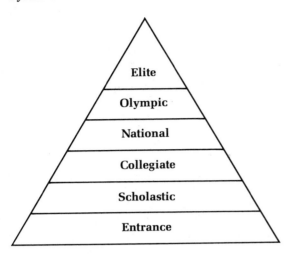

SOURCE: "Current Strategies and Problems in Personality Assessment of Athletes" by W. Kroll, 1970, in L.E. Smith, ed., *Psychology of Motor Learning* (pp. 349–371), Chicago, IL: Athletic Institute.

Figure 8.5 Morgan's Iceberg Profile

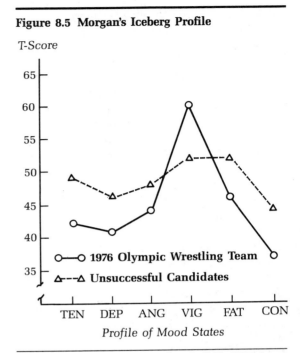

Profile of Mood States

SOURCE: "Test of Champions: The Iceberg Profile" by W.P. Morgan, 1980, *Psychology Today*, 14 (2), 92–102, 108.

and some would certainly be a function of the demands of proceeding from the entry to the elite level. Kroll calls this later phenomenon the *modification and attrition explanation* for personality similarity in top level athletes; that is, their own behaviors and personality have been modified by experience. Athletes who for whatever reason drop out of the process at some point only accentuate this homogeneity of personality. In effect, their attrition takes variability out of the formula.

Morgan's Iceberg Profile. The most creative, continuing, and collected conceptualization of elite sport performance is provided by Morgan and his various associates (Morgan, 1978a, 1978b, 1980; Morgan and Johnson, 1976; Morgan and Pollock, 1977). They conducted a series of studies of elite performers, and from these efforts the Iceberg Profile shown in figure 8.5 emerged. Morgan compared scores on a var-

iety of psychometric inventories administered to American Olympians in rowing, wrestling, and distance running. All athletes invited to the Olympic training camp in 1972 and 1976 completed a battery of physiological and psychological tests; subsequently, the athletes making the various teams were compared with those invited to camp but not selected to participate in the upcoming Olympics. The "unsuccessful" candidates were higher in tension, depression, anger, fatigue, and confusion on the Profile of Mood States (POMS) (McNair, Lorr, and Droppleman, 1971) and lower on the positive mood dimension of vigor than were the "successful" competitors. The spike effect on the vigor dimension that clearly differentiates between the successful and unsuccessful athletes constitutes the Iceberg Profile. Overall, much additional research has been generated in support of Morgan's work, and detailed accounts of more than fifty studies pertinent to the Iceberg Profile and the Profile of Mood States have been reported by Daiss and LeUnes (1986) and LeUnes, Hayward, and Daiss (1988).

Research from track, and most particularly from the distance events, has lent further substantiation to the Morgan conceptualization. Morgan and Pollock (1977) made comparisons between and among nineteen world class runners (eleven middle and long distance and eight marathoners) and eight college middle-distance runners. Among the inventories used were the STAI, EPI, POMS, and the Depression Adjective Checklist (DACL) (Lubin, 1967). No differences were found among the three groups on any of these measures. Group means can be seen in table 8.2. All things considered, the groups are remarkably similar. However, when all runners in the study were compared with college norms reported in the test manual for the POMS, substantial differences in favor of the runners were noted. Even though the instruments failed to discriminate between

world class and collegiate runners, they did discriminate between runners and a general college sample.

Morgan and Pollock concluded that their sample of elite runners (excluding the collegiate runners) were remarkably similar, affectively, to Olympic wrestlers and oarsmen studied earlier by Morgan (1968) and Morgan and Johnson (1976). National and Olympic class cyclists studied by Hagberg, Mullin, Bahrke, and Limburg (1979) also looked much like profiles isolated by Morgan and his associates for the three groups they studied. In all cases, affective superiority was achieved when these elite athletes were compared to norms from the manual. In view of observed similarities between these elite and normative samples on other psychological tests of a more enduring nature, Morgan concluded that these affective differences drawn particularly but not exclusively from the POMS are consequences of competition at a high level as opposed to antecedents for excellence (Morgan and Pollock, 1977).

Table 8.2 Raw Score Means of Three Groups of Runners on Selected Psychological Variables*

	World class runners		College runners (n = 8)	F
Variable	Middle-long distance (n = 11)	Marathon (n = 8)		
State anxiety	33.82	32.75	33.75	0.06
Trait anxiety	34.91	26.63	33.00	2.04
Tension	10.91	9.75	10.88	0.11
Depression (POMS)	9.18	3.88	6.88	1.01
Anger	8.73	6.75	8.13	0.23
Vigor	19.00	22.75	21.25	1.14
Fatigue	6.81	6.38	7.88	0.16
Confusion	8.82	5.63	7.63	1.40
Extraversion	13.27	12.75	14.88	0.44
Neuroticism	10.27	11.00	6.50	1.66
Depression (DACL)	4.73	4.13	3.13	0.81

*Differences between groups were found not to be significant (p>0.05).

SOURCE: "Psychological Characterization of the Elite Distance Runner" by W. P. Morgan and M. L. Pollock, 1977, *Annals of the New York Academy of Sciences, 301*, 382–403.

HIGHLIGHT 8.3
Dissociative
Strategies in
Distance Running

Morgan and Pollock describe elite runners in considerable detail on dimensions other than those generated from psychometric sources. Morgan had originally hypothesized that runners used *dissociative strategies* while competing in order to cope with the painful demands inherent in long distance running. Some of these so-called dissociative strategies are recounted by Morgan and Pollock:

> *Prior work conducted by the senior author revealed that marathon runners characteristically attempt to "dissociate" sensory input during competition. Previous interviews with twenty marathoners, as well as more recent interview data from long distance runners, revealed that these athletes are "cognitively active" during competition, but this cognitive activity seldom, if ever, relates to the actual running. Also, this general finding has since been observed for long distance swimmers and cyclists as well. The cognitive strategy employed by these athletes can best be regarded as "dissociative cognitive rehearsal." Many runners reconstruct images of past events throughout the 42.2 km run. For example, one of the first marathoners interviewed by the senior author routinely rehearsed or reconstructed his entire educational experience during each marathon. During the run he would age regress himself to first grade and attempt to recall as much as possible about the experience (e.g., the teacher's name and face, the names and faces of other boys and girls in the class, various experiences such as learning to read, print, work with crayons, and paste, playing an instrument in the rhythm band, recess, and so on). After a while he would proceed to second grade, recall salient "chunks" of information, and then proceed to third grade. This continued throughout grade school, high school, college, his oral defense, receipt of the Ph.D., as well as his current postdoctoral experiences. This marathoner always reconstructed his educational experience during the marathon; it was always somewhat unique, however, in that he would remember different people, events, and activities each time. In other words, the theme was always the same, but the content varied. Other runners have described remarkably similar approaches, and it would be redundant to proceed with a review of these case studies. Suffice it to say that another runner always builds a house when he marathons; another writes letters to everyone he owes a letter to; another listens to a stack of Beethoven records; another participates in extremely complex mathematical exercises; another steps on the imaginary faces of two co-workers she detests throughout the marathon; another repeatedly sings the Star Spangled Banner in crescendo fashion; another age regresses and becomes a steam locomotive at the base of heartbreak hill; and so on. The various rehearsal themes are rather different, but they all seem to be directed toward the same end—dissociating the painful sensory input. As a matter of fact, most of these runners have reported that use of these techniques helps them negotiate various pain zones and particularly the proverbial (or mythical?) wall.* (Pp. 390–391)

Morgan and Pollock had to recant the dissociative notion because of their work with the elite runners. They found that they used associated strategies as follows:

Dissociation of sensory input did not represent the principal "cognitive strategy," but rather, these elite marathon runners were found to utilize an associative strategy. These runners reported that (1) they paid very close attention to bodily input such as feelings and sensations arising in their feet, calves, and thighs, as well as their respiration; (2) whereas they paid attention to time ("the clock"), pace was largely governed by "reading their bodies"; (3) they identified certain runners they would like to stay with during a given run if possible, but they did not typically employ a "leeching" strategy; (4) during any given marathon they constantly reminded or told themselves to "relax," "stay loose," and so forth; and (5) they typically did not encounter "pain zones" during the marathon, and most of these elite runners dismissed the phenomenon referred to as "the wall" as simply a myth — that is, they did not "come up against the wall" during the marathon run. (P. 390)

An excellent summary of these cognitive strategies is provided in a *Sports Illustrated* article by Morgan (1978b).

SOURCES: "Mind of the Marathoner" by W. P. Morgan, 1978, *Sports Illustrated*, April, pp. 38–49; "Psychological Characterization of the Elite Distance Runner" by W. P. Morgan and M. Pollock, 1977, *Annals of the New York Academy of Sciences, 301*, 382–403.

Other Research on Elite Performers. In addition to Morgans' work with the Iceberg Profile, a number of studies have looked at wrestlers of high quality. Highlen and Bennett (1979) gave a questionnaire to forty elite wrestlers competing for three national-level Canadian teams. Twenty-four of the forty made one of the three teams, and comparisons were made between qualifiers and nonqualifiers. Twelve factors were isolated for study: self-confidence, thoughts under various wrestling conditions, factors affecting performance, dreams, role performance, self-talk, imagery, anxiety associated with major competitions, distraction, negative self-thoughts, blocking, and coping. The largest difference between the two groups were that the qualifiers felt that they were closer to reaching their maximum potential than were nonqualifiers and the former reported much more self-confidence than did the latter. This confidence factor was regarded by the researchers as their strongest finding.

In a separate study, Highlen and Bennett (1983) compared elite divers and wrestlers. The forty-four divers were competing for a place on the Canadian Pan American Games team; eight ultimately qualified. Self-confidence and concentration most saliently discriminated between the qualifiers and the nonqualifiers. Imagery was also a significant difference between the two groups. As for the wrestlers (N = 39), they were competing for positions on either the Canadian teams entered in the Pan American Games or the World Championships. Fifteen qualified for one or the other of the two teams. As with the divers, self-confidence and concentration differentiated between successful and unsuccessful candidates. Imagery did not differentiate between the two groups, however, although it did with the divers.

Gould, Weiss, and Weinberg (1981) have lent support to the previous findings in their study of forty-nine wrestlers competing in the 1980 Big Ten conference tournament. Nineteen place winners (first, second, third, or fourth in various weight classes) were compared with thirty wrestlers who did not place in the competition. The factors of self-confidence, proximity to reaching maximum potential, and focusing attention on match-related thoughts clearly differentiated placers from nonplacers.

In a study of elite youth wrestlers, Silva, Shultz, Haslam, and Murray (1981) found a number of differences between eight qualifiers for the 1979 United States Junior World Team and seven nonqualifiers. Qualifiers differed psychologically most significantly from nonqualifiers on the POMS dimensions of anger (qualifers were lower) and tension (qualifiers were higher).

The studies described here clearly illustrate the importance of self-confidence, performing at a near maximum capacity, and attention to the task at hand in determining elite wrestling performance. Other significant works related to elite athletes include those with U.S. Olympic gymnasts (Mahoney and Avener, 1977), Canadian Pan American games participants in ten sports (Alderman, 1970), New Zealand's top youth oarsmen (Williams, 1978), national level collegiate racquetball players (Meyers, Cooke, Cullen, and Liles, 1979), young elite American skiers (Rotella, Gansneder, Ojala, and Billing, 1980), and Olympic weight lifters (Hall, Church, and Stone, 1980). A summary of these investigations follows.

Olympic Gymnasts. Mahoney and Avener administered a broad-based questionnaire to American men gymnasts at the 1976 Olympic trials. Subsequent comparisons between those who made the team and those who did not revealed that the better gymnasts tended to be more self-confident ($r = .57$), reported a higher frequency of gymnastic dreams ($r = .45$), thought more about gymnastics in everyday situations ($r = .78$), tended to downplay the role of officiating in influencing their performance ($r = .59$), and did not rate mental attitude as greatly influencing their success ($r = -.59$). Too, the more successful participants reported slightly more anxiety prior to competition though the pattern reversed itself when competition actually commenced.

Pan American Athletes. Eighty-one male and fifty-five female Canadian athletes from ten different sports responded to Kenyon's scale for assessing attitudes toward physical activity (Kenyon, 1968). The Kenyon measure looks at six dimensions of physical activity. They are reported by Alderman (1970) as follows:

1. *Physical activity as a social experience.* A characterization of those activities whose primary purpose is to provide a medium for social intercourse, i.e., to meet new people and to perpetuate existing relationships.
2. *Physical activity for health and fitness.* A characterization of those activities in which participation is designed to improve one's health and physical fitness.
3. *Physical activity as the pursuit of vertigo.* A characterization of those activities or experiences providing, at some risk to the participant, an element of thrill and excitement through the mediums of speed, acceleration, sudden change of direction, or exposure to dangerous situations, with the participant remaining in control.
4. *Physical activity as an aesthetic experience.* A characterization of those activities which are thought of as possessing beauty or certain artistic qualities such as ballet, gymnastics, or figure skating.
5. *Physical activity as catharsis.* A characterization of those activities which provide, through some vicarious means, a release of tension precipitated by frustration.

6. *Physical activity as an ascetic experience.* A characterization of those activities that are conceived of as requiring long, strenuous, and often painful training and still competition, and which demand a deferment of many other gratifications. (P. 21)

In general, males and females had quite similar attitudes about physical activity. Additionally male athletes had a strikingly high evaluation of physical activity as an aesthetic experience. Finally, neither sex responded very strongly toward physical activity as an ascetic experience. Though many arduous hours of training are inherent in most sports at such a competitive level, few athletes appear to enjoy the pain and privation associated with asceticism.

Youth Oarsmen. New Zealand Colts (under age twenty-three) Rowing Team finalists (n = 33) participated in a variety of tests conducted by Williams. In addition to several physical measures, five psychological scales appeared to be related to rowing success and were drawn from the 16PF. Toughmindedness, emotional stability, self-sufficiency, trustfulness, and imaginativeness emerged as predictors. Trustfulness, however, was in the direction of suspiciousness, a rather unexpected finding.

Collegiate Racquetball Players. Nine members of the Memphis State University racquetball team competing in the Tennessee State Racquetball Championships were questioned by Meyers and his associates, generally in an attempt to replicate the work of Mahoney and Avener with the Olympic gymnasts. Two of the nine team members had won individual national championships, two others had won the national doubles championship, and the remaining five performed but had not won anything of national consequence. Comparisons were made between the top two individual players and the other seven players. Consistent with the findings of Mahoney on the Olympic gymnasts, Meyers et al. (1979) found that the top racquetball players tended to be more self-confident, performed more successfully in their sport-related dreams, reported more racquetball-related thoughts in everyday events, downplayed the role of officiating in their performance, reported a more structured lifestyle, and perceived themselves to be performing at nearer their own potential. Anxiety findings were similar to those for the Olympic gymnasts.

Young Skiers. Rotella and his colleagues (1980) studied twenty-six male and twenty-one female skiers ages twelve to nineteen who were enrolled in a school oriented toward producing World and Olympic caliber athletes. Again, these researchers were attempting to replicate the Mahoney and Avener approach. Only two of fifty-four items on their first inventory modeled after Mahoney and Avener correlated significantly with skiing ability as assessed by the National Ski List Ranking for 1978–1979, and they were operating close to potential and blaming inadequate training for poor performance. The better skiers saw themselves as performing nearer their maximum ability and did not believe that poor performance could be blamed on training inadequacies. The second instrument used by Rotella et al. showed that the better skiers focused much effort on remediation of weaknesses in designing training programs and thought more about actual race course strategy than did their less successful counterparts.

Olympic Weight Lifters. Hall and her associates (1980) were primarily interested in birth-order effects, though Hall and her collaborators did take into consideration achievement motives, locus of control, and anxiety. Overall, they found a very strong relationship between birth order effects and achievement motivation as measured by the Mehrabian Need Achievement

Many elite athletes view physical activity as an aesthetic experience—a belief rooted in the Greek ideal of sport as an expression of beauty.

Scale (Mehrabian, 1969). Firstborns had a very strong need to approach success whereas later-borns had a tendency to avoid failure. On Rotter's locus of control measure, firstborns and others were generally internal, though the first-borns were more external than later-borns. Both comparison groups were relatively low on trait anxiety as measured by the STAI. No attempt was made in this study to relate the variables under scrutiny to level of performance.

The rather diverse and relatively scant literature about the elite athlete reveals that self-confidence is a big factor in his or her success.

Too, the ability of elite competitors to perform at a level that is consistent with their view of their potential appears to be a solid discriminator. The role of skill-related dreams is unclear but provocative. Everyday events that are intruded upon by thoughts of competition seem relevant, also. Top-flight competitors are not prone to blame poor performance on practice inadequacies or officiating foibles; they tend to see themselves as the source and focus of success. Finally, sport as an aesthetic rather than ascetic experience has some merit in characterizing top athletes.

Our understanding of elite performers is, to quote Silva, Shultz, Haslam, and Murray (1981), "embryonic." Methodological shortcomings have been considerable; the definition of who is elite is highly variable, sample sizes are of necessity quite small in most cases, inconsistencies created by the use of a diversity of instruments are frequent, and variability in data analyses has contributed to the cloudy picture that exists. It is hoped that increasing sophistication can be brought to bear on this important area in the future so that identification and development of excellence can continue worldwide.

SUMMARY

1. The study of the relationship between personality and sport performance has generated much interest within sport psychology.
2. Personality is composed of core traits and peripheral states (what Hollander further breaks down into typical responses and role-related behaviors). Constantly exerting pressure on each of these facets of the personality is the social environment.
3. A number of competing theories attempt to explain human behavior.
4. Biological theories include the somatotype theory of Sheldon, which classifies people according to body type and temperament, and the psychobiological model of Dishman, which is used to account for exercise adherence.
5. The psychodynamic or psychoanalytic model of Sigmund Freud represents a detailed though pessimistic model for explaining human behavior. An emphasis on intrapsychic conflict, inherent badness, and determined behavior permeates the Freudian model.
6. Counter to the psychoanalytic approach is the humanistic model most closely identified with Carl Rogers and Abraham Maslow. Key concepts in the humanistic model include inherent goodness of the organism and freedom of choice. The fully functioning person of Rogers and the self-actualized individual of Maslow are key conceptualizations used to account for superior adjustment.
7. The behavioral model suggests that the goodness/badness issue is best left to the philosopher; however, behaviorists are somewhat in consonance with the analysts on the determined nature of behavior though they would suggest a very different explanation for how behavior becomes locked in. The behavioral approach has been warmly embraced by sport psychologists due to its utility in improving sport performance.
8. Trait theory has been popular in sport psychology because many researchers have felt that sport performance can be explained by trait dispositions. The model has spawned much research and controversy.
9. The interactional perspective that posits that behavior is a function of both personality and the environment is increasingly popular within sport psychology.
10. Limitations in applying the results of sport personology research have centered around conceptual, methodological, and interpretive shortcomings.
11. Conceptual problems in sport research include the tendency to conduct too much atheoretical as opposed to theoretical investigation and the failure to properly and consistently define terms, such as the elite athlete.
12. Sampling inconsistencies, an over-reliance on univariate analysis at the expense of multivariate techniques, failure to control

for response distortion, too little use of the interactional model, and the use of "one-shot" studies have all served as methodological limitations to sport research.

13. Interpretive problems include making faulty generalizations and inferring causation from correlational data.

14. The black athlete, the high risk sport participant, and the athlete who excels at the national or world level are of considerable interest to professional researchers and theorists.

15. Blacks were brought to America as indentured servants in 1619 and were enslaved until the Emancipation Proclamation of 1862. After the Civil War, they became involved extensively in baseball, boxing, and as jockeys in horse racing. Moses Fleetwood Walker and his brother Weldy Wilberforce Walker were prominent baseball players of the late 1800s, though their acceptance by whites was very poor. Tom Molineaux was the first black heavyweight boxing champion of the world, and black dominance of boxing continues unabated. Willey Simms was an early leader in jockey circles, and blacks dominated the sport of horse racing until 1900, at which time they were relegated to lesser roles in favor of white jockeys.

16. The success of black athletes in certain sports—mainly football, basketball, baseball, and boxing—is difficult to explain. Genetic or biological superiority theories abound but are hard to substantiate under critical scrutiny. Social/cultural influences that arise out of bias, prejudice, misguided preconceptions, and superstition probably constitute a more viable hypothesis for explaining black superiority in certain sports. Psychological explanations are sparse and shed very little light on the issue.

17. Sport parachuting, hang gliding, and scuba diving are popular components of the modern "risk revolution" and the psychological makeup of the participants has been intriguing to sport psychologists.

18. Thirty U.S. sport parachutists died while participating in their sport in 1986, an increase of four deaths from 1985. Deaths in sport parachuting are strongly related to inexperience. Physiologically, parachutists experience heightened reactions as well as elevated anxiety and self-reports of fear associated with jumping, but are generally low in state and trait anxiety when compared with reported test norms. Too, parachutists are above average in intelligence and are unconforming sensation seekers with a low need for order and rigidity.

19. Hang gliding is a highly dangerous activity with a death rate exceeding that of suicide for people of all ages in Canada and automobile fatalities among youth in the United States. Based on highly preliminary observational data, hang gliding participants are likely to be single, Caucasian college students who are "tuned in" to the hang gliding lifestyle. They are not unrealistic about the dangers of their sport but do not see it as overly hazardous. Reasons for leaving the sport generally center around injuries, family concerns, or career issues.

20. Scuba diving, while hazardous, appears to be a relatively safe activity when conducted properly. Overall, scuba participants appear to be rather unremarkable in personality makeup when compared with others except in the area of anxiety, where they appear to be generally low. Some evidence exists that these risks participants are also more internal and more masculine in sex role orientation.

21. Two correlates of risk taking have spawned a fair amount of research: sensation seeking and birth order effects. Clearly, high risk sport participants are sensation

seekers; they are unconventional, bored by routine, and seekers of stress through more unconventional means. As for birth effects, high risk sport participants are more likely to be laterborns than firstborn children. Apparently firstborns have their needs met in such a way that "proving" behavior through more unconventional means is not necessary for them.

22. Kroll's conceptualization of the personality performance pyramid is an intriguing way of viewing the elite athlete. Generally, however, the model is hard to support to the extent that research in the area is sparse and disconnected for the most part.

23. Morgan's notion of the Iceberg Profile as produced by the Profile of Mood States (POMS) has generated much research, and substantiation for the idea is considerable. Olympic wrestlers, oarsmen, distance runners, and cyclists all share commonalities in terms of the Iceberg Profile.

24. Wrestlers have been a fertile source of data on elite performers. In general, elite wrestlers when compared with their slightly less elite peers are most commonly differentiated by self-confidence and concentration on the task at hand. Performing at a level that is close to what they regard as their maximum potential is also a salient discriminator between the two groups of wrestlers.

25. Other studies of elite athletes from such diverse populations as Olympic weight lifters, Olympic gymnasts, Canadian Pan American Games participants from ten sports, elite New Zealand youth rowers, elite youth skiers in the United States, and national level racquetball players further substantiate the notion that elite performers are self-confident, task oriented, and actualized performers in terms of ability.

26. Studies of elite athletes are hampered by a host of methodological shortcomings

such as sample availability, sample size, definitional problems centering around what elite actually is, instrumentation selection, and data analysis variations. Nevertheless, research will continue in the hopes of shedding more light on the twin issues of identification and training of elite athletes.

SUGGESTED READINGS

Cashmore, E. (1982) *Black sportsman.* Boston, MA: Routledge & Kegan Paul.

> The trials and tribulations of being a black athlete in a largely white sports world in Great Britain are captured in this 226-page book. Brief testimonies by various black athletes are interspersed to add a more personal perspective on the issues surrounding the black athlete, a relative newcomer on the British sport scene.

Chalk, O. (1975) *Pioneers of black sport.* New York: Dodd, Mead.

> Chalk takes a look at the history of black athletes in four sports—baseball, basketball, boxing, and football. Pictures, historical chronicles, and game records of the early days of black sport serve as useful mechanisms to promote interest. This book is a must for the sport historian.

Dedera, D. (1975) *Hang gliding: The flyingest flying.* Flagstaff, AR: Northland Press.

> This book attempts to capture the essence of the sport of hang gliding through prose and a large number of color pictures. The beauty, the lifestyle, and the danger are all chronicled for the reader in a highly readable way. The photography is particularly compelling, with many of the pictures provided by the author.

Eysenck, H.J., Nias, D.K.B., & Cox, D.N. (1982) Sport and personality. *Behavior Research and Therapy, 4,* 1–56.

> Eysenck and his associates have taken an in-depth look at nearly three hundred studies related to sport personology. Topics discussed include measurement of personality in sport, antecedents of personality, the relationship of personality to

sport, differences between athletes in various sports, the state-trait distinction, sexuality, exercise and personality, somatotype theory, and strategies for learning physical skills. An excellent summary of the article is provided on pages 47 to 49.

Ravizza, K. (1984). *Qualities of the peak experience in sport.* In J. M. Silva and R. S. Weinberg (Eds.), *Psychological foundations of sport (pp. 452–461).* Champaign, IL: Human Kinetics.

Meaningful moments in sports, however elusive, are pursued by the author. Drawing from Maslow's "peak experiences" notion and Csikszentmihalyi's concept of "flow," Ravizza attempts to look at sport in terms of present awareness, complete absorption, perfection, harmony, oneness, and general transcendence of self.

REFERENCES

Alderman, R. (1970) A sociopsychological assessment of attitude toward physical activity in champion athletes. *Research Quarterly, 41,* 1–9.

Allport, G. W. (1937) *Personality—A psychological interpretation.* New York: Holt and Company.

Bachrach, A. (1970) Diver behavior. *Human Performance and SCUBA Diving, 11,* 9–137.

Ballham, A., & Allen, M. (1983) Air embolism in a sports diver. *British Journal of Sports Medicine, 17,* 7–9.

Beaumaster, E. J., Knowles, J. B., & MacLean, A. W. (1978) The sleep of skydivers: A study of stress. *Psychophysiology, 15,* 209–213.

Bem, S. (1974) The measurement of psychological androgyny. *Journal of Consulting and Clinical Psychology, 42,* 155–162.

Best, C. (1987) Experience and career length in professional football: The effect of positional segregation. *Sociology of Sport Journal, 4,* 410–420.

Brannigan, A., & McDougall, A. A. (1983) Peril and pleasure in the maintenance of a high risk sport: A study of hang-gliding. *Journal of Sport Behavior, 6,* 37–51.

Bulletin board. (1985) *NEA Now,* 5(10), 1–4.

Casher, B. (1977) Relationship between birth order and participation in dangerous sports. *Research Quarterly, 48,* 33–40.

Chu, D. (1982) *Dimensions of sport studies.* New York: Wiley.

Coakley, J. (1982) *Sport in society: Issues and controversies* (2d ed.). St. Louis, MO: C. V. Mosby.

Coakley, J. (1986) *Sport in society: Issues and controversies* (3d ed.). St. Louis, MO: Times Mirror/Mosby.

Correll, J. (1983) 1982 fatalities reflect best record since 1971. *Parachutist, 24*(4), 27–30.

Cox, R. H. (1985) *Sport psychology: Concepts and applications.* Dubuque, IA: Wm. C. Brown.

Curry, T., & Jiobu, R. (1984) *Sports: A social perspective.* Englewood Cliffs, NJ: Prentice-Hall.

Daiss, S., & LeUnes, A. (1986) The utility of the Profile of Mood States in sport research: An annotated bibliography. *Journal of Applied Research in Coaching and Athletics, 1,* 148–169.

Dishman, R. K. (1984) Motivation and exercise adherence. In J. M. Silva and R. S. Weinberg (Eds.), *Psychological foundations of sport (pp. 420–434).* Champaign, IL: Human Kinetics.

Dunn, J., & Lupfer, M. (1974) A comparison of black and white boys' performance in self-paced and reactive sports activities. *Journal of Applied Social Psychology, 4,* 24–35.

Edwards, H. (1973) *Sociology of sport.* Homewood, IL: Dorsey.

Egstrom, G., & Bachrach, A. (1971) Diver panic. *Skin Diver, 20*(11), 36–37, 54–55, 57.

Eitzen, S., & Sage, G. (1978) *Sociology of American sport.* Dubuque, IA: Wm. C. Brown.

Endler, N., & Okada, M. (1975) Multidimensional measure of trait anxiety: The S-R Inventory of General Trait Anxiousness. *Journal of Consulting and Clinical Psychology, 43,* 319–329.

Eron, L. (1987) The development of aggressive behavior from the perspective of a developing behaviorism. *American Psychologist, 42,* 435–442.

Eysenck, H. J., & Eysenck, S. B. G. (1963) *The Eysenck Personality Inventory.* San Diego, CA: Educational and Industrial Testing Service.

Eysenck, H. J., Nias, D. K. B., & Cox, D. N. (1982) Sport and personality. *Behavior Research and Therapy, 4*(1), 1–56.

Fenz, W. D., & Brown, M. (1958) Betting preferences and personality characteristics of sports parachutists. *Aerospace Medicine, 29,* 175–176.

Fenz, W. D., & Epstein, S. (1967) Changes in gradients of skin conductance, heart rate and respiration rate as a function of experience. *Psychosomatic Medicine, 29,* 33–51.

Fenz, W. D., & Jones, G. B. (1972) Individual differences in physiological arousal and performance in sport parachutists. *Psychosomatic Medicine, 34,* 1–8.

Finlayson, I. (1984) Obituary. *New Zealand Gliding Kiwi, 16*(1), 21.

Fisher, A. C. (1984) New directions in sport personality research. In J. M. Silva and R. S. Weinberg (Eds.), *Psychological foundations of sport* (pp. 70–80). Champaign, IL: Human Kinetics.

Gill, D. L. (1986) *Psychological dynamics of sport.* Champaign, IL: Human Kinetics.

Gould, D., Weiss, M., & Weinberg, R. S. (1981) Psychological characteristics of successful and nonsuccessful Big Ten wrestlers. *Journal of Sport Psychology, 3,* 69–81.

Griffiths, T. J., Steel, D. H., & Vaccaro, P. (1978) Anxiety levels of beginning SCUBA students. *Perceptual and Motor Skills, 47,* 312–314.

Griffiths, T. J., Steel, D. H., & Vaccaro, P. (1979) Relationship between anxiety and performance in scuba diving. *Perceptual and Motor Skills, 48,* 1009–1010.

Griffiths, T. J., Steel, D. H., & Vaccaro, P. (1982) Anxiety of scuba divers: A multidimensional approach. *Perceptual and Motor Skills, 55,* 611–614.

Griffiths, T. J., Steel, D. H., Vaccaro, P., & Karpman, M. (1981) The effects of relaxation techniques on anxiety and underwater performance. *International Journal of Sport Psychology, 12,* 176–182.

Hagberg, J., Mullin, J., Bahrke, M., & Limburg, J. (1979) Physiological profiles and selected physiological characteristics of national class American cyclists. *Journal of Sports Medicine, 19,* 341–346.

Hall, E., Church, G., & Stone, M. (1980) Relationship of birth order to selected personality characteristics of nationally ranked Olympic weight lifters. *Perceptual and Motor Skills, 51,* 971–976.

Hammerton, M., & Tickner, A. (1968) An investigation in to the effects of stress upon skilled performance. *Ergonomics, 12,* 851–855.

Hathaway, S., & McKinley, J. (1943) *MMPI Manual.* New York: Psychological Corporation.

Heyman, S. R., & Rose, K. G. (1979) Psychological variables affecting scuba performance. In C. H. Naudeau, W. R. Halliwell, K. M. Newell, & G. C. Roberts (Eds.), *Psychology of motor behavior and sport — 1979* (pp. 180–188). Champaign, IL: Human Kinetics.

High jump. (1985) *Track and Field News, 37*(12), 38.

Highlen, P., & Bennett, B. (1979) Psychological characteristics of successful and nonsuccessful elite wrestlers: An exploratory study. *Journal of Sport Psychology, 1,* 123–137.

Highlen, P., & Bennett, B. (1983) Elite divers and wrestlers: A comparison between open- and closed-skill athletes. *Journal of Sport Psychology, 5,* 390–409.

Hollander, E. P., (1967) *Principles and methods of social psychology.* New York: Oxford University Press.

Hymbaugh, K., & Garrett, J. (1974) Sensation seeking among skydivers. Perceptual and Motor Skills, 38, 118.

Johnsgard, K. W., Ogilvie, B. C., & Merritt, K. (1975) The stress seekers: A psychological study of sports parachutists, racing drivers, and football players. *Journal of Sports Medicine, 15,* 158–169.

Johnson, C. (1980) Heart rates in boat racers. *The Physician and Sportsmedicine, 8*(6), 86–93.

Jones, J., & Hochner, A. (1973) Racial differences in sports activities: A look at the self-paced versus reactive hypothesis. *Journal of Personality and Social Psychology, 27,* 86–95.

Kenyon, G. (1968) A conceptual model for characterizing physical activity. *Research Quarterly, 39,* 96–105.

Kroll, W. (1970) Current strategies and problems in personality assessment of athletes. In L. E. Smith (Ed.), *Psychology of motor learning* (pp. 349–367). Chicago, IL: Athletic Institute.

Kroll, W. (1976) Reaction to Morgan's paper: Psychological consequences of vigorous physical activity and sport. In M. G. Scott (Ed.), *The academy papers* (pp. 30–35). Iowa City, IA: American Academy of Physical Education.

Lazarus, R. S., & Monat, A. (1979) *Personality* (3rd ed.). Englewood Cliffs, NJ: Prentice-Hall.

Leonard, W. M. (1984) *A sociological perspective of sport* (2d ed). Minneapolis, MN: Burgess.

Leonard, W. M., & Reyman, J. E. (1988) The odds of attaining professional athlete status: Refining the computation. *Sociology of Sport Journal, 5,* 162–169.

LeUnes, A., Hayward, S. A., & Daiss, S. (1988) Annotated bibliography on the Profile of Mood States in sport, 1975–1988. *Journal of Sport Behavior, 11,* 213–219.

LeUnes, A., & Nation, J. R. (1982) Saturday's heroes: A psychological portrait of college football players. *Journal of Sport Behavior, 5,* 139–149.

Lewin, K. (1935) *A dynamic theory of personality.* New York: McGraw-Hill.

Longstreth, L. (1970) Birth order and avoidance of dangerous activities. *Developmental Psychology, 2,* 154.

Loy, J., & McElvogue, J. (1970) Racial segregation in American sport. *International Review of Sport Sociology, 5,* 5–24.

Lubin, B. (1967) Manual for the *Depression Adjective Checklist.* San Diego, CA: Educational and Industrial Testing Service.

Mahoney, M. J., & Avener, M. (1977) Psychology of the elite athlete. *Cognitive Therapy and Research, 1,* 135–141.

Martens, R. (1975) The paradigmatic crisis in American sport personology. *Sportswissenschaft, 5,* 9–24.

Martens, R. (1981) Sport personology. In G. R. F. Luschen & G. H. Sage (Eds.), *Handbook of social science of sport* (pp. 492–508). Champaign, IL: Stipes.

McNair, D. M., Lorr, M., & Droppleman, L. F. (1971) *Profile of Mood States Manual.* San Diego, CA: Educational and Industrial Testing Service.

Medoff, M. H. (1986) Positional segregation and the economic hypothesis. *Sociology of Sport Journal, 3,* 297–304.

Mehrabian, A. (1969) Measures of achieving tendency. *Educational and Psychological Measurement, 29,* 445–451.

Meyers, A., Cooke, C., Cullen, J., & Liles, L. (1979) Psychological aspects of athletic competitors: A replication across sports. *Cognitive Therapy and Research, 3,* 361–366.

Morgan, W. P. (1968) Personality characteristics of wrestlers participating in the world championships. *Journal of Sports Medicine, 8,* 212–216.

Morgan, W. P. (1978a) Sport personology: The credulous–skeptical argument in perspective. In W. F. Straub (Ed.), *An analysis of athletic behavior* (pp. 218–227). Ithaca, NY: Mouvement.

Morgan, W. P. (1978b) Mind of the marathoner. *Sports Illustrated,* April, pp. 38–49.

Morgan, W. P., & Johnson, R. (1976) Personality characteristics of successful and unsuccessful oarsmen. *International Journal of Sport Psychology, 9,* 119–133.

Morgan, W. P., & Pollock, M. L. (1977) Psychological characteristics of the elite distance runner. *Annals of the New York Academy of Sciences, 301,* 382–403.

Nation, J. R., & LeUnes, A. (1983) A personality profile of the black athlete in college football. *Psychology, 20,* 1–3.

Nisbett, R. E. (1968) Birth order and participation in dangerous sports. *Journal of Personality and Social Psychology, 8,* 351–353.

Nixon, H. L. (1981) Birth order and preference for risky sports among college students. *Journal of Sport Behavior, 4,* 12–23.

Ogilvie, B. C. (1974) The sweet psychic jolt of danger. *Psychology Today,* Oct., pp. 88–91.

Ottley, W. (1983) USPA secretary killed while making stunt jump. *Parachutist, 24*(3), 35.

Peterson, R. (1970) *Only the ball was white.* Englewood Cliffs, NJ: Prentice-Hall.

Phillips, J. C. (1976) Toward an explanation of racial variations in top-level sports participation. *International Review of Sport Sociology, 11* (3), 39–55.

Phillips, J. C. (1988) A further comment on the 'economic hypothesis' of positional segregation in baseball. *Sociology of Sport Journal, 5,* 63–65.

Powell, F. M., & Verner, J. P. (1982) Anxiety and performance relationships in first time parachutists. *Journal of Sport Psychology, 4,* 184–188.

Rader, B. (1983) *American sports from the age of folk games to the age of spectators.* Englewood Cliffs, NJ: Prentice-Hall.

Robertson, I. (1981) *Sociology* (2d ed.) New York: Worth.

Rotella, R., Gansneder, B., Ojala, D., & Billing, J. (1980) Cognitions and coping strategies of elite skiers: An exploratory study of young developing athletes. *Journal of Sport Psychology, 2,* 350–354.

Ruffer, W. A. (1975) Personality traits in athletes. *Physical Educator, 32,* 105–109.

Ruffer, W. A. (1976a) Personality traits in athletes. *Physical Educator, 33,* 50–55.

Ruffer, W. A. (1976b) Personality traits in athletes. *Physical Educator, 33,* 211–214.

Ryan, E. D. (1968) Reaction to "sport and personality dynamics." In *Proceedings* (pp. 70–75). Minneapolis, MN: National College Physical Education Association for Men.

Sheldon, W. H. (1940) *The varieties of human physique.* New York: Harper.

Sheldon, W. H. (1942) *The varieties of human temperament.* New York: Harper.

Silva, J. M. (1984) Personality and sport performance: Controversy and challenge. In J. M. Silva & R. S. Weinberg (Eds.), *Psychological foundations of sport* (pp. 59–69). Champaign, IL: Human Kinetics.

Silva, J. M., Shultz, B., Haslam, R., & Murray, D. (1981) A psychophysiological assessment of elite wrestlers. *Research Quarterly for Exercise and Sport, 52,* 348–358.

Straub, W. F. (1982) Sensation seeking among high and low-risk male athletes. *Journal of Sport Psychology, 4,* 246–253.

Tangen-Foster, J. W., & Lathen, C. W. (1983) Risk sports in basic instruction programs: A status assessment. *Research Quarterly for Exercise and Sport, 54,* 305–308.

Weltman, G., & Egstrom, G. H. (1969) Personal autonomy of scuba diver trainees. *Research Quarterly, 40,* 613–618.

Wiggins, D. (1977) Good times on the old plantation: Popular recreations of the black slave in Antebellum South, 1810–1860. *Journal of Sport History, 4,* 260–281.

Willard, N. (1978) Testing the limits. *World Health,* Nov., pp. 22–26.

Williams, L. (1978). Prediction of high-level rowing ability. *Journal of Sports Medicine, 18,* 11–17.

Williams, R., & Youssef, Z. (1975) Division of labor in college football along racial lines. *International Journal of Sport Psychology, 6,* 1–13.

Worthy, M., & Markle, A. (1970) Racial differences in reactive versus self-paced sports activities. *Journal of Personality and Social Psychology, 16,* 439–443.

Yetman, N. R. (1987) "Positional segregation and the economic hypothesis:" A critique. *Sociology of Sport Journal, 4,* 274–277.

Yiannakis, A. (1976) Birth order and preference for dangerous sports among males. *Research Quarterly, 47,* 62–67.

Zuckerman, M. (1971) Dimensions of sensation-seeking. *Journal of Consulting and Clinical Psychology, 36,* 45–52.

Zuckerman, M. (1984) Experience and desire: A new format for Sensation Seeking Scales. *Journal of Behavioral Assessment, 6,* 101–114.

Zuckerman, M., Kolin, E. A., Price, L., & Zoob, I. (1964) Development of a Sensation-seeking Scale. *Journal of Consulting Psychology, 28,* 477–482.

Psychological Assessment

INTRODUCTION

Psychological testing is big business in the United States today; the role of testing in athletics is substantial, also. Tests may be administered to individuals or groups and cover such diverse aspects of human behavior as intelligence, aptitude, achievement, personality, and interests. One type of testing alone, academic aptitude, involves well over 2 million people annually (Kaplan and Sacuzzo, 1982). Of that number, 1.8 million take the Scholastic Aptitude Test (SAT), another 120,000 the Law School Admission Test (LSAT), and 75,000 a special test for admission to business school. Coupled with the considerable use of various other aptitude and interest tests in the public high schools and colleges, and the use of personality tests in our employment/clinical psychology/criminal justice networks, they are a multibillion dollar enterprise of considerable significance.

Important, sometimes critical, decisions are made about people based on test results. Children with intellectual deficits are assigned to special education classes or schools for the mentally retarded; other children are placed in gifted and talented classes in order to capitalize on their mental abilities; individuals are classified as schizophrenic or psychopathic because of test results that substantiate their behavioral idiosyncrasies. Tests have been with us for most of the twentieth century and will have an important role, despite their controversial status, in events of the foreseeable future.

For all of these reasons, the highest degree of ethical behavior must be brought to bear on the use of psychological tests. Later in this chapter we will look at test ethics as applied to the sport psychologist and then the broader ethical issues in sport.

A BRIEF HISTORY

Testing currently is, by and large, an American enterprise. However, Kaplan and Sacuzzo (1982) tell us that the Chinese four thousand years ago had a reasonably sophisticated system of testing that was used in work evaluation and job promotion decisions. Subsequent developments extended into many facets of Chinese life to include examinations to determine who was qualified to serve in public office, a precursor of our civil service testing program in this country. Kaplan and Sacuzzo point out that the Western world probably learned about testing through interactions with the Chinese in the nineteenth century.

Though rudimentary attempts were made at testing in the late 1800s, and considerable theorizing about individual differences was starting to emerge, the first major breakthrough came at the turn of the century through the work of two Frenchmen, A. Binet and T. Simon. Initially, Binet was commissioned by the French ministry of education to design a paper-and-pencil test to separate the mentally fit from the intellectually subnormal. Out of this initial effort the two men developed the Binet-Simon Scale, which was published in 1905, revised in 1908, and again in 1911. A Stanford psychologist, Lewis Terman, adapted the scale for use in the United States in 1916, and the testing movement as a major force in psychology was under way. World Wars I and II intensified interest in testing, and led to many important improvements.

On another front, personality testing was given its initial impetus about the time of World War I. Early tests included the Rorschach Inkblot Test, developed in 1921. These first efforts led to a proliferation of paper and pencil instruments designed to measure both global and isolated traits of personality. Of these tests, none has achieved the stature of the Minnesota Multiphasic Personality Inventory (MMPI). Its impact across a number of areas of personality research and application extends to sport psychology, as we shall see shortly. A brief history of the testing movement is provided in table 9.1.

Psychological tests remain one of the most salient aspects of psychology. They have not been without critics, however, and some of the criticisms are justified. Tests have many uses and, as a consequence, are susceptible to abuse. Proper selection, use, and reporting of tests is a challenge for all psychologists, sport psychologists among them.

WHAT IS A TEST?

To Cronbach (1970, p. 26) a *test* is "a systematic procedure for observing a person's behavior and describing it with the aid of a numerical scale or a category-system." The emphasis here is on avoiding unsystematic, spur-of-the-moment procedures for evaluation, such as casual conversation. To Anastasi (1982, p. 22), a psychological test is "essentially an objective and standardized measure of a sample of behavior." Emphasis in this case is placed on the use of objective measurement and on the important notion that test responses are merely a sample of a person's overall behavior. It is hoped, of course, that the sample will be representative of the totality; this is the essence of creating a valid testing instrument. A third definitional stance is taken by Kaplan and Sacuzzo (1982, p. 4): "A psychological test is a device for measuring characteristics of human beings that pertain to behavior." Kaplan and Sacuzzo add that these behaviors include both the overt, or observable, and the covert, or internal and unobservable (feelings and thoughts). They also point to the fact that tests can be used to measure past, present, and future behaviors. For example, a test over this text material might be representative. How much you have studied (i.e., the past) is tapped, your level of current functioning is measured, and some predictions for future performance can be made. We suspect your professor will be concurrently doing all three of these things with his or her tests! In any event, the emphasis on the objective study of behavior that is implied in all three definitions will serve as our guide for the rest of the material in this chapter.

RELIABILITY, VALIDITY, AND NORMS

Three critical dimensions of any psychological test are *reliability, validity,* and *norms;* that is, is a test consistent in what it is measuring and does it measure what it was designed to measure and is our reference group relevant? Tests lacking these qualities are of little use.

Reliability

A *reliable test* is one that yields consistency, or to quote Aiken (1982):

> To be useful, psychological and educational tests, and other measuring instruments, must be fairly consistent or reliable in what they measure. The concept of the reliability of a test refers to its relative freedom from unsystematic errors of measurement. A test is reliable if it measures consistently under varying conditions that can produce measurement errors. Unsystematic errors affecting test scores vary in a random, unpredictable manner from situation to situation; hence, they lower test reliability. On the other hand, systematic (constant) errors may inflate or deflate test scores, but they do so in a fixed way and hence do not affect test reliability. Some of the variables on which unsystematic error depends are the particular sample of questions on the test, the conditions of administration, and the internal state of the examinee at testing time. (P. 72)

Table 9.1 Selected Events in the History of Psychological and Educational Measurement

2200 B.C.	Mandarins set up civil-service testing program in China.		R. Woodworth's Personal Data Sheet, the first standardized personality inventory, used in military selection.
1219 A.D.	First formal oral examination in law held at University of Bologna.	1919	L. Thurstone's Psychological Examination for College Freshmen published.
1575	J. Huarte publishes book, *Examen de Ingenios*, concerned with individual differences in mental abilities.	1920	National Intelligence Scale published; H. Rorschach's Inkblot Test first published.
1636	Oral examination for degree certification used at Oxford University.	1921	Psychological Corporation, first major test publishing company, founded by Cattell, Thorndike, and Woodworth.
1860s	Beginning of use of written examination in schools and governmental organizations in Great Britain, continental Europe, and the United States.	1923	First achievement test battery, Stanford Achievement Tests, published.
		1924	T. L. Kelley's *Statistical Method* published.
1869	Scientific study of individual differences begins with publication of Galton's "Classification of Men According to Their Natural Gifts."	1927	First edition of Strong Vocational Interest Blank for Men published.
		1936	Soviet Union bans psychological tests; first volume of Psychometrika published.
1879	Founding of first psychological laboratory in the world by Wilhelm Wundt at Leipzig, Germany.	1938	H. Murray publishes *Explorations in Personality;* O. K. Buros publishes first *Mental Measurements Yearbook*.
1884	F. Galton opens Anthropometric Laboratory in London for International Health Exhibition.	1939	Wechsler-Bellevue Intelligence Scale published.
1888	J. M. Cattell opens testing laboratory at the University of Pennsylvania.	1942	Minnesota Multiphasic Personality Inventory published.
1893	J. Jastrow displays sensorimotor tests at the Columbian Exposition in Chicago.	1949	Wechsler Intelligence Scale for Children published.
1897	J. Rice publishes research findings on spelling abilities of U.S. school children.	1969	A. Jensen's paper on racial inheritance of IQ published in *Harvard Educational Review.*
1904	C. Spearman describes his two-factor theory of mental abilities.		
1905	First Binet-Simon Intelligence Scale published; C. Jung uses word-association test for analysis of mental complexes.	1970	Increasing use of computers in designing, administering, scoring, analyzing, and interpreting tests.
1908	C. Stone's Arithmetic Tests are published.	1971	Federal court decision requiring tests used in personnel selection to be job relevant (*Griggs v. Duke Power*).
1908-1914	E. L. Thorndike develops standardized tests of arithmetic, handwriting, language, and spelling.	1974	Wechsler Intelligence Scale for Children Revised.
1916	Stanford-Binet Intelligence Scale published by L. Terman.	1975	Growth of behavioral assessment techniques.
1917	Army Alpha and Army Beta, first group intelligence tests, constructed and administered to U.S. army recruits;	1978	Eighth edition of the *Mental Measurements Yearbook* published.
		1980	Wechsler Adult Intelligence Scale (Revised) published.

SOURCE: *Psychological Testing and Assessment* (pp. 5–6) by L. Aiken, 1982, Boston, MA: Allyn & Bacon.

Psychologists generally use three methods of determining reliability, namely, *test-retest, parallel forms,* and *internal consistency.* Simply stated, the test–retest format requires the same group of examinees to respond to a given test on two separate occasions. In parallel forms, two equivalent forms in terms of content and difficulty are administered to the same subjects. Parallel forms do exist, but are difficult to put together, and are often expensive and, as a consequence, are rare in much of psychology and in sport psychology in particular. Finally, the internal consistency method is achieved through several statistically based procedures (split-half method, Kuder-Richardson reliability, and Coefficient Alpha) in which internal properties of tests are scrutinized. The reliability of a particular instrument is expressed numerically from a *perfect positive relationship* between two or more variables (+1.00) to a *perfect negative relationship* (−1.00), with a correlation coefficient of .00 indicating *no relationship.*

Validity

The generally accepted definition of *validity* is couched in terms of the degree to which a test measures what it is created to measure. This definition, according to Aiken (1982), assumes that validity is rather unidimensional, which is not the case at all. Aiken says:

> Among the methods for studying the validity of a test are analyzing its content, relating scores on the test to scores on a criterion of interest, and investigating the particular psychological characteristics or constructs measured by the test. All of these procedures for assessing validity are useful to the extent that they increase understanding of what a test is measuring so that the scores will represent more accurate information on which to base decisions. (P. 80)

This broadened definition sets the stage for a discussion of the three dimensions of validity: content, concurrent, and predictive.

Content Validity. Content validity is the extent to which the behaviors sampled on a given test are representative of the totality of all possible behaviors that could be assessed. The most obvious example here would be the tests taken in a classroom. It is hoped that the questions asked will be representative of the course content.

Concurrent Validity. Concurrent validity is a type of criterion-related validity in which the diagnosis of existing status rather than prediction of performance is paramount. This is particularly relevant to sport psychology, as we shall see, because of the need for "sport specific" tests. There is a growing mood of disenchantment over tests being used in sports that have dubious validity based on their being intended for use with nonsport samples; that is, concurrent validity appears to be questionable.

Predictive Validity. Predictive validity is a second type of criterion-related validity. Here the critical issue is the degree to which the test is predictive of performance. A highly valid test in sport psychology, for instance, would be one that relates closely to performance. A test battery administered on Thursday that would yield a coefficient of performance for a given individual or team on Saturday would indeed possess predictive validity. Examples such as this, however, are much more theoretical than actual at this time.

Norms

Most tests give good coverage to a summary of the individuals that make up the sample for which the test was normed and is therefore intended. Any speculation beyond this is suspect until research indicates that further applications are justified. The MMPI, normed on mental patients, has been used with graduate students, medical students, law enforcement officers, and athletes, and the violation of the norms that is inherent here has not gone unnoticed or uncontested.

Selecting valid, reliable, and applicable psychological tests remains a trying task for psychologists in all fields of the discipline; the sport psychologist is not at all exempt from this challenge!

USES OF TESTS IN SPORT: AN INTRODUCTION

In the broadest sense, testing can include structured interviews, systematic behavioral observations, and a host of other techniques. However, for the purposes of our discussion, testing will unless otherwise indicated be restricted largely to paper-and-pencil measures, and primarily but not exclusively to those dealing with personality traits and states.

At this juncture, a look at several specific types of tests that are used in sport research and counseling would seem appropriate. Primary emphasis will be placed on the measurement of personality variables, both enduring and temporary. Secondary emphasis will be assigned to sport-specific tests, an area of increasing interest to sport psychologists. Finally, a brief mention will be made of attitude measures used in sport.

TESTS OF ENDURING PERSONALITY TRAITS

Three standardized measures of enduring traits have dominated research in sport for the past forty years, beginning with the *Minnesota Multiphasic Personality Inventory (MMPI)* in 1943 (Hathaway and McKinley). Two other in-

struments of somewhat more recent vintage that have been utilized often are the *16 Personality Factor Questionnaire (16PF)* (Cattell, 1949) and the *Eysenck Personality Inventory (EPI)* (Eysenck and Eysenck, 1963). Each will be discussed in terms of its origin and its application to sport.

Minnesota Multiphasic Personality Inventory (MMPI)

The MMPI, 550 items long and answered "yes," "no," or "cannot say," was created by S.R. Hathaway, a psychologist, and J.C. McKinley, a physician, in 1943. The original purpose of the test was to differentiate among various psychiatric categories. No particular theoretical approach characterizes the MMPI; rather, it represents an example of criterion keying. The criterion groups (N = 50 per group) used in the development of the MMPI were psychiatric inpatients at the University of Minnesota Hospital. They were as follows (Kaplan and Sacuzzo, 1982, p. 323):

1. hypochondriacs, individuals preoccupied with the body and fears of illness;
2. depressed patients;
3. hysterics, primarily individuals who showed a physical problem with no physical cause, such as hysterical blindness;
4. psychopathic deviates, delinquent, criminal or antisocial individuals;
5. paranoids, individuals who showed symptoms including poor reality testing (for example, delusions in which they falsely believed that people were plotting against them);
6. psychasthenics, individuals with a neurotic disorder characterized by excessive doubts and unreasonable fear;
7. schizophrenics, individuals with a psychotic disorder involving dramatic symptoms such as hallucinations (seeing things that aren't there) and thinking problems such as illogical reasoning; and
8. hypomanics, individuals with a disorder characterized by hyperactivity and irritability.

The four hundred criterion individuals were then compared to approximately seven hundred control subjects consisting (unfortunately) of relatives and friends of the criterion cases. Critics of the MMPI have not let this point go unnoticed.

In addition to the eight so-called clinical scales derived from and labeled according to the types of patients, two others were subsequently added: the masculinity-femininity (MF) scale and the social-introversion (SI) scale. The MF was designed to assess male-female differences, the SI to assess the tendency to be (or not to be) outgoing. Finally, scales to measure test-taking attitudes, honesty in test taking, carelessness, misunderstanding, malingering, or the operation of special response sets were created; these were called the L (Lie), F (Frequency or Infrequency), and K (Correction) scales.

The MMPI is easily the most used personality test, having been the subject of approximately six thousand research studies (Kaplan and Sacuzzo, 1982); in addition, it has been translated into all European languages (Blaser and Schilling, 1976), the only personality instrument having that distinction.

Predictably, the MMPI is not without its shortcomings. Charges have been leveled that the size and representativeness of the normative sample is questionable. Other criticisms include item overlap among the various scales, imbalance in true-false keying, high scale intercorrelations, relatively weak reliability, and generalizability problems across demographic variables (Kaplan and Sacuzzo, 1982). Despite these weaknesses, the MMPI continues to enjoy immense popularity in clinical psychology, and its reception among sport psychologists has been considerable.

Perhaps the first sport study in which the MMPI was utilized was conducted by LaPlace (1954). In this instance, the MMPI was administered to forty-nine major league baseball players and sixty-four of their minor league counterparts. The major league players, as predicted, demonstrated a generally healthier profile with significantly lower scores on the schizophrenia and psychopathic deviate scales. Whether or not these mental states were present prior to entering baseball or came about in the interim, of course, is not known. A subsequent study by Booth in 1958 gave further credibility to the MMPI. Booth, using freshman and varsity athletes, team and individual sport participants, and athletes rated as good or poor performers, found several differences. Chief among these differences was the finding that varsity athletes who participated in individual sports scored significantly higher on the depression (D) scale and that varsity athletes competing in individual sports scored significantly higher than athletes competing in both team and individual sports on the psychasthenia (Pt) variable. Twenty-two items that discriminated good from poor athletes were identified from among the total item pool of 550 items. Booth (p. 136) concludes: "The MMPI has demonstrated merit as an instrument of measurement of personality traits of participants in programs of physical education and athletics." Booth's 22-item scale and the MMPI came under criticism by Rasch, Hunt, and Robertson (1960) when they failed to replicate Booth's findings using varsity wrestlers from the University of California at Los Angeles and the University of Oklahoma. Booth (1961) rebutted the contention of Rasch and associates by pointing to critical methodological and sampling differences between his work and theirs. Finally, Slusher (1964) showed that high school athletes and nonathletes respond quite differently to the MMPI. In his study, the two groups were different on all MMPI clinical scales except hypomania. Also, a difference was noted on the validity scale. The important thing here is that the MMPI did in fact differentiate clearly between the two groups.

Studies continued into the 1970s with a variety of athletes. Williams and Youssef (1972),

Psychological testing in sports focuses extensively on personality variables. Studies of Olympic wrestlers, for example, show that successful participants are lower in anger, tension, depression, and fatigue than their less successful counterparts.

in looking at the relationship of personality variables to personality stereotypes based on position played, administered the MMPI to 251 football players from four different colleges in Michigan. No differences were found across thirteen positions that the authors used to categorize football players. In a series of studies of gifted athletes, William Morgan and various associates have demonstrated the efficacy of a trait approach to personality assessment in athletics, and one of the tests they commonly use has been the MMPI. Beginning with a study of collegiate wrestlers over a five-year period, Morgan (1968) found that successful wrestlers (those

who entered as freshmen and went on to win two or three letters) demonstrated superior adjustment when compared with their less successful peers (freshmen going on to win one or no letters). Morgan and Johnson (1978), in a similar vein, followed up on fifty college oarsmen after four years of competition and found, again, that the successful competitors (two or three varsity letters) had a more favorable MMPI profile than the less successful oarsmen (one or no letters). All eight clinical subscales yielded a more desirable profile for the successful oarsmen.

A rather interesting comparison was made by Johnsgard, Ogilvie, and Merritt (1975) in their study of elite sports parachutists, race drivers, and football players. In order to be a part of the research, all parachutists (N = 43) must have made at least one thousand free fall jumps; the race drivers were considered to be the top thirty participants in the world at that time; the football players (N = 50) were all professionals with five or more years of experience and at least one selection as an All-Pro performer. MMPI differences among the three groups were relatively small; table 9.2 discloses what few differences existed. According to Johnsgard and his associates, there were no differences between parachutists and race drivers on any of the scales. Football players did score significantly higher on the psychasthenia (Pt) scale than either of the other two groups suggesting, along with the hypochondriasis (Hs) differences between them and parachutists, that football players are more concerned with physical health and body functions. The

difference between football players and race drivers on the psychopathic deviate (Pd) scale is interesting, suggesting authority concerns among footballers. Finally, the paranoia (Pa) difference between football players and parachutists may be suggestive of greater social awareness on the part of the first group. More recently, Geron, Furst, and Rotstein (1986) administered the MMPI to 273 male athletes and 379 male nonathletes. In general, the utility of the MMPI in discriminating among various groups of athletes was upheld.

All in all, the MMPI has an interesting history within sport research. Though it has had its moments, there is no ground swell of movement at this time to suggest that it is *the* instrument for sport research. The broad issue of validity, the usefulness of nonsport normed tests for sport research, and the highly clinical nature of the instrument are all problematical. Nevertheless, it may be a bit premature to

Table 9.2 Mean Raw Scores with K Added, Mean Derived Scores, and T-Test Confidence Levels for the MMPI

	Groups						Confidence levels between means (two-tail)		
Scales	P Parachutists		R Race drivers		F Football players		P-R	P-F	R-F
	R-S	DER	R-S	DER	R-S	DER			
L	3.2		3.5		3.7				
F	5.0	55	5.9	57	4.5	54			
K	14.1	54	13.4	52	14.9	55			
Hs	10.7	48	11.0	49	12.2	52		.02	
D	17.8	52	18.4	55	17.2	51			
Hy	18.2	53	19.1	55	19.2	55			
Pd	22.9	60	21.4	55	23.6	61			.05
Mf	24.1	57	24.7	58	23.9	57			
Pa	9.2	54	9.0	53	10.4	57		.05	
Pt	24.4	53	24.1	52	27.0	59		.01	.05
Sc	24.5	54	23.4	52	26.3	57			
Ma	21.3	61	22.1	63	22.6	64			
Si	24.9	50	24.0	49	22.9	48			

SOURCE: "The Stress Seekers: A Psychological Study of Sports Parachutists, Racing Drivers, and Football Players" by K. Johnsgard, B. C. Ogilvie, and K. Merritt, 1975, *Journal of Sports Medicine, 15,* 158–169.

totally dismiss the MMPI from our trait psychology armamentarium. Certainly, its historical significance for personality research in sport is considerable.

Sixteen Personality Factor Questionnaire (16PF)

As opposed to the criterion-based approach found in the MMPI, the 16PF (Cattell, 1949) represents an attempt to develop a personality test through the use of the sophisticated statistical technique known as factor analysis. Cattell, its creator, began his work with nearly 18,000 adjectives found in the dictionary by Allport and Odbert (1936). By consistent refinement, Cattell arrived at 180 items that measure sixteen factors assumed to be descriptive of personality. These factors are listed in table 9.3.

Though not as popular a research instrument overall as the MMPI, the 16PF has many advocates and users in sport circles. One index of its popularity is offered by Thakur and Thakur (1980), who have studied differences between athletes and nonathletes in India using a Hindi version. An early study using the 16PF was conducted by Heusner (1952), who looked at the personality of forty-one Olympic athletes as part of his master's degree requirements at the University of Illinois. For an extensive review of subsequent studies through the next fifteen years, consult Hardman (1973), who amassed the results of forty-two studies through 1969 involving sports such as cross country, swimming, gymnastics, climbing, tennis, riflery, golf, judo, wrestling, karate, association football, rugby football, American football, and basketball. Hardman found a great deal of variability in the results of these works.

Interest in the 16PF continued unabated into the 1970s. For example, Williams, Hoepner, Moody, and Ogilvie (1970) studied thirty national-level female fencers using the 16PF. In general, the subjects could be described, when compared with national collegiate norms, as intelligent, experimenting, self-sufficient,

independent, and creative. Straub and Davis (1971), in a study of football athletes playing at four different levels of competition (Ivy League, small private school, small state-supported college, Big Ten university), found considerable differences within their samples. These investigators concluded that football players involved in major college football are very different from those taking part in football at a lower level. In a somewhat similar vein, Rushall (1972) studied the 1966, 1967, and 1968 football teams at Indiana University using the 16PF. Rushall isolated few differences among the squads from those three years even though performance varied considerably over time (1966 team was 1–8–1, 1967 team 9–1, and 1968 team 6–4). In a separate study reported in the same article, Rushall administered the 16PF to five college and six high school football squads. Upon analysis, he again found few personality differences and concluded that no football player personality exists. A third study, again in the same report, generally supported Rushall's previous conclusions.

Studies from the mid-1970s include King and Chi (1974) and Foster (1977). In general, King and Chi found track athletes to be most similar to nonathletes, football players to be least similar to nonathletes, with swimmers and basketball players generally falling in between the extremes. Foster studied athletes from four sports—football, baseball, basketball, and track. His six-part groupings of athletes (successful-unsuccessful athletes, outstanding-other, successful-unsuccessful football, successful-unsuccessful baseball, successful-unsuccessful basketball, and successful-unsuccessful track) yielded few significant differences on the 16PF. Factor F, surgency, and Factor H, adventurousness, differentiated between the two football groups, and Factor G, imaginativeness, separated the two track groups. Otherwise there were no significant differences.

As testimony to the continuing popularity of the 16PF, a spate of more recent studies are

Table 9.3 The Primary Source Traits Covered by the 16PF Test

Factor	Low Sten score description (1–3)	High Sten score description (8–10)
A	Reserved, detached, critical, aloof, stiff Sizothymia	Outgoing, warmhearted, easygoing, participating Affectothymia
B	Dull Low intelligence	Bright High intelligence
C	Affected by feelings, emotionally less stable, easily upset, changeable Lower ego strength	Emotionally stable, mature, faces reality, calm Higher ego strength
E	Humble, mild, easily led, docile, accommodating Submissiveness	Assertive, aggressive, competitive, stubborn Dominance
F	Sober, taciturn, serious Desurgency	Happy-go-lucky, enthusiastic Surgency
G	Expedient, disregards rules Weaker superego strength	Conscientious, persistent, moralistic, staid Stronger superego strength
H	Shy, timid, threat-sensitive Threctia	Venturesome, uninhibited, socially bold Parmia
I	Tough-minded, self-reliant, realistic Harria	Tender-minded, sensitive, clinging, overprotected Premsia
L	Trusting, accepting conditions Alaxia	Suspicious, hard to fool Protension
M	Practical, "down-to-earth" concerns Praxernia	Imaginative, bohemian, absent minded Autia
N	Forthright, unpretentious, genuine but socially clumsy Artlessness	Astute, polished, socially aware Shrewdness
O	Self-assured, placid, secure, complacent, serene Untroubled adequacy	Apprehensive self-reproaching, insecure, worrying, troubled Guilt proneness
Q_1	Conservative, respecting traditional ideas Conservatism of temperament	Experimenting, liberal, free-thinking Radicalism
Q_2	Group dependent, a "joiner" and sound follower Group adherence	Self-sufficient, resourceful, prefers own decisions Self-sufficiency
Q_3	Undisciplined, self-conflict, lax, follows own urges, careless of social rules Low self-sentiment integration	Controlled, exacting will power, socially precise, compulsive High strength of self-sentiment
Q_4	Relaxed, tranquil, torpid, unfrustrated, composed Low ergic tension	Tense, frustrated, driven, overwrought High ergic tension

SOURCE: *Handbook for the Sixteen Personality Factor Questionnaire (16 PF)* (pp. 77–109) by R. B. Cattell, H. W. Eber, and M. M. Tatsuoka, 1970, Champaign, IL: Institute for Personality and Ability Testing.

available. In a study of outstanding Indian table tennis and badminton players, Bhushan and Agarwal (1978) found considerable differences between outstanding international competitors and low achieving participants; too, they found substantial differences between outstanding male and female participants. In a study of physical education majors and nonmajors, Gruber and Perkins (1978) concluded that the 16PF was not effective in discriminating among various categories that they had created. In a 1979 report, Renfrow and Bolton (1979a) compared 16PF responses of twenty-three adult male exercisers with an equal number of nonexercisers. Differences were found on six primary and four secondary factors. The exercisers were found to be more reserved, expedient, suspicious, forthright, liberal, and self-sufficient on the primary traits and more alert, more independent, less discreet, and showed lower superego strength on the secondary patterns. In a related study, the same authors (1979b) report data in which they compared twenty-seven adult female joggers with twenty-five female nonexercisers. In contrast to their study of males, only two primary factors and one secondary dimension achieved statistical significance. The authors defend these differences with the arguable point that "there appears to be a substantial divergence between males and females in the motivational factors that lead to the adoption of an aerobic jogging program" (p. 507).

Use of the 16PF as a research tool continues in the 1980s. For example, Williams and Parkin (1980) studied eighty-five male field hockey players in New Zealand and found the 16PF to be useful in discriminating among three groups of varying ability and experience. In India, Pestonjee, Singh, Singh, and Singh (1981) compared male and female athletes with nonathletes and found consistent personality differences. Also in India, Thakur and Ojha (1981) administered the 16PF to thirty table tennis, thirty badminton, and thirty football players, and found the footballers to be different from the other two groups, who were rather similar in personality. Finally, Evans and Quarterman (1983) compared successful black female basketball players (N = 20) with forty unsuccessful basketball players and an equal number of nonathletes. Evans and Quarterman found only two significant differences among all comparisons.

All things considered, the 16PF has been a most popular psychometric device for sport psychology researchers. However, the literature generates a picture of somewhat inconsistent results due to a multiplicity of reasons involving statistical treatments, widely varying athletic groups, cultural inconsistencies, interpretative error, and a host of more subtle problems. Too, critics of the 16PF point out that it is easily faked (Irvine and Gendreau, 1974; Odell 1971; Winder, O'Dell and Karson, 1975). Morgan (1980) pointed out that forms C and D of the 16PF have a Motivational Distortion scale, but Forms A and B do not. Unfortunately, Forms A and B have been used most often in sport research. In any event, the 16PF represents a general success story for trait psychology and merits further use, criticism, and refinement.

Eysenck Personality Inventory (EPI)

The EPI, made up of fifty-seven yes-no items, emerged in 1963 as a product of many years of work by the Eysencks, and while similar in etiology to the 16PF, it is considerably more parsimonious. The EPI purports to measure only two personality dimensions, neuroticism and introversion-extroversion. As a validity check, a third scale made up of eight MMPI Lie items is included. To give the reader an idea of what might constitute a Lie item, the following examples are offered:

1. Have you ever been late for an appointment or work?

2. Do you sometimes gossip?
3. Do you sometimes talk about things you know nothing about?
4. Are all your habits good and desirable ones?

The transparency of these questions is obvious, but is much less so when they are imbedded in the other items designed to measure neuroticism or extroversion. Scores of four or above on the Lie items are considered suspect on the EPI.

The EPI has not been as popular a research instrument as the MMPI or the 16PF, but sport researchers have made liberal use of it. Morgan's research with wrestlers at the 1966 World Tournament (Morgan, 1968) was perhaps the first usage of the EPI in athletics. Morgan found a significant correlation (r = .50) between extroversion and success at that event. Though a correlation of .50 only accounts for 25 percent of the variance, Morgan (1980) asserts that the coupling of this data with other sources of psychological or physical data can make a significant contribution to the prediction of sport performance. Support for this finding is given by Brichin and Kochian (1970) who studied accomplished female athletes in Czechoslovakia. Brichin and Kochian found a significant difference between their accomplished athletes (N = 81) and eighty-six female performers of lesser interest and accomplishment on the extroversion dimension. Delk (1973) found a significant difference between forty-one experienced male skydivers and the norms reported in the manual on extroversion. Kirkcaldy (1980) found similar results in a study of German sportsmen. On the other hand, researchers such as Reid and Hay (1979) and Fuchs and Zaichkowsky (1983) failed to find this difference in their respective studies. Nevertheless, Eysenck, Nias, and Cox (1982) conclude that sportsmen and sportswomen, regardless of level of expertise, do tend to be characterized by an extroverted temperament. They do emphasize that the relationship is a tendency and not an incontrovertible fact. Eysenck and his associates also point to a tendency for athletes, particularly outstanding ones, to be low on the EPI neuroticism measure.

In summary, the EPI offers reasonably sound measurement of two traits, extroversion and neuroticism, that are predictive of athletic participation and success in cases where the former is high and the latter is low. It is anticipated that the EPI will continue to be a useful tool in psychological and sport research and application.

STATE MEASURES IN SPORT PERSONOLOGY

As opposed to enduring traits, there are other measures of a more transient or temporary nature. Foremost among them are the *State-Trait Anxiety Inventory (STAI)* (Spielberger, Gorsuch and Lushene, 1970) and the *Profile of Mood States (POMS)* (McNair, Lorr, and Droppleman, 1971).

State-Trait Anxiety Inventory (STAI)

Spielberger and his associates make a distinction between anxiety that is relatively enduring (trait) and that which is more a function of recent events (state). Spielberger et al. attempt to measure each dimension of anxiety through responses to brief statements, twenty for state and twenty for trait.

Attesting to the overall popularity of the STAI is the fact that since its creation it has been the subject of more than two thousand archival publications (Spielberger, 1983). Too, Spielberger, Gorsuch, Lushene, Vagg, and Jacobs (1983) report research on such diverse populations as the learning disabled, psychiatric patients, psychosomatic sufferers, coronary patients, and neurotics.

In the realm of sport, Klavora (1975) reported results from a study of high school football and basketball players. In response to competitive stress, all subjects showed significant increases in state anxiety. High trait subjects exhibited significantly higher elevations than did low trait competitors. The STAI also discriminated between practice and game conditions and, overall, lent support to Spielberger's theory. Sanderson and Ashton (1981), in a study of the top eighteen- to twenty-one-year-old badminton players in England (what they call "colts"), concluded that the efficacy of the STAI lies in individual as opposed to group applications. Other applications of the STAI to sport research that are generally supportive include Griffiths, Steel and Vaccaro (1978; 1979; 1982) and Griffiths, Steel, Vaccaro, and Karpman (1981), with scuba divers; Powell and Verner (1982) with first time parachutists; Simon and Martens (1979) with nine- to fourteen-year-old males; and research in the area of motor performance (Hall, 1980; Pemberton and Cox, 1981; and Weinberg, 1979).

Profile of Mood States (POMS)

Another test that purports to measure transient states is the *Profile of Mood States (POMS)* (McNair, Lorr, and Droppleman, 1971). The POMS, made up of sixty-five words or phrases, measures six transient mood states: Tension-Anxiety, Depression-Dejection, Anger-Hostility, Vigor-Activity, Fatigue-Inertia, and Confusion-Bewilderment. By subtracting the Vigor-Activity score from the sum of the other five subscale totals, a Total Mood Disturbance (TMD) score can be computed. The authors of the test caution that the TMD score is highly tentative at this time, however.

The original intent of the POMS was to provide a tool for assessing mood states and mood changes in psychiatric outpatients, and its usefulness in that area has been demonstrated

(McNair, Lorr, and Droppleman, 1971). Further testimony as to its utility is found in sport psychology.

Morgan has been at the forefront in demonstrating the validity of the POMS in sport research. As mentioned in chapter 8, Morgan served as a consultant to the U.S. Olympic Committee in 1972 and 1976 and was able to test fifty-six contenders for positions on the Olympic wrestling team. From the results, he was able to differentiate successful from nonsuccessful team candidates; individuals who made the team were lower in tension, depression, anger, confusion, and fatigue and higher on vigor (Morgan, 1968; 1980). This configuration of scores represents the Iceberg Profile, also discussed at length earlier. Further efforts by Morgan have shown that Olympic oarsmen and top marathoners have the same Iceberg configuration (Morgan, 1978; Morgan and Pollock, 1977).

Based on the success of Morgan and other researchers, a study of college football players was initiated to see if the POMS and the Iceberg Profile would hold up in exceptional university-level athletes (LeUnes and Nation, 1982). Sixty varsity football players at Texas A&M University were compared with sixty individuals from the same university who had lettered in football in high school, and sixty peers who had never won a high school letter in any sport. In general, support was lent to the POMS and Morgan's concept; the college athletes exhibited significantly less depression, fatigue, and confusion while scoring significantly lower on total mood disturbance. Additionally, the athletes had a significantly higher vigor score than the other two groups. Actual group scores are summarized in table 9.4.

In general, the POMS has proven to be an effective state measure with considerable utility in research involving eighteen different sport populations (Daiss and LeUnes, 1986; LeUnes, Hayward, and Daiss, 1988).

Table 9.4 Profile of Mood States: Mean Scores across Groups

POMS Factor	Group		
	Nonathletes	High school athletes	College athletes
Tension	13.84$_A$	13.78$_A$	12.90$_A$
Depression	11.63$_A$	14.33$_A$	7.10$_B$
Anger	12.67$_A$	12.35$_A$	9.52$_A$
Vigor	17.80$_A$	16.23$_A$	19.60$_B$
Fatigue	10.95$_A$	11.65$_A$	6.36$_B$
Confusion	9.92$_A$	10.23$_A$	5.65$_B$
Total mood disturbance	57.58$_A$	66.33$_A$	42.40$_B$

NOTE: Row means with different subscripts are significantly different (p<.05).

SOURCE: "Saturday's Heroes: A Psychological Portrait of College Football Players" by A. LeUnes and J. R. Nation, 1982, *Journal of Sport Behavior*, 5, 139–149.

SPORT-SPECIFIC TESTS

Global tests of personality that measure relatively stable traits may have problems of applicability to athletes due to the situational nature of sport performance (Carron, 1980). None of the commonly used test batteries in psychology discussed earlier (MMPI, EPI, 16PF, POMS, STAI) were standardized on or intended for use with athletes, and the results when these tests have been used in sport have been mixed. Because of this, a call has been put out for assessment devices that are developed with and for athletes, or what are known as sport-specific tests (e.g., Carron, 1980; Kroll, 1970; Nideffer, 1981).

Athletic Motivation Inventory (AMI)

Though the call for sport-specific assessment devices is relatively recent, Tutko, Lyon, and Ogilvie actually developed the first major sport-specific test in 1969, the *Athletic Motivation Inventory (AMI)*. That the AMI is sport-specific is accentuated by the test authors in the preliminary technical manual:

The inventory assesses *only* athletic behavior and attitudes. Its use should be confined to those directly involved in athletics, and its results should not be generalized to other areas of the athlete's life. (P. 3)

The initial AMI reference groups were professional athletes (4,003 males and 1,026 females), college athletes (10,286 males and 1,843 females), and high school athletes (23,305 males and 1,855 females). The AMI, 190 items long, is answered in a basic "true," "in between," "false" or "often," "sometimes," "never" format. Sample questions include such items as:

1. When I was young, I thought about breaking a sports record.
2. Sometimes I feel like I just don't give a damn about anybody.
3. I try to think about unexpected things that might come up during competition.
4. I rarely think that training rules inhibit my personal freedom.
5. Hustle is important, but it can't compensate for lack of talent.
6. One problem with athletics is that the individual athlete has so little to say in what happens.
7. I am sometimes hurt more by how the coach says things than by what he says.

8. If asked to follow a rigid off-season training schedule, I would stick to it religiously.
9. I need the encouragement of the coach.
10. I seldom stay after practice to work out.

The 190 items fall into three categories (Ogilvie, Tutko, and Lyon, 1973):

1. Desire to be successful in athletics
2. Ability to withstand the emotional stress of competition
3. Dedication to the coach and sport

Early reliability and validity data are presented by Lyon (1972). Lyon indicated that college athletes and nonathletes differed significantly on all subtests of the AMI. Fosdick (1972), in a study of twenty-six collegiate swimmers, found two significant correlations between the AMI and the 16PF: Factor E-Assertiveness and Leadership (.50) and Factor Q-Tense and Emotional Control (−.72). In research comparing starting athletes with substitutes, Hammer and Tutko (1974), Hightower (1973), Hirst (1972), and Stewart (1970) all found consistent differences between the two groups. In a similar vein, Ogilvie (1974) and Tombor (1970) both found differences among professional, college, and high school athletes.

Despite an early burst of enthusiasm, interest in the AMI appears to have cooled. Morris (1975), in a study of highly skilled female field hockey players in Canada, found them to be significantly more aggressive, more seeking of the role of leadership, and mentally tougher than their counterparts not selected to represent their country in international play. The Morris study apparently represents the last published paper on the AMI. It seems that the instrument has seen its day, though Ogilvie has issued a call for its resurrection (Straub, 1986).

Sport Competition Anxiety Test (SCAT)

A more contemporary attempt at devising a sport-specific test is the *Sport Competition Anxiety Test (SCAT)* of Martens (1977). Based on the more general work of Spielberger and his associates, the SCAT is an attempt to measure competitive A-Trait or what Rupnow and Ludwig (1981, p. 35) call "the tendency to perceive competitive situations as threatening and to respond to the situations with feelings of apprehension or tension." Martens (1977) would add to this definition the point that some degree of state anxiety would accompany the response to whatever threat was being confronted.

Martens bases his SCAT on four factors:

1. An awareness that an interactive paradigm for studying personality is superior to trait or situational explanations
2. The recognition that situation-specific instruments are superior to general A-trait measures
3. The distinction between A-trait and A-state in the trait-state theory of anxiety
4. The desirability of developing a conceptual model for studying the social process of competition

The original work on the SCAT was begun by modifying items from the *Manifest Anxiety Scale* (Taylor, 1953), the *State-Trait Anxiety Inventory for Children* (Spielberger, 1973) and the *General Anxiety Scales* of Sarason, Davidson, Lighthall, Waite, and Ruebush (1960). After considerable refinement, which was guided by the *Standards for Educational and Psychological Tests and Manuals* of the American Psychological Association ("Standards," 1974), two forms of the instrument have emerged. One, for use with children from ten to fourteen years, is the SCAT-C, and the other is the adult form for fifteen years and up, the

Recent sport-specific tests have centered on pre-performance anxiety, often correlating it with subsequent achievement in competitive situations.

SCAT-A. Each is made up of fifteen brief statements that are answered "hardly ever," "sometimes," or "often." Items from the SCAT-A are represented in figure 9.1.

There has been no shortage of interest in the SCAT, and this is reflected in the frequency with which it is used in current research. For example, the area of preperformance anxiety and its consequences for later sport behavior is quite popular. Gerson and Deshaies (1978) studied 107 female college softball players participating in a national tournament. These researchers found a significant relationship between the SCAT and results of a precompetitive state anxiety measure, and a significant relationship between the pregame anxiety measures and batting average. Substantiation was made for the predictive validity of the

SCAT. Additional support for the SCAT is offered by Weinberg and Genuchi (1980), who studied competitive collegiate golfers. Ten high, ten moderate, and ten low scorers on the SCAT were monitored during a practice round and the first and last days of a golf tournament. Two things stand out about Weinberg and Genuchi's study; one is the utility of the SCAT and the other is the support given Oxendine's hypothesis concerning the anxiety-performance relationship.

Oxendine (1970) generally states that sports requiring precise, fine muscle coordination such as golf are best performed at low levels of anxiety. In the case of golf, the players scoring low on the SCAT performed significantly better than did the other two groups. Similarly, Wandzilak, Potter, and Lorentzen (1982) found

---

Figure 9.1 Sport Competition Anxiety Test (SCAT) Items

1. Competing against others is socially enjoyable.
2. Before I compete I feel uneasy.
3. Before I compete I worry about not performing well.
4. I am a good sportsman when I compete.
5. When I compete I worry about making mistakes.
6. Before I compete I am calm.
7. Setting a goal is important when competing.
8. Before I compete I get a queasy feeling in my stomach.
9. Just before competing I notice my heart beats faster than usual.
10. I like to compete in games that demand considerable physical energy.
11. Before I compete I feel relaxed.
12. Before I compete I am nervous.
13. Team sports are more exciting than individual sports.
14. I get nervous wanting to start the game.
15. Before I compete I usually get uptight.

SOURCE: *Sport Competition Anxiety Test* (p. 93) by R. Martens, 1977, Champaign, IL: Human Kinetics.

the SCAT to be highly predictive of preperformance state anxiety in high school female volleyball players. Interestingly, Wandzilak and associates accounted for 50 percent of the variance in performance in one of the two experimental groups they created with data from a state anxiety measure and the SCAT administered three hours before their first match. In another study involving female college basketball players, Sonstroem and Bernardo (1982) found the SCAT to be significantly related to pregame state anxiety but not significantly related to subsequent performance. Martens, Rivkin, and Burton (1980) asked 105 female high school volleyball players and their predominantly female coaches to rate each other on anxiety prior to competition. Coaches and players did not differ significantly on trait anxiety, coaches were comparable in anxiety

when compared with the SCAT norms, and again the SCAT was predictive of pregame state anxiety.

Other research in which the SCAT has been an integral part includes studies by Gould, Horn, and Spreeman (1983a; 1983b) with elite junior wrestlers; Passer (1983), who was looking at the interrelationship of trait anxiety, fear of success, fear of evaluation, perceived competence, and self-esteem of 316 ten- to fifteen-year-old soccer players, and Blais and Vallerand (1986), who looked at the interplay between electromyographic biofeedback and precompetitive anxiety in ten- to thirteen-year-old males.

Competitive State Anxiety Inventory (CSAI)

A relative of the SCAT is another creation of Martens, the *Competitive State Anxiety Inventory (CSAI)* (Martens, 1977). As with the SCAT, the CSAI has been adapted from Spielberger's work in an effort to have a measure of state anxiety related specifically to sport. Items on the CSAI, ten in number, are presented in table 9.5.

Representative pieces of research with the CSAI include that of Gruber and Beauchamp (1979) and Martens, Burton, Rivkin, and Simon (1980). The first study concluded that the CSAI is most suitable for repeated assessment of athletes in competitive settings. Gruber and Beauchamp based their conclusion on results with twelve University of Kentucky female basketball players who were administered the CSAI on sixteen separate occasions. Gruber and Beauchamp found high internal consistency on the instrument, noted changes before and after competition, revealed that state anxiety was significantly reduced after wins but remained high after losses, and found differences in state anxiety among games varying in importance. In the second study, Martens et al. reported reliability coefficients ranging between .76 and

Table 9.5 Competitive State Anxiety Inventory (CSAI) Items

The Competitive State Anxiety Inventory lists a number of statements that people have used to describe themselves. Subjects are asked to read each statement and then indicate to the right of the statement how they feel at the moment. They are instructed not to spend too much time on any one statement. There are no right or wrong answers. The list of items and a sample response are given below.

	Not at all	Somewhat	Moderately so	Very much so
1. I feel at ease				X
2. I feel nervous	X			
3. I feel comfortable				X
4. I am tense	X			
5. I feel secure		X		
6. I feel anxious	X			
7. I am relaxed		X		
8. I am jittery	X			
9. I feel calm.			X	
10. I feel over-excited and "rattled".	X			

SOURCE: "Who Predicts Anxiety Better: Coaches or Athletes?" by R. Martens, F. Rivkin, and D. Burton, 1980, in C. H. Nadeau, W. R. Halliwell, K. M. Newell, and G. C. Roberts, eds., *Psychology of Motor Behavior and Sport—1979* (p. 86), Champaign, IL: Human Kinetics.

.97 for both the adult and children's forms. Concurrent validity was established for the CSAI by correlating it with the *Activation-Deactivation Adjective Checklist (AD-ACL)* of Thayer (1967). Similarities were such that confidence in the CSAI was furthered.

Competitive State Anxiety Inventory—II (CSAI-II)

Unlike the CSAI, which is a unidimensional measure of state anxiety associated with competition, the *CSAI–II* (Martens, Burton, Vealey, Bump, and Smith, 1982) is a multidimensional scale that purports to assess somatic anxiety, cognitive anxiety, and state self-confidence. The CSAI–II is composed of twenty-seven items (three nine-item subscales) arranged on a four-point Likert scale, which will be discussed shortly. The CSAI-II has held up well under research scrutiny; for example, Burton (1988) reports strong support for the instrument in a study of two samples of swimmers at the national caliber and intercollegiate levels.

Test of Attentional and Interpersonal Style (TAIS)

Yet another test that has come to be sport-related is the *Test of Attentional and Interpersonal Style (TAIS)* (Nideffer, 1976a). Nideffer's contention is that athletic performance is closely related to attentional style or focus and, once this is isolated, predicting athletic performance in a variety of situations becomes possible. Nideffer suggests that attention can be viewed in terms of both width and direction. Width, in turn, exists on a broad to narrow continuum; athletes with a broad focus will probably be quarterbacks, linebackers, or point guards, positions all requiring a wide perspective. Narrow focus, on the other hand, is required for driving a golf ball or hitting a baseball; here the athlete must be able to shut out distractions and focus narrowly on the task at hand. As for directionality, Nideffer talks of internal and external focus. Internals are thought to be wrapped up in their own thought processes, such as world class distance runners (see Morgan, 1978). Externals, of course, would be more tuned in to forces outside themselves. Nideffer suggests that a balance between internality and externality is the optimum; flexibility is important in Nideffer's approach. A visual representation of Nideffer's model with examples from sport can be seen in figure 9.2.

The TAIS is a 144-item self-report that requires approximately twenty-five minutes to complete. It purports to measure the seventeen attentional and interpersonal factors described in table 9.6.

De Palma and Nideffer (1977) demonstrated the versatility of the TAIS in an early study of seventy-eight psychiatric patients who were compared with thirty control subjects. In general, the TAIS was acquitted quite nicely. In the area of sport, Richards and Landers (1981), in testing 159 elite and subelite shooters of various types, found that the TAIS was capable of discriminating among a number of conditions involving types of shooters (pistol, rifle,

trap, skeet), sex (male and female), and experience (experienced and inexperienced). Van Schoyck and Grasha (1981), in an interesting variant, devised a tennis-specific version of the TAIS, and they found the T-TAIS, as they called their instrument, to be more related to tennis performance than the parent TAIS. Van Schoyck and Grasha concluded that their test supported the notion that sport-specific instruments are superior for sport research to more general instruments (though the TAIS lies somewhere between the two points). In a similar vein, Albrecht and Feltz (1987) developed a baseball/softball batting version known as the B-TAIS. Like Van Schoyck and Grasha, Albrecht and Feltz found their more sport-specific variant of the TAIS to be sounder psychometrically.

Finally, Vallerand (1983) related the TAIS to decision-making processes. Using fifty-nine male basketball players as subjects (mean age 18.62 years) who were either junior college or university competitors, Vallerand asked judges to place them in three groups based on their ability to properly decide what to do on a decision-making task, in this case repeated three-on-two or two-on-one fast breaks. The players were placed in good, average, or poor decision-making groups. It was hypothesized that good decision makers, as compared to the other groups, would display a more positive scan factor (higher BET, BIT, INFP) and a more adequate focus factor (low OET, OIT, high NAR). Analysis of variance results showed no differences. A later analysis of good and poor decision makers using discriminant analysis also yielded no clear results. Vallerand believes that the TAIS may not be sensitive enough to pick up attentional differences in athletic situations, but does feel that a number of problems must be unraveled through research before the TAIS can be abandoned.

The somewhat sport-specific TAIS has provoked a great deal of interest and has spawned sport-specific variants in baseball/softball and tennis. Also, Nideffer (1986) has developed a

Figure 9.2 Nideffer's Model of Attentional Focus

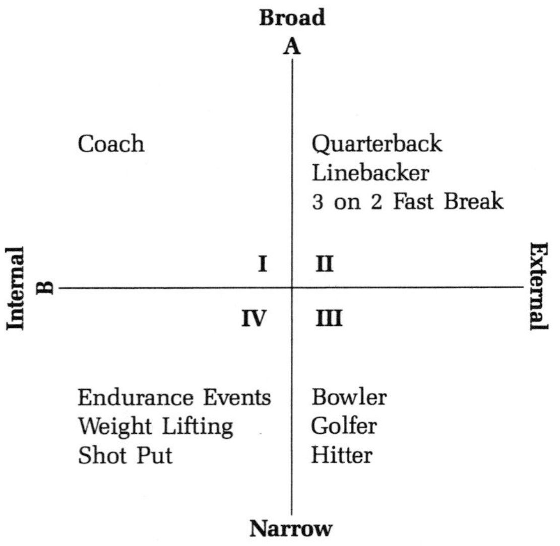

SOURCE: *The Inner Athlete* (p. 49) by R. M. Nideffer, 1976, New York: Crowell.

Table 9.6 Scales on the Test of Attentional and Interpersonal Style (TAIS)

Scale	Abbreviation	Description
Broad external attentional focus	BET	High scores on this scale are obtained by individuals who describe themselves as being able to effectively integrate many external stimuli at one time.
Overloaded by external stimuli	OET	The higher the score, the more athletes make mistakes because they become confused and overloaded with external stimuli.
Broad internal attentional focus	BIT	High scores indicate that athletes see themselves as able to effectively integrate ideas and information from several different areas. They are analytical.
Overloaded by internal stimuli	OIT	The higher the score, the more mistakes athletes make because they confuse themselves by thinking about too many things at once.
Narrow attentional focus	NAR	The higher the score, the more effective athletes see themselves with respect to being able to narrow their attention when they need to.
Reduced attentional focus	RED	A high score on this scale indicates the athletes make mistakes because they narrow attention too much.
Information processing	INFP	High scorers tend to process a great deal of stimulus information. They have high energy levels. Their perceptual-cognitive worlds are busy.
Behavior control	BCON	A high score indicates that athletes tend to be somewhat impulsive. In addition, they engage in behavior that could be considered antisocial, though not necessarily harmful.
Interpersonal control	CON	A high score indicates the athlete is in control of most situations. Leaders score high. Extremely high scores are associated with authority conflicts.
Self-esteem	SES	The higher the score, the more highly the athletes think of themselves and the more highly they feel others would see them.
Physical orientation	P/O	High scorers enjoy, and participate in, competitive athletics.
Obsessiveness	OBS	High scores are associated with rumination and worry. The scale indicates speed of decision making. Low scorers make decisions very quickly.
Extroversion	EXT	A high score indicates the athlete is warm, outgoing, and needs to be with other people.
Introversion	INT	High scorers enjoy being alone, need personal space and privacy.
Intellectual expression	IEX	High scorers express their thoughts and ideas to other people.
Negative affect expression	NAE	A high score indicates that the athletes express their anger and negative feelings to others.
Positive affect expression	PAE	A high score indicates that the individuals express their feelings of affection to others in both physical and verbal ways.

SOURCE: *The Ethics and Practice of Applied Sport Psychology* (pp. 78-79) by R. M. Nideffer, 1981, Ithaca, NY: Mouvement Publications.

set of training procedures based on his model known as attentional control training. These are shown in figure 9.3.

Figure 9.3 Training Procedures for Attentional Control Training

1. Athletes need to be able to engage in at least four different types of attention.
2. Different sport situations will make different attentional demands on an athlete. Accordingly, it is incumbent upon the athlete to be able to shift to different types of concentration to match changing attentional demands.
3. Under optimal conditions, the average person can meet the attentional demands of most sport situations.
4. There are individual differences in attentional abilities. Some of the differences are learned, some are biological, and some are genetic. Thus different athletes have different attentional strengths and weaknesses.
5. As physiological arousal begins to increase beyond an athlete's own optimal level, there is an initial tendency for the athlete to rely too heavily on the most highly developed attentional ability.
6. The phenomenon of "choking," of having performance progressively deteriorate, occurs as physiological arousal continues to increase to the point of causing an involuntary narrowing of an athlete's concentration and to the point of causing attention to become more internally focused.
7. Alterations in physiological arousal affect concentration. Thus, the systematic manipulation of physiological arousal is one way of gaining some control over concentration.
8. Alterations in the focus of attention will affect physiological arousal. Thus, the systematic manipulation of concentration is one way to gain some control over arousal (e.g., muscle tension levels, heart rate, respiration rate).

SOURCE: "Concentration and Attention Control Training" by R. M. Nideffer, 1986, in J. M. Williams, ed., *Applied Sport Psychology: Personal Growth to Peak Experience* (pp. 258–259), Palo Alto, CA: Mayfield.

Other Sport-Specific Measures

A number of relatively recent sport-specific measures show promise in assessing various aspects of personality as they relate to performance.

Psychological Skills Inventory for Sports (PSIS). Mahoney, Gabriel, and Perkins (1987) created the *Psychological Skill Inventory for Sports (PSIS)*, a fifty-one-item measure couched in a true–false format of sport skills pertinent to exceptional athletic performance. More than seven hundred male and female athletes from twenty-three different sports took part in the original scale development. There were 126 elite athletes, 141 pre-elite athletes, and 446 nonelite collegiate athletes in their sample. Sixteen leading sport psychologists also responded to the questionnaire as they thought an elite athlete would. Out of this work came a scale that measures concentration, anxiety management, self-confidence, mental preparation, and motivation.

Sport Pressure Checklist. Rushall and Sherman (1987) created the *Sport Pressure Checklist,* designing the psychometric device to assess self-perceived pressure in sport situations. The instrument is a sixteen-item checklist arranged on a seven-point Likert format, and is deemed applicable by the authors to sport participants over the age of eleven years. Highly preliminary evidence indicates that the instrument is sensitive to changes in pressure in age-group swimmers, national team cross-country skiers from Canada, male intercollegiate basketball players, and Olympic athletes from Canada. Clearly, much remains to be done with the checklist, but it represents an attempt to assess behaviors in an important part of sport, that of pressure in competitive situations.

Sport-Confidence Measurement. Vealey (1986), in an attempt to measure various aspects of sport self-confidence, has created what amounts to three instruments, the *Trait Sport-Confidence Inventory (TSCI)*, the *State Sport-Confidence Inventory (SSCI)*, and the *Competitive Orientation Inventory (COI)*. Vealey's contention is that sport self-confidence has been conceptualized in the past in terms of Bandura's (1977) *self-efficacy theory*, in terms of *perceived competence* as advocated by Harter (1978) and Nicholls (1980), or as *performance expectancies* (Corbin, 1981; Scanlan and Passer, 1979, 1981). However, Vealey feels that each of the preceding formulations lacks a bit in terms of sport-specificity; hence the development of her scales. Again, preliminary evidence is encouraging with regard to the Vealey measures; however, much research is called for in an effort to support or refute her work in a trait essential to sport success, self-confidence.

ATTITUDE MEASUREMENT IN SPORT

In addition to personality assessment, there has been a fair amount of interest in measuring various attitudes in sport. Some of the more prominent examples include the Attitudes Toward Physical Activity Scale (ATPA) (Kenyon, 1968) and the Physical Estimation and Attraction Scales (PEAS) (Sonstroem, 1978).

A major conceptual framework for looking at attitudes has been proposed by Triandis (1971), who believes that attitudes can be viewed as having three dimensions, *cognitive*, *affective*, and *behavioral*. The cognitive dimension deals with beliefs, the affective with feelings, and the behavioral with intended behavior toward the attitude object. Though not without its critics, the Triandis conceptualization serves to illustrate the multidimensional nature of attitudes. Attitude measurement in sport psychology has taken three paths, drawn from the works of Thurstone (1928), Likert (1932), and Osgood, Suci, and Tannenbaum (1957). A sport-related summary of these assessment procedures may be seen in table 9.7.

Table 9.7 Sport-Related Summary of Various Attitude Measures

One-Item Rating Scale

How much do you like jogging for exercise?

not at all __ __ __ __ __ __ __ very much
(1) (2) (3) (4) (5) (6) (7)

Thurstone Scale (The scale values in parentheses are contrived for this example.)

Check the statements with which you agree.

_____ 1. Jogging is the best way to start a day. (10.7)

_____ 2. Jogging helps a person stay fit and healthy. (7.3)

_____ 3. Jogging is unnecessary and a waste of time for most people. (3.4)

_____ 4. Jogging is distasteful and unpleasant. (2.3)

Likert Scale

For each statement, check the extent to which you agree.

1. Jogging is a good activity for most people.

_____ strongly agree (+2)

_____ moderately agree (+1)

_____ neutral (0)

_____ moderately disagree (-1)

_____ strongly disagree (-2)

2. Jogging is boring.

_____ strongly agree (-2)

_____ moderately agree (-1)

_____ neutral (0)

_____ moderately disagree (+1)

_____ strongly disagree (+2)

Semantic Differential Scale

Rate how you feel about jogging for exercise on each of the scales below:

foolish	(-3) (-2) (-1) (0) $(+1)$ $(+2)$ $(+3)$	wise
good	$(+3)$ $(+2)$ $(+1)$ (0) (-1) (-2) (-3)	bad
beneficial	$(+3)$ $(+2)$ $(+1)$ (0) (-1) (-2) (-3)	harmful
unpleasant	(-3) (-2) (-1) (0) $(+1)$ $(+2)$ $(+3)$	pleasant
valuable	$(+3)$ $(+2)$ $(+1)$ (0) (-1) (-2) (-3)	worthless

SOURCE: *Psychological Dynamics of Sport* (p. 98) by D. L. Gill, 1986, Champaign, IL: Human Kinetics.

Thurstone Scaling

In Thurstone scaling, ratings provided by judges are at the heart of the procedure. Initially, the judges are provided with a large pool of items about an issue from which the ultimate scale will be forged. Once the pool of items is shrunk through these judgments, the remaining statements are assigned numerical weights that are reflective of various attitudinal dispositions along a continuum from favorable to unfavorable. It is hoped that the numerical weights assigned to each of the possible responses will be reasonably equally distributed along the favorable-unfavorable continuum. In general, the Thurstone procedure is cumbersome to carry out.

Likert Scales

In response to the difficulties associated with the Thurstone method, Likert (1932) created a somewhat similar but simpler procedure that bears his name. In the Likert scheme, judges are not necessary and the determination of scale item values is not made. Basically, subjects are asked to respond to a pool of items along a five-point scale, and those that discriminate most effectively between subjects scoring high or low are retained as the final Likert Scale.

Semantic Differential Scales

Osgood and his associates (1957) have developed a most popular technique in the Semantic Differential Scale. The ATPA of Kenyon, mentioned earlier, is a prominent scale in sport based on the semantic differential method. Subjects in this procedure are asked to respond to a series of bipolar adjectives on a five- or seven-point scale. To Osgood et al., attitudes have evaluative (good-bad), potency (strong-weak), and activity (active-passive) compo-

nents. In practice, only the evaluative component is used in much of the existing attitude research.

Despite the sophisticated nature of the attitude measurement techniques, their popularity of late has been greater in the larger area of psychology than with sport psychology. In view of the multitude of attitudinal issues surrounding the sport realm, we may see greater use of Thurstone's, Likert's, and Osgood's procedures in the future.

SOURCES OF ERROR IN TESTING

An implicit assumption generally made with regard to the various tests is that the subject is a cooperative and honest respondent. Sport psychologists tend to compound this error by assuming that athletes will be even more cooperative and honest than other test populations. Unfortunately, no evidence supports this notion. Therefore, each of us in testing situations must be aware of possible sources of error that are subject related.

In and of itself, no test is perfect; compounding the problem is the tendency of subjects to try to enhance themselves through their responses to the test or, conversely, to look as bad as possible. Other problems are conservative response style, defensiveness, fear, ignorance, and misinformation about testing in general. An exploration of three of these problems—faking good, faking bad, and conservative response style—seems appropriate.

Faking Good

We all are prone to project self-enhancing images in social situations, and this phenomenon is not unusual in psychological assessment. Athletes are no exception. They will try to outguess the test, and one way to do this is

HIGHLIGHT 9.1
Test Information
Sources

Though testing is a dynamic and ever-changing area, the inquisitive user can consult a number of resources with a considerable degree of confidence. Foremost among them is the series of *Mental Measurement Yearbooks (MMY)*, a sterling compendium of information compiled by Buros beginning in 1938 and continuing up to the most recent volume in 1986. Included in the MMY are such mundane things as price, forms, and age of persons for whom each test is intended, as well as expert reviews and a list of studies of each. The emphasis in the MMY is on commercially produced tests.

Another significant source of test information is provided by Robinson and Shaver (1973). The intent of their work is to provide a source of test information in the social sciences that is not only useful to psychologists but to sociologists and political scientists. Included in the Robinson and Shaver work are separate chapters on the measurement of self-esteem and related constructs, locus of control, alienation and anomie, authoritarianism and dogmatism, sociopolitical attitudes, values, general attitudes toward people, religious attitudes, and several scales of a methodological nature (e.g., social desirability). Though not all scales surveyed are universally applicable to sport, Robinson and Shaver have summarized a number of measures of potential relevance.

A third significant source of information about tests is the individual test manual. Test usage, norms, relevant studies, reliability and validity data, and other information are included in any good test manual. Prospective users are strongly urged to make considerable use of this most useful source.

Several other worthwhile data sources concerning tests are as follows:

1. *Tests in Print II* (Buros, 1974)
2. *Personality Tests and Reviews I & II* (Buros, 1970, 1975b)
3. *Intelligence Tests and Reviews* (Buros, 1975a)
4. *A Sourcebook for Mental Health Measures* (Comrey, Backer, and Glaser, 1973)
5. *Measures for Psychological Assessment* (Chun, Cobb, and French, 1976)
6. *Tests and Measurements in Child Development: Handbook I* (Johnson and Bommarito, 1971); *Handbook II* (Johnson, 1976).
7. *Standards for Educational and Psychological Tests* (1974)

Many of the tests in these various sources are not relevant to sport. However, many are, and the test user in sport research and application would be wise to keep open access to as many of them as possible. As time goes by, an increasing number of global and sport-specific tests of demonstrated validity and reliability may find their way into these volumes.

always to answer troublesome questions in a manner that will project the most positive image. Tests vary considerably in their transparency, so any response set on the part of a respondent is guesswork. This transparency, of course, accentuates measurement error.

Faking Bad

Obviously, faking bad is an aberrant response pattern; why anyone would want to project a poor or maladjusted image is hard to comprehend. In reality, the sport psychologist is probably not nearly as likely to see this pattern as is the psychologist working in a clinical setting. When faking bad does occur, Nideffer (1981) suggests that it should be interpreted as a cry for help. Another interpretation might be that an improper testing climate has been created by the sport psychologist. Obviously, care should be exercised to insure that an atmosphere of rapport or cooperation is generated so that fake bad protocols are avoided or, if they do occur, are not a function of hostility or rejection on the part of the athlete.

Conservative Response Style

Nideffer suggests that the tendency to respond to tests in the most conservative, middle-of-the-road, pedestrian way is largely a function of rejection of the situation, the coach, the sport psychologist, or a combination thereof. Obviously, scores that cluster near the mean for the test are going to render decisions based on the results useless or close to it.

ETHICS AND SPORT

Ethical practice within any area of human endeavor is absolutely essential to the continu-

ing expansion and ultimate survival of the enterprise. Sport psychology is no exception, and much interest has been expressed over the past decade or so in developing a working code of ethics for sport psychologists. Progress has been made, particularly in the 1980s, and an acceptable set of ethical standards has been drafted, deliberated upon, and generally accepted by sport psychology organizations in this country and Canada as well as at the international level. The everyday application of these guiding principles is a most important development within sport psychology.

Another ethical concern of the 1980s that impinges less directly upon the everyday work life of the sport psychologist but nevertheless bears continuing monitoring is the ethics of drug use within sport. Hardly a day goes by without some major drug scandal making headlines in our newspapers; of particular interest to many is the steroid controversy, which will be discussed at length. The potential for the destruction of sport lies in drug abuse.

Ethics and the Sport Psychologist

The psychologist must be aware of the importance of ethics in guiding his or her professional actions within the sport context. Without a set of guiding ethics, a dog-eat-dog sort of environment is created to the detriment of the profession of sport psychology and sport in general. Ideally, as Nideffer (1981) points out, if all of us were possessed of the highest ideals and standards of conduct, statements about ethics would be superfluous. Given that we do not live in such a perfect world, a number of concerned individuals in positions of influence have attempted to forge a code of ethics for sport psychology. After years of debate and deliberation, the North American Society for the Psychology of Sport and Physical Activity (NASPSPA) has adapted the ethical standards of the American Psychological

Association (APA) to fit the needs of sport psychology. These NASPSPA standards are delineated in two publications, *Ethical Standards for Provision of Services by NASPSPA Members* ("Ethical Standards," 1982) and *Guidelines for Psychological Testing Within Sport and Other Physical Activity Settings* ("Guidelines," 1982). Both general ethics and ethics in testing are significant issues within sport psychology and will be treated separately.

General Ethics. The standards for professional conduct are aimed above all else at making sport more rewarding for the athlete; the welfare of the individual athlete is paramount. Beyond this overall concern, the guiding philosophy for ethical conduct within sport is spelled out in the preamble to the *Ethical Standards of Psychologists* of the APA (1981).

> Psychologists respect the dignity and worth of the individual and honor the preservation and protection of fundamental human rights. They are committed to increasing knowledge of human behavior and of people's understanding of themselves and others and to the utilization of such knowledge for the promotion of human welfare. While pursuing these objectives, they make every effort to protect the welfare of those who seek their services or any human being or animal that may be the object of study. They use their skills only for purposes consistent with these values and do not knowingly permit their misuse by others. While demanding for themselves freedom of inquiry and communication, psychologists accept the freedom this responsibility requires: competence, objectivity in the application of skills and concern for the best interest of clients, colleagues, students, research participants, and society.

The preamble clearly indicates *why* we are concerned about having a code of ethics and serves as a succinct philosophical statement about the concern the sport psychologist should have for players, coaches, and sport and physical activity in general. In order to accomplish the lofty goals stated in the preamble, one should observe nine principles of conduct:

1. *Responsibility.* The sport psychologist tries to insure that his or her services are used appropriately while assuming responsibility for acts related thereto. At all times, maintaining the highest standards is of paramount importance.
2. *Competence.* The sport psychologist provides only those services for which he or she is qualified by training, concurrently always staying alert to the limits of competence. In cases where the skills required to do a job exceed those for which professional training was provided, ready referral of the client is made to a practitioner with the requisite skills.
3. *Moral and legal standards.* Sport psychologists refuse to take part in activities that are illegal, immoral, or unethical. At the same time, they remain informed on ongoing developments in matters of law and ethics.
4. *Public statements.* Sport psychologists accurately portray their credentials and professional affiliations in such a manner as to inform rather than mislead the public, and are generally prudent in representing the profession and themselves to the potential user of their services.
5. *Confidentiality.* Sport psychologists respect the confidentiality of information obtained from persons in the course of working with them, and are clear in spelling out to these individuals just what the limitations of this confidentiality are.
6. *Welfare of the client.* Sport psychologists respect the integrity and protect the welfare of individuals or groups with whom they work. At times it is not clear just who the sport psychologist is working for (e.g., when a coach hires a sport psychologist to work with an athlete it is not always clear exactly

who the client is, the coach or the athlete), and diplomacy is required in order to clarify where loyalty lies.

7. *Professional relationships.* Sport psychologists are sensitive to their relationships with professionals working in allied areas of sport (i.e., coaches, trainers, sport physicians).

8. *Assessment techniques.* Sport psychologists exert every effort to promote the best interests of their clients in matters of psychological assessment. They explain assessments in understandable language and make every effort not to confuse the client. Information superfluous to the expressed purpose of testing, if it may be upsetting or harmful to the client, need not be divulged.

9. *Research with human participants.* While keeping in mind the welfare of the research population, the sport psychologist always conducts research in line with local, state, and federal guidelines. Openness and honesty are words to live by in conducting research with sport groups or individuals.

These guidelines for ethical behavior among sport psychologists are just that, guidelines. Not everything that happens in the sport psychologist–client relationship will conform to standard ethics, and human values will necessarily come into play. Hopefully, these value judgments will fall somewhere within the spirit of the NASPSPA guidelines and the overriding matter of human goodwill.

In a bit of a disclaimer, Rotella and Connelly (1984) suggest that the APA and related NASPSPA ethics do not go far enough, failing to properly address such performance-related issues as the pros and cons of instituting mental training with athletes, overburdening athletes with too many time and mental demands, enhancing athletic performance at the expense of the inherent fun that goes with letting things take their natural course, enhancing personal self-confidence to the detriment of the involved

player or team, overemphasis on goal setting and assertiveness, and misplaced loyalty in terms of getting injured athletes back into action through mental pain-blocking strategies. Granting the validity of the Rotella and Connelly viewpoint, the NASPSPA guidelines serve as a convenient starting point for stressing the role of ethics in guiding the day-to-day work of the sport psychologist.

Test Ethics. With regard to psychologist testing with sport populations, the NASPSPA guidelines are aimed at maintaining quality control on these assessment devices. The guidelines are applicable to test development, test utilization, and the use of results obtained from such sources. They address such issues as validity, reliability, proper test manual development in the case of new instruments, user qualifications, conditions of administration, and the use of proper norms. Sport psychologists who are conducting psychological assessment with athletes or others involved in physical activity must be familiar with the guidelines. Many errors in the past could have been prevented by a greater awareness of the strengths and weaknesses of psychological tests and their ethical usage both within and outside the domain of sport psychology.

Nideffer (1981) indicates that sport psychologists are generally called upon for their expertise in psychological assessment to accomplish two basic tasks, selection and/or screening decisions and program development and/or counseling. He further suggests that test users within sport psychology should be alert to the following considerations:

1. Determining the relevance of a test to the assigned task at hand should be well within the sport psychologists' capabilities.
2. Evaluation of test validity and reliability is a critical skill.
3. Being aware of ethical considerations related to testing is essential.

4. Test interpretation skills are most important, and this process can be aided by the use of other available information, such as the case history.
5. Proper establishment of a testing climate that fosters cooperation is an invaluable asset.
6. Care must be exercised in the reporting of test results to individuals or organizations so as to minimize misunderstanding and maximize effective usage of the communicated information.

Ethics and Drug Use in Sport

Ours is a drug-oriented society; prescription drugs, over-the-counter medications, and illegal substances are commonplace aspects of our daily lives. We often endorse "a better life through chemistry" orientation to personal well-being, and athletes are no exception. Efforts to improve performance are made at all levels of competition, but the elite athlete is especially prone to look for any edge he or she can find, and the various drugs available to them are all too often viewed as providing that coveted advantage. Athletes also function at times in the presence of considerable pain or discomfort, and they may seek relief in the form of drugs. Finally, the pressures of competition, particularly at the elite amateur or professional levels, are such that drugs, including alcohol, are seen as tension reducing and their use and abuse is not at all unusual. Len Bias of the University of Maryland (basketball) and Don Rogers of the Cleveland Browns (football) represent celebrated examples in 1986 in which abuse of the supposed recreational drug of cocaine was clearly implicated as the cause of their very premature deaths.

Curry and Jiobu (1984) classify the various drugs alluded to in the preceding paragraph as *recreational, restorative,* and *additive.*

Recreational Drugs. Recreational drugs are meant to be pleasurable in general, though many tragic stories involving their use have been documented both in and out of sport. Alcohol, marijuana, and cocaine are three such drugs.

Restorative Drugs. Muscle relaxants, anti-inflammatories, and painkillers are examples of drugs ostensibly serving a restorative function. A particularly well-known and controversial restorative drug available legally only through prescription is the anti-inflammatory drug, phenylbutazone, known as "bute." Phenylbutazone was brought to greater public awareness in a 1985 *Sports Illustrated* special report on drugs when it was implicated circumstantially in the death of Augustinius Jaspers, a twenty-three-year-old world class distance runner at Clemson University (Brubaker, 1985). Though ultimately exonerated in Jaspers' death, the phenylbutazone found in his system upon autopsy triggered a series of events that blew the lid off an illegal drug delivery ring involving coaches and athletic trainers at Clemson and Vanderbilt as well as suppliers outside the two universities.

One troubling aspect of the anti-inflammatory medications is that they do not treat pain, they merely mask it. In that sense, they are not really restorative at all. At any rate, athletes with musculoskeletal aches and pains tend to play with physical discomfort, thereby placing themselves at risk for greater injury. We sense pain for very good self-preservative reasons and masking it can lead to serious injury. Certainly, the ethics involved in deciding to use anti-inflammatory drugs are dubious at best. The same can be said for painkilling medications and injections, not an uncommon practice in keeping top-flight athletes performing. Novels such as *Semi-Tough* by Dan Jenkins and *North Dallas Forty* by Pete Gent, in part, have poignantly captured the world of pain and the abuse of painkillers to control the hurt associated with professional football.

Additive Drugs. The additive drugs are aimed at performance enhancement and are often called ergogenic aids. Pate, Rotella, and McClenaghan (1984, p. 268) define an ergogenic aid as "any substance or treatment that improves, or is thought to improve, physical performance." The "thought to improve" phrase highlights the fact that the performance-enhancing effects of these various drugs may rest more in the psychology of the individual than in the chemical properties of the various ergogenics. Chief among the ergogenic aids are the amphetamines, the practice of blood boosting, and the anabolic steroids.

Pate and his associates suggest that the various *amphetamines*, particularly Dexedrine and Benzedrine, are among the most commonly used ergogenics by athletes. Their use has been documented in professional baseball (Kirschenbaum, 1980), professional football (Mandell, 1975), and track (Leonard, 1984). Leonard also reports that nine of twelve medalists in the 1970 world weight lifting championships were disqualified after urinalysis revealed the presence of amphetamines. In football, Mandell found their use to be widespread in the professional ranks, and he cited data to suggest that approximately 50 percent of NFL players were using amphetamines. The stimulating and concurrent analgesic effects of the amphetamines are perhaps best summed up by the comment made by one professional football player: "I'm not about to go out there one-on-one against a guy who is grunting and drooling and coming at me with big dilated pupils unless I'm in the same condition" (Mandell, 1975, p. 43). Jim Bouton, in his best-seller *Ball Four*, suggests that amphetamine use was widespread in major league baseball during his playing days. One player poignantly describes the amphetamine problem in baseball as follows: "At first they might take them before a big game. Then it was before every game. Then they had to take them to practice. As the players get older, they forget about how to get energy naturally and start getting it through amphetamine pills" (Oliver, 1971, p. 65). In addition to the dependency problem mentioned by Oliver, the amphetamines may produce rage, unwarranted fearlessness, and irrational feelings of omnipotence, all of which can be potential health detriments to the athlete both on and off the field.

Blood boosting, or what is more commonly known as blood doping (Rostaing and Sullivan, 1985), is not accomplished with a drug at all. However, it does fit in with Pate and associates' definition of an ergogenic aid, and it is perceived as performance-enhancing by athletes and others, hence its inclusion in the present discussion. Blood boosting was all but unheard of until 1972, when Dr. Bjorn Ekblom of Sweden announced that his research revealed significant increases in endurance through a procedure he had developed in his laboratory. In his original study, Ekblom withdrew approximately a quart of blood from four subjects, removed the red blood cells, and put the samples in cold storage for a month. Upon reinfusion of the red blood cells, all subjects were able to run on a treadmill to exhaustion for a much longer time than had been the case before. The theory behind blood boosting is that the red blood cells will carry more oxygen so essential to the muscle tissue involved in endurance sports. Though tests of the efficiency of blood boosting have been equivocal, its use has continued, culminating in the revelation that seven of the twenty-four-member 1984 U.S. Olympic cycling team had engaged in blood boosting prior to competition. The resulting furor over the doping disclosure and others involving additive drugs led to sanctions against blood boosting in April 1985 by the International Olympic Committee (IOC) and the United States Olympic Committee (USOC) ("Ethics of Blood Doping," 1985). Prior to 1985, blood boosting was against USOC policy but not the organization's rules. As a consequence, blood boosting was a matter of individual physician, coach, or athlete conscience, and abuses such as the one involving the Olympic cycling team have occurred.

The advantages of blood boosting have not been satisfactorily demonstrated, but the dangers inherent in the practice (risks of infection, possibility of disease transmission) are well documented, thereby bringing the practice under fire from a number of sources ("Ethics of Blood Doping," 1985; Gledhill, 1982; Rostaing and Sullivan, 1985). As a result, testing has been instituted to detect blood boosting, though many problems remain in the area of test accuracy ("New Techniques," 1986).

The third additive drug category is *anabolic steroids*, synthetic derivatives of the hormone testosterone, which stimulates muscle growth and tissue repair. Steroid abuse constitutes the number-one problem facing physicians involved in international athletes (Percy, 1978). They are used most often by athletes in sports where bulk and muscle are advantageous — weight lifting, bodybuilding, professional football, and weight events in track and field). They have a generally agreed upon set of negative side effects: use of anabolic steroids may result in liver damage, hypertension, and psychological changes such as increased rage and aggression. Attesting to the mood changes, Dean Steinkuhler of the NFL Houston Oilers, a self-acknowledged user of steroids during college and the earliest days of his NFL career, says that his steroid regimen "made me real moody, violent, I wanted to kill somebody" ("A Former Husker," 1987, p. 24). Steroids can also cause decreased testicular size, lowered sperm count, and resultant sterility in males, and a lowering of the voice, increased masculinization, hirsutism, and enlargement of the clitoris in females; the effects on females are most pronounced if full growth has not been attained ("Position Statement," 1978). Because of the side effects, many objections have been raised to steroid use.

The ethical issues associated with steroid use are complex, and there are contrasting points of view about the whole matter. On one hand, there are athletes like Brian Bosworth, linebacker from the University of Oklahoma, whose steroid use has been the center of much controversy (Becker, 1986; Neff, 1987; "Boz Flunks Out," 1987). Bosworth has stated that the National Collegiate Athletic Association (NCAA) engaged in persecutory acts against him because of his steroid use, which he correctly asserted was not a violation of the law. Bill Walsh, the coach of the NFL San Francisco 49ers, sides with Bosworth on his being banned from the 1987 Orange Bowl: "It's like giving someone a six-year sentence for taking money out of a phone booth" (Walsh, 1987). Ron Hale (1987), a former U.S. powerlifting champion, says that steroids should not be banned because athletes need them to compete, especially at the elite level. This sentiment is echoed by Kugler (1984), who suggests that the drug war is being lost to the Eastern bloc nations because of this country's head-in-the-sand approach to research and development in performance-enhancing drugs, including steroids. Another vocal spokesman for steroid use is Tony Millar, an Australian physician, who sees no moral, ethical, or legal problems whatsoever with open-minded and carefully supervised usage among athletes (Miller, 1986).

Many disagree with the advocates of steroid use. Ken Fitch, an eminent Australian contemporary of Millar, strongly suggests that Millar "has done sports medicine a huge disservice. He is encouraging athletes to cheat" (Miller, 1986, p. 168). The NCAA has clearly demonstrated its opposition to steroid use by banning twenty-one college football players (including Bosworth) from postseason play for testing positive for steroids at the end of the 1986 season. The University of California at Los Angeles (UCLA) has technology that permits detection of a spoonful of sugar in an Olympic-sized swimming pool (Neff, 1987). Such technology can detect one-trillionth of a gram of amphetamine in a urine sample (Leonard, 1984).

Other advocates of a hard line on steroid use include a professional football player (Cooks, 1987), a sport psychologist (Gould, 1987), an author of a book on hormonal changes and athletes (Taylor, 1987), and a writer for *Sports Illustrated* (Zimmerman, 1987), all of whom are calling for strict control measures. Yet another strong stance on the issue of steroids has been advanced by the California legislature, which has proposed more stringent measures in dealing with steroid use in that state, particularly the illegal trafficking ("California Proposes," 1986). Finally, the stance adopted by the American College of Sports Medicine (ACSM)

The controversy over the use of performance-enhancing drugs in sports reached dramatic proportions when Canadian sprinter Ben Johnson (center) tested positive for anabolic steroids at the 1988 Olympics. Johnson, who set a world record in the 100-meter dash, was stripped of his gold medal by the International Olympic Committee. "The fastest man alive" left the games a fallen hero.

is advanced for purposes of summarizing the various anti-steroid views. This formulation can be seen in figure 9.4.

The Ethical Problems. At the heart of the misuse of the various additive drugs is the willingness of the athlete to do almost anything to gain a competitive edge; this win-at-all-cost mentality is called the Faustian philosophy of the athlete by Dr. James Puffer, a sports medicine specialist ("Drug Testing in Sports," 1985). Superimposed upon this Faustian mentality at the elite amateur level in particular is the pressure to compete with the Eastern bloc countries, which have purportedly snubbed their collective noses at IOC drug sanctions. These twin pressures of always having to be number one and keeping up with the competition have created a hydra-headed ethical monster in the area of additive drug use.

A number of ethical concerns are related to the use of performance enhancing drugs. One major problem centers around questions of civil liberties and individual freedom of choice. One argument grants freedom of choice to adult athletes once they have been educated as to the pros and cons of the use of a particular drug or procedure. Fost (1983, p. A19) sums up this position as follows: "The ingestion of steroids for competitive reasons cannot be distinguished from other tortures, deprivations and risks to which athletes subject themselves to achieve success. No one is coerced into world class competition. . . . If they find the costs excessive, they may withdraw." The counterargument to this informed consent is that, by allowing freedom of choice, the athlete who prefers to remain drug-free is forced into using drugs in order to be able to compete effectively.

The physician who is called upon to prescribe steroids for an athlete represents another interesting ethical situation. Some physicians have chosen to prescribe steroids for

athletes, using the rationale that informing them about steroid use and then providing subsequent careful monitoring of the course of treatment is preferable to saying no, which may encourage athletes to seek quasi-legal or illegal

---

Figure 9.4 The American College of Sports Medicine (ACSM) Position Statement on Steroid Use: The Use of Anabolic-Androgenic Steroids in Sports

Based on a comprehensive literature and a careful analysis of the claims concerning the ergogenic effects and the adverse effects of anabolic-androgenic steroids, it is the position of the American College of Sports Medicine that:

1. The anabolic-androgenic steroids in the presence of an adequate diet can contribute to increases in body weight, often in the lean mass compartment.
2. The gain in muscular strength achieved through high-intensity exercise and proper diet can be increased by the use of anabolic-androgenic steroids in some individuals.
3. Anabolic-androgenic steroids do not increase aerobic power or capacity for muscular exercise.
4. Anabolic-androgenic steroids have been associated with adverse effects on the liver, cardiovascular system, reproductive system, and psychological status in therapeutic trials and in limited research on athletes. Until further research is completed, the potential hazards of the use of the anabolic-androgenic steroids in athletes must include those found in therapeutic trials.
5. The use of anabolic-androgenic steroids by athletes is contrary to the rules and ethical principles of athletic competition as set forth by many of the sports governing bodies. The American College of Sports Medicine supports these ethical principles and deplores the use of anabolic-androgenic steroids by athletes.

SOURCE: "The Use of Anabolic-Androgenic Steroids in Sports," 1987, *Medicine and Science in Sports and Exercise, 19*, 102.

means of obtaining the drug. At the other end of the continuum are physicians who see no justification whatsoever for prescribing drugs for athletes. One such person is Dr. Robert Voy, chief medical officer for the USOC. Yet another physician of the same persuasion is Dr. Robert Murphy, chair of the NCAA drug education committee, who says: "Over the past three or four years I've had many requests from bodybuilders and high school and college athletes to supervise their steroid programs, and I've refused them all. Because once I take one athlete as a patient, I'd have fifty in my practice. If you treat these athletes and do liver function tests, you're saying it's okay to take anabolic steroids" (Duda, 1986, p. 175).

Yet another ethical problem is posed by the question of testing for the presence of drugs in the athlete's system. The standards for what constitutes unacceptable or illegal drug use and the questions revolving around testing precision within and between the various sports and sports-governing organizations have greatly clouded this situation. Too, the fallibility of the various tests and the false positives and false negatives generated in past cases constitute a major headache for those in the drug detection, enforcement, and rehabilitation business. Finally, some elements within sport will always try to beat the system, staying just one step ahead of available technology and philosophy. Some researchers feel that the Eastern bloc countries have either used performance enhancing anabolics not known to the rest of the world or they have found ways to circumvent detection of the ones currently in existence (Kugler, 1984).

A fourth intriguing ethical dilemma involves physicians functioning as team doctors, particularly at the intercollegiate level. These professionals are often asked to wear the dual hats of ministering to the various medical problems inherent to athletic teams while concurrently serving as head of the team's drug control program. This constitutes a serious case of divided loyalties for these physicians, and places them in a precarious ethical position.

Among all of the possible ethical problems associated with performance enhancing drugs and athletics, the four examples given are the more critical ones that must be addressed by sports professionals of all persuasions. Simon (1985, p. 74) offers two suggestions representing the present consensus on the use of performance-enhancing drugs.

1. The use of performance-enhancing drugs such as steroids by some competitors violates canons of fair competition, may fail to respect the principle of informed consent, and places undue pressure on the other athletes to become users themselves.
2. Although testing for drug use does raise important questions for civil liberties, some testing at the highest levels of competitive sport may be permissible to insure fair competition and preserve the integrity of athletic contests.

SUMMARY

1. Testing in the United States is big business, involving millions of people and billions of dollars.
2. Our history of testing is apparently traceable to China some 4,000 years ago. The two world wars served as potent forces in test development.
3. Definitions of what constitutes a test vary, but emphasis is placed on systematic, objective observations of behavior.
4. Reliability, validity, and norms are three critical components of a good psychological test. A test must measure what it is designed to measure, it must do it consistently, and it must be based on sound standardization procedures, Reliability of a test

can be established through test–retest, parallel forms, and internal consistency procedures. Validity is determined through content, concurrent, and predictive means.

5. Psychological tests in sport are generally used for two purposes: for selection and/or screening decisions and for program development. The sport psychologist should therefore be alert to a variety of concerns having to do with test selection, reporting of results, and ethics in general.

6. Tests of enduring traits have been an integral part of sport psychology research. Chief among them have been the *Minnesota Multiphasic Personality Inventory (MMPI)*, the *Sixteen Personality Factor Questionnaire (16PF)*, and the *Eysenck Personality Inventory (EPI)*.

7. Personality traits of a more temporary or transient nature also have a rich if recent heritage in sport psychology. Chief among these are the *State-Trait Anxiety Inventory (STAI)* of Spielberger and associates and the *Profile of Mood States (POMS)*, which has been elevated to a state of prominence through the work of Morgan, among others. Morgan's concept of the Iceberg Profile is one of the more interesting characterizations of the elite athlete.

8. A substantial call has been made for a move away from enduring traits or broadly conceived tests of temporary states to assessment techniques that are sport-specific. The first of these was created in 1969 by Tutko, Lyon, and Ogilvie and was called the *Athletic Motivation Inventory (AMI)*. Subsequent efforts of this sort include the *Sport Competition Anxiety Test (SCAT)*, the *Competitive State Anxiety Inventory (CSAI)*, and the *CSAI–II*, all sport-related modifications by Martens of the work of Spielberger. A fourth effort of some acclaim is the *Test of Attentional and Interpersonal Style (TAIS)* of Nideffer.

Also, a number of more recent sport-specific instruments offer promise to sport psychology.

9. Attitude measurement in sport has given rise to such instruments as Kenyon's Attitude Toward Physical Activity Scale (ATPA) and Sonstroem's Physical Estimation and Attraction Scales. According to Triandis, attitudes have cognitive, affective, and behavioral components.

10. Thurstone scaling, Likert scaling, and the semantic differential technique of Osgood and associates represent three different methods for the assessment of attitudes.

11. Ethics are essential to the viability of sport psychology. In addition to being cognizant of the ethical demands of research and practice within sport psychology, the knowledgeable sport psychologist should be alert to ethical problems with regard to drugs in sport and take a stand when necessary to insure their proper use.

12. The ethical standards by which sport psychologists ply their trade are spelled out in documents published by the North American Society for the Psychology of Sport and Physical Activity (NASPSPA) in 1982. They were drawn from the basic standards of good practice of the American Psychological Association (APA). Issues related to responsibility, competence, moral and legal standards, public statements, confidentiality, welfare of the client, professional relationships, assessment techniques, and research with human subjects are addressed within the NASPSPA code of ethics.

13. Test ethics represent another important area because of the significance that psychological assessment devices have played and will continue to play in the lives of players, coaches, and sport psychologists.

14. The drug-oriented society in which we live has influenced the world of sport, and the abuse of a wide variety of drugs is a

major ethical problem for sport psychologists, physicians, and others with a stake in the future of athletics.

15. One type of abuse involves drugs considered to be recreational, such as alcohol, marijuana, and cocaine.

16. Restorative drugs represent another category of concern and include muscle relaxants, anti-inflammatories, and painkillers.

17. Additive drugs purport to enhance performance and are generally referred to as ergogenic aids. Stimulant drugs, the practice of blood boosting or doping, and anabolic steroids are three significant ergogenic aids. The use of amphetamines, such as Dexedrine and Benzedrine, was widespread in professional sports in the 1970s but is thought to be less of a problem today, although it would be naive to assume their passage from the drug scene in athletics. Blood boosting was brought to the forefront in sport with the revelation that a number of American cyclists had engaged in blood boosting during competition in the 1984 Olympics. The IOC and other governing bodies have now banned blood boosting. Steroids use is widespread among athletes, particularly elite amateur and professional performers. Because the steroids have been shown to have a number of adverse side effects for both male and female athletes, there is an increasing outcry from many sources for a ban on their future use.

18. Drug use in athletics is fostered and maintained by the win-at-all-cost Faustian mentality of the elite athlete. Ethical problems created by the search for biochemical excellence include questions of civil liberties and freedom of choice, the question faced by physicians of whether to prescribe or not to prescribe steroids (or other drugs), the substantial difficulties associated with drug testing, and the compromise

of ethics facing physicians in some sport settings.

SUGGESTED READINGS

Battles, J., & Odom, C. (1982) Predictor variables: A consideration for coaches. *Journal of Physical Education, Recreation and Dance, 53*(5), 11–12.

This brief article suggests that selecting or evaluating athletes requires a system based on a number of variables, one of which may be the use of psychological tests. The authors point out that psychological tests are far from perfect for accomplishing this task, but it behooves coaches to be informed if they use the tests as part of their player selection and/or evaluation process.

Butcher, J., & Spielberger, C. (1983). *Advances in personality assessment* (Vol. 2). Hillsdale, NJ: Lawrence Erlbaum Associates.

Included in this book of readings are up-to-date analyses of aspects of the work of Eysenck and Spielberger. Of particular interest here is information on the development of a scale to assess anger, the State-Trait Anger Scale.

Cratty, B. J., & Hanin, Y. (1980) *The athlete in the sports team: Social-psychological guidelines for coaches and athletes.* Denver, CO: Love.

Chapter 10 of this collaborative work between American (Cratty) and Russian (Hanin) sport psychologists presents a readable survey of the relevant issues having to do with assessment of athletes. It stresses ethical behavior and common sense in dealing with athletes at all levels of sophistication.

Duda, M. (1986) Female athletes: Targets for drug abuse. *Physician and Sportsmedicine, 14*(6), 142–146.

Increasingly, female athletes are becoming caught up in the win-at-all-cost Faustian mentality so prevalent among elite male performers, and they are convincing themselves or being encouraged by overzealous coaches to attempt to increase their performance through chemical means. Perhaps this better-life-through-chemistry mentality has its roots in the 1973 World Championships in swimming, which were dominated by East German women just one year after the Americans had handily defeated them in the 1972 Olympics. In that one year East German competitors had grown much bigger and stronger, a change attributable to steroid use. Discussion throughout this article centers on the increasing temptation to gain the athletic advantage through steroids. Dr. Robert Voy, chief medical officer for the USOC says: "In men, steroids offer an unfair advantage. But in women, that advantage is probably magnified ten times" (p. 146).

Heyman, S. R. (1985) Problematic issues in sport consultation with amateur boxers. *Consulting Psychology Bulletin, 37*(2), 18–22.

Heyman discusses the ethical implications associated with consulting with an amateur boxing team. The article points up the ethical dilemma associated with using psychologically based performance enhancement techniques with boxers so that they can better inflict pain, injury, or even death on an opponent. Another interesting point Heyman makes is that sport psychologists need not compromise their ethical principles in order to curry the favor of sport organizations. To quote (p. 20): "They need our services as sport psychologist more than we need them as clients, unless we have some needs about which we are not being honest."

Nelson, G. (1948) Personality and attitude differences associated with the elective substitution of ROTC for the physical education requirement in high school. *Research Quarterly, 19,* 2–17.

A lively issue for physical educators and military people has been that of the character building qualities of physical education and of ROTC. Nelson's article relates primarily to that issue but, more importantly, represents one of the first published accounts of the use of the Minnesota Multiphasic Personality Inventory (MMPI).

REFERENCES

A former Husker fesses up. (1987) *Sports Illustrated,* Jan. 5, p. 24.

Aiken, L. (1982) *Psychological testing and assessment.* Boston, MA: Allyn & Bacon.

Albrecht, R. R., & Feltz, D. L. (1987) Generality and specificity of attention related to competitive anxiety and sport performance. *Journal of Sport Psychology, 9,* 231–248.

Allport, G. W., & Odbert, H. S. (1936) Trait names: A psycho-lexical study. *Psychological Monographs, 47*(211), 1–171.

Anastasi, A. (1982) *Psychological testing* (5th ed.). New York: Macmillan.

Bandura, A. (1977) Self-efficacy: Toward a unifying theory of behavioral change. *Psychological Review, 84,* 191–215.

Becker, D. (1986) Steroids KO Bosworth. *USA Today,* Dec. 26, p. C1.

Bhushan, S., & Agarwal, V. (1978) Personality characteristics of high and low achieving Indian sports persons. *International Journal of Sport Psychology, 9,* 191–198.

Blais, M. R., & Vallerand, R. J. (1986) Multimodal effects of electromyographic biofeedback: Looking at children's ability to control precompetitive anxiety. *Journal of Sport Psychology, 8,* 283–303.

Blaser, P., & Schilling, G. (1976) Personality tests in sport. *International Journal of Sport Psychology, 7,* 22–35.

Booth, E. (1958) Personality traits of athletes as measured by the MMPI. *Research Quarterly, 29,* 127–138.

Booth, E. (1961) Personality traits of athletes as measured by the MMPI: A rebuttal. *Research Quarterly, 32,* 421–423.

The Boz flunks out. (1987) *Sports Illustrated,* Jan. 5, front cover.

Brichin, M., & Kochian, M. (1970) Comparison of some personality traits of women participating and not participating in sports. *Ceskoslovenska Psychologie, 14,* 309–321.

Brubaker, B. (1985) A pipeline full of drugs. *Sports Illustrated,* Jan. 21, pp. 18–21.

Buros, O. K. (Ed.). (1970) *Personality tests and reviews.* Lincoln: University of Nebraska, Buros Institute of Mental Measurements.

Buros, O. K. (Ed.). (1974) *Tests in print, II.* Lincoln: University of Nebraska, Buros Institute of Mental Measurements.

Buros, O. K. (Ed.). (1975a) *Intelligence tests and reviews.* Lincoln: University of Nebraska, Buros Institute of Mental Measurements.

Buros, O. K. (Ed.). (1975b) *Personality tests and reviews, II.* Lincoln: University of Nebraska, Buros Institute of Mental Measurements.

Buros, O. K. (1986) *Ninth mental measurements yearbook.* Highland Park, NJ: Gryphon Press.

Burton, D. (1988) Do anxious swimmers swim slower? Reexamining the elusive anxiety-performance relationship. *Journal of Sport and Exercise Psychology, 10,* 45–61.

California proposes tougher steroid law. (1986) *Physician and Sportsmedicine, 14*(2), 40.

Carron, A. V. (1980) *Social psychology of sport.* Ithaca, NY: Mouvement.

Cattell, R. B. (1949) Manual for the *Sixteen Personality Factor Questionnaire.* Champaign, IL: The Institute for Personality and Ability Testing.

Chun, K., Cobb, S., & French, J. (1976) *Measures for psychological assessment.* Ann Arbor, MI: Institute for Social Research, The University of Michigan.

Comrey, A., Backer, T., & Glaser, E. (1973) *A sourcebook for mental health measures.* Los Angeles, CA: Human Interaction Research Institute.

Cooks, J. (1987) Quotelines. *USA Today,* Jan. 5, p. 10A.

Corbin, C. B. (1981) Sex of subject, sex of opponent, and opponent ability as factors affecting self-confidence in a competitive situation. *Journal of Sport Psychology, 3,* 265–270.

Cronbach, L. J. (1970) *Essentials of psychological testing* (3d ed.). New York: Harper and Row.

Curry, T., & Jiobu, R. (1984) *Sports: A sociological perspective.* Englewood Cliffs, NJ: Prentice-Hall.

Daiss, S., & LeUnes, A. (1986) The utility of the Profile of Mood States in sport: An annotated bibliography. *Journal of Applied Research in Coaching and Athletics, 1,* 148–169.

Delk, J. (1973) Some personality characteristics of skydivers. *Life Threatening Behavior, 3*(1), 51–57.

DePalma, D., & Nideffer, R. (1977) Relationships between the Test of Attentional and Interpersonal Style and psychiatric subclassification. *Journal of Personality Assessment, 41,* 622–631.

Drug testing in sports. (1985) *Physician and Sportsmedicine, 13*(12), 69–82.

Duda, M. (1986) Do anabolic steroids pose an ethical dilemma for U.S. physicians? *Physician and Sportsmedicine, 14*(11), 173–175.

Ethical standards for provision of services by NASPSPA members. (1982) *NASPSPA Newsletter,* Addendum to Fall Newsletter, pp. ii–vi.

Ethical standards of psychologists. (1981) Washington, DC: American Psychological Association.

Ethics of blood doping. (1985) *Physician and Sportsmedicine, 13*(8), 151.

Evans, V., & Quarterman, J. (1983) Personality characteristics of successful and unsuccessful black female basketball players. *International Journal of Sport Psychology, 14,* 105–115.

Eysenck, H. J., & Eysenck, S. B. G. (1963) *The Eysenck Personality Inventory.* San Diego, CA: Educational and Industrial Testing Service.

Eysenck, H. J., Nias, D. K. B., & Cox, D. N. (1982) Sport and personality. *Behavior Research and Therapy, 4*(1), 1–56.

Fosdick, D. (1972) The relationship of the *Athletic Motivational Inventory* and the *16 Personality Factor Questionnaire* as measures of the personality characteristics of college varsity swimmers. Unpublished master's thesis, San Jose State University.

Fost, N. (1983) Let 'em take steroids. *New York Times,* Sept. 9, p. A19.

Foster, W. (1977) A discriminant analysis of selected personality variables among successful and unsuccessful male high school athletes. *International Journal of Sport Psychology, 8,* 119–127.

Fuchs, C., & Zaichkowsky, L. (1983) Psychological characteristics of male and female body-builders. *Journal of Sport Behavior, 6,* 136–145.

Geron, E., Furst, D., & Rotstein, P. (1986) Personality of athletes participating in various sports. *International Journal of Sport Psychology, 17,* 120–135.

Gerson, R., & Deshaies, P. (1978) Competitive trait anxiety and performance as predictors of precompetitive state anxiety. *International Journal of Sport Psychology, 9,* 16–26.

Gledhill, N. (1982) Blood doping and related issues: A brief review. *Medicine and Science in Sports and Exercise, 14*(3), 183–189.

Gould, D. (1987) Voices from across the USA. *USA Today,* Jan. 5, 10A.

Gould, D., Horn, T., & Spreeman, J. (1983a) Competitive anxiety in junior elite wrestlers. *Journal of Sport Psychology, 5,* 58–71.

Gould, D., Horn, T., & Spreeman, J. (1983b) Sources of stress in junior elite wrestlers. *Journal of Sport Psychology, 5,* 159–171.

Griffiths, T., Steel, D., & Vaccaro, P. (1978) Anxiety levels of beginning SCUBA students. *Perceptual and Motor Skills, 47,* 312–314.

Griffiths, T., Steel, D., & Vaccaro, P. (1979) Relationship between anxiety and performance in SCUBA diving. *Perceptual and Motor Skills, 48,* 1009–1010.

Griffiths, T., Steel, D., & Vaccaro, P. (1982) Anxiety of SCUBA divers: A multidimensional approach. *Perceptual and Motor Skills, 55,* 611–614.

Griffiths, T., Steel, D., Vaccaro, P., & Karpman, M. (1981) The effects of relaxation techniques on anxiety and underwater performance. *International Journal of Sport Psychology, 12,* 176–182.

Gruber, J., & Beauchamp, D. (1979) Relevancy of the Competitive State Anxiety Inventory in a sport environment. *Research Quarterly, 50,* 207–214.

Gruber, J., & Perkins, S. (1978) Personality traits of women physical education majors and non-majors at various levels of athletic competition. *International Journal of Sport Psychology, 9,* 40–52.

Guidelines for psychological testing within sport and other physical activity settings. (1982) *NASPSPA Newsletter,* Addendum to Fall Newsletter, pp. vi–viii.

Hale, R. (1987) Don't ban steroids; athletes need them. *USA Today,* Jan. 5, p. 10A.

Hall, E. (1980) Comparison of postperformance state anxiety of internals and externals following failure or success on a simple motor task. *Research Quarterly for Exercise and Sport, 51*(2), 306–314.

Hammer, W., & Tutko, T. (1974) Validation of the Athletic Motivation Inventory. *International Journal of Sport Psychology, 5,* 3–12.

Hardman, K. (1973) A dual approach to the study of personality and performance in sport. In H. T. Whiting, K. Hardman, L. B. Hendry, and M. G. Jones (Eds.), *Personality and performance in physical education and sport* (pp. 77–122). London: Henry Kimpton.

Harter, S. (1978) Effectance motivation reconsidered: Toward a developmental model. *Human Development, 21,* 34–64.

Hathaway, S., & McKinley, J. (1943) *MMPI Manual.* New York: Psychological Corporation.

Heusner, W. (1952) Personality traits of champion and former champion athletes. Unpublished master's thesis, University of Illinois.

Hightower, J. (1973) A comparison of competitive and recreational baseball players on motivation. Unpublished master's thesis, Louisiana State University.

Hirst, J. (1972) Differences in motivation between successful and unsuccessful high school basketball teams. Unpublished master's thesis, San Jose State University.

Irvine, M., & Gendreau, P. (1974) Detection of the fake "good" and "bad" response on the Sixteen Personality Factor Inventory in prisoners and college students. *Journal of Consulting and Clinical Psychology, 42,* 465–466.

Johnsgard, K., Ogilvie, B. C., Merritt, K. (1975) The stress seekers: A psychological study of sports parachutists, racing drivers, and football players. *Journal of Sports Medicine, 15,* 158–169.

Johnson, O. (1976) *Tests and measurements in child development: Handbook II* (Vols. 1 and 2). San Francisco, CA: Jossey-Bass.

Johnson, O., & Bommarito, J. (1971) *Tests and measurements in child development: Handbook I.* San Francisco, CA: Jossey-Bass.

Kaplan, R., & Sacuzzo, D. (1982) *Psychological testing: Principles, applications, and issues.* Monterey, CA: Brooks/Cole.

Kenyon, G. (1968) Six scales for assessing attitudes toward physical activity. *Research Quarterly, 39,* 566–574.

King, J., & Chi, P. (1974) Personality and the athletic social structure: A case study. *Human Relations, 27,* 179–193.

Kirkcaldy, B. (1980) An analysis of the relationship between psychophysiological variables connected to human performance and the personality variables extraversion and neuroticism. *International Journal of Sport Psychology, 11,* 276–289.

Kirschenbaum, J. (1980) Uppers in baseball. *Sports Illustrated,* July 21, p. 11.

Klavora, P. (1975) Application of the Spielberger trait-state theory and STAI in pre-competition anxiety research. Paper presented to the North American Society for the Psychology of Sport and Physical Activity, State College, Pennsylvania.

Kroll, W. (1970) Current strategies and problems in personality assessment of athletes. In L. Smith (Ed.), *Psychology of motor learning* (pp. 349–367). Chicago, IL: Athletic Institute.

Kugler, H. (1984) We're losing the drug war. *Inside Sports, 6,* 52–54.

LaPlace, J. (1954) Personality and its relationship to success in professional baseball. *Research Quarterly, 25,* 313–319.

Leonard, W. (1984) *A sociological perspective of sport* (2nd ed.). Minneapolis, MN: Burgess.

LeUnes, A., & Nation, J. R. (1982) Saturday's heroes: A psychological portrait of college football players. *Journal of Sport Behavior, 5,* 139–149.

LeUnes, A., Hayward, S. A., & Daiss, S. (1988) Annotated bibliography on the Profile of Mood States in sport, 1975-1988. *Journal of Sport Behavior, 11,* 213–239.

Likert, R. A. (1932) A technique for the measurement of attitudes. *Archives of Psychology, 140,* 1–55.

Lyon, L. (1972) A method for assessing personality characteristics in athletes: The *Athletic Motivational Inventory.* Unpublished master's thesis, San Jose State University.

Mahoney, M. J., Gabriel, T. J., & Perkins, T. S. (1987) Psychological skills and exceptional athletic performance. *The Sport Psychologist, 1,* 181–199.

Mandell, A. (1975) Pro football fumbles the drug scandal. *Psychology Today,* June, pp. 39–47.

Martens, R. (1977) *Sport Competition Anxiety Test.* Champaign, IL: Human Kinetics.

Martens, R., Burton, D., Rivkin, F., & Simon, J. (1980) Reliability and validity of the Competitive State Anxiety Inventory CSAI: A modification of Spielberger's state anxiety inventory. In C. H. Nadeau, W. R. Halliwell, K. M. Newell, and G. C. Roberts (Eds.), *Psychology of motor behavior and sport— 1979* (pp. 91–99). Champaign, IL: Human Kinetics.

Martens, R., Burton, D., Vealey, R. S., Bump, L. A., & Smith, D. (1982) Cognitive and somatic dimensions of competitive anxiety. Paper presented at the annual meeting of the North American Society for the Psychology of Sport and Physical Activity, University of Maryland, College Park.

Martens, R., Rivkin, F., & Burton, D. (1980) Who predicts anxiety better: Coaches or athletes? In C. H. Nadeau, W. R. Halliwell, K. M. Newell, & G. C. Roberts (Eds.), *Psychology of motor behavior and sport—1979* (pp. 84–90). Champaign, IL: Human Kinetics.

McNair, D., Lorr, M., & Droppleman, L. (1971) *Profile of Mood States Manual.* San Diego: Educational and Industrial Testing Service.

Miller, C. (1986) Anabolic steroids: An Australian sports physician goes public. *Physician and Sportsmedicine, 14*(11), 167–170.

Morgan, W. P. (1968) Personality characteristics of wrestlers participating in the world championships. *Journal of Sports Medicine, 8,* 212–216.

Morgan, W. P. (1978) The mind of the marathoner. *Psychology Today,* April, pp. 38–49.

Morgan, W. P. (1980) Test of champions. *Psychology Today,* July, pp. 92–108.

Morgan, W. P., & Johnson, R. (1978) Personality characteristics of successful and unsuccessful oarsmen. *International Journal of Sport Psychology, 9,* 119–133.

Morgan, W. P., & Pollock, M. (1977) Psychologic characterization of the elite distance runner. *Annals of the New York Academy of Sciences, 301,* 382–403.

Morris, L. D. (1975) A socio-psychological study of highly skilled women field hockey players. *International Journal of Sport Psychology, 6,* 134–147.

Neff, C. (1987) Bosworth faces the music. *Sports Illustrated,* Jan. 5, pp. 20–25.

New techniques may catch blood dopers. (1986) *Physician and Sportsmedicine, 14*(2), 36.

Nicholls, J. G. (1980) Striving to demonstrate and develop ability: A theory of achievement motivation. In W. U. Meyer & B. Weiner (Chair), *Attributional approaches to human motivation.* Symposium conducted at the Center for Interdisciplinary Research, University of Bielefeld, West Germany.

Nideffer, R. M. (1976) *Test of Attentional and Interpersonal Style. Journal of Personality and Social Psychology, 34,* 394–404.

Nideffer, R. M. (1981) *The ethics and practice of applied sport psychology.* Ithaca, NY: Mouvement.

Nideffer, R. M. (1986) Concentration and attention control training. In J. M. Williams (Ed.), *Applied sport psychology: Personal growth to peak experience* (pp. 257–269). Palo Alto, CA: Mayfield.

O'Dell, J. (1971) Method for detecting random answers on personality questionnaires. *Journal of Applied Psychology, 55,* 380–383.

Ogilvie, B. C. (1974) Relationship of AMI traits to three levels of baseball competitors. Unpublished research paper, San Jose State University.

Ogilvie, B. C., Tutko, T. A., & Lyon, L. (1973) *The Motivational Inventory. Scholastic Coach, 43,* 130–134.

Oliver, C. (1971) *High for the game.* New York: Morrow.

Osgood, C. E., Suci, G. J., & Tannenbaum, P. H. (1957) *The measurement of meaning.* Urbana, IL: University of Illinois Press.

Oxendine, J. (1970) Emotional arousal and motor performance. *Quest, 13,* 23–32.

Passer, M. W. (1983) Fear of failure, fear of evaluation, perceived competence, and self-esteem in competition-trait-anxious children. *Journal of Sport Psychology, 5,* 172–188.

Pate, R., Rotella, R., & McClenaghan, B. (1984) *Scientific foundations of coaching.* Philadelphia, PA: Saunders.

Pemberton, C., & Cox, R. H. (1981) Consolidation theory and the effects of stress and anxiety on motor behavior. *International Journal of Sport Psychology, 12,* 131–139.

Percy, E. (1978) Ergogenic aids in athletics. *Medicine and Science in Sports, 10,* (4), 298–303.

Pestonjee, D., Singh, R., Singh, A., & Singh, U. (1981) Personality and physical abilities: An empirical investigation. *International Journal of Sport Psychology, 12,* 39–51.

Position statement on the use and abuse of anabolic-androgenic steroids in sports. (1978) *British Journal of Sports Medicine, 12*(2), 102–104.

Powell, F., & Verner, J. (1982) Anxiety and performance in first time parachutists. *Journal of Sport Psychology, 4,* 184–188.

Rasch, P. J., Hunt, M. B., & Robertson, P. G. (1960) The Booth Scale as a predictor of competitive behavior of college wrestlers. *Research Quarterly, 31,* 117.

Reid, R., & Hay, D. (1979) Some behavioral characteristics of rugby and association footballers. *International Journal of Sport Psychology, 10,* 239–251.

Renfrow, N., & Bolton, B. (1979a) Personality characteristics associated with aerobic exercise in adult males. *Journal of Personality Assessment, 43,* 261–266.

Renfrow, N., & Bolton, B. (1979b) Personality characteristics associated with aerobic exercise in adult females. *Journal of Personality Assessment, 43,* 504–508.

Richards, D., & Landers, D. M. (1980) Test of Attentional and Interpersonal Style scores of shooters. In G. C. Roberts & D. M. Landers (Eds.), *Psychology of motor behavior and sport—1980* (p. 94). Champaign, IL: Human Kinetics.

Rostaing, B., & Sullivan, R. (1985) Triumphs tainted with blood. *Sports Illustrated,* Jan. 21, pp. 12–17.

Rotella, R. J., & Connelly, D. (1984) Individual ethics in the application of cognitive sport psychology. In W. F. Straub & J. M. Williams (Eds.), *Cognitive sport psychology: Personal growth to peak experience.* Lansing, NY: Sport Science Association.

Rupnow, A., & Ludwig, D. (1981) Psychometric note on the reliability of the Sport Competition Anxiety Test: Form C. *Research Quarterly for Exercise and Sport, 52,* 35–37.

Rushall, B. S. (1972) Three studies relating personality variables to football performance. *International Journal of Sport Psychology, 3,* 12–24.

Rushall, B. S., & Sherman, C. A. (1987) A definition and measurement of pressure in sport. *Journal of Applied Research in Coaching and Athletics, 2,* 1–23.

Sanderson, F., & Ashton, M. (1981) Analysis of anxiety levels before and after badminton competition. *International Journal of Sport Psychology, 12,* 23–28.

Sarason, I., Davidson, K., Lighthall, F., Waite, R., & Ruebush, B. (1960) *Anxiety in elementary school children.* New York: Wiley.

Scanlan, T. K., & Passer, M. W. (1979) Factors influencing the competitive performance expectancies of young female athletes. *Journal of Sport Psychology, 1,* 212–220.

Scanlan, T. K., & Passer, M. W. (1981) Determinants of competitive performance expectancies of young male athletes. *Journal of Personality, 49,* 60–74.

Simon, R. (1985) *Sports and social values.* Englewood Cliffs, NJ: Prentice-Hall.

Simon, J., & Martens, R. (1979) Children's anxiety in sport and nonsport evaluative activities. *Journal of Sport Psychology, 1,* 160–169.

Slusher, H. (1964) Personality and intelligence characteristics of selected high school athletes and non-athletes. *Research Quarterly, 35,* 539–545.

Sonstroem, R. J. (1978) Physical estimation and attraction scales: Rationale and research. *Medicine and Science in Sports, 10,* 97–102.

Sonstroem, R. J., & Bernardo, P. (1982) Intraindividual pregame state anxiety and basketball performance: A re-examination of the inverted-U curve. *Journal of Sport Psychology, 4,* 235–245.

Spielberger, C. (1973) *State-Trait Anxiety Inventory for Children:* Preliminary manual. Palo Alto, CA: Consulting Psychologists Press.

Spielberger, C. (1983) *State-Trait Anxiety Inventory:* A comprehensive bibliography, Palo Alto, CA: Consulting Psychologists Press.

Spielberger, C., Gorsuch, R., & Lushene, R. (1970) Manual for the *State-Trait Anxiety Inventory.* Palo Alto, CA: Consulting Psychologists Press.

Spielberger, C., Gorsuch, R., Lushene, R., Vagg, P., & Jacobs, G. (1983) Manual for the *State-Trait Anxiety Inventory* (form Y). Palo Alto, CA: Consulting Psychologists Press.

Standards for educational and psychological tests and manuals. (1974) Washington, DC: American Psychological Association.

Stewart, L. (1970) A comparative study measuring the psychological makeup among groups of basketball players and coaches. Unpublished master's thesis, Western Washington State College.

Straub, W. F. (1986) Conversation with Bruce Ogilvie. *AAASP Newsletter,* 1(2), 4–5.

Straub, W. F., & Davis, S. (1971) Personality traits of college football players who participated at different levels of competition. *Medicine and Science in Sports, 3,* 39–43.

Taylor, J. (1953) A personality scale of manifest anxiety. *Journal of Abnormal and Social Psychology, 48,* 285–290.

Taylor, W. (1987). There is no safe dose; impose tighter controls. *USA Today,* Jan. 5, p. 10A.

Thakur, G., & Ojha, M. (1981) Personality differences of Indian table-tennis, badminton, and football players on primary source traits of the 16PF. *International Journal of Sport Psychology, 12,* 196–203.

Thakur, G., & Thakur, M. (1980) Personality differences between the athlete and the nonathlete. *International Journal of Sport Psychology, 11,* 180–188.

Thayer, R. E. (1967) Measurement of activation through self report. *Psychological Reports, 20,* 663–678.

Thurstone, L. L. (1928) Attitudes can be measured. *American Journal of Sociology, 33,* 529–554.

Tombor, F. (1970) Personality correlates of football and basketball performances. Unpublished master's thesis, San Jose University.

Triandis, H. C. (1971) *Attitude and attitude change.* New York: Wiley.

Tutko, T. A., Lyon, L., & Ogilvie, B. C. (1969) *Athletic Motivation Inventory.* San Jose, CA: Institute for the Study of Athletic Motivation.

Vallerand, R. (1983) Attention and decision-making: A test of the predictive validity of the Test of Attentional and Interpersonal Style in a sport setting. *Journal of Sport Psychology, 5,* 449–459.

Van Schoyck, R., & Grasha, A. (1981) Attentional style variations and athletic ability: The advantage of a sports-specific test. *Journal of Sport Psychology, 3,* 9–18.

Vealey, R. S. (1986) Conceptualization of sport-confidence and competitive orientation: Preliminary investigation and instrument development. *Journal of Sport Psychology, 8,* 221–246.

Walsh, B. Quotelines. *USA Today,* Jan. 5, p. 10A.

Wandzilak, T., Potter, G., & Lorentzen, D. (1982) Factors related to predictability of pre-game state anxiety. *International Journal of Sport Psychology, 13,* 31–42.

Weinberg, R. S. (1979) Anxiety and motor performance: Drive theory vs. cognitive theory. *International Journal of Sport Psychology, 10,* 112–121.

Weinberg, R. S., & Genuchi, M. (1980) Relationship between competitive trait anxiety, state anxiety, and golf performance: A field study. *Journal of Sport Psychology, 2,* 148–154.

Williams, J., Hoepner, B., Moody, D., & Ogilvie, B. C. (1970) Personality traits of champion level female fencers. *Research Quarterly, 41,* 446–453.

Williams, L. R. T., & Parkin, W. A. (1980) Personality factor profiles of three hockey groups. *International Journal of Sport Psychology, 11,* 113–120.

Williams, R., & Youssef, Z. (1972) Consistency of football coaches in stereotyping the personality of each position's player. *International Journal of Sport Psychology, 3,* 3–11.

Winder, P., O'Dell, J., & Karson, S. (1975) New motivational distortion scales for the 16PF. *Journal of Personality Assessment, 39,* 532–537.

Zimmerman, P. (1987). Quotelines. *USA Today,* Jan. 5, p. 10A.

PART · FOUR

A WIDER
PERSPECTIVE

10

The Female Athlete

INTRODUCTION

A separate chapter is devoted to the female athlete because of the burgeoning interest in the area and also because of some historical antecedents that have traditionally set women's roles and rights apart. It has only recently become acceptable for women to compete in sport, though this acceptance is hardly universal. Women were not allowed to participate in or, in some cases, even view athletic events held by the early Greeks. Little progress was noted over the next two thousand five hundred years. Part of the problem has to do with rather widely held views of women in general. For instance, the eighteenth century French philosopher, Rousseau, wrote: "Woman was made especially to please man. . . . If woman is formed to please and to live in subjugation, she must render herself agreeable to man instead of provoking his wrath; her strength lies in her charms" (quoted in Spears, 1978, p. 7). Consistent with this view, an old adage provides further insight into the perception of sex differences:

What are little boys made of?
Snits and snails and puppy dog tails;
That's what little boys are made of.

What are little girls made of?
Sugar and spice and everything nice;
That's what little girls are made of
(cited in Curry and Jiobu, 1984, p. 163).

Leaders in physical education have not been exempt from this bias. For example, Agnes Wayman, an early leader in the physical education movement (president of the American Physical Education Association in 1933), said, "External stimuli such as cheering audiences, bands, lights, etc., cause a great response in girls and are apt to upset the endocrine balance. Under emotional stress a girl may eas-

ily overdo. There is widespread agreement that girls should not be exposed to extremes of fatigue or strain either emotional or physical" (cited in Loggia, 1973, p. 64).

Coaches and athletic directors have also displayed bias against women's participation in athletics. Woody Hayes, the long-time football coach at Ohio State University, stated a point of view that may not have been his alone:

I hear they're even letting w-o-m-e-n in their sports program now [referring to Oberlin College]. That's your Women's Liberation, boy—bunch of goddamn lesbians. . . . You can bet your ass that if you have women around—and I've talked to psychiatrists about this—you aren't gonna be worth a damn. No sir! Man has to dominate . . . the best way to treat a woman, . . . is to knock her up and hide her shoes. (Cited in Vare, 1974, p. 38)

Nor is this view held by a high school athletic director unique to him:

We tried to organize a girls' sports program but it hasn't worked out very well. . . . Unfortunately, the girls didn't show a lot of interest. Only twelve came out for the team. There were two big tomboyish girls who remained quite enthused, but the others have not been faithful about practice. I'm not blaming them because I think a normal girl at that age is going to be more interested in catching a boy than catching a basketball. (Cited in Gilbert and Williamson, 1973, p. 47)

Akin to this opinion is the following from an anonymous source:

There is hardly a real mother in this nation who would not prefer to see her daughter dressed in a cute outfit, attracting boys and being voted the most popular girl in her class and maybe marrying a football star after she graduates, rather than growing big muscles and looking like a man in some sport. (Cited by Michener, 1976)

Some would suggest that a woman athlete is less than a woman. Consider Russell Knipp's reaction to Olga Connolly's carrying the U.S. flag in the Munich Olympic parade: "The flag bearer ought to be a man, a strong man, a warrior. A woman's place is in the home" (cited in Leonard, 1984, p. 190). And, finally, "Sports is a male sanctuary, therefore any woman who tries to invade it is not really a woman" (quoted in Lipsyte, 1975, p. 217).

Even the casual comments of the everyday male sport participant are reflective of a bias against the female athlete. For instance, "throwing like a girl" is used as a highly derogatory comment on the ability of a male. How has this picture of women and women athletes come about?

A BRIEF HISTORY

The history of female involvement in sport and physical activity is almost nonexistent. Female involvement in sport is relatively recent.

Ancient Greece

Women did take part in some activities in early Greece, but they were not only barred from participating in Olympic events but even faced a death penalty for being so bold as to try to view them. Nevertheless, they had an outlet for their athletic energies in the form of the Heraean Games, named in honor of Hera, the wife of

HIGHLIGHT 10.1
The Heraean Games

The Heraean Games represented a formalized outlet for athletic skills among young women in ancient Greece. However, evidence suggests that the games were actually limited to a footrace. Pausanias describes the games as follows:

The games consist of footraces for maidens. These are not all of the same age. The first to run are the youngest; after them come the next in age, and the last to run are the oldest of the maidens. They run in the following way: Their hair hangs down, a tunic reaches to a little above the knee, and they bare a right shoulder as far as the breast. These too have the Olympic stadium reserved for their games, but the course of the stadium is shortened for them by about one-sixth of its length. To the winning maidens they give crowns of olive and a portion of the cow sacrificed to Hera. They may also dedicate statues with their names inscribed upon them. (Robinson, 1955, p. 9)

There is some evidence that the Heraean Games actually predated the Olympic Games and continued well into the first century A.D. (Spears and Swanson, 1983).

SOURCE: *Sources for the History of Greek Athletics* (p. 9) by R. S. Robinson, 1955, Cincinnati, OH: Published by Author; *History of Sport and Physical Activity in the United States* (2d ed., p. 337) by B. Spears and R. A. Swanson, 1983, Dubuque, IA: Wm. C. Brown.

Two milestones in the history of women in baseball: the Resolutes, Vassar College's first baseball team (facing page) and members of the Racine Belles (right), who from 1943 to 1954 played in the only professional women's baseball league in the United States.

Zeus. Like the Olympics, these Heraean Games were held every four years and consisted of races for unmarried girls (Mouratidis, 1984). The games were held in Olympus beginning in what Spears (1984) calls the Archaic Period (800 B.C.–500 B.C.). By way of summarizing the overall influence of sports on early Greek women, Spears has written: "The history of women's sport in ancient Greece must be viewed in the perspective of men's sport of the same period. Throughout the ancient literature *any* suggestion of sport-like activity for women becomes evidence because of its rarity" (p. 44).

Little of significance transpired in women's athletics until the inclusion of females in the Olympic Games in 1896. Prior to that time, little, if any, involvement in physical activity was expected or condoned. However, with participation in the modern Olympics came a new era in women's athletics.

The Modern Olympics

The founder of the modern Olympics, Baron Pierre de Coubertin, reinstituted the games in 1896. Women began to participate in 1900, though Coubertin was vehemently opposed to women taking part in the competition (Emery, 1984; Gerber, Felshin, Berlin, and Wyrick,

1974). Over his considerable protests, two events for women, tennis and golf, were added to the games. Archery followed in 1904, though it had unofficial status at that time. In 1908, figure skating was made an official event, and unofficial competition was staged in gymnastics, swimming, and diving. Track and field events were added in 1928, though the debut was inauspicious. Emery (1984) reports that several runners fell upon completing the 800-meter run, thereby leading the opponents of female participation to conclude that women were indeed not up to the challenge of strenuous athletics. The extent of the setback created here is reflected by the fact that the event was discontinued until the 1960 Olympics. Perhaps the ultimate in strenuousness, the marathon, was not added to the female events until 1984. For a chronology of Olympic events for women, see table 10.1.

Table 10.1 Women in the Olympic Games

	First time on program	Women on program	United States in Olympics	First United States medal
Athletics (track and field)	1968	1928	1928	1928
Basketball	1936	1976	1976	1976
Canoe	1936	1948	1960	1964
Cycling	1896	1984	1984	—
Fencing	1896	1924	1928	—
Archery	1900	1904	1904	1904
Equestrian	1900	X	X	1972
Gymnastics	1896	1928	1936	1948
Rhythmic gymnastics	1984	1984	1984	—
Team handball	1972	1976	1984	—
Field hockey	1908	1980	1984	—
Luge	1964	1964	1980	—
Rowing	1896	1976	1976	1976
Shooting	1896	1984	1984	—
Figure skating	1908	1908	1920	1920
Speed skating	1924	1960	1960	1960
Skiing—Alpine	1948	1948	1948	1948
Skiing—Nordic	1896	1952	1972	—
Diving	1896	1912	1920	1920
Swimming	1896	1912	1920	1920
Synchronized swimming	1984	1984	1984	—
Table tennis	1896	1988	1988	—
Tennis	1896	1900	1924	1924
Volleyball	1964	1964	1964	—
Sailing	1900	X	X	X

Female competitors are now an integral part of the Olympic process, and this is reflected not only in the relatively wide variety of sports in which they participate but also by their numbers. According to Johnson and Fritz (1984), some 21 to 30 percent of the participants in the 1984 games were expected to be women, or between two thousand and three thousand in number. A further attestation of the continuing development of women in the Olympics is provided by Eitzen and Sage (1982), who note that in 1976 the time of a fifteen-year-old East German girl in the 400-meter freestyle swimming event was a full 3 seconds better than American Olympian Don Schollander's winning time in the same event for men only twelve years earlier. The Olympic Games have clearly served as a vehicle for promoting feminism in general and female sport involvement in particular.

Title IX Legislation

Another significant landmark in the development of women's athletics in this country was the passage of the Higher Education Act of 1972 and its Title IX provision. Title IX essentially prohibited sex discrimination in educational institutions receiving federal funds, thereby creating an atmosphere of sex equality in sports. Though its effects were not immediately felt, some equalization of opportunity in sport at the high school and college level has come about through the provision of separate but equal women's teams, through athletic scholarship opportunity, and through a host of other perquisites previously available only to male athletes. As Coakley (1982) says, the question of what constitutes equal opportunity has been and will continue to be a hot debate topic, but the net effect of Title IX legislation so far has been that women cannot be shortchanged in terms of access to facilities, coaching, fair scheduling, equipment, and selection of sports.

Contemporary Forces in Women's Athletics

In addition to the historical antecedents, a few contemporary forces have been at work in propelling women's efforts to the athletic forefront. In addition to the Title IX legislation, Coakley (1982) cites four reasons why there has been a demonstrable increase in female participation in sport. One of them is simply an increase in *opportunity*. Greater numbers of teams in a broader array of sports are highly noticeable today. Too, the fallout created by what might be called the *women's movement* has most certainly touched women's sport. Yet a third force is the *fitness boom* of the past decade. It has become fashionable for women to work out, strive for fitness, and take part in the fitness revolution. Finally, the *presence of role models* for aspiring young female athletes is a refreshing addition. Young girls are increasingly being afforded worthy role models in track and field, golf, tennis, swimming, marathoning, and a host of other sports. As Coakley points out, professionals, such as tennis star Tracy Austin, are important role models, but they are surpassed in impact by "real life" neighborhood or school athletes with whom younger girls can identify in a sporting capacity.

Now that we have a historical and contemporary perspective on women's sports, we can turn our attention to other dimensions of female sport participation.

THE PHYSIOLOGICAL DIMENSION IN WOMEN'S ATHLETICS

The scientific community has questioned the ability of women to compete because of a variety of physiological concerns including menstrual function, reproduction, and the breasts and genitals. Some members would propose

The Olympics have become a major vehicle for promoting female participation in sports. In 1988, U.S. track star Florence Griffith Joyner won three gold medals and a silver at the summer games in Seoul. "Flo Jo" falls to her knees after taking the 200-meter Olympic final in a world record 21:34.

that involvement in strenuous physical activity is quite damaging to these various structures and/or functions.

Menstrual Functioning

Lively debate has been conducted for quite some time with regard to the issue of physical activity and the menstrual cycle. Arnold (1924), a prominent physical educator of the early 1900s, discouraged female involvement in sport because of the deleterious effects of physical exertion on the frequency and extent of menstruation, a situation that endangered the reproductive capabilities of female participants. Another prominent physical educator of that era, Mabel Lee, conducted surveys in 1923 and 1930 in which 60 percent of her respondents echoed Arnold's concern with the dangers of disrupting the menstrual process (Lee, 1924, 1931). Incidentally, Ms. Lee was the first woman president of the American Alliance for Health, Physical Education, Recreation and Dance (AAHPERD) and, at age ninety-six, wrote a book on the history of sport and physical activity (Lee, 1983).

Early Studies. The early skepticism persisted for thirty years, but evidence began to surface that countered the prevailing pessimism about the interactive effects of exercise on menstruation and reproduction. Landmark studies by Erdelyi (1962) and Zaharieva (1965) did much to demonstrate that strenuous exercise did not negatively affect the menstrual cycle nor did menstruation significantly affect physical performance in a negative way. Erdelyi conducted an intensive study of 729 Hungarian female athletes whereas Zaharieva's work was with 66 female Olympians from ten different countries taking part in four different sports (gymnastics, swimming, track and field, and volleyball). Much of the early scientific data bearing on the exercise-menstruation issue has come from their combined works. Major conclusions that might be drawn from their efforts are as follows:

1. Some athletes do in fact suffer a performance decrement during the menses, but the majority of their subjects reported similar or improved performance as the norm.
2. Of Zaharieva's subjects, 46 percent reported that they felt no differently during the menses; 32 percent reported feeling weaker at the time.
3. Ninety-two percent of Zaharieva's subjects were rhythmic with regard to the menstrual period. Length of menses was not adversely affected, and blood flow was generally normal. Among those who were irregular (6.1 percent), most were young enough for their irregularity to be more likely a function of youth than of sport participation. Erdelyi

found similar results with his Hungarian athletes, with 83.8 percent reporting no change in menstrual cycle throughout training and competition. Eleven percent reported irregularity. Further elaboration on these results is offered by Astrand, Eriksson, Nylander, Engstrom, Karlberg, Saltin, and Thoren (1963) and Ingman (1952). Astrand et al. studied 84 Swedish swimmers and found that 15.5 percent reported menstrual problems while training, though the complaints ceased upon cessation of competition. Ingman, in a study of 107 top Finnish athletes, reported unfavorable changes in 18 percent of his subjects.

Overall, it would appear that these papers from the 1960s did much to dispel misconceptions about menstruation and performance. Efforts of late have centered around the third of the three conclusions mentioned earlier. Considerable argument concerns whether the picture is as good as was portrayed by some of the early researchers. The emphasis of late has been on the cessation of menses (amenorrhea) and on irregular menstrual functioning (oligomenorrhea).

Recent Studies. Given some research (Webb, Millan, and Stolz, 1979) that has shown higher rates of menstrual disturbance than reported by earlier authorities, as well as concern with menstrual difficulties associated with overtraining (Erdelyi, 1976), the furor over the exercise-menstruation issue continues unabated. For instance, Webb et al. reported a 59 percent rate in menstrual difficulties in a group of fifty-six Olympic athletes (basketball, gymnastics, track and field, swimming, and rowing). Primary among the complaints were "missing my period" (n = 17) and "delay in onset of period" (n = 16). Foreman (see Bloomberg, 1977), in a study of the woman's AAU cross-country championships in 1971 and 1973, found 43 percent of the runners to be either irregular or very irregular in menstrual functioning. Lutter and Cushman (1982) found, in a study of thirty-five distance runners, that 19.3 percent of these women reported irregular menstrual periods and 3.4 percent reported having no period for the previous year.

A link seems to exist between strenuous physical activity and disruptions in the menstrual cycle. Why this relationship exists and what the consequences are in terms of the total health picture of the participants are the subjects of considerable speculation.

Causes of Menstrual Difficulties. A number of theories have been advanced as to why sport participation causes menstrual difficulties. One advanced by Frisch (Frisch, 1976; Frisch and McArthur, 1974) involves the relationship between body mass and percentage of body fat. She suggests that once body fat percentage drops below a certain point, a chain reaction of biochemical changes takes place that causes a cessation of menstrual periods. Though her point is seductive, evidence does not appear to support Frisch's hypothesis (Bonen and Keizer, 1984; Sanborn, Albrecht, and Wagner, 1987).

Another possible source of the problem of menstrual difficulties has been advanced from an endocrinological point of view, pointing to hormonal changes within the subjects (Bonen and Keizer, 1984; "Menstrual Changes," 1981). Also implicated as possible causes have been heavy exercise training (Dale, Gerlach, Martin, and Alexander, 1979; Feicht, Johnson, Martin, Sparkles, and Wagner, 1978; Sasiene, 1983); stress (Gendel, 1976; Russell, 1972; Sasiene, 1983); and becoming involved in strenuous physical activity prior to menarche (Frisch, Gotz-Welbergen, McArthur, Albright, Witschi, Bullen, Birnholz, Reed, and Hermann, 1981; Wakat and Sweeney, 1979).

Consequences of Menstrual Difficulties. Several sources point to disruption of the normal menstrual cycle and the effects of strenuous training as possible causes of difficulties associated with pregnancy. However, the preponderance of the data bearing on this issue are not supportive of such a stance. Erdelyi (1962) and Zaharieva (1965), in a combined study of more than 740 female athletes, showed that the athletes had shorter labor periods, fewer instances of toxemia, fewer premature deliveries, and a lower rate of Caesarean sections than did a comparable nonathletic sample. Astrand et al. (1963) found similar results in their study of eighty-four elite swimmers. Gerber, Felshin, Berlin, and Wyrick (1974) attribute this finding to superior conditioning in fit females.

The fitness associated with athletics does in fact appear to be conducive to a good pregnancy and delivery. However, is pregnancy a handicap when one is trying to perform? Anecdotal reports would have us believe that the answer is no. Juno Stover Irwin won an Olympic medal in diving (10-meter board) when she was in her fourth month of pregnancy (Kaplan, 1979); Sue Pirtle Hays successfully competed in world championship rodeo as a bareback bronc rider when she was eight months pregnant (Kaplan, 1979); three medal winning divers in the 1952 Olympics were pregnant at the time they competed (Dyer, 1982); ten of twenty Russian medal winners in the 1956 Olympics were pregnant at the time (Dyer, 1982). Reports such as these certainly give the impression that pregnancy and top-level performance are not incompatible. Evidence from Erdelyi is most supportive of the more anecdotal observations; she found that two-thirds of 172 Hungarian athletes with children continued normal sport functioning in the early phases of pregnancy, though performance decrements were typically visible beyond the third or fourth month, at which time most of these athletes stopped serious competition.

Athletes appear to return to top form rather quickly after childbirth. Zaharieva and Sigler (1963), in a combined effort involving 207

Spanish and Hungarian athletes, found that all had between one and four children and over 75 percent of them bettered their Olympic results within two years after delivery, most in the first year. Bloom (1986) interviewed the world class distance runner, Mary Decker Slaney, and reported that she was back on the track six days after giving birth, and was running almost normally at one month. Brownlee (1988) cites personal records achieved following childbirth in such world-class athletes as Valerie Brisco, Ingrid Kristiansen and Tatyana Kazankina (track), Nancy Lopez (golf), Karen Kania (speed skating), Pat McCormick (diving), and Steffi Martin Walter (luge).

All things considered, fears of menstrual problems and pregnancy complications may be largely unfounded. Perhaps Gerber et al. (1974, pp. 514–515) summarize the research best: "On the whole, female athletes can look forward to a normal, vigorous and robust life, for the most part free of menstrual disorders and complications with marriage, pregnancy, and childbirth."

Other Problems

Coakley (1982) discusses at length a number of myths that serve as means for excluding women from total participation in sport. Three that Coakley cites have already been discussed; others include *damage to the breasts and reproductive organs*, a more *fragile bone structure* in females, and the notion that *sport participation creates bulging muscles* in females. All, according to Coakley, are myths. No convincing evidence exists that either the breasts or the reproductive organs are at risk. The breasts are spared risk for the early years due to maturation and can readily be protected when potential harm is a factor. In a study of 361 colleges and universities, Gillette (1975) indicated that breast injuries associated with sport were the least common among nine areas of injury. Similarly, Hunter and Torgan (1982) found no instance of injury to a University of Washing-

ton female athlete during the period 1976 through 1981. As for the uterus, Dunkle (1974) and Eitzen and Sage (1982) both indicate that it is a most shock-resistant organ. In terms of actual risk, males are much more susceptible in that the sexual organs are external from the earliest age and thus are highly vulnerable to trauma.

As for bone structure, women are indeed smaller but not more fragile. According to Gerber et al. (1974), the average male is 20 percent stronger than the average female, has a 25 percent faster reaction time, and has a cardiovascular capacity advantage of 25 to 50 percent. These sex differences translate into more power, speed, quickness, and strength for males, according to Curry and Jiobu (1984). These same factors also contribute to what appears to be high injury rates among males. Coakley indicates that the injury rates are actually about as high for females as males, but these equal rates are more attributable to poor coaching, training, and general carelessness in the case of female competitors than to any inherent "fragile" structures.

Bulging muscles simply are not going to happen to any great extent in the absence of male sex hormones. Normal exercise has a facilitative effect on muscle tone, and females should not shy away from exertion out of fear of becoming mannish. In a study of 116 American elite female athletes from seven different sports, May, Veach, Daily-McKee, and Furman (1985) indicated that the majority of them did not feel that vigorous training resulted in a masculine appearance. Moreover, even among those who believed that their training was conducive to muscle development, the consensus was that the effects were largely positive.

PSYCHOLOGICAL VARIABLES

Though an unlimited number of psychological variables deserve mention here, only a few have a sufficient literature to justify elaboration. Chief among them are *attribution theory, fear of success*, and *psychological androgyny*. Topics omitted because there simply is a marked absence of research on them include leadership, cohesion, audience effects, aggression and violence, the black female, and high risk sport participants. The fact that so little has been done in these areas is testimony to the recency of large-scale involvement of females in athletic endeavors.

Attribution Theory

Some overlap between the discussions here and in chapter 5 will permit us to fully develop issues related to attribution theory and female participation in sport. One significant area of research has been concerned with *gender differences*. Deaux and Emswiller (1974) have suggested that sex role stereotypes are conducive to the distortion of one's cognitive processes, particularly in the area of attributions. Deaux and Farris (1977) indicated that adult males are likely to make internal attributions (e.g., ability) for success whereas females are likely to view their successes as less attributable to ability and more a function of situational factors such as luck. For example, Iso-Ahola (1979) studied the motor performance of equal numbers (n = 80) of male and female fourth graders from physical education classes and found, among other things, that boys are less likely to admit to ability deficiencies when they fail in competitive situations involving girls than in situations where they are surpassed by other boys. Too, girls tended to see the ability of boys as a more significant factor in losses to boys than in defeats by other girls. Applying generalizations generated from the preceding studies to sport led McHugh, Duquin, and Frieze (1978) to conclude the following:

1. Based on women's internalization of beliefs in their own physical inferiority, female athletes attribute success to external factors such as luck, and failure to low ability. This pattern may be found in young girl athletes or women in general, but the female that makes this type of attribution would probably not be found in advanced athletic programs.

2. Alternatively, the societal attitudes that allude to females' natural inability in sports may produce a pattern of external attributions. Thus, the female athlete that reports playing just for fun, and winning by luck or task ease conforms more to society's view than the female who admittedly tries hard.

3. A third prediction of female athletes' attributional patterns could be based on the fact that female athletes have been found to be generally self-confident, autonomous, persevering, and achievement oriented. Preliminary studies have suggested that highly motivated women imply more effort attributions for both success and failure than low achievement oriented women. (Pp. 182–183)

As a result of observations such as these, a fair amount of related research has been generated, though it is not universally supportive of the McHugh et al. position. Bird and Williams (1980) studied 192 males and an equal number of females divided into four age groups (seven to nine, ten to twelve, thirteen to fifteen, sixteen to eighteen). Subjects were asked to respond to stories about various athletic events in which failure or success themes were programmed. Based on in-depth analysis of the results, Bird and Williams concluded that by late adolescence sex role stereotypes in sport do exist and that the directional bias is positive for males and negative for females. They further concluded that by age thirteen male success was explained by effort whereas by age sixteen female success was viewed as a function of luck.

Two additional studies with adults lend further credence to sex differences in attribution. One, by Reiss and Taylor (1984), involved an analysis of 141 male and 116 female alpine ski

Sex-role stereotypes in sports start early. The consensus of players in this soccer game is likely to be that boys win because of ability and effort; if girls win, it's a function of luck.

racers of various skill levels. A second, by Riordan, Thomas, and James (1985), included fifty-four male and twenty-five female racquetball players. Both studies concluded that females were more likely to make external attributions than were males.

A second area of interest in attribution theory research with females involves the *self-serving attributional bias*. Research on the self-serving bias has been equivocal, as was pointed out in chapter 5. Recent studies related to female athletes do little to clarify the picture. Riordan et al. (1985) found partial support for the notion in their study of racquetball players whereas Reiss and Taylor (1984), in their study of alpine skiers, interpreted their findings as not supportive of the self-serving bias. In general, so many inconsistencies occur along methodological and sampling lines that, as stated earlier, it would seem premature to stop researching the topic.

A third thrust in attributions has to do with *self versus team responses*. Bird and Brame (1978), Bird, Foster, and Maruyama (1980), and Scanlan and Passer (1980a) have all taken a look at self versus team attributions. In the first of these three studies, Bird and Brame selected subjects from several collegiate basketball conferences and, among other things, found that winners perceived themselves as having less ability than they were perceived to have by their teammates. Too, winners viewed their teams as having more ability than did losers. Effort was seen to play a greater role with winners. Winners also saw their own individual task assignments as more difficult than that of the team. Finally, losers viewed luck as playing a greater role in team success than did winners. Overall, Bird and Brame concluded that their most salient finding was that the team-ability attribution most powerfully separated winners from losers.

Bird and her associates also looked at female basketball players, but added the dimension of team cohesion into the formula. In general, cohesive teams made more convergent attributions for both self and team at the end of the season. Players from less cohesive teams saw luck as more significant than did their winning counterparts. Players from cohesive teams, in the face of occasional adversity, behaved in ways that preserved the team's integrity. In general, the Bird et al. study was also supportive of the notion that the team-self distinction is an important one in sport.

Scanlan and Passer studied young female soccer players, and their overall conclusions were generally in agreement with those of Bird and her various associates. Based on the findings of the preceding study and those of three others (Scanlan and Passer, 1978, 1979, 1980b), these researchers posit that sex differences in attributional styles are more similar than dissimilar. This position, of course, runs counter to much of our earlier discussion but does point to the need for continuing research on athletes of both sexes and their attributional efforts.

Fear of Success

One aspect of the need achievement literature that has drawn a lot of recent attention has been the concept of *fear of success (FOS)* as formulated by Matina Horner (1968, 1972). Blucker and Hershberger (1983, pp. 353–354) summarize Horner's 1968 basic premises as follows:

1. The motive to avoid success is a stable characteristic of the personality acquired early in life in conjunction with sex-role standards. It is conceived as a disposition: (a) to feel uncomfortable when successful in competitive achievement situations because such behavior is inconsistent with one's femininity (an internal standard), and (b) to expect to become concerned about social rejection following success in such situations.
2. The motive is much more common in women than men.
3. It is probably not equally important for all women. Fear of success should be more strongly aroused in women who are highly motivated to achieve and/or who are highly able (e.g., who aspire to and/or are readily capable of achieving success).

4. It is more strongly aroused in competitive achievement situations than where competition is directed against an impersonal standard.

Horner apparently viewed FOS as a highly feminine characteristic that would be manifested most noticeably in competitive situations.

In her original work, Horner asked women to respond to the following verbal lead: "After first-term finals, Anne finds herself at the top of her medical school class." For men, John was substituted for Anne. In their responses, the females wrote many more negative responses to their cues than did the males; 65 percent of the women wrote fear of success themes whereas only 9 percent of the men did. For a variety of reasons subsequent research on FOS has not yielded such clear-cut results, but the construct has caught the attention of sport researchers.

One of the first efforts in this area was generated by McElroy and Willis (1979). Female varsity athletes (n = 262) in five different sports attending three large East Coast universities responded to a series of yes-no statements related to sport-specific situations, and no evidence of FOS was noted in these participants. McElroy and Willis concluded that perhaps FOS is not generalized to athletic situations, that changing women's roles may be at work, or that women have legitimized their athletic participation and feel no need for rationalizing or justifying it. Perhaps stepping a bit beyond their data, the authors summarize their results as follows: "The absence of fear of success suggested that the female athlete does not seem to be bothered by role conflicts surrounding achievement activities" (p. 246).

Silva (1982), using the Objective Fear of Success Scale (FOSS) created by Zuckerman and Allison (1976), studied 193 undergraduate athletes and nonathletes of both sexes. As was the case with Zuckerman and Allison, Silva's females (when grouped together) scored higher on the FOSS than did the males. However, because the mean scores of the female athletes were lower than both the male and female nonathletes and also those reported by Zuckerman and Allison, it does not appear that women in sport are particularly fearful of succeeding.

In view of the works of McElroy and Willis and of Silva, it seems safe to conclude that female athletes do not appear to have fear of success problems. Fear of success remains, however, an area in which all the answers are not in.

Psychological Androgyny

The measurement of sex differences in personality is not new. A number of instruments of the 1940s and 1950s (i.e., the Minnesota Multiphasic Personality Inventory, the Guilford-Zimmerman Temperament Survey, and the California Psychological Inventory) included subscales concerned with sex differences. More recent efforts from the 1970s have been oriented toward the measurement of *psychological androgyny* (Bem, 1974; Spence, Helmreich, and Stapp, 1974).

Expressive and Instrumental Components. Androgyny is generally viewed as a mixture of the best of both sexes, that is, "combining assertiveness and competence with compassion, warmth, and emotional expressiveness" (Anastasi, 1982, p. 557). Duquin (1978) differentiates among these various traits by talking of *expressive* and *instrumental* behaviors. Expressive behaviors are associated with women, who may be seen as understanding, sympathetic, affectionate, compassionate, tender, sensitive, warm, and shy. On the other hand, males are expected to act instrumentally by being independent, ambitious, assertive, aggressive, competitive, and risk taking. Duquin further states that, while society generally attributes instrumentality to males and expressiveness to

females, the validity and desirability of the ascriptions are questionable. This sort of situation, however, is at the heart of the role conflict female athletes face in the traditionally male proving ground of sport.

Bem (1974) asserts that masculinity and femininity have long been viewed as bipolar ends of a single continuum, or as dichotomous variables. Bem's contention is that the manifestation of both is entirely possible in members of both sexes. To put it another way, Bem feels that people with healthy self-concepts will be capable of freely engaging in both "masculine" and "feminine" behaviors and will not be restrained by traditional sex role definitions. This perception is shared by Spence, Helmreich, and Stapp (1974). As a result of their combined speculations, both Bem and Spence and her associates have devised scales aimed at measuring this propensity toward expressing both the masculine and feminine aspects of the self, or what is popularly known as psychological androgyny.

Measures of Androgyny. The two most notable of the measures of androgyny are the *Bem Sex-Role Inventory (BSRI)* (Bem, 1974) and the *Personal Attributes Questionnaire (PAQ)* (Spence, Helmreich, and Stapp, 1974). Of the two measures, the BSRI has been accorded a more positive reception in sport. Before looking at the BSRI, however, research involving the PAQ should be mentioned.

Spence, Helmreich, and Stapp (1974) developed the PAQ in response to what they perceived to be a need for an instrument that would add to our understanding of masculinity, femininity, and androgyny. The PAQ is a fifteen-item five-choice response format instrument yielding a male valued (MV) score and a female valued (FV) score. In turn, the MV and FV can be subdivided through a four-way median split into the following categories: (1) *androgynous*, operationally defined as scores above the median on both MV and FV, (2) stereotypically *masculine*, consisting of a score at or above the median on MV and below the median on FV, (3) stereotypically *feminine*, defined as a median score or above on FV and below median on MV, and (4) *undifferentiated*, defined as scores below the median on both MV and FV.

In a study using the PAQ, Del Rey and Sheppard (1981) administered the instrument to 119 female athletes from three universities covering ten sports. Collapsing across the three universities, 33 percent of the athletes were androgynous, 23 percent masculine, 22 percent feminine, and 23 percent undifferentiated (100 percent is surpassed here due to rounding errors). Of more importance, a highly significant relationship was seen between the androgynous description and athlete self-esteem as measured by the Texas Social Behavior Instrument (TSBI) (Helmreich, Stapp, and Ervin, 1974).

A more recent investigation involving the PAQ was conducted by Hochstetler, Rejeski, and Best (1985). Their subjects were 149 undergraduate students, all of whom were moderate to low in cardiovascular fitness and not participating in intercollegiate sport. Thirty-three of the original 149 females were then randomly selected for further testing, eleven in each of the androgynous, masculine, and feminine conditions. The exertion tasks used in the experiment involved a treadmill task and a 30-minute jog, and the subjects were asked to rate their perceptions of the exertion involved therein. Feminine women perceived the rate of physical exertion higher than did masculine and androgynous subjects though all subjects worked at the same intensity. Interestingly, the feminine subjects were also the least fit of the three groups. Hochstetler et al. suggest that feminine-type women who enter fitness or rehabilitation programs may be at high risk for noncompliance.

Both studies cited here lend validity to the use of the PAQ in sport-related research. They further suggest that androgyny and related issues are important ones within the female sport domain. Bem's work in the area lends even more substantiation to the findings.

The Bem Sex-Role Inventory (BSRI) (Bem, 1974) is a sixty-item scale made up of twenty masculine, twenty feminine, and twenty neutral statements requiring responses based on a seven-point continuum from "Never or almost never true" to "Always or almost always true." Scoring is essentially similar to that of the PAQ in that one's position above or below the median determines classification as masculine, feminine, androgynous, or undifferentiated. Sample items from the BSRI include:

Masculine	Feminine
____ self-reliant	____ yielding
____ defends own beliefs	____ cheerful
____ independent	____ sly
____ athletic	____ affectionate
____ assertive	____ flatterable

Neutral
____ helpful
____ moody
____ conscientious
____ theatrical
____ happy

Research in female sport in which the BSRI has been used is considerable, and a summary of relevant studies can be seen in table 10.2. A number of conclusions can be drawn. One is that female athletes do not express a feminine sex role orientation. Rates such as 17 percent of elite racquetball players (Myers and Lips, 1978), 13 percent of elite field hockey players in New Zealand (Chalip, Villiger, and Duignan, 1980), 22 percent of gymnasts taking part in the NCAA championships (Edwards, Gordin, and Henschen, 1984), and 17 percent of individual sport participants (Colley, Roberts, and Chipps, 1985) lend credence to such a notion. Myers and Lips did find a 43 percent femininity rate in a group of Canadian badminton, handball, and squash players, thereby suggesting that the issue is not totally conclusive. Nevertheless, a strong trend exists toward a less feminine sex role orientation among widely diverse female athletes.

A second conclusion is that a masculine sex role orientation is indeed an integral part of female participation in sport. Gackenbach (1982) reported that collegiate swimmers view themselves as significantly more masculine in sex role orientation than do nonathletes. Kane (1982) reported 39 percent of junior college athletes in three sports score masculine on the BSRI. Twenty-five percent of eighty-four gymnasts reported a masculine orientation in the study of Edwards, Gordin, and Henschen (1984). Again, these rates were not without exceptions. Colley et al. report only a 17 percent rate among individual sport participants in their study. Henschen, Edwards, and Mathinos (1982) found no differences between rates of femininity and masculinity in their study of high school track athletes and nonathletes, though masculinity was significantly related to the need to achieve.

A third conclusion is that the picture related to androgyny as measured by the BSRI is mixed. The range of androgynous responses in female athletes is from 65 percent reported by Chalip and associates (1980) to 17 percent of the individual sport subjects studied by Colley et al. (1985). In between are percentages of 25 percent (Edwards et al.), 42 percent (team sport participants, Chalip et al.), 43 percent (Henschen et al.), and 44 percent (Myers and Lips). Given the substantial heterogeneity of these various samples, these discrepancies are possibly to be expected.

The sex role orientation of female athletes would appear to be substantially more androgynous or masculine than feminine or undifferentiated. Holding athletic ability constant, this would suggest that the androgynous or masculine female should succeed in sport without experiencing the sex role conflict that the feminine scorer would feel. Duquin (1978, p. 271) sums the issue up: "Sport, when perceived as an instrumental, cross sex-typed activity has little overall appeal to women and has a low appeal to the feminine female who, in fact, has the greatest need for experiencing such instrumental activities." Duquin further suggests that, in the best of all possible worlds, sport would be regarded not as masculine or feminine, but as androgynous. In this ideal setting, androgynous and masculine females would find sport to be a great outlet for their expressive and instrumental energies. Best of all, perhaps, is the fact that in Duquin's view feminine females would also find reinforcement in physical activity and competition. Sport perceived as an androgynous activity is portrayed in table 10.3.

SOCIALIZATION INTO SPORT

Rees and Andres (1980) have indicated that no significant grip strength differences are found in four- to six-year-old boys and girls; however, 72 percent of their respondents reported that boys are stronger. Csikszentmihalyi and Bennett (1971) have suggested that game complexity and skill levels demanded for various activities favor young males. These writers suggest that the "ceiling" on boys' games is higher than that of girls. For example, tee ball baseball may be most captivating for six- or seven-year-olds. Athletes who stick with the sport for the next several years and who acquire the necessary skills will continue to find the game of baseball intriguing. On the other hand, games that first grade girls enjoy, such as jumping rope or playing tag, will still be played four or five years later, but with little enjoyment. In effect, the girls reached their ceiling of skill long ago. These sorts of differences are at the heart of the

Table 10.2 Summary of BSRI Studies in Female Sport

Myers & Lips (1978)	Study 1: 25 males and 23 females in Canadian National Racquetball Championships	44% of females androgynous, 24% of males; 40% of males masculine, 17% of females feminine
	Study 2: 27 females and 24 males in badminton, squash, and handball tournaments in Winnipeg	26% of females androgynous, 20% of males; 44% of males masculine, 43% of females feminine
Wark & Wittig (1979)	61 introductory psychology students; 32 males endorsing masculine sex-role, 29 females endorsing feminine role—all administered the Sport Competition Anxiety Test (SCAT)	Masculine males significantly less anxious than feminine females
Chalip, Villiger, & Duignan (1980)	23 elite field hockey players registered with New Zealand Women's Hockey Association	65% androgynous, 13% feminine, 13% masculine, 9% undifferentiated
Gackenbach (1982)	13 females, 14 males involved in intercollegiate swimming—all administered the Multiple Affect Adjective Checklist (MAACL); also compared with 50 male and female nonathletes	Swimmers of both sexes saw themselves as more masculine than did nonathletes, females significantly so; male swimmers significantly less anxious and hostile than female swimmers
Henschen, Edwards, & Mathinos (1982)	67 high school track and field athletes and 67 nonathletes—also administered Mehrabian's Scale of Achieving Tendency	43% of athletes androgynous, 30% of nonathletes; virtually no differences in masculinity or femininity dimensions; female athletes significantly higher in achievement motivation; androgyny and masculinity associated with high achievement, femininity with low achievement
Kane (1982)	33 junior college athletes in volleyball, softball, and basketball and 65 nonathletes—also administered Webb's Socialization of Play Scale	39% of athletes scored masculine; 49% of nonathletes were androgynous and 47% feminine; masculine women scored significantly higher on professional end of Webb Scale than did feminine women
Edwards, Gordin, & Henschen (1984)	84 gymnasts from NCAA Championships	25% androgynous, 25% masculine, 22% feminine
Segal & Weinberg (1984)	166 female and 125 male undergraduates; also administered SCAT	19% of males and 34% of females androgynous; 38% of males and 10% of females masculine; 10% of males and 34% of females feminine; males significantly lower on competitive trait anxiety regardless of sex role orientation

Table 10.2 Summary of BSRI Studies in Female Sport—*Continued*

Butcher (1985)	213 adolescent girls observed from grade 6 through grade 10; complete data after five years on 66% of the original sample	Significant increase over five-year period in both independent and expressive descriptors
Colley, Roberts, & Chipps (1985)	48 male and female under-graduates participating in individual sports, 48 team sport athletes, and 48 nonathletes; and 12 females in noncompetitive individual sports also adminis-tered SCAT, Eysenck Personality Questionnaire, and Rotter's I-E Scale	42% of team sport females androgynous, 38% feminine; 17% of individual sport females androgynous, 33% feminine, 17% masculine; 13% of female non-athletes androgynous, 71% feminine; 33% of male team sport athletes androgy-nous, 46% masculine, 4% feminine; 25% of individual sport participants androgynous, 58% masculine, 4% feminine; 13% of nonathletes androgy-nous, 42% masculine, 17% feminine
Wittig, Duncan, & Schurr (1987)	151 female and 119 male university undergraduates; also administered the SCAT and the Physical Self-Efficacy Scale (Ryckman, Robbins, Thornton, and Cantrell, 1982)	Males and females endorsing a masculine role showed more physical satisfaction than did other groups, with males higher than females on satisfac-tion index

Table 10.3 Sport Perceived as an Androgynous Activity

Females Classified on the BSRI	Expected Performance	Expected Attraction
Masculine	moderate-high	moderate-high
Androgynous	high	high
Feminine	moderate	moderate

SOURCE: "The Androgynous Advantage" by M. Duquin, 1978, in C. Oglesby, ed., *Women and Sport: From Myth to Reality* (p. 103), Philadelphia, PA: Lea & Febiger.

issue of sex role socialization and sport. Males are rewarded for competing whereas females are seen as sacrificing femininity if they throw themselves into competitive situations, such as sport. In an effort to explain some of the more relevant findings in women's sports participa-tion, we shall, in turn, look at four dimensions that appear to be salient, namely, role conflict, agents of socialization, the acceptability of var-ious sports, and why females compete.

Role Conflict

Oglesby (1984) cites various sources of evidence indicating that parents consistently perceive sex differences between their male and female children even though no objective differences exist. Oglesby further indicates that bipolar trait definitions of the two sexes imply that males are active, aggressive, public, cultural, rule-governed, instrumental, goal oriented, organized, dominating, competitive, and controlled. On the other hand, females are viewed as passive, submissive, private, natural, idiosyncratic, expressive, chaotic, disorganized, subordinate, cooperative, and controlled. This sort of thinking has dominated sex differences in general and female sport participation in particular.

One of the earliest investigations in this area was conducted by Brown (1965). Using the semantic differential technique (Osgood, Suci, and Tannenbaum, 1957) in which concepts are evaluated through responses to words arranged in a bipolar fashion (e.g., weak-strong, hot-cold, beautiful-ugly), Brown investigated attitudes toward such female roles as cheerleader, sexy girl, twirler, tennis player, feminine girl, swimmer, and basketball player. The female athletic roles were consistently viewed by both college males and females as less desirable. Griffin (1973), in summarizing results of her 1972 master's thesis, reported that semantic differential responses to the concepts of ideal woman, girlfriend, mother, housewife, woman professor, and woman athlete indicated that the latter two concepts were least favorably viewed by 279 undergraduate students (128 males, 151 females). A model representing the semantic distance between these six roles is reported in figure 10.1. Griffin viewed these results as indicative of no shift in attitudes toward nontraditional roles for women.

Snyder, Kivlin, and Spreitzer (1975) found that 65 percent of college women respondents reported feeling that a stigma is attached to female participation in sport. Sage and Loudermilk (1979), in a study of 268 college female athletes, reported that 26 percent of these women reported great or very great role conflict.

Subsequent reports have been more encouraging. For instance, Snyder and Spreitzer (1978), in a comparison of the attitudes of 500 high school girls participating in sports or music, found no real stigma attached to female participation in sports. Female athletes were as

Figure 10.1 A Model Representing the Semantic Distance between Six Women's Roles

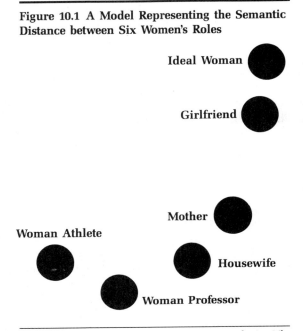

SOURCE: "What's a Nice Girl Like You Doing in a Profession Like This," by P. Griffin, 1973, *Quest, 19,* 96–101.

well-adjusted as the female nonathletes in this study. Kingsley, Brown, and Seibert (1977) compared college students' (120 athletes and 120 nonathletes) attitudes toward the concepts of dancer with high and low success aspirations with softball player with high and low success aspirations. Results indicated that athletes, regardless of sport, rated the softball player as more acceptable than the dancer; nonathletes did not rate the dancer significantly higher than the softball player concept; and, for all subjects, the softball player was rated significantly higher than the dancer. Vickers, Lashuk, and Taerum (1980) used a semantic differential technique to evaluate four concepts: male, male athlete, female, and female athlete. Subjects were 264 students from the seventh grade, tenth grade, and college classes, and all subjects were positive toward both male and female athletes. In fact, female athlete was the highest rated of the four concepts. Michael, Gilroy, and Sherman (1984) asked equal numbers of male and female athletes and nonathletes to evaluate hypothetical female athletes and nonathletes. Athletes and nonathletes of both sexes found the athletic stimulus person to be more attractive than the nonathletic figure.

Brown (1988), in summarizing a survey conducted under the auspices of the Women's Sport Foundation and Wilson Sporting Goods, found that as girls get older, they view girls who play sports as either very popular (55 percent) or a little popular (41 percent). Seventy-eight percent of the respondents did not think that boys made fun of girls who play sports. Apparently, female involvement in sports is increasingly being accepted by both sexes and may actually be positively related to popularity in high-school-age girls. Overall there have been positive changes toward female involvement in athletics. However, much remains to be done to insure that women are accorded proper respect for sport participation.

Agents of Socialization

The family is the primary socialization force in the early years. In the area of women's athletics, this is certainly true. Malumphy (1970) has indicated that the family is the primary source of socialization into sport, not only for females but also for males. Greendorfer (1977) states that the family is most influential in childhood, but this influence becomes weaker in adolescence and adulthood. Snyder and Spreitzer (1978) support this notion, indicating that parental interest is a big factor in sport involvement by females. Weiss and Knoppers (1982), in a study of collegiate volleyball players, found that parents, peers, and teachers/coaches were most influential in childhood, but the influence of brothers was most salient in college. The latter finding, as might be expected, has not been corroborated by prior or subsequent research. Finally, Hig-

ginson (1985), in a study of 587 participants in the Empire State Games in Syracuse, New York, found that parents were the most influential socialization forces prior to age thirteen, being replaced in adolescence by coaches and physical education teachers.

Parents are very important in the early sport socialization of females, with some indication that the father is particularly crucial. When children reach adolescence, coaches and physical educators take on increased significance. Beyond adolescence, the socialization agents become nebulous and more research here is warranted.

Acceptability of Various Sports

Early studies indicated that individual sports were more acceptable than team sport insofar as women were concerned (DeBacy, Spaeth, and Busch, 1970; Harres, 1968; Layman, 1968). Support for this conclusion of sport acceptance was suggested by Snyder and Kivlin (1975). They asked 328 college female athletes, "Do you feel that there is a stigma attached to women who participate in the sport you specialize in?" Fifty-eight percent of basketball players said yes, followed by 47 percent of track and field athletes, 38 percent of swimmers, and 27 percent of gymnasts. Following up on the notion that some sports are more acceptable for females than others, Snyder and Spreitzer (1973) asked a random sample of the citizens of Toledo, Ohio, the question, "In your opinion, would participation in any of the following sports enhance a girl's/woman's feminine qualities?" Responses indicated that 67 percent felt that swimming would, followed by 57 percent for tennis, 54 percent for gymnastics, 14 percent for softball and basketball, and 13 percent for track and field. Sage and Loudermilk (1979) reported that female athletes in what they called the less approved sports (softball, basketball, volleyball, field hockey, and track and field) experienced significantly more role

HIGHLIGHT 10.2

Women Umpires in Major League Baseball?

The cover of the March 14, 1988, edition of *Sports Illustrated* featured Pam Postema, the leading candidate to become major league baseball's first female umpire. Her situation poignantly portrayed the problems that women face in traditionally all male sports. Bob Knepper of the Houston Astros, in the lead story on the front page of the March 15, 1988, *Houston Chronicle,* viewed Postema's possible ascent to the major leagues in this way: "I don't think she should be an umpire. It has nothing to do with her qualifications. She did a great job back here today, but I believe God has ordained that there are some things women should do and some things they should not do. This (umpiring) is an occupation women should not be in." On the other hand, Ed Vargo, director of umpire supervision for the National League, said: "She's not here because she's a female. She's here because she has gotten good recommendations from minor league managers and good marks from our people who scouted her. She deserves a look, and that's what we're giving her" (Garrity, 1988, p. 26).

In anticipation of the fervor created by Postema's situation, *USA Today* (Stacey, 1987, p. 9C) sampled public opinion, and the accompanying picture emerged.

'Yer OUT!' And, 'Yer IN!'

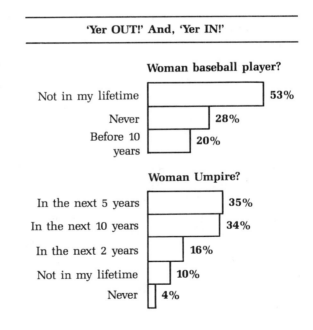

Woman baseball player?

Not in my lifetime	53%
Never	28%
Before 10 years	20%

Woman Umpire?

In the next 5 years	35%
In the next 10 years	34%
In the next 2 years	16%
Not in my lifetime	10%
Never	4%

SOURCE: "Waiting for the Call" by J. Garrity, 1988, *Sports Illustrated*, March 14, pp. 26–27; "Knepper Throws a Curve'" by N. Hohlfeld, 1988, *Houston Chronicle*, March 15, p. 1; " 'Yer Out!' and 'Yer In!' " by J. Stacey, 1987, *USA Today*, Oct. 1, p. 9C.

For many college athletes, the notion persists that some sports are significantly more "feminine" than others. Would these rugby players experience more role conflict than a group of figure skaters?

conflict than those in more accepted sports (tennis, golf, swimming, gymnastics). Ostrow, Jones, and Spiker (1981), in a study of 93 undergraduate nursing majors, isolated a number of sex appropriate sports. For example, figure skating and ballet were rated as significantly feminine; no significant differences were noted for swimming, bicycling, and bowling; marathon running, the shot put, basketball, archery, tennis, racquetball, and jogging were seen as masculine activities.

More recently, Hoferek and Hanick (1985) asked people in a town in Iowa to respond to a questionnaire related to women and sports, and compared their results with those from Ohio reported by Snyder and Spreitzer (1973). A summary of the major findings of both studies can be seen in tables 10.4a and 10.4b. Hoferek and Hanick concluded that, in general, sport participation by females was seen as neither enhancing nor detracting in terms of image. Another interesting finding was that basketball was not seen in the Iowa study as enhancing or detracting, but nevertheless was the sport of choice with the Iowa sample insofar as the responses went to the question, "If you had a daughter, what sports would you prefer that she participate in?" Fifty-three percent of the

Table 10.4a Percent Responding That Participation Enhances Feminine Qualities

"In your opinion, would participation in any of the following sports enhance a girl's/woman's feminine qualities?"

Sport	Percent Saying Yes		x^{2*}
	Ohio city	Iowa town	
Gymnastics	54	48	—
Swimming	67	42	***
Tennis	57	35	***
Basketball	14	24	**
Track	13	23	**
Softball	14	20	—

$*x^2$ based on 2 (Ohio vs. Iowa) × 2 (yes vs. no) analysis with df = 1.

$**p<.05.$

$***p<.01.$

Source: "Woman and Athlete: Toward Role Consistency" by M. Hoferek and P. Hanick, 1985, *Sex Roles, 12,* 687–695.

Table 10.4b Percent Responding That Participation Detracts from Feminine Qualities

"In your opinion, would participation in any of the following sports detract from a girl's/woman's feminine qualities?"

Sport	Percent Saying Yes		x^{2*}
	Ohio city	Iowa town	
Gymnastics	6	0	**
Swimming	2	0	—
Tennis	2	0	—
Basketball	21	7	***
Track	30	7	***
Softball	20	9	**

$*x^2$ based on 2 (Ohio vs. Iowa) × 2 (yes vs. no) analysis with df = 1.

$**p<.05.$

$***p<.01.$

Source: "Woman and Athlete: Toward Role Consistency" by M. Hoferek and P. Hanick, 1985, *Sex Roles, 12,* 687–695.

respondents cited basketball; no other sport was cited in more than 9 percent of the cases. In summation, the authors concluded that the comparison of the Ohio and Iowa results sug-

gests that traditional, rigid sex role stereotypes were transcended and the opportunity set was dominant.

Comparing responses in Toledo, Ohio, in 1973 with those from a small Iowa town in the early 1980s may be a bit like the proverbial comparison of oranges and apples. Too, the finding that basketball was so popular may very easily be attributed to the long-term popularity of the sport in Iowa. In any event, a healthy change seems to be under way in the way female participation in sport is perceived. Snyder and Spreitzer (1983, p. 7) sum up their response to the Ohio and Iowa data: "From 1972 to 1981, the popular conception of femininity vis-à-vis the athletic role has become more flexible; this openness was more evident in the relatively rural Iowa sample than in the urban Ohio sample."

Why Women Compete

Kidd and Woodman (1975) created a tripartite notion as to why females compete in sports, with "have fun," "play well," and "to win" serving as the respective parts of the formula. Nicholson (1979) used the same conditions in a study of 502 athletes and nonathletes in the eighth and ninth grades in Michigan. Generally speaking, Nicholson found few differences between the two groups concerning "having fun" and "winning"; however, sport participants placed much more emphasis on "playing well." Nicholson's results were corroborated by Siegel and Newhof (1984). Siegel and Newhof studied basketball players in Divisions I, II, and III of the Association for Intercollegiate Athletics for Women (AIAW) and found no statistically significant differences across divisions concerning participation satisfaction. Personal satisfaction was viewed most positively, followed by winning and pressures to participate.

An interesting development that bears on the issue of female competitiveness concerns the ability of women to respond to what is consid-

Are femininity and well-developed musculature incompatible? Not so, says Lisa Lyon, a graduate of UCLA and an ardent bodybuilder:

Bodybuilding . . . is definitely an evolution of the concept of feminin-ity. Musculature is something that's very animal, but it's in no way a con-tradiction with femininity. Why should muscles be considered masculine? It's redefining the whole idea of femininity. You don't have to be soft, you don't have to be weak. You can be strong, muscular—you can make that visual statement and at the same time be feminine. I think I have a very feminine body. I think of myself entirely as a woman" (Gaines and Butler, 1983, p. 67).

This sentiment is echoed by Carla Dunlap, perhaps the best known of all the female bodybuilders: "Some people think I look beautiful. Some peo-ple are disgusted. I have to detach myself from their opinions; I feel good about my muscles and about myself" (Ebert, 1985, p. 29).

Testimonials such as these do not represent a scientific view of the issue at hand, and the available data from sport psychology are limited. However, it is possible to put together a thumbnail sketch of the female bodybuilder from existing studies. In an effort to look at how these athletes are perceived, Franck (1984) asked forty-five females and thirty-one males from an introductory psychology class to rate the attractiveness of some of the lead-ing female bodybuilders shown in a slide presentation. The male subjects rated the bodybuilders as being significantly more attractive than did the females; increased exposure to the bodybuilders also enhanced their attrac-tiveness ratings. One caveat is in order with regard to Franck's first find-ing; it may well be that males would rate any collection of females higher than would other females.

A study by Jackson and Marsh (1986) with elite Australian female power lifters has relevance to the present discussion, though it might be argued that power lifting and bodybuilding are not made up of the same kinds of athletes. Our suspicion is that the similarities are far greater than the differences, hence their inclusion here. In any event, the elite lifters were compared with a sample of Australian high school students broken down into athlete and nonathlete subsamples. Based on a measure of role con-flict, the power-lifter group scored higher than did the other two groups; in all three groups, however, perceived role conflict was greater than experienced role conflict. An Australian adaptation of the leading Ameri-can sex role inventories (e.g., BSRI, PAQ) showed both athlete groups to be significantly higher in masculinity than the nonathlete group; however, there were no differences among the three groups on femininity. In all instances the femininity scores were higher than the masculinity scores, thereby suggesting that female power lifters can be masculine without sacrificing their femininity. With regard to self-concept, both athletic groups scored higher than did the nonathlete group. Jackson and Marsh concluded that perceived role conflict is more salient than experienced role conflict,

that masculinity can be expressed without concomitant loss of femininity, and that self-concept is high, all of which add up to healthy personal
adjustment among female power lifters.

On the downside, two points of concern have emerged that bear on
bodybuilders and weight lifters. One is the use of steroids to enhance
strength and muscularity (Gaines and Butler, 1983; Todd, 1985). The
dangers of these chemicals were chronicled in detail in the section on
sport ethics in Chapter 9; suffice it to say that steroids pose a serious threat
to builders, lifters, and female athletes in general. A second concern, and
one expressed very well by Todd (1985), is the absence of female strength
coaches in the university setting. It seems that bodybuilding and weight
lifting would serve as solid foundations for jobs related to increasing the
strength and conditioning of other athletes, and yet not one female was
working in such a position at the collegiate level as late as 1985. Apparently, men have a stranglehold on strength and conditioning coaching
positions, a situation that Todd and others would like to see changed.

SOURCE: "Flex Appeal" by R. Ebert, 1985, *Houston Chronicle*, Oct. 6, p. 29; "Exposure and Gender
Effects in the Social Perception of Women Bodybuilders" by L. Franck, 1984, *Journal of Sport
Psychology*, *6*, 239–245; "Iron Sisters" by C. Gaines and G. Butler, 1983, *Psychology Today*, *17*(11),
pp. 64–69; "Athletic or Antisocial? The Female Sport Experience" by S. A. Jackson and H. W.
Marsh, 1986, *Journal of Sport Psychology*, *8*, 198–211; "Strength Training for Female Athletes"
by J. Todd, 1985, *Journal of Physical Education, Recreation and Dance*, *56*(6), 38–39.

ered to be a standard "gut-check" in sport, coming from behind to win. Weinberg and various
associates (Weinberg, Richardson, and Jackson,
1981; Weinberg, Richardson, Jackson, and
Yukelson, 1983; Ransom and Weinberg, 1985)
have been at the forefront in studying this new
dimension. In the 1983 study, two thousand
four hundred collegiate and professional men's
and women's basketball games and one thousand nine hundred collegiate and open men's
and women's volleyball matches for 1980–1981
were dissected for sex differences in the ability to come from behind. Being behind in
basketball was determined by halftime scores,
whereas in volleyball, the loss of the first set
was considered to be the critical point for this
determination. In professional basketball, men's
teams came from behind to win 30 percent of
the time; only 7 percent of the women's teams
did. At the collegiate level, these figures were
37 percent and 24 percent, respectively. No sig-

nificant sex differences in volleyball were
noted.

In the 1981 and 1985 works, coming from
behind on the part of tennis players of both
sexes was studied. The 1981 study found that
male tennis players at both the amateur and
professional levels came from behind (i.e., they
lost the first set) more often than did female
players. The more recent of the two studies was
along the same lines. The top twenty male and
female players in the 1980 United States Tennis
Association yearbook were studied, and particularly the 242 matches in which they dropped
the first set. No sex differences in ability to
come back were noted, thereby indicating that
elite players of both sexes appear to possess
equal ability in overcoming adversity. This
equality notion is further substantiated when
these top twenty athletes are compared with
the ability to come from behind of the top five
hundred players. In this situation, 39 percent

of males and 37 percent of females in the top twenty came from behind to win; in the case of the top five hundred, the figures drop rather precipitously to 15 percent for males and 9 percent for the females.

Though not remotely researched out, this come from behind phenomenon represents an interesting aspect of competitiveness in females. Preliminary evidence from Weinberg and associates indicates that elite females are as capable of responding to potential defeat as are males, at least in tennis. Males at a lower level of competitiveness show a slight superiority to equal ability females, but both groups are inferior to the top-flight females in coming from behind to win.

ACHIEVING EQUALITY

Equal opportunity within sport is a most complex issue. Life experiences and differences in physical characteristics are only two of a number of considerations that make equality so complicated. Too, a finite number of resources are available; there is only so much money, only so many facilities, and only so much equipment to be used. A spirit of community between the sexes appears to be a part of the answer to the dilemma. And creativity is definitely called for. In this spirit of shared creativity, Coakley (1982) outlines six alternatives that have been suggested as possible answers to sport equality and they are:

1. *All teams in any program should be open to members of both sexes.* This possible solution presupposes free access to all opportunities. However, because of sex differences in experience and physical talent, many women would find themselves again on the outside looking in. Too, some sports, such as football, simply do not lend themselves at all well to equal opportunity.

2. *There should be sex-integrated teams in all sports with quota systems insuring equal representation of the sexes.* Though appealing at first glance, this proposal may guarantee equal representation but not equal opportunity to participate. Again, this idea ignores differences in interests, experience, and physical ability.

3. *There should be separate men's and women's teams in each sport offered within a program.* This is a most attractive alternative, but would most assuredly eventually run afoul of the problem of finite resources mentioned earlier. Nevertheless, this suggestion should be implemented when and wherever possible. Programs that sponsor men's volleyball, for instance, should most certainly have a corresponding team of females.

4. *There should be two coeducational teams in each sport offered in a program.* Of all the suggested solutions, this one may have the least merit. One problem is that, in reality, it does little to reduce sex discrimination or assure equal opportunity to participate. In a number of sports, men would dominate the top-level team, and women would be relegated to the second team. This would fail to provide for the needs of the females involved while it discriminated against males who possess the talent to play at the second level of competition. A second shortcoming of this suggestion is that it places the top female athlete in an environment where if she succeeds in playing at the top, male-dominated level, her relative skill level may take a sudden drop. This also greatly weakens the second-level team because its best player has been promoted. Finally, being a member of the second-level team may carry with it the problem of less allocation of coaching, training, and equipment resources.

5. *Every sport program should sponsor teams based on a size classification system.* This alternative may be of some help, but it does

not really guarantee equal opportunity for women and is most certain to be plagued by the finite resources problem.

6. *There should be an equal number of single-sex teams based on the different interests of males and females.* Though very complex, this suggestion has merit, primarily because of its feasibility economically. It implies that while boys are playing football, girls might engage in field hockey, a sport much more appropriate for females; while boys are wrestling, girls might be playing volleyball; instead of baseball, girls might play softball. In such sports as track and field, golf, and tennis, there would be men's and women's teams.

Coakley cites an idea of Fasteau (1973) that is attractive insofar as it implements this approach. The men's and women's varsity teams in basketball would collectively serve as the school's varsity team, would compete on the same day against the various other teams on the schedule, would share the various resources, and would be governed by a unified scoring system in which the overall winner would be determined by combining the scores of the two events. While having many advantages in terms of allocation of resources, social relationships, school spirit, enhancement of the role of women's sports in the overall picture, and a host of other advantages, Fasteau's proposal runs counter to sport tradition. Nevertheless, it could be implemented whenever possible as a means of enhancing equal opportunity in women's sport.

Coakley further suggests that none of his six proposals is an answer to the equal opportunity issue, but that implementing the best of them when possible should be encouraged. Finally, he suggests that commitment to the spirit of equality would do much to facilitate sport participation among women.

Thanks to the positive effects of the women's movement, technological advances, the physi-cal fitness boom, and increasingly positive added acceptance of female involvement in competitive situations, there does indeed appear to be a revolution taking place, one destined to eventually propel women to an ultimate position of equality. This achievement of equality, according to Richardson, Albury, and Tandy (1985, p. 64), will have taken place when "play skills are neutral rather than sexist."

SUMMARY

1. Because of past biases and the current developmental status of women's sport, a separate chapter has been devoted to the female athlete.

2. Though women in ancient Greece were generally oppressed athletically, they did have their own analogue to the Olympics, the Heraean Games, named after Hera, the wife of Zeus.

3. Not until 1896, with the founding of the modern Olympic Games, were women really accorded a place in sport. With each successive Olympics since then, the athletic menu for women has gradually expanded. About three thousand women took part in the 1984 Games.

4. Title IX of the Higher Education Act of 1972 has served as another landmark in women's sports. Its main effect has been to set the stage for equal opportunity in sport.

5. Contemporary factors such as increased opportunity, fallout produced by the women's movement, the recent fitness boom, and the presence of role models have all served as additional forces in enhancement of sport involvement on the part of women.

6. Physiological issues of relevance within sport include menstrual functioning, pregnancy, and childbirth, and myths related to female participation in sport.

7. Menstrual functioning has attracted much interest among sport scientists. Early speculation was that menstruation and physical exertion did not mix, thereby creating a host of problems for the involved females.

8. Early 1960s research by Erdelyi with Hungarian female athletes and by Zaharieva with Olympic athletes from ten different countries did much to dispel the earlier skepticism about menstrual function and athletic participation.

9. Recent studies have complicated our understanding of the relationship between menstruation and sport. Though not as negative as the earliest speculations, they are not quite as positive as Erdelyi and Zaharieva.

10. Causes of menstrual difficulties in athletes are numerous. Frisch has advanced a theory suggesting that these problems are reactions to a disturbed body mass to percentage of body fat ratio. Other authorities point to an endocrinological explanation, excessively strenuous training, and heavy training prior to menarche as possible etiological agents.

11. The consequences of these menstrual cycle disruptions appear to be minimal or nonexistent in terms of pregnancy or childbirth. Female athletes compete well in the early stages of pregnancy, appear to have easy, uncomplicated deliveries, and compete even more effectively in some cases after childbirth.

12. The myth that sport participation by women endangers their breasts and internal sexual structures has not been supported. Further myths lacking support include the notion that women are structurally less able to compete and the idea that sport produces bulging, unattractive muscles.

13. Three psychological variables of considerable interest to sport psychologists include attribution theory, fear of success, and psychological androgyny.

14. Research in the late 1970s showed that young females attributed success to external things, such as luck. They, like males, also attributed male success to ability, an internal attribute. Further research indicates that by age thirteen, sex role stereotypes are in effect. These stereotypes attribute male success to effort, female success to luck. A more recent area of interest, self versus team attribution, has emerged and bears more investigation.

15. Horner suggested in 1972 that females manifest a fear of success (FOS) in a variety of competitive situations. Subsequent research has not been supportive of the Horner position.

16. The concept of psychological androgyny was introduced to the literature in 1974. Androgyny is viewed as an optimal amalgamation of the best of what have been viewed as bipolar traits, masculinity and femininity. Research using both the Personal Attributes Questionnaire (PAQ) and the Bem Sex-Role Inventory (BSRI) have been provocative. In general, female athletes who are successful are either androgynous or masculine on these measures. Feminine females do not find the athletic realm particularly rewarding, though they may need its benefits most. Overall, it appears that females feel little sex role conflict in their sport involvement.

17. Socialization into sport is a most complex issue. Some of the more relevant subaspects of socialization into sport include role conflict, socialization agents, sport acceptance, and why females compete.

18. Traditional definitions of the concepts of male and female have generated much research interest within psychology. Research from the mid-1960s showed a preference for traditional female roles and a rejection of the female athlete. Even as late as 1975, 65 percent of college women saw a stigma attached to women's participation in sport. Recent research is indica-

tive of healthy changes in the perception of the female athlete.

19. Parents are the prime source of early socialization into sport. In adolescence, coaches and physical educators replace the parents. Beyond adolescence, little is known of socialization forces.

20. The acceptability of the broad array of sport for females varies. In general, the more feminine sports carry slightly more acceptance. Sports such as basketball, volleyball, and softball appear to be regarded more unfavorably. Recent research in Iowa is suggestive of positive changes concerning the acceptance of a greater number of sport activities.

21. Though the evidence is sparse, female athletes appear to place more importance on having fun and playing well than on winning. In another facet of competition, women participating in some sports seem to be less likely than men to come from behind to win. Males at lower levels of skill in tennis appear to be better than females of similar skill level at coming from behind, but this diminishes to no differences at the elite level. In professional basketball, substantial differences favor the male players; though not as pronounced, male collegiate players also come from behind to win more often. Volleyball studies show no sex differences in the ability to come from behind to win.

22. A number of proposals have been advanced that have as their ultimate goal the ending of discrimination against females in sport and the creation of equal opportunity for participation. None of the proposals to end discrimination have universal merit or acceptance. A spirit of commitment to equality should pervade future efforts to equalize opportunity.

23. The ultimate in sport opportunity may be achieved when sport is not viewed as a male or female province but as a human activity.

SUGGESTED READINGS

Caldwell, F. (1982) Menstrual irregularity in athletes: The unanswered question. *Physician and Sportsmedicine, 10*(5), 142.

   Caldwell offers a brief and intriguing review of the work at Harvard of Rose Frisch. It is Frisch's hypothesis that menstrual problems in athletes are due to fat metabolism brought about by lowering of percentage of body fat below a desirable level. A number of criticisms of Frisch's work are brought together in this informative paper.

Lammer, M. (1981) Women and sport in ancient Greece. In J. Borms, M. Hebbelink, & A. Venerando (Eds.), *Women and Sport: An historical, biological, physiological and sportsmedical approach* (pp. 16–23). Basel: S. Karger.

   Lammer provides a brief summary of the role of women in Greek athletic life. A critical review is made of the historical writings that have shaped our views of this period. Much of what we think we know of this topic comes from the writings of Pausanius, who visited Olympia some five hundred years after the inception of the Heraean Games, a fact that bothers the author.

Mechikoff, R. A., & Evans, V. (1987) *Sport psychology for women.* New York: Harper & Row.

   This book combines psychological theory as it applies to the female sport experience with practical, how-to-do-it guidance with regard to basketball, field hockey, gymnastics, softball, swimming, tennis, track and field (including cross country and long-distance running), and volleyball. The chapters dealing with the various sports are actually edited readings written by successful coaches who explain how they put psychological theory into practice in the competitive setting.

The SIRLS database (1985) Sport, women, and sexism. *Sociology of Sport Journal, 2,* 259–265.

Janis, L. (1985) Annotated bibliography on minority women in athletics. *Sociology of Sport Journal, 2,* 266–274.

   These two annotated bibliographies provide thirty and twenty-four references respectively. Many are from readily available sources. Others, from more obscure sources, will require the reader/researcher to be diligent in pursuing them for research or other purposes. The bibliography on the minority female athlete is most intriguing in view of the general paucity of available literature.

A number of recent books are available that are devoted entirely to the study of physical, psychological, social, political, economic, historical, and ethical issues surrounding women's involvement in sport and physical activity. The interested reader will find a wealth of relevant theorizing and research.

REFERENCES

Anastasi, A. (1982) *Psychological testing* (5th ed.). New York: Macmillan.

Arnold, E. H. (1924, October). Athletics for women. *American Physical Education Review*, 452–457.

Astrand, P. O., Eriksson, B. O., Nylander, I., Engstrom, I., Karlberg, P., Saltin, B., & Thoren, C. (1963). Girl swimmers with special reference to respiratory and circulatory adaptation and gynaecological and psychiatric aspects. *Acta Paediatrica Scandinavica*, Supplement 147.

Bem, S. (1974) The measurement of psychological androgyny. *Journal of Consulting and Clinical Psychology*, 42, 155–162.

Bird, A. M., & Brame, J. (1978) Self versus team attributions: A test of the "I'm OK, but the team's so-so" phenomenon. *Research Quarterly*, 49, 260–267.

Bird, A. M., Foster, C., & Maruyama, G. (1980) Convergent and incremental effects of cohesion on attributions for self and team. *Journal of Sport Psychology*, 2, 181–194.

Bird, A. M., & Williams, J. M. (1980) A developmental–attributional analysis of sex role stereotypes for sport performance. *Developmental Psychology*, 16, 319–322.

Bloom, M. (1986) You've come a long way, baby. *The Runner*, Dec., pp. 26–36.

Bloomberg, R. (1977) Coach says running affects menstruation. *Physician and Sportsmedicine*, 5(9), 15.

Blucker, J., & Hershberger, E. (1983). Causal attribution theory and the female athlete: What conclu-

sions can we draw? *Journal of Sport Psychology*, 5, 353–360.

Bonen, A., & Keizer, H. A. (1984) Athletic menstrual cycle irregularity: Endocrine response to exercise and training. *Physician and Sportsmedicine*, 12(8), 78–94, 158.

Brown, B. (1988) Study: Girls find activities for a lifetime. *USA Today*, June 8, p. 9C.

Brown, R. (1965) A use of the semantic differential to study the image of girls who participate in competitive sports and certain other school related activities. Unpublished doctoral dissertation, Florida State University.

Brownlee, S. (1988) Moms in the fast lane. *Sports Illustrated*, May, pp. 56–60.

Butcher, J. (1985) Longitudinal analysis of adolescent girls' participation in physical activity. *Sociology of Sport Journal*, 2, 130–143.

Chalip, L., Villiger, J., & Duignan, P. (1980) Sex-role identity in a selected sample of women field hockey players. *International Journal of Sport Psychology*, 11, 240–248.

Coakley, J. (1982) *Sports in society: Issues and controversies* (2d. ed.). St. Louis, MO: C. V. Mosby.

Colley, A., Roberts, N., & Chipps, A. (1985) Sex-role identity, personality, and participation in team and individual sports by males and females. *International Journal of Sport Psychology*, 16, 103–112.

Csikszentmihalyi, M., & Bennett, S. (1971) An exploratory model of play. *American Anthropologist*, 73, 45–58.

Curry, T., & Jiobu, R. (1984) *Sports: A social perspective*. Englewood Cliffs, NJ: Prentice-Hall.

Dale, E., Gerlach, D., Martin, D., & Alexander, C. (1979) Physical fitness profiles and reproductive physiology of the female distance runner. *Physician and Sportsmedicine*, 7(1), 83–95.

Deaux, K., & Emswiller, T. (1974) Explanations of successful performance on sex-linked tasks: What is skill for the male is luck for the female. *Journal of Personality and Social Psychology*, 29, 80–85.

Deaux, K., & Farris, E. (1977) Attributing causes for one's own performance: The effects of sex, norms, and outcome. *Journal of Research in Personality*, 11, 59–72.

DeBacy, D., Spaeth, R., & Busch, R. (1970) What do men really think about athletic competition for women? *Journal of Health, Physical Education, and Recreation*, 41, 28–29.

Del Rey, P., & Sheppard, S. (1981) Relationship of psychological androgyny in female athletes to self-esteem. *International Journal of Sport Psychology, 12,* 165–175.

Dunkle, M. (1974) Equal opportunity for women in sport. In B. Hoepner (Ed.), *Women's athletics: Coping with controversy.* Washington, DC: American Association for Health, Physical Education, and Recreation.

Duquin, M. E. (1978) The androgynous advantage. In C. A. Oglesby (Ed.), *Women and sport: From myth to reality* (pp. 89–106). Philadelphia, PA: Lea and Febiger.

Dyer, K. (1982) *Challenging the men: The social biology of female sporting achievement.* St. Lucia, Queensland, Australia: University of Queensland Press.

Ebert, R. (1985) Flex appeal. *Houston Chronicle.* Oct. 6, p. 29.

Edwards, S. W., Gordin, R. D., & Henschen, K. P. (1984). Sex-role orientations of female NCAA championship gymnasts. *Perceptual and Motor Skills, 58,* 625–626.

Eitzen, D. S., & Sage, J. (1982). *Sociology of American sport* (2d. ed.). Dubuque, IA: Wm. C. Brown.

Emery, L. (1984) Women's participation in the Olympic Games. *Journal of Physical Education, Recreation and Dance, 55*(5), 62–63, 72.

Erdelyi, G. (1962) Gynecological survey of female athletes. *Journal of Sports Medicine and Physical Fitness, 2,* 174–179.

Erdelyi, G. (1976) Effects of exercise on the menstrual cycle. *Physician and Sportsmedicine, 4*(3), 79–81.

Fasteau, B. (1973) Giving women a sport chance. *Ms., 2*(1), 56–58, 103.

Feicht, C., Johnson, T., Martin, B., Sparkles, K., & Wagner, W. (1978). Secondary amenorrhea in athletes. *Lancet,* Nov. 25, pp. 1145–1146.

Franck, L. (1984). Exposure and gender effects in the social perception of women bodybuilders. *Journal of Sport Psychology, 6,* 239–245.

Frisch, R. (1976) Fatness of girls from menarche to age 18 years, with a nomogram. *Human Biology, 48,* 353–359.

Frisch, R., & McArthur, J. (1974) Menstrual cycles: Fatness as a determinant of minimal weight for height necessary for their maintenance or onset. *Science, 185,* 949–951.

Frisch, R., Gotz-Welbergen, A., McArthur, J., Albright, T., Witschi, J., Bullen, B., Birnholz, J., Reed, R., & Hermann, H. (1981) Delayed menarche and amenorrhea of college athletes in relation to age of onset of training. *Journal of American Medical Association, 246,* 1559–1563.

Gackenbach, J. (1982) Collegiate swimmers: Sex differences in self-reports and indices of physiological stress. *Perceptual and Motor Skills, 55,* 555–558.

Gendel, E. (1976) Psychological factors and menstrual extraction. *Physician and Sportsmedicine, 4*(3), 72–75.

Gerber, E., Felshin, J., Berlin, P., & Wyrick, W. (Eds.). (1974) *The American woman in sport.* Reading, MA: Addison-Wesley.

Gilbert, B., & Williamson, N. (1973) Are you being two-faced? *Sports Illustrated, 38,* 45–54.

Gillette, J. (1975) When and where women are injured in sport. *Physician and Sportsmedicine, 3*(5), 61–63.

Greendorfer, S. (1977) Role of socializing agents in female sport involvement. *Research Quarterly, 48,* 304–310.

Griffin, P. (1973) What's a nice girl like you doing in a profession like this? *Quest, 19,* 96–101.

Harres, R. (1968) Attitudes of students toward women's athletic competition. *Research Quarterly, 39,* 278–284.

Helmreich, R., Stapp, J., & Ervin, C. (1974) The Texas Social Behavior Inventory (TSBI). *Journal Supplement Abstract Service Catalog of Selected Documents in Psychology, 4,* 79. (Ms. No. 681)

Henschen, K., Edwards, S., & Mathinos, L. (1982) Achievement motivation and sex-role orientation of high school female track and field athletes versus nonathletes. *Perceptual and Motor Skills, 55,* 183–187.

Higginson, D. (1985) The influence of socializing agents in the female sport-participation process. *Adolescence, 20,* 73–82.

Hochstetler, S., Rejeski, W. J., & Best, D. (1985) The influence of sex-role orientation on ratings of perceived exertion. *Sex Roles, 12,* 825–835.

Hoferek, M., & Hanick, P. (1985) Woman and athlete: Toward role consistency. *Sex Roles, 12,* 687–695.

Horner, M. (1968) Sex differences in achievement motivation and performance in competitive and non-competitive situations. Unpublished doctoral dissertation, University of Michigan.

Horner, M. (1972) Toward an understanding of achievement-related conflicts in women. *Journal of Social Issues, 28,* 157–175.

Hunter, L. Y., & Torgan, C. (1982) The bra controversy: Are sports bras a necessity? *Physician and Sportsmedicine, 10*(11), 75–76.

Ingman, O. (1952) Menstruation in Finnish top class sportswomen. International symposium of the medicine and physiology of sports and athletes. Finnish Association of Sports Medicine.

Iso-Ahola, S. (1979) Sex-role stereotypes and causal attributions for success and failure in motor performance. *Research Quarterly, 50,* 630–640.

Johnson, K., & Fritz, H. (1984) The phenomenon of the Olympic Games: Women in the games. *Journal of Physical Education, Recreation, and Dance, 55*(5), 61.

Kane, M. (1982) The influence of level of sport participation and sex-role orientation on female professionalization of attitudes toward play. *Journal of Sport Psychology, 4,* 290–294.

Kaplan, J. (1979) *Women and sports.* New York: Viking Press.

Kidd, T. R., & Woodman, W. F. (1975) Sex and orientations toward winning in sport. *Research Quarterly, 46,* 476–483.

Kingsley, J., Brown, F., & Seibert, M. (1977) Social acceptance of female athletes by college women. *Research Quarterly, 48,* 727–733.

Layman, E. (1968) Attitudes towards sports for girls and women in relation to masculinity-femininity stereotypes of women athletes. Paper presented at Symposium of American Association for the Advancement of Science, Dallas, Texas.

Lee, M. (1924) The case for and against intercollegiate athletics for women and the situation as it stands today. *American Physical Education Review, 29,* 13–19.

Lee, M. (1931) The case for and against intercollegiate athletics for women and the situation since 1923. *Research Quarterly, 2,* 93–127.

Lee, M. (1983) *A history of physical education and sports in the U.S.A.* New York: Wiley.

Leonard, W. (1984) *A sociological perspective of sport* (2d ed.). Minneapolis, MN: Burgess.

Lipsyte, R. (1975) *Sports world: An American dreamland.* New York: Quadrangle Books.

Loggia, M. (1973) On the playing fields of history. *Ms.,* July, pp. 62–65.

Lutter, J., & Cushman, S. (1982) Menstrual patterns in female runners. *Physician and Sportsmedicine, 10*(9), 60–72.

Malumphy, T. (1970) The college woman athlete—questions and tentative answers. *Quest, 14,* 18–27.

May, J. R., Veach, T. L., Daily-McKee, D., & Furman, G. (1985) A preliminary study of elite adolescent women athletes and their attitudes toward training and femininity. In N. K. Butts, T. T. Gushiken, & B. Zarins (Eds.), *The elite athlete* (pp. 163–169). New York: Spectrum Pub.

McElroy, M., & Willis, J. (1979) Women and the achievement conflict in sport: A preliminary study. *Journal of Sport Psychology, 1,* 241–247.

McHugh, M. C., Duquin, M. E., & Frieze, I. H. (1978) Beliefs about success and failure: Attribution and the female athlete. In C. A. Oglesby (Ed.), *Women and sport: From myth to reality* (pp. 173–191). Philadelphia, PA: Lea and Febiger.

Menstrual changes in athletes: A round table. (1981) *Physician and Sportsmedicine, 9*(11), 99–112.

Michael, M., Gilroy, F., & Sherman, M. (1984) Athletic similarity and attitudes towards women as factors in the perceived physical attractiveness and liking of a female varsity athlete. *Perceptual and Motor Skills, 59,* 511–518.

Michener, J. A. (1976) *Sports in America.* New York: Fawcett Crest.

Mouratidis, J. (1984) Heracles at Olympia and the exclusion of women from the ancient Olympic games. *Journal of Sport History, 11*(3), 41–55.

Myers, A., & Lips, H. (1978) Participation in competitive amateur sports as a function of psychological androgyny. *Sex Roles, 4,* 571–578.

Nicholson, C. (1979) Some attitudes associated with sport participation among junior high school females. *Research Quarterly, 50,* 661–667.

Oglesby, C. A. (1984) Interactions between gender identity and sport. In J. M. Silva and R. S. Weinberg (Eds.), *Psychological foundations of sport* (pp. 387–399). Champaign, IL: Human Kinetics.

Osgood, C., Suci, G., & Tannenbaum, P. (1957) *The measurement of meaning.* Urbana: University of Illinois Press.

Ostrow, A. G., Jones, D. C., & Spiker, D. D. (1981) Age role expectations and sex role expectations for selected sport activities. *Research Quarterly for Exercise and Sport, 52,* 216–227.

Ransom, K., & Weinberg, R. S. (1985) Effect of situation criticality on performance of elite male and female tennis players. *Journal of Sport Behavior, 8,* 144–148.

Rees, C., & Andres, F. (1980) Strength differences: Real and imagined, *Journal of Physical Education and Research, 2,* 61.

Reiss, M., & Taylor, J. (1984) Ego-involvement and attribution for success and failure in a field setting. *Personality and Social Psychology Bulletin, 10,* 536–543.

Richardson, P., Albury, K., & Tandy, R. (1985) Mirror, mirror, on the wall . . . *Journal of Physical Education, Recreation and Dance, 56*(6), 62–65.

Riordan, C., Thomas, J., & James, M. (1985) Attributions in a one-on-one sports competition: Evidence for self-serving biases and gender differences. *Journal of Sport Behavior, 8,* 42–53.

Russell, G. (1972) Premenstrual tension and psychogenic amenorrhea: Psychological interactions. *Journal of Psychosomatic Research, 16,* 279–287.

Ryckman, R. M., Robbins, M. A., Thornton, B., & Cantrell, P. (1982) Development and validation of a physical self-efficacy scale. *Journal of Personality and Social Psychology, 42,* 891–900.

Sage, G. H., & Loudermilk, S. (1979) The female athlete and role conflict. *Research Quarterly, 50,* 88–96.

Sanborn, C. F., Albrecht, B. H., & Wagner, W. W. (1987) Athletic amenorrhea: Lack of association with body fat. *Medicine and Science in Sports and Exercise, 19,* 207–212.

Sasiene, G. (1983) Secondary amenorrhea among female athletes: Current understandings. *Journal of Physical Education, Recreation and Dance, 54*(6), 61–63.

Scanlan, T. K., & Passer, M. W. (1978) Factors related to competitive stress among male youth sport participants. *Medicine and Science in Sports, 10,* 103–108.

Scanlan, T. K., & Passer, M. W. (1979) Sources of a competitive stress in young female athletes. *Journal of Sport Psychology, 1,* 151–159.

Scanlan, T. K., & Passer, M. W. (1980a) The attributional responses of young female athletes after winning, trying, and losing. *Research Quarterly for Exercise and Sport, 51,* 675–684.

Scanlan, T. K., & Passer, M. W. (1980b) Self-serving biases in the competitive sport setting: An attribu-

tional dilemma. *Journal of Sport Psychology, 2,* 124–136.

Segal, J., & Weinberg, R. S. (1984) Sex, sex role orientation, and competitive trait anxiety. *Journal of Sport Behavior, 7,* 153–159.

Siegel, D., & Newhof, C. (1984) The sports orientation of female collegiate basketball players participating at different competitive levels. *Perceptual and Motor Skills, 59,* 79–87.

Silva, J. M. (1982) An evaluation of fear of success in male and female athletes and nonathletes. *Journal of Sport Psychology, 4,* 92–96.

Snyder, E. E., & Kivlin, J. (1975) Woman athletes and aspects of psychological well-being and body image. *Research Quarterly, 46,* 191–199.

Snyder, E. E., Kivlin, J., & Spreitzer, E. A. (1975) The female athlete: An analysis of objective and subjective role conflict. In D. Harris and R. Christina (Eds.), *Psychology of sport and motor behavior* (pp. 165–180). University Park: Pennsylvania State University.

Snyder, E. E., & Spreitzer, E. A. (1973) Family influence and involvement in sports. *Research Quarterly, 44,* 249–255.

Snyder, E. E., & Spreitzer, E. A. (1978) Socialization comparisons of adolescent female athletes and musicians. *Research Quarterly, 49,* 342–350.

Snyder, E. E., & Spreitzer, E. A. (1983) Change and variation in the social acceptance of female participation in sports. *Journal of Sport Behavior, 6,* 3–8.

Spears, B. (1978) Prologue: The myth. In C. A. Oglesby (Ed.), *Women and sport: From myth to reality* (pp. 3–15). Philadelphia, PA: Lea & Febiger.

Spears, B. (1984) A perspective of the history of women's sport in ancient Greece. *Journal of Sport History, 11*(2), 32–45.

Spence, J., Helmreich, R., & Stapp, J. (1974) The Personal Attributes Questionnaire: A measure of sex role stereotypes and masculinity-femininity. *Journal Supplement Abstract Service Catalog of Selected Documents in Psychology, 4,* 43. (Ms. No. 617)

Spence, K., Helmreich, R., and Stapp, J. (1975) Ratings of self and peers on sex-role attributes and their relation to self esteem and concepts of masculinity and femininity. *Journal of Personality and Social Psychology, 32,* 29–39.

Vare, R. (1974) *Buckeye: A study of coach Woody*

Hayes and the Ohio State Football Machine. New York: Harper.

Vickers, J., Lashuk, M., & Taerum, T. (1980) Differences in attitude toward the concepts "male," "female," "male athlete," and "female athlete." *Research Quarterly for Exercise and Sport, 51,* 407–416.

Wakat, D., & Sweeney, K. (1979) Etiology of athletic amenorrhea in cross country runners. *Medicine and Science in Sport, 11*(1), 91.

Wark, K., & Wittig, A. (1979) Sex role and sport competition anxiety. *Journal of Sport Psychology, 1,* 248–250.

Webb, J., Millan, D., & Stolz, C. .(1979) Gynecological survey of American female athletes competing at the Montreal Olympic Games. *Journal of Sports Medicine, 19,* 405–412.

Weinberg, R. S., Richardson, P., & Jackson, A. V. (1981) Effect of situation criticality on tennis performances of males and females. *International Journal of Sport Psychology, 12,* 253–259.

Weinberg, R. S., Richardson, P., Jackson, A. V., & Yukelson, D. (1983) Coming from behind to win: Sex differences in interacting sport teams. *International Journal of Sport Psychology, 14,* 79–84.

Weiss, M., & Knoppers, A. (1982) The influence of socializing agents on female collegiate volleyball players. *Journal of Sport Psychology, 4,* 267–279.

Wittig, A. F., Duncan, S. L., & Schurr, K. T. (1987) The relationship of gender, gender-role endorsement, and perceived self-efficacy to sport competition anxiety. *Journal of Sport Behavior, 10,* 192–199.

Zaharieva, E. (1965) Survey of sportswomen at the Tokyo Olympics. *Journal of Sports Medicine and Physical Fitness, 5,* 215–219.

Zaharieva, E., & Sigler, J. (1963) Maternidad y deporte. *Tokogenic Pract.,* 144–149.

Zuckerman, M., & Allison, S. (1976) An objective measure of fear of success: Construction and validation. *Journal of Personality Assessment, 40,* 422–430.

11

Youth Sport

Whatever happened to the good old days when if you felt like playing baseball you would round up your buddies, get a bat and a ball and would go out and play. What do we do now? We dress up our kids in uniforms, give them professional equipment, tell them where to play, when to play, organize their games for them, give them officials, and put them in the hands of a coach who doesn't know the first thing about the sport or what's good for an eight year old. (Joe Paterno, football coach at Penn State, as quoted by Dorothy Harris, 1973.)

INTRODUCTION

Perhaps no area of physical activity is as controversial as youth sport. On the one hand, early participation in sport is widely held to serve as a mechanism for building character, encouraging sportsmanship, and promoting overall personality development. On the other hand, this early sport involvement has also been viewed as an emotional pressure cooker in which children are subjected to a host of unusual and undesirable stresses. Where the truth actually lies, of course, is a matter of conjecture.

Most agree that youth sport is high drama. The cast is varied and includes the following actors: (a) *The athletes.* Some are very young participants who are merely striving to acquire the most rudimentary of skills. Others, perhaps at a plateau somewhat beyond entry status, are trying to have fun and meet a variety of social and physical needs. At a more advanced level, others are working on perfecting skills that will allow them to continue participation at points far beyond their current states of sophistication. (b) *The coaches.* These volunteers come in all sizes, shapes, and descriptions and are vital to the immediate enjoyment and later involvement of their young charges. Probably most mean well but too few are prepared in the strictest sense of the word for properly providing

for meaningful sport experiences for young athletes. Much remains to be done in training these volunteers, and some of the more innovative approaches in this connection will be discussed later in chapter 12. (c) *Extras.* Foremost among these actors are parents and other spectators, though program administrators are also vital cogs in the youth sport network. Mix this varied cast of characters together and what unfolds is the intense drama known as youth sport.

A BRIEF HISTORY

Youth sport as an organized entity is a relatively new phenomenon. By the second decade of the 1900s, sport had attained a firm foothold in the fabric of everyday America, and this movement was to have significant effects on youth sport. A second significant force in this sport awakening was an increasing awareness throughout society of the rights of children. Prior to the 1900s, children were exploited in the workplace and were accorded little status generally. A third positive agent of change with regard to the youth sport movement was the emergence of social agencies such as the Boy Scouts, Boys Club, and the YMCA. These youth-oriented organizations took it upon themselves to provide a broad array of programming aimed at constructive use of leisure time. Prominently displayed were organized athletic activities, which were believed to be useful in keeping young people off the streets and out of trouble. Too, these social agencies saw character building as a significant duty, and sports were thought to facilitate this process. The impact of all of these agencies was further enhanced because the public schools largely took the view that sports prior to age twelve were too physically and mentally strenuous; as a consequence, little was offered to meet the

Social agencies such as the YMCA have contributed greatly to the development of youth sports in the United States. Summer camps, an early and important part of YMCA work, were part of a broad array of programs designed to keep boys off the streets and out of trouble.

sporting needs of the preadolescent. This philosophy was to gradually change in the 1940s and 1950s, and a significant force in this alteration in point of view was Little League baseball, which began in Williamsport, Pennsylvania, in 1939.

Little League Baseball

A Pennsylvania businessman, Carl Stotz, was the architect of *Little League baseball*. So popular was his product that by 1954 there were four thousand leagues nationwide (Hale, 1956) involving some 70,000 young men (Skubic, 1955). Today, there are 2.5 million youngsters aged eight to twelve playing on more than 42,000 teams in twenty-eight countries (White, 1987). This rather meteoric rise of youth baseball was not traveled on a hazard-free highway, however. Critics were vociferous in their opposition to the Little League program, and their views were reflective of concern among educators, physical educators, and laymen over possible mental and physical harm that might result from early, intense athletic competition.

Slowly but surely, many of the critics of youth baseball were quieted by research extolling the benefits of organized competition. Perhaps the first of these research efforts was reported by Scott (1953) in a paper in *Research Quarterly*, which was to publish a series of articles over the next decade that generally were supportive of Little League baseball. Scott generally suggested, based on results of a questionnaire, that parents of Little League players approved of their sons' participation. Skubic (1955), in an attempt to debunk the claim that intense competition was too physically strenuous for young athletes, carried out an interesting study of players and nonplayers. Skubic observed 206 boys, ages nine through fifteen (75 Little Leaguers, 51 Middle Leaguers, and 80 nonplayers) in several stress conditions and measured their responses through the Galvanic Skin Response (GSR) procedure. Based on her observations, Skubic concluded that GSR variations were not significant regardless of whether boys were competing in league games, championship contests, or games generated in physical education classes. To put the results in her own words, Skubic said, "Insofar as the GSR can be taken to be a valid measure of the emotional excitation of boys of this age level, the results of the present study suggest that youngsters were no more stimulated by competition in league games than they were by competition in physical education games" (pp. 350–351).

In 1956, Skubic reported results of four questionnaires aimed at ascertaining parental attitudes toward Little League play. In general, parental attitudes were quite positive toward the activity, though some concern was expressed that not all boys got to play in league games. Other results from her study showed that Little League participants were higher achievers in school and showed better overall personal adjustment than did nonparticipants. These positive findings were corroborated by Seymour (1956) in a study of five leagues in Atlanta, Georgia.

Interest in the Little League games had grown to the point that, in 1947, a national championship playoff was created. This Little League World Series has continued and now has an international flavor and considerable press and television coverage. By the early 1970s interest had greatly increased, but male domination of the game was not to go unchallenged.

All of the early reports, of course, centered around the benefits of sport participation for young boys. However, Little League baseball was not exempt from the effects of the growing women's movement of the 1970s. In 1973, a young girl from Hoboken, New Jersey, named Maria Pepe attempted to become the first girl to compete in Little League baseball. Though Maria Pepe's efforts were rebuffed, she paved the way for Amy Dickinson to become the first female Little Leaguer. According to Jennings

HIGHLIGHT 11.1
Little League
Baseball Comes to
Russia

In 1992, baseball becomes an official Olympic sport. This development led the Soviet Union to petition Little League Baseball and its President, Dr. Creighton J. Hale, to set up a franchise arrangement with that country. Accordingly, the first Little League teams in Russia were expected to officially begin play in 1989. In 1988 there were thirty teams of college-age competitors and two of youngsters between the ages of eight and twelve years. As a goodwill gesture, Hale attempted to raise $250,000 from corporations in the United States to build six or seven fields, probably in the Moscow area. Also, advisors from the United States were scheduled to go to the Soviet Union to conduct training sessions for the Russian coaches.

SOURCE: "Soviets Ready to Build Their Diamonds in the Rough" by L. Gutierrez, 1988, *USA Today*, Jan. 26, p. 8C; "Soviets in Little League," *Houston Chronicle*, Jan. 26, Sect. 2, p. 3.

(1981, p. 81), Amy Dickinson was characterized as follows: "First player selected in town draft in 1974; All-Star for three years; 1976—starting pitcher (4–2 record including a 1-hitter and another game with 13 strikeouts) and shortstop; excellent at completing the double play; .382 batting average."

Though the Dickinson case was a breakthrough for girls wishing to participate in Little League activities, there has been no landslide in that direction. Jennings (1981) cites 1980 statistics from Little League national headquarters indicating that less than 1 percent of all Little Leaguers are girls.

Concerns about Youth Fitness

A second historical force that served to promote youth sport and fitness resulted from research conducted in the early 1950s in which American children were shown to be generally unfit when compared with similar samples of European youth. Kraus and Hirschland (1954) were the prime architects of this legendary research, and their findings were ultimately brought to the attention of President Dwight Eisenhower. Alarmed at the fitness gap presented to him, Eisenhower convened a 1955 meeting aimed at responding to this fitness crisis. Out of these

deliberations involving 149 national educational and fitness leaders and chaired by Vice President Richard Nixon came, among other things, the President's Council on Youth Fitness (now known as the President's Council on Physical Fitness and Sports), which has served since that time as a moving force behind national youth fitness.

In addition to generating a national-level concern with youth fitness, Eisenhower's actions led the American Alliance for Health, Physical Education and Recreation (AAHPER) to develop its Youth Fitness Test. As the components of the AAHPER test make clear, physical educators at that time viewed fitness in a motoric sense, and this philosophy was to dominate thinking for the next twenty years. In the mid-1970s an awareness was reached that fitness involved more than speed, strength, or endurance. Flexibility, body composition, and cardiorespiratory fitness came to be a part of the fitness formula (Blair, Falls, and Pate, 1983). This transition from the Kraus-Weber approach of the 1950s to the more modern definition of fitness can be seen in table 11.1.

The concern with youth fitness and its measurement have not resulted in concomitant rises in fitness, however. Although the overall picture is probably better than that reported to

Table 11.1 Comparison of 1958 and 1980 Youth Fitness Tests

Test Item	Fitness Components
AAHPER youth fitness test (1958)	
Pull-ups (boys) or modified pull-ups (girls)	Muscular strength/endurance
Sit-ups	Muscular strength/endurance
Shuttle run	Agility, speed
Standing broad jump	Power
50-yard dash	Speed
Softball throw	Skill/muscular strength
600-yard run-walk	Cardiorespiratory endurance, speed
AAHPERD health-related physical fitness test (1980)	
Mile run or 9-minute run	Cardiorespiratory fitness
Sum of triceps and subscapular skinfolds	Body composition
Sit-ups	Muscular strength/endurance
Sit-and-reach	Flexibility

SOURCE: "A New Definition of Youth Fitness" by Russell R. Pate, 1983, *Physician and Sportsmedicine, 11* (4), 87–95.

President Eisenhower, much remains to be accomplished. Of particular concern is the problem of a leveling-off phenomenon. For example, Legwold (1983) cites data showing that fitness in boys stays the same or decreases after age fourteen. For girls, the figure is age twelve.

Irrespective of the debate surrounding youth fitness, the impetus given the youth sport movement by the data from the 1950s clearly has been considerable. Most significantly, it sent out an alert that emphasized the need for constructive exercise and physical activity, thereby serving as a significant force in shaping our views of the interaction between sport and fitness in children.

MOTIVES FOR PARTICIPATING IN SPORT

That children do take part in sporting activities is unarguable; estimates are that nearly 20 million of them between the ages of six and sixteen are involved in nonschool-sponsored programs and yet another 6 million take part in activities that are school-sponsored (Martens, 1978; Shaffer, 1980). What, then, prompts this fascination with sport?

Having Fun

Thirty years ago, Skubic (1956) found that a high priority for youth participation in sport was having fun. Little has transpired since 1956 to change this perception. Studies conducted with diverse youth groups by Gill, Gross and Huddleston (1981), Gould, Feltz, Weiss, and Petlichkoff (1982), Griffin (1978), and Sapp and Haubenstricker (1978) have all lent support to the fact that having fun is of paramount importance. Of these research efforts, the study by Sapp and Haubenstricker merits further elaboration. These investigators looked at the participation objectives of 579 boys and 471 girls ages eleven to eighteen, participating in eleven non–school-related sports, and found that the most common reason for participation in their sample was to have fun. Recent work by Gould, Feltz, and Weiss (1985) indicates that fun is still very important to youth athletes. Gould, Feltz, Weiss, and Petlichkoff (1982) studied 365 swimmers from ages eight to nineteen. Fun was first in importance out of thirty variables studied. Sex differences were noted; girls rated having fun as significantly more important. Scanlan and Lewthwaite (1986), in a study of youth wrestlers from ages nine to fourteen, found sport enjoyment to be closely linked to parental and coach satisfaction, with a lack of maternal pressure and negative reactions to performance, and positive adult involvement in their sport. To quote Kleiber (1981, p. 83): "Winning is important, but fun is more important—at least for children."

Skill Improvement

Another reason that young people choose sport participation is to improve their skills. In the Sapp and Haubenstricker report, skill improvement was second only to "having fun" and was mentioned by 80 percent of the respondents. Other studies have not accorded skill development quite as lofty a state, but nevertheless are supportive. Wankel and Kreisel (1985), in a study of 310 soccer, 338 hockey, and 174 baseball participants, found that youth in all three groups rated improving game skills as fourth in importance. On a related note, however, comparing their skills with those of others was rated highest of ten enjoyment factors by soccer and baseball players and second by the hockey contingent. Gould et al. (1985), in their study of youth swimmers, also found the skill development factor to be ranked fourth of fourteen factors studied. No appreciable differences were noted by either sex or age considerations in the Gould et al. (1985) sample.

One study in which personal performance was paramount was conducted by McElroy and

Kirkendall (1980). More than two thousand participants in the summer portion of the 1979 National Youth Sports Program (average age 11.9 years) responded to a questionnaire about their reasons for taking part in sport. A particularly pertinent question asked of the subjects was:

> In playing a sports game, which of the following is most important?
>
> (a) to defeat your opponent or the other team (winning orientation)
> (b) to play as well as you can (personal performance)
> (c) to play fairly, by the rules at all times (fair play)
> (d) everyone on the team should get to play (total participation)

The results of the responses to this question are summarized in table 11.2.

Table 11.2 Competitive Orientation Among Youth Sport Participants

	Males (N = 1236)	Females (N = 1096)
Winning orientation	13.5%	4.6%
Personal performance	51.0	48.3
Fair play	24.4	37.6
Total participation	11.0	9.4
	100.0%	100.0%

SOURCE: "Significant Others and Professionalized Sport Attitudes" by M. A. McElroy and D. R. Kirkendall, 1980, *Research Quarterly for Exercise and Sport, 51,* 645–653.

Clearly, to play as well as one can was overwhelmingly most important in this investigation. Other points of interest include the fact that a winning orientation was endorsed by less than 5 percent of the sample. Too, fun per se was not listed as an alternative, hence its absence from the data.

In summary, its relative rank can be argued, but skill development obviously is an important aspect of youth sports, and coaches and others should be alert to its significance with children.

Fitness Benefits

Fifty-six percent of the Sapp and Haubenstricker respondents saw fitness benefits as an important aspect of sport participation, thereby ranking it third behind having fun and skill development. Gould, Feltz, Weiss, and Petlichkoff (1982), in their study of competitive youth swimmers, reported that their subjects actually saw fitness benefits as a close second to having fun. Others who have stressed the fitness aspect in their research include Gill et al. (1981), Gould et al. (1985), and Griffin (1978).

Team Atmosphere

Sapp and Haubenstricker (1978) found team atmosphere to be fourth in importance with their respondents. Wankel and Kreisel (1985) found that being on a team was fifth in importance for each of the sport groups in their study. Closely allied with this aspect is the social dimension of making friends, and this is a consistent finding across virtually all of the studies. Clearly, the social dimension of youth sport participation cannot be overlooked by those who are in the business of providing sport experience for young people.

Other Reasons

In addition to the reasons for participating already cited, others are perhaps less salient but nevertheless worth mentioning. Among them are sportsmanship, excitement or challenge, travel, and such extrinsic rewards as trophies, citations in the newspapers, and feeling important.

MOTIVES FOR DISCONTINUING PARTICIPATION IN SPORT

Clearly, youth sport is popular and participation is multidimensionally determined; however, it is not rewarding to equal degrees for all who participate. As a consequence, a substantial dropout problem is associated with the various youth activities. Among them are not getting to play enough, not having fun, too much emphasis on winning or on competition, too much stress generated by parents or peers, poor coaching (or what at least is perceived to be poor coaching), and general conflict of interest with other life activities. We shall address each of these issues in turn.

Not Getting to Play Enough

Because of the emphasis placed on winning by coaches, by parents of youth athletes, and by society as a whole, a strong tendency exists always to play the best athletes in order to satisfy the hunger, however misguided, for victory. Lost in the shuffle are the less talented performers. Some of them will never become athletes of any consequence; however, the distressing fact is that a fair number will be turned off long before they ever find out the ultimate verdict on their sport skills. Knowing what we do about the tremendous variability in physical maturation rates, it seems ludicrous to make premature assessments of talent, judgments with far-reaching implications for future sport participation. One can only wonder how many potentially fine athletes have been turned off before the age of eight or ten or twelve because some coach or administrator decided that winning was more important than total participation of all involved.

Not Having Fun

Closely overlapping with not getting to play enough is not enjoying sports. All too easily overlooked is the fact that up to adolescence, fun is the main reason why young people participate in sport. This fact, in turn, should dictate that all involved in setting up youth programs must do their best to guarantee that fun is awarded the highest priority when planning takes place. Although this is easy to say, the doing is more complicated. Again, the "win at all cost" mentality tends to dominate.

Too Much Emphasis on Winning or on Competition

As can easily be seen, the notion of winning pervades virtually all of the reasons why sport is not always fun for an all too numerous group of children. Orlick (1974), in a study of sixty dropouts from five sports, noted that 67 percent

cited competitive emphasis as the major reason for their discontinuation of competition. Pooley (1981), in a study of youth soccer players, found that 33 percent of his respondents dropped out because of too much emphasis on competition. Gould, Feltz, Horn, and Weiss (1982) found this figure to be 16 percent in a group of dropouts from competitive swimming. Results from these three studies should serve as fair warning that too much emphasis can indeed be placed on the competitive aspects of youth sports.

Too Much Pressure from Parents and Peers

Youth participants are greatly swayed by parents and peers in both initiating and discontinuing sport involvement. Probably everyone

Ideally, sport activities should be rewarding events for children rather than vicarious experiences for their parents.

"Please, Mrs. Enright, if I let you pinch-hit for Tommy, all the mothers will want to pinch-hit."

is familiar with the parent who reacts to every sport event in which his or her child plays as if it were the Super Bowl and the World Series wrapped into one. Undoubtedly, the chemistry at work here is part ego and part genuine concern for the happiness and well-being of the child. Irrespective of where the true motivation lies, this parental reaction serves as a potential source of stress for the child involved (and for those around him or her, too). The issue of the role of the spectators has been the subject of more than one heated debate in both lay and professional groups. Martens and Seefeldt (1979), reacting to the problems caused by overzealous parent/spectators, have suggested a number of steps that can be taken to curb potentially stress-inducing and embarrassing displays. Among the suggested steps are (1) requiring parents to remain seated in the specified spectator viewing area during all contests; (2) restricting the yelling of instructions, and more particularly criticisms, during the events; (3) not allowing parents to make any derogatory comments to opposing players, officials, and league administrators; and (4) brooking no parental interference with the coach(es) of their children. Parents should have the character to temporarily relinquish their child to the coach for the duration of the event at hand. Though the measures suggested by Martens and Seefeldt may seem unduly harsh, experience has shown that they are not without justification. Games should always be oriented philosophically toward making sport physically healthy and psychosocially rewarding for the participants rather than as a means for parents to live out their lives vicariously through their children.

Poor Coaching

The potential for misperception of what the coach may be trying to accomplish is considerable. Too, the potential for bad coaching procedures is equally possible. Not enough has been done in terms of training coaches to work with youth; coaches are often very interested in young people and have the best of intentions but simply lack the interpersonal and sport-related skills to be successful. Also, a minority are probably frustrated Vince Lombardis living out some sort of fantasy through the use of strong-arm methods, badgering of officials, and other tactics used or perceived to have been used by their coaching idols. Young people deserve coaches who have the best training available, those with an appreciation of the principles of child development, and those with a soft touch in dealing with people. Many of the other reasons for dropping out could be avoided or greatly buffered by an informed and sensitive coach.

Conflict of Interest with Other Life Activities

One of the more consistent findings with regard to why young people drop out of sports is conflict with other life demands. It is unreasonable to think that sports is the be-all and end-all for everyone, and it would be naive to assume that other priorities do not exist. In the earliest years of athletic performance, little else is available to do and parents pretty much dictate the course of organized activities, sporting or otherwise. However, with increasing maturation comes a rather natural progression toward some degree of independence. This greater independence is reflected in a number of ways, not the least of which is dropping out of sport. The skill selection process is partly responsible, but equally powerful are the pulls of growing heterosocial needs, part-time employment, debating, drama, music, and an endless array of other valuable and valued human endeavors.

A number of studies have substantiated the significance of this conflict of interest finding. For instance, Fry, McClements, and Sefton (1981), in a study of two hundred hockey dropouts in Canada, found that 31 percent

HIGHLIGHT 11.2
Adult Verbalizations
at Youth Sport
Events

Most of us are familiar with the obnoxious sports fan, and nowhere is this person more noticeable than at youth sporting events. Data from a number of studies, however, appear to support the notion that these loud, obnoxious types are actually in the minority. They stand out precisely because they are so vociferous in expressing their dislike for players, coaches, officials, and other fans.

Recent youth sport studies by Faucette and Osinski (1987) and Walley, Graham, and Forehand (1982) in baseball, Crossman (1986) in hockey, and Randall and McKenzie (1987) in soccer, all point to a generally well-behaved spectator. In the Faucette and Osinski study, spectators at a youth baseball Mustang World Series served as subjects. During a four-day period, sixty-four spectators attending eleven different games were observed by two trained researchers. Results showed that spectators spend over 80 percent of their time silently watching the proceedings or conversing with friends. When verbal comments were made, they were predominantly neutral or positive in tone. Negative comments accounted for slightly over 1 percent of all verbalizations. Walley et al. found virtually identical behaviors in their observations of youth T-ball spectators. Four male raters observed four fans at eighteen different games; they found that 92 percent of the fans offered no verbalizations and far less than 1 percent of them were of a negative variety. Walley and associates did suggest, however, that negative verbalizations may be a linear function; that is, as the stakes go up, so may negativity.

Crossman (1986) had observers view 272 spectators at ninety-one minor league hockey games in Canada. Spectator behavior varied according to the level of the athletes involved, the importance of the competition, and sex of the onlooker, but did not support the stereotype of the verbally abusive fan. In the Randall and McKenzie (1987) investigation involving youth soccer, nearly 75 percent of the verbalizations made by fans were instructive while 5.8 percent were considered to be negative in tone.

These studies have served to shed light on a fascinating aspect of youth sport, that of spectator behavior. Apparently, the picture they have presented dispels the negative stereotype so often held with regard to spectators at youth sporting events. Most fans are quiet, neutral, or positive, with the negative spectator a statistical rarity.

SOURCES: "Spectator Behavior at Minor League Hockey Games: An Exploratory Study" by J. E. Crossman, 1986, *Perceptual and Motor Skills, 63,* 803–812; "Adult Spectator Verbal Behavior During a Mustang League World Series" by N. Faucette and A. Osinski, 1987, *Journal of Applied Research in Coaching and Athletics, 2,* 141–152; "Spectator Verbal Behavior in Organized Youth Soccer: A Descriptive Analysis" by L. E. Randall and T. L. McKenzie, 1987, *Journal of Sport Behavior, 10,* 200–211; "Assessment and Treatment of Adult Observer Verbalizations at Youth League Baseball Games" by P. B. Walley, G. M. Graham, and R. Forehand, 1982, *Journal of Sport Psychology, 4,* 254–266.

reported conflicts as the number one reason for dropping out of their sport. Similarly, Orlick (1974), in his study of five sports reported earlier, found that 31 percent cited general life conflict as the reason for dropping out of their respective sports. In a study by Gould et al. (1985), even stronger results were found with swimmers in the age range of ten to eighteen. "Other things to do" was cited by 84 percent of their subjects.

Burton and Martens (1986) address this issue in a study of youth wrestlers, ages seven to seventeen, and their parents and coaches. The dropouts in their study reported conflict of interest problems as paramount in importance. However, Burton and Martens suspect that threats to perceived ability were the actual culprits in the dropouts in their study. Despite the caveat provided by Burton and Martens, a major factor in dropping out of sport is simple conflict of interest with other activities, a not altogether unhealthy reason. However, the fact that dropping out is so tied in with increasing age does little to ameliorate the aggravations associated with dropping out in the earlier age groups, such as eight through twelve. The younger the participants, the more vulnerable they appear to be to the kinds of things over which the adult leadership has some degree of control, namely, getting to play, having fun, and developing skills with the help of an informed and sensitive coach.

STRESS AND YOUTH SPORT

Simon and Martens (1979) conducted research involving 749 boys ranging in age from nine to fourteen years with the intent to look at pre-event state anxiety responses in a variety of sport and nonsport situations. Required school activities such as classroom examinations, non-required nonsport activities such as band solos,

and several nonschool team versus individual and contact versus noncontact sports were studied. One of the more revealing findings of the Simon and Martens effort was that, of eleven activities, band solos evoked more pre-event state anxiety than any of the sports did. Results of their thought-provoking analyses can be seen in figure 11.1.

Despite the interesting data presented by Simon and Martens, in the minds of many remains a suspicion that sport may not be as stressful as is popularly assumed for all competitors though it still is threatening for too many youngsters. This supposition has, in turn, led to a great deal of theorizing and research concerning competitive stress and youth sport.

That youth sport is stressful for some youngsters is a given, and a number of factors contribute to this situation. Among the stress factors are the general emphasis on winning as the measure of success and the constant pressure of social evaluation provided by coaches, parents, and peers. Too, one's perceived ability, success expectancy, the expectation of negative evaluation, and the expectancy to feel bad in the face of poor performance are additional anxiety producers. We shall deal with each of these issues in an effort to shed light on why it is that youth sport is so stressful for some of its membership.

Competition: Product or Process?

The word *competition* comes to us from the Latin *com* and *petere*, which collectively mean "to seek together." Clearly, much of sport at all age levels has drifted away from the "seeking together" idea, and youth sport is no exception. Part of the problem in youth sport and sport in general, according to DuBois (1980), is an emphasis on sport as product rather than process. Characteristics of a *product orientation* include: (1) *Winning above all else.* Events in any contest become meaningful in this context

Figure 11.1 Children's Precompetitive State Anxiety in Eleven Sport and Nonsport Evaluative Activities

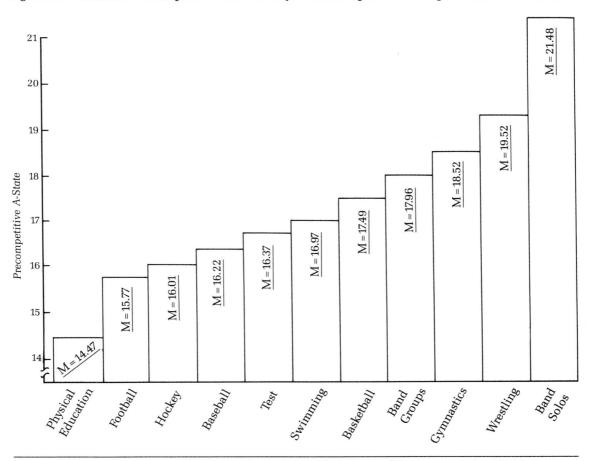

SOURCE: "Children's Anxiety in Sport and Nonsport Evaluative Activities" by J. Simon and R. Martens, 1979, *Journal of Sport Psychology*, 1, 160–169.

so long as they contribute to winning and to the concomitant feeling of domination that goes with beating an opponent. (2) *Tangible awards.* Competition is made much more significant if a prize of some kind is superordinate to competition itself. (3) *Seeking of adulation.* The product-oriented competitor plays more for the admiration of others than for the intrinsic enjoyment that competition can provide. DuBois suggests that this adulation issue may, in part,

explain the difficulties faced by women in their efforts to join the sport subculture. Women have long been viewed as providers or sources rather than recipients of adulation. (4) *Dehumanization of the opponent.* The feeling of domination of an opponent is of primary importance here. Feelings of worth are enhanced not from competing but from domination. At best, this can be viewed as a neurotic sort of motivation for play.

On the other side of the coin, and much more optimistically, the *competition-as-process* approach has much to recommend it. Key to this process point of view are the following: (1) *Participation as an end in itself.* Winning is secondary to taking part. Sport takes on the trappings of an intrinsically rewarding activity because the players participate for the sake of participation; winning is left to take care of itself. (2) *Striving for personal or team excellence.* Playing as best one can is paramount here. The old cliche, "It's not whether you won or lost, but how you played the game," exemplifies this approach to participation. (3) *Aesthetic sensitivity.* There is absolutely no reason why sport, with all its rough and tumble activities, cannot be viewed as an aesthetic experience. Harmony, "oneness," and rhythm then become integral parts of a sport-as-process experience. (4) *Rapport with competitors.* Competitors are viewed as catalytic agents in the pursuit of mutual goals, namely, excellence in personal and team performance. Without the opponent, no standard exists against which to measure one's own performance. Therefore, the opponent becomes not an enemy but a valued ally.

The competition as process approach is the one we choose to support. Competition as process is not a sentimental notion of what ought to be; it represents an attainable goal toward which all involved with youth sport should be oriented. Not only would youth sport take on new meaning for all concerned, but the lifetime carryover would be significant. We might actually end up with adults with a lifelong interest in sports and physical fitness, adults who also appreciate good ability and effort, sportsmanship, and the aesthetic properties inherent in physical activity.

Competitive Stress

The scientific study of the interaction of youth sport and stress owes a debt of gratitude to the research efforts of Rainer Martens and various associates and the separate and collaborative efforts of Michael Passer and Tara Scanlan. Accordingly, most of what transpires in the next several pages will reflect their substantial efforts in this most important aspect of youth sport.

Researchers generally agree that *competitive stress* is a negative emotional state that is generated when the child feels unable to adequately respond to competitive performance demands, thereby risking failure, subsequent negative evaluation of athletic competence, and resultant loss of self-esteem (Martens, 1977; Passer, 1984; Scanlan, 1984; Scanlan and Passer, 1978; 1981). Vital to understanding competitive stress is an awareness that the entire sequence of events is highly personal and subjective; it is not real or objective failure that matters. What is important is how competitive adequacy is perceived by the child in question. Too, great individual differences exist in response to competition; not all situations evoke a stress response, and the overall reaction is greatly mediated by a psychologically systemic stress tolerance. Suffice it to say, competitive stress is an incredibly complex phenomenon!

Competitive stress may occur at any time. It may take place at home the day of an important contest or shortly before competition. This is made much more likely where precompetition inadequacies are experienced. A second forum for competitive stress is during actual competition. If an awareness of inability becomes salient, competitive stress becomes a reality. Finally, stress may rise after the fact in situations where game performance may be viewed as inadequate. Giving up a game-winning home run or striking out with the bases loaded in the bottom of the last inning are familiar events for many who have participated in baseball, and postgame competitive stress reactions to such events are quite common.

Measures of Stress

Scanlan (1984) suggests that stress may be measured through *behavioral, physiological,* or *psychological* means. *Behaviorally,* sleep difficulties, appetite loss, digestive disturbances, or self-reports of "nerves" might be used as indices of stress. *Physiologically,* increases in heart rate, respiration, or alterations brought about through activation of the autonomic nervous system could be monitored and used to indicate the presence of stress. An example of physiological monitoring that was touched on earlier involved a Galvanic skin response (GSR) study with Little Leaguers (Skubic, 1955). Yet another effort in physiological monitoring of stress by Hanson (1967) is noteworthy. Also using Little Leaguers, Hanson reported that players' heart rates rose to an average of 166 beats per minute while they were batting. No other game situation evoked anywhere near this much stress. It is clear, however, that physiological monitoring is an important part of overall stress measurement. *Psychologically,* the standard stress assessment procedures have been various paper-and-pencil measures, particularly those capable of highlighting state and/or trait anxiety. A general example of the former is Spielberger's *State Anxiety Inventory for Children (SAIC)* (Spielberger, 1973); a sport specific measure of significance is the children's version of the *Competitive State Anxiety Inventory (CSAI-C)* (Martens, Burton, Rivkin, and Simon, 1980). Both of these tests have been used extensively within the youth sport context.

A third important test, and one that has been discussed earlier, is the *Sport Competition Anxiety Test (SCAT)* (Martens, 1977), purportedly a measure of *competitive trait anxiety (CTA).* CTA has been of considerable interest to researchers in sport-related anxiety. Martens' contention is that there will be a significant correlation between high trait anxiety and subsequent state-related anxiety responses to competition. Research by Gill and Martens (1977) and Weinberg and Genuchi (1980) as well as that reported in the various reports by Passer and Scanlan have been most supportive of this line of investigation.

In the various studies conducted on competitive trait anxiety (CTA), at least two preliminary but significant findings emerge. One is that CTA appears to increase with age, particularly in precollege samples. This increase in anxiety is, no doubt, linked with the increased importance of winning as an athlete grows older and more experienced. A second finding is that CTA is higher in females than in males. Passer (1984) issues several caveats related to these age and gender generalizations, however. One reservation has to do with the cross-sectional rather than longitudinal nature of the differences. It has not been demonstrated over time with groups of athletes that these results would be replicated. Too, laboratory and field studies of state anxiety reactions prior to competition reveal few gender differences (Passer, 1984). It would logically follow that high CTA individuals should have higher precompetitive state anxiety; this relationship has not been satisfactorily demonstrated. Clearly, a need exists for additional research in the area of age and gender differences in CTA.

Cognitive Aspects of Competitive Stress

Passer (1984) suggests that the extent to which an athlete experiences competitive stress will largely be dictated by at least four cognitive mediators, namely, *perceived ability, success expectancy, expectancy of negative evaluation,* and *expectancy of experiencing negative affect or emotion.*

Perceived Ability. How we perceive our ability is a function of some sort of a continuing comparison process that begins in the preschool years and continues unabated to varying degrees throughout the remainder of life. In their earliest years, children have a rather undifferentiated sense of self that is gradually altered by a myriad of environmental events. However, this sense of self eventually must be measured against a multidimensional rather than a unidimensional set of standards. At age four or five years, the evaluative process begins in earnest and thereafter intensifies, perhaps reaching a peak in the adolescent years, that period in which the search for personal identity is so important. One forum that provides much feedback concerning this self-perception of ability is that of sport. To be selected first (or last) in a pickup baseball game or to be the star (or goat) of an important soccer match has far-reaching consequences for the self-perception of the young athlete. Through a long series of informal and formal events within sports comes a cognitive state that is labeled perceived ability. And with varying perceptions of this ability to compete comes the potential for competitive stress in its various manifestations.

Success Expectancy. Success in youth sport means different things to different people; success may be viewed in terms of winning or losing by some and as playing well and having fun by others. Nevertheless, expectancy for success or failure is an important mediator of competitive stress. Passer (1984) reports that high-CTA youth athletes often feel that they are as physically talented as their low-CTA peers, but consistently report lower expectancy of success. Obviously, CTA is an important part of success expectancy.

Expectancy of Negative Evaluation. The sport situation offers numerous opportunities for self and other appraisal. Home runs and errors, touchdowns and fumbles, and hustling or failing to hustle all are occasions for assessing ability and effort on the part of coaches, parents, and peers. Interestingly, adult significant others appear to be more of a source of com-

petitive stress than are peers (Passer, 1983; 1984). Too, competitive trait anxiety is an integral part of this dimension of competitive stress; high-CTA youngsters do not necessarily expect more disapproval when they perform poorly but they may be more susceptible to negative feedback from significant other adults when such occurrences do transpire.

Expectancy of Negative Affect. High-CTA youth appear to expect the results of their poor performance to be more emotionally aversive than do low-CTA children. Passer (1983), in a study of youth soccer players, found that shame and being generally upset were more common among high-CTA players who performed inadequately. Passer explained these observed feelings of guilt, shame, and dejection in terms of greater expectancy of criticism for poor performance, on an overblown emphasis on success, or on a simple classically conditioned response in which past failures have been paired with negative emotional feelings, thereby eliciting a conditioned negative emotional state related to competing.

Antecedents of Competitive Stress

Obviously there must be antecedent events that create a favorable climate for the development of competitive trait anxiety or competitive stress. While it is likely, as suggested by Martens (1977), that individual variations in experiencing competitive stress have strong roots in recurring competitive sport situations, there must be other predispositional factors to consider. Passer (1984) suggests that parent-child interactions, interactions with other adults and peers, and history of success and failure are three such antecedents.

Parent-Child Interactions. There is sufficient literature both in and outside of sport psychology to suggest that parent-child relationships are a salient factor in the development of personality. Parental use of positive and negative feedback for various behaviors is a most crucial part of this child-rearing process. Children raised with substantial inconsistencies in the use of reinforcement and punishment tend to behave accordingly; they behave erratically because they are not sure just what the exact rules governing the game of life are. This inability, of course, generalizes to the games we play daily.

Children who are raised on a steady diet of punitive measures represent a different issue. They tend to become immune to the effects of punishment and represent discipline problems in school, on the playground, and in the various sport settings. Perhaps a good example can be seen in the personage of George Brett, the multitalented major league baseball player. According to Nuwer (1986, p. 64), "Young George looked like a better bet to end up in a

---

HIGHLIGHT 11.3
Child-Rearing Styles and Child-Coach Interactions

Bryant Cratty (1983) has generated an intriguing conceptualization of how youth athletes are most likely to react to their coaches based on the style of child-rearing used by their parents. The styles cited by Cratty are hardly exhaustive of all the possibilities, but his formulation is thought provoking.

1. *Absolute Authority:* A closed conceptual system. Concrete forms of parental authority are experienced, parents trust all authority, and this trust is transmitted to children.

   In sport the child raised under such a system might be comfortable and conforming to an authoritarian coach, place moral behavior and the athleticism as joined values, be unhappy with troublemakers on the team.

2. *Capriciousness:* A psychological vacuum, lacking stable guidelines. An unstable diversity of an unreliable guideline is offered to the child.

   In sport the child might be difficult to coach; may be little motivated by needs to support team, school, or coach; may shift in allegiance from time to time during the season; may be subject to mood shifts.

3. *Overindulgent Child-Rearing:* An approach in which children are protected by parents from demands of society, overindulged, given little feeling that they are responsible for their actions and consequences. Child opportunities to explore alternatives are often restricted.

   In sport these children may be friendly when not under stress but may not do well when stressed, because they are unused to stress in general, may need constant approval from coach, and may do better in individual sports than in team sports.

4. *Exploration Style:* A style that permits the child to explore environment and search for alternatives, which are not often judged harshly by parents. Nonpunitive acceptance is usually accorded the child by parents.

   In sport the child may be difficult for an authoritarian coach to understand, may be amenable to sudden changes in sports situations, tactics, and opponents' behaviors, may be sensitive to the social forces within the team, and may offer useful coaching suggestions if permitted to do so.

SOURCE: *Psychology in Contemporary Sport* (2d ed., p. 205) by B. J. Cratty, 1983, Englewood Cliffs, NJ: Prentice-Hall.

reformatory uniform than in trim Kansas City blues." What Nuwer was referring to was the love-hate relationship that existed between Brett and his extremely hard-nosed, demanding father. In speaking of some of the stories that surfaced from time to time concerning their stormy relationship, the elder Brett states, "None of the stories are fun. There was always anger" (p. 64). It was this anger that made young Brett become a bit of a rebel and discipline problem, a boy lacking in academic study habits and general ambition. Despite some early difficulties, however, George Brett developed into an apparently model citizen. Nevertheless, the early negative approach to creating excellence was not without a price. One can only wonder just how many similar cases did not have such a happy ending. The child who is exposed to a balanced ratio of positive and negative sanctions within the family will be most able to cope, whether in sport or in the game of life.

Interactions with Other Adults and Peers. The role of coaches and parents in the creation of competitive stress was discussed at length earlier, but little has been said about peer pressure. The fact that children spend the majority of their play time in situations not supervised by adults tells us something about the potential for evaluation opportunities on the part of peers. Too, sports, unlike academics, creates such an environment of interdependence that performance failures that affect others must necessarily be viewed with a jaundiced eye by those significant other peers.

History of Success and Failure. Passer (1984) indicates that failure can contribute to competitive trait anxiety in at least two ways. One is that frequent failures enhance the chances for negative adult and peer evaluations. Secondly, repeated failure may lead to the perception of all competition as unduly threatening.

Summary. Clearly, sport can be very stressful for some youngsters. The extent to which sport is stressful will be mediated by a number of interdependent factors, including whether competition is viewed as a product or as a process, the level of generalized and competitive state and trait anxiety experienced, and the extent to which cognitive mediators such as perceived ability, expectancy of success, and expectancy of negative evaluation and emotion are invoked. The role that interactions with coaches, parents, and peers play in this scenario cannot be overestimated.

RECOMMENDATIONS FOR IMPROVING YOUTH SPORT

Youth sport is a positive experience for many who participate. In the best of all possible worlds, it should be so for all youngsters. Developing an appreciation for the skills required within a particular sport, achieving and maintaining a high level of physical fitness, and developing the ability to confront and overcome adversity are all attainable through sport involvement, and these opportunities should be readily available to every participant.

A number of sport scientists have issued calls for improving youth sport. The next several pages will summarize various of these recommendations from the American Academy of Pediatrics (1981), Burke and Kleiber (1976), Duda (1985), Magill (1978), Singer and Gerson (1980), Stewart (1981), and Wood (1983). Their combined reflections cut across several sport science subspecialties including medicine, psychology, and sociology, and they offer much food for thought.

First, the medical aspects of improving youth sport must be addressed. All youth players should be monitored with periodic health status checkups. Too, professional care should be readily available in all competitive settings (including practices, where many injuries occur). The provision of proper equipment, geared to minimize chances for injury, is also important. Particular emphasis here should be on protecting the still-developing joints of the young athlete. It is also important to provide the best in arenas or playing fields. Monetary constraints often force youth activities to take place in less than optimal physical surroundings. However, given the importance we attach to participation, all of us should strive to obtain the best for our youth. Another way to reduce injury is to modify the rules to fit the age and skill level manifested. Instead of tackle football, playing the flag variety is encouraged; baskets are lowered for peewee basketballers; and extremely young pitchers are not allowed to throw the curve ball in baseball. These reasonably simple variants can reduce injury and enhance enjoyment at the same time. Finally, another recommendation that would reduce injury and promote enjoyment is to encourage and provide opportunity for proper sport conditioning for all.

On the psychological side, reinforcement of effort over the old bugaboo, win-loss, is of considerable importance. Coaches who are trained through one of the various youth coaching workshop programs to be discussed in the next chapter, ones who stress the importance of consistent improvement and skill acquisition to both players and parents, would be a most welcome addition. It would also be important for these coaches to play competitive and social evaluation aspects as low-key as possible. Setting realistic sport mastery goals is another way of shaping positive attitudes and skills. Individualizing the instruction and overall handling of youth would also be helpful. Much use of positive reinforcement is called for in dealing with young people; they respond predictably well to positive strokes and generally unpredictably or unsatisfactorily to negativism from coaches, parents, or peers. A clear focus on continual development of positive feelings about oneself is also recommended. Youth sport should be a big part of self-concept development. Positive sport experiences should result in enhanced feelings of self-worth. Impinging on these feelings of positive self-regard is the concept of locus of control. There are those who maintain that an internal locus of control is psychologically healthy. Singer and Gerson (1980) suggest that evaluating success against the backdrop of individual ability might translate into the development of an internal locus, one in which ability and effort attributions will become dominant. Though argumentative, the Singer and Gerson hypothesis is provocative.

On a more sociological note, a number of recommendations have been made. One is to structure youth sport in such a way that it only vaguely resembles big-time amateur or professional sport. This requires that league officials downplay such things as pep squads, elaborate awards ceremonies, and undue recognition of players or teams through the various media. Inappropriate spectator behavior should not be tolerated by league officials. Aggression and violence on the part of players or spectators, and temper tantrums and similar negative emotional displays on the part of players should not be tolerated. The occasional highly publicized misbehaviors of potential role models at the collegiate or professional level should not be glorified. Finally, positive social behavior on the part of parents might be facilitated by getting them involved in the conduct of some aspects of the action. Manning the concession stand or getting involved in field maintenance and improvement can serve to promote good relations among parents.

As a final note related to the issue of improving youth sport, parents would do well to reinforce involvement in sports other than the "Big Three"—baseball, basketball, and football. Sports such as golf, racquetball, or tennis involve generally lower stakes, are not played in group settings, and parental and peer pressure are less powerful.

If all of the recommendations were to be universally put into effect, the goals and hopes

Positive sport experiences promote healthy self-concept development.

we all have for youth sport would surely be realized. None of the suggestions is pie-in-the-sky. Each of them, with proper urging and support, could be implemented and would insure that our young people would be getting the best that youth sport has to offer.

HEALTH RISKS ASSOCIATED WITH YOUTH SPORT

As part of the hue and cry associated with youth sport since its inception as a formalized entity, critics have pointed the finger at physical risks and psychological trauma. Most certainly there are risks associated with rough and tumble physical activity, whether organized or informal. How many youngsters have broken an arm or a collarbone in a fall from a tree? Or dislocated a finger or injured a knee in a hastily thrown together baseball game in someone's backyard? However, it is our contention that organizers of more formalized youth activities have an opportunity and an obligation to provide proper leadership in reducing the risk of physical injury for the participants. With proper care and supervision, much of the injury potential in organized sport can be

HIGHLIGHT 11.4
Would You Want
Your Child to Play
Tennis?

Data from a recent *USA Today* survey (Finn, 1987) indicate that tennis at the highly competitive level is an expensive hobby. Participants at the Omega Easter Bowl tennis tournament in Miami, Florida, perhaps the showcase event for junior tennis players in the United States, were asked to respond to a number of questions related to tennis participation; 336 of 384 competitors responded to the mail survey from *USA Today.* Chief among the results were:

1. 85.2 percent reported family income above $40,000 per year; almost 40 percent reported income over $80,000.
2. Over 70 percent reported spending in excess of $5,000 per year on tennis alone; 31.3 percent spend over $10,000 annually.
3. Only 14.7 percent took up tennis after age ten; an equal number began playing prior to age six.
4. Over 59 percent reported practicing from two to six hours daily.
5. More than 40 percent reported that their school studies have suffered because of tennis involvement; on the other hand, only 8.3 percent had a grade average in school below a B. Less than 1 percent did not plan to go to college.
6. Parents influenced the decision to take up the game of tennis almost equally. Only 7 percent cited themselves as the reason.

If you want your child to be a top tennis player, it is imperative that you allocate the necessary financial resources to the undertaking. Your child would be best advised to pick up the game at an early age if he or she is to be competitive with other top players. Also, it is likely that they will have to devote an inordinate amount of time to the endeavor, and their grades may suffer as a result. Finally, it is important that you be the source of inspiration for taking up the game of tennis.

SOURCE: "Players to Hit Books as Well as Serves" by R. Finn, 1987, *USA Today*, April 16, p. 12C.

brought under control, a situation that does not exist in the unorganized sector.

The American Academy of Pediatrics (1981) points to the existence of several problems that increase the likelihood of injury. One potential source of difficulty is that there are such *discrepancies in the physical capabilities* among various youth, partially as a function of the fact that their strength is not proportional to their size. To compound the problem, there are such *variations in maturity* that grouping athletes for competition by chronological age becomes a questionable strategy. Gomolak (1975, p. 96) sums this situation up very well: "At thirteen . . . boys can vary physically from 90 pounds of baby fat and peach fuzz to 225 pounds of muscle and mustache." This developmental discrepancy has led Hafner (see Gomolak, 1975) to develop a program in the state of New York in which physical maturity rather than chronology dictates the grouping of young people for the purpose of athletic participation. Hafner's system is called the Selection Classification Age Maturity (SCAM) program, and its implementation led to a significant reduction in player injuries. The essence of Hafner's approach is an emphasis on matching players up physically. Such things as menarche for females and facial, axillary, and pubic hair growth in males are coupled with extensive medical examinations and tests of agility, strength, speed, and endurance in order to arrive at a proper maturity placement for each athlete. Although the long-term success of the Hafner approach has not been determined, the notion of maturity matching within junior high, junior varsity, and varsity interscholastic programs seems to be a reasonable one.

A second problem area with young athletes is *impatience with restrictions* on their activities when they are necessary for the diagnosis or treatment of an injury. Running too soon after a leg injury, removing a cast without medical approval and attention, or failure to stay off an injured knee are only a few of the many examples of things young athletes have been known to do.

Yet another troublesome concern has to do with the *musculoskeletal immaturity* of young athletes, which leaves them susceptible to joint and other injuries. A particularly controversial aspect of this problem area concerns what has come to be known as "Little League elbow." Perhaps a brief look at the injury picture in the early days of Little League baseball would set the scene for subsequent discussion.

Hale (1961), reacting to criticisms of Little League baseball, showed in a five-year study of nearly 800,000 players a relatively low injury rate. Hale's analysis reported 15,444 injuries requiring medical attention, or an incidence of around 2 percent. Given the number of exposures to potentially injurious situations that are inherent in baseball (Hale indicates that there were 148 million pitched balls alone), Little League appears to be not especially hazardous. No particular singling out of injuries to the arm or elbow was made by Hale. However,

his work arose out of concern about injuries in baseball and laid the foundation for a number of studies over the next quarter century that dealt with arm and elbow problems in particular.

In reviewing the literature as well as following up on 328 former Little Leaguers, Francis, Bunch, and Chandler (1978) assert that injury to the throwing elbow was less common in the Little League players than it was in a matched sample of seventy people who had never played the game of baseball. The injury rate in the form of residual elbow lesions for the ex-Little Leaguers was 1.5 percent whereas it was 2.8 percent for the control group. Overall, there were 7 of 398 total subjects with residual elbow difficulties. Of the 328 ex-Little Leaguers, 28 had gone on to play at the collegiate level; one of these players, a pitcher, had residual damage to the throwing arm. Francis and his associates concluded that psychological trauma might be more of a problem than physical damage in Little League baseball. In any event, the Francis et al. study suggests that "Little League elbow" does exist, but not at the alarming rate suggested by critics of the game.

A fourth problematic issue concerns the possibility of *undiagnosed or unrecognized congenital or acquired conditions* that might predispose the athlete to injury or, at the extreme, death. The concern about death is highlighted from time to time by reports in the various media of young, talented, and superbly conditioned high school or college athletes who die on the basketball court or the football field, deaths often attributed by examining medical authorities to covert, undiagnosed congenital heart conditions.

A fifth problem area has to do with *conditioning*. Considerable evidence suggests that our young people are not in optimal physical condition. The conditioning deficiency has obvious ramifications for sport; too many youngsters are not physically prepared for the demands of their chosen sport and all too often are also not willing to become properly conditioned. These liabilities with regard to fitness enhance injury risk, of course.

A sixth area of concern is *protective equipment*. Young athletes are often uninformed, indifferent, or uninterested in the fitting, adjustment, or maintenance of protective equipment.

Finally, youth participants all too often are not provided with *access to the services of qualified athletic trainers*. Less than qualified parents, coaches, or an on-call physician usually provide the services of the qualified trainer, a condition that is less than desirable.

SUMMARY

1. Youth sport is a multifaceted enterprise, one fraught with controversy as to its positive and negative consequences.
2. Sport involvement on a formal basis is a relatively new phenomenon. The growth of organized sport in general in this country and a concomitant increasing awareness of the rights of children gave considerable impetus to the youth sport movement. Too, the emergence of agencies such as the Boy Scouts, Boys Club, and YMCA pushed youth sport to the forefront of American life. The reluctance of the public schools to provide physical education and sport experiences for youngsters under the age of twelve years made the activities provided by these various agencies even more significant.
3. Little League baseball began in 1939 in Pennsylvania and has experienced meteoric rise; some seven thousand leagues now serve 2 to 3 million participants. In its earliest days, Little League baseball met with substantial resistance from a variety of critics who saw the sport as too physically dangerous and psychologically demanding.

Research published in the 1950s and 1960s countered many of these claims, and Little League baseball continues to prosper. The effects of the equal rights movement led to Amy Dickinson becoming the first female Little Leaguer.

4. A second force that propelled youth sport was an increasing concern about physical fitness. A landmark study conducted in the early 1950s indicated that American youngsters were inferior to their European peers in overall fitness. President Dwight Eisenhower was most appalled by this finding, and this led him to convene a panel of 149 education and fitness leaders in an effort to respond to what many regarded as a true national crisis. The President's Council on Youth Fitness, still operative today, and the AAHPER Youth Fitness Test, also still operative but with alterations, were two significant products of this presidential response.
5. Approximately 25 million children under age eighteen participate in nonschool and school-sponsored athletic activities.
6. Having fun consistently appears to be the primary reason why children take part in sport, followed in no particular order by improving athletic skills, achieving a higher level of fitness, and experiencing the social rewards offered by team sports. Extrinsic rewards, such as trophies or media coverage, appear to be of secondary importance.
7. The dropout rate in youth sport is, in the view of some, alarmingly high and constitutes a problem for which too few answers have been found. Significant reasons why youngsters discontinue sport participation include not getting to play enough; not having fun; too much pressure from parents, coaches, and peers; too much emphasis on winning on the part of the same sources; and unsatisfactory coaching. Another factor that assumes increased salience with age is conflict of interest with other life activities.

8. Sources of stress in youth sport include too much emphasis on winning and the pressure associated with constant social evaluation by significant others. Too, one's perceived ability and its association with expectancy of success are added sources of competitive anxiety.

9. Competition may be viewed as a product or as a process. In the product orientation, the emphasis is on winning above all else, tangible rewards, seeking of adulation, and dehumanization of one's opponent. In the process orientation, participation becomes an end in itself, personal or team excellence is sought, the activities are appreciated for their aesthetic properties, and there is respect for the opposition.

10. Competitive stress is a negative emotional state that is generated when a person feels unable to cope with competitive demands. This subjective perception of failure results in negative evaluation of athletic ability and resultant loss of self-esteem.

11. Competitive stress may be measured physiologically, behaviorally, or psychologically. Heart rate changes relate to the physiological dimension, quantified sleep loss relates to the behavioral, and using the Sport Competition Anxiety Test (SCAT) represents a psychological measurement tool.

12. Research has suggested that competitive stress is mediated by at least four cognitive variables, namely, perceived ability, expectancy of success, expectancy of negative evaluation, and expectancy of experiencing negative emotional states.

13. General parent-child interactions, interactions with other adults and peers, and history of success or failure are major antecedents of competitive stress.

14. Recommendations for improving youth sport involve attacking the problem from the medical, psychological, and sociological perspectives. Thorough physical examinations, proper equipment, and adapting the rules to fit various skill levels are a few of many medical recommendations. Psychologically speaking, reinforcement of effort (process) over the win-loss (product) standard is highly recommended. Sociologically, not tolerating inappropriate behavior and reinforcing prosocial efforts among fans and players would be valuable in making youth sport more rewarding for all involved.

15. A number of health risk factors that contribute to injury rates have been identified by the American Council of Pediatrics and others. Among these health risk factors are discrepancies in size and skill at various ages, impatience with restrictions when injured, musculoskeletal immaturity, possible undetected congenital predisposers to injury, overall physical conditioning deficits, poor utilization of protective equipment, and poor access to services of qualified trainers.

SUGGESTED READINGS

Cratty, B. J., & Pigott, R. (1984) *Student projects in sport psychology*. Ithaca, NY: Mouvement.

Cratty and Pigott have put together a collection of twenty-one projects that they suggest can be used to assist teachers and students in sport psychology classes. Project 8, the youth in sport, and Project 18, parent-child observation, are particularly relevant to youth sport. Project 8 involves interviewing a child with the goal of ascertaining some of the psychosocial forces that affect performance and enjoyment of sport. In Project 18, using a suggested checklist, the student assesses parental effects on performance and enjoyment of sport through observation of adults at youth sporting events.

Martens, R. (1978) *Joy and sadness in children's sports*. Champaign, IL: Human Kinetics.

This 360-page book is a classic reading in the literature of youth sport. Martens, a self-acknowledged proponent of youth sports, primarily attempts to portray the joy of sports but acknowledges the difficulty of addressing the issues without confronting the down side. The book was created for all who care about youth sport, and it is sufficiently scholarly and readable to be of interest to coaches, parents, and sports professionals alike. Martens chose 36 articles from a broad array of sources to address the many issues in youth sport.

Martens, R. (1982) Kid sports: A den of iniquity or a land of promise? In R. A. Magill, M. J. Ash, & F. L. Smoll (Eds.), *Children in sport: A contemporary anthology.* (2d ed.), pp. 201–216. Champaign, IL: Human Kinetics.

Martens explores the role that youth sport plays in the moral development of children. In the process, the role of reinforcement and punishment is discussed at length. Martens emphasizes the role that modeling of parental or coach action plays in shaping desirable sport behavior in young players. He elaborates on the role of winning versus competing for the more process kinds of reasons.

Orlick, T., & Botterill, C. (1975) *Every kid can win.* Chicago, IL: Nelson-Hall.

Though a bit dated, this book remains a must for all involved in youth sport. The authors have attempted to bridge the communications gap that exists between people who generate ideas and those who apply them, in this case, coaches, parents, and others who interact with young people in the athletic arena. Practical suggestions are made about how to keep children in sport and how to make the experience as rewarding as possible in the process. A chapter on the female athlete is particularly interesting given the date of the publication of this work.

Picou, J. S., McCarter, V., & Howell, F. (1985) Do high school athletics pay? Some further evidence. *Sociology of Sport Journal, 2,* 72–76.

Data collected from five southern states at several time intervals were analyzed to see if participation in high school athletics is linked to later financial reward in the work world. White males clearly benefited, but this was not the case for black males or white and black females. The discussion relates these results to other studies.

Zingale, D. (1977) "Ike" revisited on sport and physical fitness. *Research Quarterly, 48,* 12–18.

Zingale summarizes the various contributions to sport and physical fitness made by President Dwight D. Eisenhower. Prominent among these efforts were the establishment of the President's Council on Youth Fitness, his general support of fitness for people of all ages, and his promotion of the sport of golf. The latter was a consuming passion for the late president.

REFERENCES

American Academy of Pediatrics (1981) Injuries to young athletes. *Physician and Sportsmedicine, 9*(2), 107–110.

Blair, S., Falls, H., & Pate, R., (1983) A new physical fitness test. *Physician and Sportsmedicine, 11*(4), 87–95.

Burke, E., & Kleiber, D. (1976) Psychological and physical implications of highly competitive sports for children. *Physical Educator, 33,* 63–70.

Burton, D., & Martens, R. (1986) Pinned by their own goals: An exploratory investigation into why kids drop out of wrestling. *Journal of Sport Psychology, 8,* 183–197.

DuBois, P. (1980) Competition in youth sport: Process or product? *Physical Educator, 37,* 151–154.

Duda, J. (1985) Consider the children: Meeting participants' goals in youth sport. *Journal of Physical Education, Recreation and Dance, 56*(6), 55–56.

Francis, R., Bunch, T., & Chandler, B. (1978) Little League elbow: A decade later. *Physician and Sportsmedicine, 6*(4), 88–94.

Fry, D., McClements, J., & Sefton, J. (1981) *A report on participation in the Saskatoon Hockey Association.* Saskatoon, Sask., Canada: SASK Sport.

Gill, D. L., & Martens, R. (1977) The role of task type and success–failure on selected interpersonal variables. *International Journal of Sport Psychology, 8,* 160–177.

Gill, D. L., Gross, J. B., & Huddleston, S. (1981) Participation motivation in youth sport. *International Journal of Sport Psychology, 14,* 1–14.

Gomolak, C. (1975) Problems in matching young athletes: Baby fat, peach fuzz, muscle, and mustache. *Physician and Sportsmedicine, 3*(5), 96–98.

Gould, D., Feltz, D. L., Horn T., & Weiss, M. (1982) Reasons for discontinuing involvement in competitive youth swimming. *Journal of Sport Behavior, 5,* 155–165.

Gould, D., Feltz, D. L., & Weiss, M. (1985) Motives for participating in competitive youth swimming. *International Journal of Sport Psychology, 16,* 126–140.

Gould, D., Feltz, D. L., Weiss, M., & Petlichkoff, L. M. (1982) Participating motives in competitive youth swimmers. In T. Orlick, J. T. Partington, & J. H. Salmela (Eds.) *Mental training for coaches and athletes* (pp. 57–58). Ottawa: Coaching Association of Canada.

Griffin, L. (1978) *Why children participate in youth sports.* Paper presented at American Alliance for Health, Physical Education and Recreation (AAHPER) Convention, Kansas City, Missouri.

Hale, C. J. (1956) Physiological maturity of Little League baseball players. *Research Quarterly, 27,* 276–284.

Hale, C. J. (1961) Injuries among 771,810 Little League baseball players. *Journal of Sports Medicine and Physical Fitness, 1,* 80–83.

Hanson, D. (1967) Cardiac response to participation in Little League baseball competition as determined by telemetry. *Research Quarterly, 38,* 384–388.

Harris, D. V. (1973) Physical activities for children: Effects and affects. Paper presented at American Alliance for Health, Physical Education and Recreation (AAHPER) Convention, Minneapolis, Minnesota.

Jennings, S. (1981) As American as hot dogs, apple pie, and Chevrolet: The desegregation of Little League baseball. *Journal of American Culture, 4*(4), 81–91.

Kleiber, D. (1981) Searching for enjoyment in children's sports. *Physical Educator,* May, 77–84.

Kraus, H., & Hirschland, P. (1954) Minimum muscular fitness tests in young children. *Research Quarterly, 25,* 178–188.

Legwold, G. (1983) New verse, same chorus: Children aren't fit. *Physician and Sportsmedicine, 11*(55), 153–155.

Magill, R. A. (1978) Critical periods: Relation to youth sports. In R. A. Magill, M. J. Ash, & F. L. Smoll (Eds.), *Children in sport* (pp. 38–47). Champaign, IL: Human Kinetics.

Martens, R. (1977) *Sport Competition Anxiety Test.* Champaign, IL: Human Kinetics.

Martens, R. (1978) *Joy and sadness in children's sports.* Champaign, IL: Human Kinetics.

Martens, R., & Seefeldt, V. (1979) *Guidelines for children's sports.* Washington, DC: Alliance for Health, Physical Education, Recreation and Dance.

Martens, R., Burton, D., Rivkin, F., & Simon, J. (1980) Reliability and validity of the Competitive State Anxiety Inventory (CSAI). In C. H. Nadeau, W. R. Halliwell, K. M. Newell, & G. C. Roberts (Eds.), *Psychology of motor behavior and sport — 1979* (pp. 91–99). Champaign, IL: Human Kinetics.

McElroy, M. A., & Kirkendall, D. R. (1980) Significant others and professionalized sport attitudes. *Research Quarterly for Exercise and Sport, 51,* 645–653.

Nuwer, H. (1986) The new improved George Brett. *Inside Sports, 8,* (June), pp. 60–70.

Orlick, T. (1974) The athletic dropout — A high price of inefficiency. *CAHPER Journal,* Nov.-Dec., pp. 21–27.

Passer, M. W. (1983) Fear of failure, fear of evaluation, perceived competence, and self-esteem in competitive-trait-anxious children. *Journal of Sport Psychology, 5,* 172–188.

Passer, M. W. (1984) Competitive trait anxiety in children and adolescents. In J. M. Silva & R. S. Weinberg (Eds.), *Psychological foundations of sport* (pp. 130–144). Champaign, IL: Human Kinetics.

Pooley, J. (1981) *Dropouts from sport: A case study of boys' age-group soccer.* Paper presented at American Alliance for Health, Physical Education, Recreation and Dance (AAHPERD) Convention, Boston, Massachusetts.

Sapp, M., & Haubenstricker, J. (1978) Motivation for joining and reasons for not continuing in youth sports programs in Michigan. Paper presented at American Alliance for Health, Physical Education, and Recreation (AAHPER) Convention, Kansas City, Missouri.

Scanlan, T. K. (1984) Competitive stress and the child athlete. In J. M. Silva & R. S. Weinberg (Eds.), *Psychological foundations of sport* (pp. 118–129). Champaign, IL: Human Kinetics.

Scanlan, T. K., & Lewthwaite, R. (1986) Social psychological aspects of competition for male youth participants: IV. Predictors of enjoyment. *Journal of Sport Psychology, 8,* 25–35.

Scanlan, T. K., & Passer, M. W. (1978) Factors related to competitive stress among male youth sport participants. *Medicine and Science in Sports, 10,* 103–108.

Scanlan, T. K., & Passer, M. W. (1981) Competitive stress and the youth sport experience. *Physical Educator, 38,* 144–151.

Scott, P. (1953) Attitudes toward athletic competition in elementary schools. *Research Quarterly, 24,* 352–361.

Seymour, E. (1956) Comparative study of certain behavior characteristics of participant and non-participant boys in Little League baseball. *Research Quarterly, 27,* 338–346.

Shaffer, T. (1980) The uniqueness of the young athlete: Introductory remarks. *American Journal of Sports Medicine, 8,* 370–371.

Simon, J., & Martens, R. (1979) Children's anxiety in sport and nonsport evaluative activities. *Journal of Sport Psychology, 1,* 160–169.

Singer, R. N., & Gerson, R. (1980) Athletic competition for children: Motivational considerations. *International Journal of Sport Psychology, 11,* 249–262.

Skubic, E. (1955) Emotional responses of boys to Little League and Middle League competitive baseball. *Research Quarterly, 26,* 342–352.

Skubic, E. (1956) Studies of Little League and Middle League baseball. *Research Quarterly, 27,* 97–110.

Spielberger, C. (1973) *Preliminary test manual for the State-Trait Anxiety Inventory for Children.* Palo Alto, CA: Consulting Psychologists Press.

Stewart, M. (1981) Youth sport participation and the physiological functions of the child. *Physical Educator, 38,* 59–64.

Wankel, L. M., & Kreisel, P. (1985) Factors underlying enjoyment of youth sports: Sport and age group comparisons. *Journal of Sport Psychology, 7,* 51–64.

Weinberg, R. S., & Genuchi, M. (1980) Relationship between competitive trait anxiety, state anxiety, and golf performance: A field study. *Journal of Sport Psychology, 2,* 148–154.

White, C. (1987) Little League is big the world over. *USA Today,* Aug. 25, pp. 1C-2C.

Wood, R. (1983) Thoughts on reducing the fear of failure in young children. *Physical Educator, 40,* 219–221.

The Coach and Sport Psychology

Dear Coach Rockne:

As you may know, I have been interested for some years in many of the problems of psychology and athletics. I am writing you now because during the past season I heard a few comments about you and your team that were of interest to my work, having always taken the point that men on a team play best when they love the game they are playing. I have said that I did not believe such a team would have to be keyed up to its games. A team that is keyed up is bound to have a slump. Men who are always playing their best because they like the game are far more apt to go through a season without a serious slump. Now the point I am getting at is this: I have heard it said that you do not key your men up to their games: that you select such men as play the game joyously for its own sake and that you try to develop in them as much of this spirit as you can.

I am wondering if you care to tell me directly about these things? I am asking for information only because of my psychological interest in athletic sports.

Cordially yours,

Coleman R. Griffith

Dear Mr. Griffith:

I feel very grateful to you for having written me, although I do not know a great deal about psychology.

I do try to pick men who like the game of football and who get a lot of fun out of playing it. I never try to make football hard work. I do think your team plays good football, because they do like to play and I do not make any effort to key them up, except on rare, exceptional occasions. I keyed them up for the Nebraska game this year, which was a mistake, as we had a reaction the following Saturday against Northwestern. I try to make our boys take the game less seriously than, I presume, some others do, and we try to make the spirit of the game one of exhilaration and we never allow hatred to enter into it, no matter against whom we are playing.

Thanking you for your kindness, I am

Yours cordially,

[Knute Rockne]

My dear Mr. Rockne:

Let me thank you most heartily for your comments about the play spirit in football. If you are so inclined, I would like to hear about the plans you make for playing a post-season game and what efforts you have to make to reawaken the interest of the men. I doubt very much whether teams that have to be keyed up to a game will be able to do so well weeks after the season is closed as a team which plays in the spirit in which yours seems to play. I do not mean, of course, to trouble you about this before your trip to the coast but I will be most grateful for any comments you may have to make after you come back.

Cordially yours,

Coleman R. Griffith

Dear Mr. Griffith:

Regarding our trip to the coast, we took it mostly in the way of a pleasure trip and an educational trip, and we made the workouts short and snappy, so as not to make them hard work in any sense of the word. We had just one real hard workout and that was at Tucson, which served to sort of get the boys in a mood for a game. The climate of California sort of took the resiliency and drive out of their legs before the second half began. However, the spirit of play manifested itself and the boys were so alert that they took advantage of every mistake made by Stanford. I think a keyed-up team would have been too tense and too excited to have profited by these opportunities.

From an educational point of view, we had a very profitable trip and the boys missed but one day of classes.

Yours sincerely,

[Knute Rockne]

My dear Mr. Rockne:

I am doubly indebted to you for your letter of February 10. I was almost sure that the plan which you say you followed would bring success. I know that other teams have gone to the coast so keyed-up and excited that their own mental states fought against them.

Cordially yours,

Coleman R. Griffith

INTRODUCTION

The exchange of letters in 1924–1925 between one of college football's most successful coaches, Knute Rockne of Notre Dame, and the father of sport psychology, Coleman Griffith at the University of Illinois, serves as a poignant reminder that the coaching practices of sixty years ago and those of today have little in common (LeUnes, 1986). Coaching at any level, but particularly in the collegiate or professional ranks, has become a pressure-laden enterprise, one in which win–loss record is generally viewed as the standard by which all success is measured. Our quest here is for a better understanding of the kinds of people who choose this enigmatic profession and what psychology has to offer coaches in their pursuit of excellence for themselves and their players.

FEATURES OF COACHING: PROS AND CONS

Undoubtedly, a great many rewards are associated with coaching. Prevailing in one-to-one competition with your peers has a tremendous amount of appeal. Equally attractive is the pride in taking a group of individuals and molding them into a productive and cohesive team. Another source of great satisfaction has to be watching young people master skills and, at the same time, grow up to be useful contributing citizens. For some coaches, substantial monetary rewards and fame accompany such success. Though these various incentives hardly exhaust the myriad possibilities, they serve as reminders that coaching can be a most exhilarating calling.

Fuoss and Troppmann (1981) indicate that those who go into coaching will also confront a number of unique features of their chosen field that fall into the category of hazards of the profession. For one thing, *everyone is an expert on sport!* Few will tell a watchmaker, a welder, and a wizard in electronics how to do their respective jobs, yet most of us are quite willing to tell an athletic coach how to run his or her team. Second-guessing by the so-called Monday-morning quarterback is a well-documented phenomenon in the coaching experience.

Another pitfall comes in the form of *endless work hours.* Coaches put in many arduous hours in their search for the winning formula. Coaches seem to wholeheartedly subscribe to the work ethic, and this is seen in the various slogans they use to guide their own work and that of their players. "The will to win is the will to work," "success is 99 percent perspiration and 1 percent inspiration," "by failing to prepare yourself, you are preparing to fail," "there is no substitute for hard work," "alertness plus hard work equals a winner," and "winners are workers" are slogans that personify the work ethic in coaching. Because these ideas are so deeply ingrained in the coaching mentality, they contribute to the idea that the coach who works longest will prevail over those who are not so diligent. Craig Morton, when coaching the Denver Gold of the now defunct United States Football League, was branded as being not very diligent, because he worked only a forty-hour week. His feeling was that coaches spend far more time at the job than is required. Morton may or may not have been correct, but he violated a time-honored coaching norm that the person who works longest and hardest prevails.

A third occupational hazard of coaching is *constant evaluation,* and this appraisal is largely based on the performance of other people (players). The coach's record is a matter of public record and the pressure to notch wins over losses seems eternal. Few of us in other professions are so unfailingly scrutinized. The college professor's product is difficult to measure; we often operate in a vacuum as to our proficiency. Not so the coach; the record is out there for all to see.

Another negative feature of the coaching business is the *lack of security* associated with it. The coach is only as good as last year's record insofar as management is concerned. To quote Norm Sloan, the former head basketball coach at North Carolina State University: "Coaching is the only profession in which you have to prove yourself as much in the thirtieth year as in the first year" (Sloan, 1977; p. 2). "What have you done for me lately?" seems to sum up the way coaches are viewed by those in positions of authority. All one has to do to substantiate the frailties of coaching tenure is look at statistics from the various amateur and professional leagues. In 1986 and 1987, there were twenty managerial changes in major league baseball, seventeen coaching changes in the National Basketball Association (NBA), eight in the National Football League (NFL), and twenty-one in the National Hockey League (NHL) (Wulf, 1988). The picture is as negative in big-time college football, where twenty-five coaching changes were made at the Division 1-A level in 1986 ("Changing," 1987). Perhaps the situation is worse in college basketball, where 123 changes in head coaches were made in 1985 and 1986; this represents nearly a 40 percent turnover over a two-year period ("Basketball Coaches," 1986). And when one considers the ripple effect created among assistant coaches when the head coach is fired, the unsettled nature of the profession of coaching takes on even more significant proportions. Because of the lack of security, frequent moves are common. Too, getting ahead in coaching calls for additional moves that are not dictated by failure to win.

The unsettled nature of the business and the frequent moving brings us to a fifth drawback, and that is that coaching takes a *toll on family life.* Supportive of this position is a study by Sabock and Jones (1978) in which they asked high school coaches' wives to respond to a survey on problems they faced. Chief among the problems cited were excessive time demands that interfered with family life, health problems among their spouses due to job stress, and a generally irregular schedule involving travel, meals, and other family considerations. Though Sabock and Jones were also able to address the issue of husbands whose wives were coaches, little else has been done in this regard. Certainly, female coaches are subject to the same strains and stresses as the male coach, and it follows that their husbands would be affected to somewhat the same degree as the wives of male coaches.

A final concern to be addressed here is *coaching as a terminal career.* Very few coaches actually retire from coaching at the usual retirement age of sixty-five or seventy. One can count on one hand, for instance, the number of college football coaches over the age of fifty-five. (Joe Paterno of Penn State, and Bo Schembechler of Michigan are ones that readily come to mind. Can you name others?) To put the issue in data-based terms, Fred Jacoby (1978), Commissioner of the Mid-American Conference, found that only six of eighty-four assistant coaches in football were over fifty years of age; only one of the ten head coaches was over fifty. Clearly, the coaching of football is a young man's game. Parallels are likely to exist in most other sports. It would appear that coaches, like players, should be aware that they are in a career with a short life expectancy and should prepare for that eventuality, both psychologically and financially.

All things considered, individuals who choose coaching stand to reap many rewards but they should also be aware of another side of the coin. Having to deal with the multiple pressures of many critics, working seemingly endless hours, having the future rest as much on what others do as on what the coach does himself or herself, having little job security, living a sometimes disjointed family life, and being a member of a career with a short life expectancy are things that have to be dealt with in order to persist and thrive in the profession of coaching.

Qualities of a Good Coach

Though there may be a few diehards in the group, the majority of coaches are aware that coaching is more than X's and O's. This is not to downplay the importance of the intellectual side of the world of sports, but more an attempt to underscore the importance of being able to properly motivate athletes to do their best. Perhaps a personal experience from the background of your senior author would be instructive. In the ninth grade, we found ourselves without a football coach, only a short time before fall practice was to start. For whatever reason, a young (and most capable) science teacher named Carl Davidson was assigned the extra duties as junior high football coach.

Despite vehement protests based on the fact that he had never touched a football nor even attended a football game, he took over the coaching reins two weeks prior to the first game. He was referred to several of the ninth graders as resources on what to do, and as a result he read Bud Wilkinson's then very popular book on the split-T formation (Wilkinson, 1952) and installed it as our offense. Despite this inauspicious debut, Mr. Davidson was able to survive and, ultimately, excel. He lost no games that year and only five in the next seven years. He demonstrated that excellence is perhaps achieved more through motivation than sheer knowledge of the game. All in all, I am convinced that I owe my fascination with the psychological side of sport to those serendipitous events of the early 1950s, and I am deeply indebted to Carl Davidson for proving invaluable insights into the importance of motivation in athletic performance.

What is it, then, that makes for a good coach? Inasmuch as *coaches are teachers and,*

HIGHLIGHT 12.1
A Coach's Bill of Rights

Tutko (1988) has proposed that the coach is in an unusual position in that the job can be, at the same time, one of the most rewarding and yet demanding vocations. Dr. Tutko suggests that coaches need a Bill of Rights both to help them clarify their own roles and to help those in administrative positions (hire and fire positions) better understand what it is that a coach is and does. Accordingly, a Coach's Bill of Rights has been created.

Bill of Rights

1. The right to determine strategy
2. The right to a motivated style
3. The right to discipline [players]
4. The right to evaluate talent
5. A right to personal teaching technique
6. The right to select a support staff
7. The right to be free from outside influences
8. The right to be free from personal scrutiny
9. The right to be yourself
10. The right to objective evaluation

SOURCE: "The Coach's Bill of Rights" by T. A. Tutko, 1988, *Sports Psychology, 3*(2), 1–4.

Good coaches are tuned in to their performers. Knowing when to cajole, when to exhort, and when to pat athletes on the back is vital to successful coaching.

ultimately, all coaching is nothing more than teaching, the coach should be knowledgeable about the activity being taught. Athletes need to be taught the basic skills or fundamentals essential to excellent performance. A technology for accomplishing this skill acquisition has been provided in chapter 3 (Behavior Principles and Applications), and it behooves all coaches to become familiar with the behavioral approach to coaching. Coaches who are methodical and orderly in the teaching of skills and who are expert in the proper application of positive reinforcement and punishment (with emphasis on reinforcement) are miles ahead of their lesser informed contemporaries. At the same time, coaches should have sessions in which the knowledge aspects of the game are stressed. For example, sessions on proper utilization of the rules of a particular activity could be most helpful.

In addition to being a good teacher who knows his or her sport, the coach should also be a *good student*. Studying various sport periodicals on how to improve one's product, attending seminars that have the same goals in mind, and attending university courses in sport or in sport psychology are readily accessible activities for the coach who wants to grow and improve.

The successful coach is a *motivator*. Successful coaches are successful wherever they may go. Programs in the doldrums are continually given new life by coaches who have been successful elsewhere. The ability to motivate is part and parcel of this success formula. Getting athletes to run through the proverbial brick wall seems to come far easier for some coaches than others. Clearly, the former group are motivators, people who are able to generate the desire to excel in their athletes. Perhaps Mike Vreeswyk, a basketball player at Temple University, captures the essence of the coach as motivator in the following quote about his mentor, John Chaney: "If Coach says a flea can pull a plough, we say hitch him up" (Kirkpatrick, 1988, p. 30).

Being aware of *individual differences* in athletes is also an important ingredient in coaching excellence. Some athletes are turned on by yelling, screaming, throwing things, and other emotional displays. Others are turned off by these shows of emotion, preferring a more serene, meditative approach to getting ready to participate. Individualizing motivation becomes important here. Knowing which athletes to pat on the back and which ones to cajole and emotionally exhort to perform is vital to coaching. Too, watching for signs of under- or overarousal is important. As we saw in our discussion of the inverted-U hypothesis in chapter 4, there is an optimum level of arousal that is conducive to good performance. The good coach has a responsibility to acquire some sense of what this optimum level is for the team and for individual players as well. Though numbers cannot be attached to the individual levels of arousal in the sport context, some skillful assessment of the appropriate level for each player can be made by coaches who are tuned in to their performers.

The good coach is also a *good listener*, keeping an eye open and an ear to the ground to achieve a sense of individual and team subtleties and undercurrents. Consistent with being a good listener, the coach should be a sensitive sounding board for problems, complaints, and wishes of the players. Too, the good coach is going to utilize the team leaders as allies in providing keys to more ably working with other participants. Finally, the good coach will be forceful but democratic, allowing for considerable individual input into the everyday management of the sport at hand, whether team or individual. Players certainly should not run the operation, but they should have considerable input because they are invaluable sources of insights and information.

At times, people step out of line, and sport is obviously no exception to the rule. When misbehavior occurs, the coach must become a *disciplinarian*. Players need to adhere to a reasonable set of rules both on and off the field of play, and penalties must be meted out for violations of the conduct code. The good coach clearly states the code of player conduct up front, and adheres to it with reasonable regularity. When violations occur, punishment should be levied. Consistent with the time-honored rules learned in both the animal laboratory and in human research, if punishment is to be successful in changing behavior, it must be *mild, prompt,* and *consistent. Mildness* means that counterproductive emotionality will be minimal, thereby allowing the intended message to get through. *Promptness* means that the punishment and behavior will be tied together temporally in such a way that no mixed messages are sent; to wit, this is the transgression and here is the specified penalty. Finally, punishment that is *consistent* conveys a firm message that there are rules, no one is above the law, and all violations will carry a uniform punishment. Athletes, like the rest of us, can live within a punitive policy that is applied only when absolutely necessary and meets the tripartite standards of mildness, promptness, and consistency.

The good coach also *leads by example*. This implies that the coach who demands hard work from others is also a hard worker. It means that the coach who demands fitness is an exemplar of fitness. Obviously, coaches need not be in as good a condition as their players, but they should serve as fitness role models for their athletes. It means that the coach who commands respect should show respect for others. It means that the coach who expects unbridled enthusiasm should be an enthusiastic person. It means that the coach who asks that the players be good listeners also listens when players and assistant coaches are communicating. Finally, though this list is by no means exhaustive, the coach who expects athletics to build character should be a role model and facilitator of the character-building aspects of athletic participation.

Finally, the good coach must be a *goal setter*. Quite a bit of research on goal setting has emerged of late in the sport psychology literature, and the up-to-date coach would do well to incorporate the best of these findings into his or her motivational repertoire.

SETTING PERFORMANCE GOALS
IN SPORT

The application of goal setting to sport is discussed at length by Locke and Latham (1985). These authorities, after surveying more than one hundred studies across a broad variety of work and laboratory settings, have arrived at five conclusions that they feel are sound with regard to goal setting. They are:

1. specific, difficult goals lead to better performance than vague, easy goals;
2. short-term goals can facilitate the achievement of long-term goals;
3. goals affect performance by affecting effort, persistence, and direction of attention, and by motivating strategy development;
4. feedback regarding progress is necessary for goal setting to work; and
5. goals must be accepted if they are to affect performance. (P. 205)

Using these five general conclusions as a point of departure, Locke and Latham elabo-

rated on ten specific hypotheses of their own, all generated with the overall guiding hypothesis that goal setting theory is as applicable to sport as it is in the business or research laboratory settings.

Chief among their suggestions was the use of *goal setting* in the practice and competitive environments. For example, table 12.1 contains a suggested list of goals for the development of certain skills within a variety of sporting contexts. Specific suggestions for skill attainment are made; all are clear-cut and, at the same time, attainable. The suggestions also serve as specific feedback sources to coaches and athletes. The results of the goal setting are measurable, and thus the goals are far superior to the sort of general advice so often given: "Let's go hard for ten or fifteen minutes" or "Work on your free throws. You've had trouble with them lately."

Table 12.2 offers concrete ways of assessing performance in football and basketball. Players are provided with measurable and attainable goals that push them to greater performance. This goal setting, in turn, should translate into better overall team performance, an obvious goal of coaches of team sports.

Crucial to the success of goal setting is the concept of *reinforcement*, which was discussed at length in chapter 3. In brief, reinforcement must convey to the athletes that it is contingent on very specific behavior on their part. Reinforcement should be used to accurately portray degrees of skill acquisition.

By way of summary, Cox (1985) offers the following *suggestions for coaches* who are interested in improving individual and team performance through goal setting:

1. Set short-term goals as a part of long-term improvement.
2. Set tough but realistic goals.
3. Set measurable goals.
4. Delineate clear-cut strategies for goal attainment.
5. Constantly monitor and evaluate goal-setting programs.

Table 12.1 Examples of Goals for Subcomponents of Skilled Tasks

Tennis

10 backhands in a row down the line

10 volleys in a row alternating left and right corners

5 first serves in a row in left third of service court; 5 in middle third; 5 in right third

5 returns of serve in a row deep to the add court

Football

Wide receiver:

5 over-the-head catches in a row of a 40-yard pass

5 one-handed catches in a row of a 15-yard pass

Defensive back:

5 interceptions in a row with receiver using pre-announced route

2 or fewer completions allowed out of 5 tries with receiver running unknown route

Kicker: 10 field goals in a row from 40-yard line

Baseball

Infielder: 10 hard grounders in a row fielded without error, 5 to left and 5 to right

Outfielder: 20 fly balls caught on the run without error (5 to left, 5 to right, 5 in back, 5 in front)

Hitter: 5 curve balls in a row hit out of infield

Wrestling

6 takedowns using at least two techniques against an inferior but motivated opponent in (?) minutes

6 escapes using at least 3 different techniques in (?) minutes against same opponent

Basketball

20 foul shots in a row

30 uncontested lay-ups in a row

10 jump shots in a row from 10 feet

5 out of 10 jump shots from 40 feet

Dribbling 2 minutes man-on-man against best defensive player without losing ball

Soccer

10 shots into left corner of goal from 30 feet with goalie not moving from center of goal

5 goals out of 10 shots from 20 feet with goalie free to move

Hockey

Goalie:

stops 10 of 15 shots from 20 feet

stops 5 of 10 one-on-one situations

Forward: passes successfully 8 out of 10 times to open man in front of net with one defender in between

Lacrosse

Similar to soccer and hockey

Golf

6 drives in a row over 200 yards and landing on fairway

15 putts in a row of 12 feet

10 9-irons in a row onto green from 75 yards

SOURCE: "The Application of Goal Setting to Sports" by E. Locke and G. Latham, 1985, *Journal of Sport Psychology, 7,* 205–222.

ROLES OF THE COACH

Coaches, regardless of whether they are working with individuals or teams, live a pressure-laden, fishbowl kind of existence. Coaches are expected to win, be a positive reflection on the organization for which they toil, build character in young athletes, and make money for the organization. Frank Kush, while head football coach at Arizona State University, said: "My job is to win football games. I've got to put people in the stadium, make money for the university, keep the alumni happy, and give the school a winning reputation. If I don't win, I'm gone" (Michener, 1976). The coach, in this context, becomes a slave to many masters.

A glance at figure 12.1 will afford some additional insight into the role complexity

Table 12.2 Concrete Ways of Assessing Performance in Football and Basketball

A. Sample Point System for Defensive Lineman in Football

Point value	Action
20	Touchdown
10	Interception or fumble recovery
5	Cause fumble
5	Sack
3	Block pass
3	Pressure passer (e.g., within 3 feet of passer when ball released)
5	Tackle runner for 5 yard loss or more
4	Tackle runner for 1 to 4 yard loss
3	Tackle runner after gain of 0 to 3 yards
2	Tackle runner after gain of 4 to 5 yards
3	Tackle after lineman runs more than 10 yards
1	Any other tackle
—	Assist on any of above: 1/2 the number of points indicated
—	Bonus points (0 to 20): Any key 4th-quarter play in a winning effort: judgment of coaches

Possible comparison standards for setting goals

1) Own performance (number of points in previous game and/or against same opponent last time played)
2) Own best previous performance (same season)
3) Performance of other team's best lineman in previous week
4) Average of all defensive linemen on same team in previous week

B. Sample Point System for Basketball Players

Point value	Action
2	Field goal
1	Assist
1	Foul shot
1	Rebound
1	Steal
1	Blocked shot
Number of points held below average	Hold opposing player to less than season average (one-on-one defense)

Possible comparison standards for setting goals

1) Own season average
2) Own performance against same opponent that year
3) Own performance in last 3 games

SOURCE: "The Application of Goal Setting to Sports" by E. Locke and G. Latham, 1985, *Journal of Sport Psychology, 7,* 205–222.

facing the typical coach. There are multiple pressures impinging on the coach, and success in large part will depend on how well these pressures are handled.

At the *administrative level,* the coach must get along with owners, general managers, athletic directors, and other administrators, depending on the level at which the coaching is being done. This serving of many masters is no small task; often, much money and even bigger egos are involved, greatly increasing the pressure to win at all costs. Too, the prerogatives of the coach can be measurably circumvented by a meddling administrator. For

example, chronic failures to win among several organizations in professional baseball, basketball, and football are testimonials to mismanagement. One needs little imagination to figure which organizations these are.

Players are another demand on the resources of the coach. If the coach is not successful in dealing with the players, the other roles are largely inconsequential. The coach must care about the athletes, must be able to motivate them, and must be concerned with their overall welfare. Equally important, the players must sense this commitment to their athletic and personal well-being.

Figure 12.1 Roles Coaches Are Expected to Play

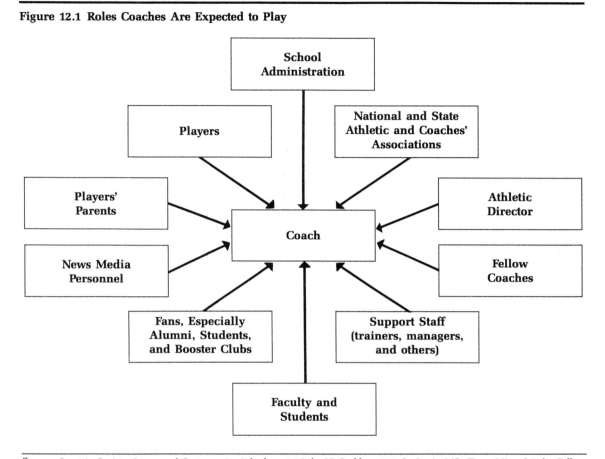

SOURCE: *Sport in Society: Issues and Controversies* (3d ed., p. 303), by J.J. Coakley, 1986, St. Louis, MO: Times Mirror/Mosby College Publishing.

Assistant coaches are factors also to be reckoned with. These aides are invaluable in terms of ultimate success and must be treated accordingly. Assistants should be paid what they are worth in terms of the free market, must be given a free rein to coach their various specialties, and should always be treated as trusted allies. Where feasible, they should be groomed for better jobs. It must be very rewarding to look around and see proteges everywhere. Tom Landry, head football coach of the NFL Dallas Cowboys, has Dan Reeves of the Denver Broncos, Gene Stallings of the Phoenix Cardinals, and Mike Ditka of the Chicago Bears all coaching against him after serving mentorships in Dallas. In the case of the late Bear Bryant of the University of Alabama, his former players who are now coaches are too numerous to mention, and undoubtedly were a continuing source of immense satisfaction to him. In basketball, Bobby Knight of Indiana had fifteen proteges coaching in major programs at the end of 1986 (Allen, 1987).

The *media* demand yet another role of the coach. Media people are paid to promote listeners, viewers, or subscribers for the organi-

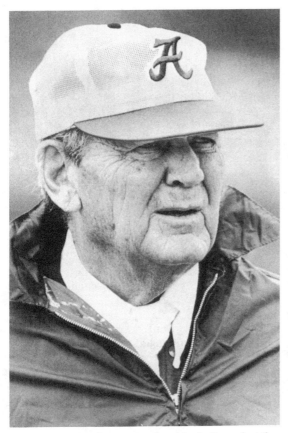

During his twenty-five years as head football coach at the University of Alabama, the legendary "Bear" Bryant served as mentor for countless players who are now coaches.

zations for which they work and put a lot of pressure on coaches for interesting, salable material. The Monday morning interviews, the pre- and postgame interviews, the midweek interviews, and interviews to explain wins or losses, the interviews related to exceptional players, and continuous media speculation as to team prospects and the ultimate fate of the coaches themselves all require the ability to express oneself under pressure. Too, the coaches' diplomacy and tact will be taxed at these times. Media exposure is important to the welfare of the teams and athletes, but the inherent pressures create further role demands for the coaches involved.

Dealing with fans is still another challenge to coaches. There would be few sports if there were not fans, and they can greatly determine the fate of a particular program, either through support or the failure to support it. As a consequence, a good relationship with the fans is important. At the professional level, their support is essential to the financial success of the organization. At the intercollegiate level, this financial dependence is also there in terms of ticket sales, alumni contributions, and overall program support. At the interscholastic level, the fans are often parents with much ego involvement with the activities at hand, and they require a delicate, supportive touch.

Of particular interest in the collegiate area of late has been the *"booster,"* often an over-zealous university supporter. Boosters have subverted the very educational goals for which their universities were created through illegal payments to players or prospects, unethical inducements to perform, and, in some cases, blatantly illegal actions, such as plying athletes with cocaine. It is absolutely essential to the academic-athletic balance in universities that these kinds of people not be allowed to function with university sanction, and the coach must be the first to champion the cause of anti-boosterism. At the same time, well-meaning alumni have much to offer university athletic programs, and it would not be prudent for the coach to turn these people away. Knowing the good guys from the guys in black unfortunately is not an easy distinction for the coach to make, and no program is available to tell which is which. Needless to say, alumni should be encouraged to support their teams and universities; they should never be encouraged or allowed to subvert the ultimate reason why universities exist, namely academics.

Undoubtedly other role demands are made on coaches, depending on the level at which they function. The roles described here at least create some idea of why coaching is such a demanding profession. By way of summary, perhaps Sabock (1979) says it best when he suggests that the good coach will be all of the following: teacher, disciplinarian, salesperson, public relations specialist, diplomat, organizer, role model, psychologist, leader, judge and jury, mother or father figure, dictator, politician, actor, fund-raiser, director, field general, equipment manager, trainer, community citizen, and citizen of the school, university, or organization. With these challenges in mind, it is easy to see why coaches undertake such a career. It is equally easy to see why there are not many old, venerable salts in the sometimes stormy seas of coaching.

COACHING BURNOUT

As one example of the stress of coaching, an early study by Gazes, Sovell, and Dellastatious (1969) revealed that football and basketball coaches' heart rates average sixty-three beats per minute above resting level during game competition. McCafferty, Gliner and Horvath (1978) have lent support to the heart rate change noted by Gazes and associates. For example, one cross country coach had a heart rate elevation as high as 100 beats above base level. In water polo, the rate for one coach was 108 beats above resting level. For a volleyball coach, the rate was 69 beats above normal. Clearly, if heart rate changes are valid measures of stress, we can say that coaching is a stressful experience.

One possible outcome of prolonged stress is exhaustion; this exhausted state has often been referred to as *burnout*. It is most certainly not restricted to coaches; it is a well-documented phenomenon in many work settings.

Causes of Burnout

Taking the Job Too Seriously. Probably the single biggest causative factor in coaching burnout

is taking oneself too seriously. Coaching is an important challenge, but there is more to life than work. Achieving a balance in life's various demands, and keeping work in perspective, would seem to be a highly preventive first step in avoiding burnout.

Problem Parents. Parents, as stated earlier, constitute a considerable source of stress. When the coach–parent relationship gets out of proportion, stress is generated that can ultimately be a part of coaching burnout.

Problem Athletes. Darrell Royal, a most successful football coach in a winning tradition established at the University of Texas, retired from coaching at a relatively early age, professing symptoms of burnout. One of the contributing factors was the loss of interest in coddling eighteen-year-old prima donnas during recruiting. Getting young people to choose the particular coach's school, keeping them academically eligible, and getting the most out of their often immense athletic talents is a challenging task, and is made considerably more demanding by problem athletes.

Disenchantment. When the thrill of coaching disappears for whatever reason, burnout cannot be far behind. The notion of a career change becomes prominent in the coach's thoughts.

Pressure to win. Losing seasons (or strings of them) are frustrating for people with the preexisting fascination with winning that characterizes coaches. Too, a losing season when preseason expectancies have been extremely high is disconcerting.

Other Pressures. Lack of appreciation by administrators, family pressures, too many coaching and teaching duties, little monetary reward, and having to share strained resources with other programs in and out of athletics all take their toll on coaches. When paired with other demands, a recipe for coaching burnout is being mixed.

Smith's Cognitive-Affective Model of Athletic Burnout

One of the more detailed and innovative approaches to the conceptualization of athletic burnout has been formulated by Smith (1986). According to Smith, burnout is a reaction to chronic stress and is made up of physical, mental, and behavioral components. The interaction of this assortment of environmental and personal variables causes burnout. Smith has laid out his model showing the parallel relationships among *situational, cognitive, phys-*

iologic, and *behavioral* components of stress and burnout. This conceptual model can be seen in figure 12.2. Essentially, Smith states that burnout occurs when the available resources are insufficient to meet the demands being placed on the system by the various sources of life stress. Concurrently, there will be a cognitive appraisal of the stress, and the resultant emotional responses will be tempered by how the demands are assessed, an appraisal of what resources are available to deal with the demands, the likely consequences if the demands are not met, and the personal meaning of the demands for the individual. *Self-efficacy, expectancy of success, self-concept,* and a host of other variables discussed in earlier chapters all come into play at this point in the Smith

Figure 12.2 A Conceptual Model for Burnout

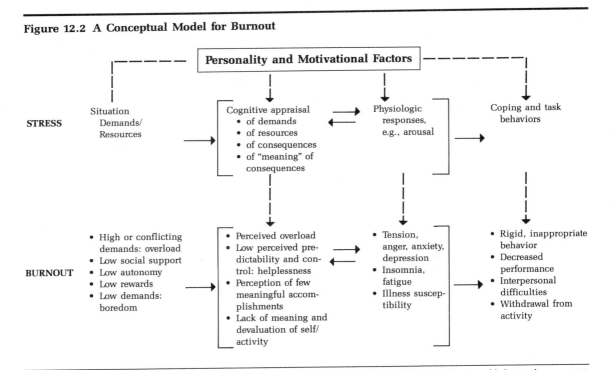

NOTE: This model shows the parallel relationships assumed to exist among situational, cognitive, physiologic, and behavioral components of stress and burnout. Individual differences in motivation and personality are assumed to influence all of the components.

SOURCE: "Consultation in Sport Psychology" by R.E. Smith, 1986, *Consulting Psychology Bulletin, 38,* (1), 17–20.

model. The third part of the model is manifested if danger or harm is feared, and this is the physiologic component. Finally, a variety of coping behaviors, some positive and others counterproductive, will be manifested as moderated by other components of the model. One of these counterproductive behaviors is burnout. In offering his model, Smith has raised some interesting questions concerning the operationalizing of burnout, its measurement, its epidemiological properties, and related causative and moderator variables.

Effects of Burnout

According to Pate, Rotella, and McClenaghan (1984), the effects of burnout will be seen in the two areas closest to the coach—athletes and family—and the two interact in a circular fashion that multiplies as both relationships deteriorate. Pate et al. further state that *three strategies for coping* with alienation resulting from burnout will become dominant. The first tendency is to *blame the athletes* for the existing problems, looking at them as being low in ability or low in motivation. The second blaming response is to look inward (self-blame), thereby attributing the problems to *lack of coaching ability*. The third available blaming strategy is to point the accusing finger at *the situation itself*. Administrators, lack of overall support, and emphasis on more preferred sport programs become sources of blame for difficulties. The net result of these three blaming strategies is that the coach will sink into a career of despondent mediocrity or make a career change aimed at restoring motivation and mental well-being.

Prevention of Burnout

A *well-rounded life* is the key to avoiding burnout. Taking various aspects of one's life equally seriously is most important; letting coaching duties take over to the exclusion of family, friends, and other aspects of life simply will not work in the long run. Burnout in the face of unidimensionality of perspective is, if not inevitable, highly likely.

Maintaining an awareness that *no coach is immune to burnout* is an important preventive measure. Winners and losers alike can burn out; minor sport coaches are not exempt from the burnout so often associated with coaching in major sports; too, burnout is not the exclusive province of collegiate or professional coaches. It can happen at all levels of coaching. Finally, burnout is not an exclusively male phenomenon; Caccese and Mayerberg (1984), in a study of 138 male and 93 female coaches from NCAA and AIAW Division I, found that female coaches reported significantly higher levels of emotional exhaustion and lower levels of personal accomplishment than did members of a comparable male sample. Clearly, female coaches are susceptible to coaching burnout, perhaps even more so than their male counterparts.

Keeping one's *physical health* at an optimal level is an important inoculation against burnout. Coaches who are healthy and stay in reasonable shape are likely to feel good, radiate enthusiasm, and serve as an inspiration to their athletes. This overall sense of well-being is contagious; others sense their enthusiasm, take it in, return it to them, and a cycle of enthusiasm is generated and reinforcement of good health is provided on a good maintenance schedule.

Having *associations with others* who understand the coaching situation is important. Other coaches know only too well what the individual coach is going through, and they can serve as sources of tension release. Pate et al. (1984) calls this "blowing out," referring to the process as one whereby coaches selectively release tension by letting out frustrations and stresses in the presence of others who will understand these occasional outbursts.

HIGHLIGHT 12.2
A Measure of
Burnout

Maslach and Jackson have developed a measure of burnout, the Maslach Burnout Inventory (MBI) (Maslach and Jackson, 1981), that has received much attention in assessing the presence of the condition among coaches and athletes. The MBI is composed of twenty-two items designed to measure both frequency and intensity of feelings, and consists of three subscales: Emotional Exhaustion (EE), Depersonalization (D), and Personal Accomplishment (PA). By reversing the direction of the scoring of PA, which is the inverse of EE and D, the result is that the higher the score, the greater the degree of burnout on all three subscales.

Caccese and Mayerberg (1984) indicated that female coaches in their study reported significantly higher levels of emotional exhaustion (EE) and significantly lower levels of personal accomplishment (PA) than did the male coaches they surveyed. The largest gender differences were found on the item, "I feel frustrated by my job," insofar as frequency was concerned. In terms of intensity, "I feel burned out by my job" showed the largest difference. Overall, however, none of the two groups reported any excessive amount of burnout. Due to limitations in the development of the MBI, comparisons by occupations are not possible, and so no statement as to burnout in coaches relative to other career groups is possible.

Capel (1986) studied athletic trainers using the MBI and found little evidence for burnout among these allied professionals. Capel, Sisley, and Desertrain (1987), in a study of high school basketball coaches from six western states, found burnout to be at a low to medium level. Nevertheless, there were burned out coaches in the Capel et al. sample.

Smith (1986), pointing to other successful sport-specific measures that have been outgrowths of assessment devices aimed at nonsport populations, has issued a call for a sport-specific conceptualization and measurement of burnout.

Source: "Gender Differences in Perceived Burnout of College Coaches," by T. Caccese and C. Mayerberg, 1984, *Journal of Sport Psychology, 6,* 279–288; "Psychological and Organizational Factors Related to Burnout in Athletic Trainers" by S. A. Capel, 1986, *Athletic Training, 21,* 322–327; "The Relationship of Role Conflict and Role Ambiguity to Burnout in High School Basketball Coaches" by S. A. Capel, B. L. Sisley, and G. S. Desertrain, 1987, *Journal of Sport Psychology, 9,* 106–117; "The Measurement of Experienced Burnout" by C. Maslach and S. E. Jackson, 1981, *Journal of Occupational Behavior, 2,* 99–113; "Toward a Cognitive-Affective Model of Athletic Burnout" by R. Smith, 1986, *Journal of Sport Psychology, 8,* 36–50.

Maintaining a sense of humor is crucial to preventing burnout. Being able to laugh at oneself and the frailties and foibles of others in and out of athletics can be a real tension reducer. There is much humor in athletics, and athletes and coaches are rich sources of such material. Daily quotes and a plethora of books on the lighter side of sports are commonplace. The coach who contributes to this literature and who appreciates it when coined by others has to be a step up in burnout avoidance.

Undoubtedly, other ingredients of the mentally healthy person could be elaborated on. Suffice it to say, however, that the points covered here are quite basic to keeping one's head on the old shoulders when all others around seem to be losing theirs, and the end result will be an enjoyable athletic experience for players, coaches, and fans alike.

PERSONALITY OF THE COACH

In all frankness, little is known about the personality of coaches. Early studies of the subject have taken two directions, one having to do with the supposed authoritarian nature of coaches and the other to do with their Machiavellian or manipulative qualities in social situations.

Authoritarianism

Ogilvie and Tutko (1966) started the ball rolling with their study of sixty-four coaches from the four major American sports, football, basketball, baseball, and track. Based on his earlier work with Ogilvie, Tutko and an associate (Tutko and Richards, 1971) identified five types of coaches, one being the hard-nosed or authoritarian coach. Gallon (1980) summarizes the authoritarian coach of Tutko and Richard as follows:

> These coaches leave no doubt about who is boss. They possess well-formulated goals, know exactly what they are trying to achieve, and expect and demand certain responses from those under them. They take the credit or blame for both achievement and mistakes. The advantages and disadvantages of authoritarianism are the same as those for any dictatorship. Most coaches fall into this category. (P. 19)

The veracity of Gallon's assertions is subject to question, but the last statement about most coaches being authoritarians has been a popularly accepted one for many years.

Scott (1971) has stated that the relaxed and understanding coach is far outnumbered by those who are rigid and authoritarian. He also indicates that extensive psychological testing has shown coaches to be among the most authoritarian vocational groupings, often outscoring policeman and career military officers on measures of the trait. The "extensive psychological testing" alluded to by Scott refers to conclusions drawn from Ogilvie's and Tutko's 1966 work cited earlier. However, many conclusions from Ogilvie and Tutko's work have been overdrawn and may not be at all representative of coaches beyond the sixty-four in their study.

Research by LeUnes and Nation (1982) may have relevance to the issue of coaching authoritarianism. One source of coaches are the players who choose to coach upon graduation. Our 1982 study of one group of collegiate football players shows that, when compared with non-football-playing peers, the football players are overwhelmingly authoritarian. These data are presented in table 12.3.

If one assumes that a potential coaching pool is represented in the sample of football players, it follows that the likelihood that such a personality is authoritarian is fairly high. On the other hand, there were a number of low-authoritarian players in the sample, and these players may go into coaching rather than the authoritarian ones. More research on this issue is needed. For the time being, it seems sufficient to say that the stereotype of a coach as an authoritarian personality is not strongly supported, but the issue warrants further investigation.

Machiavellianism

Christie and Geis (1970) are responsible for furthering scientific interest in the *Machiavellian personality*. Drawing from the writings of Machiavelli (*The Prince* and *The Discourses*), Christie and Geis devised a scale purporting to measure Machiavellianism, or what Robinson and Shaver (1973, p. 590) see as "a person's strategy for dealing with people, especially the

Table 12.3 Authoritarian Dimensions: Mean Scores Across Groups

F-Scale Factor	Groups		
	Nonathletes	High School Athletes	College Athletes
Conventionalism	11.25$_A$	12.20$_B$	12.77$_B$
Authoritarian Submission	22.32$_A$	23.34$_B$	25.00$_B$
Authoritarian Aggression	22.75$_A$	26.29$_B$	26.52$_B$
Anti-Intraception	10.87$_A$	11.56$_{A,B}$	11.91$_B$
Superstition and Stereotypy	15.42$_A$	16.02$_A$	18.07$_B$
Power and Toughness	20.58$_A$	21.64$_{A,B}$	22.79$_B$
Destructiveness and Cynicism	6.28$_A$	6.15$_A$	6.84$_B$
Projectivity	13.00$_A$	13.05$_A$	16.18$_B$
Sex	8.57$_A$	9.61$_B$	10.13$_B$
Total Score	131.17$_A$	139.95$_B$	149.84$_C$

NOTE: Row means with different subscripts are significantly different (p<.05).

SOURCE: "Saturday's Heroes: A Psychological Portrait of College Football Players" by A. LeUnes and J. R. Nation, 1982, *Journal of Sport Behavior, 5*, 139–149.

degree to which he feels other people are manipulable in interpersonal situations." Scott (1971) has stated that coaches as a group are rather insensitive in their dealings with others and are prone to manipulate players and others in order to win. This assertion has been challenged by Sage in a pair of studies conducted in the mid-1970s. In the first study (Sage, 1972a), Sage administered the Machiavellian Scale to 496 college and high school coaches and a sample of male college students from fourteen different universities. No significant differences were found among the various coaching groups and the university students except on age and years of experience; interestingly, the relationship was negative with older more experienced coaches scoring lower than their younger contemporaries. Additionally, there was no indication of even a mild relationship between win-loss record and Machiavellianism, a finding also substantiated by Walsh and Carron (1977) in their survey of a Canadian coaching sample.

Sage's second study (Sage, 1972b) took a slightly different tack, with the Machiavellian measure being replaced by the Polyphasic Values Inventory (PVI) (Roscoe, 1965), a scale designed to assess conservatism on a variety of philosophical, political, economic, educational, social, religious, and personal-moral issues. A group of randomly selected coaches (n = 246) were then compared with large numbers of college students (n = 4,005) and businessmen (n = 479). Coaches were found to be considerably more conservative than the college students and generally more liberal than the businessmen. Sage concluded that coaches are in fact conservative but probably no more so than males in most other professions.

When all is said and done, coaches are probably a bit authoritarian and conservative, but probably no more so than members of other professions. Too, being authoritarian is not all bad. At times, one firm hand has to be in control of things. The meetings between coaches and players at critical times in athletic contests call for someone taking control, and that person often is and should be the coach. Finally, coaches may be authoritarian or conservative in the job situation because it serves them well, but they may not be that way at all in dealings with others.

The preceding discussion summarizes two avenues of research into the coaching personality and are not compelling in terms of conclusiveness. Also, *authoritarianism* and *Machiavellianism* represent only two of many personality dimensions that characterize coaches and saliently point up the need for much more extensive research in the area of personality and coaching.

COACHING AND YOUTH SPORT

Much of the discussion to this point has centered around the male coach working at a fairly sophisticated level in the male-dominated major team sports. However, there are other demanding coaching situations not involving older male players and coaches. One of the more prominent of these situations is the *coaching of children*. Youth athletes have become more significant in the sport world, and good coaching is vital to their successful participation.

Lombardo (1986) indicates that there are more than 4 million youth coaches in the United States, many of whom are not qualified to properly deal with children regardless of how well intentioned they may be. To quote Lombardo: "Many leagues are totally dependent upon volunteers and, short of being a convicted felon, are all welcomed" (p. 199). Perhaps things are not quite so grim as portrayed by Lombardo, but his position probably contains an element of truth.

The Coaching Behavior Assessment System (CBAS)

In an effort to reduce the magnitude of the problem of well-intentioned but poorly pre-pared coaches in youth sport, a number of coaching improvement schemes have been developed. One of the leaders in coaching improvement is the innovative *Coaching Behavior Assessment System (CBAS)* developed by Smith, Smoll, and Hunt (1977). The CBAS was developed to allow for direct observation and subsequent coding of coaching behaviors. The twelve behavioral categories in the CBAS were divided into two subcategories, *reactive or elicited* and *spontaneous or emitted behaviors*. The *reactive category* refers generally to player behaviors whereas the *spontaneous category* refers primarily to game-related or game-irrelevant acts. These various behaviors can be seen in detail in table 12.4.

Smoll and Smith (1984) have summarized the later research on the CBAS. After refining the CBAS, Smoll and Smith used it in a study of fifty-one male coaches and 542 players in the Seattle, Washington, area. Trained observers coded an average of 1,122 behaviors per coach over a four-game period. Results indicated, among other things, that two-thirds of the coaches' behaviors fell within the three instructional and support categories, and the rate of punitive behaviors was generally quite low. The correlation between coaches' ratings of the frequency with which they used a particular behavior and their awareness of the fact was low and insignificant except for the category of punishment. Coaches do seem aware of their use of punitive approaches but are less aware of other behaviors.

Other conclusions drawn from the Smoll and Smith study were that players evaluated their teammates and the sport of baseball more positively if they played for coaches who used high levels of reinforcement and support, self-esteem was enhanced by the positive coaches, positive coaches were liked much better than the more punitive ones, and win-loss record was generally unrelated to the youngster's feelings about their coaches.

The logical outgrowth of this research was the creation of a training program for youth

Table 12.4 CBAS Response Categories

Class I. Reactive Behaviors

Responses to desirable performance

Reinforcement	A positive, rewarding reaction, verbal or nonverbal, to a good play or good effort
Nonreinforcement	Failure to respond to a good performance

Responses to mistakes

Mistake-contingent encouragement	Encouragement given to a player following a mistake
Mistake-contingent technical instruction	Instructing or demonstrating to a player how to correct a mistake
Punishment	A negative reaction, verbal or nonverbal, following a mistake
Punitive technical instruction	Technical instruction that is given in a punitive or hostile manner following a mistake
Ignoring mistakes	Failure to respond to a player mistake

Response to misbehavior

Keeping control	Reactions intended to restore or maintain order among team members

Class II. Spontaneous Behaviors

Game-related

General technical instruction	Spontaneous instruction in the techniques and strategies of the sport (not following a mistake)
General encouragement	Spontaneous encouragement that does not follow a mistake
Organization	Administrative behavior that sets the stage for play by assigning duties, responsibilities, positions, etc.

Game-irrelevant

General communication	Interactions with players unrelated to the game

SOURCE: "Leadership Research in Youth Sport" by F. L. Smoll and R. E. Smith, 1984, in J. M. Silva and R. S. Weinberg, eds., *Psychological Foundations of Sport* (p. 375), Champaign, IL: Human Kinetics.

coaches; Smoll and Smith have labeled their training program *Coach Effectiveness Training (CET)*. To validate the effectiveness of CET, a three-hour program, thirty-one Little League baseball coaches were randomly assigned to an experimental (training) group and to a control group that did not receive the purported benefits of CET. Interviews with 325 players at the end of the season were supportive of CET. The trained coaches used more reinforcement and less punishment, were liked better by the players, and were seen as better teachers. Additionally, self-esteem gains were seen in the players who had CET-trained coaches. Significantly, there were no differences in win-loss records of the two groups, indicating that the gains afforded by CET are primarily expressed in the psychosocial domain.

Coach training programs such as that developed by Smoll and his associates can be

HIGHLIGHT 12.3
Behavioral
Guidelines of Youth
Sports Coaches

Ron Smith and Frank Smoll have generated some of the more useful research in the area of coaching youth participants. One important outcome of their work has been the creation of a set of guidelines for working with young athletes that are everyday, sensible applications of behavioral principles discussed earlier in chapter 3.

I. *Reactions to player behaviors and game situations:*
A. *Good plays*
Do: Reinforce!! Do so immediately. Let the players know that you appreciate and value their efforts. Reinforce effort as much as you do results. Look for positive things, reinforce them, and you'll see them increase. Remember, whether the kids show it or not, the positive things you say and do stick with them.
Don't: Take their efforts for granted.
B. *Mistakes, screw-ups, boneheaded plays, and all the things that pros seldom do*
Do: Encourage immediately after mistakes. That's when the kid needs encouragement most. Also, give *corrective instruction* on how to do it right, but always do so in an encouraging manner. Do this by emphasizing not the bad thing that just happened, but the good things that will happen if the kid follows your instruction (the "why" of it). This will motivate the player positively to correct the mistake rather than motivate him/her negatively to avoid failure and your disapproval.
Don't: Punish when things go wrong. Punishment isn't just yelling at kids; it can be any indication of disapproval, tone of voice, or action. Kids respond much better to a positive approach. Fear of failure is reduced if you work to reduce fear of punishment.
C. *Misbehaviors, lack of attention*
Do: Maintain order by establishing clear expectations. Emphasize that during a game all members of the team are part of the game, even those on the bench. Use reinforcement to strengthen team participation. In other words, try to prevent misbehaviors from occurring by using the positive approach to strengthen their opposites.
Don't: Constantly nag or threaten the kids in order to prevent chaos. Don't be a drill sergeant. If a kid refuses to cooperate, quietly remove him or her from the bench for a while. Don't use physical measures (e.g., running laps). The idea here is that if you establish clear behavioral guidelines early and work to build team spirit in achieving them, you can avoid having to repeatedly *keep control*. Remember, kids want clear guidelines and expectations, but they don't want to be regimented. Try to achieve a healthy balance.

II. *Getting positive things to happen:*
Do: Give instruction. Establish your role as a teacher. Try to structure participation as a learning experience in which you're going to help the kids develop their abilities. Always give instruction in a positive

fashion. **Satisfy your players' desire to become the best athletes they can be. Give instruction in a clear, concise manner; if possible, demonstrate how to do it.**

Do: Give encouragement. **Encourage effort; don't demand results. Use it selectively so that it is meaningful. Be supportive without acting like a cheerleader.**

Do: Concentrate on the game. **Be "in the game" with the players. Set a good example for team unity.**

Don't: Give either instruction or encouragement in a sarcastic or degrading manner. **Make a point, then leave it. Don't let "encouragement" become irritating to the players.**

SOURCE: "Leadership Research in Youth Sport" by F. L. Smoll and R. E. Smith, 1984, in J. M. Silva and R. S. Weinberg, eds., *Psychological Foundations of Sport* (pp. 385–386), Champaign, IL: Human Kinetics.

influential in improving coaching success at the youth level. As a result, there have been a number of other systems developed to improve youth coaching, and we shall discuss them now.

Other Approaches to Improving Youth Coaching

Murphy (1985) mentions four other programs beyond the CET. One of these is the *National Youth Sport Coaches Association (NYSCA)*, founded in 1981 and headquartered in West Palm Beach, Florida. The NYSCA, an agency of the United Way, involves five to six hours of training through the use of videotapes. Items such as first aid, the psychology of children, and how to organize effective practices are only a few of the topics covered by NYSCA. As of 1985, more than 30,000 youth coaches have participated in the NYSCA training.

Another well-conceived and well-received training program is the *American Coaching Effectiveness Program (ACEP)*, the brainchild of Rainer Martens of the University of Illinois. Founded by Martens in 1981, ACEP has as its motto, "Athletes first, winning second," and had reached 25,000 youth coaches as of 1985. Attesting to the popularity of the ten-hour ACEP is its adoption by such organizations as the YMCA, Boys Clubs of America, and Pony baseball.

The *Youth Sport Institute (YSI)*, an outgrowth of the 1978 Senate-mandated Michigan study concerning youth sport mentioned in chapter 11, is located at Michigan State University. The primary function of YSI is to enhance the enjoyment of sport by young people.

In Canada, the *Canadian National Certification Program (CNCP)* serves as an invaluable source of guidance for coaches of youth. CNCP is a five-level program ranging from Level 1, the grass roots level, to Level 5, in which youth are being trained to represent their home country in international competition. Emphasis at all levels is placed on theory, technique, and application. More and more provinces and municipalities in Canada are requiring CNCP training for youth coaches.

It is apparent that a healthy movement is afoot in the United States and Canada to insure that young people are provided with as good an early sport experience as is possible. Training of volunteer coaches through the various available programs is a necessary step in the process of improving youth sport. It is hoped that all youth coaches in the not too distant future will be graduates of one of the training programs in operation today.

THE FEMALE COACH

With the implementation of Title IX in 1976, women were expected to rapidly achieve parity in sport. Although gains have been made, areas of concern still exist. One of them has to do with female coaches. At a time when the number of female athletes has increased, the percentage of women in coaching positions has declined. For example, nearly 2 million girls participated in interscholastic sports in 1983–1984, while 150,000 competed at the intercollegiate level during the same academic year (Perry, 1986). Both of these figures represent five- to sixfold increases over 1970–1971. However, the picture for female coaches is not so rosy.

In the early 1970s, most of the coaches of women's sports were women. One big reason for this preponderance of female coaches is related to the fact that these women's programs were largely outgrowths of girls' physical education classes and girls' athletic associations (Sisley and Capel, 1986).

As interest in women's athletics has increased, there has been a concomitant and substantial decrease in the number of female coaches. This trend toward the reduction in female coaches was first noted by Holmen and Parkhouse (1981). They report that the number of intercollegiate coaching positions for women increased 37 percent from 1974 to 1979. However, during the same time period, the number of female intercollegiate coaches dropped 20 percent. At the same time, the number of male coaches increased by 137 percent. Recent data from Brewington and White

(1988) offer little solace; since the early 1970s, the number of female sport administrators had dropped from 90 percent to 15 percent, and the number of female coaches from 90 percent to 50 percent.

At the interscholastic level, Hart and Mathes (1982) reported that, in 1975, women coached 92 percent (1,402) of the girls' teams in Wisconsin; by 1981, this figure had dropped to 943, or 46.2 percent. In another interscholastic study, Schafer (1984) reported that 89 percent of coaches of high school women's teams in 1973–1974 were women, whereas this number dropped to 33 percent by 1983–1984. Another study by True (1983) found similar trends; data from eight states indicate a 40 to 50 percent decrease in female coaches depending on which state was being considered. Acosta and Carpenter (1985), in a study of the states of Illinois, Kansas, Nebraska, and Wisconsin, found nearly identical declines, generally in the 40 to 50 percent range. Clearly, there has been a substantial reduction in the percentage of female coaches over the past ten years at both intercollegiate and interscholastic levels.

Why has a reduction in the number of female coaches come about? Hart, Hasbrook, and Mathes (1986) suggest that at least three explanations have credibility: (a) role conflict, (b) incomplete occupational socialization, and (c) outright sex discrimination. *Role conflict* is an attractive explanation because balancing the multiple demands of teacher, coach, wife, and mother represents quite a challenge. However, research by Locke and Massengale (1978) and Massengale (1980, 1981a, 1981b) suggests that role conflict is not the exclusive domain of female coaches; in fact, male coaches find the varying demands upon their time and energy to be quite conflicting and stressful.

Burlingame (1972) has suggested that failure in various occupations may be a function of *incomplete occupational socialization.* In cases where this model may be true, the

In recent years the numbers of female athletes at all levels have increased. Somewhat paradoxically, the percentage of women in coaching positions has declined. University of Texas track and field coach Terry Crawford is currently one of a dwindling number of female coaches at the intercollegiate level.

involved individuals simply have not acquired the knowledge, skills, and values to be successful at their jobs. The lack of expectancy of becoming a coach, the dearth of good female role models for coaching, and a shortage of top competitive experience would all contribute to the failure of female coaches to acquire the knowledge, skills, and values so fundamental to success. Though appealing intellectually, virtually no research has been done to support or refute this model.

The third possible explanation, *sex discrimination*, is also an attractive one, but little again has been done to substantiate or refute such a position. Mathes (1982) reported that female coaches feel restricted to minor sports, believe their mobility to be limited in terms of becoming head coaches or athletic directors, and generally see coaching as a limited source of job opportunity. Mathes also reported other areas in which inequities are seen, particularly in pay, general support, and facilities.

In an attempt to expand on this tripartite framework, Hart et al. (1986) asked 256 present and 105 former interscholastic coaches in Wisconsin to respond to a forty-five-item questionnaire designed to ascertain why women enter and leave coaching. Based on their data, Hart and her associates cited *value orientations toward coaching* as part of the explanation. Present coaches entered coaching primarily for the sporting and competitive experience. They reported they would leave the profession when their performances were no longer acceptable. Former coaches, on the other hand, entered coaching because they had been asked to do so, and because they wanted to work with advanced, more motivated students. These same coaches left the profession due to time and role conflicts. Although the Hart et al. research raises more questions than it answers, it does suggest that the decline in female coaches is real and must be dealt with constructively in the future if women are to take their rightful place in the coaching profession.

A final point concerns male and female coaches and how they are perceived by athletes. Parkhouse and Williams (1986), in a study of eighty male and eighty female interscholastic basketball players in California, found a substantial sex bias favoring male coaches. Though this discovery of possible sex bias is somewhat at variance with earlier research (Cottle, 1982; Rikki and Cottle, 1984; Weinberg, Reveles, and Jackson, 1984), it may suggest that the decline in the number of female coaches is partially due to a "male is better" bias in evaluating coaching ability.

THE BLACK COACH

Black coaches are rare. This is particularly true in the collegiate ranks. Nowhere is the lack of black coaches more pronounced than in football at the Division I level. Latimer and Mathes (1985) studied the racial makeup of forty-seven Division I colleges and found only eighty black coaches at work (one head, seventy-nine assistants). Fifty-three (66 percent) of the black coaches responded to their questionnaires. Results indicated that the social and educational background of black coaches were similar to that of white coaches, but black coaches were overrepresented at the peripheral positions. Most of these coaches also played peripheral positions when they were participants.

According to one study ("Black Head Coaches," 1982), there were only thirty black head coaches in all major sports at predominantly white universities. Yetman, Beghorn, and Thomas (1980) indicated that slightly over 5 percent of the head coaches in Division I college basketball were black. In 1987, of 1,102 men's and women's programs in the top three divisions of intercollegiate competition, only 4.2 percent had blacks for head coaches in football, basketball, baseball, and track ("Black Hiring," 1987). No head coaches are found in the National Football League (NFL), one is employed in major league baseball, and only a smattering are heading teams in the National Basketball Association (NBA). Clearly, black coaches are in short supply at the intercollegiate and professional levels in the so-called major sports.

In view of these facts, a call for more black coaches at the top levels of athletic competition seems appropriate. Accordingly, it would seem appropriate to expend more energy in behalf of the identification and recruitment of black coaches.

COMMUNICATION AND COACHING

In all likelihood, the coach who communicates best is most often the winner in athletic contests. All coaches should become acquainted with the best ways of reaching their athletes. Traditional theory in the psychology of communication indicates that there are *four elements in the communication process:* the source, the message, the channel, and the receiver. The *source* is the person originating the communication, the coach in this case. The effectiveness of the coach will depend on such factors as credibility with his or her players, perceived competence, personal and psychological attractiveness, status, and power. The *message* pertains to the meaning being conveyed and may involve shrugs, facial expressions, vocal inflections, and the use of sarcasm or sincerity. The *channel* refers to the method used, either verbal or nonverbal. The *receiver* obviously is the target for whom the message is intended, and such variables as intelligence, motivation, and personality will dictate how much and what is perceived. A pictorial representation of the interaction of these four

components of communication can be seen in figure 12.3.

Figure 12.3 Interaction of Four Components of Communication

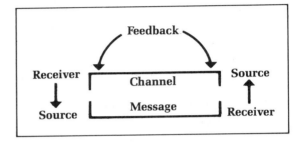

Mehrabian (1971) has indicated that message transmission is only slightly weighted by what is actually said; he says that any message is *7 percent verbal, 38 percent vocal emphasis,* and *55 percent facial expression.* Coaches should be aware that a lot of what they transmit to their players is nonverbal. Such things as *kinesics* (body language), *proxemics* (social distance or territoriality), and *paralanguage* (inflection or tone) become significant determinants of what is communicated. With regard to *kinesics,* visual gaze, posture, facial gestures, and hand movements are involved; in *proxemics,* personal space issues are paramount; in *paralanguage,* slow speech, fast speech, high pitch, sarcasm, and variable use of phrases are manipulated for desired effect. The effective coach motivates and educates through verbalizations, but is also aware of the strategic use of the various elements of kinesics, proxemics, and paralanguage.

THE COACH AND THE SPORT PSYCHOLOGIST

The role of the sport psychologist in assisting coaches is a highly ambiguous one. Traditionally, coaches have been skeptical of psychology in general. Others who have had contact with well-intentioned sport psychologists who were not able to produce or with outright charlatans using the title have added fuel to the anti-psychologist fire. However, there are signs that coaches are becoming increasingly aware of the role of psychological factors in physical performance and are also admitting that they do not have all the answers in this area. At the same time, sport psychologists have increasingly become attuned to their own assets and liabilities, and are offering their services to coaches and athletic teams in areas in which they can truly produce. Too, sport psychologists are increasingly cognizant of the need for extreme diplomacy in dealing with coaches and athletes. All of these attitudinal improvements should result in much more cooperation in the future between coaches and sport psychologists.

Rushall, Morris, Glencross, and Smith (1979) indicate that coaches are becoming increas-ingly aware of the advantages of working with a sport psychologist. One reason Rushall and his associates cite for this growing use of sport psychological services is that some problems are beyond the coach's competence and require the attention of a professional. Secondly, because of the many demands made on their time, coaches may not always recognize problems or, if alert to them, may not institute measures to resolve them. Hence, the need for specialized assistance.

A necessary first step in the process of providing sport psychology services is *establishing credibility* with coaches. Lanning (1980), Rushall et al. (1979), and Suinn (1986) offer a number of suggestions for effectiveness in the sport environment. The guidelines that follow are a synthesis of their various suggestions:

1. The interest of the sport psychologist in the problems of sport should be clearly evident.

HIGHLIGHT 12.4
In a Slump? Call a Slumpbuster!

Jim Taylor has elaborated on a procedure he has developed to help players and coaches to avoid or break out of performance decrements, or "slumps," in sports. Certainly, slumps are well-known in the world of sports, and Taylor has suggested that what is needed in these cases is a slumpbuster. To Taylor (1988, p. 40), a slump is "an unexplained decline in performance from a previously determined baseline level of a particular athlete that extends longer than would be expected from normal noncyclic variations in performance in a given sport." Once slumps are defined and causal factors identified, slumpbusting may then proceed. One important step is to take time out, time away from the aversive emotional properties associated with the slump. Another procedure is to engage in goal-setting strategies such as those discussed in this chapter. It may also be useful to engage in individual or group counseling as a part of slumpbusting. In brief, Taylor has generated a framework for understanding athletic slumps; systematic application and evaluation of slumpbusting would seem to be the next step in preventing or alleviating the effects of the performance decrements in sport known as slumps.

SOURCE: "Slumpbusting: A Systematic Analysis of Slumps in Sports" by J. Taylor, 1988, *Sport Psychologist, 2*, 39–48.

2. The ability to objectively evaluate sport situations is critical to success.

3. An awareness is needed that, as the level of performance escalates, the problems of the coach and the sport psychologist concurrently increase.

4. The sport psychologist, as an outsider to athletes and coaches, must prove his or her skills to them.

5. The sport psychologist can have a substantial impact on assistant coaches, athletes, and others related to a team; diplomacy in dealing with these various persons is necessary.

6. A realization that each player and team is unique should guide the efforts of the sport psychologist.

7. Maximization of strengths and recognition of limitations is essential to effective functioning.

8. The role of the sport psychologist is always as psychologist and not as coach.

9. The sport psychologist serves as consultant not as expert; he or she is a collaborator with others involved with the team or individual athlete.

10. The ability to listen is one of the most valuable tools of the sport psychologist.

If these guidelines are adhered to in a consistent fashion, the sport psychologist should increasingly become a contributing member in the attainment of athletic excellence. The future can be bright for the sport psychologist working hand in hand with coaches in an effort to make sport even more fun through increased standards of performance.

SUMMARY

1. With so much premium placed at all levels on winning, coaching has become a pressure-laden profession. The many pluses are offset by occupational hazards. Second-guessing by everyone who feels he or she is an expert on sport, the endless work schedule, the pressures of constant evaluation, the lack of job security, the strain on family life, and the fact that coaching is a terminal career are all drawbacks to entering and staying in the coaching business.

2. The qualities of the good coach include being knowledgeable about the sport, being a student of the game, having the ability to motivate athletes, being aware of individual differences in athletes, being a good listener, exercising discipline when necessary, leading by example, and being a goal setter.

3. Roles of the coach include getting along with management; being committed to the athletes; having a good working relationship with assistant coaches and being an advocate in their behalf; establishing contact with the various media; dealing with parents, fans, and boosters; and meeting a broad variety of other demands necessary to success in coaching. The role of the coach in goal setting is a most important one.

4. Burnout is a common problem in many vocations, and the coaching profession is not exempt from the phenomenon.

5. Taking the job too seriously, having to deal with problem parents and problem athletes, loss of the thrill of coaching, feeling the constant pressure always to win, and being underpaid and underappreciated are some of the more prominent causes of coaching burnout.

6. The cognitive-affective model of athletic burnout proposed by Smith represents an attempt to add sophistication to the definition and assessment of the phenomenon.

7. Athletes and the immediate family will be most seriously affected by the burnout of a coach, and the two interact to exacerbate the problem.

8. Living a broadly based, rewarding life outside of work is an important preventive

measure related to coaching burnout. Being aware that burnout can happen to anyone regardless of level of coaching or sex of the coach, keeping one's physical health at an optimum level, having friends with whom one can release tension, and maintaining a sense of humor are other important preventive measures.

9. Coaches have been widely assumed to be authoritarian, dogmatic, and Machiavellian. Research conducted in the 1970s and 1980s has not supported this widely accepted contention. Coaches appear to be generally conservative but probably are no more so than adults of similar age and education in other vocations.

10. Many of the more than 4 million youth coaches in the United States are poorly qualified for the duties of coaching youth, but several programs have been created to improve the situation.

11. The Coaching Behavior Assessment System (CBAS) has been developed with the ultimate goal of upgrading youth coaching. An outgrowth of the CBAS research with Little League coaches and players in Seattle, Washington, was Coach Effectiveness Training (CET). CET was tried with a sample of coaches matched with a group of coaches who were not given CET. Results indicated that the trained coaches used more reinforcement and less punishment when coaching, were liked better by their players, and were seen as better teachers. Self-esteem gains were noted in their players, though no win–loss advantage occurred as a result of training.

12. Other approaches to improving youth coaching include the National Youth Sport Coaches Association (NYSCA) in Florida, Rainer Martens' American Coaching Effectiveness Program (ACEP), the Youth Sport Institute (YSI) program at Michigan State, and the Canadian National Certification Program (CNCP), a program with five levels ranging from instructing novices to coaching Canada's elite youth.

13. Two million girls participated in interscholastic sports in 1983–1984, and 150,000 women competed at the intercollegiate level. Although female sport participation is on a substantial upswing, female coaches are not faring nearly so well. Their numbers decreased at a rate as high as 40 to 50 percent in many states in a recent ten-year period. Role conflict, incomplete occupational socialization, and discrimination have all been cited as possible explanations for this decline in the number of women in coaching.

14. Black coaches at the highest levels of the sport of football are virtually nonexistent, particularly as head coaches. The picture is somewhat brighter in basketball, though baseball also lags behind. Black coaches, like black athletes, are overrepresented at the peripheral and underrepresented at the central positions.

15. Communication in and out of coaching involves four components: the source, the message, the channel, and the receiver. The source originates the communication, the message refers to meaning being conveyed by a communication, the channel refers to verbal or nonverbal mechanisms in communication, and the receiver is the target of the communication. By becoming more familiar with the nuances of communication theory, coaches could substantially improve their ability to relate to players and others.

16. Sport psychologists can be of considerable service in supplementing the efforts of a coach. Areas of expertise in the repertory of a skilled psychologist are found to varying degrees in coaching, and coaches could profit from taking advantage of these capabilities. The insightful sport psychologist should make his or her interest in sport very clear, should be capable of

objective evaluation of problems to be solved, should be aware of psychological demands at all levels of competition, should be aware that he or she is an outsider to coaches and athletes and must exert measures to change this perception, should be aware that his or her impact extends beyond the head coach to the assistants, should appreciate the unique aspects and commonalities among athletes and coaches, should maximize strengths and recognize limitations, should always be cognizant of the fact that his or her role is as psychologist, not as coach, should be a collaborator, not an expert, and should be a constantly tuned-in listener.

SUGGESTED READINGS

Bruns, B., & Tutko, T. A. (1986) Dealing with the emotions of childhood sports. In R. E. Lapchick, (Ed.), *Fractured focus: Sport as a reflection of society* (pp. 207–219). Lexington, MA: D. C. Heath.

The authors elaborate on some of the problems facing youth athletes and offer suggestions on how parents can best deal with them. The problem of being a perennial substitute or bench-warmer is addressed, as are peer group troubles, the fear of injury, and the child who wants to stop participating in sport. The numerous suggestions for dealing with these problem areas make this a very useful and practical article for parents of youth sport participants.

Gould, D. (1986) Goal setting for peak performance. In J. M. Williams (Ed.), *Applied sport psychology: Personal growth to peak performance* (pp. 133–148). Palo Alto, CA: Mayfield.

In addition to providing an excellent summary of goal setting research and theory, Gould discusses a goal setting system for coaches and some common problems in setting goals. Among the latter are setting too many goals too soon, failing to be cognizant of individual differences, setting goals that are too general, failing to modify unrealistic or outdated goals, failing to set performance goals, and failing to create an environment conducive to goal attainment.

Horn, T. S. (1986) The self-fulfilling prophecy theory: When coaches' expectations become reality. In J. M. Williams (Ed.), *Applied sport psychology: Personal growth to peak performance* (pp. 59–73). Palo Alto, CA: Mayfield.

Horn illustrates how Rosenthal and Jacobson's 1968 research study on self-fulfilling prophecy can be turned to the advantage of the youth coach. Emphasis is placed on how the expectations set at the beginning of a sport season by youth coaches can become reality. Additionally, behavioral recommendations that will assist coaches in the expectancy-performance process are delineated.

Mechikoff, R. A., & Kozar, B. (Eds.). (1983) *Sport psychology: The coach's perspective.* Springfield, IL: Charles C. Thomas.

Twenty-two prominent amateur and professional coaches and athletic administrators from seven different sports have contributed articles on how their use of psychological tactics relates to their particular coaching philosophies. The purpose of the volume overall is not to enhance theory or research but to give a view of the practice of psychology within the sporting domain.

Smoll, F. L. (1986) Coach-parent relationships: Enhancing the quality of the athlete's sport experience. In J. M. Williams (Ed.), *Applied sport psychology: Personal growth to peak performance* (pp. 47–58). Palo Alto, CA: Mayfield.

Smoll attempts to outline the objectives of youth sport, the role and responsibilities of parents in the process, and the relationship of the coach to parents and young sport participants. Coaches are offered suggestions for handling problem parents, including those who are disinterested, overcritical, screamers, overprotective, or prone to try to assume the prerogatives of the coach. It is shown how they can facilitate understanding through coach–parent meetings. This reading, though brief, provides many useful tips for youth coaches.

REFERENCES

Acosta, R., & Carpenter, L. (1985) Women in athletics: A status report. *Journal of Physical Education, Recreation and Dance, 56*(7), 30–34.

Allen, K. (1987) Coaches too close to go head-to-head too often. *USA Today,* March 20, p. 4C.

Basketball coaches shift jobs at a record pace: 123 in top division have moved in 2 years. (1986) *Chronicles of Higher Education, 33*(13), 27.

Black head coaches: Taking charge on major campuses. (1982) *Ebony,* May, pp. 57–62.

Black hiring issue subject to scrutiny. (1987) *USA Today,* Sept. 28, p. 2C.

Brewington, P., & White, C. (1988) Women fight to keep the door from closing. *USA Today,* Feb. 4, p. 1C.

Burlingame, M. (1972) Socialization constructs and the teaching of teachers. *Quest, 18* (Winter), 40–56.

Caccese, T., & Mayerberg, C. (1984) Gender differences in perceived burnout of college coaches, *Journal of Sport Psychology, 6,* 279–288.

Changing of the guard. (1987) *USA Today,* Jan. 22, p. 7C.

Christie, R., & Geis, F. (1970) *Studies in Machiavellianism.* New York: Academic Press.

Cottle, S. (1982) Sex bias and professional status level effects in the evaluations of coaching ability. Unpublished master's thesis, California State University, Fullerton.

Cox, R. H. (1985). *Sport psychology: Concepts and applications.* Dubuque, IA: Wm. C. Brown.

Fuoss, D., & Troppmann, R. (1981) *Effective coaching: A psychological approach.* New York: Wiley.

Gallon, A. (1980). *Coaching: Ideas and ideals.* Boston: Houghton-Mifflin.

Gazes, P., Sovell, B., & Dellastatious, J. (1969) Continuous radioelectrocardiographic monitoring of football and basketball coaches during games. *American Heart Journal, 78,* 509–512.

Hart, B., Hasbrook, C., & Mathes, S. (1986) An examination of the reduction in the number of female interscholastic coaches. *Research Quarterly for Exercise and Sport, 57,* 68–77.

Hart, B., & Mathes, S. (1982) Women coaches— Where are they? Paper presented at 1982 Wisconsin Association for Health, Physical Education and Recreation, Glendale, Wisconsin.

Holmen, M., & Parkhouse, B. (1981) Trends in the selection of coaches for female athletes: A demographic inquiry. *Research Quarterly for Exercise and Sport, 52,* 9–18.

Jacoby, F. (1978) Where is your next job? *Summer Manual,* American Football Coaches Association, 73–75.

Kirkpatrick, C. (1988) Freshman at work. *Sports Illustrated,* Feb. 1, pp. 28–31.

Lanning, W. (1980) Applied psychology in major college athletics. In R. M. Suinn (Ed.), *Psychology in sports: Methods and applications* (pp. 362–367). Minneapolis, MN: Burgess.

Latimer, S., & Mathes, S. (1985) Black college football coaches' social, educational, athletic, and career pattern characteristics. *Journal of Sport Behavior, 8,* 149–162.

LeUnes, A. (1986) A sport psychologist and a football legend discuss the psychology of coaching: Coleman Griffith and Knute Rockne. *Journal of Applied Research in Coaching and Athletics, 1,* 127–134.

LeUnes, A., & Nation, J. R. (1982) Saturday's heroes: A psychological portrait of college football players. *Journal of Sport Behavior, 5,* 139–149.

Locke, E., & Latham, G. (1985) The application of goal setting to sports. *Journal of Sport Psychology, 7,* 205–222.

Locke, L., & Massengale, J. (1978) Role conflict in teacher/coaches. *Research Quarterly, 49,* 162–174.

Lombardo, B. F. (1986) The behavior of youth sport coaches: Crisis on the bench. In R. E. Lapchick (Ed.), *Fractured focus: Sport as a reflection of society* (pp. 199–205). Lexington, MA: D.C. Heath.

Massengale, J. (1980) Role conflict and the occupational milieu of the teacher/coach: Some real working world perspectives. In *National Association for Physical Education in Higher Education Proceedings, II,* 47–52.

Massengale, J. (1981a) Researching role conflict. *Journal of Physical Education, Recreation and Dance, 52*(9), 23.

Massengale, J. (1981b) Role conflict and the teacher/ coach: Some occupational causes and considerations for the sport sociologist. In S. Greendorfer and A. Yiannakis (Eds.), *Sociology of sport: Diverse perspectives* (pp. 149–157). West Point, NY: Leisure Press.

Mathes, S. (1982) Women coaches: Endangered species? Paper presented at the American Alliance for Health, Physical Education, Recreation and Dance National Convention, Houston, Texas.

McCafferty, W., Gliner, J., & Horvath, S. (1978) The stress of coaching. *Physician and Sportsmedicine, 6*(2), 67–71.

Mehrabian, A. (1971) *Silent messages.* Belmont, CA: Wadsworth.

Michener, J. A. (1976) *Sports in America.* New York: Fawcett Crest.

Murphy, P. (1985) Youth sport coaches: Using hunches to fill a blank page. *Physician and Sportsmedicine, 13*(4), 136–142.

Ogilvie, B. C., & Tutko, T. A. (1966) *Problem athletes and how to handle them.* London: Pelham Books.

Pate, R., Rotella, R., & McClenaghan, B. (1984) *Scientific foundations of coaching.* Philadelphia, PA: Saunders.

Parkhouse, B. L., & Williams, J. M. (1986) Differential effects of sex and status on evaluation of coaching ability. *Research Quarterly for Exercise and Sport, 57,* 53–59.

Perry, J. (1986) Five-on-one: Should men coach women's sports? *Journal of Physical Education, Recreation and Dance, 57*(3), 62–63.

Rikki, R., & Cottle, S. (1984) Sex bias in evaluation of coaching ability and physical performance research. *Perspectives, 6,* 32–41.

Robinson, J., & Shaver, P. (1973) *Measures of social psychological attitudes.* Ann Arbor, MI: Institute for Social Research.

Roscoe, J. (1965) The construction and applications of the Polyphasic Values Inventory. Unpublished doctoral dissertation, Colorado State College.

Rushall, B., Morris, H., Glencross, D., and Smith, R. (1979) Coaches and sport psychology. *International Journal of Sport Psychology, 10,* 164–167.

Sabock, R. (1979) *The coach.* Philadelphia, PA: Saunders.

Sabock, R., & Jones, D. (1978) The coaching profession: Its effects on the coaches' family. *Athletic Journal, 58*(9), 42, 44–45, 62.

Sage, G. H. (1972a) Machiavellianism among college and high school coaches. *Seventy-fifth Proceedings of the National College Physical Education Association for Men,* pp. 45–60.

Sage, G. H. (1972b) Value orientations of American college coaches compared to male college students and businessmen. *Seventy-fifth Proceedings of the National College Physical Education Association for Men,* pp. 174–186.

Schafer, S. (1984) *Sports needs you. A working model for the equity professional.* Denver, CO: Colorado Department of Education.

Scott, J. (1971) *The athletic revolution.* New York: Macmillan.

Sisley, B., & Capel, S. (1986) High school coaching: Filled with gender differences. *Journal of Physical Education, Recreation and Dance, 57*(3), 39–43.

Sloan, N. (1977) Opinions out loud. *NCAA News, 14*(7), 2.

Smith, R. E. (1986) Toward a cognitive–affective model of athletic burnout. *Journal of Sport Psychology, 8,* 36–50.

Smith, R. E., Smoll, F. L., & Hunt, E. (1977) A system for the behavioral assessment of athletic coaches. *Research Quarterly, 48,* 401–407.

Smoll, F. L., & Smith, R. E. (1984) Leadership research in youth sports. In J. M. Silva and R. S. Weinberg (Eds.), *Psychological foundations of sport* (pp. 371–386). Champaign, IL: Human Kinetics.

Suinn, R. M. (1986) Consultation in sport psychology. *Consulting Psychology Bulletin, 38*(1), 17–20.

True, S. (1983) *Data on the percentage of girls' high school athletic teams coached by women.* Kansas City, MO: National Federation of State High School Associations.

Tutko, T. A., & Richards, J. W. (1971) *Psychology of coaching.* Boston, MA: Allyn and Bacon.

Walsh, J., & Carron, A. V. (1977) Attributes of volunteer coaches. Paper presented at the annual meeting of the Canadian Association of Sport Sciences, Winnipeg, Canada.

Weinberg, R. S., Reveles, M., & Jackson, A. (1984) Attitudes of male and female athletes toward male and female coaches. *Journal of Sport Psychology, 6,* 448–453.

Wilkinson, C. (1952) *Oklahoma Split T football.* New York: Prentice-Hall.

Wulf, S. (1988) Another one bites the dust. *Sports Illustrated,* June 6, pp. 48–55.

Yetman, N., Beghorn, F., & Thomas, F. (1980) Racial participation and integration in intercollegiate basketball, 1958-1960. Paper presented at the annual program of the North American Society for the Sociology of Sport, Denver, Colorado.

Sport and Physical Activity for All

INTRODUCTION

Thus far, the more formalized aspects of sport for men, women, and children have been the center of attention. However, quite a number of sport psychologists have devoted their time and energy to promoting an understanding of sport and fitness apart from the orthodox world of athletics. Of primary concern in this chapter will be issues of general fitness, exercise adherence, prevention or alleviation of anxiety and depression through exercise, and peak experiences related to physical activity. Of secondary interest will be discussions of an admixture of athletes, including runners, ex-athletes, and elderly citizens interested in competition and fitness.

Our collective fascination with physical fitness has led to a rush of activity that can be measured, informally at least, by a concurrent explosion of facilities dedicated to fitness, fitness equipment and paraphernalia, television shows demonstrating or extolling the virtues of fitness, and other related fitness enterprises.

The available statistics on adherence to the various exercise regimens are not particularly good. Why exercise adherence is poor and some recommendations to improve it will be discussed. The relationship of exercise adherence to cardiac rehabilitation will come under scrutiny, largely as a product of the concern expressed at all levels within the health professions over coronary heart disease, cardiovascular fitness, and cardiac rehabilitation.

The relationship of exercise and fitness to mood states constitutes a third area of considerable fascination to psychologists, including those with an interest in sport and fitness. There are many advocates of the use of fitness activities for the prevention or alleviation of anxiety and depression.

Finally, the psychological aspects of participation by various populations of fitness seekers will be elaborated on. These selected populations include runners and senior participants. The runners who will be scrutinized are recreational joggers, marathon runners, and ultramarathoners. Much interest recently has been generated in the exercise habits of senior citizens; a discussion of their involvement in sport and fitness is warranted.

PHYSICAL FITNESS

We are experiencing a fitness boom in North America. Attesting, at least partially, to the fascination with fitness are statistics from a national information clearinghouse in New York City cited by Legwold (1985). Estimates from Legwold's source point to 1983 expenditures on the part of exercise and fitness enthusiasts of approximately $8 billion on activewear, $1 billion for exercise equipment, yet another $1 billion on athletic footwear, and $50 million on books concerned with exercise and diet. Additionally, corporate fitness centers and health clubs spent $5 billion on various programs and paraphernalia to support their operations.

Above and beyond the money that has been spent on fitness enterprises, physical involvement on the part of people interested in exercise and fitness appears to be at an all-time high. Silva and Weinberg (1984), drawing on statistics from the National Running and Fitness Association in 1981, found a 50 percent increase in that organization's membership from 1980 to 1981, with the 1981 roster showing some 30 million members. Dishman (1984) cites combined data from a National Center for Health Statistics survey and the Harris Poll that places the number of exercisers in this country at 50 to 60 million. Legwold (1985) indicates that there were upward of 85 million exercisers in this country as of 1983, a 14 percent increase in numbers over the previous year.

"*And what do you do to maintain your cardiovascular fitness, Miss Holt?*"

The current rage for fitness in the United States often seems to have a stronger verbal than behavioral component.

Before we become too excited about these data related to money expended and numbers of exercisers, some word of caution is in order. Just because a person buys a pair of running shoes does not mean that running will take place. A waitress I know is the proud owner of expensive running shoes because they are comfortable to work in; a friend has an equally expensive pair of shoes that he bought because they provide maximum comfort when he drives his automobile. And how many unused exercise bicycles must there be in this country, equipment that was purchased with the best of intentions in mind? Related to the present discussion are data proffered by Dishman (1984) and Stephens (1985). Dishman suggests that only one-third of exercisers actually work out sufficiently to realize the benefits of their fitness regimen; less optimistically, Stephens places this figure at 20 percent. Clearly, we have a fascination with fitness in this country, but one that seems to have a

stronger verbal than behavioral component. We shall look at this discrepancy between what is said and what is done later in this chapter.

A Definition of Physical Fitness

Physical activity, exercise, and physical fitness tend to be used interchangeably by professionals and laymen alike. However, Caspersen (1985) suggests that the three terms actually connote quite different things and should be treated accordingly. To Caspersen, physical activity refers to any bodily movement produced by the skeletal muscles that results in an expenditure of energy. Physical activity may be expended as a function of exercise, but the housewife chasing after three young children and the meter reader attempting to elude a dog are also expending energy. Hence, physical activity is not at all synonymous with the other two terms under present consideration. *Exercise* is a subset of physical activity characterized by planned, organized, and repetitive components aimed at improving or maintaining physical fitness. Finally, *physical fitness* refers to a set of attributes that are either health- or skill-related. The discussion in this chapter will be guided by the definitional distinctions suggested by Caspersen.

Benefits of Physical Fitness

Proponents of physical fitness are adamant in their claims about the benefits to be gained from physical activity in the sport and exercise context. Many authorities point to a host of both physical and psychological benefits.

Physical Benefits. Silva and Weinberg (1984) mention several physical benefits associated with physical fitness. They include increased blood flow to the heart, lowered blood pressure, increased lung capacity which allows for more efficient delivery of oxygenated blood to all parts of the body, and lower blood lactate levels. Several authorities (e.g., LaPorte, Dearwater, Cauley, Slemenda, and Cook, 1985; Powell, 1985; and Siscovick, 1985) add to the list by citing control of hypertension, diabetes mellitus, and osteoporosis. Finally, Williams and Long (1983) suggest that digestive and excretory functioning may be enhanced by being physically fit, and that weight control may also be a decided benefit for many who exercise regularly.

A physical fitness benefit often cited (Silva and Weinberg, 1984; Williams and Long, 1983) that does not appear to be a benefit after all is a lowered resting heart rate. Authorities such as LaPorte et al. (1985), Legwold (1985), and Rogers (1985) argue that there is little or no evidence that a low resting heart rate is, in and of itself, an indicator of superior cardiac functioning, and it probably tells us nothing more about the person than that he or she is still alive.

Psychological Benefits. Among the positive psychological gains associated with physical fitness, a number of investigators point to anxiety- or stress-reduction (Folkins and Sime, 1981; Powell, 1985; Williams and Long, 1983), a topic we shall discuss in detail later. Also, there may well be benefits in terms of socialization, that is, meeting new people and creating new friendships and acquaintances and maintaining old ones. How many of us who exercise regularly have our exercise behavior maintained by getting to work out with a friend or several friends? And how many of us would continue our exercise regimen if our partner(s) suddenly stopped going?

Many people find physical fitness a convenient way to meet others. How many of us who exercise regularly maintain our routine by working out with a group of friends?

HIGHLIGHT 13.1
Rest and Meditation:
Good as Exercise?

Many sport (and health) psychologists are of the opinion that exercise causes a reduction in tension. Raglin and Morgan (1985) suggest that the distraction or diversion associated with exercise may account for the purported anxiety reduction. In an earlier test of this hypothesis, Bahrke and Morgan (1978) randomly assigned seventy-five males to three conditions, one involving *aerobic exercise,* another *meditation,* and a third *quiet rest.* Predictions were that the aerobic exercise and meditation conditions would result in reduced state anxiety as measured by the State-Trait Anxiety Inventory (STAI); in fact, both treatments resulted in reduced anxiety. Surprisingly, however, the quiet rest group experienced similar reductions in state anxiety.

Morgan and his associates point out that their findings may suggest a *quantitative* difference in state anxiety that in no way addresses the *qualitative* issues associated with exercise. A number of physiological changes, such as lowered blood pressure, may not occur as a result of quiet rest or meditation. Also, it is likely that the desirable effects associated with exercise may be much more long lasting than those related to meditation or rest.

SOURCES: "Anxiety Reduction Following Exercise and Meditation" by M. S. Bahrke and W. P. Morgan, 1978, *Cognitive Therapy and Research, 2,* 323–333; "Influence of Vigorous Exercise on Mood State" by J. Raglin and W. P. Morgan, 1985, *Behavior Therapist, 8,* 179–183.

A third psychological plus to fitness, suggested by Legwold (1985, p. 136), is "ageless confidence and cool control." Legwold also suggests a fourth fitness benefit in terms of one's sex life, a notion also mentioned by Williams and Long (1983). A final psychological benefit for the more serious fitness buff is the thrill of competition. All one has to do to see this quality in action is to line up any Saturday in the nearest 10-kilometer or marathon run. One of the virtues of such events is that they serve as a showcase for most of the other physical and psychological benefits of exercise and fitness. Unfortunately, physical activity can also serve as a forum for inappropriate proving behavior. This issue we shall attend to a bit later.

EXERCISE ADHERENCE/COMPLIANCE

One of the more interesting paradoxes associated with human behavior is the issue of exercise adherence/compliance, terms we shall use interchangeably (Brawley, 1987; Dishman, 1982). Perhaps as many as 60 million people in the United States exercise on a regular basis and most extol its many physical, psychological, and social virtues. Substantial numbers of others would like to obtain the alleged benefits of exercise but cannot stay with a program long enough to do so. This inability to stick with an exercise regimen is one of the more perplexing problems facing professionals in the various health-related enterprises.

Statistics from a number of adherence studies indicate that about 50 percent of the individuals who start a fitness campaign will drop out in six months or less (Dishman, 1986; Shephard, 1985). These statistics refer to individuals with no known cardiovascular problems. In individuals with a documented history of cardiovascular problems, adherence rates to postmyocardial infarction exercise prescriptions are equally poor. Sanne (1973) studied 148 post-MI patients in Sweden and found that 29 percent of the group never began prescribed exercise programming; at the end of two years, 29 percent of the original 148 patients were working out under a hospital administered exercise program (another 17 percent said they were working out at home on their own). By the four-year mark, 14 percent were still working out at the hospital and 18 percent reported exercising on their own, an overall adherence rate for four years of 32 percent. In a more recent study, Andrew, Oldridge, Parker, Cunningham, Rechnitzer, Jones, Buck, Kavanagh, Shephard, Sutton, and McDonald (1981) found an exercise noncompliance rate of over 44 percent in their longitudinal study of 728 postcoronary men in Ontario, Canada. While some of the patients in each of these studies either never started or dropped out of prescribed exercise due to valid medical contraindications, the adherence rate in MI patients appears to be less than satisfactory.

Inasmuch as adherence rates are low for both "healthy" individuals and those with a history of heart problems, it seems worthwhile at this point to take a look at predictors of exercise adherence, why people fail to comply with exercise programs, and some ways that exercise adherence might be improved.

Predictors of Exercise Adherence/Compliance

There are a number of physical, psychological, and social predictors of exercise adherence. Perhaps the most salient of these predictors is *physical proximity to the exercise area*, which, as Roth (1974) points out, underscores the importance of practical considerations in exercise adherence. Studies in which geographical proximity to the exercise area has been cited include Teraslinna, Partanen, Koskela, Partanen, and Oja (1969) with Finnish business executives; Andrew et al. (1981) with Canadian heart patients; and Hanson (1977) with American college professors. In each of the studies,

proximity was important to the continuance of exercise; in the Teraslinna et al. study, proximity was the single biggest determinant.

Another continuous finding is that *spousal support* is important in exercise adherence. McCready and Long (1985) point to a positive though not overwhelming correlation between spousal support and continuance in exercise programs. Dishman (1984, p. 425) states that "a spouse's attitude toward a participant's involvement is a greater influence in the participant's behavior than is his or her own attitude."

It has been suggested that *exercising in small as opposed to large groups* is conducive to exercise continuance (Dishman, 1984). It seems logical that most of the reinforcement associated with exercise should be realized when groups are small and attention from instructors and peers is maximized. Shephard (1985) indicates that many people are intimidated by mixed classes, so provisions should be made in certain instances to have male and female groupings for exercise.

Another mild indicator of exercise adherence is apparently *socioeconomic status*. That exercise may not be reaching an optimal number of people is a challenge issued by Shephard (1985), who states that greater targeting of blue-collar workers and people at the lower end of the white-collar work strata should be carried out by the exercise leadership.

At a psychological level, preliminary and thus tentative research data has implicated an *internal locus of control* as a correlate of exercise adherence. Levenson (1981) has intimated that subjects engaged in health-related activities tend to be more internal on her IPC scale (discussed at several other points in this book), a finding corroborated by McCready and Long (1985) and Noland (1981).

Why People Drop Out of Exercise Programs

A number of negative predictors of exercise adherence have been identified. From the discussion of positive predictors, it seems abundantly clear that poor accessibility to the exercise area, a lack of spousal support, and exercising in large and potentially impersonal groups have considerable impact on whether one complies with an exercise regimen. Beyond these problems, *time* appears to be a significant determinant of exercise compliance (Andrew et al., 1981; Dishman, 1986; Gettman, Pollock, and Ward, 1983; Oldridge, 1982; Shephard, 1985). Combining time and accessibility probably constitutes a grouping that accounts for much of the variance in exercise compliance. The extent to which the time-accessibility interaction is true, however, remains to be determined. Sime, Whipple, Stamler, and Berkson (1978) found that dropouts in their study perceived time and accessibility to be problems even though they actually lived closer to their workout environment than did the exercise compliers with whom they were compared!

Another problem in exercise adherence concerns *smoking*. Several authorities have noted the tendency of smokers to drop out of exercise programs (e.g., Massie and Shephard, 1971) and, at the other extreme, the equal tendency on the part of nonsmokers to comply (McCready and Long, 1985).

A third negative predictor concerns *poor choice of exercise*. Persons beginning an exercise program should weigh the merits of various forms of exercise and choose one that is within their physical capabilities and their general interests. A poorly chosen exercise program is destined to fail. A listing of eight of the more popular forms of exercise and their advantages and disadvantages can be seen in table 13.1.

Related to choice of exercise is the issue of *injury*. All too often, the beginning exerciser is looking for a "quick fix" and this misplaced emphasis often results in an injury that, in turn, dampens enthusiasm for further exercise. Poor choice of type of exercise, a misguided emphasis on too much exercise too soon, and poor equipment selection all interact to produce the injury effect. The beginning exerciser should choose appropriate exercise, opt for a proper workout environment (to include proper instruction), and select suitable equipment.

Two psychological constructs that, like the locus of control dimension of internality mentioned earlier, have been positively though weakly linked to the exercise adherence literature are the *Type A personality* and *extraversion*. The Type A personality is associated with an aggressive, hard-driving, hard-working, time-pressured, and highly competitive individual who is prone, among other things, to being at high risk for coronary heart disease (Friedman and Rosenman, 1974). According to research reported by Oldridge, Wicks, Hanley, Sutton, and Jones (1978), Type A individuals appear to have relatively poor exercise compliance rates. Dishman (1984) interprets the results reported by Oldridge and his colleagues as reflective of either a lack of patience with the slow pace so characteristic of the typical fitness program or as a result of setting other competing goals that eventually take priority over exercise because these competing activities may provide the more immediate feedback necessary to the psychological sustenance of the Type A personality.

As for *extraversion*, at least two studies have mentioned higher compliance rates for extraverted as opposed to introverted personalities (Blumenthal, Williams, Wallace, Williams, and Needles, 1982; Massie and Shephard, 1971). Inasmuch as extraverts derive much reinforcement from group interactions, exercise groups readily meet the affiliative needs of these typically outgoing people.

While the conceptions of the Type A personality and the extravert are interesting ones, they are in need of further research. Any number of other personality dimensions surely are pertinent to exercise compliance, and studies

Table 13.1 Benefits and Disadvantages of Eight Popular Forms of Physical Activity

Activity	Benefits	Disadvantages	Warnings
Jogging	Excellent conditioner for endurance, lung, and heart capacity. Builds leg strength. Equipment inexpensive, requires no special facilities.	Requires preliminary start-up program. Does nothing for flexibility or strength (except legs). Tightens muscles in back of leg and calf, shortens Achilles tendon.	Persons 30 and older should have a physical examination first. Wear good running shoes. Watch out for dogs.
Walking	Good beginning exercise, especially for people out of shape. When done briskly, maintains heart and lung capacity. No equipment or facilities needed.	Walking speed of 5 to 6 miles per hour necessary for conditioning effect on heart.	Don't expect fast results from walking only.
Swimming	Excellent conditioner for endurance. Exercises virtually all muscles in body. Especially suitable for persons recovering from hip, knee, or ankle problems. Considered best all-around exercise.	Requires a body of water.	Do not swim alone.
Tennis	Excellent for body shaping, flexibility, and agility. May develop endurance if played vigorously. Strengthens arm muscles.	Requires a court and an opponent. Equipment and accessories moderately expensive. Activity is sporadic. Only improves endurance if players run for the balls: doubles play does not develop endurance.	May cause anxiety in players who worry about their game.
Cross-country skiing	Perhaps the best sport for developing endurance. Develops arm and shoulder muscles. Injuries less common than in downhill skiing.	Requires preconditioning program to develop muscles. Requires snow and proper terrain. Moderate equipment costs.	Be prepared for cold and high altitude.
Calisthenics	Good for flexibility and muscle tone. Good warm-up for other activities. No equipment necessary.	Boring. Does not develop endurance unless done very vigorously.	
Bicycling	Develops endurance if done vigorously. Develops leg and back muscles. Can see scenery while exercising.	Only builds endurance if done vigorously. Moderate equipment cost. Will not give maximum benefit to muscles in legs, ankles, and feet unless leg is fully extended when pedal is at bottom of circle.	Use a bicycle path if possible. Watch out for cars if not possible.
Weight training	Excellent for developing muscular strength. Can enhance performance in other athletic activities, including volleyball, basketball, and golf. Can be done at home with homemade or low-cost equipment.	Does not aid flexibility or endurance. Lifting heavy weights narrows blood vessels in muscles and reduces circulation. Advanced weight lifting requires access to gymnasium.	Start light: start slowly; warm up first. May be hazardous to persons with tendency toward high blood pressure.

SOURCE: "I Was a 49-Pound Weakling" by Don Akchin, 1977, in *Insider: Ford's Continuing Series of College Newspaper Supplements* © 1977 13-30 Corporation.

should be undertaken with the goal of expanding our knowledge base about psychological constructs and fitness.

Improving Exercise Adherence/Compliance

Dishman (1984) has provided us with an intriguing behavioral approach for promoting exercise adherence, and much of the ensuing discussion will be based on his ideas. Dishman suggests that while we may have little or no control over some situational variables such as spousal support, socioeconomic class, professional or blue-collar status, and so forth, we must live within these multiple realities and work within the constraints they provide, both in and outside of the exercise environment. It follows that we should concentrate on events over which we actually have some degree of control to help us adhere to our chosen physical fitness regimen.

One of the approaches suggested by Dishman is *behavioral contracting*. In this situation, exercise specifics are spelled out with the cooperation of both the person doing the exercise and the person(s) supervising it. Once the details are worked out to the satisfaction of all parties, a behavioral contract is signed that more or less publicly binds the exerciser to the mutually determined agreement.

Lotteries represent a second behavioral technique for maximizing exercise adherence. Exercise is determined on a daily basis through a lottery system, or what might be referred to as "luck of the draw." Various exercise programs might be thrown into the lottery formula, and the person using this approach would simply work out according to what was drawn on any particular day. Here an attempt is being made in the case of the lottery to reward the exerciser on a random basis, which should relieve some of the boredom found in more ritualistic programs of exercise.

Self-monitoring and stimulus-cueing are two *goal setting techniques* that have much to recommend them. In *self-monitoring*, objective records are kept that serve as highly identifiable reinforcers for exercise. Such general things as weight loss and heart rate or blood pressure can be monitored for feedback purposes. Examples of event-specific items include mileage in jogging and resistances, repetitions, and sets in weight programs. *Stimulus-cueing* involves exercising using the same activity at the same time and place every day. There is much to be said for the adherence potential in such regimentation; exercise can then become a part of everyday activities. Thompson and Wankel (1980) have pointed out that ritualistic approaches to exercise may have their drawbacks. These authorities have found evidence counter to the general theme of the various goal-setting techniques, which points up the problems in exercise adherence at both the research and the practice levels.

Crucial to an understanding of the various behavioral approaches is the concept of reinforcement or reward. The more reinforcement that can be brought to bear on persons who are exercising, the more likely they are to repeat the desired response of exercise adherence. This relationship between reinforcement and response, of course, is at the heart of conditioning and learning, discussed in detail in chapter 3. Shephard (1985), at a very practical level, suggests that exercise rewards may be *symbolic* (badge, T-shirt), *material* (money, time off from work), or *psychological* (friendship, recognition). Regardless of how the various rewards may be structured and dispensed, they are essential in some form or fashion if the goal of exercise compliance is to be achieved.

COGNITIVE AND AFFECTIVE CONSEQUENCES OF EXERCISE

A regular program of exercise has long been maintained to have positive cognitive and affective consequences for both normal and clinical populations. The actual data bearing on this important and complex issue of fitness and its psychological benefits are less compelling. Not all research has found the purported benefits, and many of the existing studies have been plagued with a host of theoretical and methodological ills. The end result is a cloudy picture concerning the relationship between fitness and psychological well-being. (The various theoretical and methodological shortcomings and recommendations for their remediation will be discussed later in this chapter.)

In the next several pages, an attempt will be made to shed light on what we think we know about exercise and its consequences for cognitive and affective functioning. Much of what will follow is an amalgamation of excellent review articles by Folkins and Sime (1981) and Tomporowski and Ellis (1986).

Effects of Exercise on Cognitive Processes

The pioneering work of Jean Piaget (1936) on the relationship between motor development and cognitive development in children has sparked considerable research in various areas of psychology for more than fifty years. More recently within the psychology and exercise domain and in an attempt to shed light on this contentious issue, Folkins and Sime (1981) reviewed the available literature on the relationship between exercise and cognitive functioning and concluded that while success has been achieved with geriatric mental patients, the picture was much less clear with normal children and adults, where conflicting results dominate. On an even more contemporary note, Tomporowski and Ellis (1986) have reviewed several dozen studies and have generally arrived at the same conclusions as Folkins and Sime. In their extensive review, Tomporowski and Ellis categorized the available studies in one of four ways: (1) very brief, high-intensity anaerobic exercise; (2) short duration, high-intensity

anaerobic exercise; (3) short duration, moderate-intensity aerobic exercise; and (4) long duration aerobic exercise.

Very Brief, High-Intensity Anaerobic Exercise. By the very nature of the type of exercise used in anaerobic studies, the physical measures involved a variety of strength tests (e.g., hand dynamometers, weights suspended on pulleys). Most of the research was aimed at testing the inverted-U hypothesis. Results generally indicated that moderate levels of anaerobic exercise facilitate cognitive performance as measured by such things as addition problems, digit-span tests, perception of geometric figures, and paired-associate learning. High and low levels of tension, on the other hand, did not facilitate cognitive functioning.

Short Duration, High-Intensity Anaerobic Exercise. The results here are most inconclusive. Six of eleven studies surveyed showed no effects; several showed facilitation of cognitive functioning up to a ten or fifteen minutes of exercise, at which time impaired performance became dominant. One additional study showed cognitive impairment at all points. Bicycle pedaling, step-up tasks, or treadmill running were paired with discrimination or arithmetic tasks in these various studies.

Short Duration, Moderate-Intensity Aerobic Exercise. Calisthenics, step-up tasks, bicycle pedaling, treadmill running, and run-jog-walk tasks were used as exercises, and a host of cognitive tasks were employed in this group of studies. Studies in which moderate levels of exercise were used tended to report improved cognitive functioning with increases in arousal. Also, highly fit subjects performed better than less physically fit people on cognitive tasks that were administered in the moderate intensity exercise condition.

Long Duration Aerobic Exercise. Tomporowski and Ellis (1986) cite only three studies within this category. A marathon race, a five-mile march carrying a 40-pound pack, and a treadmill task to fatigue were used as long duration aerobic events, with signal detection, perceptual organization, and a free-recall memory test serving as the cognitive measures. Facilitation was found in two studies (Gliner, Matsen-Twisdale, Horvath, and Maron, 1979; Lybrand, Andrews, and Ross, 1954) and no effect was found in the third (Tomporowski, Ellis, and Stephens, 1985). Clearly, there is a dearth of research related to assessing the effects of long-duration aerobic exercise and cognitive functioning.

The inability of the various research conclusions to create a consensus concerning exercise and cognitive functioning has been brought about by a variety of problems. Little of what has been done has been tied to theory, and methodological flaws are numerous. For example, selection bias is found in many studies; that is, subjects are volunteers who are often physically fit and highly motivated prior to any interventions. These volunteers are often compared with themselves or with control groups who differ greatly in fitness, motivation, and many other attributes. Folkins and Sime (1981, p. 386) sum up the selection bias problem as follows: "Self-selected, motivated volunteers may demonstrate improvement in psychological functioning simply because they are motivated for overall self-improvement. It is therefore necessary to arrange for control groups that have time exposure equal to that of trainees, as well as equal and justified expectations for benefit."

Both Folkins and Sime and Tomporowski and Ellis enumerate proposals for improving future research in fitness and cognitive functioning. One suggestion is to pay more attention to the measurement of the physical effects brought about by exercise. An example would be the measurement of lactic acid produced by exercise (Fox, 1984). Another is the perceived exertion methodology of Borg (1973). Yet a third

measure of precision is cardiovascular functioning. A fourth improvement suggestion has to do with assessing preintervention levels of fitness. Comparing highly fit, highly motivated subjects with less fit, perhaps even unmotivated individuals undoubtedly contributes little to our understanding of the important issues at hand. Fifth, greater attention should be devoted to systematic analysis of the intensity and duration of exercise and the placement of the measures of cognitive functioning (that is, during or after exercise). Finally, the veritable smorgasbord of cognitive tests used across the variable research studies has contributed to the currently inconclusive picture of the exercise-cognition issue. In all likelihood, many dimensions of cognition have been tapped in the past, and greater selectivity in choosing future cognitive tasks might well yield more valid results.

Effects of Exercise on Mood

Affect and mood have long been used synonymously in the psychological literature, and they shall be used interchangeably in the ensuing discussion of the relationship between exercise and affective states. Of the various mood states, two that have come under considerable scrutiny in the exercise literature are anxiety and depression, and we shall confine our discussion to the relevant findings concerning each construct.

Exercise and Anxiety. One of the generally assumed outcomes of exercise is anxiety reduction, and the literature is largely supportive of this claim. Folkins and Sime (1981) cite fourteen studies dealing with exercise and affect and thirteen of them reported improvement in mood. Of the thirteen positive reports, seven dealt with anxiety and all pointed to improvement related to that particular affective dimension.

As noted earlier, one of the more popular measures of anxiety has been the *State-Trait*

HIGHLIGHT 13.2
Hypotheses Used to Account for Anxiety Reduction Associated with Exercise

Morgan (1985) and Raglin and Morgan (1985) have suggested that the anxiolytic properties of exercise may be associated with at least four factors:

1. *The Distraction Hypothesis.* This hypothesis hinges on the proposition that various exercise strategies serve to divert or distract subjects from anxiety-producing stressors. It thus serves as a psychological explanation for the anxiety-reducing properties of exercise.
2. *The Endorphin Hypothesis.* Here, the emphasis is on the release of "morphine-like" chemicals within the pituitary gland and the brain that serve to reduce the painful effects while concurrently enhancing the euphoric aspects of exercise.
3. *The Thermogenic Hypothesis.* In essence, the tension reduction associated with exercise is thought to be produced by the elevation of body temperature. Among other things, this hypothesis works in favor of the tension-reducing properties of, for example, sauna baths.
4. *The Monoamine Hypothesis.* Largely a model based on research with animals, the monoamine hypothesis asserts that anxiety reduction is brought about by exercise through its alteration of various neurotransmitter substances within the brain.

SOURCES: "Affective Beneficence of Vigorous Physical Activity" by W. P. Morgan, 1985, *Medicine and Science in Sports and Exercise, 21,* 94–99; "Influence of Vigorous Exercise on Mood State" by J. Raglin and W. P. Morgan, 1985, *Behavior Therapist, 8,* 179–183.

Anxiety Inventory (STAI) (Spielberger, Gorsuch, and Lushene; 1970), and the STAI has been used widely in the exercise and affective state research. For example, Long (1984) studied sixty-one volunteers from a selected community using the STAI, among other things. Long's subjects were administered the STAI prior to being assigned to an aerobics conditioning program involving jogging, a waiting list control group, or a stress inoculation training group that was treated for ten weeks in accordance with the system popularized by Meichenbaum (1977). A post-treatment and a three-month follow-up testing session were also used in Long's research. Results indicated that self-report statements concerning anxiety (the STAI) decreased in both the jogging and the stress inoculation training groups. These changes were still in effect for both groups at the three-month measurement. In a fifteen-month follow-up study, Long (1985) reported data from forty-five of her original sixty-one subjects, and continued reports of less anxiety were noted. Consistent with data reported earlier in this chapter, only 40 percent of the jogging treatment group were still working out at the time the fifteen-month follow-up was conducted. Generally supportive of Long's findings is the work of Berger (1987), who found decreases in state but not trait anxiety in a study of individuals trying to achieve fitness through swimming.

It thus appears that anxiety reduction can be achieved through a regular program of exercise. However, some critics point either to negative findings found elsewhere but not reported here or to research flaws in the studies reporting positive effects. Accordingly, Raglin and Morgan (1985) assert that it would be best at this time to view the relationship between exercise and anxiety reduction as correlational. Their view is that "physical activity of a vigorous nature is *associated* with improved mood state but available research does not support the commonly held view that exercise *causes* their observed alterations in mood" (p. 182). Until such time as causative links are clearly delineated, it seems appropriate to accept the Raglin and Morgan caveat as illustrative of the current state of the art related to exercise and anxiety reduction.

Exercise and Depression. Depression is a well-documented source of human psychic suffering in our society. According to data from the President's Committee on Mental Health, one of every four Americans suffers from depression at any given time (Monahan, 1986). Depression is, as might be expected, at the root of most suicides, with perhaps 80 percent or more being depression related (Monahan, 1986). Depression is characterized by withdrawal, inactivity, and feelings of hopelessness and loss of control. By acting on each of these symptoms, physical exercise has become popular as a therapeutic intervention in depression.

The use of physical exercise as part of the treatment of depression received much impetus in the late 1970s from a scientific report by Greist, Klein, Eischens, and Faris (1978) and from popular books extolling the virtues of running as a means of promoting overall mental and physical well-being (Fixx, 1977).

The popularity of running as a therapeutic intervention has been propelled to the forefront of the exercise-as-therapy literature through a number of research efforts. This is certainly not intended to suggest that other exercises might not be useful, but merely that running has received the most favorable press. Greist et al. are quick to point out that while other exercise modalities are probably quite useful, they used only running in their treatment and research programs. Bearing on this point, Brown, Rami-

rez, and Taub (1978) found decreases in depression in their study of high school and college students with wrestling, mixed exercise, and jogging. Tennis produced marginal but positive effects, while softball had no effect at all on depression scores. The greater reduction in depression in the Brown et al. study was in the subjects who engaged in a ten-week program of jogging that required the subjects to work out five times per week.

Considering the pivotal role the work of Greist and his associates has played in the exercise-as-therapy for depression movement, a brief elaboration on their work seems timely. In their study, subjects (men and women) who had been diagnosed as clinically depressed were assigned to one of three groups, a time-limited psychotherapy group (n = 9), a time-unlimited psychotherapy group (n = 7), and a running treatment group (n = 8). The time-limited psychotherapy group received ten therapy sessions emphasizing immediate change strategies; the time-unlimited group was given psychodynamic-oriented therapy; and the eight runners met with a running therapist (not a psychologist or psychiatrist). Stretching, thirty to forty-five minutes of walking and running, discussions while exercising with little emphasis on the depression itself, and further stretching characterized the intervention for the running group. According to Greist and his colleagues, six of the eight patients were essentially well at the end of three weeks, another at the end of the sixteenth week, and one neither improved nor deteriorated although her overall fitness level improved. The overall conclusion was that running was as successful as traditional psychotherapy and at a considerable saving in terms of money and time for the clients. Though the Greist et al. study is not above criticism, the work has been well-received concerning the possible utility of exercise as a means of dealing with depression. Brown (see Monahan, 1986, p. 197), in a burst of considered enthusiasm, says: "It's almost too good to be true. If you could bottle it and sell it over the counter, you'd make hundreds."

Despite the strength of the research findings and the exuberance of the various testimonials by practitioners, the depression research suffers from many of the same problems as does that in the area of anxiety. Better use of theory and more focused attention to methodological issues is clearly called for. Too, the link between exercise and depression is, as was the case in anxiety discussed earlier, more correlational than causal at this point. More research is needed to establish the supposed causal link between the two.

Considerations in Using Exercise as Therapy for Anxiety or Depression. A number of issues need to be addressed when prescribing exercise as therapy for either anxiety or depression, and a careful delineation of these concerns has been made by Buffone (1984). One issue brought up is that of proper psychological diagnosis and a corresponding *individually tailored exercise prescription.* Choice of type of exercise enters in here, as does the notion of combining running with other possible therapeutic modalities, such as stress inoculation training mentioned earlier in the Long studies (1984; 1985). A second issue to consider is the *proficiency of the exercise therapist.* This person should have mental health training as well as skill in conducting proper exercise. Too, this individual should serve as a *model* for the advantages of exercise and ideally possess expertise in the prevention and treatment of exercise-related injuries. Finally, *reinforcement of exercise behaviors* must be a concern of all involved parties. Care in this area should be exercised to insure that the exercise regimen, once introduced, becomes a positive therapeutic force and not a negative addiction for the client. The consequences of negative addiction to exercise may be such that the client ends up merely trading one problem for another.

SPECIAL FITNESS POPULATIONS

The intent of this section is to address some of the remaining important issues within sport and fitness. At times the emphasis will be more on sport than fitness; at other times, the reverse will be true. One of these special groups is made up of *runners,* individuals whose search for fitness is manifested through jogging or competitive running done outside the high school or college environment. Runners, marathoners, and ultramarathoners will be discussed within the context of the notions of positive and negative addiction. Second, there has been an explosion of interest of late in exercise, fitness, and competitive activities for *senior citizens,* and we shall survey what is going on with this increasingly numerous segment of our population.

The Runner

Whatever the explanation, running has become exceedingly popular as a means of achieving fitness. Some people approach running (and other forms of exercise) with reason, and this is referred to as a *positive addiction to exercise.* Other exercisers seem to lose sight of what exercise is all about, and the rabidity with which they pursue the elusive goal of fitness is so noticeably excessive that *negative addiction* can be readily inferred.

Positive Addiction. The popularization of running as the exercise of choice and the idea of *positive addiction* have been attributed to the eminent psychiatrist, William Glasser (1976). Glasser discusses his notion of positive addiction in a book by the same name; he suggests that running, among all possible exercises, is most likely to result in the highly prized positive addiction. To quote Glasser (p. 104):

I believe that running creates the optimal condition for positive addiction because it is our most ancient and still most effective survival mechanism. We are descended from those who ran to stay alive, and this need to run is programmed genetically into our brains. When we have gained the endurance to run long distances easily, then a good run reactivates the ancient neural program. As this occurs, we reach a state of mental preparedness that leads to a basic feeling of satisfaction that is less-critical than any other activity that we can do alone.

Though there are many who would argue with Glasser as to the origin of our propensity to run, he does make a compelling case for his point of view with regard to the positive and addictive qualities of running.

Just what is this quality known as positive addiction to running/exercise? Positive addiction is characterized, first of all, by an element of controllability; that is, the person involved controls the exercise regimen. As we shall soon see, exercise can control the person; this is called negative addiction. Beyond the control factor, the positively addicted person carefully programs exercise into his or her daily life. Careful organization of competing activities takes place so as to reduce possible sources of

In 1988, the 77th annual Bay to Breakers race, a 7.5 mile "mini-marathon" across San Francisco, drew an estimated 85,000 enthusiasts. Part foot race, part parade, Bay to Breakers attracted runners dressed as celebrities, couch potatoes, and, in at least one instance, a giant pair of tennis shoes.

interference with the exercise program. Exercise is blended in with work and family life in such a way as to add to rather than detract from those important life dimensions. As one becomes more positively addicted, feelings of control, competence, and physical and psychological well-being increase. Conversely, if the positively addicted person is forced by scheduling conflicts, illness, or injury to miss working out, there is a sense of loss, guilt, and physical and mental discomfort. One runner who responded to Glasser (1976) summed up his feelings about missing his running workouts as follows: "When I miss my workouts I feel as though I have let myself down. My personal integrity suffers a blow. Guilt feelings mount continuously until I run again. . . . I am glad, however, that I feel this way because it is the watchdog that makes sure I do my running." If all potential exercisers could arrive at such a point of positive addiction, exercise compliance would rapidly become a nonissue.

One of the first studies aimed at substantiating the positive addictive qualities of running was conducted by Carmack and Martens (1979). These researchers, among other things, administered a Commitment to Running Scale to 250 male and 65 female runners of various competence and experience levels, and support for both the validity of the scale and the positive addiction notion was demonstrated.

Perhaps the most consistent research effort related to runners of various persuasions is found in nine unrelated studies that used the *Profile of Mood States (POMS)*. A summary of these nine studies can be found in table 13.2. Several conclusions about runners can be drawn from the various studies. One is that running appears to have a facilitative effect on mood. In all studies in which runners were compared with groups of nonrunners, there were clear differences in mood state in favor of the runners. Second, the two studies in which an attempt was made to tease out the role of endogenous opiates (endorphins) were equivocal, which is representative of the overall literature on the exercise-endorphin relationship. Finally, it appears that runners of all levels of competence share somewhat equally in the mood benefits associated with their selected exercise medium. The research on this latter point, however, is scant, and any conclusions drawn at this time should be considered as tentative.

Negative Addiction. If exercise is viewed as bipolar, as suggested by Sachs (1984), noncompliance would represent one end of the continuum and addiction the other. In turn, addiction might also be viewed as bipolar, with the range running from the positive to the negative dimensions. All of us who have exercised for any length of time have been exposed to persons for whom exercise has become their master. Their behavior is so out of the ordinary that it is noticeable to all observers. They run until they drop. Their life is dominated by running. They fail to use good judgment as to their strengths and weaknesses as a runner. They run to the detriment of their health, career, family, and interpersonal relationships.

Research and speculation about the idea of negative addiction was initiated by Morgan (1979), who felt that such a state had been reached when the person believed that running was necessary in order to cope with everyday life and if withdrawal symptoms emerged when running was withdrawn.

One index of running gone awry is found in injury statistics. Diekhoff (1984), in a study of sixty-eight committed male and female runners, administered a Type A/B Scale, an Addiction to Running Scale, and a Commitment to Running Scale. He found that those who had suffered injuries while running tended to be Type A personalities, addicted to running, committed to running, ran more miles, and were more likely to run in fun runs and races than were the noninjured runners. A significant correlation was found between addiction to running and number of doctor visits and between the use of drugs or physical therapy and commitment to running. Layman and Morris (1986) studied more than one thousand runners of all levels of ability and experience and found a highly significant relationship between addiction to running and injuries. Almost 60 percent of the runners in their study

Table 13.2 Mood State Profiles of Runners

Researcher(s)	Subjects	Results
Farrell, Gates, Maksud, & Morgan (1982)	6 experienced distance runners	Mood states improved after treadmill task
Gondola & Tuckman (1982)	348 nonelite marathoners, 856 college students	Marathoners less tense, depressed, fatigued, confused, more vigorous than college sample
Gondola & Tuckman (1983)	68 marathoners, 210 10-Kers, 186 aspiring 10-Kers	10-Kers less tense, depressed than other two groups; 10-Kers less angry, fatigued than marathoners; 10-Kers more vigorous, less confused than aspiring 10-Kers
Joesting (1981)	50 sailors, 130 runners	Male runners less depressed, angry, fatigued than male sailors; female runners less fatigued than female sailors
Markoff, Ryan, & Young (1982)	11 male, 4 female marathoners	Less anger and depression on pre- and post-running POMS administration
Morgan and Pollock (1977)	World class middle and long distance runners, world class marathoners, college middle distance runners	Athletes less tense, depressed, fatigued, confused, higher vigor than norm group from POMS manual; elite and college runners not different
Porter (1985)	Average female runners	Profiles similar to those of young elite male runners
Thomas, Zebas, Bahrke, Araujo, & Etheridge (1983)	24 college distance runners, 20 jumpers and sprinters	Similar profiles for both groups; overall profile similar to elite performers in other sports
Wilson, Morley, & Bird (1980)	10 marathoners, 10 joggers, 10 nonexercisers	Both exercise groups less depressed, angry, confused, more vigorous than nonexercisers; marathoners less depressed, angry, confused, more vigorous than joggers

SOURCE: "Annotated Bibliography on the Profile of Mood States in Sport" by S. Daiss and A. LeUnes, 1986, *Journal of Applied Research in Coaching and Athletics, 1,* 148–169; Manual for the *Profile of Mood States,* by D. McNair, M. Lorr, and L. Droppleman, 1971, San Diego, CA: Educational and Industrial Testing Service.

reported running-related injuries in the preceding twelve months. Sixty percent of the injured runners considered themselves to be addicted to running. Hailey and Bailey (1982), as part of their attempt to validate the Negative Addiction Scale, found a linear relationship between years of running and negative addiction; addiction scores on their scale were significantly higher for runners who had run from one to four years than for those who had been running for less than a year.

Runner's High. Much interest has been shown among runners and sport scientists alike concerning what, for lack of a better term, has come to be known as the "runner's high." The runner's high is characterized most by an unexpected and heightened sense of well-being that may vary from runner to runner in frequency, intensity, and duration. It apparently occurs only in distance runners and will likely not be experienced by runners who log only six to ten miles per week (Weltman and Stamford, 1983).

Wagemaker and Goldstein (1980) indicate that the runner's high will occur only in individuals who run for twenty-five or thirty minutes. Sachs (1984) says that at least thirty minutes of running is necessary; in addition, he thinks that distances of six miles or more are required. There is lively argumentation as to whether many distance runners experience the phenomenon at all. Estimates of the occurrence of the runner's high range from 9 to 10 percent of all runners (Weinberg, 1980) to 77 or 78 percent (Lilliefors, 1978; Sachs, 1980). As Sachs (1984) has pointed out, a range of 9 to 78 percent indicates that we have much to learn about the mysterious phenomenon of the runner's high.

The diversity of descriptive terms used to flesh out the runner's high illustrates just how complex and elusive the phenomenon is. To Csikszentmihalyi (1975), the runner's high is described as "flow." To Henderson (1977) it is a "natural laxative" that throws off the waste in the body and mind. "Transcendence" and "euphoric sensation" are descriptive terms used

---

HIGHLIGHT 13.3
Runner's High: A Case Study

As mentioned in the preface, JRN and I visited Bruce Ogilvie for three days in 1981 at his home in Los Gatos, California. On the morning of the second day, we joined Bruce and several of his friends for a six-mile run at 5:30 A.M. The first two miles of the chosen cross-country course involved the ascent of a steep incline, most certainly what would be called a mountain in most of Texas, and the toll extracted on a sore knee left me far behind the pack. Eventually, I lost sight of the other joggers. In the process, I missed a critical turn up the side of a mountain that ultimately led back down to the starting point in Los Gatos. This error added an additional five or six miles to the overall trip. Somewhere along the way, a mixture of exhaustion, cool early morning California air, the excitement of the trip to California, the beauty of the landscape, the smell of anise, and an unscheduled tour of the various wineries along the way produced what must have been the elusive "runner's high" so often referred to by runners and researchers. Though the distance covered far exceeded anything I had covered before, the feeling at the end of the track was one of light-headed giddiness as well as disappointment and frustration because no one wanted to continue the run. Was this the "runner's high"? I suspect so, and I doubt that it will ever happen again. I'm just glad I was there to be a part of what may be, for most of us, a once-in-a-lifetime experience.

by Sachs (1980; 1984). Peoples (1983) talks in terms of "steady state stimulation." For Ravizza (1984), the runner's high is merely one example of "peak experience" associated with sport. Johnsgard (1985) draws parallels between the runner's high and the tranquil state often thought to be a part of transcendental meditation, and he uses terms like "centering state" and "existential drift" for purposes of enhancing his explanation. Agreement exists that the runner's high is a real but esoteric phenomenon that almost defies description. Problems in operationally defining the experience are a result of this verbal richness, and research in the area is thereby hampered. Nevertheless, further investigation into the runner's high is warranted in view of the fascination it has provided individuals who have been fortunate enough to have had the experience.

Marathon Runners. Tradition has it that the marathon event was named in honor of the city of Marathon, some twenty-six miles from Athens and the scene of one of the most significant battles between the Greeks and the invading Persians in the year 490 B.C. The Greeks inflicted a great defeat on the numerically superior Persian forces, and the news of the victory was carried from Marathon to Athens by a runner named Pheidippides. Pheidippides reportedly died of exhaustion after his victory announcement (Howell, 1983). Grogan (1981), in a bit of a disclaimer, suggests that the legendary runner was probably named Pheidippides, may or may not have run from Marathon to Athens, and most probably did not die after his victory announcement because he was an accomplished ultramarathoner. Well-documented accounts indicated that Pheidippides had run from Athens to Sparta and back, a distance of 200 miles, in three or four days, in search of support troops for the upcoming battle at Marathon shortly before his relatively short run from Marathon to Athens.

Arguments as to the origin of the marathon aside, it was a part of the first modern Olympics in 1896, with a field of twenty-five entrants. Only nineteen ran in 1900 and fourteen finished the event in 1904. With each successive Olympics, however, the number of runners has increased. Women participated in the marathon for the first time in the 1984 Olympics in Los Angeles.

Several studies related to personality variables have pointed to marathoners being introverted as opposed to extraverted personalities (e.g., Clitsome and Kostrubala, 1977; Gontang, Clitsome, and Kostrubala, 1977; Morgan and Costill, 1972; Silva and Hardy, 1986). Others have pointed to low anxiety levels as being characteristic (Morgan and Costill, 1972; Silva and Hardy, 1986). Still others have found superior mood profiles, primarily using the POMS (Gondola and Tuckman, 1982; Markoff, Ryan, and Young, 1982; Morgan and Pollock, 1977; Silva and Hardy, 1986; Wilson, Morley, and Bird, 1980). Although the evidence is insufficient at this time in terms of creating a marathon runner personality profile, a number of psychological benefits appear to be associated with such an undertaking, a finding that is consistent with claims made about the positive effects of running and exercise in general.

Ultramarathoners. McCutcheon and Yoakum (1983) define an ultramarathon as any race that exceeds the official marathon distance of 26 miles, 385 yards. Maron and Horvath (1978) divide ultramarathons into those that require repetitive days of running long distances and those that are continuous for distances up to 100 miles. Maron and Horvath, in a study of runners participating in the first type of ultramarathon, were interested in physiological variables only. The race in question was run in 1928, and involved running the 3,484 miles between Los Angeles and New York City. The twenty-five entrants who finished the event averaged 41 miles a day for eighty-four consecutive days; interestingly, few and only minor physiological problems were found at the end of the grueling competition. A study of the second type suggested by Maron and Horvath involved six hundred participants in a 54-mile race run annually in South Africa. Again, no physiological problems were noted in the participants.

Psychological reports of these athletes are scant. Folkins and Wieselberg-Bell (1981), in a study of entrants in what they consider to be the toughest endurance run in the United States (a 100-mile trail over the crest of the Sierra Nevada mountains and known as the Western States Endurance Run), found deviant MMPI scores on several subscales in comparisons of finishers and nonfinishers. The finishers had higher Psychopathic deviate (Pd), Depression (D), and Schizophrenia (Sc) scores. On the whole, however, Folkins and Wieselberg-Bell concluded that the ultramarathoners as a group appeared to be reasonably normal, and they interpreted the deviant MMPI patterns as being perhaps necessary for completion of basically what may be a deviant task. Another study of ultramarathoners by McCutcheon and Yoakum (1983) revealed no personality differences between their subjects and a matched group of runners who had never competed at distances over 10 miles.

Clearly little is known about the psychological makeup of these interesting athletes. Perhaps future research will be directed toward gaining an understanding of a phenomenon that may, as suggested by Folkins and Wieselberg-Bell, require a little deviance.

Exercise and Competition for Senior Citizens

A 1987 front page graphic in *USA Today* indicated that the median age of the American population was 31.7 years in 1986 and will rise to 41.6 by the year 2050. One repercussion of this "graying of America" has to do with the role of fitness and competition as means of adding to the quality of life for senior citizens. Fitness advocates and sport scientists have spent very little time studying the physical fitness and competitive needs, wishes, and talents of people forty-five years of age and older. More attention will be paid to these older citizens in the future, with the goal of improving the quality if not the quantity of life.

Myths permeate the literature concerning the effects of exercise on the aging process. In the next several pages, we shall look at what we know about exercise and competition for senior citizens.

Fitness Issues of Seniors. Veschi (1963) has quoted Rousseau, the esteemed eighteenth century French philosopher: "When a body is strong, it obeys; when it is weak, it gives orders." Perhaps this observation is nowhere more applicable than to our generally less-fit seniors. We have all seen an overweight older person who has a so-called beer belly, or who shuffles, a characteristic of older people who have suffered the inevitable shrinkage of connective tissue that so greatly limits length and resiliency of stride. One can go on and on about the effects of sedentary living; suffice it to say that many of these results of physical deterioration could have been fended off or ameliorated with a good physical activity program.

We have some measure of control over the biological dimension of the aging process. We can apparently moderate the effects of aging through diet, exercise, and prudence in everyday matters generally. Smith and Gilliam (1983) and Stamford (1984) all indicate that 50 percent of the physical decline associated with age is due to disuse rather than senescence. Satchel Paige, the legendary baseball pitcher who played major league baseball in his fifties, summed up the chronological/biological distinction (and age discrimination, also) as follows: "How old would you be if you didn't know how old you was?"

All wishes to the contrary aside, there are legitimate physiological changes associated

HIGHLIGHT 13.4
The Interplay
between Exercise
and Aging

Waneen Wyrick Spirduso of the University of Texas has carved out a most significant research niche in the area of aging and exercise. In a comprehensive survey of the available literature up to 1980, she concluded that there is, methodological shortcomings aside, indirect evidence to suggest that the decline in some aspects of brain functioning in the motoric sense may be substantially allayed by chronic exercise. Inasmuch as it is largely inexpensive, unobtrusive, and self-imposed, exercise may actually offer significant intervention in the aging process, according to Spirduso. The psychological and societal ramifications of this assertion are considerable and merit further attention.

It would appear that simple reaction time as measured by reaction to a visual stimulus is affected not so much by age as physical condition. Clifford and Spirduso (1978) looked at young runners, young racket-sports competitors, older racket-sports competitiors, older runners, young inactives, and older inactives (young was defined as twenty to thirty years of age, while older was fifty to seventy). The linear relationship between extent of physical involvement and simple reaction and movement time is graphically displayed in figure 13.1.

Figure 13.1 Age, Physical Fitness, and Reaction Time*

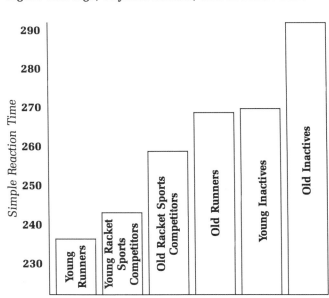

*Ordinal values are in milliseconds.

SOURCE: "Neuromuscular Speed and Consistency of Performance as a Function of Age, Physical Activity Level and Type of Physical Activity" by W. W. Spirduso and P. Clifford, 1978, *Journal of Gerontology, 33,* 26–30.

> The significant differences are most noticeable between inactive young and old people and the other four groups. This suggests that differences in simple reaction and movement time are more a function of fitness level than of age.
>
> SOURCES: "Physical Fitness, Aging, and Psychomotor Speed: A Review" by W. W. Spirduso, 1980, *Journal of Gerontology, 35*, 850–865; "Exercise and the Aging Brain" by W. W. Spirduso, 1983, *Research Quarterly for Exercise and Sport, 54*, 208–218; "Neuromuscular Speed and Consistency of Performance as a Function of Age, Physical Activity Level and Type of Physical Activity" by W. W. Spirduso and P. Clifford, 1978, *Journal of Gerontology, 33*, 26–30.

with age and we would be remiss to ignore them. There are unassailable declines in muscle mass and increases in weight and body fat due to a slowing of basal metabolism. Flexibility is affected by aging, as is bone mineral content. Cardiovascular changes involving the heart, the blood vessels, lung surface area, and elasticity are real (Smith and Zook, 1986). These must all be taken into account when drawing up an exercise prescription for an older client. At the same time, we should encourage lifelong fitness as a means for altering the course of deterioration of these various bodily systems.

At the psychological level, little is known about people who either have exercised throughout their lives or have only recently begun such a program. Physical benefits have been found in the case of people who have begun an exercise regimen after age sixty (e.g., Sager, 1984; Sidney and Shephard, 1976). The comparable data on psychological benefits of such efforts is scant. Supposition of improved well-being and higher self-esteem are easily invoked, but actual supportive data are rare. Sidney and Shephard (1976) did find a decrease in anxiety levels in a sample of men and women over sixty years of age who underwent a fourteen-week conditioning program. Much more research needs to be conducted to help substantiate the notion that there are, in fact, psychological benefits to exercise for senior citizens.

The Competitive Senior. Beyond accounts found largely in the popular press, not a great deal more is known about competitive seniors —those athletes who choose to enter various sporting events for the thrill and challenge provided. Rudman (1986), in an attempt to assess how sports are viewed by three different age groups (eighteen to thirty-four, thirty-five to fifty-four, fifty-five plus), queried 1,319 subjects about their participation in fourteen different athletic events. Age, marital status, income, occupational status, and geographic location served as independent variables in the Rudman study. Among the more notable, though not surprising, results was a clear age-related bias in sport involvement. A steady age-related decrease was found; only golf was exempt from differential participation as a function of chronology. The largest drop-off in sport involvement occurred between the eighteen to thirty-four and the thirty-five to fifty-four age groups, suggesting that discontinuation from competition takes place fairly early in life.

An interesting approach to fostering competition among senior athletes over the age of fifty-five has been put together by the fitness coordinator for Baltimore (Maryland) County and described by Zeigler and Michael (1985). The competition, known as the Maryland Senior Olympics, was instituted in 1980 with three hundred entrants, a figure that doubled by the 1984 games. Thirty events encompassing seventeen different sports comprise the

Hundreds of Maryland residents over fifty-five gather annually to compete in over thirty events in the state's Senior Olympics.

HIGHLIGHT 13.5
The Retired Athlete

Retirement from athletics can occur at a number of junctures and for several reasons. One popular point of departure for discussing career termination is retirement from intercollegiate athletics and another is termination of a professional career. In turn, these retirements may occur for at least three reasons—the selection process, chronological age, or incapacitating injury (Ogilvie and Howe, 1986).

The selection process is particularly brutal. According to Paul Dietzel (1983), a former head football coach and athletic director, only 1 out of every 235 high school players will ever "start" for a Division 1 college team. Even more remote is the possibility of a professional football career; only 1 out of each 5,635 (.018 percent) high school football players will play for a professional team. To compound this problem, only a few of those who make it into the professional ranks will stay long. The average career in the National Football League is 4.2 years; in the National Basketball Association, the statistics are even more grim. The career expectancy of an NBA player is 3.4 seasons. Making it to the professional level is a long shot at best, and survival in such a "Darwinian sports world" (Ogilvie and Howe, 1986, p. 366) is a gargantuan undertaking in its own right. Another view of the selection process discussed so far is provided by Ogilvie and Howe (1986, p. 366):

	Basketball	Football
High school	700,000	1,300,000 +
College (NCAA Varsity)	15,000	75,000
Draft	200(NBA)	320(NFL)
Final selection	50	150

What becomes of people who retire from sports? The answer to this question is best understood in terms of two perspectives, that of the collegiate athlete who is terminating an athletic career and that of the professional player who is leaving what may amount to a lifetime of sports involvement.

The Collegiate Athlete. Two recent studies (Greendorfer and Blinde, 1985; Kleiber, Greendorfer, Blinde, and Samdahl, 1987) have generated some understanding of the dynamics concerning the collegiate athlete who "hangs it up" after expiration of eligibility. Reviewing these two research efforts, we can draw several conclusions. One is that termination of athletics at this level is far from traumatic for the majority of athletes involved. In the Greendorfer and Blinde study of 1,123 male and female athletes, 89 percent of the 697 females and 90 percent of the 426 males looked forward to life after college; additionally, 55 percent of the women and 57 percent of the men indicated that they were quite or extremely satisfied with themselves upon career termination; too, 75 percent of the athletes were still participating in their sport at some less formal level. Finally, 81 percent of the men and 55 percent of the women continued to follow their respective sports through the media on a "regular" or "religious" basis.

A second conclusion from the two studies is that there were no sex differences in adjustment to termination. Past research has completely neglected the adjustment of female athletes to career termination, so these two studies represented a significant point of departure concerning research about this issue.

Third, career termination by way of injury resulted in a feeling of less life satisfaction for those athletes. Apparently, a sense of unfulfilled promise permeated the mentality of these injured athletes, resulting in less life satisfaction scores on the measure used. Finally, a shifting of priorities over the collegiate years took place in the majority of the athletes, with sport becoming less significant in their lives and education assuming an increasingly prominent role. These data support the earlier findings of Haerle (1975), who studied professional baseball players and found a strong relationship between amount of education and postplaying occupational achievement.

The Professional Athlete. Presumably, the adjustment to career termination is more complex at the professional level because the stakes are higher. The money involved is substantially greater, with the average 1985 salary in the NBA at $231,000 and that of the NFL $160,000 (Ogilvie and Howe, 1986). Too, the "sports only" identification is probably more operational at this stratified performance level. Partial support for the unidimensionality of professional athletes is provided by Ogilvie and Howe (1986), who indicate that only 20 percent of NBA players and 32 percent of NFL athletes had a college degree.

The popular literature is rife with reports of brain-damaged boxers, football players who cannot get out of bed without assistance, and athletes from all sport persuasions who are wife-battering, drug-addicted, alcoholic deadbeats. It is all too easy to infer from these sensationalized accounts that adjustment problems are rampant among ex-athletes. Little, of course, is made of the ex-athlete who quietly goes to work and becomes an adjusted and contributing citizen. Few statistics are available with which to accurately arrive at a composite of what the retired professional athlete is really like.

One of the first studies of athletic termination, and one with problems of extrapolation to our professional athletes, was conducted by Mihovilovic (1968) with retired Yugoslavian soccer players. Ninety-five percent of these athletes were forced to retire and 53 percent reported missing the camaraderie afforded by team members; 39 percent took up smoking for the first time and 16 percent increased their alcohol consumption upon retirement.

Adaptation to family life constitutes another challenge to athletic retirement; Ogilvie and Howe (1986) cite statistics from the NFL Players Association in which 50 percent of all marriages of ex-NFL players end in divorce. Mihoces (1988) sets this divorce figure at 33.5 percent, still a high number. Inability to adjust to incapacitating injury associated with contact sports such as football is a consideration. Mihoces (1988) indicates that 66 percent of all NFL players retire with permanent injury. Underwood (1979, p. 80), in discussing football injuries, poignantly portrays the plight of the seriously injured retiree: "Statistics do not show, however, how many ex-pros can no longer tie their shoe laces, or curl their fingers about a golf club. Statistics do not show many can't sleep without narcotics and have to call their wives for help to get out of bed."

Though we have much to learn about the adjustment of professional athletes to retirement, it seems obvious that all is not a bed of roses. Inadequate education, a paucity of job skills beyond those necessary to athletic performance, physical infirmity, and interpersonal difficulties variously contribute to the problems facing all too many retired athletes. Athletic administrators, counselors, agents, coaches, sport psychologists, and the athletes themselves all have a vested interest in doing all they can to smooth the transition from what clearly is a brief career as an athlete to the more long-term endeavor of contributing human being. Perhaps Dietzel (1983, p. 162) sums the situation up best: "The 'average' NFL player will have 42.4 years remaining after his playing career. That means that even if he does 'make it' in the pros, he will have to earn a living for the remaining two-thirds of his life. He has a .018 percent chance of being a pro but he has a solid 100 percent chance of being a 'breadwinner' for the overwhelming majority of his life."

SOURCE: "There Is Life After Football" by P. Dietzel, 1983, *Physical Educator, 40,* 161–162; " 'Retirement' from Intercollegiate Sport: Theoretical and Empirical Considerations" by S. Greendorfer and E. Blinde, 1985, *Sociology of Sport Journal, 2,* 101–110; "Career Patterns and Career Contingencies of Professional Baseball Players: An Occupational Analysis" by R. K. Haerle, 1975, in D. W. Ball and J. W. Loy, eds., *Sport and Social Order* (pp. 461–519), Reading, MA: Addison-Wesley; "Quality of Exit from University Sports and Life Satisfaction in Early Adulthood" by D. Kleiber, S. Greendorfer, E. Blinde, and D. Samdahl, 1987, *Sociology of Sport Journal, 4,* 28–36; "Less-visible Players Find Little Glory after Football" by G. Mihoces, 1988, May 10, *USA Today,* p. 12C; "The Status of Former Sportsmen" by M. A. Mihovilovic, 1968, *International Review of Sport Sociology, 3,* 73–93; "The Trauma of Termination From Athletics" by B. Ogilvie and M. Howe, 1986, in J. Williams, ed., *Applied Sport Psychology: Personal Growth to Peak Experience* (pp. 365–382), Mountain View, CA: Mayfield; *The Death of an American Game* (p. 80) by J. Underwood, 1979, Boston: Little, Brown.

games, with separate male and female competition, except for the three coeducational activities: square dancing and doubles in tennis and badminton. Continual revamping of the competition has been done to stay within reasonable safety limits that might be specific to seniors. Games such as those of Baltimore County offer fun and safe competition for older athletes.

A Final Note. As sport scientists, we can ignore the needs and wishes of our older citizens for fitness and competitive outlets or we can respond to the challenges at hand. More research is needed to help gain insight into our older citizens so that a greater quality of life can be provided through carefully chosen exercise or physical activity. Increasingly, professionals in the health business are reassessing the fascination with running and superior cardiovascular functioning as the major indicators of fitness. Brisk walking, ardent gardening, enthusiastic carpentry, or physical activity of any kind may well be as healthy for those who enjoy them as jogging, calisthenics, or aerobic dancing are for others. Much remains to be done in tailoring exercise or physical activity to individuals' needs, wishes, and capabilities.

SUMMARY

1. Our fascination with fitness had led to much speculation and research aimed at promoting a better understanding of exercise and its relationship to mental and physical fitness. Why people value fitness, why others cannot adhere to fitness regimens, and the consequences of exercise for prevention and alleviation of anxiety and depression are some of the more significant issues confronting health professionals. The psychology of running, the adjustment of athletes to retirement, and the exercise and competitive needs of senior citizens have sparked interest among sport and exercise scientists.

2. An apparent fitness boom of major proportions has seen 50 to 60 million Americans involved in some kind of exercise. However, a large number of so-called exercisers may not work out regularly enough to realize the possible gains in level of fitness. The commitment to fitness may be more verbal than behavioral.

3. Caspersen (1985) suggests that there are differences among physical activity, exercise, and physical fitness, and these distinctions have served as a guiding philosophy for the present discussion.

4. Among the more prominent physical benefits of physical fitness are increased blood flow to the heart, lowered blood pressure, increased lung capacity, lower blood lactate levels, more effective digestive and excretory functioning, and weight control. Whether or not a lowered resting heart rate is actually a benefit remains contentious.

5. The psychological benefits of exercise are less well documented but are thought to include reductions in anxiety and depression, increased socialization, self-confidence, improved sex life, and the thrill of competition against oneself, external standards, or other competitors.

6. Statistics on exercise adherence/compliance are generally not good. Exercise dropout rates of up to 50 percent are seen in both exercisers with no history of coronary problems who want to become more fit and those who are postmyocardial infarction patients.

7. Predictors of exercise adherence/compliance include geographical proximity to the exercise area, support from the spouse, exercising in small as opposed to large groups, higher socioeconomic status, and, more tentatively, an internal locus of control.

8. Negative predictors of adherence/compliance include lack of time, accessibility, being a smoker, poor choice of exercise, early injury, Type A personality, and being more introverted.

9. A number of behavioral approaches to increase exercise compliance that have been used with some success are behavioral contracts, lotteries, self-monitoring, stimulus-cueing, and everyday reinforcement of exercise behavior.

10. Concerned professionals have shown much interest in the contribution of exercise to cognitive and affective functioning.

11. Many studies have been conducted concerning various kinds of exercise as they relate to cognitive functioning, and the results are highly equivocal at this point. This is generally true for both anaerobic and aerobic exercise conducted at varying degrees of intensity and time. Flaws in methodology and a failure to tie the research to any theoretical base have hampered studies.

12. Exercise is thought to have an impact on both anxiety and depression, two affective states that have been of considerable interest to scientists across many professional fields.

13. In an extensive review of the literature, Folkins and Sime (1981) cite studies pointing to improved affective functioning as a result of exercise. Evidence also suggests that reductions in anxiety can be achieved by pairing exercise with other approaches, such as stress inoculation training.

14. Depression is a major mental health problem in the United States, and a variety of approaches have been used in an attempt to deal with the condition. Greist and his colleagues (1978) brought the use of running as therapy for depression to the forefront from the scientific perspective, whereas Fixx (1977) served the same function for the larger community with his popular book on the many virtues of running. Like the link between anxiety and exercise, the one involving depression is best thought of as correlational as opposed to causative at this point. More research is needed to make the desired causal connection between exercise and improved affect.

15. In using exercise as therapy for anxiety or depression, first priority should be given to making an accurate psychological diagnosis of the client(s). Exercises should be carefully tailored to the individual and should be performed under the guidance of a skilled exercise therapist who serves as an adjustment and fitness model. The therapy situation requires liberal use of reinforcement.

16. Runners, ex-athletes, and senior citizens represent three populations of interest to sport and exercise professionals.

17. Much has been made, and with some justification, about the merits of running as a means of promoting physical fitness. Some runners (and other exercisers) form a positive addiction and others a negative addiction to their exercise regimen.

18. The notion of positive addiction was popularized in 1976 by psychiatrist William Glasser. To Glasser, the positively addicted person has a healthy attitude toward exercise, has it worked nicely into everyday life, and does not let exercise control his or her life. Evidence from a number of sources supports a generally healthy psychological state among runners, who Glasser would say are most likely to become positively addicted because they are using the exercise of choice.

19. The negatively addicted person has relinquished control of exercise. Work, family life, and health may be sacrificed for the sake of the search for fitness. Injury statistics indicate that addicted runners are at higher risk of injury while working out or competing.

20. The phenomenon of the "runner's high" is generally agreed to exist, but attempts to operationalize it have not been successful. Estimates indicate that from 9 percent to 78 percent of all runners have experienced the "runner's high."

21. The marathon event was named after a small Greek town in which a prominent battle was fought between the Greeks and the Persians in 490 B.C. The marathon was introduced as an Olympic event in 1896, and its popularity has increased ever since. The event was added to the slate of activities for women in the 1984 Olympics. Studies of marathoners suggest that they are introverts, have low anxiety levels, and have superior mood profiles in general.

22. Ultramarathoners run distances above the 26 miles, 385 yards found in the marathon event. Ultramarathons may involve long distances over several days or weeks or distances up to 100 miles in a given day. Little is known about the psychology of ultramarathoners. Highly preliminary evidence suggests that they are generally psychologically healthy with just enough personality deviance to help them run what may itself be a deviant event.

26. There will be an increase in the median age of the typical American of ten years by the year 2050. This "graying of America" is a phenomenon that will place added pressure on a variety of services, not the least of which is exercise and fitness for senior citizens.

27. Chronological age is unalterable; biological age can be modified to an unknown extent, and it remains the task of the exerciser and the exercise and fitness specialists to determine just what this limit is. It seems likely that exercise offers one point of intervention in this biological aging issue.

28. Seniors who still have a competitive streak are increasingly being provided with outlets for their energies and talents. One such example is the Maryland Senior Olympics, a thirty-event competition for men and women over age fifty-five.

29. Although exercise may represent one way to achieve fitness, physical activities of any kind that keep people occupied, interested, and moving about may be just as productive in promoting health.

SUGGESTED READINGS

Cash, T., Winstead, B., & Janda, L. (1986) The great American shape-up. *Psychology Today*, April, pp. 30–37.

Reporting results from a 1985 survey, the authors indicate that less satisfaction with body image was reported by a higher proportion of their 30,000 respondents than in a similar 1972 study. Women reported less satisfaction than did men, placed less importance on fitness, and did less to achieve fitness. A decrease in body satisfaction as a function of increasing age was also noted. A very positive relationship was found between concern for fitness and health and approval of overall appearance.

Lerch, S. (1984) The adjustment of athletes to career ending injuries. *Arena Review*, 8(1), 54–67.

Consistent with the text treatment of reasons why athletic careers are brought to an end, Lerch discusses at length a number of the considerations related to one cause of termination, namely serious injury. He elaborates on four types of disability and seven potential positive contributors to postcareer adjustment. The article is liberally sprinkled with anecdotes from well-known athletes concerning their injuries and the problems they had in making the transition from athlete to ex-athlete and everyday citizen.

Rees, C.R., Andres, F., & Howell, F. (1986) On the trail of the "turkey trotters": The effect of previous sport involvement and attitudes on commitment to and skill in running. *Sociology of Sport Journal*, 3, 134–143.

This study was conducted on 141 male and female runners competing in a 5-mile race. Attitudes toward previous sport involvement and actual previous sport involvement did not seem to affect current skill level or commitment to running. Present attitude toward running, on the other hand, was predictive.

Reiter, M. (1985) What makes older athletes go. *Parade*, December 1, pp. 7–9.

In 1985, there were 61.4 million Americans over the age of fifty, and their favorite activities were, in order, general exercise, swimming, cycling, golf, bowling, walking, running, and tennis. Using these data as a point of departure, Reiter describes four physically elite senior competitors: an eighty-two-year-old male tennis player of considerable renown, a fifty-six-year-old female distance runner known as the "running nun" because of her occupation, a fifty-seven-year-old male amateur champion golfer, and a fifty-two-year-old female cyclist of world class caliber. This article is good fare for those seeking inspirational senior athletic models.

Rejeski, W.J. (1985) Perceived exertion: An active or passive process? *Journal of Sport Psychology*, 7, 371–378.

Rejeski makes the point that exercise prescriptions should take into account individual subjective reports of work intensity, or what he calls rate of perceived exertion (RPE). How one perceives the exertion involved in a particular activity rather than the actual work output may well be a critical determinant of exercise adherence/compliance.

REFERENCES

Andrew, G., Oldridge, N., Parker, J., Cunningham, D., Rechnitzer, P., Jones, N., Buck, C., Kavanagh, T., Shephard, R., Sutton, J., & McDonald, W. (1981) Reasons for dropout from exercise programs in post-coronary patients. *Medicine and Science in Sports and Exercise, 13*(3), 164–168.

Berger, B. (1987) Swimmers report less stress: A series of investigations. In W. P. Morgan & S. E. Goldston (Eds.), *Exercise and mental health* (pp. 139–143). New York: Hemisphere Pub.

Blumenthal, J., Williams, R., Wallace, A., Williams, R., & Needles, T. (1982) Physiological and psychological variables predict compliance to prescribed exercise therapy in patients recovering from myocardial infarction. *Psychosomatic Medicine, 44*, 519–527.

Borg, G. (1973) Perceived exertion: A note on history and methods. *Medicine and Science in Sports, 5*, 90–93.

Brawley, L. R. (1987) Some thoughts on adherence to health-related programs in applied sport psychology. *AAASP Newsletter, 2*(1), 5–6.

Brown, R., Ramirez, D., & Taub, J. (1978) The prescription of exercise for depression. *Physician and Sportsmedicine, 6*(12), 35–45.

Buffone, G. W. (1984) Exercise as a therapeutic adjunct. In J. M. Silva & R. S. Weinberg (Eds.), *Psychological foundations of sport* (pp. 445–451). Champaign, IL: Human Kinetics.

Carmack, M. A., & Martens, R. (1979) Measuring commitment to running: A survey of runners' attitudes and mental states. *Journal of Sport Psychology, 1*, 25–42.

Caspersen, C. (1985) Physical activity, exercise, and physical fitness: Definitions and distinctions for health-related research. *Physician and Sportsmedicine, 13*(5), 162.

Clitsome, T., & Kostrubala, T. (1977) A psychological study of 100 marathoners using the Myers-Briggs Type indicator and demographic data. In P. Milvey (Ed.), *The marathon: Physiological, medical, epidemiological, and psychological studies. Annals of the New York Academy of Sciences, 301*, 1010–1019.

Csikszentmihalyi, M. (1975) *Beyond boredom and anxiety.* San Francisco, CA: Jossey-Bass.

Diekhoff, G. (1984) Running amok: Injuries in compulsive runners. *Journal of Sport Behavior, 7*, 120–129.

Dishman, R. K. (1982) Compliance/adherence in health-related exercise. *Health Psychology, 1*, 237–267.

Dishman, R. K. (1984) Motivation and exercise adherence. In J. M. Silva & R. S. Weinberg (Eds.), *Psychological foundations of sport* (pp. 420–434). Champaign, IL: Human Kinetics.

Dishman, R. K. (1986) Exercise compliance: A new view for public health. *Physician and Sportsmedicine, 14*(5), 127–145.

Farrell, P., Gates, W., Maksud, M., & Morgan, W. (1982) Increases in plasma B-endorphin/B-lipotropin immunoreactivity after treadmill running in rats. *Journal of Applied Psychology, 52*, 1245–1249.

Fixx, J. (1977) *The complete book of running.* New York: Random House.

Folkins, C., & Sime, W. (1981) Physical fitness training and mental health. *American Psychologist, 36*, 373–389.

Folkins, C., & Wieselberg-Bell, N. (1981) A personality profile of ultramarathon runners: A little deviance may go a long way. *Journal of Sport Behavior, 4*, 119–127.

Fox, E. (1984) *Sports physiology.* Philadelphia, PA: Saunders.

Friedman, M., & Rosenman, R. (1974) *Type A behavior and your heart.* New York: Knopf.

Gettman, L., Pollock, M., & Ward, A. (1983) Adherence to unsupervised exercise. *Physician and Sportsmedicine, 11*(10), 56–66.

Glasser, W. (1976) *Positive addiction.* New York: Harper & Row.

Gliner, J. A., Matsen-Twisdale, J. A., Horvath, S. M., & Maron, M. B. (1979) Visual evoked potentials and signal detection following a marathon race. *Medicine and Science in Sports, 11*, 155–159.

Gondola, J., & Tuckman, B. (1982) Psychological mood states in "average" marathon runners. *Perceptual and Motor Skills, 55*, 1295–1300.

Gondola, J., & Tuckman, B. (1983). Extent of training and mood enhancement in women runners. *Perceptual and Motor Skills, 57*, 333–334.

Gontang, A., Clitsome, T., & Kostrubala, T. (1977) A psychological study of 50 sub-3 hour marathoners. In P. Milvey (Ed.), *The marathon: Physiological, medical, epidemiological, and psychological studies. Annals of the New York Academy of Sciences, 301*, 1020–1046.

Greist, J., Klein, M., Eischens, R., & Faris, J. (1978) Running out of depression. *Physician and Sportsmedicine, 6*(12), 49–56.

Grogan, R. (1981) Run, Pheidippides, run! The story of the battle of Marathon. *British Journal of Sports Medicine, 15*, 186–189.

Hailey, B. J., & Bailey, L. (1982) Negative addiction in runners: A quantitative approach. *Journal of Sport Behavior, 5*, 150–153.

Hanson, M. (1977) Coronary heart disease, exercise, and motivation in middle aged males. Doctoral dissertation, University of Wisconsin, Madison, 1976. *Dissertation Abstracts International, 37*, 2755B.

Henderson, J. (1977) Running commentary. *Runner's World, 13*(9), 15.

Howell, R. (1983) History of the Olympic marathon. *Physician and Sportsmedicine, 11*(11), 153–158.

Joesting, J. (1981) Comparison of personalities of athletes who sail with those who run. *Perceptual and Motor Skills, 52*, 514.

Johnsgard, K. (1985) The motivation of the long distance runner: I. *Journal of Sports Medicine, 25*, 135–143.

LaPorte, R., Dearwater, S., Cauley, J., Slemenda, C., & Cook, T. (1985) Physical activity or cardiovascular fitness: Which is more important for health? *Physician and Sportsmedicine, 13*(3), 145–150.

Layman, D., & Morris, A. (1986) Addiction and injury in runners: Is there a mind-body connection? Paper presented at the annual convention of the North American Society for the Psychology of Sport and Physical Activity, Scottsdale, Arizona.

Legwold, G. (1985) Are we running from the truth about the risks and benefits of exercise? *Physician and Sportsmedicine, 13*(5), 136–148.

Levenson, H. (1981) Differentiating among internality, powerful others, and chance. In H. Lefcourt (Ed.), *Research with the locus of control construct: Assessment methods* (Vol. 1, pp. 1–39). New York: Academic Press.

Lilliefors, F. (1978) *The running mind.* Mountain View, CA: World Publications.

Long, B. C. (1984) Aerobic conditioning and stress inoculation: A comparison of stress-management interventions. *Cognitive Therapy and Research, 8*, 517–542.

Long, B. C. (1985) Stress-management interventions: A 15-month follow-up of aerobic and stress inoculation training. *Cognitive Therapy and Research, 9*, 471–478.

Lybrand, W. A., Andrews, T. G., & Ross, S. (1954) Systematic fatigue and perceptual organization. *American Journal of Psychology, 67*, 704–707.

Markoff, R., Ryan, P., & Young, T. (1982) Endorphins and mood changes in long-distance running. *Medicine and Science in Exercise and Sport, 14*, 11–15.

Maron, M., & Horvath, S. (1978) The marathon: A history and review of the literature. *Medicine and Science in Sports, 10*, 137–150.

Massie, J., & Shephard, R. (1971) Physiological and psychological effects of training: A comparison of individual and gymnasium programs, with a characterization of the exercise 'drop-out.' *Medicine and Science in Sports, 3*, 110–117.

McCready, M., & Long, B. C. (1985) Locus of control, attitudes toward physical activity, and exercise adherence. *Journal of Sport Psychology, 7*, 346–359.

McCutcheon, L., & Yoakum, M. (1983) Personality attributes of ultramarathoners. *Journal of Personality Assessment, 47*, 178–180.

Meichenbaum, D. (1977) *Cognitive-behavior modification: An integrated approach.* New York: Plenum.

Monahan, T. (1986) Exercise and depression: Swapping sweat for serenity? *Physician and Sportsmedicine, 14*(9), 192–197.

Morgan, W. P. (1979) Negative addiction in runners. *Physician and Sportsmedicine, 7*(2), 56–70.

Morgan, W. P., & Costill, D. (1972) Psychological characteristics of the marathon runner. *Journal of Sports Medicine and Physical Fitness, 12*, 42–46.

Morgan, W. P., & Pollock, M. (1977) Psychologic characterization of the elite distance runner. In P. Milvey (Ed.), *The marathon: Physiological, medical, epidemiological, and psychological studies. Annals of the New York Academy of Sciences, 301*, 382–403.

Noland, M. (1981) The efficacy of a new model to explain leisure exercise behavior. Unpublished doctoral dissertation, University of Maryland.

Oldridge, N. (1982) Compliance and exercise in primary and secondary prevention of coronary heart disease: A review. *Preventive Medicine, 11,* 56–70.

Oldridge, N., Wicks, J., Hanley, R., Sutton, J., & Jones, N. (1978) Noncompliance in an exercise rehabilitation program for men who have suffered a myocardial infarction. *Canadian Medical Association Journal, 118,* 361–375.

Peoples, C. (1983) A psychological analysis of the "runner's high." *Physical Educator, 40,* 38–41.

Piaget, J. (1936) *The origins of intelligence in children.* New York: New York University Press.

Porter, K. (1985) Psychological characteristics of the average female runner. *Physician and Sportsmedicine, 13*(5), 171–175.

Powell, K. (1985) Workshop on epidemiologic and public health aspects of physical activity and exercise. *Physician and Sportsmedicine, 13*(3), 161.

Raglin, J., & Morgan, W. P. (1985) Influence of vigorous exercise on mood state. *Behavior Therapist, 8,* 179–183.

Ravizza, K. (1984) Qualities of the peak experience in sport. In J. M. Silva & R. S. Weinberg (Eds.), *Psychological foundations of sport* (pp. 452–461). Champaign, IL: Human Kinetics.

Rogers, C. (1985) Of magic, miracles, and exercise myths. *Physician and Sportsmedicine, 13*(5), 156–166.

Roth, W. (1974) Some motivational aspects of exercise. *Journal of Sports Medicine, 14,* 40–47.

Rudman, W. (1986) Sport as a part of successful aging. *American Behavioral Scientist, 29,* 453–470.

Sachs, M. (1980) On the trail of the runner's high — A descriptive and experimental investigation of characteristics of an elusive phenomenon. Unpublished doctoral dissertation, Florida State University.

Sachs, M. (1984) Psychological well-being and vigorous physical activity. In J. M. Silva & R. S. Weinberg (Eds.), *Psychological foundations of sport* (pp. 435–444). Champaign, IL: Human Kinetics.

Sager, K. (1984) Exercises to activate seniors. *Physician and Sportsmedicine, 12*(5), 144–151.

Sanne, H. (1973) Exercise tolerance and physical training of non-selected patients after myocardial infarction. *Acta Medica Scandinavica, 551,* 1–124.

Shephard, R. (1985) Motivation: The key to exercise compliance. *Physician and Sportsmedicine, 13*(7), 88–101.

Sidney, K., & Shephard R. (1976) Attitudes toward health and physical activity in the elderly. Effects of a physical training program. *Medicine and Science in Sports, 4,* 246–252.

Silva, J., & Hardy, C. (1986) Discriminating contestants at the United States Olympic marathon trials as a function of precompetitive anxiety. *International Journal of Sport Psychology, 17,* 100–109.

Silva, J. M., & Weinberg, R. S. (1984) Exercise and psychological well-being. In J. M. Silva & R. S. Weinberg (Eds.), *Psychological foundations of sport* (pp. 415–419). Champaign, IL: Human Kinetics.

Sime, W. E., Whipple, I. T., Stamler, J., & Berkson, D. M. (1978) Effects of long-term (38 months) training on middle-aged sedentary males: Adherence and specificity of training. In F. Landry & W. A. R. Orban (Eds.), *Exercise and well-being: Exercise physiology* (pp. 456–464). Miami, FL: Symposium Specialists.

Siscovick, D. (1985) The disease-specific benefits and risks of physical activity and exercise. *Physician and Sportsmedicine, 13*(3), 164.

Smith, E. L., & Gilliam, C. (1983) Physical activity prescription for the older adult. *Physician and Sportsmedicine, 11*(8), 91–101.

Smith, E. L., & Zook, S. K. (1986) The aging process: Benefits of physical activity. *Journal of Physical Education, Recreation and Dance,* Jan., pp. 32–34.

Spielberger, C., Gorsuch, B., & Lushene, R. (1970) Manual for the *State-Trait Anxiety Inventory.* Palo Alto, CA: Consulting Psychologists Press.

Stamford, B. (1984) Exercise and longevity. *Physician and Sportsmedicine, 12*(6), 209.

Stephens, T. (1985) A descriptive epidemiology of leisure-time physical activity. *Physician and Sportsmedicine, 13*(3), 162.

Teraslinna, P., Partanen, T., Koskela, A., Partanen, K., & Oja, P. (1969) Characteristics affecting willingness of executives to participate in an activity program aimed at coronary heart disease prevention. *Journal of Sports Medicine and Physical Fitness, 9,* 224–229.

Thomas, T., Zebas, C., Bahrke, M., Araujo, J., & Etheridge, G. (1983) Physiological and psychological correlates of success in track and field athletes. *British Journal of Sports Medicine, 17,* 102–109.

Thompson, C., & Wankel, L. (1980) The effects of perceived activity choice upon frequency of exercise behavior. *Journal of Applied Social Psychology, 10,* 436–444.

Tomporowski, P. D., & Ellis, N. R. (1986) Effects of exercise on cognitive processes: A review. *Psychological Bulletin, 99,* 338–346.

Tomporowski, P. D., Ellis, N. R., & Stephens, R. (1985) The immediate effects of strenuous exercise on free-recall memory. *Ergonomics, 30,* 121–129.

Veschi, R. (1963) Longevity and sport. *Journal of Sports Medicine and Physical Fitness, 3,* 44–49.

Wagemaker, H., & Goldstein, L. (1980) The runner's high. *Journal of Sports Medicine, 20,* 227–228.

Weinberg, R. S. (1980) Relationship of commitment to running scale to runners' performances and attitudes. In *Abstracts: Research papers 1980 AAHPERD Convention.* Washington, DC: AAHPERD.

Weltman, A., & Stamford, B. (1983) Psychological effects of exercise. *Physician and Sportsmedicine, 11*(1), 175.

Williams, R., & Long, J. (1983) *Toward a self-managed lifestyle* (3rd ed.). Boston: Houghton-Mifflin.

Wilson, V., Morley, N., & Bird, E. (1980) Mood profiles of marathon runners, joggers, and non-exercisers. *Perceptual and Motor Skills, 50,* 117–118.

Zeigler, R. G., & Michael, R. H. (1985) The Maryland Senior Olympic Games: Challenging older athletes. *Physician and Sportsmedicine, 13*(8), 159–163.

AUTHOR INDEX

SUBJECT INDEX

Additional Copyright Information

p. xiv: From *The Face Is Familiar* by Ogden Nash. Copyright 1937 by Ogden Nash. Copyright © renewed 1964 by Ogden Nash. First appeared in *The New Yorker*. By permission of Little, Brown and Company.

p. 8, fig.1.1: Adaptation of Table 1-1 from *Introduction to Psychology*, Eighth Edition, by Rita L. Atkinson, Richard C. Atkinson, and Ernest Hilgard, copyright © 1983 by Harcourt Brace Jovanovich, Inc., reprinted by permission of the publisher.

p. 9, table 1.2: Adaptation of Table 1-2 from *Psychology: Understanding Behavior* by Robert Baron et al., copyright © 1980 by Holt, Rinehart and Winston, Inc., reprinted by permission of the publisher.

p. 73, fig. 3.3: Copyright 1980 by the Society for the Experimental Analysis of Behavior, Inc.

p. 108, fig 4.5: Reprinted with permission of Macmillan Publishing Company. Copyright © 1987 by Macmillan Publishing Company.

p. 126, table 5.1: Adaptation of Table 8-1 from *Human Motivation* by Bernard Weiner, copyright © 1980 by Holt, Rinehart and Winston, Inc., reprinted by permission of the publisher.

p. 134, table 5.3: Reprinted by permission. Copyright © 1943 by The President and Fellows of Harvard College; Copyright © 1971 by Henry A. Murray.

p. 159, fig 6.1: Reprinted with permission of The Free Press, a Division of Macmillan, Inc. from *Leadership Dynamics: A Practical Guide to Effective Relationships* by Edwin P. Hollander. Copyright © 1978 by The Free Press.

p. 171, table 6.2; p. 173, fig. 6.6; p. 178, fig. 6.7: From Richard H. Cox, *Sport Psychology Concepts and Applications*. Copyright © 1985 Wm. C. Brown Publishers, Dubuque, Iowa. All Rights Reserved. Reprinted by permission.

p. 180, table 6.4: Reprinted from *Social Forces*, 55 (March 1977). "The Home Advantage" by Barry Schwartz and S. F. Barsky. Copyright © The University of North Carolina Press.

p. 181, table 6.5; p. 182, table 6.6: Copyright 1984 by the American Psychological Association. Adapted by permission of the publisher and author.

pp. 217–18, highlight 7.4: Copyright 1979. Reproduced by permission of McGraw-Hill Book Company.

p. 233, fig 8.1: Adapted from *Principles and Methods of Social Psychology* by E. P. Hollander. Copyright © 1967 by Oxford University Press, Inc. Reproduced by permission.

p. 258, fig 8.4: From "Personality and Sport Performance" by J. M. Silva, in J. M. Silva and R. S. Weinberg, Eds., *Psychological Foundations of Sport*. Champaign, Ill.: Human Kinetics, 1984.

p. 276, table 9.1: Copyright © 1982 by Allyn & Bacon, Inc.

p. 283, table 9.3: Adapted from pages 77–109, *Handbook for the Sixteen Personality Questionnaire (16PF)*, copyright © 1970 by the Institute for Personality and Ability Testing, Inc. Reproduced by permission.

p. 305, fig 9.4: Copyright American College of Sport Medicine 1984. Reproduced by permission.

p. 332: Reproduced by special permission of the Publisher, Consulting Psychologists Press, Inc., Palo Alto CA 94306, from *Bem Sex-Role Inventory* by Sandra Lipsitz Bem, PhD, © 1978. Further reproduction is prohibited without the Publisher's consent.

Photo Credits

p. 4 G. Giansanti/Sygma
p. 5 Evan Johnson/Jeroboam
p. 13 Courtesy U.S. Olympic Committee
p. 14 News and Publications Service, Stanford University
p. 36 Bettmann Archive
p. 42 Bettmann Archive
p. 50 Courtesy of the Harvard University Archives
p. 53 From John Grafton, *New York in the Nineteenth Century*, Dover Publications, 1977
p. 64 (top) Courtesy Naismith Memorial Basketball Hall of Fame; (bottom) UPI/Bettmann Newsphotos
p. 70 Tom Ballard/EKM-Nepenthe
p. 87 Focus on Sports
p. 88 AP/Wide World Photos
p. 100 Mike Malyszko/Stock, Boston
p. 111 Courtesy U.S. Olympic Committee
p. 117 G. Giansanti/Sygma
p. 130 Robert Ginn/EKM-Nepenthe
p. 133 Michael Hayman/Stock, Boston
p. 145 © Billy E. Barnes
p. 157 Courtesy Dallas Cowboys
p. 168 AP/Wide World Photos
p. 175 Joseph Schuyler/Stock, Boston
p. 195 Anestis Diakopoulos/Stock, Boston
p. 197 AP/Wide World Photos
p. 207 Stuart Franklin/Sygma
p. 212 UPI/Bettmann Newsphotos
p. 221 © Charles M. Schulz/United Media
p. 242 (left) National Baseball Library, Cooperstown, N.Y.; (right) Culver Pictures
p. 253 Robert Burroughs/Jeroboam
p. 264 Library of Congress
p. 280 UPI/Bettmann Newsphotos
p. 289 © Warren Morgan
p. 304 AP/Wide World Photos
p. 320 Courtesy Vassar College Library
p. 321 National Baseball Library, Cooperstown, N.Y.
p. 324 AP/Wide World Photos
p. 329 © Billy E. Barnes
p. 339 Steve Malone/Jeroboam
p. 355 YMCA Archives/University of Minnesota
p. 361 Drawing by Mulligan; © 1979 the New Yorker Magazine, Inc.
p. 372 Vince Compagnone/Jeroboam
p. 386 Tom Carter/Jeroboam
p. 392 Courtesy University of Alabama
p. 404 Courtesy University of Texas
p. 415 Drawing by Koren, © 1979 The New Yorker Magazine, Inc.
p. 416 © Warren Morgan
p. 427 Brant Ward/San Francisco Chronicle
p. 435 Courtesy Maryland Office on Aging and Maryland Senior Olympics Commission